T3-ANT-230

INTRODUCING
MODERN CURRICULUM PRESS MATHEMATICS

A COMPLETE, ECONOMICAL MATH SERIES TEACHING PROBLEM-SOLVING STRATEGIES, CRITICAL-THINKING SKILLS, ESTIMATION, MENTAL-MATH SKILLS, AND ALL BASIC MATH CONCEPTS AND SKILLS!

Modern Curriculum Press Mathematics is an alternative basal program for students in grades K-6. This unique developmental series is perfect for providing the flexibility teachers need for ability grouping. Its design encourages thinking skills, active participation, and mastery of skills within the context of problem-solving situations, abundant practice to master those skills, developed models students actively work with to solve problems, and reinforcement of problem-solving and strategies. Other features like these provide students with solid math instruction.

- Each lesson begins with a developed model that teaches algorithms and concepts in a problem-solving situation.

- Students are required to interact with the model by gathering data needed to solve the problem.

- A developmental sequence introduces and extends skills taught in the basal curriculum—including statistics, logic, and probability.

- An abundant practice of math skills ensures true mastery of mathematics.

- Estimation and mental math skills are stressed in all computational and problem-solving activities.

- Calculator activities introduce students to basic calculator skills and terms.

- Comprehensive **Teacher's Editions** provide abundant additional help for teachers in features like **Correcting Common Errors, Enrichment,** and **Extra Credit,** and the complete **Table of Common Errors.**

Modern Curriculum Press Mathematics is a comprehensive math program that will help students develop a solid mathematics background. This special sampler will show you how:

- **Developed Models** begin each lesson, demonstrate the algorithm and concept in a problem-solving situation, and get students actively involved with the model.

- **Getting Started** provides samples of the concept or skill that is taught and allows the teacher to observe students' understanding.

- **Practice, Apply,** and **Copy and Do** activities develop independent skills where students practice the algorithm and apply what they have learned in the lesson or from a previous lesson. **Excursion** activities extend the math skill and are fun to do.

- **Problem Solving** pages introduce students to the techniques of problem solving using a four-step model. **Apply** activities on these pages allow students to use problem-solving strategies they have learned in everyday situations. The second half of the page focuses on higher-order thinking skills.

- **Chapter Test** pages provide both students and teachers with a checkpoint that tests all the skills taught in the chapter. There are alternative Chapter Tests based on the same objectives at the end of each student book.

- **Cumulative Review** pages maintain skills that have been taught not only in the previous chapter, but all skills taught up to this point. A standardized test format is used beginning at the middle of the second grade text.

- **Calculator** pages teach students the various functions and the basic skills needed to use calculators intelligently.

- **Teacher Edition** pages feature reduced student pages with answers, objectives, suggestions for **Teaching the Lesson, Materials, Correcting Common Errors, Enrichment,** and more.

A Developed Model Gets Students To Think, Actively Participate, And Understand Math Skills!

The major difference between *Modern Curriculum Press Mathematics* and other math programs is the developed model in which students actively work. Every lesson of *Modern Curriculum Press Mathematics* features concept development based on this developed model. Students are required to interact with this model discriminating what data is needed to solve the problem. This process teaches and reinforces their thinking skills and gets them actively involved providing the motivation to read and understand. The four-step teaching strategy of SEE, PLAN, DO, CHECK successfully increases students' understanding and provides a firm foundation for total math master of skills.

■ One major objective is the focus of every two-page lesson.

■ An algorithm or a model word problem keeps students interested and involved and provides a purpose for learning.

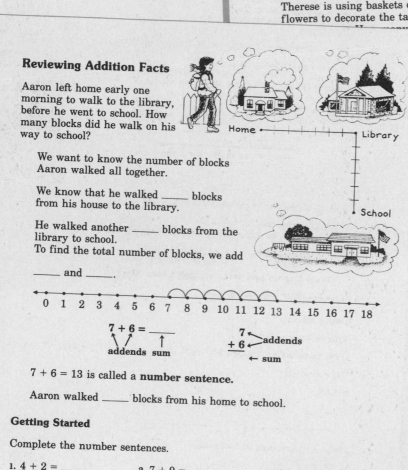

Reviewing Addition Facts

Aaron left home early one morning to walk to the library, before he went to school. How many blocks did he walk on his way to school?

We want to know the number of blocks Aaron walked all together.

We know that he walked _____ blocks from his house to the library.

He walked another _____ blocks from the library to school.
To find the total number of blocks, we add

_____ and _____.

$7 + 6 =$ _____
addends   sum

7
$+ 6$ ← addends
← sum

$7 + 6 = 13$ is called a **number sentence.**

Aaron walked _____ blocks from his home to school.

Getting Started

Complete the number sentences.

1. $4 + 2 =$ _____   2. $7 + 9 =$ _____   3. $8 + 3 =$ _____

4. $2 + 9 =$ _____   5. $5 + 6 =$ _____   6. $8 + 8 =$ _____

Add.

7. 8
   $+ 7$

8. 4
   $+ 1$

9. 9
   $+ 9$

10. 5
    $+ 5$

11. 3
    $+ 6$

12. 9
    $+ 4$

Dividing by 4

Therese is using baskets of flowers to decorate the tables

r of flowers that asket.

make up.

the baskets.

rs, we divide

ers into each basket.

plete the number sentences.

2.

How many in all? _____

How many groups? _____

How many in each group? _____

$12 ÷ 4 =$ _____

nces.

$4 =$ _____   5. $8 ÷ 4 =$ _____   6. $32 ÷ 4 =$ _____

3

MCP All rights reserved

MODERN CURRICULUM PRESS
MATHEMATICS

Teacher's Edition   Level E

Royce Hargrove   **Richard Monnard**

Acknowledgments

Content Writers   Babs Bell Hajdusiewicz
Phyllis Rosner
Laurel Sherman

Contributors   Linda Gojak
William Hunt
Christine Bhargava
Jean Laird
Roger Smalley
Erdine Bajbus
Rita Kuhar
Vicki Palisin
Jeanne White
Kathleen M. Becks
Jean Antonelli
Sandra J. Heldman
Susan McKenney
Nancy Toth
Nancy Ross
Connie Gorius
Denise Smith

Project Director   Dorothy A. Kirk

Editors   Martha Geyen
Phyllis Sibbing

Editorial Staff   Sharon M. Marosi
Ann Marie Murray
Patricia Kozak
Ruth Ziccardi

Design   The Remen-Willis
Design Group

Cover Art © 1993 Adam Peiperl

Modern Curriculum Press
An imprint of Pearson Learning
299 Jefferson Road, P.O. Box 480
Parsippany, NJ 07054-0480

www.pearsonlearning.com

1-800-321-3106

Copyright © 1994 by Modern Curriculum Press, an imprint of Pearson Learning, a division of Pearson Education, Inc. All rights reserved. Printed in the United States of America. This publication is protected by Copyright, and permissions should be obtained from the publisher prior to any prohibited reproduction, storage in a retrieval system, or transmission in any form or by any means, electronic, mechanical, photocopying, recording, or likewise. For information regarding permission(s), write to Rights and Permissions Department. This edition is published simultaneously in Canada by Pearson Education Canada.

ISBN 0-8136-3120-3 (Teacher's Edition)   **ISBN 0-8136-3113-0** (Pupil's Edition)

9 10 11 12 13 14 15 16 17 PO 06 05 04 03 02 01 00

K
Modern Curriculum Press

Mathematics

A
Modern Curriculum Press

Mathematics

B
Modern Curriculum Press

Mathematics

D
Modern Curriculum Press

Mathematics

E
Modern Curriculum Press

Mathematics

F
Modern Curriculum Press

Mathematics

C
Modern Curriculum Press

Mathematics

Teacher's Guide

C
Modern Curriculum Press

Mathematics

- Students interact with the artwork to gather data needed to solve problems. This interaction helps develop higher-order thinking skills.

- Each objective is introduced in a problem-solving setting developing problem-solving thinking skills.

- The four-step teaching method of SEE, PLAN, DO, CHECK guides students easily through the development of each skill.

- Students SEE the "input" sentences and the artwork and use them to help solve the problems. This allows them to be actively involved in their work.

- Students PLAN how they are going to solve problems using their reasoning skills to determine what operations are needed.

- Students use the model to help DO the problem. Each developed model shows students how to do the algorithm.

- To CHECK understanding of the math skill, a concluding sentence reinforces the problem-solving process.

- Important math vocabulary is bold-faced throughout the text and defined in context and in the glossary.

- A check (√) points out important concepts to which students should give special attention.

Subtracting Fractions with Unlike

Duncan is feeding the chickens on his uncle's farm. When he started, there were $4\frac{1}{2}$ buckets of chicken feed. How much feed has he used?

We want to know how much chicken feed Duncan has used.

We know that he started with ____ buckets

of feed, and he has ____ buckets left.

To find the amount used, we subtract the amount left from the original amount.

We subtract ____ from ____.

To subtract fractions with unlike denominator follow these steps:

Rename the fractions as equivalent fractions with the least common denominator	Subtract the fractions.
$4\frac{1}{2} = 4\frac{2}{4}$ $-1\frac{1}{4} = 1\frac{1}{4}$	$4\frac{1}{2} = 4\frac{2}{4}$ $-1\frac{1}{4} = 1\frac{1}{4}$ $\frac{1}{4}$

Duncan has used ____ buckets of feed.

Getting Started

Subtract.

1. $15\frac{5}{8}$
$-7\frac{1}{3}$

2. $87\frac{2}{3}$
$-39\frac{1}{6}$

3.

Copy and subtract.

5. $\frac{7}{8} - \frac{1}{4} =$ ____

6. $\frac{5}{6} - \frac{1}{2} =$ ____

7. $\frac{9}{10} - \frac{6}{15} =$ ____

127

Place Value through Thousands

The government space agency plans to sell used moon buggies to the highest bidders. What did Charley pay for the one he bought?

We want to understand the cost of Charley's moon buggy.

Charley paid exactly _____.
To understand how much money this is, we will look at the place value of each digit in the price.

✔ The numbers 0, 1, 2, 3, 4, 5, 6, 7, 8 and 9 are called **digits**. The position of the digit decides its place value.

thousands	hundreds	tens	ones
___	___	___	___

In 7,425, the digit 4 represents hundreds, and the

digit 7 represents _____.
Numbers can be written in **standard** or **expanded form**.

Standard Form   Expanded Form
7,425   7,000 + 400 + 20 + 5

We say Charley paid **seven thousand, four hundred twenty-five dollars**. We write _____.

Getting Started

Write in standard form.

1. five thousand, six hundred fifty-eight _____

2. 3,000 + 50 + 8 _____

Write in words.

3. 6,497

4. 823

5. 9,045

Write the place value of the red digits.

6. 3,9 8

7. 9 ,603

8. 7 29

9. $5,3 0

7

T-5

TEACHER-GUIDED PRACTICE ACTIVITIES CHECK STUDENTS' UNDERSTANDING OF MATH CONCEPTS!

Getting Started activities provide the opportunity for students to try to do what they've just learned and for teachers a chance to check understanding. These activities also allow the teacher to evaluate students' progress in a particular objective before continuing on in the lesson. A complete **Table of Common Errors** can be found in the **Teacher's Editions.** This list helps the teacher diagnose and correct those errors identified by research to be the most common. Lesson plans offer specific suggestions for dealing with each individual error, so the teacher can concentrate on those area where students need help. Showing th teacher ways to keep errors from happening by alerting to common mistakes, will make teaching math go more smoothly.

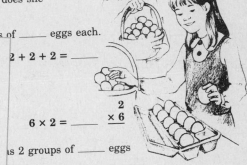

Multiplying, the Factor 2

Sun Li is helping her mother pack eggs in cartons. How many eggs does she pack into each carton?

_____ has 6 groups of _____ eggs each.

$2 + 2 + 2 =$ _____

$6 \times 2 =$ _____ $\begin{array}{r} 2 \\ \times 6 \\ \hline \end{array}$

_as 2 groups of _____ eggs

$2 \times 6 =$ _____ $\begin{array}{r} 6 \\ \times 2 \\ \hline \end{array}$

_s into each carton.

_ltiplication to show how many

2.
$2 + 2 + 2 + 2 + 2 =$ _____

$5 \times 2 =$ _____

$2 \times 5 =$ _____

4. $2 \times 6 =$ _____   5. $\begin{array}{r} 4 \\ \times 2 \\ \hline \end{array}$ 6. $\begin{array}{r} 2 \\ \times 2 \\ \hline \end{array}$

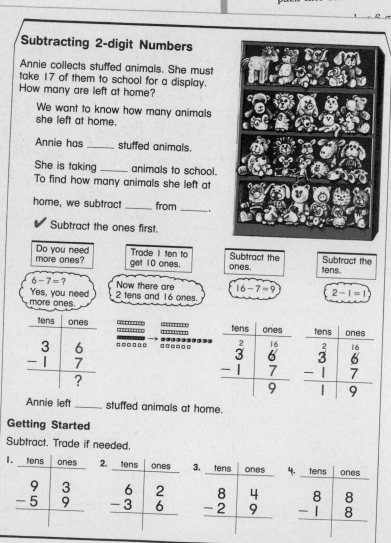

Subtracting 2-digit Numbers

Annie collects stuffed animals. She must take 17 of them to school for a display. How many are left at home?

We want to know how many animals she left at home.

Annie has _____ stuffed animals.

She is taking _____ animals to school. To find how many animals she left at

home, we subtract _____ from _____.

✔ Subtract the ones first.

Do you need more ones?	Trade 1 ten to get 10 ones.	Subtract the ones.	Subtract the tens.
$6 - 7 = ?$ Yes, you need more ones.	Now there are 2 tens and 16 ones.	$16 - 7 = 9$	$2 - 1 = 1$

tens	ones
3	6
−1	7
	?

tens	ones
$\overset{2}{3}$	$\overset{16}{6}$
−1	7
	9

tens	ones
$\overset{2}{3}$	$\overset{16}{6}$
−1	7
1	9

Annie left _____ stuffed animals at home.

Getting Started

Subtract. Trade if needed.

1.
tens	ones
9	3
−5	9

2.
tens	ones
6	2
−3	6

3.
tens	ones
8	4
−2	9

4.
tens	ones
8	8
−1	8

MCP All rights reserved

Subtracting 2-digit numbers, with trading

- Samples that the students work allow the teacher to check students' understanding of the skill.

- Students gain both confidence and competence in working these problems.

- If the objective is not fully grasped by the student, the **Table of Common Errors** will help the teacher deal with each individual type of error.

- Students gain a deeper understanding of the basic algorithm introduced in the developed model.

- New skills are reinforced through the sample problems students work right on the spot.

- Teachers observe any typical student errors before continuing additional work in the lesson.

- Teacher-guided practice activities will encourage classroom discussion.

- **Getting Started** activities help the teacher to single out predictable errors quickly.

- All samples found in the **Getting Started** activities prepare students to work the exercises found in the next part of the lesson.

Using Customary Units of Length

Robert, Janis and Jonathan are being measured for band uniforms. What is Robert's height in inches?

We want to rename Robert's height in inches.

We know that he is _____ feet _____ inches tall.

____ches as inches, we multiply ___ the number of inches in a ___ extra inches.

_____ and add _____.

| 12 inches (in.) = 1 foot (ft) |
| 3 feet = 1 yard (yd) |
| 36 inches = 1 yard |
| 5,280 feet = 1 mile (mi) |
| 1,760 yards = 1 mile |

___ll.

___ber like $5\frac{1}{2}$ feet as inches, we

_____ inches

___ as larger units, like 48 inches

___ rename larger units as
___ name smaller units as larger ones.

___ easurements of length.

3 yd 1 ft	1 yd = 3 ft
− 1 yd 2 ft	3 ft + 1 ft = 4 ft
1 yd 2 ft	

Add or subtract.

3. 6 ft 9 in.
   − 2 ft 11 in.

4. 7 yd 2 ft 3 in.
   − 5 yd 1 ft 6 in.

$1\frac{8}{9}$ yd

2 in.

217

Addition and Subtraction Properties

Properties are like special tools. They make the job of adding and subtracting much easier.

Twelve minus nine is three.

That's right because nine plus three is twelve.

Addition

Order Property
We can add in any order.

$5 + 2 = 7$ $2 + 5 = 7$

$3 + 6 + 7 = $ _____ $7 + 3 + 6 = $ _____

Grouping Property
We can change the grouping.

✔ Remember to add the numbers in parentheses first.

$(6 + 3) + 5 = 14$ $6 + (3 + 5) = 14$

$(8 + 2) + 4 = $ _____ $8 + (2 + 4) = $ _____

Zero Property
Adding zero makes the sum the same as the other addend.

$5 + 0 = 5$ $0 + 7 = 7$

$0 + 1 = $ _____ $8 + 0 = $ _____

Subtraction

Subtracting Zero
Subtracting zero makes the difference the same as the minuend.

$9 - 0 = 9$ $7 - 0 = $ _____

Subtracting a Number from Itself
Subtracting a number from itself leaves zero.

$8 - 8 = 0$ $3 - 3 = $ _____

Checking Subtraction
Subtracting is the reverse of adding.

$15 - 9 = 6$ because $6 + 9 = 15$

$12 - 7 = $ _____

because _____ + _____ = _____

✔ **Solving for** n is finding the value for the n in the equation.

Getting Started

Solve for n.

1. $0 + 0 = n$ 2. $0 + 6 = n$

$n = $ _____ $n = $ _____

Subtract. Check by adding.

3. 15
   − 9

4. 12
   − 7

5. 18
   − 9

Add. Check by grouping the addends another way.

6. 5
   3
  + 4

7. 2
   6
  + 3

8. 6
   3
  + 4

9. $(5 + 2) + 6 = n$

$n = $ _____

10. $3 + (5 + 4) = n$

$n = $ _____

3

INDEPENDENT PRACTICE ACTIVITIES PROVIDE PLENTY OF DRILL, PRACTICE, AND EXTENSION IN A VARIETY OF FORMATS!

The purpose of building skills is to ensure that students can use and apply those skills. That goal can only be reached when skills are clearly and systematically taught and then practiced. With *Modern Curriculum Press Mathematics,* the teacher can be as-sured that students will have abundant opportunities to practice their newly-learned math skills. The variety of practice activities allows the teacher to meet the needs of every student. Working independently helps students strengthen new skills, become more confident, and increase their under-standing. Practice helps students learn Some students need more practice tha others to help them catch on. *Modern Curriculum Press Mathematics* offers a variety of practice situations so that students stay on target with what they are learning.

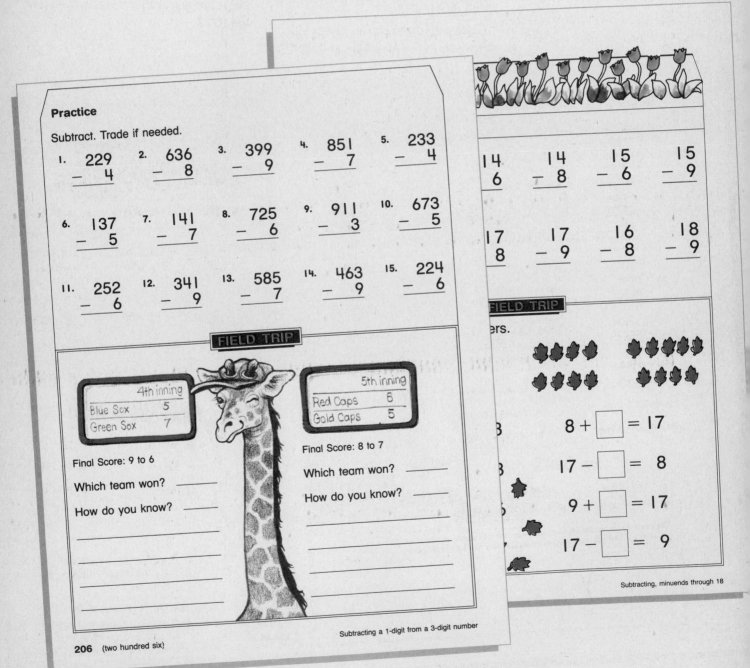

Practice

Subtract. Trade if needed.

1. 229 − 4
2. 636 − 8
3. 399 − 9
4. 851 − 7
5. 233 − 4

6. 137 − 5
7. 141 − 7
8. 725 − 6
9. 911 − 3
10. 673 − 5

11. 252 − 6
12. 341 − 9
13. 585 − 7
14. 463 − 9
15. 224 − 6

FIELD TRIP

4th inning
| Blue Sox | 5 |
| Green Sox | 7 |

Final Score: 9 to 6

Which team won? _____

How do you know? _____

_____

_____

5th inning
| Red Caps | 6 |
| Gold Caps | 5 |

Final Score: 8 to 7

Which team won? _____

How do you know? _____

_____

_____

206 (two hundred six)

Subtracting a 1-digit from a 3-digit number

14 − 6   14 − 8   15 − 6   15 − 9

17 − 8   17 − 9   16 − 8   18 − 9

FIELD TRIP

...ers.

8 + □ = 17

17 − □ = 8

9 + □ = 17

17 − □ = 9

Subtracting, minuends through 18

T-8

The teacher can begin the process of individual mastery by assigning **Practice** exercises that students can work independently.

■ *Modern Curriculum Press Mathematics* integrates problem solving into the practice activities with **Apply** problems. Some of these problems relate to the algorithm. However, some require previously-learned skills encouraging students to think and maintain skills.

■ Both vertical and horizontal forms of problems are used making students more comfortable with forms found in standardized test formats.

■ An emphasis on practical skills encourages learning by applying math to everyday situations.

■ Independent practice provides more opportunities for application and higher-order thinking skills.

■ The variety of practice activities keeps students motivated and interested in learning.

■ **Copy and Do** exercises check students' ability to assemble an algorithm from an equation and gives them practice in transferring information.

■ **Excursion** activities extend the basic skill work and are fun to do. The teacher can challenge the more capable students with these mind-stretching activities.

■ Giving students ample opportunities to practice and strengthen new skills builds solid skill development and helps the teacher more easily measure the results.

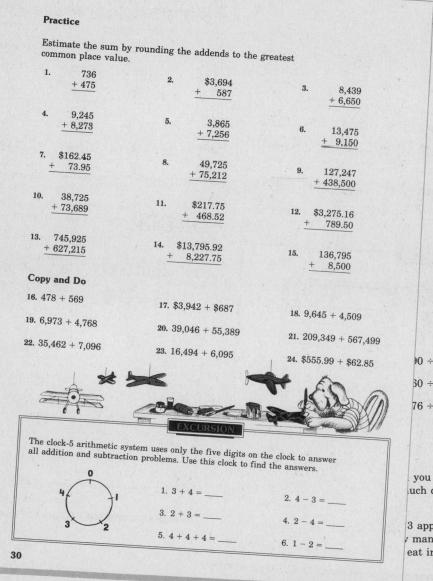

Practice

Estimate the sum by rounding the addends to the greatest common place value.

1. 736
    + 475

2. $3,694
    +   587

3.   8,439
    + 6,650

4.   9,245
    + 8,273

5.   3,865
    + 7,256

6.   13,475
    + 9,150

7. $162.45
    +   73.95

8.   49,725
    + 75,212

9.   127,247
    + 438,500

10. 38,725
    + 73,689

11. $217.75
    + 468.52

12. $3,275.16
    +   789.50

13. 745,925
    + 627,215

14. $13,795.92
    +   8,227.75

15.   136,795
    +   8,500

Copy and Do

16. 478 + 569

17. $3,942 + $687

18. 9,645 + 4,509

19. 6,973 + 4,768

20. 39,046 + 55,389

21. 209,349 + 567,499

22. 35,462 + 7,096

23. 16,494 + 6,095

24. $555.99 + $62.85

EXCURSION

The clock-5 arithmetic system uses only the five digits on the clock to answer all addition and subtraction problems. Use this clock to find the answers.

1. 3 + 4 = ____

2. 4 − 3 = ____

3. 2 + 3 = ____

4. 2 − 4 = ____

5. 4 + 4 + 4 = ____

6. 1 − 2 = ____

30

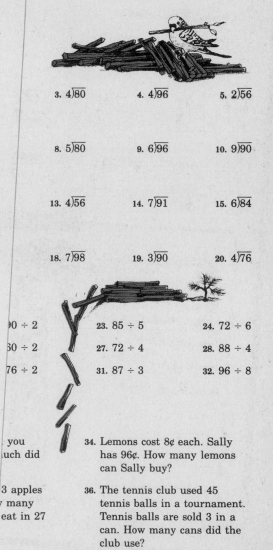

3. 4)80   4. 4)96   5. 2)56

8. 5)80   9. 6)96   10. 9)90

13. 4)56   14. 7)91   15. 6)84

18. 7)98   19. 3)90   20. 4)76

90 ÷ 2   23. 85 ÷ 5   24. 72 ÷ 6

60 ÷ 2   27. 72 ÷ 4   28. 88 ÷ 4

76 ÷ 2   31. 87 ÷ 3   32. 96 ÷ 8

you much did

3 apples many eat in 27

34. Lemons cost 8¢ each. Sally has 96¢. How many lemons can Sally buy?

36. The tennis club used 45 tennis balls in a tournament. Tennis balls are sold 3 in a can. How many cans did the club use?

MATH COMES ALIVE WHEN STUDENTS LEARN TO INTEGRATE COMPUTATION, PROBLEM-SOLVING STRATEGIES, AND REASONING TO MAKE DECISIONS FOR THEMSELVES!

Problem-solving pages present lessons that increase understanding with a four-step teaching strategy: SEE, PLAN, DO, CHECK. *Modern Curriculum Press Mathematics* offers step-by-step instruction in how to understand word problems as well as varied practice in actually using the skills learned. Each lesson focuses on a different problem-solving strategy. These strategies develop students' higher-order thinking skills and help them successfully solve problems. Step-by-step, students will understand the question, find the information needed, plan a solution, and then check it for accuracy. This develops students' critical-thinking skills and ability to apply what they've learned to solve problems that go beyond basic operations.

■ Word problems utilize high-interest information and focus on everyday situations.

PROBLEM SOLVING

Drawing a Picture

A parking lot has 9 rows of 8 parking spaces each. The fourth and fifth spaces in every third row have trees in them. The outside spaces in every row are reserved for the handicapped or for emergency vehicles. How many regular parking spaces are there in the lot?

★ SEE
We want to know how many spaces are left for regular parking.

There are _____ rows of parking spaces.

There are _____ spaces in each row.

In every third row, _____ spaces are lost to trees.

In every row _____ spaces are used for special vehicles.

★ PLAN
We can draw a picture of the parking lot, crossing out the closed parking spaces. Then we can count the regular spaces left.

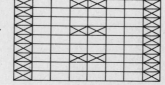

★ DO
We count _____ spaces left for regular parking.

★ CHECK
We can check by adding the spaces open in each row.

$4 + 6 + 6 + 4 + 6 + 6 + 4 + 6 + 6 =$ _____

MCP All rights reserved

173

...ach problem.
...n.

2. A Super-Duper ball bounces twice its height when it is dropped. Carl dropped a Super-Duper ball from the roof of a 12-foot garage. How high will the ball bounce after 5 bounces?

4. The distance around a rectangle is 10 centimeters. The length of each of the two longer sides is 3 centimeters. What is the length of each of the two shorter sides?

6. What 7 coins together make 50 cents?

- Step by step, students learn to understand the question, find the information they need, plan a method of solution, find an answer, and check it for accuracy.

- Every step of the process is organized so that students truly understand how to arrive at the solution.

- The problem-solving banner alerts students that they are involved in a problem-solving lesson. These focused lessons remind students how to approach problems and how to use skills and specific strategies already learned.

- Learning to integrate computation, problem-solving strategies, and reasoning makes math come alive for students.

- Problems incorporate previously taught computational skills—focusing students' minds on the problem-solving process itself.

- Problem-solving applications appear in every problem-solving lesson. This frequent practice reduces apprehension and builds confidence.

- Practice in applying the strategies gives students a chance to use skills in routine and non-routine problems.

- In every chapter, problem-solving strategies and critical-thinking skills are developed, applied, and reinforced.

- Students choose appropriate strategies to solve problems and are challenged to formulate their own problems and to change the conditions in existing problems.

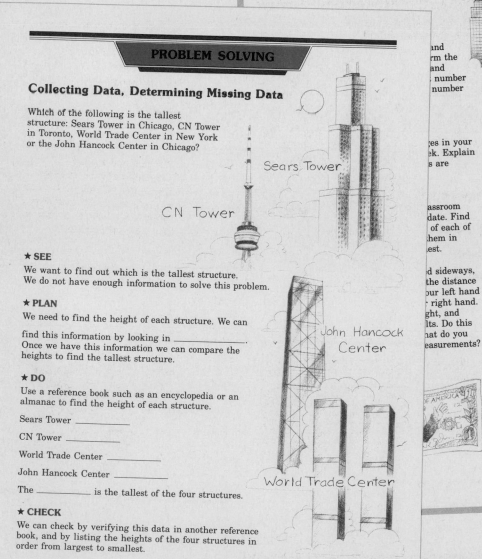

PROBLEM SOLVING

Collecting Data, Determining Missing Data

Which of the following is the tallest structure: Sears Tower in Chicago, CN Tower in Toronto, World Trade Center in New York or the John Hancock Center in Chicago?

★ SEE

We want to find out which is the tallest structure.
We do not have enough information to solve this problem.

★ PLAN

We need to find the height of each structure. We can

find this information by looking in _____.
Once we have this information we can compare the heights to find the tallest structure.

★ DO

Use a reference book such as an encyclopedia or an almanac to find the height of each structure.

Sears Tower _____

CN Tower _____

World Trade Center _____

John Hancock Center _____

The _____ is the tallest of the four structures.

★ CHECK

We can check by verifying this data in another reference book, and by listing the heights of the four structures in order from largest to smallest.

2. Roll a pair of dice 30 times and record the number of times each sum appears. Perform the experiment a second time. What sum appears most often? What sum appears least often?

4. Toss a coin 50 times and record the number of heads and tails. Which side of the coin appears most often?

6. Record the dates of the coins available in your classroom. How many years difference exist between the newest and oldest coin?

8. An arithmetic game is created by adding the values of certain U.S. currency. Since a portrait of George Washington appears on a $1 bill and a portrait of Abraham Lincoln appears on the $5 bill, we say that George Washington + Abraham Lincoln = $6. Find the value of Thomas Jefferson + Alexander Hamilton + Woodrow Wilson.

CHAPTER TEST PAGES PROVIDE A VEHICLE FOR STUDENT EVALUATION AND FEEDBACK!

Every chapter in *Modern Curriculum Press Mathematics* concludes with a **Chapter Test.** These tests provide the opportunity for students to demonstrate their mastery of recently acquired skills. **Chapter Test** pages enable the teacher to measure all the basic skills students have practiced in the lesson and evaluate their understanding. The focus of these pages is the assessing of mastery of algorithms. An adequate number of sample problems are provided to accomplish this. This important checkpoint helps the teacher to better meet individual student-computational needs.

■ **Chapter Test** pages are carefully correlated to what has been taught throughout the entire series.

■ **Chapter Test** pages assess students' mastery of all the skills taught in the lesson.

■ All directions are written in an easy-to-follow format.

■ Both vertical and horizontal forms of problems are used making students more comfortable with exercises found in standardized tests.

■ In the back of each student book, there is an alternate **Chapter Test** for each chapter based on the same objectives covered in the first test.

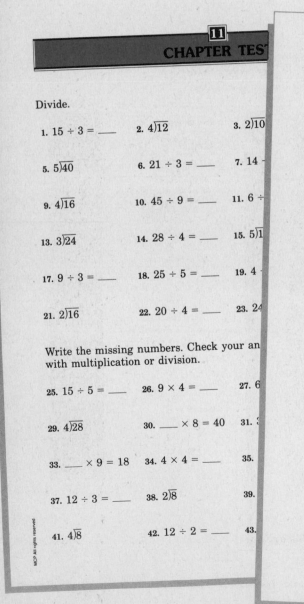

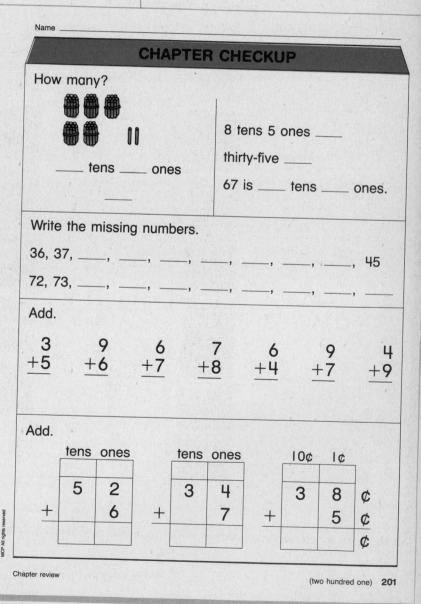

Systematic Maintenance Is Provided At Every Level With Cumulative Review Pages!

Every chapter contains a **Cumulative Review** page that provides an on-going refresher course in basic skills. These pages maintain the skills that have been taught in the chapter plus the skills learned in previous chapters.

Cumulative Review pages actually reach back into the text for a total maintenance of skills. **Cumulative Review** pages are progressive instruction because they build on the foundation laid earlier for a thorough and sequential program of review. A standardized test format is used beginning at the middle of the second grade. Students will benefit by gaining experience in dealing with this special test format.

■ A variety of problems done in standardized test format give students a better chance to score well on these tests.

■ Directions are minimal and easy to understand.

■ Design elements on every test are the same found on standardized tests.

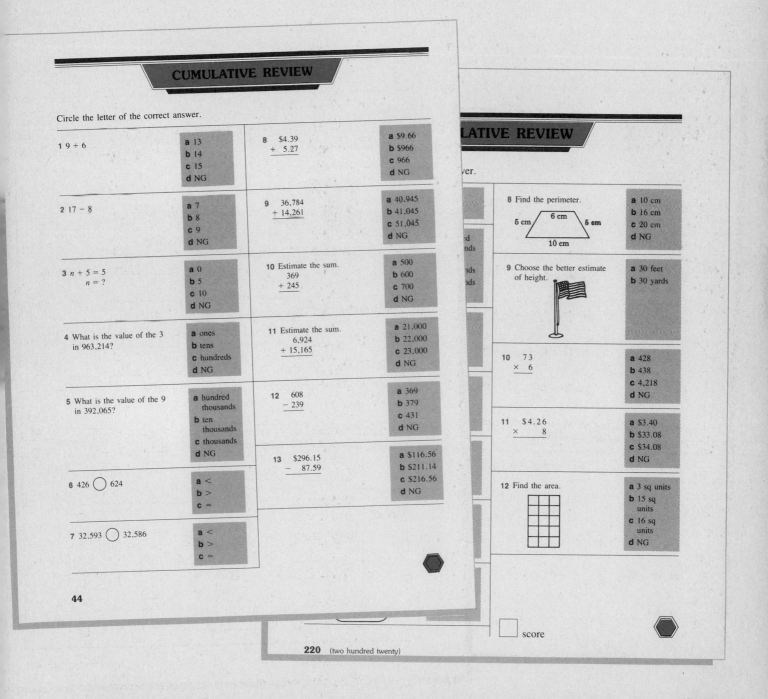

CUMULATIVE REVIEW

Circle the letter of the correct answer.

1 9 + 6
   a 13
   b 14
   c 15
   d NG

2 17 − 8
   a 7
   b 8
   c 9
   d NG

3 $n + 5 = 5$
   $n = ?$
   a 0
   b 5
   c 10
   d NG

4 What is the value of the 3 in 963,214?
   a ones
   b tens
   c hundreds
   d NG

5 What is the value of the 9 in 392,065?
   a hundred thousands
   b ten thousands
   c thousands
   d NG

6 426 ◯ 624
   a <
   b >
   c =

7 32,593 ◯ 32,586
   a <
   b >
   c =

8 $4.39 + 5.27
   a $9.66
   b $966
   c 966
   d NG

9 36,784 + 14,261
   a 40,945
   b 41,045
   c 51,045
   d NG

10 Estimate the sum.
   369 + 245
   a 500
   b 600
   c 700
   d NG

11 Estimate the sum.
   6,924 + 15,165
   a 21,000
   b 22,000
   c 23,000
   d NG

12 608 − 239
   a 369
   b 379
   c 431
   d NG

13 $296.15 − 87.59
   a $116.56
   b $211.14
   c $216.56
   d NG

44

...LATIVE REVIEW

8 Find the perimeter.
   (trapezoid: 5 cm, 6 cm, 5 cm, 10 cm)
   a 10 cm
   b 16 cm
   c 20 cm
   d NG

9 Choose the better estimate of height.
   a 30 feet
   b 30 yards

10 73 × 6
   a 428
   b 438
   c 4,218
   d NG

11 $4.26 × 8
   a $3.40
   b $33.08
   c $34.08
   d NG

12 Find the area.
   a 3 sq units
   b 15 sq units
   c 16 sq units
   d NG

☐ score

CALCULATOR LESSONS PROVIDE EXCITING LEARNING ACTIVITIES AND ADD INTEREST AND PRACTICALITY TO MATH!

Calculator lessons are found throughout *Modern Curriculum Press Mathematics*. The activities are used in many ways—to explore number patterns, to do calculations, to check estimations, and to investigate functions. Each **Calculator** lesson is designed to help students learn to use and operate calculators while they reinforce and improve their mathematical skills.

■ **Calculator** lessons teach students to use simple calculators while reinforcing chapter content.

■ **Calculator** lessons introduce student to basic calculator skills and terms.

■ Practical calculator activities promot student involvement as they take an active part in what they are learning.

■ Students learn, practice, and apply critical-thinking skills as they use calculators.

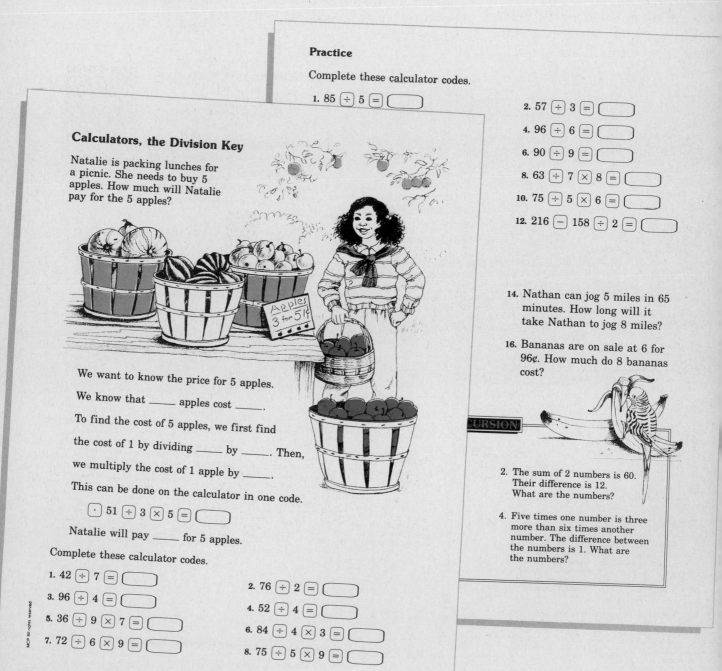

Practice

Complete these calculator codes.

1. 85 ÷ 5 = ☐

2. 57 ÷ 3 = ☐
4. 96 ÷ 6 = ☐
6. 90 ÷ 9 = ☐
8. 63 ÷ 7 × 8 = ☐
10. 75 ÷ 5 × 6 = ☐
12. 216 − 158 ÷ 2 = ☐

14. Nathan can jog 5 miles in 65 minutes. How long will it take Nathan to jog 8 miles?

16. Bananas are on sale at 6 for 96¢. How much do 8 bananas cost?

EXCURSION

2. The sum of 2 numbers is 60. Their difference is 12. What are the numbers?

4. Five times one number is three more than six times another number. The difference between the numbers is 1. What are the numbers?

Calculators, the Division Key

Natalie is packing lunches for a picnic. She needs to buy 5 apples. How much will Natalie pay for the 5 apples?

Apples 3 for 51¢

We want to know the price for 5 apples.

We know that ____ apples cost ____.

To find the cost of 5 apples, we first find the cost of 1 by dividing ____ by ____. Then, we multiply the cost of 1 apple by ____.

This can be done on the calculator in one code.

· 51 ÷ 3 × 5 = ☐

Natalie will pay ____ for 5 apples.

Complete these calculator codes.

1. 42 ÷ 7 = ☐
3. 96 ÷ 4 = ☐
5. 36 ÷ 9 × 7 = ☐
7. 72 ÷ 6 × 9 = ☐

2. 76 ÷ 2 = ☐
4. 52 ÷ 4 = ☐
6. 84 ÷ 4 × 3 = ☐
8. 75 ÷ 5 × 9 = ☐

MCP All rights reserved

139

T-14

PLAN CLASSROOM-READY MATH LESSONS IN MINUTES WITH COMPREHENSIVE TEACHER'S EDITIONS!

The **Teacher's Editions** of *Modern Curriculum Press Mathematics* are designed and organized with the teacher in mind. The full range of options provides more help than ever before and guarantees efficient use of the teacher's planning time and the most effective results for efforts exerted.

Each **Teacher's Edition** provides an abundance of additional **Enrichment, Correcting Common Errors** and application activities. Plus they contain a complete **Error Pattern Analysis.** The teacher will also find reduced student pages with answers, objectives, suggestions for teaching lessons, materials, **Mental Math** exercises, and more.

■ There's no need for the teacher to struggle with two separate books because student pages are reduced in the **Teacher's Edition.**

■ Clear headings and notes make it easy for the teacher to find what is needed before teaching the lesson.

■ The teacher will be more effective with lesson plans that are always complete in two pages and include everything needed.

■ Student **Objectives** set a clear course for the lesson goal.

Time to the Half-hour
pages 163-164

Objective
To practice telling time to the hour and half-hour

Materials
* Demonstration clock
* Two pencils of different lengths

Mental Math
Which is less?
1. 2 dimes or 5 nickels (2 dimes)
2. 14 pennies or 2 nickels (2 nickels)
3. 5 nickels or 4 dimes (5 nickels)
4. 1 quarter or 2 dimes (2 dimes)
5. 6 nickels or 1 quarter (1 quarter)

Skill Review
Show times to the hour and half hour on the demonstration clock. Have students write the time on the board. Now have a student set the clock to show an hour or half-hour. Have the student ask another student to write the time on the board. Have a student write a time for the hour or half-hour and invite another student to place the hands on the clock to show the times.

Name _____

Match the clocks

MCP All rights reserved.

Telling time to the hour and half-hour

Teaching page 163
On the demonstration clock, start at 12:00 and slowly move the minute hand around the clock. Ask students to tell what the hour hand does as the minute hand moves slowly around the clock face. (moves slowly toward the next number) Tell students the minute hand moves around the clock face 60 minutes while the hour hand moves from one number to the next. Tell students there are 60 minutes in 1 hour.

Ask students to tell where the hour hand is on the first clock. (between 5 and 6) Ask where the minute hand is. (on 6) Ask the time. (5:30) Tell students to find 5:30 in the center column and trace the line from the clock to 5:30. Tell students to draw a line from each clock to its time.

Multiplying, the Factor 5
pages 125-126

Objective
To multiply by the factor 5

Materials
none

Mental Math
Ask students to multiply 4 by:
1. the number of ears one person has. (4 × 2 = 8)
2. the number of feet two students have. (4 × 4 = 16)
3. the number of noses in a crowd of 7. (4 × 7 = 28)
4. the number of their toes. (4 × 10 = 40)

Skill Review
Have students make up a multiplication chart. Tell them to write 2, 3, 4 along the top, 2 through 10 along the side. Tell them to fill in the chart by multiplying each top number by each side number.

Multiplying, the Factor 5

Each key on a calculator has a special job to do. How many keys are there on the calculator keyboard?

We need to find the total number of keys on the calculator.

We can see there are __5__ rows of keys.

Each row has __5__ keys.

We can add. $5 + 5 + 5 + 5 + 5 =$ __25__

We can also multiply.

$5 \times 5 =$ __25__ $\begin{array}{r} 5 \\ \times 5 \\ \hline 25 \end{array}$

There are __25__ keys on the calculator keyboard.

Getting Started

Use both addition and multiplication to show how many are in the picture.

1.
$5 + 5 + 5 + 5 =$ __20__
$4 \times 5 =$ __20__
$5 \times 4 =$ __20__

Multiply.

2. $\begin{array}{r} 3 \\ \times 5 \\ \hline 15 \end{array}$ 3. $\begin{array}{r} 8 \\ \times 5 \\ \hline 40 \end{array}$ 4. $5 \times 6 =$ __30__   5. $9 \times 5 =$ __45__

(one hundred twenty-five) **125**

Teaching the Lesson

Introducing the Problem Have students look at the calculator illustrated while you read the problem. Identify the question and explain that there are several ways they could answer it. Have students read the information sentences, filling in the information required. (5 rows, 5 keys) Read each sentence and tell students to do the indicated operation in their text while one student writes it on the board. Read the solution sentence aloud and have a student give the answer while the others complete that sentence in their texts. (30)

Developing the Skill Have students start at 5 and count aloud by five's through 50. Ask a volunteer to continue through 100. Explain that this may seem easy because they are used to counting out nickels. Because five is also half of ten, and when counting by fives, every other number will be a multiple of ten. Now write these addition problems on the board and have students work them: **5 + 5 =** , **5 + 5 + 5 =** , **5 + 5 + 5 + 5 =** . (10, 15, 20) Next to each of these problems write the multiplication problem that corresponds. (5 × 2, 5 × 3, 5 × 4) Have volunteers put the rest of the addition and multiplication problems for the factor five on the board, 5 × 5 through 5 × 10.

- A list of **Materials** helps the teacher reduce class preparation time.
- The **Mental Math** exercise gives the teacher an opportunity to brush-up on skills at the beginning of each day's lesson.
- **Skill Review** bridges new skills with previously-taught skills for total reinforcement.

- The **Teaching the Lesson** section is meant to give practical suggestions for introducing the problem and developing the skill. Specific suggestions for an effective presentation of the model are made in **Introducing the Problem.**

- In **Developing the Skill,** the teacher is given suggestions for presenting and developing the algorithm, skill, and/or concept. Where practical, recommendations are made for the use of manipulatives.

Zeros in Minuend

pages 69-70

Objective

To subtract 4- or 5-digit numbers when minuends have zeros

Materials

* thousands, hundreds, tens, ones jars
* place value materials

Mental Math

Tell students to answer true or false:

1. 776 has 77 tens. (T)
2. 10 hundreds < 1,000. (F)
3. 46 is an odd number. (F)
4. 926 can be rounded to 920. (F)
5. 72 hours = 3 days. (T)
6. 42 ÷ 6 > 7 × 1. (F)
7. 1/3 of 18 = 1/2 of 12. (T)
8. perimeter = L × W. (F)

Skill Review

Write 4 numbers of 3- to 5-digits each on the board. Have students arrange the numbers in order, from the least to the greatest, and then read the numbers as they would appear if written from the greatest to the least. Repeat for more sets of 4 or 5 numbers.

Subtracting, More Minuends with Zeros

The Susan B. Anthony School held its annual fall Read-a-Thon. How many more pages did the fifth grade read than the second-place class?

We want to know how many more pages the fifth grade read than the second-place class.

We know the fifth grade read __5,003__ pages.

The second-place class is the __sixth__ grade.

It read __4,056__ pages.
To find the difference between the number of pages, we subtract __4,056__ from __5,003__.

✔ Remember to trade from one place value at a time.

$$\begin{array}{r} 9\ \ 9 \\ 5,0\overset{\scriptstyle 9\ \ 9}{0}3 \\ -\ 4,056 \\ \hline 947 \end{array}$$

The fifth grade read __947__ more pages than the sixth grade.

Class Reading Records

Fourth Grade	3,795 pages
Fifth Grade	5,003 pages
Sixth Grade	4,056 pages

Getting Started

Subtract.

1.
$$\begin{array}{r} 3,005 \\ -\ 1,348 \\ \hline 1,657 \end{array}$$

2.
$$\begin{array}{r} \$40.09 \\ -\ \ \ 9.75 \\ \hline \$30.34 \end{array}$$

3.
$$\begin{array}{r} 3,300 \\ -\ 1,856 \\ \hline 1,444 \end{array}$$

4.
$$\begin{array}{r} \$50.00 \\ -\ \ 27.26 \\ \hline \$22.74 \end{array}$$

5.
$$\begin{array}{r} 8,512 \\ -\ 7,968 \\ \hline 544 \end{array}$$

6.
$$\begin{array}{r} \$90.17 \\ -\ \ 20.87 \\ \hline \$69.30 \end{array}$$

Copy and subtract.

7. 26,007 − 18,759
7,248

8. 70,026 − 23,576
46,450

9. $900.05 − $267.83
$632.22

69

MCP All rights reserved

Teaching the Lesson

Introducing the Problem Have a student read the problem. Ask students what 2 problems are to be solved. (which class read the second-highest number of pages and how many more pages the first-place fifth graders read) Ask students how we can find out which class came in second place. (arrange numbers from the table in order from greatest to least) Ask a student to write the numbers from greatest to least on the board. (5,003, 4,056, 3,795) Have students complete the sentences and work through the model problem with them.

Developing the Skill Write **4,000−2,875** vertically on the board. Ask students if a trade is needed to subtract the ones column. (yes) Tell students that since there are no tens and no hundreds, we must trade 1 thousand for 10 hundreds. Show the 3 thousands and 10 hundreds left. Now tell students we can trade 1 hundred for 10 tens. Show the trade with 9 hundreds and 10 tens left. Tell students we can now trade 1 ten for 10 ones. Show the trade so that 9 tens and 10 ones are left. Tell students we can now subtract each column beginning with the ones column and working to the left. Show students the subtraction to a solution of **1,125.** Remind students to add the subtrahend and the difference to check the work. Repeat for more problems with zeros in the minuend.

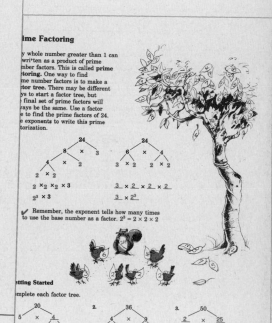

Prime Factoring

Any whole number greater than 1 can be written as a product of prime number factors. This is called **prime factoring.** One way to find the prime number factors is to make a factor tree. There may be different ways to start a factor tree, but the final set of prime factors will always be the same. Use a factor tree to find the prime factors of 24. Use exponents to write this prime factorization.

$$\begin{array}{ccc} 24 & & 24 \\ 4 \times 6 & & 6 \times 4 \\ 2 \times 2 & 3 \times 2 & 2 \times 3 \quad 2 \times 2 \\ \\ 2 \times 2 \times 2 \times 3 & & 3 \times 2 \times 2 \times 2 \\ 2^3 \times 3 & & 3 \times 2^3 \end{array}$$

✔ Remember, the exponent tells how many times to use the base number as a factor. $2^3 = 2 \times 2 \times 2$

Getting Started

Complete each factor tree.

1.
20
5 × 4
2 × 2

2.
36
4 × 9
2 × 2 3 × 3

3.
50
2 × 25
5 × 5

Write each prime factorization using exponents if possible.

4. 8
2^3

5. 35
5×7

6. 48
$2^4 \times 3$

7. 72
$2^3 \times 3^2$

8. 400
$2^4 \times 5^2$

99

...composite ...ctors. Tell ...e factor- ...h aloud, ...he tree ...r tree on ...t a num- ...of prime ...d. Have ...f each

Developing the Skill Point out that when a prime number is used more than once in the prime factoring, it can be expressed with an **exponent.** Remind students that 2^3 is the same as $2 \times 2 \times 2$. Stress that the 3 in 2^3 is an exponent, and that this exponent tells the number of times 2 is used as a factor. Have students complete each of the following factor trees and then write each prime factorization using exponents:

$$\begin{array}{cc} 50 & 28 \\ 2 \times (25) & 7 \times (4) \\ (2) \times (5) \times (5) & (7) \times (2) \times (2) \\ (2 \times 5^2) & (7 \times 2^2) \end{array}$$

s the

FREQUENT ATTENTION IS GIVEN TO CORRECTING COMMON ERRORS, ENRICHMENT AND OPTIONAL EXTRA-CREDIT ACTIVITIES!

These comprehensive **Teacher's Editions** are intended to provide the teacher with a convenient, well-structured approach to teaching mathematics. From motivating introductory exercises to challenging extension activities, *Modern Curriculum Press*

Mathematics **Teacher's Editions** suggest a complete step-by-step plan to insure successful learning. The succinct lesson plans help the teacher provide solid math instruction to students.

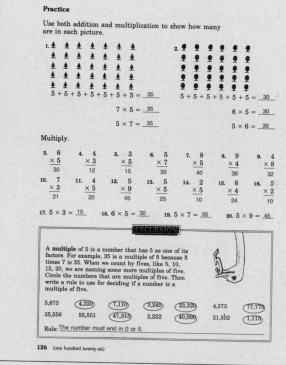

Practice

Use both addition and multiplication to show how many are in each picture.

1. 5 + 5 + 5 + 5 + 5 + 5 = ___35___

   7 × 5 = ___35___

   5 × 7 = ___35___

2. 5 + 5 + 5 + 5 + 5 + 5 = ___30___

   6 × 5 = ___30___

   5 × 6 = ___30___

Multiply.

3. 6 ×5 = 30	4. 4 ×3 = 12	5. 3 ×5 = 15	6. 5 ×7 = 35	7. 8 ×5 = 40	8. 9 ×4 = 36	9. 4 ×8 = 32	
10. 7 ×3 = 21	11. 4 ×5 = 20	12. 5 ×9 = 45	13. 5 ×5 = 25	14. 2 ×5 = 10	15. 6 ×4 = 24	16. 5 ×2 = 10	

17. 5 × 3 = __15__   18. 6 × 5 = __30__   19. 5 × 7 = __35__   20. 5 × 9 = __45__

EXCURSION

A **multiple** of 5 is a number that has 5 as one of its factors. For example, 35 is a multiple of 5 because 5 times 7 is 35. When we count by fives, like 5, 10, 15, 20, we are naming some more multiples of five. Circle the numbers that are multiples of five. Then write a rule to use for deciding if a number is a multiple of five.

5,673   (4,220)   (7,110)   (3,245)   (23,320)   4,373   (77,770)

35,556   55,551   (47,315)   2,222   (40,000)   21,502   (1,115)

Rule: The number must end in 0 or 5.

126   (one hundred twenty-six)

Correcting Common Errors

If students have difficulty learning facts of 5, have them practice with partners. Have them draw a vertical number line from 0 through 50, marking it in intervals of 5. Have one partner write the addition problem to the left of each multiple of five on the number line while the other partner writes the corresponding multiplication problem.

```
            ⌐0
        5  ⌐5    (5 × 1)
      5 + 5 ⌐10   (5 × 2)
    5 + 5 + 5 ⌐15   (5 × 3)
  5 + 5 + 5 + 5 ⌐20  (5 × 4)
```

Enrichment

Ask students how many fives are in 55 if, there are 10 fives in 50. (11) Tell them to complete a multiplication table for fives that goes up to the product 150. Have them use the table to figure the number of nickels in $4.00. (80)

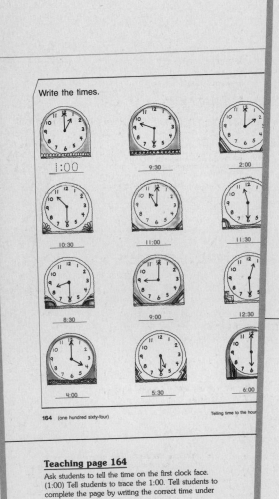

Write the times.

1:00   9:30   2:00

10:30   11:00   11:30

8:30   9:00   12:30

4:00   5:30   6:00

164   (one hundred sixty-four)   Telling time to the hour

Teaching page 164

Ask students to tell the time on the first clock face. (1:00) Tell students to trace the 1:00. Tell students to complete the page by writing the correct time under each clock.

Practice

Have students do all the problems on the page. Remind the class that they can use addition to figure out any multiplication facts they are not sure of.

Excursion

Have students write the multiples of 5 through 200. Help students to see that any number that ends in 0 or 5 is a multiple of 5. Have students write the rule. Now write several 4- and 5-digit numbers on the board and ask students to circle the numbers that are multiples of 5.

Extra Credit   *Logic*

Write the following on the board:

WOW	TOT	POP	BIB
525	969	343	5445

Ask students what all of these have in common. Explain they are palindromes, or words or numbers which are the same whether they are read forward or backward. Also, explain 302 is not a palindrome, but if you reverse the numbers and add, it will make a palindrome:

```
  302
+ 203
  505
```

Using this method, ask students what palindrome they can make with these numbers: 36; (99) 342; (585) 4,205; (9,229) 3,406 (9,449). Have students list some other numbers which, when reversed and added, will form a palindrome.

- Follow up activities f ... ing **Common Errors, Er** ... **Extra Credit** suggestions.

- In the **Correcting Common Errors** feature, a common error pattern is explored and a method of remediation is recommended. Collectively, all the **Correcting Common Errors** features in any chapter constitute a complete set

n **Correct- ent,** and of the common errors likely to be committed by the students when working in that area of mathematics.

- **Enrichment** activities are a direct extension of the skills being taught. Students can do these activities on their own while the teacher works with those students who need more help.

- **Extra Credits** are challenging independent activities to expand the mathematical experiences of the students. The **Extra Credit** section encompasses a wide variety of activities and projects and introduces and extends skills taught in the normal basal curriculum—including statistics, logic, and probability.

Practice

Subtract.

1. 3,004 − 2,356 **648**
2. 8,002 − 5,096 **2,906**
3. 3,891 − 1,750 **2,141**
4. $20.08 − 15.99 **$4.09**
5. 4,020 − 1,865 **2,155**
6. $87.00 − 28.59 **$58.41**
7. 3,007 − 2,090 **917**
8. $50.06 − 37.08 **$12.98**
9. 19,006 − 8,275 **10,731**
10. 20,006 − 14,758 **5,248**
11. $400.26 − 236.58 **$163.68**
12. $793.42 − 253.87 **$539.55**

Copy and Do

13. 4,001 − 2,756 **1,245**
14. $70.05 − $26.59 **$43.46**
15. 8,060 − 7,948 **112**
16. 7,007 − 2,468 **4,539**
17. 21,316 − 12,479 **8,837**
18. 14,000 − 8,396 **5,604**
19. $100.21 − $93.50 **$6.71**
20. 60,004 − 51,476 **8,528**
21. 52,006 − 9,037 **42,969**
22. $800.00 − $275.67 **$524.33**
23. 34,612 − 29,965 **4,647**
24. 50,010 − 36,754 **13,256**

Apply

Use the chart on page 69 to help solve these problems.

25. How many pages did the three classes read all together? **12,854 pages**

26. How many more pages did the sixth grade read than the fourth grade? **261 pages**

70

Correcting Common Errors

Some students may bring down the numbers that are being subtracted when there are zeros in the minuend.

INCORRECT	CORRECT
3,006 − 1,425 = 2,421	3,006 − 1,425 = 1,581

Have students work in pairs and use play money to model a problem such as $300 − $142, where they see that they must trade 3 hundreds for 2 hundreds, 9 tens, and 10 ones before they can subtract.

Enrichment

Tell students to find out the year in which each member of their family was born, and make a chart to show how old each will be in the year 2000.

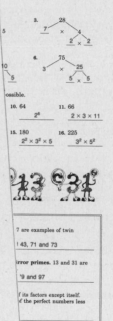

Practice

Remind students to begin with the ones column, work to the left and trade from one place value at a time. Have students complete the page independently.

Extra Credit *Biography*

An American inventor, Samuel Morse, struggled for many years before his inventions, the electric telegraph and Morse code were recognized. Morse was born in Massachusetts in 1791, and studied to be an artist. On a trip home from Europe, Morse heard his shipmates discussing the idea of sending electricity over wire. Intrigued, Morse spent the rest of the voyage formulating his ideas about how this could be accomplished. Morse taught at a university in New York City, and used his earnings to continue development of his telegraph. After five years, Morse demonstrated his invention, but found very little support. After years of requests for support, Congress finally granted Morse $30,000 to test his invention. He dramatically strung a telegraph wire from Washington, D.C. to Baltimore, Maryland, and relayed the message, "What hath God wrought" using Morse code. Morse's persistence finally won him wealth and fame. A statue honoring him was unveiled in New York City one year before his death in 1872.

Correcting Common Errors

Some students do not write the prime factorization of a number correctly because they cannot identify prime numbers. Have them work with partners to name all the prime numbers from 1 to 50 and write them on an index card. The students can use these cards as a guide for this work.

Enrichment

Provide this alternative method of dividing to find prime factorization of a number. Tell students they must always divide by a prime number.

$$2 \underline{|\ 36} \quad\quad 36 = 2^2 \times 3^2$$
$$2 \underline{|\ 18}$$
$$3 \underline{|\ 9}$$
$$3$$

Have students use this method to find the prime factorization of: 120 ($2^3 \times 3 \times 5$); 250 ($5^3 \times 2$); 1,000 ($2^3 \times 5^3$); 72 ($3^2 \times 2^3$)

Extra Credit *Applications*

Have a student write the primary United States time zones across the board. Discuss how this pattern continues around the world. Divide students into groups and provide them with globes or flat maps. Have students choose various cities in the United States and elsewhere in the world, and determine what the time would be in those cities when it is 6:00 AM in their home city. Have students make another list of cities without times indicated to exchange with classmates to figure time comparisons.

100

Bibliography

Suggested Mathematics Software for Grades 4–6

The list that follows is only a sampling of the many interesting and effective commercial software programs that are available in the marketplace. These and many of the mathematical programs that are published every year have a high degree of correlation with the objectives, goals and content of **Modern Curriculum Press Mathematics.**

Estimation Quick Solve. Minneapolis, MN: MECC, 1990. (Apple)

This program offers practice in estimation skills in a timed game. Playing against the computer or opponents, students are given enough time to estimate an answer to problems involving operations, whole numbers, fractions, decimals, percents, and measurements.

Exploring Measurement, Time, and Money, Level III. Dayton, NJ: IBM, 1990. (IBM)

Combining a tutorial with drill and practice, this program focuses on rounding, measurements of weight, length, time, money, and temperature.

The Factory: Strategies in Problem Solving. Cappo, Marge and Mike Fish. Scotts Valley, CA: Wings for Learning, 1991.

Students make decisions on how to operate an assembly line that turns out geometric products. They choose the appropriate tools and the most logical order to create a specified end-product.

The Geometric preSupposer: Points and Lines. Education Development Center, Judah L. Schwartz, Michal Yerushalmy. Pleasantville, NY: Sunburst Communications, 1986. (Apple, IBM)

Students learn about basic geometric concepts by drawing shapes and experimenting with lengths, angles, perimeter, area, and circumference.

How the West Was One + Three × Four. Bonnie Seiler. Pleasantville, NY: Sunburst Communications, 1989. (Apple, IBM)

A train and a stagecoach race each other down a number trail. In this problem-solving game, students practice working with the order of operations and the use of parentheses.

Math Blaster Mystery. Torrance, CA: Davidson and Associates, 1991. (Apple, IBM, Mac)

Everyone loves a mystery! In four different activities, students build problem-solving skills as they use whole numbers, fractions, decimals, percents, and pre-algebraic equations.

Math Shop. Jefferson City, MO: Scholastic, 1990. (Apple, IBM, Mac)

In the familiar setting of a mall, students become clerks at stores and practice their math skills involving basic arithmetic operations, fractions, decimals, percents, ratios, linear measurement, coins, and equations with two variables.

New Math Blaster Plus. Torrance, CA: Davidson, 1990. (Apple, IBM, Mac)

Using fast-paced, arcade-like games, this program builds skills in addition, subtraction, multiplication, division, fractions, decimals, and percents. Teachers can print customized tests.

Number Maze Decimals and Fractions. Scotts Valley, CA: Great Wave Software, 1990. (Mac)

Students gain admittance to fascinating mazes by answering questions involving decimals and fractions. Students must add and subtract decimals and fractions and convert from decimals to fractions.

Number Munchers. Minneapolis, MN: MECC, 1986. (Apple, IBM, Mac)

Students control a number-munching monster. If the monster eats the correct answer, the student moves on to the next level. The program drills concepts such as multiples 2–20, factoring of numbers 3–99, prime numbers 1–99, and equality and inequality.

Return of the Dinosaurs. Oklahoma City, OK: American Educational Computer, 1988. (Apple, IBM)

A dinosaur is running through the town and someone must catch it and take it back to its home. In this problem-solving program, students use thinking, observing, and planning skills to guess the best way to catch up with the dinosaur. Along the way, they learn how to use a database and maps.

Stickybear Math 2. Norfolk, CT: Optimum Resource, Inc., 1989. (Apple, IBM)

This program features the adventures of the colorful character Stickybear. Students solve sets of multiplication and division problems of increasing difficulty.

Super Solvers: Outnumbered! Fremont, CA: The Learning Company, 1990. (IBM)

This program, part of a series, immerses students in the treachery of the Master of Mischief who wants to take over the TV station and show boring shows all day. Students use math skills to solve problems and amass enough clues to ruin his plans. This is an exciting, fun-filled program.

Scope and Sequence for MODERN CURRICULUM PRESS MATHEMATICS

Scope and Sequence

	K	1	2	3	4	5	6
READINESS							
Attributes	■						
Shapes	■	■					
Colors	■	■	■				
NUMERATION							
On-to-one correspondence	■						
Understanding numbers	■	■	■				
Writing numbers	■	■					
Counting objects	■	■	■				
Sequencing numbers	■	■	■	■	■		
Numbers before and after	■	■	■	■	■		
Ordering numbers			■	■	■	■	■
Comparing numbers	■	■	■	■	■	■	■
Grouping numbers	■	■	■	■	■		
Ordinal numbers	■	■	■	■			
Number words		■	■	■	■	■	■
Expanded numbers		■	■	■	■	■	■
Place value		■	■	■	■	■	■
Skip-counting		■	■	■	■	■	
Roman numerals			■	■	■		
Rounding numbers				■	■	■	■
Squares and square roots				■			

Scope and Sequence

	K	1	2	3	4	5	6
Primes and composites				■	■	■	■
Multiples					■	■	■
Least common multiples						■	■
Greatest common factors						■	■
Exponents							■
ADDITION							
Addition facts	■	■	■	■	■	■	■
Fact families		■	■	■	■	■	
Missing addends	■	■	■	■	■		
Adding money	■	■	■	■	■	■	■
Column addition		■	■	■	■	■	■
Two-digit addends		■	■	■		■	
Multidigit addends			■	■	■	■	■
Addition with trading		■	■	■	■	■	■
Basic properties of addition					■	■	■
Estimating sums				■	■	■	■
Addition of fractions				■	■	■	■
Addition of mixed numbers				■	■	■	■
Addition of decimals				■	■	■	■
Rule of order				■	■	■	■
Addition of customary measures						■	■

Scope and Sequence

	K	1	2	3	4	5	6
Addition of integers							■
SUBTRACTION							
Subtraction facts	■	■	■	■	■	■	■
Fact families		■	■	■	■	■	
Missing subtrahends		■	■				
Subtracting money	■	■	■	■	■	■	■
Two-digit numbers		■	■	■	■	■	
Multidigit numbers			■	■	■	■	■
Subtraction with trading		■	■	■	■	■	■
Zeros in the minuend				■	■	■	■
Basic properties of subtraction				■	■	■	■
Estimating differences				■	■	■	■
Subtraction of fractions				■	■	■	■
Subtraction of mixed numbers						■	■
Subtraction of decimals				■	■	■	■
Rule of order				■	■	■	■
Subtraction of customary measures						■	■
Subtraction of integers							■
MULTIPLICATION							
Multiplication facts			■	■	■	■	■
Fact families			■	■	■		

Scope and Sequence

	K	1	2	3	4	5	6
Missing factors					■		
Multiplying money			■	■	■	■	■
Multiplication by powers of ten				■	■	■	■
Multidigit factors				■	■	■	■
Multiplication with trading				■	■	■	■
Basic properties of multiplication			■	■	■	■	■
Estimating products				■	■	■	■
Rule of order				■	■	■	■
Multiples					■	■	■
Least common multiples						■	■
Multiplication of fractions						■	■
Factorization						■	■
Multiplication of mixed numbers							■
Multiplication of decimals					■	■	■
Exponents							■
Multiplication of integers							■
DIVISION							
Division facts				■	■	■	■
Fact families				■	■		
Divisibility rules				■		■	■
Two-digit quotients				■	■	■	■

Scope and Sequence

	K	1	2	3	4	5	6
Remainders				■	■	■	■
Multidigit quotients					■	■	■
Zeros in quotients					■	■	■
Division by multiples of ten					■	■	■
Two-digit divisors					■	■	■
Properties of division					■	■	
Averages				■	■	■	■
Greatest common factors						■	■
Division of fractions						■	■
Division of mixed numbers						■	■
Division of decimals						■	■
Division by powers of ten						■	■
MONEY							
Counting pennies	■	■	■	■	■		
Counting nickels	■	■	■	■	■		
Counting dimes	■	■	■	■	■		
Counting quarters		■	■	■	■	■	
Counting half-dollars			■	■	■	■	
Counting dollar bills		■	■	■	■		
Writing dollar and cents signs		■	■	■	■	■	■
Matching money with prices	■	■	■				

Scope and Sequence

	K	1	2	3	4	5	6
Determining amount of change	■	■	■				
Determining sufficient amount		■	■				
Determining which coins to use		■	■				
Addition	■	■	■	■	■	■	■
Subtraction	■	■	■	■	■	■	■
Multiplication			■	■	■	■	■
Division					■	■	■
Rounding amounts of money				■	■	■	■
Finding fractions of amounts					■	■	■
Buying from a menu or ad			■	■	■	■	■
FRACTIONS							
Understanding equal parts	■	■	■	■			
One half	■	■	■	■			
One fourth	■	■	■	■			
One third	■	■	■	■			
Identifying fractional parts of figures			■	■	■	■	■
Identifying fractional parts of sets			■	■	■	■	■
Finding unit fractions of numbers				■	■	■	
Equivalent fractions				■	■	■	■
Comparing fractions				■	■	■	■
Simplifying fractions					■	■	■

Scope and Sequence

	K	1	2	3	4	5	6
Renaming mixed numbers					■	■	■
Addition of fractions				■	■	■	■
Subtraction of fractions				■	■	■	■
Addition of mixed numbers					■	■	■
Subtraction of mixed numbers						■	■
Multiplication of fractions						■	■
Factorization						■	■
Multiplication of mixed numbers						■	■
Division of fractions						■	■
Division of mixed numbers						■	■
Renaming fractions as decimals							■
Renaming fractions as percents							■
DECIMALS							
Place value				■	■	■	■
Reading decimals				■	■	■	■
Writing decimals				■	■	■	■
Converting fractions to decimals				■	■	■	■
Writing parts of sets as decimals				■	■	■	
Comparing decimals				■	■	■	■
Ordering decimals							■
Addition of decimals				■	■	■	■

Scope and Sequence

	K	1	2	3	4	5	6
Subtraction of decimals				■	■	■	■
Rounding decimals				■		■	■
Multiplication of decimals					■	■	■
Division of decimals						■	■
Renaming decimals as percents							■
GEOMETRY							
Polygons	■	■	■	■	■	■	■
Sides and corners of polygons			■	■	■		
Lines and line segments					■	■	■
Rays and angles					■	■	■
Measuring angles						■	■
Symmetry			■			■	■
Congruency				■	■	■	■
Similar figures					■	■	■
Circles						■	■
MEASUREMENT							
Non-standard units of measure	■	■					
Customary units of measure		■	■	■	■	■	■
Metric units of measure	■	■	■	■	■	■	■
Renaming customary measures					■	■	■
Renaming metric measures					■	■	■

Scope and Sequence

	K	1	2	3	4	5	6
Selecting appropriate units			■	■	■	■	
Estimating measures		■	■	■	■	■	
Perimeter by counting	■	■	■				
Perimeter by formula			■	■	■	■	■
Area of polygons by counting			■	■			
Area of polygons by formula					■	■	■
Volume by counting				■			
Volume by formula					■	■	■
Addition of measures						■	■
Subtraction of measures						■	■
Circumference of circles							■
Area of circles							■
Surface area of space figures							■
Estimating temperatures				■			
Reading temperature scales			■	■			
TIME							
Ordering events	■						
Relative time	■						
Matching values	■	■	■	■	■		
Calendars	■	■	■	■			
Days of the week	■	■	■	■			

Scope and Sequence

	K	1	2	3	4	5	6
Months of the year	■	■	■	■			
Telling time to the hour	■	■	■	■			
Telling time to the half-hour		■	■	■			
Telling time to the five-minutes			■	■	■		
Telling time to the minute			■	■	■		
Understanding AM and PM					■		
Time zones					■		
GRAPHING							
Tables		■	■	■	■	■	■
Bar graphs	■	■	■	■	■	■	■
Picture graphs			■	■	■		■
Line graphs					■	■	■
Circle graphs						■	■
Tree diagrams						■	
Histograms							■
Ordered pairs				■	■	■	■
PROBABILITY							
Understanding probability					■	■	■
Listing outcomes					■	■	■
Means and medians						■	
Circle graphs						■	■

Scope and Sequence

	K	1	2	3	4	5	6
Tree diagrams						■	■
Histograms							■
RATIOS AND PERCENTS							
Understanding ratios					■	■	■
Equal ratios						■	■
Proportions							■
Scale drawings						■	■
Ratios as percents						■	■
Percents as fractions						■	■
Fractions as percents						■	■
Finding the percents of numbers						■	■
INTEGERS							
Understanding integers							■
Addition of integers							■
Subtraction of integers							■
Multiplication of integers							■
Graphing integers on coordinate planes							■
PROBLEM SOLVING							
Creating an algorithm from a word problem		■	■	■	■	■	■
Selecting the correct operation		■	■	■	■	■	■
Using data			■	■	■	■	■

Scope and Sequence

	K	1	2	3	4	5	6
Reading a chart			■	■	■	■	■
Using a four-step plan				■	■	■	■
Drawing a picture				■	■	■	■
Acting it out				■	■	■	■
Making a list				■	■	■	■
Making a tally				■	■	■	
Making a table				■	■	■	■
Making a graph				■	■	■	
Guessing and checking					■	■	■
Looking for a pattern					■	■	■
Making a model					■		
Restating the problem					■	■	■
Selecting notation					■	■	■
Writing an open sentence					■	■	■
Using a formula					■	■	■
Identifying a subgoal						■	■
Working backwards						■	■
Determining missing data						■	■
Collecting data						■	■
Solving a simpler but related problem						■	■
Making a flow chart							■

Scope and Sequence

CALCULATORS	K	1	2	3	4	5	6
Calculator codes				■	■	■	■
Equal key				■	■	■	■
Operation keys				■	■	■	■
Square root key				■			
Clear key				■	■	■	■
Clear entry key				■	■	■	■
Money				■	■	■	■
Unit prices				■	■	■	
Fractions				■	■		
Percents					■		
Banking				■	■	■	
Inventories					■		
Averages					■		
Rates						■	■
Formulas						■	■
Cross multiplication							■
Functions							■
Binary numbers							■
Repeating decimals							■
Statistics							■

Table of Common Errors

This **Table of Common Errors** is designed to help the teacher understand the thinking patterns and potential errors that students commonly commit in the course of learning the content in *Modern Curriculum Press Mathematics*. Familiarity with this list can help the teacher forestall errant thinking and save much time used in reteaching.

In the **Correcting Common Errors** feature in each lesson in this **Teacher's Guide,** one of the errors that is relevant to that lesson is discussed in detail and a suggestion is given for its remediation. Collectively, in any chapter, all of the common errors for that mathematical topic are discussed and abundant assistance is given to the teacher for rectifying the situations.

Numeration

1. The student mistakes a number for another because it has been carelessly written.

2. When writing numerals for a number that is expressed in words, a student fails to use zeros as placeholders where they are needed.

   Write forty thousand, fifty-two in numerals.

   ▶ **4,052**

3. The student confuses the names of place values.

4. The student confuses the names of periods with those of place values.

   Write 42,652 in words.

   ▶ Four **thousand** two, six hundred fifty-two

5. The student fails to write the money sign and/or decimal point in an answer involving money.

   $$\begin{array}{r} \$5.65 \\ +\ 3.39 \\ \hline \end{array}$$
   ▶ **904**

6. When ordering whole numbers, the student incorrectly compares single digits regardless of place value.

   The student thinks that 203 is less than 45 because 2 is less than 4 and 3 is less than 5.

7. The student rounds down when the last significant digit is 5.

   ▶ $7,546 \approx$ **7,000**

8. The student rounds progressively from digit to digit until the designated place value is reached.

   Round 3,456 to thousands.

   ▶ $3,460 \approx 3,500 \approx 4,000$

9. The student changes the common interval when skip-counting.

   ▶ 2, 4, 6, 8, **11, 14, 17**

10. When evaluating a base number raised to an exponent, the student multiplies the base number by the exponent.

    ▶ $2^4 =$ **2 × 4** $= 8$

Addition and Subtraction

1. The student is unsure of the basic facts of addition and/or subtraction.

2. The student copies the problem incorrectly.

3. The student makes simple addition errors when adding numbers with two or more digits.

$$\begin{array}{r} 64 \\ +28 \\ \hline 95 \end{array}$$ ▶

4. The student thinks that a number plus zero is zero.

▶ $6 + 0 = \mathbf{0}$

5. The student adds during a subtraction computation, or vice versa.

$$\begin{array}{r} 46 \\ -27 \\ \hline 23 \end{array} \qquad \begin{array}{r} 28 \\ +42 \\ \hline 66 \end{array}$$ ▶

6. The student computes horizontal equations from left to right regardless of the operations.

▶ $3 + 2 \times 5 = \mathbf{25}$

7. When doing a computation involving several numbers, the student omits a number.

*Find the sum of 23, 36, **54**, 88, and 75.*

▶ $$\begin{array}{r} 23 \\ 36 \\ 88 \\ +75 \\ \hline 222 \end{array}$$

8. The student forgets the partial sum when adding a column of addends.

▶ $$\begin{array}{r} \mathbf{6} \\ \mathbf{9} \\ +\ \mathbf{3} \\ \hline 12 \end{array}$$

9. The student omits the regrouped value.

▶ $$\begin{array}{r} 47 \\ +\ 23 \\ \hline 60 \end{array}$$

10. The student fails to rename and places more than one digit in a column in an addition problem.

▶ $$\begin{array}{r} 56 \\ +78 \\ \hline 1{,}214 \end{array}$$

11. In an addition problem, the student writes the tens digit as part of the answer and regroups the ones.

▶ $$\begin{array}{r} 4 \\ 56 \\ +78 \\ \hline 161 \end{array}$$

12. The student rounds the answer rather than the components of the problem.

Estimate the sum of 356 and 492.

▶ $$\begin{array}{r} 356 \\ +492 \\ \hline \mathbf{848 \approx 800} \end{array}$$

13. The student does not align the numbers properly when adding or subtracting whole numbers.

▶ $$\begin{array}{r} 43 \\ +\ 29 \\ \hline 659 \end{array} \qquad \begin{array}{r} 307 \\ +1\ 2 \\ \hline 409 \end{array}$$

14. The student incorrectly adds or subtracts from left to right.

▶ $$\begin{array}{r} 1 \\ 47 \\ +\ 91 \\ \hline 39 \end{array}$$

15. The student confuses addition and subtraction by one with either addition and subtraction of zero or with multiplication by one.

▶
$$6 + 1 = 6$$
$$6 - 1 = 6$$

16. The student adds or subtracts digits from different columns.

$$
\begin{array}{cc}
67 & 35 \\
+\ 2 & -\ 2 \\
\hline
89 & 13
\end{array}
$$
▶

17. The student makes simple subtraction errors when subtracting numbers with two or more digits.

$$
\begin{array}{r}
514 \\
6\,4 \\
-28 \\
\hline
37
\end{array}
$$
▶

18. The student thinks that a number minus zero is zero.

▶ $6 - 0 = 0$

19. The student thinks that zero minus another number is zero.

▶ $0 - 6 = 0$

20. When creating fact families, the student applies commutativity to subtraction.

$$8 - 5 = 3 \qquad \mathbf{5 - 8 = 3}$$
$$8 - 3 = 5 \qquad ▶ \quad \mathbf{3 - 8 = 5}$$

21. The student brings down the digit in the subtrahend when the corresponding minuend digit is a zero.

$$
\begin{array}{r}
20 \\
-13 \\
\hline
13
\end{array}
$$
▶

22. In multidigit subtraction problems, the student correctly renames the zero in the tens place but does not decrease the digit to the left of the zero.

$$
\begin{array}{r}
9 \\
1012 \\
6\,\emptyset\,2 \\
-4\,3\,7 \\
\hline
2\,6\,5
\end{array}
$$
▶

23. In a multidigit subtraction problem, the student ignores the zero and renames from the digit to the left of the zero.

$$
\begin{array}{r}
5\ 1012 \\
\emptyset\,\emptyset\,2 \\
-4\,3\,7 \\
\hline
1\,7\,5
\end{array}
$$
▶

24. In a multidigit subtraction problem, the student correctly trades from the digit to the left of the zero and renames the zero as 10 but fails to reduce the 10 by one when the second regrouping is done.

▶
$$
\begin{array}{r}
5\ 1012 \\
\emptyset\,\emptyset\,2 \\
-4\,3\,7 \\
\hline
1\,7\,5
\end{array}
$$

25. The student does not trade in a subtraction problem but finds the difference between the smaller digit and the larger regardless of their positions.

$$
\begin{array}{r}
537 \\
-182 \\
\hline
455
\end{array}
$$
▶

26. In a subtraction problem, the student does not decrease the digit to the left after trading.

▶
$$
\begin{array}{r}
12 \\
5\,2 \\
-3\,8 \\
\hline
2\,4
\end{array}
$$

Multiplication

1. The student is unsure of the basic multiplication facts.

2. The student mistakes a multiplication sign for an addition sign, or vice versa.

3. The student thinks that one times any number is one.

$$6 \times 1 = 1$$

▶
```
    36
  ×31
    11
  108
 1,091
```

4. The student confuses multiplication by zero with multiplication by one, thinking that any number times zero is that number.

$$6 \times 0 = 6$$

▶
```
    26
  ×30
    26
   78
  806
```

5. The student ignores the parentheses in a horizontal equation and does not distribute multiplication over addition or subtraction.

▶ $3 \times (5 + 2) = 15 + 2 = 17$

6. The student makes simple multiplication mistakes in multidigit multiplication problems.

▶
```
    234
  × 12
    498
    234
  2,838
```

7. The student is unsure of how many zeros are in the product when multiplying by a multiple of ten.

▶
```
    756
  × 500
  37,800
```

8. The student makes simple addition errors in multidigit multiplication problems.

▶
```
    234
  × 12
    468
    234
  2,838
```

9. The student misaligns the digits in the partial products in a multiplication problem.

▶
```
    234
  × 12
    468
    234
    702
```

10. The student writes the tens digit as part of the answer and regroups the ones.

▶
```
     5
    47
  ×  5
   253
```

11. The student does not regroup or fails to add the regrouped value.

▶
```
    36
  × 7
   212
```

12. When multiplying whole numbers, the student adds the renamed digit before multiplying.

▶
```
     4
    56
  × 7
   632
```

13. In a multidigit multiplication problem, the student confuses the regrouped digit for the second partial product with that of the first partial product.

▶
```
     1
     4
    36
  ×27
   252
   102
  1,272
```

Division

1. The student is unsure of the basic division facts.

2. In a division problem, if either term is one, the student thinks the answer is one.

   ▶ $6 \div 1 = 1$
     $1 \div 6 = 1$

3. The student does not realize that division by zero has no meaning.

   ▶ $6 \div 0 = 6$
     $0 \div 0 = 0$

4. The student places the initial quotient digit over the wrong digit in the dividend.

   ▶ $\begin{array}{r} 7{,}231 \\ 2\overline{)1{,}462} \end{array}$

5. The student ignores initial digits in the dividend that are less than the divisor.

   ▶ $\begin{array}{r} 231 \\ 2\overline{)1{,}462} \end{array}$

6. The student does not align the digits carefully and consequently misses one of the digits in the dividend.

   ▶ $\begin{array}{r} 4\,7 \text{ R1} \\ 3\overline{)1{,}462} \\ \underline{1\,2} \\ 22 \\ \underline{21} \\ 1 \end{array}$

7. The student fails to record a zero in a quotient.

   ▶ $\begin{array}{r} 3\,9 \text{ R7} \\ 12\overline{)3{,}715} \\ \underline{3\,6} \\ 115 \\ \underline{108} \\ 7 \end{array}$

8. The first estimated partial quotient is too low so the student subtracts and divides again and places an extra digit in the quotient.

   ▶ $\begin{array}{r} 3{,}106 \text{ R7} \\ 23\overline{)9{,}345} \\ \underline{6\,9} \\ 24 \\ \underline{23} \\ 145 \\ \underline{138} \\ 7 \end{array}$

9. The student fails to subtract the last time or fails to record the remainder as part of the quotient.

   $\begin{array}{r} 309 \\ 12\overline{)3{,}715} \\ \underline{3\,6} \\ 115 \\ \underline{108} \end{array}$

   ▶

10. The student records the remainder as the last digit of the quotient.

   ▶ $\begin{array}{r} 571 \\ 3\overline{)172} \\ \underline{15} \\ 22 \\ \underline{21} \\ 1 \end{array}$

11. The student records a remainder that is larger than the divisor.

   ▶ $\begin{array}{r} 155 \text{ R5} \\ 4\overline{)625} \end{array}$

12. The student incorrectly subtracts in a division problem.

   $\begin{array}{r} 73 \text{ R1} \\ 3\overline{)230} \\ \underline{21} \\ 10 \\ \underline{9} \\ 1 \end{array}$

   ▶

13. The student fails to subtract before bringing down the next digit in a division problem.

▶
```
      41
   6)256
     24
      6
      6
```

14. The student incorrectly multiplies in a division problem.

▶
```
      86 R2
   3)230
     21
     20
     18
      2
```

15. The student stops dividing before all the digits in the dividend have been divided.

▶
```
      1,257
   6)75,421
```

16. When factoring for primes, the student lists a composite number for a prime number.

▶ $64 = 8 \times 4 \times 2 \times 2$

Measurement

1. The student is confused about how to read fractional measures on a ruler.

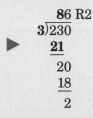

▶ **7 inches**

2. The student does not properly align the object to be measured with the point that represents zero on the ruler.

3. The student reads the small hand of a standard clock as minutes and the large hand as hours.

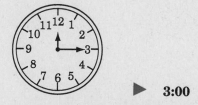

▶ **3:00**

4. The student reads the time on a standard clock incorrectly when the hour hand is between two numbers.

▶ **7:53**

5. The student confuses the meaning of 12:00 AM and 12:00 PM.

6. The student selects an incorrect time zone for a designated city.

7. The student is confused about whether the time is earlier to the east or to the west.

8. When converting from one measure to another, the student uses the incorrect equivalent unit.

▶ *The student thinks that 1 foot = 10 inches, or that 1 meter = 1000 centimeters.*

9. When converting from one measure to another, the student incorrectly divides when he or she should have multiplied, or vice versa.

Change 36 yards to feet.

▶ 36 yards = **12 feet**

10. The student compares measurements expressed in different units.

> 3 ft < 15 in.
> 6 m > 2 km

11. The student fails to simplify measures after adding denominate numbers.

> 6 ft 8 in.
> +4 ft 10 in.
> 10 ft **18 in.**

12. The student finds the difference between the two numbers instead of regrouping denominate numbers.

> 6 ft 8 in.
> −4 ft 10 in.
> 2 ft **2 in.**

13. The student regroups an incorrect value when subtracting denominate numbers.

> $\overset{5}{\cancel{6}}$ ft $\overset{18}{\cancel{8}}$ in.
> −4 ft 10 in.
> 1 ft 8 in.

Geometry

---

1. The student confuses the meanings of line and line segment.

2. The student confuses perpendicular lines with parallel lines.

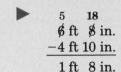

3. The student confuses the diameter of a circle with its radius.

4. The student does not name the vertex of an angle by the middle of the three letters.

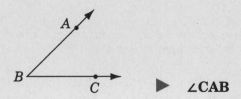

> ∠**CAB**

5. The student uses the opposite scale on a protractor when measuring an angle.

6. When bisecting a line or angle, the student uses the incorrect point for the compass point and fails to find the midpoint.

7. The student changes the setting of the compass when the construction calls for identical settings.

8. The student calculates the measure of a missing angle of a triangle by subtracting only one of the given angles from 180°.

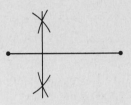

> **90°**

9. The student confuses the names of basic polygons.

10. The student thinks the geometrical term *similar* applies to two figures that are somewhat like each other.

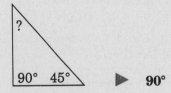

11. The student confuses the meaning of *similar* and *congruent*.

12. The student identifies a line as a line of symmetry, even though it doesn't create two congruent parts.

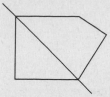

13. The student confuses corresponding parts of congruent figures with different orientations.

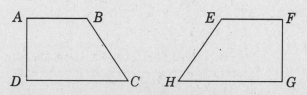

14. The student confuses the formula for finding the perimeter with that for finding the area.

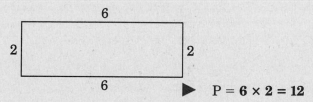

$$P = 6 \times 2 = 12$$

15. The student omits one or more of the dimensions of a polygon when computing its perimeter.

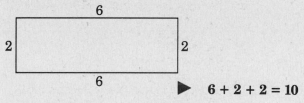

$$6 + 2 + 2 = 10$$

16. When computing the circumference of a circle, the student multiplies the radius by *pi*.

17. When computing the circumference of a circle, the student squares the radius and multiplies by *pi*.

18. When calculating the area of a parallelogram, the student uses the slant height for one of the measures.

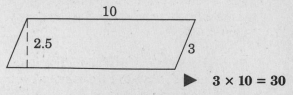

$$3 \times 10 = 30$$

19. When computing the area of a triangle, the student forgets to divide by 2.

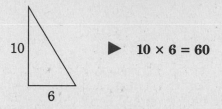

$$10 \times 6 = 60$$

20. When computing the area of a circle, the student multiplies the diameter by *pi*.

21. When computing the area of a circle, the student squares the diameter and multiplies by *pi*.

22. When computing the area of a circle, the student multiplies the radius by pi and then squares that product.

23. The student confuses the names of basic space figures.

24. The student uses the area formula for finding volume, or vice versa.

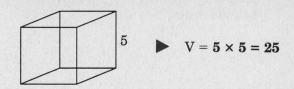

$$V = 5 \times 5 = 25$$

25. The student confuses the concepts of surface area and volume of space figures.

26. The student finds the surface area of only the visible faces of space figures.

Fractions

1. The student counts the wrong number of parts of a picture when naming equivalent fractions.

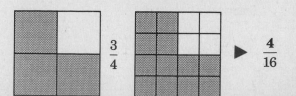

$$\frac{3}{4} \quad \blacktriangleright \quad \frac{4}{16}$$

2. The student transposes the numerator and the denominator of a fraction.

3. The student confuses the meanings of greatest common factor and least common multiple.

4. To find equivalent fractions, the student uses addition or subtraction instead of multiplication or division.

▶ $\dfrac{3+4}{4+4} = \dfrac{7}{8}$

$\dfrac{9-8}{12-8} = \dfrac{1}{4}$

5. When raising fractions to a common denominator, the student uses a number that is not a multiple of all the denominators.

$\dfrac{3}{4} = \dfrac{}{8}$

▶ $\dfrac{2}{3} = \dfrac{}{8}$

6. When simplifying a fraction the student does not divide by the greatest common factor.

▶ $\dfrac{16 \div 4}{24 \div 4} = \dfrac{4}{6}$

7. When the denominator is a multiple of the numerator, the student simplifies the fraction by dividing the denominator by the numerator.

▶ $\dfrac{3}{9} = 3$

8. When renaming an improper fraction as a mixed number, the student writes the tens digit in the numerator as the whole number.

▶ $\dfrac{17}{9} = 1\dfrac{7}{9}$

9. When renaming an improper fraction as a mixed number, the student writes only the whole number and ignores the fraction.

▶ $\dfrac{13}{4} = 3$

10. When converting mixed numerals to improper fractions, the student multiplies the whole number by the denominator but fails to add the numerator to this product.

▶ $3\dfrac{1}{2} = \dfrac{6}{2}$

11. When renaming a whole number as a mixed number in a subtraction problem, the student fails to reduce the whole number by one.

▶ $3 = 3\dfrac{5}{5}$

12. When comparing fractions with the same numerator, the student compares only the denominators.

▶ $\dfrac{1}{3} < \dfrac{1}{4}$

13. When using cross multiplication to compare two fractions, the student confuses the products and reverses the sign.

$\dfrac{2}{3} > \dfrac{3}{4}$

▶ 9   8

14. When renaming a fraction as a decimal, the student divides the denominator by the numerator instead of vice versa.

▶ $\dfrac{3}{4} = 1.33\dfrac{1}{3}$

15. When adding or subtracting fractions, the student adds or subtracts both the numerators and the denominators.

▶ $\dfrac{3}{5} + \dfrac{2}{3} = \dfrac{5}{8}$

16. When adding fractions, the student finds a common denominator but does not rename the numerators.

▶ $\dfrac{2}{3} + \dfrac{1}{5} = \dfrac{2}{15} + \dfrac{1}{15} = \dfrac{3}{15} = \dfrac{1}{5}$

17. When adding mixed numbers, the student fails to recognize an opportunity to simplify an answer.

$$3\frac{2}{3} = 3\frac{4}{6}$$
$$+4\frac{1}{2} = 4\frac{3}{6}$$

▶ $\quad\quad 7\frac{7}{6}$

18. When adding or subtracting mixed numbers, the student works only with the fractions.

$$5\frac{1}{2} = \frac{3}{6}$$
$$+6\frac{1}{3} = \frac{2}{6}$$

▶ $\quad\quad \frac{5}{6}$

19. When regrouping a mixed number in a subtraction problem, the student regroups the whole number but simply affixes a one to the existing numerator.

$$5\frac{1}{3} = 5\frac{5}{15} = 4\frac{15}{15}$$
$$-2\frac{3}{5} = 2\frac{9}{15} = 2\frac{9}{15}$$

$$\quad\quad 2\frac{6}{15} = 2\frac{2}{5}$$

20. The student adds the one regrouped from the whole number to the numerator of the fraction.

$$7\frac{2}{5} = 6\frac{3}{5}$$
$$-\quad\frac{3}{5} = \quad\frac{3}{5}$$

$$\quad\quad 6$$

21. When finding a fractional part of a number, the student fails to either multiply by the numerator or divide by the denominator.

▶ $\quad \frac{3}{7}$ of $21 = 63$

$\quad \frac{3}{7}$ of $21 = 3$

22. The student confuses multiplication of fractions with addition and finds a common denominator before operating only on the numerators.

▶ $\quad \frac{2}{3} \times \frac{3}{4} = \frac{8}{12} \times \frac{9}{12} = 72$

23. When multiplying two fractions, the student cross multiplies to find the product.

▶ $\quad \frac{2}{3} \times \frac{3}{4} = \frac{8}{9}$

24. The student confuses multiplication of fractions with division and inverts the second factor.

▶ $\quad \frac{2}{3} \times \frac{3}{4} = \frac{2}{3} \times \frac{4}{3} = \frac{8}{9}$

25. When multiplying or dividing mixed numbers, the student operates on the whole numbers and the fractions separately.

▶ $\quad 2\frac{3}{5} \times 4\frac{1}{6} = 8\frac{3}{30} = 8\frac{1}{10}$

$\quad 6\frac{3}{7} \div 2\frac{3}{5} = \frac{3}{7} \times \frac{5}{3} = 3\frac{15}{21} = 3\frac{5}{7}$

26. The student fails to invert the second fraction in a division problem.

▶ $\quad \frac{3}{4} \div \frac{2}{3} = \frac{3}{4} \times \frac{2}{3} = \frac{1}{2}$

27. When dividing fractions, the student inverts the first fraction instead of the second one.

▶ $\quad \frac{3}{4} \div \frac{2}{9} = \frac{4}{3} \times \frac{2}{9} = \frac{8}{27}$

28. When dividing by a mixed number, the student reciprocates only the fraction.

▶ $\quad 2\frac{2}{3} \div 1\frac{1}{2} = 2\frac{2}{3} \times 1\frac{2}{1} = \frac{8}{3} \times \frac{3}{1} = \frac{24}{3} = 8$

29. When the divisor is a mixed number, the student renames it as an improper fraction but fails to invert it before multiplying.

▶ $\quad \frac{3}{4} \div 1\frac{1}{2} = \frac{3}{4} \times \frac{3}{2} = \frac{9}{8} = 1\frac{1}{8}$

Ratios, Proportion, and Percents

1. The student transposes the terms of a ratio.

   The student thinks that a 7 to 5 ratio is the same as a 5 to 7 ratio.

2. The student does not multiply or divide the terms of a ratio by the same number when finding equal ratios.

   ▶ $3:5 = 9:\mathbf{25}$

3. When calculating a missing term in two equal ratios, the student multiplies by the other term.

   ▶ $\dfrac{3}{4} = \dfrac{\mathbf{12}}{24}$

4. When finding a distance based on a scale, the student uses the actual distance and ignores the scale.

5. When solving a proportion for a missing term, the student confuses the means and the extremes of the proportion.

   $\mathbf{2:3} :: 4:x$
   ▶ $\mathbf{2} \times \mathbf{3} = 4 \times x$
   $6 = 4x$
   $1\dfrac{1}{2} = x$

6. The student renames a ratio or fraction as a percent but fails to write the percent sign.

   ▶ $\dfrac{1}{2} = 0.50 = \mathbf{50}$

7. When renaming a percent as a decimal, the student simply omits the percent sign.

   ▶ $3.5\% = \mathbf{3.5}$

8. When renaming a decimal number with more than two decimal places as a percent, the student moves the point as far right as the last place.

   ▶ $0.275 = \mathbf{275\%}$

9. When renaming a fraction as a percent, the student renames the fraction as a decimal and then simply affixes a percent **sign** to the decimal equivalent.

   ▶ $\dfrac{3}{4} = 0.75 = \mathbf{.75\%}$

10. When finding the percent of a number, the student multiplies by the percent without renaming it as a decimal or fraction.

    20% of 45

    ▶ $\mathbf{20} \times 45 = 900$

Decimals

1. The student confuses the terms used for place values of decimals with those of whole numbers.

   Find the place value of the underlined digit in 4.6̲39.

   ▶ **tens**

2. When writing decimal numbers, the student does not place the nonzero digits in the correct places.

   Write three and four thousandths in numerals.

   ▶ 3.040

3. The student omits the decimal point in a decimal number.

   Write fourteen hundredths in numerals.

   ▶ 14

4. When ordering decimals, the student's answer is based on the number of digits.

   The student thinks that because 0.2381 has five digits and 0.47 has only three, the first number is larger.

5. The student rounds to the wrong decimal place.

   Round 0.6524 to the nearest thousandths.

   ▶ **0.65**

6. When rounding decimal numbers, the student replaces values beyond the designated place value with zeros.

   Round 0.6548 to hundredths.

   ▶ **0.6500**

7. The student places the repeating bar over digits which don't repeat in a decimal number.

   ▶ $0.91\ldots = 0.\overline{91}$

8. When interpreting a repeating decimal, the student thinks the next digit to the right of the overlined digit is always zero.

9. When adding or subtracting decimals, the student operates on the whole number parts and the decimal parts of the numbers separately.

   $$\begin{array}{r} 22.3 \\ +17.9 \\ \hline \end{array}$$
   ▶ 39.**12**

10. The student confuses multiplication of decimals with addition and aligns the decimal point of the product with the decimal points of the factors.

    $$\begin{array}{r} 2.6 \\ \times 3.2 \\ \hline 5\ 2 \\ 78 \\ \hline \end{array}$$
    ▶ 83.2

11. The student counts decimal places in the factors in a multiplication problem from the left instead of from the right.

   $$\begin{array}{r} 3.01 \\ \times 1.12 \\ \hline 6\ 02 \\ 30\ 1 \\ 301 \\ \hline \end{array}$$
   ▶ **33.**712

12. The student annexes zeros to the right of a nonzero digit in a product.

    $$\begin{array}{r} 0.3 \\ \times 0.02 \\ \hline \end{array}$$
    ▶ 0.**600**

13. When dividing a number by a decimal number, the student ignores the decimal point in the divisor and places the decimal point in the quotient over that in the dividend.

    ▶ $0.3\overline{)1.68}$ with quotient 0.56

14. The student fails to use a zero as a place holder in a quotient.

    ▶ $5\overline{)0.230}$ with quotient $.46$

15. The student moves the decimal point to the left when multiplying by a power of 10 or to the right when dividing by a power of 10.

    ▶ $7.6 \times 100 = \mathbf{0.076}$
    $7.6 \div 100 = \mathbf{760}$

16. The student moves the decimal point in the divisor but fails to move it accordingly in the dividend.

    ▶ $0.05_\wedge\overline{)6.25}$ with quotient 1.25

17. The student fails to divide to at least one place beyond the place value to which the answer is to be rounded.

    Express $\frac{1}{3}$ as a decimal to the nearest hundredths.

    ▶ $3\overline{)1.00}$ with quotient $\mathbf{0.33}$

Integers

1. When comparing integers, the student ignores the signs and compares absolute values.

   ▶ $^-3 > {}^+1$

2. When adding a positive and negative number, the student adds absolute values and uses the sign of the greater.

   ▶ $^-4 + {}^+7 = {}^+\mathbf{11}$

3. When adding a positive and negative number, the student finds the difference between them but always makes the answer either positive or negative.

   ▶ $^+7 + {}^-6 = {}^-\mathbf{1}$
   $^-3 + {}^+2 = {}^+\mathbf{1}$

4. When subtracting integers, the student adds them and uses the sign of the greater absolute value.

   ▶ $^+5 - {}^-7 = {}^-\mathbf{2}$

5. When subtracting integers, the student changes the operation sign to addition but fails to change the sign of the subtrahend.

   ▶ $^-7 - {}^-5 = {}^-7 + {}^-5 = {}^-\mathbf{12}$

6. When multiplying or dividing any negative numbers, the student always makes the answer negative.

   ▶ $^-2 \times {}^-2 \times {}^-2 \times {}^-2 = {}^-\mathbf{16}$
   $^-15 \div {}^-3 = {}^-\mathbf{5}$

7. When graphing integers, the student becomes confused about which quadrant to use for any given pair.

Graphing and Probability

1. The student fails to divide by the number of addends when computing the average.

2. The student confuses the meanings of mean and median.

3. The student reverses the numbers in an ordered pair.

   The student thinks (3,2) is the same as (2,3).

4. The student locates points on a grid by first counting up and then over.

   Graph (2,3) and label it point A.

   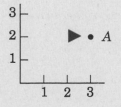

5. The student uses the next larger interval on the scale when reading data on a bar graph.

    ▶ **A is 3.**

6. The student confuses the data from the two categories in creating a double-bar graph.

7. The student reads a point on a line graph by counting forward from the next higher interval.

   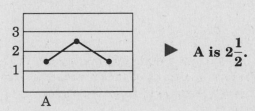 ▶ **A is $2\frac{1}{2}$.**

8. The student does not refer to a key when interpreting a picture graph.

How many books does Bob own?

$2\frac{1}{2}$

9. The student interprets percents on a circle graph as amounts of the whole rather than as rates.

10. The student confuses the number of possible outcomes with the number of chances not to get the outcome.

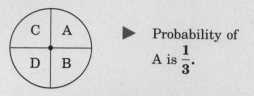

Probability of A is $\frac{1}{3}$.

11. The student may fail to write all possible combinations for each and every choice.

Problem Solving Errors

1. The student uses the wrong operation or operations to solve a problem.

2. The student chooses the operation based on the relative size of the numbers in the problem.

3. The student thinks that all numbers in a word problem must be used to get the solution.

4. The student does not use all the relevant information given in a problem.

5. The student does not read the problem carefully, but selects key words to determine the operation or operations.

6. The student does not answer the question posed in the problem.

7. The student is confused because the problem contains unfamiliar words or situations.

8. The student does not find all the possible solutions because he or she is not systematic when making a list.

9. The student does not collect enough data to establish a pattern.

10. The student misreads a chart or table used in a problem.

11. The student's diagram does not faithfully depict the situation in the problem.

12. The student does not check if the data that is being tested makes sense in the problem.

Calculators

1. The student enters incorrect codes into the calculator.

2. When entering a percent in a calculator, the student forgets to enter the percent sign.

3. When entering a subtraction into a calculator, the student enters the subtrahend before the minuend.

4. When entering a division into a calculator, the student enters the divisor before the dividend.

5. The student fails to enter decimal points at the appropriate places in a calculator code.

MODERN CURRICULUM PRESS
MATHEMATICS
Level E

Richard Monnard

Royce Hargrove

Project Editor .... Dorothy A. Kirk
Editor .... Martha Geyen
Design and Production .... Remen-Willis Design Group
Illustration .... Jane McCreary, Sharron O'Neil,
Susan Jaekel, Doug Roy, Dennis Noble, Lauren Mills,
Valerie Felts
Cover Art .... © 1993 Adam Peiperl

This book is the property of:

Book No. _____ Enter information in spaces below as instructed.

State _____

Province _____

County _____

Parish _____

School district _____

Other _____

Issued to	Year Used	CONDITION ISSUED	RETURNED

PUPILS to whom this textbook is issued must not write on any page or mark any part of it in any way, consumable textbooks excepted.
1. Teachers should see that the pupil's name is clearly written in ink in the spaces above in every book issued.
2. The following items should be used in recording the condition of this book: New; Good; Fair; Poor; Bad.

Modern Curriculum Press
An imprint of Pearson Learning
299 Jefferson Road, P.O. Box 480
Parsippany, NJ 07054-0480

www.pearsonlearning.com

1-800-321-3106

Copyright © 1994 by Modern Curriculum Press, an imprint of Pearson Learning, a division of Pearson Education, Inc. All rights reserved. Printed in the United States of America. This publication is protected by Copyright, and permissions should be obtained from the publisher prior to any prohibited reproduction, storage in a retrieval system, or transmission in any form or by any means, electronic, mechanical, photocopying, recording, or likewise. For information regarding permission(s), write to Rights and Permissions Department. This edition is published simultaneously in Canada by Pearson Education Canada.

ISBN 0-8136-3113-0 (Pupil's Edition)
ISBN 0-8136-3120-3 (Teacher's Edition)

8 9 10 11 12 13 14 15 16 17 PO 06 05 04 03 02 01 00

Table of Contents

Basic Facts

pages 1-2

Objective

To review addition and subtraction fact families

Materials

*addition and subtraction cards
one-inch graph paper

Mental Math

Ask students the result of:

1. $3 + 4 + 1 + 0 =$ (8)
2. $7 + 4 - 2 =$ (9)
3. $5 + 5 + 5 - 1 =$ (14)
4. $8 - 3 + 5 - 6 =$ (4)
5. $10 + 10 - 4 - 1 =$ (15)
6. $10 + 2 - 0 - 5 =$ (7)
7. $0 + 4 + 5 - 4 =$ (5)

Skill Review

Use flash cards to review addition and subtraction facts. Have students give an answer to the problem on the flash card and then make up another problem with the same numbers. For example, if the card reads $3 + 4$, the student will answer that $3 + 4 = 7$. Making up another problem, the student might say that $4 + 3 = 7$ or even that $7 - 3 = 4$.

Addition and Subtraction Facts

The fifth grade class has entered 13 animals in the school pet show. Write two addition and two subtraction equations using the numbers of puppies, kittens and pets.

We are looking for the two addition and two subtraction facts that make a **fact family.**

We know the **sum** or total number of pets in the show is _13_.

There are _8_ puppies and _5_ kittens entered.

To write the addition facts, we add the addends, _8_ and _5_.

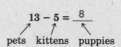

$$8 + 5 = \underline{13}$$
puppies kittens pets

$$5 + 8 = \underline{13}$$
addends sum

To write the subtraction facts, we subtract _8_ and _5_ from the total number of pets.

$$13 - 5 = \underline{8}$$
pets kittens puppies

subtrahend
$$13 - 8 = \underline{5}$$
minuend difference

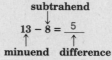

The fact family for 5, 8 and 13 is made of two _addition_ facts and two _subtraction_ facts.

8	5	13	13
+5	+8	− 8	− 5
13	13	5	8

Getting Started

Write the fact family for each set of numbers.

1. 2, 4, 6

$2 + 4 = 6$ $6 - 4 = 2$

$4 + 2 = 6$ $6 - 2 = 4$

2. 7, 15, 8

$7 + 8 = 15$ $15 - 8 = 7$

$8 + 7 = 15$ $15 - 7 = 8$

Add or subtract.

3. $16 - 9 = \underline{7}$

4.
7
+ 3
10

MCP All rights reserved

Teaching the Lesson

Introducing the Problem Read the problem aloud while students examine the illustration. Have students read and complete the information sentences. Read the next sentence aloud and write on the board $8 + 5 = 13$, $5 + 8 = 13$, labeling problems as they appear in the text. Ask a student to point to addends and sum in each sample. Read the next sentence aloud with students and write the subtraction facts on the board. Have a student label them as they appear in the book. Have students complete the fact family.

Developing the Skill Use an overhead projector to show this chart. Find an addend (3) along the top and another (5) along the side. Read along the lines until they cross at the sum (8). Repeat, finding 5 along the top, 3 along the side. Do a subtraction problem. Find the subtrahend along the top, read down to find the minuend, read to the left-hand edge to find the difference. Have students practice finding fact families on the chart.

	0	1	2	3	4	5	6	7	8	9
0	0	1	2	3	4	5	6	7	8	9
1	1	2	3	4	5	6	7	8	9	10
2	2	3	4	5	6	7	8	9	10	11
3	3	4	5	6	7	8	9	10	11	12
4	4	5	6	7	8	9	10	11	12	13
5	5	6	7	8	9	10	11	12	13	14
6	6	7	8	9	10	11	12	13	14	15
7	7	8	9	10	11	12	13	14	15	16
8	8	9	10	11	12	13	14	15	16	17
9	9	10	11	12	13	14	15	16	17	18

1

Write the fact family for each set of numbers.

1. 3, 4, 7

$3 + 4 = 7$

$4 + 3 = 7$

$7 - 4 = 3$

$7 - 3 = 4$

2. 2, 9, 7

$2 + 7 = 9$

$7 + 2 = 9$

$9 - 7 = 2$

$9 - 2 = 7$

3. 6, 7, 13

$6 + 7 = 13$

$7 + 6 = 13$

$13 - 7 = 6$

$13 - 6 = 7$

4. 8, 0, 8

$8 + 0 = 8$

$0 + 8 = 8$

$8 - 0 = 8$

$8 - 8 = 0$

5. 12, 5, 7

$5 + 7 = 12$

$7 + 5 = 12$

$12 - 7 = 5$

$12 - 5 = 7$

6. 9, 17, 8

$8 + 9 = 17$

$9 + 8 = 17$

$17 - 9 = 8$

$17 - 8 = 9$

7. 7, 1, 8

$7 + 1 = 8$

$1 + 7 = 8$

$8 - 1 = 7$

$8 - 7 = 1$

8. 11, 6, 5

$5 + 6 = 11$

$6 + 5 = 11$

$11 - 5 = 6$

$11 - 6 = 5$

Add or subtract.

9. $7 + 2 = \underline{9}$

10. $3 + 1 = \underline{4}$

11. $11 - 5 = \underline{6}$

12. $14 - 7 = \underline{7}$

13. $7 + 6 = \underline{13}$

14. $8 - 5 = \underline{3}$

15. $8 + 0 = \underline{8}$

16. $10 - 8 = \underline{2}$

17. $15 - 8 = \underline{7}$

18. $9 + 6 = \underline{15}$

19. $5 + 9 = \underline{14}$

20. $16 - 8 = \underline{8}$

21. $\begin{array}{r} 11 \\ -\ 8 \\ \hline 3 \end{array}$	**22.** $\begin{array}{r} 8 \\ +7 \\ \hline 15 \end{array}$	**23.** $\begin{array}{r} 10 \\ -\ 4 \\ \hline 6 \end{array}$	**24.** $\begin{array}{r} 9 \\ -0 \\ \hline 9 \end{array}$	**25.** $\begin{array}{r} 10 \\ -\ 7 \\ \hline 3 \end{array}$	**26.** $\begin{array}{r} 1 \\ +5 \\ \hline 6 \end{array}$
27. $\begin{array}{r} 6 \\ +6 \\ \hline 12 \end{array}$	**28.** $\begin{array}{r} 9 \\ -3 \\ \hline 6 \end{array}$	**29.** $\begin{array}{r} 7 \\ +0 \\ \hline 7 \end{array}$	**30.** $\begin{array}{r} 15 \\ -\ 6 \\ \hline 9 \end{array}$	**31.** $\begin{array}{r} 8 \\ +9 \\ \hline 17 \end{array}$	**32.** $\begin{array}{r} 8 \\ +4 \\ \hline 12 \end{array}$
33. $\begin{array}{r} 6 \\ +9 \\ \hline 15 \end{array}$	**34.** $\begin{array}{r} 6 \\ -1 \\ \hline 5 \end{array}$	**35.** $\begin{array}{r} 12 \\ -\ 6 \\ \hline 6 \end{array}$	**36.** $\begin{array}{r} 7 \\ +5 \\ \hline 12 \end{array}$	**37.** $\begin{array}{r} 9 \\ +9 \\ \hline 18 \end{array}$	**38.** $\begin{array}{r} 2 \\ +6 \\ \hline 8 \end{array}$
39. $\begin{array}{r} 4 \\ +9 \\ \hline 13 \end{array}$	**40.** $\begin{array}{r} 9 \\ -1 \\ \hline 8 \end{array}$	**41.** $\begin{array}{r} 7 \\ +3 \\ \hline 10 \end{array}$	**42.** $\begin{array}{r} 8 \\ -8 \\ \hline 0 \end{array}$	**43.** $\begin{array}{r} 11 \\ -\ 4 \\ \hline 7 \end{array}$	**44.** $\begin{array}{r} 6 \\ +5 \\ \hline 11 \end{array}$
45. $\begin{array}{r} 1 \\ +0 \\ \hline 1 \end{array}$	**46.** $\begin{array}{r} 14 \\ -\ 5 \\ \hline 9 \end{array}$	**47.** $\begin{array}{r} 5 \\ +7 \\ \hline 12 \end{array}$	**48.** $\begin{array}{r} 3 \\ -2 \\ \hline 1 \end{array}$	**49.** $\begin{array}{r} 10 \\ -\ 1 \\ \hline 9 \end{array}$	**50.** $\begin{array}{r} 7 \\ +8 \\ \hline 15 \end{array}$

2

Correcting Common Errors

Some students may have difficulty mastering their addition and subtraction facts. Have these students work with partners. Give each pair a set of cards with an addition or subtraction fact on each. Partners take turns saying or writing the other three facts in the fact family.

Enrichment

Have students make a set of domino-like cards representing fact families using 3×5 cards, pencils and crayons. Show them a card of the $3 + 2$ family. Explain that it shows that $3 + 2 = 5$ and that $5 - 3 = 2$. Tell them to make similar cards for all the fact families represented on the addition/subtraction chart used in teaching the lesson. (There are 54 such families.)

Practice

Have students complete the practice problems. Point out that they are working with fact families.

Extra Credit *Measurement*

Have students measure distances around specified objects (ex. books, desks, etc.) with non-standard units of measure which they have devised and named, using sticks, toothpicks, straws or pencils. Have them measure the objects again using standard units of measure. Have them compare the ease and accuracy of both methods.

Addition and Subtraction Properties

pages 3-4

Objective

To review properties of addition and subtraction

Materials

*two sets of number cards 0 through 9
Cuisinaire rods, Sterns blocks, or similar manipulatives

Mental Math

Ask students which is larger:

1. $2 + 1$ or $2 + 2$? $(2 + 2)$
2. $5 + 3$ or $5 - 2$? $(5 + 3)$
3. $6 - 1$ or $6 - 2$? $(6 - 1)$
4. $4 - 2$ or $4 - 1$? $(4 - 1)$
5. $9 - 1$ or $9 + 1$? $(9 + 1)$
6. $10 - 1$ or $8 + 1$? (same)

Skill Review

Dictate these problems to students and ask them to give one other problem in the same fact family.

1. $3 + 6 = 9$, $(6 + 3 = 9, 9 - 3 = 6, 9 - 6 = 3)$
2. $7 - 5 = 2$ $(7 - 2 = 5, 2 + 5 = 7, 5 + 2 = 7)$
3. $4 + 1 = 5$
4. $10 - 4 = 6$
5. $7 + 4 = 11$

Addition and Subtraction Properties

Properties are like special tools. They make the job of adding and subtracting much easier.

Twelve minus nine is three.

That's right because nine plus three is twelve.

Addition

Order Property
We can add in any order.

$5 + 2 = 7$ $\qquad$ $2 + 5 = 7$

$3 + 6 + 7 = \underline{16}$ $\qquad$ $7 + 3 + 6 = \underline{16}$

Grouping Property
We can change the grouping.
✔ Remember to add the numbers in parentheses first.

$(6 + 3) + 5 = 14$ $\qquad$ $6 + (3 + 5) = 14$

$(8 + 2) + 4 = \underline{14}$ $\qquad$ $8 + (2 + 4) = \underline{14}$

Zero Property
Adding zero makes the sum the same as the other addend.

$5 + 0 = 5$ $\qquad$ $0 + 7 = 7$

$0 + 1 = \underline{1}$ $\qquad$ $8 + 0 = \underline{8}$

Subtraction

Subtracting Zero
Subtracting zero makes the difference the same as the minuend.

$9 - 0 = 9$ $\qquad$ $7 - 0 = \underline{7}$

Subtracting a Number from Itself
Subtracting a number from itself leaves zero.

$8 - 8 = 0$ $\qquad$ $3 - 3 = \underline{0}$

Checking Subtraction
Subtracting is the reverse of adding.

$15 - 9 = 6$ because $6 + 9 = 15$

$12 - 7 = \underline{5}$ because

$\underline{5} + \underline{7} = \underline{12}$

✔ **Solving for *n*** is finding the value for the *n* in the equation.

Getting Started

Solve for *n*.

1. $0 + 0 = n$
$n = \underline{0}$

2. $0 + 6 = n$
$n = \underline{6}$

Subtract. Check by adding.

3. $\begin{array}{r} 15 \\ -\ 9 \\ \hline 6 \end{array}$

4. $\begin{array}{r} 12 \\ -\ 7 \\ \hline 5 \end{array}$

5. $\begin{array}{r} 18 \\ -\ 9 \\ \hline 9 \end{array}$

Add. Check by grouping the addends another way.

6. $\begin{array}{r} 5 \\ 3 \\ +\ 4 \\ \hline 12 \end{array}$

7. $\begin{array}{r} 2 \\ 6 \\ +\ 3 \\ \hline 11 \end{array}$

8. $\begin{array}{r} 6 \\ 3 \\ +\ 4 \\ \hline 13 \end{array}$

9. $(5 + 2) + 6 = n$
$n = \underline{13}$

10. $3 + (5 + 4) = n$
$n = \underline{12}$

MCP All rights reserved

3

Teaching the Lesson

Introducing the Problem Have students read the introduction and examine the illustration. Beginning with addition, have students read aloud with you the order property grouping property and the zero property. Have students complete each sample problem. Continue with subtraction: subtracting zero, subtracting a number from itself and checking subtraction. Have students complete the sample problems. Point out that **solving for n** is a short way of saying that they are to find the numerical value for an unknown number.

Developing the Skill Use Cuisinaire rods, Sterns blocks or other manipulatives to demonstrate these concepts.

order property:

$2 + 3 = 5$ $\quad$ $3 + 2 = 5$

grouping property:

$(2 + 3) + 1 = 6$ $\quad$ $2 + (3 + 1) = 6$

zero, adding and subtracting:
$2 + 0 = 0$ $\quad$ $4 - 0 = 4$

subtracting a number from itself:
$6 - 6 = 0$

checking subtraction:
$7 - 2 = 5$ $\quad$ $2 + 5 = 7$

Give students additional problems of each kind to work with manipulatives.

Practice

Solve for *n*.

1. $5 + 0 = n$
   $n = \underline{5}$
2. $6 - 0 = n$
   $n = \underline{6}$
3. $0 - 0 = n$
   $n = \underline{0}$
4. $9 - 9 = n$
   $n = \underline{0}$

5. $5 + 8 = n$
   $n = \underline{13}$
6. $8 + 5 = n$
   $n = \underline{13}$
7. $9 + 7 = n$
   $n = \underline{16}$
8. $9 + n = 16$
   $n = \underline{7}$

Subtract. Check by adding.

9.	10.	11.	12.	13.	14.
11	15	14	16	14	6
− 6	− 7	− 5	− 8	− 7	− 6
5	8	9	8	7	0

15.	16.	17.	18.	19.	20.
17	12	13	15	11	14
− 8	− 5	− 6	− 6	− 8	− 9
9	7	7	9	3	5

Add. Check by grouping the addends another way.

21.	22.	23.	24.	25.	26.
4	7	8	4	5	7
3	2	1	3	2	1
+ 2	+ 6	+ 4	+ 5	+ 6	+ 7
9	15	13	12	13	15

27. $(8 + 0) + 6 = n$
    $n = \underline{14}$
28. $2 + (4 + 5) = n$
    $n = \underline{11}$
29. $(4 + 4) + 5 = n$
    $n = \underline{13}$

30. $6 + (2 + 3) = n$
    $n = \underline{11}$
31. $(1 + 6) + 3 = n$
    $n = \underline{10}$
32. $7 + (3 + 5) = n$
    $n = \underline{15}$

EXCURSION

Arrange the numbers 1 through 10 into 5 pairs of numbers so that the paired numbers have the sums of 6, 7, 9, 16 and 17.

$\underline{5} + \underline{1} = 6$ $\underline{3} + \underline{4} = 7$ $\underline{7} + \underline{2} = 9$

$\underline{10} + \underline{6} = 16$ $\underline{9} + \underline{8} = 17$

4

Correcting Common Errors

Some students may have difficulty understanding the order property. Have them work with partners on a set of column addition problems with three addends. For each problem, one partner adds from top to bottom, and the other adds from bottom to top. Then they compare answers to make sure that they are the same.

Enrichment

Have students solve for the missing number.

1. $n + 4 = 11$ ($n = 7$)
2. $14 - n = 5$ ($n = 9$)
3. $8 + n = 12$ ($n = 4$)
4. $n - 10 = 0$ ($n = 10$)
5. $14 = n + 8$ ($n = 6$)
6. $7 = n - 3$ ($n = 10$)
7. $2 + x = 5$ ($x = 3$)
8. $5 + a = 9$ ($a = 4$)
9. $13 = q + 4$ ($q = 9$)
10. $6 = 9 - b$ ($b = 3$)

Practice

Have students complete the practice problems. Remind them that when solving for **n,** they are to find a number that when substituted for the letter will make the problem correct.

Excursion

Take the numbers 1 through 10 and divide them into 5 pairs, so that the paired numbers have the sums of 16, 7, 6, 17 and 9.

Extra Credit   *Applications*

Ask students to solve the following problem: (Making a diagram may be helpful to them.) If a single-celled organism divided once every 30 minutes, how many organisms would there be at the end of 4 hours? Have them draw a picture that illustrates their answer. Display their mathematical art.

Reviewing Facts

Objective

To review addition and subtraction facts

Materials

*addition and subtraction flash cards

Mental Math

Have students solve for n.

1. 3 + 2 = n (5)
2. 2 + 0 = n (2)
3. 6 + 6 = n (12)
4. 5 + 8 = n (13)
5. 12 − 2 = n (10)
6. 11 − 7 = n (4)
7. 8 − 8 = n (0)

Skill Review

Use flash cards to review addition and subtraction facts. Divide the class into two teams. Show a flash card to one team. If they give the correct answer, show a different card to the other team. If a student misses a fact, he must sit down. The team with the most players at the end is the winner.

Practicing Addition Facts

Add.

2 +1 = 3	7 +2 = 9	7 +4 = 11	1 +3 = 4	1 +8 = 9	2 +3 = 5	3 +2 = 5	7 +9 = 16	1 +4 = 5	4 +4 = 8
3 +0 = 3	5 +5 = 10	8 +6 = 14	6 +0 = 6	0 +6 = 6	2 +9 = 11	3 +1 = 4	6 +3 = 9	6 +5 = 11	6 +8 = 14
9 +1 = 10	7 +0 = 7	5 +2 = 7	2 +2 = 4	1 +2 = 3	2 +6 = 8	9 +4 = 13	5 +3 = 8	7 +3 = 10	7 +6 = 13
0 +9 = 9	9 +9 = 18	3 +3 = 6	1 +6 = 7	9 +0 = 9	0 +2 = 2	7 +7 = 14	0 +3 = 3	4 +7 = 11	0 +5 = 5
7 +8 = 15	5 +6 = 11	1 +1 = 2	2 +4 = 6	5 +9 = 14	2 +5 = 7	5 +4 = 9	1 +0 = 1	7 +1 = 8	3 +5 = 8
8 +8 = 16	9 +2 = 11	5 +7 = 12	1 +7 = 8	5 +8 = 13	0 +4 = 4	6 +9 = 15	6 +7 = 13	4 +9 = 13	7 +5 = 12
9 +6 = 15	5 +1 = 6	4 +3 = 7	6 +1 = 7	8 +1 = 9	2 +0 = 2	8 +2 = 10	3 +8 = 11	6 +2 = 8	3 +7 = 10
6 +4 = 10	4 +0 = 4	9 +5 = 14	0 +7 = 7	3 +4 = 7	4 +1 = 5	8 +9 = 17	4 +8 = 12	0 +1 = 1	9 +3 = 12
8 +7 = 15	1 +5 = 6	6 +6 = 12	3 +9 = 12	8 +4 = 12	4 +2 = 6	3 +6 = 9	8 +3 = 11	5 +0 = 5	2 +8 = 10
1 +9 = 10	0 +8 = 8	8 +0 = 8	0 +0 = 0	2 +7 = 9	4 +5 = 9	9 +7 = 16	9 +8 = 17	4 +6 = 10	8 +5 = 13

MCP All rights reserved

5

Teaching the Lesson

Introducing the Problem Tell students this lesson will help them review addition and subtraction facts.

Developing the Skill

	0	1	2	3	4	5	6	7	8	9
0	0	1	2	3	4	5	6	7	8	9
1	1	2	3	4	5	6	7	8	9	10
2	2	3	4	5	6	7	8	9	10	11
3	3	4	5	6	7	8	9	10	11	12
4	4	5	6	7	8	9	10	11	12	13
5	5	6	7	8	9	10	11	12	13	14
6	6	7	8	9	10	11	12	13	14	15
7	7	8	9	10	11	12	13	14	15	16
8	8	9	10	11	12	13	14	15	16	17
9	9	10	11	12	13	14	15	16	17	18

Review addition and subtraction facts using the addition/subtraction chart. Give each student a copy.
Dictate several problems. Have students find the addends and then read in to the sum. Then have them find the subtrahend, read in to the minuend and left to the difference.

Practicing Subtraction Facts

Subtract.

3 −1 **2**	1 −0 **1**	12 −4 **8**	9 −4 **5**	10 −7 **3**	7 −7 **0**	8 −1 **7**	14 −5 **9**	6 −0 **6**	9 −8 **1**
15 −9 **6**	8 −7 **1**	10 −8 **2**	18 −9 **9**	8 −0 **8**	13 −4 **9**	7 −0 **7**	3 −2 **1**	12 −5 **7**	14 −8 **6**
8 −4 **4**	11 −3 **8**	8 −6 **2**	4 −0 **4**	9 −0 **9**	10 −4 **6**	11 −4 **7**	5 −3 **2**	1 −1 **0**	8 −3 **5**
8 −2 **6**	6 −3 **3**	6 −2 **4**	4 −1 **3**	7 −3 **4**	3 −3 **0**	11 −8 **3**	2 −1 **1**	10 −1 **9**	10 −2 **8**
9 −2 **7**	7 −1 **6**	5 −5 **0**	5 −0 **5**	15 −8 **7**	4 −3 **1**	13 −5 **8**	10 −3 **7**	5 −1 **4**	4 −4 **0**
6 −5 **1**	13 −9 **4**	9 −6 **3**	12 −8 **4**	11 −2 **9**	9 −1 **8**	2 −2 **0**	10 −6 **4**	7 −6 **1**	13 −6 **7**
16 −9 **7**	15 −7 **8**	7 −5 **2**	14 −9 **5**	17 −8 **9**	12 −6 **6**	8 −5 **3**	12 −7 **5**	5 −4 **1**	10 −9 **1**
6 −4 **2**	9 −9 **0**	12 −9 **3**	16 −8 **8**	9 −5 **4**	6 −1 **5**	8 −8 **0**	16 −7 **9**	9 −7 **2**	5 −2 **3**
11 −9 **2**	11 −7 **4**	4 −2 **2**	11 −6 **5**	11 −5 **6**	15 −6 **9**	7 −4 **3**	2 −0 **2**	14 −6 **8**	17 −9 **8**
6 −6 **0**	13 −8 **5**	10 −5 **5**	3 −0 **3**	14 −7 **7**	9 −3 **6**	0 −0 **0**	7 −2 **5**	13 −7 **6**	12 −3 **9**

6

Correcting Common Errors

If students have difficulty mastering their basic facts, have them work with partners and a set of flash cards. Have them take turns quizzing each other to practice the facts. Be sure the student reads the entire fact along with giving the answer.

Enrichment

Have students conduct their own Arithmetic Bee. Using the addition and subtraction flash cards, have one student stand up while a director shows the cards. Explain that students must give the correct answer before the contest "director" moves on to the next card. If a contestant makes a mistake, the student is eliminated. The last student standing is the winner.

Practice

Have students complete the addition and subtraction problems independently

Extra Credit *Sets*

List these items on the board and ask students what they have in common: golf clubs, chess pieces, a chemistry set, china dishes. (They all come in sets.) Point out that sets of items go by a variety of names, such as team, group, herd. Have students list as many words as they can in five minutes, that are different names for sets of things. Have the student who lists the most words write his list on the board.

Thousands

pages 7-8

Objective

To review place values through thousands

Materials

Mental Math

Give students these number pairs to use in sentences using is greater than or is less than.

1. 4, 12 (4 is less than 12)
2. 42, 24 (42 is greater than 24)
3. 2, [10 − 1] (2 is less than [10 − 1])
4. [3 + 3], [6 − 1] ([3 + 3] is more than [6 − 1])
5. [13 − 12], 0 ([13 − 12] is greater than 0)

Skill Review

Put these problems on the board. Have students work them at their desks, encouraging speed by timing them.

1. **7 + 5** (12)   8. **7 − 6** (1)
2. **10 − 2** (8)   9. **9 − 3** (6)
3. **8 + 4** (12)   10. **16 − 7** (9)
4. **5 + 6** (11)   11. **5 + 2** (7)
5. **13 − 5** (8)   12. **9 + 9** (18)
6. **15 − 9** (6)   13. **4 + 9** (13)
7. **6 + 8** (14)   14. **16 − 8** (8)

Place Value through Thousands

The government space agency plans to sell used moon buggies to the highest bidders. What did Charley pay for the one he bought?

We want to understand the cost of Charley's moon buggy.

Charley paid exactly __$7,425__.
To understand how much money this is, we will look at the place value of each digit in the price.

✔ The numbers 0, 1, 2, 3, 4, 5, 6, 7, 8 and 9 are called **digits.** The position of the digit decides its place value.

thousands	hundreds	tens	ones
7	4	2	5

In 7,425, the digit 4 represents hundreds, and the digit 7 represents __thousands__.
Numbers can be written in **standard** or **expanded form.**

Standard Form	Expanded Form
7,425	7,000 + 400 + 20 + 5

We say Charley paid **seven thousand, four hundred twenty-five dollars.** We write __$7,425__.

Getting Started

Write in standard form.

1. five thousand, six hundred fifty-eight __5,658__   2. 3,000 + 50 + 8 __3,058__

Write in words.

3. 6,497   4. 823   5. 9,045

__six thousand, four__   __eight hundred__   __nine thousand,__

__hundred ninety-seven__   __twenty-three__   __forty-five__

Write the place value of the red digits.

6. 3,948   7. 9,603   8. 7,529   9. $5,370

__tens__   __thousands__   __hundreds__   __ones__

MCP All rights reserved

7

Teaching the Lesson

Introducing the Problem Have students read the problem silently while you read it aloud. Have a student read and complete the information sentence. (paid $7,425) Read the next sentences aloud, explaining digits. Put a four column place value chart on the board and write in the number **7,425.** Ask a student to read the next sentence and explain the place value for the digit 7. (thousands) Read the next sentence aloud and write **standard** and **expanded form** on the board. Ask a student to explain how both can be used to represent the same number. (The expanded form shows the whole value of each digit in the standard form.) Reading the final sentences, point out that we use the expanded form when we read numbers aloud and standard form when we write $7,425.

Developing the Skill Write the vertical expanded form of these numbers on the board:

```
29 = 20          355 = 300          4,721 = 4,000
   + 9                  50                     700
                      +  5                      20
                                             +   1
```

Ask students to point to ones, tens, hundreds and thousands. Read each number vertically, starting at the top, so that students will see how the expanded version is also the way we read numbers aloud. Dictate several three- and four-digit numbers and have students write the numbers in vertical, expanded form.

7

Practice

Write in standard form.

1. eight hundred fifty-three
   <u>853</u>

2. six thousand, two hundred twenty-five
   <u>6,225</u>

3. four thousand, nine hundred
   <u>4,900</u>

4. three thousand, six hundred six
   <u>3,606</u>

5. seven thousand, twenty
   <u>7,020</u>

6. nine thousand, four hundred seventeen
   <u>9,417</u>

7. six hundred sixty-six
   <u>666</u>

8. three thousand, thirty-eight
   <u>3,038</u>

9. $7,000 + 300 + 30 + 9 =$ <u>7,339</u>

10. $4,000 + 60 + 2 =$ <u>4,062</u>

11. $500 + 6 =$ <u>506</u>

12. $2,000 + 700 + 8 =$ <u>2,708</u>

Write in words.

13. 6,257 <u>six thousand, two hundred fifty-seven</u>

14. 3,209 <u>three thousand, two hundred nine</u>

15. 765 <u>seven hundred sixty-five</u>

16. 8,050 <u>eight thousand fifty</u>

17. 89 <u>eighty-nine</u>

18. 4,961 <u>four thousand, nine hundred sixty-one</u>

19. 2,006 <u>two thousand, six</u>

20. 8,863 <u>eight thousand, eight hundred sixty-three</u>

21. 7,210 <u>seven thousand, two hundred ten</u>

22. 9,176 <u>nine thousand, one hundred seventy-six</u>

23. 1,311 <u>one thousand, three hundred eleven</u>

24. 5,320 <u>five thousand, three hundred twenty</u>

Write the place value of the red digits.

25. 9,650
    <u>hundreds</u>

26. 8,639
    <u>thousands</u>

27. 136
    <u>tens</u>

28. $4,257
    <u>hundreds</u>

29. 97
    <u>ones</u>

30. 7,348
    <u>tens</u>

31. 5,090
    <u>hundreds</u>

32. 3,748
    <u>thousands</u>

33. 7,516
    <u>ones</u>

34. $3,259
    <u>hundreds</u>

35. 831
    <u>hundreds</u>

36. 6,547
    <u>ones</u>

8

Correcting Common Errors

Some students may forget to use zero as a place holder when they write numbers in standard form and write 647 for "six thousand forty-seven." Have students practice writing numbers on a place-value chart, being aware that there must be a digit in every place to the right of the digit in the farthest left place.

Enrichment

Show students how the expanded form of a number can be used to simplify multi-digit addition:
$$24 + 54 = 20 + 4 + 50 + 4 =$$
$$20 + 50 + 4 + 4 =$$
$$70 + 8 = 78$$
Ask students to use expanded form to complete these problems:

1. $45 + 91$ (136)
2. $335 + 462$ (797)
3. $821 + 34$ (855)
4. $65 + 51$ (116)
5. $7,324 + 1,203$ (8,527)
6. $668 + 321$ (989)

Practice

Ask students what they are asked to do in each section. Have them complete the page independently.

Extra Credit *Measurement*

Using the daily newspaper and/or televised weather broadcasts, have students record the daily high and low temperature in their city and another city on a different continent, for one week. These temperatures can be logged in Fahrenheit and Celsius degrees. At the end of the week, have students find the average high and low temperatures for each city. Then have students make a bar graph of their results and compare graphs. Discuss any similarities in temperatures that occur in various parts of the world.

Comparing and Ordering

pages 9-10

Objective

To review comparing and ordering numbers

Materials

Mental Math

Have students tell whether the middle number in each set is closer to the first or to the last.

1. 0, 3, 10 (3 is closer to 0)
2. 10, 12, 20 (12 closer to 10)
3. 0, 5, 10
4. 0, 61, 100
5. 60, 61, 70
6. 50, 57, 60
7. 200, 240, 300

Skill Review

Put a four-digit place value chart on the board and review the meaning of each place with the class. Write the following numbers on the board and ask students to identify the place value of the underlined digits.

1. **324**
2. **5,622**
3. **95**
4. **3,778**
5. **776**
6. **892**
7. **34**
8. **207**
9. **4,879**
10. **3,677**
11. **401**
12. **8**

Comparing and Ordering Numbers

The two highest mountains on earth are Mount Everest and K2. Which mountain ranks first as the highest point on earth?

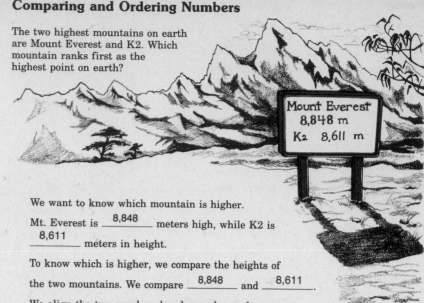

Mount Everest 8,848 m
K2 8,611 m

We want to know which mountain is higher.

Mt. Everest is ___8,848___ meters high, while K2 is ___8,611___ meters in height.

To know which is higher, we compare the heights of the two mountains. We compare ___8,848___ and ___8,611___.

We align the two numbers by place value and, starting at the left, compare the digits.

8,848	8,848
8,611	8,611
8 = 8	8 > 6

We say 8,848 **is greater than** 8,611 or 8,611 **is less than** 8,848.

We write **8,848 > 8,611** or **8,611 < 8,848.**

___Mt. Everest___ is the highest mountain on earth.

Getting Started

Write < or > in the circle.

1. 73 $<$ 76
2. 246 $<$ 426
3. 3,287 $>$ 3,247
4. 5,275 $<$ 6,796
5. 4,572 $>$ 4,562
6. 9,205 $<$ 9,215

Write the numbers in order from least to greatest.

7. 5,246 4,375 6,295
   4,375 5,246 6,295

8. 6,203 6,245 6,196
   6,196 6,203 6,245

9. 3,058 3,028 3,167
   3,028 3,058 3,167

MCP All rights reserved

9

Teaching the Lesson

Introducing the Problem Read the problem aloud and ask students to examine the illustration. Ask students what information is given. (Mt. Everest, 8,848 m; K-2 is 8,611 m) Ask another to read and complete the plan sentence. (We compare 8,848 and 8,611.) Write these numbers on the board. Pointing to the thousands column, ask students which is larger (neither, each is an 8) Point to the hundreds column and ask which is larger. (8) Ask students which is larger: 8,848 or 8,611. (8,848) Read the next sentences aloud and write the symbols < and > on the board. Have students complete the solution sentence.

Developing the Skill Put this number line on the board:

110 115 120 125 130 135 140 145

Give students the following number pairs and ask them to tell which is larger: 125, 135; 120, 115; 140, 145; 125, 120. Have students write a number line from 1,000 to 2,000 marked in hundreds. Ask them to use the number line to compare 1,300 and 1,400; 1,545 and 1,598; 1,870 and 1,900.

Practice

Write < or > in the circle.

1. 67 $>$ 63   2. 92 $<$ 95   3. 126 $>$ 123

4. 562 $<$ 652   5. 309 $>$ 299   6. 417 $<$ 471

7. 3,644 $<$ 4,564   8. 5,947 $<$ 5,949   9. 3,699 $>$ 3,000

10. 7,243 $>$ 7,234   11. 1,006 $<$ 1,008   12. 9,450 $>$ 9,350

13. 6,225 $>$ 6,224   14. 8,500 $<$ 8,600   15. 4,060 $>$ 4,059

Write the numbers from least to greatest.

16. 349 285 351
    _285 349 351_

17. 603 596 728
    _596 603 728_

18. 400 399 401
    _399 400 401_

19. 2,659 2,650 2,670
    _2,650 2,659 2,670_

20. 7,810 7,920 7,890
    _7,810 7,890 7,920_

21. 5,236 4,868 4,976
    _4,868 4,976 5,236_

22. 3,965 3,695 3,569
    _3,569 3,695 3,965_

23. 8,196 8,194 8,190
    _8,190 8,194 8,196_

24. 4,210 4,021 4,110
    _4,021 4,110 4,210_

Apply

Use the chart to answer questions 25 through 30.

25. Which mountain is the highest?
    Elbert

26. Which mountain is the lowest?
    La Plata

27. Which mountain is the fourth highest? _Blanca_

28. How many mountains are higher than Harvard? _2_

29. How many mountains are less than 14,350 feet? _1_

Mountain	Height in Feet
Blanca	14,345
Elbert	14,433
Harvard	14,420
LaPlata	14,336
Massive	14,421

30. List the mountains from highest to lowest.
    Elbert, Massive, Harvard, Blanca, La Plata

10

Correcting Common Errors

Some students may have difficulty comparing numbers when they are written side-by-side. Have them rewrite the numbers on a place-value chart, one above the other. They can then compare the digits in each place starting at the left. Ask them to work in pairs to compare the following numbers, identifying the place that determines which number is larger and then identifying the larger number.

1. 1,341 and 1,449 (hundreds; 1,449)
2. 39 and 32 (ones; 39)
3. 49 and 51 (tens; 51)
4. 448 and 442 (ones; 448)
5. 6,339 and 7,458 (thousands, 7,458)

Enrichment

Ask students to find and compare the following quantities:

1. the number of students in their class; the number in a neighboring class
2. the number of students in their school; the number in another school in the community
3. the number of people in their community; the number in a nearby community

Practice

Have students complete the practice problems. Review the meaning of the symbols < and >.

Extra Credit *Numeration*

Remind students that parentheses in a mathematical statement tell them which operation in a series to compute first. Where parentheses are placed determines the value of the statement.

For example: $(4 + 4) \times 2 = 16$, but $4 + (4 \times 2) = 12$. Have students decide where to place parentheses in the following problems to reach the given solution.

1. $13 - 2 + 1 = 10$ $[13 - (2 + 1) = 10]$
2. $3 \times 2 + 2 = 12$ $[3 \times (2 + 2) = 12]$
3. $16 - 4 \times 2 = 24$ $[(16 - 4) \times 2 = 24]$
4. $2 + 2 \times 2 = 8$ $[(2 + 2) \times 2 = 8]$
5. $6 \times 6 \div 3 = 12$ $[(6 \times 6) \div 3 = 12$ or $6 \times (6 \div 3) = 12]$
6. $12 - 8 - 1 = 3$ $[12 - (8 - 1) = 3]$

Hundred Thousands

pages 11-12

Objective

To review place values through hundred thousands

Materials

Mental Math

Ask students the place value of the 6 in:

1. 61 (tens)
2. 116 (ones)
3. 600 (hundreds)
4. 6 (ones)
5. 6,336 (thousands and ones)
6. 7,369 (tens)
7. 467 (tens)
8. 36 (ones)

Skill Review

Have students identify the place value of the digits that must be compared to find the larger of each number pair:

1. (338; 337) (ones)
2. (24; 38) (tens)
3. (7,576; 7,612) (hundreds)
4. (8; 12) (tens)
5. (43; 48) (ones)
6. (552; 589) (tens)
7. (3,472; 5,334) (thousands)

MCP All rights reserved

Place Value through Hundred Thousands

Two of the three largest islands in the world are in the Southwest Pacific Ocean. Which of these two islands is larger in area?

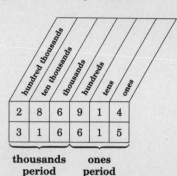

Borneo
286,914
sq mi

New Guinea
316,615
sq mi

We need to find which island is larger.

Borneo has __286,914__ square miles.

New Guinea has __316,615__ square miles.
To find the larger island, we extend the place value grid to hundred thousands and compare __286,914__ to __316,615__.

✔ Every three place values, beginning on the right, are grouped in **periods**. Knowing the periods helps us to read large numbers.

hundred thousands	ten thousands	thousands	hundreds	tens	ones
2	8	6	9	1	4
3	1	6	6	1	5

thousands period   ones period

We say Borneo has an area of **two hundred eighty-six thousand, nine hundred fourteen** square miles. New Guinea's area is **three hundred sixteen thousand, six hundred fifteen** square miles.

3 is __greater__ than 2, therefore 316,615 is __greater__ than 286,914.

The larger island is __New Guinea__ because __316,615__ square miles is greater than __286,914__ square miles.

Getting Started

Write the number in standard form.

1. three hundred twenty thousand, nine hundred fifty-eight __320,958__

Write the place value of the red digit.

2. 74**3**,869
  __ten thousands__

3. 296,**1**58
  __hundreds__

Write < or > in the circle.

4. 329,476 (>) 326,483

11

Teaching the Lesson

Introducing the Problem Have a student read the problem aloud and identify the question being asked. Read the information sentences and have students provide the numbers. (Borneo, 286,914 sq mi; New Guinea, 316,615 sq mi) Read both numbers aloud to show that the new place value is read as hundred thousands. Draw attention to the 6-digit place value chart in their texts. Point out that starting from the left, there is a difference in the numbers in the first column, hundred thousands. Have students complete the solution sentences. (3 is greater than 2; 316,615 is greater than 286,914; larger island is New Guinea because 316,615 is greater than 286,914)

Developing the Skill

Write 345,819 in expanded form: Read each line to remind the class of each place value and the way the place values are read. Give them these numbers and ask them to write each in expanded form: 439,100; 102,823; 833,781; 23,881. Have students make a six-digit place value chart and put the same numbers in it.

300,000
40,000
5,000
800
10
9

Practice

Write the number in standard form.

1. six hundred seventy-two thousand, five hundred eleven ___672,511___

2. thirty-eight thousand, two hundred eighty-three ___38,283___

3. four hundred six thousand, five hundred ___406,500___

4. one hundred fourteen thousand, ninety-one ___114,091___

5. seventy thousand, seventeen ___70,017___

6. two hundred thousand, three hundred thirty-five ___200,335___

Write the place value of the red digit.

7. 39**4**,157
___thousands___
_____

8. 63,**2**06
___hundreds___
_____

9. **9**86,154
___hundred___
___thousands___

10. 321,71**5**
___ones___
_____

11. 7**0**4,397
___ten thousands___
_____

12. **2**43,826
___hundred___
___thousands___

13. **4**5,375
___ten thousands___
_____

14. 832,**5**96
___hundreds___
_____

Write < or > in the circle.

15. 492,738 ⊘ 482,375

16. 692,587 ⊘ 694,437

17. 823,421 ⊘ 82,754

18. 199,965 ⊘ 200,048

19. 387,248 ⊘ 384,596

20. 524,137 ⊘ 542,137

Apply

Use the chart to answer questions 21 through 24.

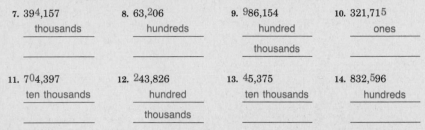

21. Which Great Lake is the largest? ___Superior___

22. How many Great Lakes have areas greater than 15,000 square miles? ___3___

23. How many Great Lakes have less area than Lake Michigan? ___2___

24. List the Great Lakes in order from the largest to the smallest. ___Superior, Huron, Michigan, Erie, Ontario___

Area of Great Lakes in Square Miles			
Erie	9,930	Ontario	7,520
Huron	23,010	Superior	31,820
Michigan	22,400		

12

Correcting Common Errors

Some students may have trouble identifying the place value of a particular digit when they are working with larger numbers. Have them write the numbers on a place-value chart, reading the names of the places to find the place of the red digit.

Enrichment

Ask students to tell whether they would estimate the following numbers in tens, hundreds, thousands, ten thousands or hundred thousands. Remind them that an estimate is a good guess.

1. pages in a book (100's)
2. pupils in the school (100's)
3. eggs in a carton (10's)
4. stars in the sky (100,000's)
5. houses in your community (answers will vary)
6. jellybeans in a quart jar (100's)

Practice

Have students complete the practice problems independently. Remind them of the meaning of standard form.

Mixed Practice

1. 7 + 5 + 8 (20)
2. 15 − 9 (6)
3. 9 + 5 (14)
4. 12 − 8 (4)
5. 1,000 + 300 + 7 (1,307)
6. 6 + 8 (14)
7. 300,000 + 2,000 + 600 + 20 (302,620)
8. 17 − 8 (9)
9. 50,000 + 2,000 + 10 + 5 (52,015)
10. 7 + 9 + 8 (24)

Extra Credit *Numeration*

Tell students they must develop a secret number code to be used in a national security project. Tell them to devise a symbol code, having a different symbol for each number 0 through 9. (for example, Δ = 1; □ = 2, etc.) Have them devise 3-digit addition and subtraction problems, using the code symbols, and have another student work them. The other student must be sure to also write their answer in the number code. Then have them correct each other's work.

Rounding Numbers

pages 13-14

Objective

To review rounding numbers to the
nearest 100 or 1,000

Materials

Mental Math

Ask students to find two addends in
each problem that have the sum of 10
and then add the third number:

1. 1 + 3 + 9 (13)
2. 3 + 2 + 8 (13)
3. 5 + 7 + 5 (17)
4. 8 + 2 + 5 (15)
5. 9 + 9 + 1 (19)
6. 3 + 7 + 4 + 6 (20)
7. 8 + 4 + 6 + 2 (20)

Skill Review

Put this number line on the board:

0 1 2 3 4 5 6 7 8 9 10

Point to several numbers and ask students to tell whether the number is
closer to 0 or to 10. Explain that this
is the same as rounding numbers to
the nearest 10. Remind them that
while 5 is not closer to either end, it is
always rounded up. Repeat with a
number line from 30 to 40.

Rounding Numbers

Soccer has become the world's most
popular sport. Matches often attract
huge crowds of people. Approximately
how many thousands of people
attended this soccer match?

We are looking for the number of thousands of
people who attended the soccer match.

The exact attendance was ___104,647___.
To approximate the number of people, we can round the
attendance number.

> To round a number to a
> particular place value,
> locate the digit to be
> rounded.

If the digit to the right is 0, 1, 2, 3 or
4, the digit we are rounding stays the
same. All the digits to the right are
replaced by zeros.

Rounded to hundreds,

104,647 is ___104,600___.

If the digit to the right is 5, 6, 7, 8 or
9, the digit we are rounding is raised
one. All digits to the right are
replaced by zeros.

Rounded to thousands,

104,647 is ___105,000___.

Rounded to the nearest thousand, there were
___105,000___ people at the soccer match.

Getting Started

Round to the nearest hundred.

1. 864	2. 15,143	3. 609,056	4. 12,450
900	15,100	609,100	12,500

Round to the nearest thousand.

5. 37,295	6. 126,529	7. 53,816	8. 756,500
37,000	127,000	54,000	757,000

MCP All rights reserved

13

Teaching the Lesson

Introducing the Problem Read the problem aloud
while students follow in their texts. Ask what information is
given in the picture. (attendance was 104,647) Explain that
this number can be rounded to hundreds or thousands in
order to estimate the number of people. Read the sentence
in the box, explaining that in order to round a number, they
must first locate the significant digit. Ask one student to
round 104,647 to hundreds (104,600) and another to
round it to thousands (105,000) Have a student read and
complete the solution sentence. (105,000)

Developing the Skill Ask a student to list the five digits
that signal that a number will be rounded down. (0, 1, 2, 3,
4) and another to list the five that mean a number will be
rounded up. (5, 6, 7, 8, 9) Write on the board: **452,449.**
Remind students that to round this to the nearest thousand,
they must look at the hundreds column. Ask one student to
underline the digit in the hundreds column, ask another to
identify the digit in that column as one that is rounded up
or down, and ask a third to round the number to the nearest thousand. (452,000) Repeat this three-part process for
the following numbers: 885,278 (885,000), 205,910
(206,000), 3,818. (4,000)

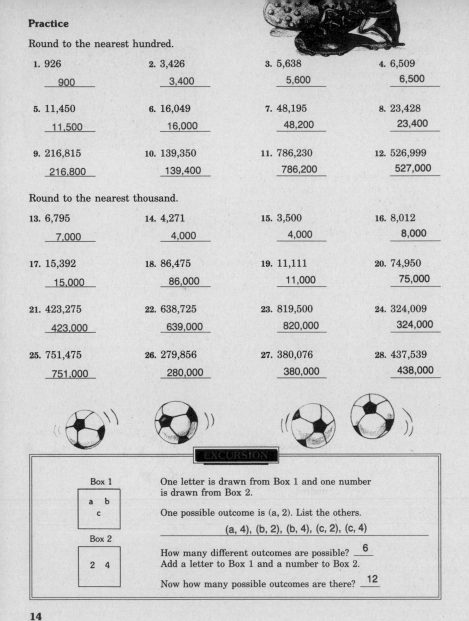

Practice

Round to the nearest hundred.

1. 926	2. 3,426	3. 5,638	4. 6,509
900	3,400	5,600	6,500
5. 11,450	6. 16,049	7. 48,195	8. 23,428
11,500	16,000	48,200	23,400
9. 216,815	10. 139,350	11. 786,230	12. 526,999
216,800	139,400	786,200	527,000

Round to the nearest thousand.

13. 6,795	14. 4,271	15. 3,500	16. 8,012
7,000	4,000	4,000	8,000
17. 15,392	18. 86,475	19. 11,111	20. 74,950
15,000	86,000	11,000	75,000
21. 423,275	22. 638,725	23. 819,500	24. 324,009
423,000	639,000	820,000	324,000
25. 751,475	26. 279,856	27. 380,076	28. 437,539
751,000	280,000	380,000	438,000

EXCURSION

Box 1

a b
  c

One letter is drawn from Box 1 and one number is drawn from Box 2.

One possible outcome is (a, 2). List the others.

(a, 4), (b, 2), (b, 4), (c, 2), (c, 4)

Box 2

2 4

How many different outcomes are possible? 6

Add a letter to Box 1 and a number to Box 2.

Now how many possible outcomes are there? 12

14

Correcting Common Errors

Some students may use the digit in the place to which they are rounding instead of the digit to the right to determine how to round the number. As these students do each problem, have them put an arrow over the digit in the place to which they are rounding. Next, have them identify the digit to the right and explain how it would affect the digit in the place under the arrow. Lastly, have them write the rounded number.

Enrichment

Give students the following prices. Tell them to round each to the nearest ten dollars. Point out that this is the same as rounding to the nearest thousand pennies.

1. $34.90 ($30.00)
2. $120.35 ($120.00)
3. $89.45 ($90.00)
4. $28.00 ($30.00)
5. $3,452.90 ($3,450.00)
6. $809.25 ($810.00)

Practice

Have students complete the practice problems independently. Point out that in one section they will round to the nearest hundred and in the other to the nearest thousand.

Excursion

With only two boxes, either the array form or the tree diagram can be used to find the Cartesian product.

	2	4
a	a2	a4
b	b2	b4
c	c2	c4

or

a < 2 .... a2
    4 .... a4
b < 2 .... b2
    4 .... b4
c < 2 .... c2
    4 .... c4

With more than two boxes, the tree diagram is best.

Extra Credit *Applications*

Have students take their pulse rate to count the number of times their hearts beat in one minute. (count the number of beats in 15 seconds and multiply by four.) Ask them to compute the following based on their own heart rate: How many times does your heart beat in one hour? How many times does your heart beat in one day? How many times does your heart beat in one week?

Hundred Billions

pages 15-16

Objective

To learn place value through hundred billion

Materials

*overhead projector
12-digit place value charts

Mental Math

Ask students to find a number exactly halfway between:

1. 3 and 5 (4)
2. 4 and 10 (7)
3. 1 and 11 (6)
4. 20 and 22 (21)
5. 14 and 18 (16)
6. 15 and 21 (18)
7. 1 and 2 (1½)

Skill Review

Write these numbers on the board and have students identify the place value of the 2 in each.

1. **20** (tens)
2. **204** (hundreds)
3. **1,342** (ones)
4. **8,267** (hundreds)
5. **424,800** (ten thousands)
6. **200,981** (hundred thousands)
7. **542,640** (thousands)
8. **934,882** (ones)
9. **56,520** (tens)
10. **8,286** (hundreds)

Place Value through Hundred Billions

Japan is the seventh most populated country in the world. How does its population compare with that of Nigeria?

We want to compare the population of Japan with that of Nigeria.

To understand large numbers, we need to extend the place value grid to include the billions and millions periods.

To compare these two numbers, we begin at the left and compare each pair of digits in the same place value.

POPULATION	
Japan	124,017,000
Nigeria	122,471,000

The first two digits of each number are the same.

billions			millions			thousands			ones		
hundreds	tens	ones	hundreds	tens	ones	hundreds	tens	ones	hundreds	tens	ones
1	2	4	0	1	7	0	0	0			
1	2	2	4	7	1	0	0	0			

In the one millions place, the 4 is greater than the 2.

We say   124,017,000 is ___greater___ than 122,471,000.

We write   124,017,000 _>_ 122,471,000.

We say the population of Japan is **one hundred twenty-four million, seventeen thousand,** and that of Nigeria is **one hundred twenty-two million, four hundred seventy-one thousand.**

Getting Started

1. Write in standard form: thirty-six billion, eighty-five million, two hundred fifty-three thousand, seven hundred nine. ___36,085,253,709___

2. Write in words: 209,326,250,086 ___two hundred nine billion, three hundred twenty-six million, two hundred fifty thousand, eighty-six___

Write the place value of the red digits.

3. 6 39,276,439,140
   ___hundred billions___

4. 49,6 57,394
   ___hundred thousands___

Write < or > in the circles.

5. 6,968,215 (>) 6,944,318

6. 13,276,493 (<) 13,726,493

15

MCP All rights reserved

Teaching the Lesson

Introducing the Problem   Have a student read the problem aloud and identify the question being asked. (how the two populations compare) Read the plan section aloud. Use the overhead projector to show the place value chart. Move from right to left, identifying each place value for the class. Write the population of the Soviet Union on the chart and then the population of the United States. (272,308,000; 233,200,000) Remind students that to compare two such large numbers, they will start at the left. Work through the rounding off with the students. Ask a student to read and complete the solution sentences. (say **272,308,000 is greater than 233,200,000; write 272,308,000> 233,200,000**) Read the final sentence and explain that this is the way these large numbers are written and read.

Developing the Skill   Project a 12-digit place value chart on the board. Give students a copy and have them label each place. Ask a student to tell how many tens there are in 100 (10), how many hundreds in 1,000 (10), how many thousands in 10,000 (10). Now ask how many millions in 10,000,000 (10), in 100,000,000 (100), and in a billion (1,000). Continue with questions about similar numbers. Dictate several six- to twelve- digit numbers for students to enter in their place value chart.

Write in standard form.

1. six billion, two hundred fifteen million, three hundred thousand, twenty-nine.

   6,215,300,029

2. three hundred twelve billion, six hundred twenty-seven million, fifty-five thousand

   312,627,055,000

3. ninety-six million, seven hundred forty-five thousand, eight hundred twenty-six

   96,745,826

4. eleven billion, four hundred eleven million, sixty-three   11,411,000,063

Write in words.

5. 5,002,939   five million, two thousand, nine hundred thirty-nine

6. 49,000,153,007   forty-nine billion, one hundred fifty-three thousand, seven

7. 13,819,000,506   thirteen billion, eight hundred nineteen million, five hundred six

8. 100,300,016   one hundred million, three hundred thousand, sixteen

Write the place value of the red digits.

9. 94,679,250   millions

10. 1,236,946,000   billions

11. 47,392,165   ten millions

12. 126,739,475,321   millions

13. 113,196,256   hundred thousands

14. 87,209,000,000   ten billions

15. 326,437,792   ten thousands

16. 675,964,286,000   hundred billions

17. 127,096,358   millions

18. 39,475,139,471   billions

19. 59,736,285   ten millions

20. 425,000,000,000   ten billions

Write < or > in the circle.

21. 37,349,246 ⊘ 37,459,680

22. 196,475,857,216 ⊘ 196,547,857,216

23. 39,758,427,511 ⊘ 39,758,427

24. 715,426,823,976 ⊘ 751,798,156,392

16

Correcting Common Errors

Some students may confuse period names and place-value names. Have them practice by writing the numbers on a place-value chart. As they read the number, they point to and use the period name to identify each set of three digits.

Enrichment

Give students a cup of salt, a teaspoon and some graph paper. Tell them to make an estimate of the number of grains of salt in the cup. Allow them to work together to figure out a plan for counting the grains. One solution is to measure out a teaspoon of salt, spread it evenly on the graph paper, count one square and multiply or add to find the number on the entire sheet. Then they can measure (or look up) the number of teaspoons in the cup.

Practice

Have students complete the practice problems, referring to their 12-digit place value charts.

Extra Credit *Numeration*

Write on the board two rows of column addition problems suitable for the ability level of your group. Each student will need a pencil and paper. Tell the students instead of working the problems as shown, but to round off the addends in row one to the nearest tenth, in row two to the nearest hundred, and in row three to the nearest thousand. Then work each problem in the usual way.
Example:

4751	=	4800
3643	=	3600
6444	=	6400
8988	=	9000
		23,800

Problem Solving Using a Plan

pages 17-18

Objective

To use a plan to solve a problem

Materials

Mental Math

Have students find two ways to make these problems correct:

1. 2 + 4 = 7 (2 + 4 = 6 or 2 + 5 = 7, or 3 + 4 = 7)
2. 10 − 5 = 6 (10 − 5 = 5 or 10 − 4 = 6 or 11 − 5 = 6)
3. 3 × 5 = 12 (3 × 5 = 15 or 3 × 4 = 12)
4. 15 − 7 = 9 (15 − 7 = 8 or 15 − 6 = 9 or 16 − 7 = 9)
5. 7 + 13 = 19 (7 + 13 = 20 or 6 + 13 = 19 or 7 + 12 = 19)
6. 6 × 7 = 36 (6 × 6 = 36 or 6 × 7 = 42)
7. 5 + 21 = 25 (5 + 21 = 26 or 4 + 21 = 25 or 5 + 20 = 25)

Using a Plan

Kathleen's goal is to successfully solve all thirty-six sets of Honor Problems. There are eight problems in a set. If it takes Kathleen about one and one-half hours to solve six problems, how many hours will it take her to solve all the problems?

★ SEE

We want to know how long it will take Kathleen to solve all of the problems.

There are __36__ sets of problems. There are __8__ problems in each set.

It takes Kathleen one and one-half hours, or __90__ minutes

to complete __6__ problems.

★ PLAN

To find the total number of problems Kathleen will solve, we multiply the number of sets by the number of

problems in each. We multiply __36__ by __8__.
To find how many groups of six problems there are, we divide the total number of problems by the number

she can work in the given time. We divide __288__ by ____.
To find the number of minutes it will take to solve all the problems, we multiply the number of groups of six by the number of minutes in an hour and a half.

We multiply __48__ by __90__. To rename minutes as

hours, we divide the number of minutes by 60. We divide __4,320__ by __60__.

★ DO

```
      36                      48 groups of 6          48                    72 hours
    ×  8                   6)288                     × 90                 60)4320
    ------                                          ------                  420
    288 total problems                              4320 minutes            ----
                                                                            120
                                                                            120
```

It will take __72__ hours to solve all of the problems.

★ CHECK

We can check our work by reworking our computation and asking ourselves if each answer seems reasonable.

MCP All rights reserved

17

Teaching the Lesson

Read the problem aloud. Point to the four stages: SEE, PLAN, DO, CHECK. Explain that in this lesson students will learn to follow these steps. Ask a volunteer to read the SEE section in the text. (36 sets of problems, 8 problems in each set, takes 90 minutes to complete 6 problems) Point out that at this stage they look over the problem, identify the question that must be answered and organize the information included in the problem. The next step is to plan a strategy for solving the problem. Have a student read the PLAN section. (multiply 36 by 8) Wait for students to do the multiplication. (288) Ask the student to continue reading. (divide 288 by 6) Wait for students to divide. (48) Read the next section of the PLAN aloud. (multiply 48 by 90). Point out that this problem has three stages and so formulating a plan to organize the steps is very important. Direct students' attention to the DO section. Point out that they have already done the first two steps. Have them complete the multiplication (48 × 90 = 4,320) and then show them

how to divide the total number of minutes by 60 to get the number of hours. (4320 ÷ 60 = 72 hours) Read the solution sentence aloud. Point out that the CHECK may be done in different ways. They can do each step of the problem again, to see that the computation was correct. Or they may work backward from 72 hours, to 4,320 minutes, to 48 sets of problems at 90 minutes each, to 288 problems if each group has 6 problems, to 36 sets of problems if each set has 8 problems.

Apply

1. Jennifer has saved $18 and Carl has saved $5. If each saves $2 more a month, how many more months will it take Jennifer to have exactly twice as much as Carl?
   4 months

2. A phone call costs 50 cents for the first three minutes and 10 cents for each additional minute. If the total cost of the call was $3.50, how many minutes long was it?
   33 minutes

3. Design a plan of how it would be possible to plant 10 trees in 5 rows, and have 4 trees in each row.
   See Solution Notes.

4. A letter costs 29 cents to mail and a post card costs 19 cents. Jason sent mail to eight friends and the cost was $2.12. How many letters did Jason send?
   6 letters

5. I have some jelly beans. When I count them by fives, I have three left over, but when I count them by sevens, there are six left over. I have fewer than 50 beans. How many jelly beans do I have?
   13 or 48 jelly beans

6. Darlene had some marbles before she won an additional 17 from Joe. Darlene then lost one third of her marbles to her brother. If Darlene now has 34 marbles, how many had she when she started?
   34 marbles

7. Read Exercise 2 again. What if the cost of the call were $4.00 instead of $3.50? Now how many minutes long would the phone call have been?
   38 minutes

8. When can an eight-digit number with a 9 in the millions place be less than an eight-digit number with an 8 in the millions place?
   See Solution Notes.

9. Manny Moneybucks won one million dollars in a contest. The prize would be paid at the rate of one thousand dollars a month. How many months would it take for Manny to get all of his prize money?
   1,000 months

10. Suppose you win a contest. You have a choice of two ways to be paid the prize: $10,000 a year for the rest of your life or $1,000 a month for 1,000 months. Which way would you choose and why?
    Answers may vary.

18

Extra Credit *Numeration*

Duplicate or write the following problems on the board. Tell students to use the four basic operations of +, −, × and ÷ to fill in each of the missing operations. Remind students that operations within parentheses are done first.

1. (5 _ 5) _ 5 _ 5 = 15 [(5 × 5) − 5 − 5 = 15]
2. (3 _ 3) _ 3 _ 3 = 15 [(3 × 3) + 3 + 3 = 15]
3. (2 _ 2 _ 2) _ 2 = 3 [(2 + 2 + 2) ÷ 2 = 3]
4. 6 _ 6 _ 6 _ 6 = 0 [6 + 6 − 6 − 6 = 0]
5. (4 _ 4) _ (4 _ 4) = 8 [(4 × 4) − (4 + 4) = 8]
6. (3 _ 3) _ 3 _ 3 _ 3 = 10 [(3 ÷ 3) + 3 + 3 + 3 = 10]

Note: Sometimes there may be more than one solution.

Solution Notes

1. Jennifer $18 - $20 - $22 - $24 - $26
   Carl $5 - $7 - $9 - $11 - $13
   Increases equal number of months.

2. Subtract cost of first three minutes from the total. Divide $3.00 by $.10 to equal 30 minutes. The first 3 minutes + 30 = 33 min.

3. Suggest a star shape.

4. Divide $2.12 by 29¢ until a remainder is found that is a multiple of 19¢.

5. Arrange number lines showing multiples of 5 and 7:

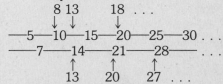

   Show remainders with arrows. Places where two arrows meet are solutions.

6. Start with 34 and work backward. Take half of 34 and add it to 34. (34 is ⅔ of the unknown; half of 34 is ⅓ of that number; together they make up the unknown amount) Divide: 34 ÷ 2 = 17. Add: 34 + 17 = 51. And subtract 17.

Higher-Order Thinking Skills

7. Analysis: $4.00 is 5 × 10¢ more than $3.50; so the time is 5 minutes longer than the first answer.

8. Synthesis: An eight-digit number goes to ten millions; so the answer is when one number has a digit in the ten millions place with a value less than the digit in the ten millions place of another.

9. Analysis: There are 1,000 thousands in 1 million.

10. Evaluation: Monthly payments yield a million dollars in a little more than 83 years. To get the same million with the annual payment, students would have to live 100 more years.

Calculator Codes

pages 19-20

Objective

To review the calculator keyboard and addition and subtraction

Materials

calculators

Mental Math

Ask students to give the operation:

1. 12 ☐ 3 = 15 (+)
2. 25 = 27 ☐ 2 (−)
3. 4 ☐ 4 = 0 (−)
4. 9 ☐ 5 = 4 (−)
5. 21 ☐ 7 = 14 (−)
6. 15 ☐ 6 = 21 (+)
7. 19 ☐ 9 = 10 (−)

Skill Review

Ask students to find these keys: +, −, ×, −, =, CE and C. Have them explain what the symbol on each key means. Put these problems on the board and have students fill in the blanks.

1. 3 ☐ 2 = 1 (−)
2. 8 ☐ 5 = 13 (+)
3. 15 ☐ 10 + 5 (=)
4. 16 − 4 ☐ 12 (=)

Calculator Codes

A calculator can make many operations easier. Numbers and operations are entered by pressing the **keys** on the **keyboard.** We use a **calculator code** to show the order in which to press the keys. Turn your calculator on, enter the codes, and write the results on the empty screens.

5 (+) 8 (=) (13)

16 (−) 9 (=) (7)

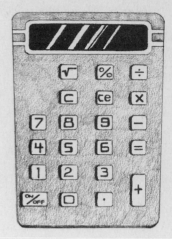

Sometimes a key is pressed by mistake. The **clear key** (C) clears all entries in the calculator, and starts it over at 0. The **clear-entry key** (CE) cancels only the most recent entry.

Complete these codes.

9 (+) 8 (+) 6 (C) (=) (0)   12 (−) 6 (−) 2 (C) (=) (0)

9 (+) 8 (+) 6 (CE) (=) (17)   12 (−) 6 (−) 2 (CE) (=) (6)

15 (−) 3 (CE) (+) 6 (=) (21)   27 (÷) 9 (C) + 3 (=) (3)

The equal key (=) is also called the **constant key.** It remembers the last operation and number entered.

Complete these codes.

3 (+) 3 (=) (=) (=) (=) (15)   12 (−) 4 (=) (=) (=) (0)

7 (+) 7 (=) (=) (=) (=) (=) (42)   25 (−) 5 (=) (=) (=) (=) (5)

8 (+) 8 (=) (=) (=) (=) (40)   6 (+) 8 (=) (=) (=) (=) (=) (46)

21 (−) 7 (=) (=) (=) (0)   36 (−) 6 (=) (=) (=) (=) (=) (6)

MCP All rights reserved

19

Teaching the Lesson

Introducing the Problem Have a student read the problem aloud. Point out any differences between your calculators and the model shown in the text. Remind students that the operations shown in boxes represent the keys on the calculator. Have them complete the first two problems and enter the answers as indicated. (13, 7) Explain the clear key and the clear-entry key. Have students do the next six problems. (0, 0, 17, 6, 21, 3) Ask a student to explain the difference between the action of the two keys. (one clears the entire problem, the other only the last entry) Explain that the = key remembers the last operation and the last number and will repeat it until you enter a new number and operation. Have students work the last eight problems. (15, 0, 42, 5, 40, 46, 0, 6)

Developing the Skill Put the following problems on the board for students to work. Have students come to the board and complete the codes.

2 + 5 = (7)   **13 + 27 =** (40)
15 + 3 = (18)   **38 − 28 =** (10)

Ask students to give the answer to each of these calculator codes:

5 + 5 CE + 4 = (9)
3 + 5C 6 + 5 = (11)

Now have students add 5 to itself four times. (+ 5 = = = =; 20) Have them start with 26 and subtract 3 four times. (26 − 3 = = = = =; 14) Put solutions on the board.

Practice

Complete these codes. Write each result on the screen.

1. 7 $+$ 6 $=$ (13)
2. 17 $-$ 8 $=$ (9)
3. 8 $+$ 7 $=$ (15)
4. 8 $-$ 6 $=$ (2)
5. 3 $+$ 8 $+$ 4 $=$ (15)
6. 15 $-$ 9 $+$ 4 $=$ (10)
7. 8 $+$ 6 $+$ 7 $=$ (21)
8. 21 $-$ 7 $-$ 6 $=$ (8)
9. 17 $-$ 9 $+$ 6 $=$ (14)
10. 8 $-$ 5 $+$ 9 $=$ (12)
11. 14 $-$ 3 $+$ C $=$ (0)
12. 9 $+$ 4 $-$ 5 $+$ 7 C $=$ (0)
13. 13 $+$ 7 $-$ 7 $+$ 5 CE $=$ (13)
14. 9 $+$ 6 $-$ 4 CE $-$ 7 $=$ (8)

Apply

Use your calculator to solve these problems.

15. Tom rode his bike 9 miles on Monday, 6 miles on Wednesday and 7 miles on Friday. How far did Tom ride his bike?
22 miles

16. Ann tried 25 free throws and made 13. Rhonda tried 20 free throws, and made 5 more than Ann. How many free throws did Rhonda make?
18 free throws

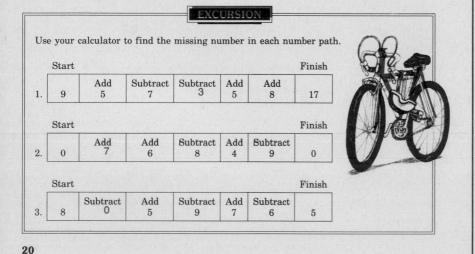

EXCURSION

Use your calculator to find the missing number in each number path.

1.

Start	Add 5	Subtract 7	Subtract 3	Add 5	Add 8	Finish
9						17

2.

Start	Add 7	Add 6	Subtract 8	Add 4	Subtract 9	Finish
0						0

3.

Start	Subtract 0	Add 5	Subtract 9	Add 7	Subtract 6	Finish
8						5

20

Correcting Common Errors

Some students may get incorrect answers when using their calculators because they accidentally push the incorrect key. Have them work with partners, taking turns to name the keys out loud as they enter the calculator codes.

Enrichment

Show students that + 3 = = is the same as 3 × 2. Ask them to work these problems using = instead of ×. Have them write out the way they solved each problem as well as the answer. (There will be two ways to do each problem.)

1. 5 × 9 (+ 5 = = = = = = = = = =; 45)
2. 10 × 5
3. 8 × 4
4. 6 × 6

Practice

Have students work the practice problems with calculators. Remind them that accuracy is important and they should check each step on the screen to see that they have entered the number correctly.

Excursion

Students will see they can work each code, skipping over the missing number, arriving at an answer. Finding the difference between that answer and the one given, will give them the missing number.

Extra Credit *Logic*

Have students solve the following math riddles. What three numbers 1 through 9 have a:

1. product of 210 and a sum of 18? (5, 6, 7)
2. product of 40 and a sum of 11? (2, 4, 5)
3. product of 144 and a sum of 17? (3, 6, 8)
4. product of 42 and a sum of 12? (2, 3, 7)
5. product of 160 and a sum of 17? (4, 5, 8)
6. product of 72 and a sum of 18? (1, 8, 9)
7. product of 216 and a sum of 19? (4, 6, 9)
8. product of 48 and a sum of 13? (2, 3, 8)

Have students make math riddles of their own using three numbers.

Chapter Test

page 21

Item	Objective
1-9	Recall basic addition and subtraction facts (See pages 1-6)
10	Add three 1-digit addends (See pages 3-4)
11-14	Identify place value in a number less than 100,000,000,000 (See pages 7-8, 11-12)
15-20	Compare and order numbers through hundred thousands (See pages 11-12)
21-24	Round numbers to the nearest 100 or 1,000 (See pages 13-14)
25-28	Read and write numbers through billions (See pages 15-16)

Add or subtract.

1. $5 + 9 = \underline{14}$ 2. $7 + 8 = \underline{15}$ 3. $15 - 6 = \underline{9}$ 4. $7 - 7 = \underline{0}$

5. $\begin{array}{r} 4 \\ +\ 7 \\ \hline 11 \end{array}$
6. $\begin{array}{r} 16 \\ -\ 9 \\ \hline 7 \end{array}$
7. $\begin{array}{r} 14 \\ -\ 8 \\ \hline 6 \end{array}$
8. $\begin{array}{r} 9 \\ -\ 0 \\ \hline 9 \end{array}$
9. $\begin{array}{r} 7 \\ +\ 0 \\ \hline 7 \end{array}$
10. $\begin{array}{r} 6 \\ 2 \\ +\ 3 \\ \hline 11 \end{array}$

Write the place value of the red digits.

11. 17,291   12. 603,201   13. 35,916   14. 815,960,000

  hundreds   hundred   ones   hundred

  _____   thousands   _____   millions

Write < or > in the circle.

15. 86 $<$ 96   16. 357 $>$ 351   17. 367,040 $<$ 376,400

18. 3,954 $>$ 3,594   19. 86,751 $>$ 68,975   20. 275,386 $>$ 275,097

Round to the nearest hundred.   Round to the nearest thousand.

21. 3,265   22. 6,500   23. 15,638   24. 75,475

  3,300   6,500   16,000   75,000

Write in standard form.

25. sixteen million, four hundred fifty-seven thousand, nine hundred four

  16,457,904

26. two hundred billion, sixty-four million, seven thousand, thirty-seven

  200,064,007,037

Write in words.

27. 31,405,000 _____ thirty-one million, four hundred five thousand _____

28. 16,008,000,000 _____ sixteen billion, eight million _____

MCP All rights reserved

21

21

Circle the letter of the correct answer.

1 7 + 8
a 14
(b) 15
c 16
d NG

2 16 − 7
a 7
b 8
(c) 9
d NG

3
   6
   2
  + 7
a 8
b 9
c 17
(d) NG

4 $n + 3 = 9$
   $n = ?$
a 3
(b) 6
c 12
d NG

5 $4 + n = 4$
   $n = ?$
(a) 0
b 4
c 8
d NG

6 What is the place value of the 6 in 4,639?
a ones
b tens
(c) hundreds
d NG

7 What is the place value of the 7 in 37,186?
a ones
b tens
c hundreds
(d) NG

8 What is the place value of the 0 in 208,596?
a thousands
(b) ten thousands
c hundred thousands
d NG

9 379 ◯ 397
(a) <
b >
c =

10 7,929 ◯ 7,992
(a) <
b >
c =

11 673,291 ◯ 672,391
a <
(b) >
c =

12 Round 13,743 to the nearest hundred.
a 13,000
(b) 13,700
c 13,800
d NG

13 Round 46,257 to the nearest thousand.
(a) 46,000
b 46,200
c 47,000
d NG

14 Round 259,500 to the nearest thousand.
a 259,000
(b) 260,000
c 261,000
d NG

☐ score

22

Cumulative Review

page 22

Item	Objective
1-2	Recall basic addition and subtraction facts (See pages 1-6)
3	Add three 1-digit numbers (See pages 3-4)
4-5	Find missing addends (See pages 1-2)
6	Identify place value in a number less than 10,000 (See pages 7-8)
7-8	Identify place value in a number less than 1,000,000 (See pages 11-12)
9-10	Compare and order numbers through thousands (See pages 9-10)
11	Compare and order numbers through hundred thousands (See pages 11-12)
12-14	Round numbers to the nearest 100 or 1,000 (See pages 13-14)

Alternate Cumulative Review

Circle the letter of the correct answer.

1 6 + 7
a 12
(b) 13
c 14
d NG

2 17 − 9
a 6
b 7
(c) 8
d NG

3
   4
   1
  + 9
a 13
b 16
c 12
(d) NG

4 $6 + n = 7$
   $n = ?$
a 3
(b) 1
c 2
d NG

5 $n + 4 = 8$
   $n = ?$
(a) 4
b 2
c 6
d NG

6 Give the place value of the 4 in 9,482.
a ones
b tens
(c) hundreds
d NG

7 Give the place value of the 0 in 680,473.
a ones
b tens
c hundreds
(d) NG

8 Give the place value of the 8 in 85,206.
a thousands
(b) ten thousands
c hundred thousands
d NG

9 245 ◯ 254
(a) <
b >
c =

10 9,773 ◯ 9,737
a <
(b) >
c =

11 124,973 ◯ 123,973
a <
(b) >
c =

12 Round 18,876 to the nearest hundred.
a 19,000
(b) 18,900
c 18,800
d NG

22

Adding 2- and 3-digit Numbers

pages 23-24

Objective

To review addition of 2- and 3-digit numbers

Materials

*addition flash cards

Mental Math

Have students give the total value of the following coins:

1. 1 dime, 1 nickel, 2 pennies (17¢)
2. 1 quarter, 10 pennies (35¢)
3. 1 nickel, 1 quarter, 9 pennies (39¢)
4. 10 dimes ($1.00)
5. 2 quarters, 5 nickels (75¢)
6. 5 pennies (5¢)

Skill Review

Write a 3-digit place value chart on the board. Have a student label each place. (hundreds, tens, ones) Write the number 734 in the chart and ask students how many hundreds (7), how many tens (3), and how many ones (4). Have students copy the place value chart and dictate the following numbers for them to put in their charts: 552, 901, 52, 610, 848, 5 and 80.

2

ADDITION AND SUBTRACTION OF WHOLE NUMBERS

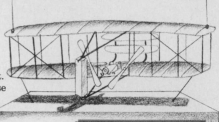

Adding 2- and 3-digit Numbers

The Wright brothers made the world's first airplane flights on December 17, 1903, at Kitty Hawk, North Carolina. Orville made the first flight but Wilbur made the longest. How far did the Wright brothers fly on those two flights?

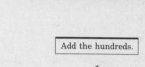

Orville   120 feet
Wilbur   852 feet

We need to find the total distance the Wright brothers flew.

Orville flew __120__ feet and Wilbur flew __852__ feet.

To find the total distance, we add __120__ and __852__.

Add the ones.		Add the tens.	Add the hundreds.
$\begin{array}{r} 1\,2\,0 \\ +\ 85\,2 \\ \hline 2 \end{array}$	$0 + 2 = 2$	$\begin{array}{r} 1\,20 \\ +\ 8\,52 \\ \hline 72 \end{array}$	$\begin{array}{r} 1\,20 \\ +\ 852 \\ \hline 972 \end{array}$

The Wright brothers flew a total of __972__ feet in their first two flights.

Getting Started

Add.

1. $\begin{array}{r} 56 \\ +48 \\ \hline 104 \end{array}$
2. $\begin{array}{r} 18 \\ +74 \\ \hline 92 \end{array}$
3. $\begin{array}{r} 32 \\ +49 \\ \hline 81 \end{array}$
4. $\begin{array}{r} 56 \\ +83 \\ \hline 139 \end{array}$

5. $\begin{array}{r} 134 \\ +\ 57 \\ \hline 191 \end{array}$
6. $\begin{array}{r} 24 \\ +269 \\ \hline 293 \end{array}$
7. $\begin{array}{r} 284 \\ +\ 53 \\ \hline 337 \end{array}$
8. $\begin{array}{r} 896 \\ +\ 73 \\ \hline 969 \end{array}$

Copy and add.

9. 117 + 359
   476
10. 636 + 338
    974
11. 485 + 394
    879

23

MCP All rights reserved

Teaching the Lesson

Introducing the Problem   Read the problem aloud. Have a student read the information sentences. (Orville, 120 feet; Wilbur, 852 feet) Read the plan sentence and direct their attention to the problem worked in three steps in the model. Illustrate the steps on the board, adding ones, then tens, then hundreds. Have a student fill in the solution sentence. (972 feet)

Developing the Skill   Ask a student to explain the place value in a 3-digit number. (hundreds, tens, ones) Explain that two 3-digit numbers can be added if like digits are added: hundreds to hundreds, tens to tens, and so on. Point out that they will start each addition with the ones column and add from right to left. Put these problems on the board. Have one student label the place values and have another do each addition.

387	108	447	704	56	806
+141	+891	+222	+643	+842	+ 85
(528)	(999)	(669)	(1,347)	(898)	(891)

Practice

Add.

1. 63 + 29 92	2. 51 + 26 77	3. 37 + 19 56	4. 68 + 81 149	5. 54 + 73 127
6. 215 + 83 298	7. 68 + 471 539	8. 537 + 49 586	9. 617 + 62 679	10. 694 + 84 778
11. 215 + 326 541	12. 409 + 376 785	13. 632 + 185 817	14. 328 + 467 795	15. 515 + 284 799

Copy and Do

16. 611 + 243
854

17. 319 + 432
751

18. 708 + 248
956

19. 573 + 284
857

20. 79 + 80
159

21. 326 + 47
373

22. 58 + 306
364

23. 212 + 448
660

24. 327 + 192
519

25. 76 + 517
593

26. 843 + 195
1,038

27. 754 + 236
990

Apply

Solve these problems.

28. On Tuesday, 143 fifth graders visited the air museum. On Wednesday, 218 sixth graders toured the art museum. How many students went on field trips to the two museums?
361 students

29. One hundred twelve fifth graders took bag lunches on their field trip. Ninety-six sixth graders carried their lunches on their tour. How many students took their lunches to the museums?
208 students

30. How many bottle caps between them would two boys have collected, if one had saved 65 and the other had saved 349?
414 bottle caps

31. Is the sum of 852 and 475 greater or less than the sum of 799 and 499?
greater

24

Correcting Common Errors

Some students may correctly rename when they are adding but then forget to add the renamed number.

INCORRECT   CORRECT

34	1 34
+ 79	+ 79
103	113

Have these students practice by using place-value materials to model each problem.

Enrichment

Ask students to work in pairs. Mark off a starting line and give each group a tape measure. Explain that each student will jump as far as possible from the starting line and measure the jump. The two partners add their distances together. See which team gets the highest score. This is a good activity for outdoors.

Practice

Have students complete the practice problems independently. Point out that when copying problems they will have to be careful to keep the columns straight.

Extra Credit *Applications*

Have students bring in grocery store register tapes. Number the tapes. Cut off the total amounts and number the total to correspond with its tape. Then put the totals and tapes into separate envelopes. Tell students to independently practice their addition by adding the prices on a tape and checking their total by matching the total in the envelope. Extend the activity by using tapes with the totals left on, but with a price on the tape covered. Have students find the missing price.

24

Column Addition

Objective

To review column addition, addends less than 10,000

Materials

Mental Math

Have students complete each fact family:

1. 3 + 4 = 7 (4 + 3 = 7, 7 − 3 = 4, 7 − 4 = 3)
2. 9 + 1 = 10 (1 + 9 = 10, 10 − 1 = 9, 10 − 9 = 1)
3. 5 + 5 = 10 (10 − 5 = 5)
4. 3 + 0 = 3 (0 + 3 = 3, 3 − 0 = 3, 3 − 3 = 0)
5. 8 − 2 = 6 (8 − 6 = 2, 2 + 6 = 8, 6 + 2 = 8)

Skill Review

Dictate these column addition problems for students to copy and complete.

1. 3 + 1 + 6 (10)
2. 5 + 4 + 10 (19)
3. 11 + 4 + 8 (23)
4. 6 + 6 + 6 (18)
5. 9 + 4 + 8 (21)
6. 7 + 7 + 5 (19)

MCP All rights reserved

Column Addition

The state of Maine is larger than Vermont, New Hampshire and Massachusetts put together. What is the total area of these three smaller states?

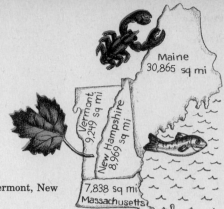

Maine 30,865 sq mi

Vermont 9,249 sq mi

New Hampshire 8,969 sq mi

7,838 sq mi Massachusetts

We need to find the total area of Vermont, New Hampshire and Massachusetts.

Vermont covers __9,249__ square miles, New Hampshire __8,969__ square miles and Massachusetts __7,938__ square miles.

To find the total area, we add the areas of all three states. We add __9,249__, __8,969__ and __7,838__.

Add the ones.	Add the tens.	Add the hundreds.	Add the thousands.
$\overset{2}{9,249}$	$\overset{1\,2}{9,249}$	$\overset{2\ 1}{9,249}$	$\overset{2}{9,249}$
8,969	8,969	8,969	8,969
+ 7,838	+ 7,838	+ 7,838	+ 7,838
6	56	056	26,056

The total area of Vermont, New Hampshire and Massachusetts is __26,056__ square miles.

Getting Started

Add.

1. 736
    458
  + 695
  _____
  1,889

2. 498
     76
  + 625
  _____
  1,199

3. 8,216
      987
  +   43
  _____
  9,246

4. 1,917
    6,212
    3,965
  + 2,468
  _____
  14,562

Copy and add.

5. 896 + 3,248 + 652
   4,796

6. 96 + 2,795 + 865
   3,756

7. 8,485 + 6,458 + 5,216
   20,159

25

Teaching the Lesson

Introducing the Problem Read the problem aloud and have students survey the map. Have one student read and complete the information sentences. (Vermont, 9,249; New Hampshire, 8,969; Massachusetts, 7,838) Read the plan sentence aloud. Direct students' attention to the problem worked in four stages in their texts. Copy the problem on the board and have different students add each column while the others follow in their texts. Have students transfer the answer to the solution sentence. (total area, 26,056 sq mi)

Developing the Skill Explain that column addition is simply adding three or more numbers. Ask students if it is different from adding two numbers. (no) Put a sample problem on the board within a 4-digit place value chart. (4,550 + 3,225 + 1,134) Emphasize importance of keeping columns straight. Ask students where you should start to add. (ones column) Have a volunteer do the ones addition.

Ask other students to complete the addition of tens, hundreds and thousands. (8,909) Remind students they may have to trade ones for tens, tens for hundreds, or hundreds for thousands when they add. Have students do these problems on the board:

3,558	5,234	7,859	3,961
1,492	463	2,616	5,462
+3,933	+ 74	+ 127	+3,653
(8,983)	(5,771)	(10,602)	(13,076)

Practice

Add.

1.	596 428 + 74 **1,098**	**2.**	318 79 + 654 **1,051**	**3.**	483 727 + 851 **2,061**	**4.**	547 685 + 219 **1,451**
5.	3,247 1,656 + 947 **5,850**	**6.**	7,225 74 + 858 **8,157**	**7.**	412 3,639 + 4,725 **8,776**	**8.**	59 753 + 6,257 **7,069**
9.	5,286 1,394 + 6,475 **13,155**	**10.**	9,275 6,450 + 7,096 **22,821**	**11.**	6,352 874 628 + 5,395 **13,249**	**12.**	8,216 4,728 3,219 + 6,853 **23,016**

Copy and Do

13. 1,475 + 9,654 + 3,617
14,746

14. 3,872 + 6,593 + 76
10,541

15. 4,232 + 7,912 + 825
12,969

16. 396 + 975 + 856
2,227

17. 3,279 + 85 + 7,293
10,657

18. 654 + 96 + 8,455
9,205

19. 8,273 + 4,176 + 6,228
18,677

20. 7,593 + 2,483 + 5,312
15,388

21. 8,948 + 7,316 + 9,286
25,550

Apply

Use the chart to answer questions 22 through 24.

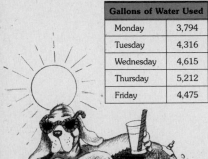

Gallons of Water Used	
Monday	3,794
Tuesday	4,316
Wednesday	4,615
Thursday	5,212
Friday	4,475

22. How much water was used on Monday, Wednesday and Friday?
12,884 gallons

23. How much water was used on Tuesday, Wednesday and Thursday?
14,143 gallons

24. How much water was used in the five days?
22,412 gallons

26

Correcting Common Errors

Some students may add incorrectly when working with column addition because they cannot remember the partial sum. Have them practice by writing the sum of the first two numbers in the column next to the second number and then adding that sum to the third number, and continue in like manner to the bottom of the column. They can repeat the procedure with each column in the problem.

Enrichment

Give students the following information: The planet Mars has two moons, Phobos and Deimos. Phobos is 5,585 miles from Mars and Deimos is 8,744 miles from Phobos. Have them calculate the distance from Mars to its furthest moon. (14,329 miles)

Practice

Have students complete the practice problems. Remind them to keep their columns straight when they copy problems.

Extra Credit *Applications*

Use a typewriter to give students experience in setting up and solving division and multiplication problems. Explain that typewriters can be set to type a certain number of letters or spaces per line. Show students how this is done using the margin set of a typewriter. Then give students the following problems:

1. If the typewriter is set for 50 spaces or letters per line, how many lines will it take to type 200 spaces or letters? (4 lines)

2. If your typewriter is set for 50 letters or spaces per line, how many letters or spaces will there be in 6 lines of type? (300 spaces)

3. If a person can type 60 words per minute, how many words can be typed in 10 minutes? (600 words)

Have students actually type the problems on the typewriter to see if their calculations are correct.

26

Adding Greater Numbers

pages 27-28

Objective

To add numbers to one million

Materials

graph paper

Mental Math

Ask students to tell which sum is larger:

1. 2,000 + 15,000 or 9,000 + 4,000
   (17,000 > 13,000)
2. 500 + 900 or 300 + 1,200
   (1,400 < 1,500)
3. 7,000 + 1,000 or 5,000 + 3,000
   (same, 8,000)
4. 8,000 + 8,000 or 14,000 + 1,000
   (16,000 > 15,000)
5. 17,000 + 10,000 or
   5,000 + 20,000 (27,000 > 25,000)

Skill Review

Put this chart on the board for students to complete:

How many?

10's in 100 _____ (10)
100's in 1000 _____ (10)
1000's in 10,000 _____ (10)
10,000's in 100,000 _____ (10)
100,000's in 1,000,000 _____ (10)

Ask students to label their own 7-digit place value chart.

Adding Greater Numbers

The Dakota Territory was first opened for homesteading in 1863. How many people live in the states of North and South Dakota today?

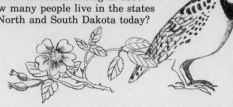

NORTH DAKOTA
POP. 635,717

SOUTH DAKOTA
POP. 703,768

We want to find the present population of North and South Dakota.

The population of North Dakota is 635,717 ,

and that of South Dakota is 703,768 .

To find the total population, we add 635,717

and 703,768 .

✔ Remember to start adding the ones, and continue adding each column to the left.

$$\begin{array}{r} 635,717 \\ +703,768 \\ \hline 1,339,485 \end{array}$$

There are 1,339,485 people presently living in North and South Dakota.

✔ Remember when adding any numbers, including money, align the place values carefully. In the case of money, be sure to include the dollar sign and decimal point in the sum.

Getting Started

Add.

1.	2.	3.
67,294	$6,243.15	267,395
+ 38,615	+ 756.28	+ 538,246
105,909	$6,999.43	805,641

Copy and add.

4. $11,275.85 + $16,984.36
   $28,260.21

5. 984,247 + 651,426
   1,635,673

6. 327,128 + 49,765 + 4,386
   381,279

MCP All rights reserved

27

Teaching the Skill

Introducing the Problem   Have a student read the problem aloud and ask the class to look at the illustration. Read the information sentences aloud and have students follow in their texts. Continue with the plan sentence and write the problem on the board as it appears in the text. Have a student work the problem. Explain that as with smaller numbers they are to start with ones and move to the left as they add. Have a student read and complete the solution sentence. (1,343,485 people) Ask a student to read the last sentences.

Developing the Skill   Explain that keeping the digits in straight columns is very important. Give each student graph paper and have them copy this problem, putting one digit in each square:

$$\begin{array}{r} 347,992 \\ +810,694 \end{array}$$

Work the problem on the board while students do it on graph paper. (1,158,686) Dictate these problems and have them use graph paper to practice keeping columns straight.

382,448	273,129	403,028
+171,365	+367,701	+527,372
(553,813)	(640,830)	(930,400)

27

Add.

1.
```
  34,739
+  6,726
  41,465
```

2.
```
   4,757
+ 75,839
  80,596
```

3.
```
  57,265
+ 18,491
  75,756
```

4.
```
  112,536
+ 455,392
  567,928
```

5.
```
  648,257
+ 316,826
  965,083
```

6.
```
$2,169.85
+  795.37
$2,965.22
```

7.
```
$4,256.48
+ 3,817.52
$8,074.00
```

8.
```
  196,275
+ 827,385
1,023,660
```

9.
```
  453,750
+ 936,248
1,389,998
```

10.
```
$16,375.37
+  9,683.82
$26,059.19
```

11.
```
  756,385
+ 836,298
1,592,683
```

12.
```
$47,384.36
+ 26,428.75
$73,813.11
```

Copy and Do

13. 13,751 + 8,475
22,226

14. $9,275.16 + $3,186.36
$12,461.52

15. 16,750 + 11,240 + 9,126
37,116

16. 32,756 + 9,748 + 14,755
57,259

17. $4,725.50 + $876.39 + $2,175.29
$7,777.18

18. 136,795 + 56,726
193,521

19. 212,750 + 3,968 + 11,265
227,983

20. $485.27 + $16,295 + $3,705.83
$20,486.10

21. 326,758 + 246,720 + 613,953
1,187,431

22. 487,350 + 927,375 + 867,426
2,282,151

Apply

Use the map to answer questions 23 through 25.

23. How many people live in the cities of San Francisco and Oakland?
1,096,201 people

24. What is the total population of Oakland, Fremont and San Jose?
1,327,829 people

25. How many people live in all four cities on the map?
2,051,788

Oakland 372,242
San Francisco 723,959
Fremont 173,339
San Jose 782,248

28

Correcting Common Errors

Watch for students who rename incorrectly or forget to rename entirely. Have them practice by doing the addition on a place-value chart where they show all the renamed numbers.

```
   T HTO
   1 1 1
   4,637
 + 2,498
   7,135
```

Enrichment

Give students the following information: The planet Neptune has two moons, Triton and Nereid. Triton is 219,000 miles from Neptune and Nereid is 3,242,000 miles from Triton. Ask students to calculate the distance from Neptune to Nereid. (219,000 + 3,242,000 = 3,461,000 mi)

Practice

Have students complete the practice problems independently.

Mixed Practice

1. 13 − 8 (5)
2. 652 + 927 (1,579)
3. 30,000 + 7,000 + 6 (37,006)
4. 6,203 + 28 + 495 (6,726)
5. $530.95 + 657.38 ($1,188.33)
6. 11 − 5 (6)
7. 7 + 6 + 9 (22)
8. $25.93 + $178.36 + $596.09 ($800.38)
9. 500,000 + 20,000 + 7,000 + 500 + 3 (527,503)
10. 14 − 6 (8)

Extra Credit *Applications*

Divide students into groups. Have each group choose a sport to research that requires a specific playing field or area. Remind them to include indoor sports. Have each group find the exact dimensions of the field for their sport and put their information on a class chart. Draw a class chart on the board, divided into four columns, recording: sport name, diagram of field, length and width. Have students then calculate the perimeters of all the fields and chart that data.

Estimating Sums

pages 29-30

Objective

To round to the nearest 100 or 1,000 in order to estimate sums

Materials

Mental Math

Ask students to tell all values for a and b that will make these number sentences true:

1. a + b = 12 (12,0; 11,1; 10,2; 9,3; 8,4; 7,5; 6,6)
2. a + b = 2
3. a + b = 10
4. a + b = 14

Skill Review

Put a number line on the board:

0—1—2—3—4—5—6—7—8—9—10

Indicate with an arrow that numbers to the right of 5 are rounded up, to the left, down. Give students these numbers to round to the nearest 10:

1. 24 (20)   4. 32 (30)
2. 38 (40)   5. 45 (50)
3. 15 (20)   6. 81 (80)

MCP All rights reserved

Estimating Sums

Larry is a flight attendant for a major airline. He keeps track of the number of miles he flies each month. Estimate the distance Larry has flown since September.

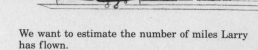

LOG BOOK	
September	8,465 miles
October	11,878 miles
November	9,312 miles
December	12,744 miles

We want to estimate the number of miles Larry has flown.

To estimate the distance, we round each monthly distance to the nearest thousand and add.

✔ Notice that the numbers are all rounded to thousands place because that is the greatest place value they all have in common.

8,465 is rounded to __8,000__.

11,878 is rounded to __12,000__.

9,312 is rounded to __9,000__.

12,744 is rounded to __13,000__.

The estimated sum is __42,000__.

Larry has flown about __42,000__ miles.

Getting Started

Estimate the sum by rounding the addends to the greatest common place value.

1.	687	700	2.	16,350	16,000	3.	37,852	38,000
	+ 793	+ 800		+ 7,275	+ 7,000		+ 6,275	+ 6,000
		1,500			23,000			44,000

4.	$758.16	$800	5.	$3,742.38	$4,000	6.	$38,215.39	$38,000
	+ 186.50	+ 200		+ 6,849.26	+ 7,000		+ 7,812.06	+ 8,000
		$1,000			$11,000			$46,000

Copy and add.

7. 557 + 678
   1,235

8. 4,329 + 3,592
   7,921

9. $47,615.83 + $75,589.45
   $123,205.28

29

Teaching the Lesson

Introducing the Problem   Have a student read the problem aloud and tell what is to be found. (estimated distance flown). Have students look at the log book. Have a student read the plan sentences. Explain that they will round to the nearest thousand because even the smallest numbers have thousands. Put each distance on the board and have students round the numbers to the nearest thousand. (8,000; 12,000; 9,000; 13,000) Ask students to add 8, 12, 9 and 13; and have a volunteer put the estimated sum on the board. (42,000) Read the solution sentence aloud.

Developing the Skill   Write this chart on the board and ask students to round them to the nearest 10, 100 and 1,000.

	nearest 10	nearest 100	nearest 1000
5,684	5,680	5,700	6,000
34,375	34,380	34,400	34,000
667,498	667,500	667,500	667,000

Explain that to decide how to round numbers, students will consider what place value the numbers have in common, and why they are being rounded. Point out that if they are being rounded so that they can be added mentally, students will want to round so that the resulting numbers are easy to add. Give them the following number triplets and ask students what place value they would round to: 34,800; 59,023; 9,448 (thousands); 38; 52; 428 (tens); 328; 992; 2,318 (hundreds).

Practice

Estimate the sum by rounding the addends to the greatest common place value.

1.	736 + 475	700 + 500 1,200	2.	$3,694 + 587	$3,700 + 600 $4,300	3.	8,439 + 6,650	8,000 + 7,000 15,000
4.	9,245 + 8,273	9,000 + 8,000 17,000	5.	3,865 + 7,256	4,000 + 7,000 11,000	6.	13,475 + 9,150	13,000 + 9,000 22,000
7.	$162.45 + 73.95	$160 + 70 $230	8.	49,725 + 75,212	50,000 + 80,000 130,000	9.	127,247 + 438,500	100,000 + 400,000 500,000
10.	38,725 + 73,689	40,000 + 70,000 110,000	11.	$217.75 + 468.52	$200 + 500 $700	12.	$3,275.16 + 789.50	$3,300 + 800 $4,100
13.	745,925 + 627,215	700,000 + 600,000 1,300,000	14.	$13,795.92 + 8,227.75	$14,000 + 8,000 $22,000	15.	136,795 + 8,500	137,000 + 9,000 146,000

Copy and Do

16. 478 + 569
    1,047
17. $3,942 + $687
    $4,629
18. 9,645 + 4,509
    14,154
19. 6,973 + 4,768
    11,741
20. 39,046 + 55,389
    94,435
21. 209,349 + 567,499
    776,848
22. 35,462 + 7,096
    42,558
23. 16,494 + 6,095
    22,589
24. $555.99 + $62.85
    $618.84

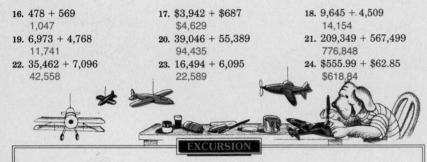

EXCURSION

The clock-5 arithmetic system uses only the five digits on the clock to answer all addition and subtraction problems. Use this clock to find the answers.

1. 3 + 4 = __2__
2. 4 − 3 = __1__
3. 2 + 3 = __0__
4. 2 − 4 = __3__
5. 4 + 4 + 4 = __2__
6. 1 − 2 = __4__

30

Correcting Common Errors

Some students may estimate incorrectly because they always round down or always round up when rounding the addends. For each addend, have the students write the two multiples of ten or a hundred or a thousand, as appropriate, that the addend is between, circling the closer multiple. Then they can rewrite the problem using the correctly rounded addends.

Enrichment

Have students examine a newspaper. Explain that reporters frequently round numbers for large statistics. For example, if it is reported that 54,960 fans watched the Reds beat the Phillies, it is likely that the original number was rounded to the nearest ten. Ask students to find at least five reported numbers and guess to what place the numbers were rounded.

Practice

Have students complete the practice problems. Remind them to keep place value columns straight.

Excursion

Addition sums are found by working clockwise around the clock. For example, 1 + 3 = 4. Subtraction differences are found by working in a counterclockwise direction; 4 − 2 = 1.

Extra Credit *Sets*

Remind students that instead of saying the elements of Set A are red, white and blue, you would write: A = [Red, White, Blue]. Duplicate or write the following on the board, and ask students how they would write the contents of each, correctly:

1. A is the set of all numbers divisible by 5 up to and including 25.
2. B is the set of the letters of the alphabet which spell your first name.
3. D is the set of 5 of your favorite foods.
4. E is the set of the members of your family.
5. F is the set of all the even numbers less than 20.
6. G is the set of months of the year which contain the letter 'R'.

Subtracting, 2- and 3-digits

pages 31-32

Objective

To review subtraction with 2- and 3-digit minuends

Materials

*subtraction flash cards

Mental Math

Ask students to make up a fact family for each number:

1. 9 (2 + 7 = 9, 7 + 2 = 9, 9 − 2 = 7, 9 − 7 = 2)
2. 4 (2 + 2 = 4, 4 − 2 = 2 or 3 + 1 = 4, 1 + 3 = 4, 4 − 3 = 1, 4 − 1 = 3)
3. 12 (Answers will vary.)
4. 18 (Answers will vary.)

Skill Review

Use flash cards to review subtraction facts. Emphasize quick recognition. As you move about the room, save any cards that students miss and go through those facts a second time.

Subtracting, 2- and 3-digit Minuends

The North and South Platte Rivers join to form the Platte River in Nebraska. The North Platte was part of the famous Oregon Trail. How much longer is the North Platte River than the South Platte River?

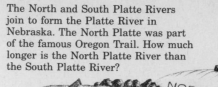
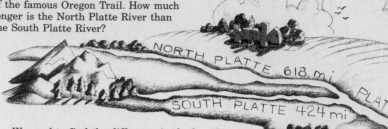

We need to find the difference in the lengths of the two Platte Rivers.

The North Platte is __618__ miles long while the

South Platte is __424__ miles long.

To find the difference, we subtract __424__ from __618__ .

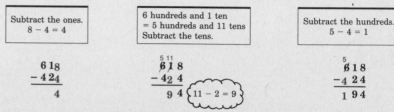

Subtract the ones. 8 − 4 = 4	6 hundreds and 1 ten = 5 hundreds and 11 tens Subtract the tens.	Subtract the hundreds. 5 − 4 = 1

$$\begin{array}{r} 6\,1\,8 \\ -\,4\,2\,4 \\ \hline 4 \end{array} \qquad \begin{array}{r} {}^{5\ 11}6\,1\,8 \\ -\,4\,2\,4 \\ \hline 9\,4 \end{array} \quad (11 - 2 = 9) \qquad \begin{array}{r} {}^{5}6\,1\,8 \\ -\,4\,2\,4 \\ \hline 1\,9\,4 \end{array}$$

The North Platte is __194__ miles longer than the South Platte.

Getting Started

Subtract.

1. $\begin{array}{r} 94 \\ -\,48 \\ \hline 46 \end{array}$
2. $\begin{array}{r} 76 \\ -\,43 \\ \hline 33 \end{array}$
3. $\begin{array}{r} 416 \\ -\,52 \\ \hline 364 \end{array}$
4. $\begin{array}{r} 683 \\ -\,47 \\ \hline 636 \end{array}$

5. $\begin{array}{r} 916 \\ -\,324 \\ \hline 592 \end{array}$
6. $\begin{array}{r} 483 \\ -\,165 \\ \hline 318 \end{array}$
7. $\begin{array}{r} 715 \\ -\,286 \\ \hline 429 \end{array}$
8. $\begin{array}{r} \$8.27 \\ -\,4.88 \\ \hline \$3.39 \end{array}$

Copy and subtract.

9. 862 − 591 271
10. $7.93 − $2.81 $5.12
11. 553 − 196 357

MCP All rights reserved

31

Teaching the Lesson

Introducing the Problem Read the problem aloud and have a student read the lengths of the rivers on the map. As you read the information sentence, have students supply the appropriate numbers. (North Platte, 618 miles; South Platte, 424 miles) Ask a volunteer to read the plan sentence. Illustrate the problem on the board and ask students to follow in their texts as you work the problem. Explain that they will subtract ones first, tens next and hundreds last. Have students do each subtraction paying special attention to the tens as they change 6 hundreds and 1 ten to 5 hundreds and 11 tens. Ask a student to read the solution sentence.

Developing the Skill Put a 2-digit place value chart on the board. Write this problem: **83 − 37.** Ask students to look at the ones column and tell if it is possible to subtract. (no) Have a student show the trade and complete the subtraction; first ones, then tens. (46) Remind students that no matter how many digits, the method of subtraction will be the same. Write on the board: **226 − 193.** Have one student subtract ones, have another trade a hundred for tens and subtract. Explain that in each problem they will first examine each column to see if the subtraction can be done without trade, then they will trade if necessary and then subtract.

Practice

Subtract.

1. 76 − 42 34	2. 88 − 79 9	3. 327 − 83 244	4. 723 − 18 705
5. 474 − 281 193	6. 717 − 225 492	7. $8.83 − 5.37 $3.46	8. 945 − 219 726
9. 653 − 486 167	10. $5.18 − 3.99 $1.19	11. 924 − 687 237	12. 457 − 378 79
13. 721 − 389 332	14. 684 − 399 285	15. 832 − 496 336	16. $5.15 − 3.49 $1.66

Copy and Do

17. 89 − 16
73
18. 92 − 27
65
19. 138 − 57
81
20. 148 − 63
85
21. 214 − 59
155
22. 675 − 281
394
23. $9.71 − $6.28
$3.43
24. 487 − 273
214
25. 721 − 583
138
26. $825 − $196
$629
27. 532 − 476
56
28. 894 − 249
645
29. $4.28 − $1.75
$2.53
30. 672 − 496
176
31. 816 − 197
619
32. $3.19 − $1.79
$1.40

Apply

Use the chart to answer questions 33 and 34.

33. How much more coastline does Texas have than Oregon?
71 miles

34. Texas has how much less coastline than the combined coastlines of New York and Oregon?
56 miles

United States Coastlines	
New York	127 miles
Oregon	296 miles
Texas	367 miles

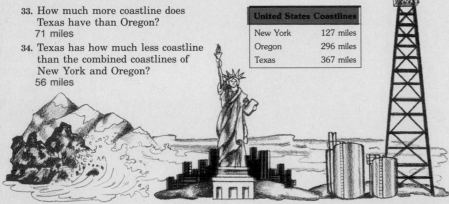

32

Correcting Common Errors

Some students may subtract incorrectly because they always subtract the smaller digit from the larger one.

INCORRECT   CORRECT

$$\begin{array}{r} 84 \\ -27 \\ \hline 63 \end{array} \qquad \begin{array}{r} ^{7}8^{1}4 \\ -27 \\ \hline 57 \end{array}$$

Have these students first identify places where they will need to trade, or rename, and then show the trading so that they will subtract correctly.

Enrichment

Give students the advertising sections of the Sunday newspaper. Have them find at least four items that are on sale. They are to find the original price, the sale price and then subtract to calculate the difference. Explain that the difference is the amount saved when they buy something on sale.

Practice

Have students complete the practice problems. Point out the importance of keeping columns aligned when they copy problems.

Extra Credit   *Logic*

Duplicate the following, or write on the board for students to solve:

1. What number between 1 and 100, when spelled out, has its letters in alphabetical order? (forty)
2. Spelling numbers again, what is the first number to have the letter 'A' in it? (one thousand)

Challenge students to devise two number/word problems to exchange with a partner to solve.

Zeros in the Minuends

pages 33-34

Objectives

To subtract numbers with 4 digits
To subtract with zeros in the minuend

Materials

Mental Math

Ask students to solve for n.

1. $12 + n = 17$ (5)
2. $12 + n = 16$ (4)
3. $n + 6 = 14$ (8)
4. $n + 9 = 16$ (7)
5. $8 + n = 18$ (10)
6. $7 + n = 15$ (8)
7. $n + 7 = 19$ (12)

Skill Review

Put this problem on the board and label the parts:

$$\begin{array}{r} 45 \\ -\ 18 \\ \hline 27 \end{array}$$ minuend
subtrahend
difference

Dictate these problems. Ask students to work them on paper and to label each part.

84	345	572	926
-57	-84	-153	-379
(27)	(261)	(419)	(547)

Subtracting, Zeros in the Minuends

In 1699, Louisiana became a royal colony of France. How many years later did Louisiana become a territory of the United States?

We need to find how long it took Louisiana to become a part of the United States.

Louisiana became a colony of France in ___1699___.
It became a territory of the United States when it

was purchased in ___1803___.
To find the number of years between its becoming a French colony and its becoming a part of the United States, we subtract the earlier date from the more

recent one. We subtract ___1699___ from ___1803___.

Subtract the ones.	Subtract the tens.	Subtract the hundreds.	Subtract the thousands.
800 = 7 hundreds and 10 tens 10 tens = 9 tens and 10 ones	9 tens − 9 tens = 0 tens	7 hundreds − 6 hundreds = 1 hundred	1 thousand − 1 thousand = 0 thousands

$$\begin{array}{r} 9 \\ 7\ 1013 \\ 1\,8\cancel{0}\cancel{3} \\ -1699 \\ \hline 4 \end{array} \qquad \begin{array}{r} 7\ 9 \\ 1\,8\cancel{0}3 \\ -1699 \\ \hline 04 \end{array} \qquad \begin{array}{r} 7 \\ 1\cancel{8}03 \\ -1699 \\ \hline 104 \end{array} \qquad \begin{array}{r} 1803 \\ -1699 \\ \hline 104 \end{array}$$

It was ___104___ years after it became a French colony, that Louisiana became part of the United States.

Getting Started

Subtract.

1.	870	2.	$4.08	3.	3,056	4.	9,308
	-496		-3.59		$-2,684$		$-4,675$
	374		$0.49		372		4,633

5.	$40.05	6.	9,302	7.	8,001	8.	$60.00
	-16.87		$-1,875$		$-3,975$		-9.75
	$23.18		7,427		4,026		$50.25

Copy and subtract.

9. $70.65 − $24.79 $45.86   10. 4,703 − 4,656 47   11. 9,030 − 4,798 4,232

MCP All rights reserved

33

Teaching the Lesson

Introducing the Problem Read the problem aloud and have students examine the map. Have one student read the information sentences. Read the plan sentence and explain the meaning of earlier and more recent. Ask students to follow in their texts as you work the problem on the board. Explain that they can subtract the dates just as they would any other numbers. Subtract each column, starting with ones. Show students when they trade for ones and find no tens, they must go to the hundreds column to trade. When you have completed the subtraction, have a student read the solution sentence. (104 years)

Developing the Skill Explain that a zero in the subtrahend poses no problem because zero subtracted from any number leaves the number itself. Ask a student to explain why a zero in the minuend is more difficult. (because you cannot subtract anything from zero without trading first, and because if you have to trade with a column containing

a zero you are forced to trade twice) Put these two problems on the board as samples of these two possible difficulties:

$$\begin{array}{r} 309 \\ -182 \\ \hline (127) \end{array} \qquad \begin{array}{r} 602 \\ -238 \\ \hline (364) \end{array}$$

Point out that in the first problem ones can be subtracted, but a trade is needed to subtract tens. But show students that in the second problem, a trade is required in the ones column, and that the trade will involve hundreds, tens and ones. Have a student work each problem.

Subtract.

1. 3,905 − 2,659 1,246	2. 8,063 − 2,785 5,278	3. 6,247 − 3,968 2,279	4. 5,710 − 2,396 3,314
5. 6,070 − 2,985 3,085	6. $37.08 − 29.89 $7.19	7. 7,006 − 2,589 4,417	8. $40.37 − 9.56 $30.81

Copy and Do

9. 8,704 − 3,596
5,108

10. $70.09 − $32.58
$37.51

11. 6,000 − 852
5,148

12. 4,398 − 4,029
369

13. $58.08 − $29.59
$28.49

14. 8,757 − 6,458
2,299

15. 3,050 − 1,976
1,074

16. $80.08 − $37.85
$42.23

17. 4,082 − 2,697
1,385

18. $70.00 − $29.56
$40.44

19. 8,104 − 3,976
4,128

20. 9,054 − 6,780
2,274

Apply

Use the chart to answer questions 21 and 22.

21. How much longer than the Illinois River is the Ohio/Allegheny River?
1,426 km

22. What is the total length of these four tributaries of the Mississippi River?
8,852 km

Major Tributaries of the Mississippi River	
Arkansas	2,348 kilometers
Illinois	676 kilometers
Missouri	3,726 kilometers
Ohio/Allegheny	2,102 kilometers

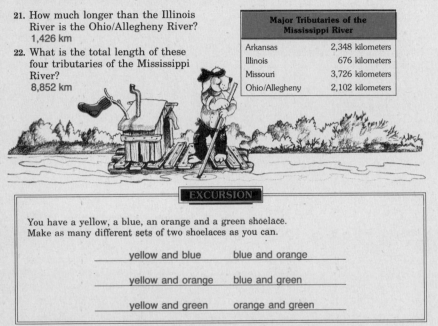

EXCURSION

You have a yellow, a blue, an orange and a green shoelace.
Make as many different sets of two shoelaces as you can.

yellow and blue	blue and orange
yellow and orange	blue and green
yellow and green	orange and green

34

Correcting Common Errors

Some students may have difficulty subtracting when they have to rename a place twice because there is a zero in the minuend, such as in 506 − 227. Have these students practice by writing the problem in expanded form,

$$500 + 0 + 6$$
$$− 200 + 20 + 7$$

trade for a hundred,

$$400 + 100 + 6$$
$$− 200 + 20 + 7$$

and then trade for a ten and subtract.

$$400 + 90 + 16$$
$$− 200 + 20 + 7$$
$$200 + 70 + 9 = 279$$

Enrichment

Ask students to subtract the following Roman numerals and illustrate their method for subtracting. Point out that because Roman numerals have no place value, subtracting them is like using an expanded form for Arabic numbers.

1. MCMLXVI − MCM (1,966 − 1,900 = 66)
2. MMDII − MCCLIV (2,502 − 1,254 = 1,248)
3. CDXX − CCCIX (420 − 309 = 111)

Practice

Have students complete the practice problems. Suggest that they show each trade above the problem. Remind them to keep columns aligned when they copy problems.

Excursion

Remind students they are working only with single shoelaces, not pairs. You could discuss how the problem would change if there were a pair of each colored lace. Have students research the meaning of **permutations.**

Extra Credit *Applications*

Tell students to bring newspaper grocery ads to class. Have them plan a 3-meal menu for a day, for their family using items they see advertised. Tell them to list the groceries they would need to buy to prepare each meal, in the correct quantities, omitting things they would have on hand such as salt & pepper, ketchup, etc. Then have them list the cost of each grocery item and a daily total. Have them multiply to find a sample weekly food budget. Discuss differences in their totals.

Subtracting Greater Numbers

pages 35-36

Objective

To subtract numbers with six digits

Materials

Mental Math

Ask students to tell which is larger:

1. 3 tens or 19 ones (3 tens)
2. 25 tens or 2 hundreds (25 tens)
3. 1 thousand or 14 hundreds (14 hundreds)
4. 243 ones or 15 tens (243 ones)
5. 72 hundreds or 10 thousands (10 thousands)
6. 5 tens or 80 ones (80 ones)

Skill Review

Review multi-digit subtraction by having volunteers work these problems on the board:

507	7,076	5,804	$80.08
−279	− 987	−2,586	− 17.96
(228)	(6,089)	(3,218)	($62.12)

Encourage them to show any trades above each problem.

Subtracting Greater Numbers

In 1953, Auguste Piccard and his son Jacques set a record, by exploring the Mediterranean Sea in a bathyscaph lowered to about 10,299 feet. Seven years later, Jacques Piccard and Don Walsh descended just over 35,798 feet in the Pacific Ocean to set a new record. By how many feet was the record extended?

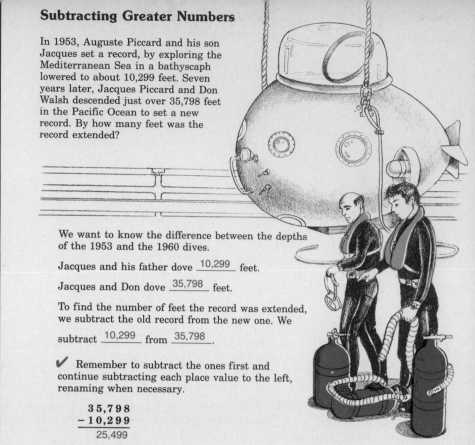

We want to know the difference between the depths of the 1953 and the 1960 dives.

Jacques and his father dove __10,299__ feet.

Jacques and Don dove __35,798__ feet.

To find the number of feet the record was extended, we subtract the old record from the new one. We subtract __10,299__ from __35,798__.

✔ Remember to subtract the ones first and continue subtracting each place value to the left, renaming when necessary.

$$
\begin{array}{r}
35{,}798 \\
-10{,}299 \\
\hline
25{,}499
\end{array}
$$

The Piccard-Walsh team bettered the record by __25,499__ feet.

Getting Started

Subtract.

1.
$$
\begin{array}{r}
73{,}246 \\
-\ 9{,}563 \\
\hline
63{,}683
\end{array}
$$

2.
$$
\begin{array}{r}
127{,}086 \\
-\ 56{,}796 \\
\hline
70{,}290
\end{array}
$$

3.
$$
\begin{array}{r}
\$8{,}752.38 \\
-\ 4{,}615.19 \\
\hline
\$4{,}137.19
\end{array}
$$

Copy and subtract.

4. 612,672 − 572,375 40,297

5. $4,075.08 − $1,796.29 $2,278.79

MCP All rights reserved

35

Teaching the Lesson

Introducing the Problem Have a student read the problem aloud and identify the key word in the problem. (how many feet was the record **extended**) Read the information sentences and continue with the plan sentence, explaining that they will subtract to find the difference. Have a student put the problem on the board, show any trades necessary and do the subtraction. Point out that no matter how many digits there are, they will always start subtracting in the ones column and move to the left. Have a student read and complete the solution sentence. (bettered the record by 25,499 ft)

Developing the Skill Remind students how to write numbers in an expanded form. For example: 5,292 can be written 5000 + 200 + 90 + 2. Show the class how the expanded form can help them subtract.

$$65{,}364 - 27{,}192 =$$

$$
\begin{array}{r}
60{,}000 + 5{,}000 + 300 + 60 + 4 \\
-20{,}000 + 7{,}000 + 100 + 90 + 2
\end{array}
$$

is the same as

$$
\begin{array}{r}
50{,}000 + 15{,}000 + 200 + 160 + 4 \\
-20{,}000 + \ 7{,}000 + 100 + \ 90 + 2 \\
\hline
30{,}000 + \ 8{,}000 + 100 + \ 70 + 2 \text{ or} \\
38{,}172
\end{array}
$$

Have them do these two problems the same way:
120,463 − 86,795 = (33,668)
$652.04 − 238.75 = ($413.29)

35

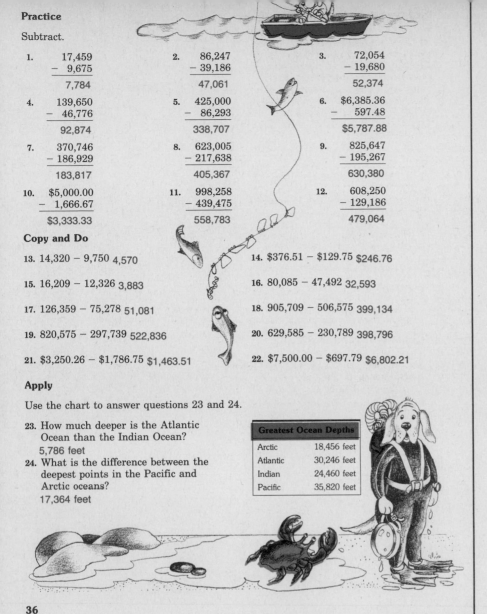

Practice

Subtract.

1. 17,459
    − 9,675
    _____
    7,784

2. 86,247
    − 39,186
    _____
    47,061

3. 72,054
    − 19,680
    _____
    52,374

4. 139,650
    − 46,776
    _____
    92,874

5. 425,000
    − 86,293
    _____
    338,707

6. $6,385.36
    − 597.48
    _____
    $5,787.88

7. 370,746
    − 186,929
    _____
    183,817

8. 623,005
    − 217,638
    _____
    405,367

9. 825,647
    − 195,267
    _____
    630,380

10. $5,000.00
    − 1,666.67
    _____
    $3,333.33

11. 998,258
    − 439,475
    _____
    558,783

12. 608,250
    − 129,186
    _____
    479,064

Copy and Do

13. 14,320 − 9,750 4,570

14. $376.51 − $129.75 $246.76

15. 16,209 − 12,326 3,883

16. 80,085 − 47,492 32,593

17. 126,359 − 75,278 51,081

18. 905,709 − 506,575 399,134

19. 820,575 − 297,739 522,836

20. 629,585 − 230,789 398,796

21. $3,250.26 − $1,786.75 $1,463.51

22. $7,500.00 − $697.79 $6,802.21

Apply

Use the chart to answer questions 23 and 24.

23. How much deeper is the Atlantic Ocean than the Indian Ocean?
    5,786 feet

24. What is the difference between the deepest points in the Pacific and Arctic oceans?
    17,364 feet

Greatest Ocean Depths	
Arctic	18,456 feet
Atlantic	30,246 feet
Indian	24,460 feet
Pacific	35,820 feet

Correcting Common Errors

Some students subtract incorrectly because they do not carefully align their columns or do not place their renaming digits properly. Have them perform their work on grid paper and encourage them to check each subtraction problem by adding.

Enrichment

Ask students to write the mileage shown on the family car odometer on a 3 × 5 card and do the following activities: 1. Arrange the cards on a table from the lowest mileage to the highest. 2. Calculate the difference between the mileage on their car and the mileage on the car next in the order. 3. Have the highest mileage student calculate the range of all the numbers, subtracting the lowest mileage from the highest. 4. Explain what happens after the car has gone 100,000 miles. (Most odometers have only 5 whole mile digits and drop back to zero.)

Practice

Have students complete the practice problems. Ask them to show any trades, copy carefully and use dollar signs when required.

Mixed Practice

1. $76.38 + $137.93 + $396.38 ($610.69)
2. 7,291 − 5,350 (1,941)
3. 9 + 8 (17)
4. $200.58 − $69.95 ($130.63)
5. 8,000 − 4,376 (3,624)
6. 20,000 + 5,000 + 200 + 30 + 7 (25,237)
7. 257,908 + 326,493 (584,401)
8. 9 + 3 + 7 (19)
9. 6,050 − 4,327 (1,723)
10. 11 − 8 (3)

Extra Credit   *Logic*

Explain that logic problems give pieces of information and require students to match various facts to solve the problem.

Dictate the following problem: Larry, Curly and Moe are married to Laverne, Shirley and Mary. Laverne's sister is married to Moe. Larry has never met Mary. Mary is an only child. Who is married to whom?

(Mary cannot be married to Moe since she is an only child, and she never met Larry so Mary must be married to Curly. Laverne cannot be married to Moe or Curly so she must be married to Larry which leaves Moe married to Shirley.

Note: Be aware that there is more than one way to reason out this solution.)

Estimating Differences

pages 37-38

Objective

To estimate, rounding numbers through thousands

Materials

Mental Math

Have students add:

1. 20 + 40 + 10 (70)
2. 40 + 40 + 40 (120)
3. 60 + 20 + 20 (100)
4. 50 + 50 + 90 (190)
5. 20 + 40 + 80 (140)
6. 70 + 70 + 30 (170)
7. 100 + 20 + 10 (130)

Skill Review

Have students identify the place value these number pairs should be rounded to before they add. Then have them round and add.

1. 228 and 56 (tens; 290)
2. 62 and 37 (tens; 100)
3. 19 and 5 (tens; 30)
4. 302 and 448 (hundreds; 700)
5. 4,429 and 8,208 (thousands; 12,000)
6. 3,471 and 557 (hundreds; 4,100)

Estimating Differences

The moon travels in an oval-shaped orbit around the earth every $29\frac{1}{2}$ days. Estimate to the nearest thousand miles, the difference between the moon's closest and farthest points from earth.

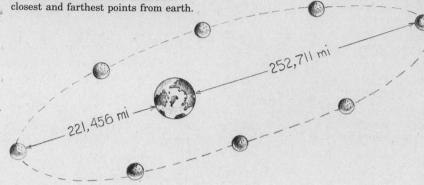

252,711 mi

221,456 mi

We want to estimate the difference between the two distances, to the nearest thousand miles.

To estimate a difference, we round the minuend and subtrahend and subtract.

252,711 rounded to the nearest thousand is __253,000__ .

221,456 rounded to the nearest thousand is __221,000__ .

The estimated difference is __32,000__ .

There are approximately __32,000__ miles between the closest and farthest points of the moon's orbit.

Getting Started

Estimate the difference by rounding to the greatest common place value.

1.	926	900
	− 275	− 300
		600

2.	15,650	16,000
	− 9,427	− 9,000
		7,000

3.	46,750	47,000
	− 7,210	− 7,000
		40,000

4.	$475.39	$500
	− 126.15	− 100
		$400

5.	$4,294.86	$4,300
	− 847.58	− 800
		$3,500

6.	$9,285.17	$9,000
	− 1,721.15	− 2,000
		$7,000

MCP All rights reserved

37

Teaching the Lesson

Introducing the Problem Read the problem aloud and have students look at the chart. Explain that because the moon's orbit is an oval, it is sometimes nearer the earth, sometimes farther away. Have a student read the information and the plan sentences. Put the distances on the board and ask students to round them to the nearest thousand. (252,711 to 253,000; 221,456 to 221,000) Have another student subtract the rounded distances. (estimated difference is 32,000) Read the solution sentence aloud.

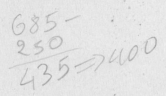

Developing the Skill Explain that in this lesson each number pair will be rounded to the greatest common place value. Point out that this means they must compare the numbers, find the largest place value they have in common, and then round to that place value. Write **32,003** and **4,394** on the board. Starting with ones move to the left in each number and have students tell the greatest common place value. (thousands) Have them identify the greatest common place value in each of these number pairs, round and subtract:

1. 685 − 250 (hundreds, 400)
2. $735.16 − $412.45 (hundreds, $300)
3. 6,099 − 3,721 (thousands, 2,000)
4. 23,844 − 4,882 (thousands, 19,000)

Estimate the difference by rounding to the greatest common place value.

1.	962 − 315 **700**	1,000 − 300	2.	836 − 297 **500**	800 − 300	3.	850 − 335 **600**	900 − 300	

4.	4,325 − 2,686 **1,000**	4,000 − 3,000	5.	9,720 − 3,819 **6,000**	10,000 − 4,000	6.	6,075 − 1,750 **4,000**	6,000 − 2,000	

7.	12,615 − 7,279 **6,000**	13,000 − 7,000	8.	52,651 − 16,235 **30,000**	50,000 − 20,000	9.	839,750 − 214,210 **600,000**	800,000 − 200,000	

10.	$679.18 − 213.75 **$500**	$700 − 200	11.	$872.39 − 365.79 **$500**	$900 − 400	12.	$4,765.16 − 426.52 **$4,400**	$4,800 − 400	

13.	$4,275.35 − 2,961.46 **$1,000**	$4,000 − 3,000	14.	$15,748.57 − 6,214.12 **$10,000**	$16,000 − 6,000	15.	$215,560 − 6,957 **$209,000**	$216,000 − 7,000	

16.	$5,675.49 − 3,899.42 **$2,000**	$6,000 − 4,000	17.	$10,648 − 7,493 **$4,000**	$11,000 − 7,000	18.	$416,698 − 32,455 **$390,000**	$420,000 − 30,000	

EXCURSION

Write true or false after each statement.

Anteaters
Martians
Kookoos

1. All Martians are anteaters. _true_
2. Some kookoos are Martians. _true_
3. At least one kookoo is an anteater. _true_
4. If it is a kookoo, then it is an anteater. _false_
5. If it is a Martian, then it is an anteater. _true_
6. If it is not a Martian, then it is not an anteater. _false_
7. If it is not an anteater, then it is not a Martian. _true_

Correcting Common Errors

Some students may estimate differences incorrectly because they round incorrectly. Have them work with partners on numbers such as the following. Have them take turns rounding, first to the nearest 100, and then to the nearest 1,000.
1. 3,678 (3,700; 4,000)
2. 57,296 (57,300; 57,000)
3. 425,915 (425,900; 426,000)

Enrichment

Newspapers are a good source of estimated numbers. Have students look in a newspaper for a pair of rounded numbers and then make up a word problem. Give them this example: "Total hog sale this week in Chicago was 34,000 heads compared to 23,000 heads a week ago." How many more hogs were sold this week than last? (11,000)

Practice

Have students complete the practice problems. Tell them to determine the greatest common place value before they round and subtract.

Excursion

Remind students they are working with a Venn diagram. In this case, each circle represents all of one kind of creature. If two circles overlap, it signifies that some of the creatures belong to both groups. Have students write additional sentences related to the diagram.

Extra Credit   *Applications*

Invite a representative from a local bank to discuss savings accounts. Ask the representative to bring a sample savings account book page to show how to keep track of dates, withdrawals, deposits and balances. Have them define these terms and demonstrate the math used to arrive at these figures. Then supply students with a sample account sheet showing a list of deposits and withdrawals and have students supply correct figures in the balance column. Ask the speaker to discuss other types of accounts the bank offers its customers.

Problem Solving
Acting It Out

pages 39-40

Objective

To solve problems by acting parts out

Materials

play money
marbles
3 dimes, 5 pennies
ruler, yardstick or meterstick
500 sheets of paper
model clocks

Mental Math

Have students add:

1. 31 + 29 = (60)
2. 56 + 18 = (74)
3. 15 + 19 = (34)
4. 22 + 71 = (93)
5. 40 + 13 = (53)
6. 52 + 59 = (111)
7. 71 + 30 = (101)

Acting It Out

Frank bought a pair of ski boots from Patty for $60. Two weeks later he sold them to his friend, Scott, for $70. At the end of the ski season Frank bought the boots back for $80. The next fall he sold the boots to Ronnie for $90. How much money did Frank make or lose in buying and selling the ski boots?

★ SEE

We want to know the amount of money Frank will make or lose.

Frank originally bought the ski boots for _$60_.

He sold the boots to Scott for _$70_.

He bought the boots back for _$80_.

He sold the boots to Ronnie for _$90_.

★ PLAN

Keeping track of the money spent and earned is difficult to do. We can make it simpler by acting the problem out. We will need four students to act the parts of Frank, Patty, Scott and Ronnie. Each actor will need to start with $100 in play money.

★ DO

Follow the actions of the problem as the actors play their roles. Frank starts with $100.

He buys the boots from Patty for _$60_.

Frank sells the boots to Scott for _$70_.

He buys the boots back for _$80_.

He sells the boots to Ronnie for _$90_.

Have Frank count his money. He now has _$120_.

Since he started with $100, he _made $20_.

★ CHECK

After Frank buys the ski boots for $60, he has _$40_ left.

He sells the boots for $70. He then has _$110_.

He buys the boots back for $80. He has _$30_.

He sells the ski boots for $90. He has _$120_.

MCP All rights reserved

39

Teaching the Lesson

Read the problem aloud. Remind students of the SEE, PLAN, DO, CHECK method for solving problems. Ask a student to read the SEE section. Explain that in this section they will restate the problem and list the information the problem provides. (originally bought boots for $60; sold to Scott for $70; bought back for $80; sold to Ronnie for $90) Read the PLAN section aloud. Ask four students to come up and pretend to be Patty, Frank, Scott and Ronnie. Give each $100 in $10 bills and have them act out the series of sales. Ask a student to read the DO section while the actors follow. (buys for $60, sells to Scott for $70, buys back for $80, sells to Ronnie for $90) Now ask Frank to count his money. ($120) Ask how much more he has now. ($20) Explain that to check the problem, they can follow Frank's finances exclusively. Ask a student to read the CHECK section. Remind students that they have decided to have Frank start out with $100 as a point of reference. (After he buys boots, has $40; sells for $70, has $110; buys back for $80, has $30; sells for $90, has $120)

Solve these problems.

1. Tony has less than 30 marbles. When he puts them in groups of five he has one left. When he puts them in groups of three he has none left. How many marbles does he have?

   21 marbles

2. Show that it is not practical to fold a piece of paper in half more than eight consecutive times.

   See Solution Notes.

3. Three brothers give their sister a total of 30 cents to buy an apple. Each brother pays 10 cents for his share. When the sister discovers that the apple only costs 25 cents, she returns the five cents to her brothers. They each take one cent and give their sister the remaining two cents for her trouble. Therefore each brother only paid nine cents for a total of 27 cents, and the sister was given two cents. What happened to the other penny?

   See Solution Notes.

4. Nine lockers all in a row are closed. Nine students line up and perform the following actions: the first student goes to every locker and opens each door. The second student then goes to every second locker, opens it if it is closed, and closes it if it is open. The third student goes to every third locker, opens it if it is closed, and closes it if it is open. If this continues for all nine students, what lockers are open at the conclusion of the ninth student's trip?

   Lockers 1, 4 and 9

5. Use a common measuring device such as a ruler, yardstick or meter stick to determine the thickness of one sheet of paper.

   Answers will vary.

6. The hour hand and minute hand of a clock cross at noon. How many times will the hands cross between noon and midnight? Do not count noon, but do count midnight.

   12 times

7. What is the greatest number and what is the least number that would be represented by 6,400 if rounded to the nearest hundred?

   See Solution Notes.

8. What is the greatest and what is the least amount of money that would be represented by $3,000 if rounded to the nearest thousand dollars?

   See Solution Notes.

9. Ten flowers grow in a circle. A butterfly gathers nectar from one, and then continues to visit every third flower around the circle. Tell whether the butterfly visits all 10 flowers and prove your answer.

   Yes

10. Suppose Don Noe has some dimes, nickels, and pennies. He has exactly 12 coins and they are worth exactly 25¢. What coins does Don have? Explain how you got your answer.

    See Solution Notes.

40

Extra Credit *Numeration*

Have one student come to the board to write the basic Roman numerals for 1–100 (I = 1, V = 5, X = 10, L = 50, C = 100) as a review. Then tell students to write five 4-digit addition or subtraction problems, using Roman numerals, to exchange with a friend and solve. Have them correct each other's work. As an extension, have them write 5 column addition problems having at least 4 addends, using Roman numerals.

Solution Notes

1. Try this with marbles. Notice multiples of 5 with 1 left over to form a series: 6, 11, 16, 21, 26. Groups of three form another: 3, 6, 9, 12, 15, 18, 21, . . . Both 6 and 21 work.

2. Point out each time paper is folded, the thickness doubles. Show that it goes from 2 to 64 thicknesses of paper in only 6 folds. Seven folds would require 128 thicknesses!

3. Let students act the problem out with 3 dimes, an apple and 5 pennies. In the end they should see each boy gave a dime toward an apple that costs 25¢. The nickle change was divided as described, with 1¢ going to each brother, and the remaining 2¢ to the sister. This accounts for all 30¢.

4. Act this out. Use lockers or draw a series of long rectangles on the board labeled open or closed. When the ninth student is done, 1, 4 and 9 will be open.

5. Suggest students measure the height of a stack of 500 sheets of paper, and divide the height by 500 to find the thickness of one sheet. The division will give a decimal answer. Have them measure the stack twice, loose and compressed. Ask if it makes a difference. (yes)

6. Give each student a model clock. Let them start at noon and turn the hands until they read midnight. (The hands cross 12 times.)

Higher-Order Thinking Skills

7. Analysis: The greatest would be 6,449 and the least would be 6,350.

8. Analysis: The greatest would be $3,499 and the least would be $2,500, round midway amounts up.

9. Analysis and Evaluation: Proofs will vary; e.g., draw 10 dots in a circle and connect every third one with a line segment without lifting the pencil.

10. Synthesis: The coins are 10 pennies, 1 nickel, and 1 dime. Act it out with real or play coins.

Calculators and Savings Accounts

pages 41-42

Objective

To use calculators to balance a savings account

Materials

calculators

Mental Math

Have students tell the place value of the digit these pairs have in common:

1. 12 and 2 (ones)
2. 448 and 43 (tens)
3. 5,702 and 12,740 (hundreds)
4. 9,228 and 9,445 (thousands)
5. 14,881 and 24,323 (thousands)
6. 63 and 243 (ones)
7. 775 and 970 (tens)

Skill Review

Review number and function keys with the class. Ask them to work the following problems with calculators:

1. 34 + 92 (126)
2. $286 + 448 ($734)
3. 2,836 + 4,489 (7,325)
4. 14,882 + 45,670 (60,552)
5. 772 + 409 (1181)
6. 4,470 + 9,037 (13,507)
7. $337 + 1,391 ($1,728)

Calculators and Savings Accounts

Ling is depositing money into his savings account. He has already saved $115.75. How much will Ling have after he makes this deposit?

SAVINGS DEPOSIT	
ACCOUNT HOLDER	ACCOUNT NUMBER
Ling Kwan	123-456-789
Date Stamp	CURRENCY	$16	00
	COIN		
	CHECKS	$12	50

Ling had __$115.75__ in his account.

This deposit is made up of __$16.00__ in currency and __$12.50__ in a check.

To find the new balance in Ling's account, we add the previous balance to the total amount being deposited. We add __$115.75__ to the sum of __$16.00__ and __$12.50__.

Balance		Currency		Check		New Balance
115.75	+	16	+	12.5	=	144.25

✔ Remember the calculator does not print zeros to the far right of the decimal point and you don't have to key them in. $12.50 is thus keyed in as 12.5.

Ling will have __$144.25__ in his account after he makes the deposit.

If Ling then makes a withdrawal of $8.85, how much will he have left in his account?

Balance		Withdrawal		New Balance
144.25	−	8.85	=	135.4

Ling will have __$135.40__ in his account after he makes the withdrawal.

MCP All rights reserved

41

Teaching the Lesson

Introducing the Problem Read the problem aloud. Have students examine the savings deposit slip illustrated. Ask a student to read the information sentences and provide the amounts required. Explain that to find the new total, students will have to add the deposit, both currency and check, to the previous balance. Read the plan sentence. Have students look at the calculator codes and work the problem on their calculators. (new balance, $144.25) Read the next sentence and explain that they do not have to enter terminal zeros. Explain that calculators do not print any zeros at the far right of the decimal. Have a student read the solution sentence. Continue reading the next portion of the problem aloud. Have students complete the subtraction on their calculators. (new balance, $135.40) Have a volunteer read and complete the solution sentence.

Developing the Skill Explain that adding and subtracting money on the calculator is just like adding and subtracting other numbers. They must, however, be careful to put in the decimal point. Remind students that zeros at the end of a number with a decimal point are not necessary and are not printed by calculators. Ask students to translate these calculator numbers into dollars and cents: 12.5 ($12.50); 3.5 ($3.50); 450.3 ($450.30); 1.5 ($1.50); 44.3 ($44.30)

Complete these codes. Write the answers on the screen.

1. 56 + 49 + 16 = (121)   2. 67 − 25 − 12 = (30)

3. 75.75 + 19.63 = (95.38)   4. 52.4 + 86.57 = (138.97)

5. 96.82 − 47.92 = (48.9)   6. 61.59 − 37.59 = (24)

7. 82.35 + 16.5 − 63.59 = (35.26)   8. 868.47 − 429.48 + 2.5 = (441.49)

Use a calculator to add or subtract. Estimate to see if the answer seems reasonable.

9. 24,265	10. 39,215	11. $416.58	12. $8,715.85
− 6,987	+ 29,875	+ 238.75	− 5,615.85
17,278	69,090	$655.33	$3,100.00

Apply

Use these bank books to answer questions 13 and 14.

13. How much does Mary have after she makes a withdrawal of $63.85?
$332.94

14. How much will Chuck have after he deposits $16.75?
$193.60

Use a calculator to complete these accounts.

SAVINGS ACCOUNT 246-315

Date	Deposit	Withdrawal	Balance
10-10			$415.00
10/26		$18.21	$396.79
		$63.85	

SAVINGS ACCOUNT 139-125

Date	Deposit	Withdrawal	Balance
10/2			$176.85
10/21	$16.75		

15.

Deposit	Withdrawal	Balance
		$300.00
$26.55		$326.55
	$48.95	$277.60
	$125.00	$152.60
$75.85		$228.45
	$96.50	$131.95
$112.00		$243.95

16.

Deposit	Withdrawal	Balance
		$600.00
	$86.15	$513.85
$125.50		$639.35
$38.75		$678.10
	$49.95	$628.15
$125.85		$754.00
	$75.50	$678.50

42

Correcting Common Errors

Some students may balance a savings account incorrectly because they confuse deposits and withdrawals. Have them think of deposit as "add" and withdraw as "subtract" when they read or hear the words. Then have them work with their calculators as you dictate a series of deposits and withdrawals beginning with a balance of $100. Say, "Deposit $40; deposit $13.50; withdraw $50; deposit $2.25; deposit $10; withdraw $25. ($90.75)

Enrichment

Give students a newspaper. Ask them to find an advertised sale and list 5 items on sale. Ask them to use their calculators to determine the original price. For example: A dishwasher is on sale for $288. The ad explains that you save $41. Have them determine the price of the dishwasher before the sale. ($288 + 41 = $329)

Practice

Have students complete the practice problems. Explain that when they balance accounts they should remember that deposit means add to, and withdraw means subtract from.

Extra Credit *Applications*

Ask students to list things in their natural environment that would be difficult to count because of their large numbers; for example: grains of sand, ants in a hill, leaves on a tree, etc. Using this list as a starting point for discussion, challenge students to find another, specific example of something natural to count that they would like to learn more about. Have them research that topic, gathering information to report to the class. Tell them that within their report, they must explain a system they have devised to count that natural object.

Chapter Test

page 43

Item	Objective
1-4	Add two numbers with sums less than 1,000, one regrouping (See pages 23-24)
5	Add two or more numbers less than 10,000 (See pages 25-26)
6-8	Add two or more numbers less than 1,000,000 (See pages 27-28)
9-16	Estimate sums by rounding to nearest 100 or 1,000 and adding (See pages 29-30)
17-19	Subtract two numbers up to 3 digits (See pages 31-32)
20-23	Subtract up to 4-digit numbers, zeros in the minuend (See pages 33-34)
24	Subtract two numbers less than 1,000,000 (See pages 35-36)
25-36	Estimate differences by rounding to nearest 100 or 1,000 and subtracting (See pages 37-38)

Add.

1.
$$\begin{array}{r} 36 \\ + 46 \\ \hline 82 \end{array}$$

2.
$$\begin{array}{r} 56 \\ + 29 \\ \hline 85 \end{array}$$

3.
$$\begin{array}{r} 126 \\ + 85 \\ \hline 211 \end{array}$$

4.
$$\begin{array}{r} \$4.26 \\ + 2.59 \\ \hline \$6.85 \end{array}$$

5.
$$\begin{array}{r} 3,675 \\ + 6,978 \\ \hline 10,653 \end{array}$$

6.
$$\begin{array}{r} 13,659 \\ + 48,263 \\ \hline 61,922 \end{array}$$

7.
$$\begin{array}{r} 121,965 \\ + 758,246 \\ \hline 880,211 \end{array}$$

8.
$$\begin{array}{r} 18,279 \\ 38,657 \\ + 92,158 \\ \hline 149,094 \end{array}$$

Estimate each sum after rounding to the greatest common place value.

9.
$$\begin{array}{r} 386 \\ + 148 \\ \hline \end{array} \quad \begin{array}{r} 400 \\ + 100 \\ \hline 500 \end{array}$$

10.
$$\begin{array}{r} 6,736 \\ + 2,651 \\ \hline \end{array} \quad \begin{array}{r} 7,000 \\ + 3,000 \\ \hline 10,000 \end{array}$$

11.
$$\begin{array}{r} 15,974 \\ + 7,338 \\ \hline \end{array} \quad \begin{array}{r} 16,000 \\ + 7,000 \\ \hline 23,000 \end{array}$$

12.
$$\begin{array}{r} 49,150 \\ + 21,896 \\ \hline \end{array} \quad \begin{array}{r} 50,000 \\ + 20,000 \\ \hline 70,000 \end{array}$$

13.
$$\begin{array}{r} 489 \\ + 652 \\ \hline \end{array} \quad \begin{array}{r} 500 \\ + 700 \\ \hline 1,200 \end{array}$$

14.
$$\begin{array}{r} 4,095 \\ + 5,758 \\ \hline \end{array} \quad \begin{array}{r} 4,000 \\ + 6,000 \\ \hline 10,000 \end{array}$$

15.
$$\begin{array}{r} 87,502 \\ + 6,298 \\ \hline \end{array} \quad \begin{array}{r} 88,000 \\ + 6,000 \\ \hline 94,000 \end{array}$$

16.
$$\begin{array}{r} 48,493 \\ + 36,094 \\ \hline \end{array} \quad \begin{array}{r} 50,000 \\ + 40,000 \\ \hline 90,000 \end{array}$$

Subtract.

17.
$$\begin{array}{r} 93 \\ - 47 \\ \hline 46 \end{array}$$

18.
$$\begin{array}{r} 749 \\ - 51 \\ \hline 698 \end{array}$$

19.
$$\begin{array}{r} 976 \\ - 387 \\ \hline 589 \end{array}$$

20.
$$\begin{array}{r} 4,085 \\ - 993 \\ \hline 3,092 \end{array}$$

21.
$$\begin{array}{r} 7,626 \\ - 2,498 \\ \hline 5,128 \end{array}$$

22.
$$\begin{array}{r} 16,750 \\ - 8,974 \\ \hline 7,776 \end{array}$$

23.
$$\begin{array}{r} \$120.08 \\ - 96.79 \\ \hline \$23.29 \end{array}$$

24.
$$\begin{array}{r} 413,696 \\ - 49,739 \\ \hline 363,957 \end{array}$$

Estimate each difference after rounding to the greatest common place value.

25.
$$\begin{array}{r} 832 \\ - 279 \\ \hline \end{array} \quad \begin{array}{r} 800 \\ - 300 \\ \hline 500 \end{array}$$

26.
$$\begin{array}{r} 7,540 \\ - 2,659 \\ \hline \end{array} \quad \begin{array}{r} 8,000 \\ - 3,000 \\ \hline 5,000 \end{array}$$

27.
$$\begin{array}{r} 15,270 \\ - 8,312 \\ \hline \end{array} \quad \begin{array}{r} 15,000 \\ - 8,000 \\ \hline 7,000 \end{array}$$

28.
$$\begin{array}{r} 88,659 \\ - 61,236 \\ \hline \end{array} \quad \begin{array}{r} 90,000 \\ - 60,000 \\ \hline 30,000 \end{array}$$

29.
$$\begin{array}{r} 751 \\ - 479 \\ \hline \end{array} \quad \begin{array}{r} 800 \\ - 500 \\ \hline 300 \end{array}$$

30.
$$\begin{array}{r} 4,659 \\ - 2,388 \\ \hline \end{array} \quad \begin{array}{r} 5,000 \\ - 2,000 \\ \hline 3,000 \end{array}$$

31.
$$\begin{array}{r} 86,454 \\ - 7,652 \\ \hline \end{array} \quad \begin{array}{r} 86,000 \\ - 8,000 \\ \hline 78,000 \end{array}$$

32.
$$\begin{array}{r} 49,602 \\ - 27,499 \\ \hline \end{array} \quad \begin{array}{r} 50,000 \\ - 30,000 \\ \hline 20,000 \end{array}$$

33.
$$\begin{array}{r} 685 \\ - 397 \\ \hline \end{array} \quad \begin{array}{r} 700 \\ - 400 \\ \hline 300 \end{array}$$

34.
$$\begin{array}{r} 7,647 \\ - 4,892 \\ \hline \end{array} \quad \begin{array}{r} 8,000 \\ - 5,000 \\ \hline 3,000 \end{array}$$

35.
$$\begin{array}{r} 93,247 \\ - 61,983 \\ \hline \end{array} \quad \begin{array}{r} 90,000 \\ - 60,000 \\ \hline 30,000 \end{array}$$

36.
$$\begin{array}{r} 69,458 \\ - 3,901 \\ \hline \end{array} \quad \begin{array}{r} 69,000 \\ - 4,000 \\ \hline 65,000 \end{array}$$

MCP All rights reserved

43

Circle the letter of the correct answer.

1 9 + 6
a 13
b 14
c) 15
d NG

2 17 − 8
a 7
b 8
c) 9
d NG

3 $n + 5 = 5$
$n = ?$
a) 0
b 5
c 10
d NG

4 What is the place value of the 3 in 963,214?
a ones
b tens
c hundreds
d) NG

5 What is the place value of the 9 in 392,065?
a hundred thousands
b) ten thousands
c thousands
d NG

6 426 ◯ 624
a) <
b >
c =

7 32,593 ◯ 32,586
a <
b) >
c =

8 $4.39
+ 5.27
a) $9.66
b $966
c 966
d NG

9 36,784
+ 14,261
a 40,945
b 41,045
c) 51,045
d NG

10 Estimate the sum.
369
+ 245
a 500
b) 600
c 700
d NG

11 Estimate the sum.
6,924
+ 15,165
a 21,000
b) 22,000
c 23,000
d NG

12 608
− 239
a) 369
b 379
c 431
d NG

13 $296.15
− 87.59
a $116.56
b $211.14
c $216.56
d) NG

☐ score

44

Cumulative Review

Item	Objective
1-2	Recall basic addition and subtraction facts (See pages 1-2, 5-6)
3	Find missing addends (See pages 1-2)
4-5	Identify place value in a number less than 1,000,000 (See pages 11-12)
6	Compare and order numbers through thousands (See pages 9-10)
7	Compare and order numbers through hundred thousands (See pages 11-12)
8	Add two numbers with sums less than 1,000, one regrouping (See pages 23-24)
9	Add two or more numbers less than 1,000,000 (See pages 27-28)
10-11	Estimate sums by rounding to the nearest 100 and adding (See pages 29-30)
12	Subtract up to 4-digit numbers with zeros in the minuend (See pages 33-34)
13	Subtract two numbers up to 6-digits (See pages 35-36)

Alternate Cumulative Review

Circle the letter of the correct answer.

1 8 + 9
a 15
b 16
c) 17
d NG

2 16 − 7
a 7
b 8
c) 9
d NG

3 $4 + n = 4$
$n = ?$
a) 0
b 4
c 8
d NG

4 Give the place value of the 7 in 57,832.
a ones
b tens
c hundreds
d) NG

5 Give the place value of the 2 in 428,073.
a hundred thousands
b) ten thousands
c thousands

6 379 ◯ 973
a) <
b >
c =

7 45,662 ◯ 45,653
a <
b) >
c =

8 $3.28
+ 6.49
a) $9.77
b $97.7
c $977
d NG

9 27,660
+ 43,395
a 70,955
b 61,055
c) 71,055
d NG

10 Estimate the sum after rounding to the nearest hundred.
458
+ 349
a 700
b) 800
c 900
d NG

11 Estimate the sum after rounding to the nearest hundred.
7,850
+ 16,274
a 24,100
b) 24,200
c 24,300
d NG

12 507
− 248
a) 259
b 269
c 341
d NG

44

Multiplying Whole Numbers

pages 45-46

Objective

To review basic multiplication facts and properties

Materials

counters
*multiplication flashcards

Mental Math

Ask students to tell which difference is smaller:

1. 300 − 100 or 500 − 200 (300 − 100)
2. 90 − 20 or 100 − 90 (100 − 90)
3. 1,000 − 500 or 800 − 100 (1,000 − 500)
4. 40 − 10 or 50 − 10 (40 − 10)
5. 80 − 70 or 30 − 0 (80 − 70)

Skill Review

Have students do the following addition on paper:

1. 2 + 2 + 2 + 2 (8)
2. 5 + 5 + 5 (15)
3. 8 + 8 + 8 + 8 (32)
4. 9 + 9 + 9 (27)
5. 4 + 4 + 4 + 4 + 4 (20)
6. 7 + 7 + 7 + 7 + 7 (35)
7. 1 + 1 + 1 + 1 + 1 + 1 + 1 (7)

Basic Facts and Properties

Jogging is a great form of aerobic exercise. On Saturday, Jewel plans to jog 4 miles, at the same rate of speed she is jogging today. How long will it take Jewel to jog the 4 miles?

We want to find the total time it will take Jewel to jog 4 miles.
We know she jogged 1 mile in __9__ minutes.

She is going to jog __4__ miles on Saturday. To find the time it will take Jewel to jog the

total distance, we multiply __9__ × __4__.

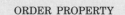

factor	factor	product		9 ← factor
↓	↓	↓		× 4 ← factor
9	× 4	= 36		36 ← product

It will take Jewel __36__ minutes to jog 4 miles. Multiplication has several basic properties that help you to understand it.

ORDER PROPERTY
Factors can be multiplied in any order.

6 × 4 = 24   5 × 7 = __35__

4 × 6 = 24   7 × 5 = __35__

GROUPING PROPERTY
Factors can be grouped in any way.

(4 × 2) × 3 = 24   (5 × 1) × 6 = __30__

4 × (2 × 3) = 24   5 × (1 × 6) = __30__

ZERO PROPERTY
If one factor is 0, the product is 0.

4 × 0 = 0   8 × 0 = __0__

0 × 4 = 0   0 × 8 = __0__

IDENTITY PROPERTY
If one factor is 1, the product is the same as the other factor.

7 × 1 = 7   5 × 1 = __5__

1 × 9 = 9   1 × 3 = __3__

Getting Started

Multiply.

1. 0
    × 8
    ___
    0

2. 1
    × 3
    ___
    3

3. 9 × 6 = __54__

4. (4 × 2) × 7 = __56__

MCP All rights reserved

45

Teaching the Lesson

Introducing the Problem Read the problem aloud. Ask a student to tell how long it took Jewel to run one mile. (9 minutes) Read the information sentences aloud. Have a volunteer read and complete the plan sentence. Put the multiplication on the board and label the parts. (factor, factor, product) Have a student read the solution sentence. (36 minutes) Point out the two groups of problems below. Explain that in multiplication, as in addition, factors can be listed in any order. Have a student read and complete the problems. Point out that the factors can be grouped in any way. Have another student read the problems. Have students read and complete the sections on the zero property and identity properties.

Developing the Skill Give students strategies for learning multiplication facts. Remind them that multiplication is repeated addition: 4 × 5 = 4 + 4 + 4 + 4 + 4. Explain how basic properties can help. Remembering that n × 0 = 0 and n × 1 = n will solve all facts involving 0 or 1 as a factor. Point out that the order property means that even if they cannot remember 7 × 5, they may be able to remember 5 × 7. Even the grouping property can help them remember difficult facts. For example: 8 × 7 = (2 × 4) × 7 = 2 × (4 × 7) = 2 × 28 = 56. Quiz students with multiplication flashcards.

Multiply.

1 ×1 = 1	0 ×5 = 0	8 ×1 = 8	1 ×6 = 6	3 ×6 = 18	9 ×3 = 27	1 ×7 = 7	3 ×2 = 6	8 ×0 = 0
5 ×2 = 10	1 ×9 = 9	1 ×4 = 4	0 ×1 = 0	7 ×1 = 7	4 ×4 = 16	1 ×2 = 2	0 ×0 = 0	2 ×9 = 18
3 ×0 = 0	7 ×4 = 28	7 ×0 = 0	2 ×0 = 0	3 ×3 = 9	3 ×1 = 3	8 ×3 = 24	5 ×4 = 20	5 ×7 = 35
4 ×8 = 32	9 ×0 = 0	5 ×9 = 45	8 ×2 = 16	2 ×3 = 6	0 ×2 = 0	6 ×9 = 54	5 ×6 = 30	2 ×7 = 14
5 ×8 = 40	7 ×5 = 35	7 ×8 = 56	4 ×0 = 0	2 ×6 = 12	1 ×5 = 5	6 ×6 = 36	6 ×7 = 42	0 ×8 = 0
3 ×8 = 24	1 ×0 = 0	4 ×1 = 4	9 ×8 = 72	7 ×9 = 63	3 ×5 = 15	6 ×2 = 12	9 ×0 = 0	3 ×7 = 21
4 ×7 = 28	3 ×9 = 27	6 ×3 = 18	6 ×4 = 24	7 ×7 = 49	7 ×2 = 14	9 ×5 = 45	9 ×2 = 18	4 ×6 = 24
6 ×1 = 6	2 ×2 = 4	6 ×5 = 30	2 ×4 = 8	2 ×5 = 10	5 ×0 = 0	5 ×1 = 5	8 ×8 = 64	0 ×3 = 0
9 ×7 = 63	8 ×7 = 56	4 ×9 = 36	7 ×6 = 42	8 ×5 = 40	0 ×4 = 0	3 ×4 = 12	6 ×0 = 0	9 ×1 = 9
1 ×3 = 3	4 ×3 = 12	0 ×7 = 0	9 ×6 = 54	4 ×2 = 8	8 ×6 = 48	9 ×9 = 81	5 ×5 = 25	2 ×8 = 16
2 ×1 = 2	6 ×8 = 48	7 ×3 = 21	8 ×9 = 72	0 ×9 = 0	1 ×8 = 8	9 ×4 = 36	0 ×6 = 0	5 ×3 = 15

46

Correcting Common Errors

If students continue to have difficulty mastering their multiplication facts, have them work with partners and a set of flash cards. Have them take turns quizzing each other, noting the facts with which their partner has difficulty and practicing these facts more often.

Enrichment

Give students a set of array cards. Each card should show one array, for example 4 rows of 5 dots with the total number of dots in an upper corner. Cut off the bottom of the array and tell students to figure out what the dimensions of the array were before you cut off the bottom.

Practice

Instruct students to complete the practice problems as quickly but accurately as possible. You may want to copy this page and use it more than once as a timed multiplication test.

Mixed Practice

1. 708,103 − 298,176 (409,927)
2. $596.83 + $427.89 + $19.36 ($1,044.08)
3. 700,000 + 80,000 + 700 + 40 + 8 (780,748)
4. 9 + 8 + 5 (22)
5. 65 + 48 + 93 + 68 (274)
6. $2,000.000 − $858.39 ($1,141.61)
7. 285,963 + 362,896 (648,859)
8. 15 − 8 (7)
9. 1,708 − 956 (752)
10. 3,965 + 18,195 + 1,940 (24,100)

Extra Credit *Creative Drill*

Remind students that a magic square is a square array of numbers such that the sum of each row, column and diagonal is the same. Have the students complete each of the magic squares below using only the digits 1 through 9.

8	(1)	6
(3)	5	(7)
4	(9)	(2)

2	(9)	(4)
(7)	(5)	3
(6)	1	8

(2)	(3)	6
9	5	(1)
(4)	7	(8)

Ask students to look for any similarities between each of the magic squares above, for example the 5 is always in the center square, the even digits are in the corners, etc. Have the students construct a different 3 × 3 magic square of their own.

Finding Common Multiples

Objective

To find the least common multiple of two numbers

Materials

graph paper
100 basic multiplication facts
   test

Mental Math

Have students solve for n:

1. $2 \times n = 8$ (4)
2. $n \times 6 = 30$ (5)
3. $3 \times 7 = n$ (21)
4. $n \times 5 = 10$ (2)
5. $n \times n = 49$ (7)
6. $0 \times n = 0$ (n could be any number)
7. $1 \times n = 9$ (9)

Skill Review

Use a sheet of 100 multiplication facts as a 3-minute timed test. Encourage students to work quickly, but to be as accurate as they can. Have them check each other's work at the end. Review with the entire class any multiplication facts missed by a number of students.

Multiples and Common Multiples

The fifth graders are comparing sets of **non-zero multiples**. The first six non-zero multiples of 2 shown on the board are 2, 4, 6, 8, 10 and 12. The three dots indicate that the set of multiples of 2 keeps on going. The students compare this set with the set of multiples of 5. What will be the **least common multiple** of 2 and 5?

Number	Multiples
2	0, 2, 4, 6, 8, 10, 12 . . .
3	0, 3, 6, 9, 12, 15, 18 . . .
4	0, 4, 8, 12, 16, 20, 24 . . .
5	0, 5, 10, 15, 20, 25, 30 . . .

We are looking for the least common multiple of 2 and 5.
The **least common multiple** of two or more numbers is the smallest number that can be evenly divided by those numbers.
We know the multiples of 2 are 2, __4__, __6__, __8__, __10__, __12__ . . .
The multiples of 5 are __5__, __10__, 15, __20__, __25__, __30__ . . .
The multiples of 2, and the number 0, are also called **even** numbers. The other whole numbers are called **odd** numbers.

✔ Notice that although the first multiple of any number is zero, it is not listed here. Zero would never be a least common multiple.

The common multiples of 2 and 5 are __10__, __20__, __30__ . . .
The least common multiple of 2 and 5 is __10__.

Getting Started

1. Write the first 8 multiples of 6.
   __6__, __12__, __18__, __24__,
   __30__, __36__, __42__, __48__

2. Write the first 8 multiples of 9.
   __9__, __18__, __27__, __36__,
   __45__, __54__, __63__, __72__

3. Write the common multiples of 6 and 9 that you listed.
   __18__, __36__

4. Write the least common multiple of 6 and 9.
   __18__

Write the least common multiple.

5. 2, 6 __6__
6. 5, 7 __35__

Write even or odd for each number.

7. 3 __odd__
8. 0 __even__

MCP All rights reserved

47

Teaching the Lesson

Introducing the Problem Read the problem aloud while students examine the chart. Explain that multiples of a number are the products of that number with the numbers 0, 1, 2, 3 and so on. Point out that the least common multiple means the smallest number common to both sets of multiples. Explain that the least common multiple will be the smallest number that can have both numbers as a factor. Have a student read and complete the information sentences. Read the next sentences, and explain that the zero multiple (0) of every number is trivial because it is common to all numbers. Have a student read the solution sentences aloud. (Common multiples are 10, 20, 30; least common multiple is 10.)

Developing the Skill Explain that a number multiplied by the numbers 0 through 9 forms a family of multiplication facts. Ask a student to recite the family for the number 3. $(3 \times 0 = 0, 3 \times 1 = 3, 3 \times 2 = 6, \ldots 3 \times 9 = 27)$ Point out that the family for 3 will have products, or multiples, in common with the family for 5. Have another student recite the family of multiplication facts for 5. $(5 \times 0 = 0, 5 \times 1 = 5, 5 \times 2 = 10, \ldots 5 \times 9 = 45)$ Ask the class to identify the smallest product these families have in common. (15) Put both sets of multiples on the board and circle the least common multiple. Ask students to find the least common multiple of 6 and 8. (24)

Practice

1. Write the first 8 multiples of 4.
   <u>4</u>, <u>8</u>, <u>12</u>, <u>16</u>,
   <u>20</u>, <u>24</u>, <u>28</u>, <u>32</u>

2. Write the first 8 multiples of 8.
   <u>8</u>, <u>16</u>, <u>24</u>, <u>32</u>,
   <u>40</u>, <u>48</u>, <u>56</u>, <u>64</u>

3. Write the common multiples of 4 and 8 that you listed.
   <u>8</u>, <u>16</u>, <u>24</u>, <u>32</u>

4. Write the least common multiple of 4 and 8.
   <u>8</u>

Write the least common multiple.

5. 2, 3 <u>6</u>   6. 2, 4 <u>4</u>   7. 3, 9 <u>9</u>   8. 4, 5 <u>20</u>

9. 3, 5 <u>15</u>   10. 5, 6 <u>30</u>   11. 7, 8 <u>56</u>   12. 4, 6 <u>12</u>

13. 4, 10 <u>20</u>   14. 9, 12 <u>36</u>   15. 10, 15 <u>30</u>   16. 8, 12 <u>24</u>

Write even or odd for each number.

17. 7   18. 10   19. 15   20. 35   21. 28   22. 83
   <u>odd</u>   <u>even</u>   <u>odd</u>   <u>odd</u>   <u>even</u>   <u>odd</u>

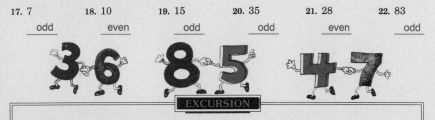

EXCURSION

A number is **even** if it has 2 as one of its factors.
A number is **odd** if 2 is *not* one of its factors.
Write a set of factors for each multiplication problem. Write the product. Then identify each product as odd or even.

Ex: $7 \times 6 = 7 \times (3 \times 2) = 42$ **even**   (2 is a factor of 42.)

1. $5 \times 14 = $ <u>$5 \times (2 \times 7)$</u> $=$ <u>70</u>   <u>even</u>

2. $6 \times 18 = $ <u>$(2 \times 3) \times (2 \times 3 \times 3)$</u> $=$ <u>108</u>   <u>even</u>

3. $15 \times 21 = $ <u>$(3 \times 5) \times (3 \times 7)$</u> $=$ <u>315</u>   <u>odd</u>

Decide if the product of these numbers would be even or odd.

4. even × odd = <u>even</u>

5. odd × odd = <u>odd</u>

6. even × even = <u>even</u>

48

Correcting Common Errors

Some students may have difficulty listing multiples of a number without first writing the multiplication facts. Have them work in small groups to practice seeing and saying multiples. Members take turns being the slippery finger. Draw a number line from 0 to 81 on the chalkboard showing a point for each whole number. To practice multiples of 3, for example, the member who is the slippery finger dips his finger in water and, as the other members say the multiples of 3, starts at 0 and draws loops to every third number. Have members take turns at the chalkboard until all have had a chance to be the slippery finger.

Enrichment

Have students find the least common multiple of these sets of three numbers:

1. 2, 3, 4 (12)
2. 2, 4, 8 (8)
3. 3, 5, 6 (30)
4. 3, 5, 7 (105)
5. 8, 5, 3 (120)

Practice

Have students complete the practice problems. Remind them that a pair of numbers will have many common multiples but that they are to find the least common multiple. Explain again that least means smallest.

Excursion

Dictate several odd and even numbers for students to identify the ones that have two as a factor, and those that do not. Review the example with them and have them complete the excursion. Have them insert numbers in problems 4, 5 and 6 to prove them correct.

Extra Credit   *Statistics*

Remind students that ancient civilizations had ways of graphing and counting things that were of importance in their lives. One of these methods was by using **pictographs.** Ask students to research what a pictograph is. Then have them imagine that they are prehistoric people. Ask them to write a story about a day in their lives and to include a pictograph cave drawing of important things that happened to them, for example, the number of elk killed in a recent hunt, the weather, etc.

Multiples of 10 through 10,000

pages 49-50

Objective

To multiply a multiple of 10, 100, 1,000 and 10,000 by a 1-digit factor

Materials

1-inch graph paper

Mental Math

Ask students to insert the correct sign, either <, > or =.

1. $3 + 5$ ( ) $7 + 1$ (=)
2. $10 - 2$ ( ) $4 + 5$ (<)
3. $4 + 4$ ( ) 4×2 (=)
4. $6 + 1$ ( ) $9 - 3$ (>)
5. $18 - 9$ ( ) $5 + 3$ (>)
6. $5 + 5$ ( ) 10×1 (=)

Skill Review

Give each student one-inch graph paper to write the ten multiples of the numbers 1 through 9 horizontally:

1	2	3	4	5	6	7	8	9
2	4	6	8	10	12	14	16	18
3	6	9	12	15	18	21	24	27
4	8	12	16	20	24	28	32	36 . . .

Point out that this forms a multiplication chart. If they read across and down from the numbers on top and side (factors), they will find the correct product.

Multiples of 10, 100, 1,000 and 10,000

Computer printers work very fast. How many characters can this one print in 6 minutes of steady use?

We want to find the total number of characters the printer can make in 6 minutes.

The printer makes ___5,000___ characters per minute.

The printer is used for ___6___ minutes.
To find the total number of characters printed, we multiply ___5,000___ by ___6___.
Study the pattern in these multiplication equations.

$6 \times 1 = 6$	$6 \times 5 = 30$
$6 \times 10 = 60$	$6 \times 50 = 300$
$6 \times 100 = 600$	$6 \times 500 = 3,000$
$6 \times 1,000 = 6,000$	
$6 \times 10,000 = 60,000$	$6 \times 5,000 =$ ___30,000___

The printer can make ___30,000___ characters in 6 minutes.

✔ To multiply by multiples of 10, 100 and 1,000 mentally, we find the product of the non-zero digits and follow it by the number of zeros in the multiple.

$5 \times 1 =$ ___5___ $5 \times 10 =$ ___50___ $5 \times 100 =$ ___500___

$5 \times 6 =$ ___30___ $5 \times 60 =$ ___300___ $5 \times 600 =$ ___3,000___

$5 \times 1,000 =$ ___5,000___ $5 \times 10,000 =$ ___50,000___

$5 \times 6,000 =$ ___30,000___ $5 \times 60,000 =$ ___300,000___

Getting Started

Multiply. Use mental math.

1. $7 \times 800 =$ ___5,600___   2. $3,000 \times 9 =$ ___27,000___   3. $40 \times 6 =$ ___240___

4. $4 \times 7,000 =$ ___28,000___   5. $900 \times 8 =$ ___7,200___   6. $5 \times 30 =$ ___150___

7. $60 \times 3 =$ ___180___   8. $4 \times 300 =$ ___1,200___   9. $3,000 \times 3 =$ ___9,000___

10. $6 \times 6,000 =$ ___36,000___   11. $700 \times 9 =$ ___6,300___   12. $5 \times 70 =$ ___350___

MCP All rights reserved

49

Teaching the Lesson

Introducing the Problem Read the problem aloud. Ask a student to read and complete the next three sentences. (makes 5,000 characters/minute; used for 6 minutes) Read the plan sentence aloud (multiply 5,000 by 6) and direct students' attention to the multiplication below. Copy these patterns on the board, completing the last problem. ($6 \times 5,000 = 30,000$) Explain that as one factor increases by a factor of 10, the multiple also increases by a factor of ten, or by one zero. Point out this means that multiplying by 10, 100, 1,000 or 10,000 allows them to multiply the non-zero digits and simply add the same number of zeros to the product as were in the factor. Have a student read the solution sentence. (30,000 characters) Have students complete the problems below and put the results on the board.

Developing the Skill

Remind students of the grouping property of multiplication. Put this example on the board:
$4 \times 600 = 4 \times (6 \times 100) = (4 \times 6) \times 100 = 2400$.
Have students regroup and multiply these numbers:

1. $5 \times 7,000$ [$= 5 \times (7 \times 1,000) = (5 \times 7) \times 1,000 = 35,000$]
2. 8×400 [$= 8 \times (4 \times 100) = (8 \times 4) \times 100 = 3,200$]
3. 7×80 [$= 7 \times (8 \times 10) = (7 \times 8) \times 10 = 560$]
4. $6,000 \times 8$ [$= (6 \times 1,000) \times 8 = 1,000 \times (6 \times 8) = 48,000$]

49

Multiply. Use mental math.

1. $5 \times 300 = $ ___1,500___   2. $20 \times 9 = $ ___180___   3. $100 \times 6 = $ ___600___

4. $1,000 \times 7 = $ ___7,000___   5. $6 \times 5,000 = $ ___30,000___   6. $60 \times 3 = $ ___180___

7. $8 \times 40,000 = $ ___320,000___   8. $3 \times 2,000 = $ ___6,000___   9. $3,000 \times 7 = $ ___21,000___

10. $600 \times 6 = $ ___3,600___   11. $8 \times 40 = $ ___320___   12. $10,000 \times 9 = $ ___90,000___

13. $90,000 \times 7 = $ ___630,000___   14. $3 \times 300 = $ ___900___   15. $5,000 \times 8 = $ ___40,000___

16. $6,000 \times 2 = $ ___12,000___   17. $4 \times 40,000 = $ ___160,000___   18. $700 \times 5 = $ ___3,500___

19. $6 \times 50 = $ ___300___   20. $900 \times 3 = $ ___2,700___   21. $20,000 \times 8 = $ ___160,000___

22. $3,000 \times 4 = $ ___12,000___   23. $60,000 \times 6 = $ ___360,000___   24. $4 \times 8,000 = $ ___32,000___

25. $2 \times 70,000 = $ ___140,000___   26. $4 \times 500 = $ ___2,000___   27. $60 \times 9 = $ ___540___

28. $9 \times 90,000 = $ ___810,000___   29. $3 \times 700 = $ ___2,100___   30. $7 \times 60,000 = $ ___420,000___

31. $5,000 \times 2 = $ ___10,000___   32. $90 \times 3 = $ ___270___   33. $2,000 \times 9 = $ ___18,000___

34. $4 \times 80,000 = $ ___320,000___   35. $3 \times 4,000 = $ ___12,000___   36. $9 \times 80,000 = $ ___720,000___

Apply

Solve these problems.

37. Name tags for the sales convention come in boxes of 500. How many name tags are there in 7 boxes?
3,500 name tags

38. The convention manager put 40 chairs in each of the meeting rooms. How many chairs are there in 9 meeting rooms?
360 chairs

39. A sales person for a computer company flies 5,000 miles each month. How far does he fly in 6 months?
30,000 miles

40. Company cars for each sales team cost $30,000. How much will company cars for 8 sales teams cost?
$240,000

50

Correcting Common Errors

Some students may write the incorrect number of zeros when they are multiplying multiples of 10; 100; 1,000; or 10,000. Have them practice patterns of numbers, such as those shown below, and compare the numbers of zeros in the products with those in the factors.

4×10 4×50
4×100 4×500
$4 \times 1,000$ $4 \times 5,000$
$4 \times 10,000$ $4 \times 50,000$

It will help them see the pattern more readily if, for each example, they circle the basic fact in color. For example:

Enrichment

Show students this multiplication shortcut:
$309 \times 6 = (300 + 9) \times 6 = 300 \times 6 + 9 \times 6 = 1,800 + 54 = 1,854$. Explain that it can be used to do seemingly difficult problems without pencil and paper. Give students these problems and ask them to work them mentally.

1. $4,005 \times 4$ (16,020)
2. $70,200 \times 4$ (280,800)
3. 905×8 (7,240)

Practice

Have students complete the practice problems. Remind them to count zeros carefully.

Mixed Practice

1. $7,000.00 - $3,407.91 ($3,592.09)
2. $657,909 + 273,486$ (931,395)
3. $10,000 \times 8$ (80,000)
4. $427.95 + $365.28 + $39.72 ($832.95)
5. 7×9 (63)
6. $309.73 - $285.41 ($24.32)
7. $32 + 57 + 95 + 48$ (232)
8. $8 + 9$ (17)
9. $6 \times 6,000$ (36,000)
10. $15 - 6$ (9)

Extra Credit *Measurement*

Making sure students have been exposed to the world's system of time zones, display a map of the United States with the four time zones clearly marked. Duplicate or write on the board the following:

1. I am in the capital of Ohio. When it is 3 PM in Boston, Massachusetts, what time is it here?
2. A flight from the Chesapeake Bay area to San Francisco, California takes four hours. If I left Pittsburgh at 10:30 AM, what time would I arrive in San Francisco?
3. It is 10 PM in Wichita, Kansas. What time is it in Miami, Florida?

Have students make up their own time zone problems to exchange with a partner to solve.

Estimating Products

pages 51-52

Objective

To estimate multiplication products

Materials

Mental Math

Have students provide an answer to each sequence:

1. $30 + 40 - 10$ (60)
2. $400 - 200 + 700$ (900)
3. $50 + 50 + 100$ (200)
4. $3,000 + 5,000 - 100$ (7,900)
5. $4,000 - 2,000 + 7,000$ (9,000)
6. $50 + 200 - 20$ (230)
7. $5,000 - 500 - 300$ (4,200)

Skill Review

Ask students to round these numbers to the nearest 10:

1. 42 (40)   4. 371 (370)
2. 119 (120)   5. 166 (170)
3. 69 (70)   6. 3,441 (3,440)

Have them round these to the nearest 100:

1. 338 (300)   4. 1,992 (2,000)
2. 682 (700)   5. 227 (200)
3. 949 (900)   6. 7,394 (7,400)

Estimating Products

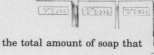

A water pipe broke in Simon's grocery store, and 23 boxes of soap were completely soaked. About how many grams of soap were ruined?

We want to estimate the total amount of soap that was ruined.

We know each box contained ___1,875___ grams of soap.

There were ___23___ boxes damaged by water. To estimate, we round each factor and multiply.

1,875 rounded to the nearest 1,000 is ___2,000___.

23 rounded to the nearest 10 is ___20___.

✔ To multiply two multiples of 10, 100, 1,000 or 10,000, we mentally multiply the non-zero whole numbers. The product will have as many zeros as there are in both factors together.

$2 \times 2 = 4$ 3 zeros + 1 zero = 4 zeros

$$2,000 \times 20 = 40,000$$

✔ In multiplication, we round each factor to its greatest place value. In 756×24, we estimate 800 times 20.

About ___40,000___ grams of soap were ruined.

Getting Started

Multiply. Use mental math.

1. $8,000 \times 200 =$ ___1,600,000___   2. $40 \times 10,000 =$ ___400,000___

3. $6,000 \times 3,000 =$ ___18,000,000___   4. $500 \times 3,000 =$ ___1,500,000___

Round the factors and estimate the products.

5. 9×63
$10 \times 60 = 600$

6. 38×72
$40 \times 70 = 2,800$

7. 43×165
$40 \times 200 = 8,000$

8. 425×688
$400 \times 700 = 280,000$

9. $1,526 \times 65$
$2,000 \times 70 = 140,000$

10. $4,321 \times 788$
$4,000 \times 800 = 3,200,000$

MCP All rights reserved

51

Teaching the Lesson

Introducing the Problem Read the problem aloud. Have a student read the information sentences. (each contained 1,875 grams; 23 boxes damaged) Have students read the plan sentence and round each factor. Direct the students' attention to the highlighted material. Explain that the multiplication can be simplified. Put the following on the board:

$2,000 \times 20 = (2 \times 2) \times (1,000 \times 10) = 4 \times 10,000 = 40,000$. Have a student read the solution sentence. (about 40,000 grams)

Developing the Skill Show students how to regroup problems in order to solve them more easily. Write on the board:

$400 \times 7,000 = (4 \times 100) \times (7 \times 1,000) = (4 \times 7) \times (100 \times 1,000) = 28 \times 10,000 = 280,000$. Explain that all that is required is that they multiply the single digits and that they

count zeros correctly. Ask students to tell how many zeros in each of these products:

1. 30×20 (two zeros; 600)
2. 400×700 (four zeros; 280,000)
3. $5,000 \times 9$ (three zeros; 45,000)
4. $70 \times 7,000$ (four zeros; 490,000)
5. $8,000 \times 6,000$ (six zeros; 48,000,000)

When they have counted the number of zeros expected, have each student regroup these problems in the way you have shown and multiply.

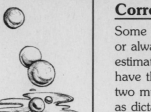

Practice

Multiply. Use mental math.

1. $500 \times 30 = $ __15,000__   2. $70 \times 800 = $ __56,000__

3. $3,000 \times 80 = $ __240,000__   4. $60 \times 6,000 = $ __360,000__

5. $10,000 \times 50 = $ __500,000__   6. $900 \times 7,000 = $ __6,300,000__

7. $4,000 \times 2,000 = $ __8,000,000__   8. $9,000 \times 800 = $ __7,200,000__

9. $50 \times 90 = $ __4,500__   10. $300 \times 3,000 = $ __900,000__

11. $400 \times 200 = $ __80,000__   12. $500 \times 6,000 = $ __3,000,000__

Round the factors and estimate the products.

13. 56×43
$60 \times 40 = 2,400$

14. 67×16
$70 \times 20 = 1,400$

15. 9×439
$10 \times 400 = 4,000$

16. 237×15
$200 \times 20 = 4,000$

17. 623×32
$600 \times 30 = 18,000$

18. 87×482
$90 \times 500 = 45,000$

19. 128×256
$100 \times 300 = 30,000$

20. 389×721
$400 \times 700 = 280,000$

21. 796×593
$800 \times 600 = 480,000$

22. $3,258 \times 6$
$3,000 \times 10 = 30,000$

23. $2,847 \times 9$
$3,000 \times 10 = 30,000$

24. $43 \times 3,159$
$40 \times 3,000 = 120,000$

25. $8,225 \times 33$
$8,000 \times 30 = 240,000$

26. $6,215 \times 215$
$6,000 \times 200 = 1,200,000$

27. 387×465
$400 \times 500 = 200,000$

28. $7,096 \times 583$
$7,000 \times 600 = 4,200,000$

29. $289 \times 5,653$
$300 \times 6,000 = 1,800,000$

30. $7,850 \times 68$
$8,000 \times 70 = 560,000$

31. 175×8
$200 \times 10 = 2,000$

32. 785×302
$800 \times 300 = 240,000$

33. $9 \times 5,276$
$10 \times 5,000 = 50,000$

34. 57×48
$60 \times 50 = 3,000$

35. $4,796 \times 78$
$5,000 \times 80 = 400,000$

36. $3,475 \times 2,758$
$3,000 \times 3,000 = 9,000,000$

Apply

Solve these problems.

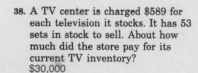

37. The Speedy Bike Company orders bolts in barrels that hold 4,260 bolts each. About how many bolts will they receive if they order 9 barrels?
40,000 bolts

38. A TV center is charged $589 for each television it stocks. It has 53 sets in stock to sell. About how much did the store pay for its current TV inventory?
$30,000

52

Correcting Common Errors

Some students may always round low or always round high when they are estimating a product. To correct this, have them write for each factor the two multiples of 10; 100; or 1,000—as dictated by the problem—and then choose the one to which it is closer. They can use a number line as a visual aid to confirm their choice. Then have them multiply the two rounded factors to estimate the product.

Enrichment

Give each student graph paper and have them write numbers 1 through 100, in ten rows of ten. Tell them to go through all the multiplication tables, crossing out numbers on the chart when they appear as products in the multiplication. Have them use a different color for each factor: red for 2, blue for 3, and so on.
Some numbers will be crossed with more than one color. Ask students to describe any patterns they see in the finished chart.

Practice

Have students complete the problems on the page. Explain that when they round, they may round one factor to tens and another to hundreds.

Mixed Practice

1. 6×7 (42)
2. $30,106 - 24,378$ (5,728)
3. 50×90 (4,500)
4. $12,146 + 8,072 + 25,396$ (45,614)
5. $300,000 + 80,000 + 1,000 + 20 + 6$ (381,026)
6. $\$872.63 + \$2,765.36$ ($3,637.99)
7. 200×40 (8,000)
8. $\$873.80 - \$612.95$ ($260.85)
9. $497,163 + 347,694$ (844,857)
10. $117 + 346 + 295 + 406$ (1,164)

Extra Credit   Estimation

Have students make a four-column chart with the following headings: less than 1 gram, 1-10 grams, 1-10 kilograms, more than 10 kilograms. Using newspapers and magazines, have students use their powers of estimation to find pictures of objects that fit into each column, and cut and paste them accordingly. Display the finished charts.

Multiplication with Renaming

pages 53-54

Objective

To review multiplying 1- and 2-digit numbers with renaming

Materials

2-digit place value charts
*overhead projector
*ten-strips and single counters

Mental Math

Ask students to identify the larger product:

1. 2×8 or 3×4 (16)
2. 9×5 or 6×6 (45)
3. 9×3 or 5×5 (27)
4. 7×1 or 3×2 (7)
5. 10×0 or 2×1 (2)
6. 8×4 or 5×6 (32)
7. 6×9 or 5×10 (54)

Skill Review

Ask students to multiply and then identify how many tens and ones there are in each product.

1. 6×7 (42; 4 tens, 2 ones)
2. 3×8 (24; 2 tens, 4 ones)
3. 6×6 (36; 3 tens, 6 ones)
4. 9×5 (45; 4 tens, 5 ones)
5. 7×9 (63; 6 tens, 3 ones)
6. 2×2 (4; no tens, 4 ones)
7. 8×2 (16; one ten, 6 ones)
8. 9×9 (81; 8 tens, 1 one)

Multiplication with Renaming

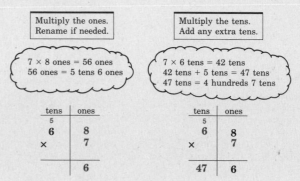

Miss Evans drives one of the 7 buses that carry students to school every day. If each bus has the same capacity, what is the largest number of students that can be brought to school by bus each day?

We want to find the largest number of students that can be bussed to school each day.

We know there is a capacity of __68__ students for each bus.
There are __7__ buses which make runs every day.

To get the total capacity of all the buses, we multiply the capacity of one, by the number of buses.

We multiply __68__ by __7__.

Multiply the ones. Rename if needed.	Multiply the tens. Add any extra tens.
7×8 ones = 56 ones 56 ones = 5 tens 6 ones	7×6 tens = 42 tens 42 tens + 5 tens = 47 tens 47 tens = 4 hundreds 7 tens

tens	ones		tens	ones
5			5	
6	8		6	8
×	7		×	7
	6		47	6

The buses can transport up to __476__ students each day.

Getting Started

Multiply. Check by estimation.

1. 56	2. 49	3. 38	4. 57
× 3	× 6	× 2	× 9
168	294	76	513

Copy and multiply.

5. 27×5
135

6. 94×7
658

7. 60×4
240

8. 71×8
568

53

MCP All rights reserved

Teaching the Lesson

Introducing the Problem Read the problem aloud. Ask a student to read the information sentences. Read the plan sentences aloud (multiply 68 by 7) and use the overhead projector to show students the problem worked in their texts. Tell them to begin to multiply in the ones column. Ask a student for the product of 8 and 7 (56). Point out that there are 5 tens, 6 ones in the product. Explain that you can put the 6 ones in the column for ones, but will have to write the 5 tens above the tens column and remember to add it in when you have multiplied tens. Have a student multiply tens. ($6 \times 7 = 42$) Remind them that there are 5 more tens and ask a student to add. ($42 + 5 = 47$) Write 47 in the hundreds and tens columns and have a student read the entire answer. (476) Read the solution sentence aloud.

Developing the Skill Give each student a page of 2-digit place value charts. Tell them to work the following problems within the charts in this way:

tens	ones
3	
2	6
×	5
13	0

1. 48×5 (240)
2. 39×7 (273)
3. 54×4 (216)
4. 82×2 (164)

53

Practice

Multiply. Check by estimation.

1.	2.	3.	4.
21 × 3 —— 63	45 × 2 —— 90	53 × 6 —— 318	75 × 4 —— 300

5.	6.	7.	8.
36 × 7 —— 252	49 × 9 —— 441	26 × 3 —— 78	37 × 8 —— 296

9.	10.	11.	12.
96 × 5 —— 480	63 × 7 —— 441	82 × 6 —— 492	40 × 9 —— 360

Copy and Do

13. 16 × 8
128

14. 48 × 2
96

15. 59 × 3
177

16. 24 × 4
96

17. 75 × 8
600

18. 28 × 7
196

19. 63 × 9
567

20. 39 × 5
195

21. 65 × 7
455

22. 93 × 4
372

23. 74 × 6
444

24. 68 × 4
272

25. 86 × 5
430

26. 61 × 9
549

27. 49 × 3
147

28. 98 × 2
196

Apply

Solve these problems.

29. Many students come to school by car pool. If each car transports 6 pupils, how many students are in 12 car pools?
72 students

30. A total of 57 boys and 38 girls come to school by train. How many students come to school by train?
95 students

31. Mrs. Chen has 31 students in her class. Nine of her students walk to school. How many of her students use transportation to get to school?
22 students

32. Most of the spectators who attended the basketball game came in 4 buses. Each bus held 57 passengers. How many spectators rode the buses?
228 spectators

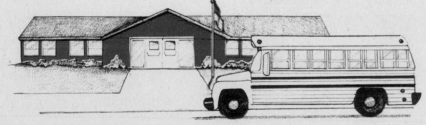

54

Correcting Common Errors

Some students may rename incorrectly when they are multiplying. Have them work with partners and place-value materials to model problems. They can use ten-strips and unit squares, for example, or white counters for ones and red counters for tens. They should recognize that, for example, 7 × 68 means 7 groups of 8 ones and 7 groups of 6 tens and then work together to trade, or rename, the 56 ones for tens and ones. Have the partners take turns to explain how they trade ones for tens and tens for hundreds when working with similar-type problems.

Enrichment

Give students graph paper and colored markers. Remind them that multiplication problems can be represented by arrays. Ask students to illustrate these problems with an array of markers arranged in squares. Encourage creativity in the way they color each array.
1. 15 × 6 2. 20 × 3 3. 6 × 6

Practice

Have students complete the page. Suggest that they show any extra tens above each problem. Remind students to work the copy and do problems carefully.

Extra Credit *Numeration*

Explain to students that before our numeral system was invented, the Egyptians used a system called hieroglyphics. In the hieroglyphic numeral system, different pictures were used to represent a given quantity:

1 = | (a vertical staff or stick)
10 = ∩ (a heel bone)
100 = ? (a coil of rope)
1,000 = ⚘ (a lotus flower)

These symbols were repeated as often as necessary to represent a given quantity. For example, 132 would have been expressed in hieroglyphics as ?∩∩∩||, one 100, three 10's and two 1's. Write several numbers, up to 4 digits on the board, for students to write in hieroglyphics.

54

Multiplying Larger Numbers

pages 55-56

Objective

To review multiplication of up to 6-digit by 1-digit numbers

Materials

Mental Math

Ask students to balance their savings account if they start with $100 each time.

	Deposit	Withdraw	Balance
1.	$50	$20	($130)
2.	$10	$100	($10)
3.	$100	$50	($150)
4.	$90	$80	($110)
5.	$300	$50	($350)
6.	$0	$25	($75)
7.	$75	$50	($125)

Skill Review

Have students work the following problems. Remind them that when they have a product that exceeds 9 in any place, they will have to rename and add to the next column.

1. $35 \times 6 = $ (210)
2. $60 \times 8 = $ (480)
3. $29 \times 7 = $ (203)
4. $52 \times 6 = $ (312)
5. $44 \times 9 = $ (396)
6. $17 \times 5 = $ (85)

Multiplying Larger Numbers

Pierre has saved exactly enough money to buy 2 pairs of running shoes at the annual shoe sale. How much has Pierre saved?

ONCE - A - YEAR
SHOE SALE!
RUNNING SHOES $39.97
TENNIS SHOES $19.97
BASKETBALL SHOES $24.49

We are looking for the total amount of money Pierre has saved.

We know a pair of running shoes costs $39.97 .

Pierre has saved enough to buy __2__ pairs.

To find the amount of money Pierre has saved, we multiply the cost of one pair of shoes by the number of pairs he will buy.

We multiply $39.97 by __2__.

✔ To multiply money, we multiply as we do whole numbers and place the decimal point between the second and the third digits from the right.

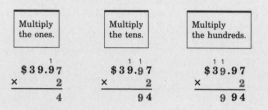

Multiply the ones.	Multiply the tens.	Multiply the hundreds.	Multiply the thousands. Place the decimal point and write the dollar sign.
$\overset{1}{\$3}9.97$ $\times \quad\quad 2$ $\quad\quad 4$	$\overset{1\;1}{\$3}9.97$ $\times \quad\quad 2$ $\quad 9\,4$	$\overset{1\;1}{\$3}9.97$ $\times \quad\quad 2$ $9\;9\,4$	$\overset{1}{\$3}9.97$ $\times \quad\quad 2$ $\$79.94$

Pierre has saved $79.94 .

Getting Started

Multiply. Check by estimation.

1. 257
    × 7
    1,799

2. $3.96
    × 5
    $19.80

3. 6,247
    × 3
    18,741

4. $27.48
    × 6
    $164.88

Copy and multiply.

5. $12,426 \times 4$
   49,704

6. $\$315.07 \times 8$
   $2,520.56

7. $615,210 \times 2$
   1,230,420

8. $\$1,512.38 \times 9$
   $13,611.42

55

MCP All rights reserved

Teaching the Lesson

Introducing the Problem Have a student read the problem aloud. Read the information sentences and have students supply the cost of each pair and the number of pairs. Have a student read the plan sentences. (multiply $39.97 by 2) Explain that multiplying money is like multiplying whole numbers. Direct their attention to the problem worked in the model. Ask a student to work the problem step by step on the board. Suggest that they write any regrouped numbers above the problem. Explain that thousands in this problem refer to cents. Ask how many dollars are in a 1,000¢ ? ($10) Have a student read the solution sentence. ($79.94)

Developing the Skill Remind students that they always start multiplying in the ones column and move to the left. When they have a 2-digit product, they will write down the right-hand digit and rename. Have them write each renaming in this lesson. Suggest that when they multiply money, they do the multiplication first and write in the decimal point at the end. Have them do these problems at their seats while a student works them on the board:

1. $1.46
    ×   4
      ($5.84)

2. $45.23
    ×   6
     ($271.38)

3. $357.27
    ×   9
    ($3,215.43)

4. $3,256.74
    ×   7
    ($22,797.18)

Practice

Multiply. Check by estimation.

1. $$\begin{array}{r} 859 \\ \times\ 4 \\ \hline 3{,}436 \end{array}$$

2. $$\begin{array}{r} 937 \\ \times\ 7 \\ \hline 6{,}559 \end{array}$$

3. $$\begin{array}{r} \$3.47 \\ \times\ 8 \\ \hline \$27.76 \end{array}$$

4. $$\begin{array}{r} \$7.28 \\ \times\ 2 \\ \hline \$14.56 \end{array}$$

5. $$\begin{array}{r} 1{,}276 \\ \times\ 3 \\ \hline 3{,}828 \end{array}$$

6. $$\begin{array}{r} \$32.67 \\ \times\ 6 \\ \hline \$196.02 \end{array}$$

7. $$\begin{array}{r} 4{,}758 \\ \times\ 4 \\ \hline 19{,}032 \end{array}$$

8. $$\begin{array}{r} \$75.45 \\ \times\ 5 \\ \hline \$377.25 \end{array}$$

9. $$\begin{array}{r} 17{,}246 \\ \times\ 9 \\ \hline 155{,}214 \end{array}$$

10. $$\begin{array}{r} \$215.37 \\ \times\ 2 \\ \hline \$430.74 \end{array}$$

11. $$\begin{array}{r} 36{,}256 \\ \times\ 5 \\ \hline 181{,}280 \end{array}$$

12. $$\begin{array}{r} \$409.27 \\ \times\ 7 \\ \hline \$2{,}864.89 \end{array}$$

Copy and Do

13. $3,036.58 \times 3$
    $9,109.74$
14. $8,174.58 \times 6$
    $49,047.48$
15. $212,639 \times 7$
    $1,488,473$
16. $857,916 \times 8$
    $6,863,328$
17. 796×5
    $3,980$
18. $4 \times 3,275$
    $13,100$
19. $9 \times \$12.07$
    $\$108.63$
20. $8,712 \times 2$
    $17,424$
21. $5 \times \$15.75$
    $\$78.75$
22. $32,751 \times 8$
    $262,008$
23. $\$165.81 \times 3$
    $\$497.43$
24. $6 \times 217,816$
    $1,306,896$

Apply

Solve these problems.

25. There are 1,760 yards in 1 mile. How many yards are there in 6 miles?
    10,560 yards

26. A truck holds 2,475 gallons of milk. How many gallons will 3 trucks hold?
    7,425 gallons

27. Tennis shoes cost $19.97 and basketball shoes are $24.49. How much more do the basketball shoes cost?
    $4.52

28. The paint and supplies needed to paint 1 house cost $129.35. How much will it cost to paint 5 houses?
    $646.75

29. The space shuttle can carry 11,456 pounds of equipment in one trip. How many pounds can the space shuttle carry in 8 trips?
    91,648 pounds

30. The distance around the globe at the equator is 24,900 miles. How much farther is that distance, than the 2,825 mile distance between Los Angeles and New York City?
    22,075 miles more

56

Correcting Common Errors

When multiplying larger numbers, some students may have difficulty keeping track of all the renaming. Have them practice by writing the partial products as shown below.

$$\begin{array}{r} 1{,}237 \\ \times\ 6 \\ \hline 42 \leftarrow 6 \times 7 \\ 180 \leftarrow 6 \times 30 \\ 1\ 200 \leftarrow 6 \times 200 \\ 6\ 000 \leftarrow 6 \times 1{,}000 \\ \hline 7{,}422 \end{array}$$

Enrichment

Have students calculate the total cost of the following items:

1. 4 pounds of hamburger at $1.89 per pound ($7.56)
2. 8 pounds of chicken at $1.29 per pound ($10.32)
3. a 4-pound wheel of Swiss cheese at $3.29 per pound ($13.16)
4. a 2-pound lobster at $12.95 per pound ($25.90)

Practice

Have students complete the practice problems. Remind them to include the dollar signs and decimal points. Have them write in any renaming they do.

Mixed Practice

1. $8,707 - 868$ (7,839)
2. 23×7 (161)
3. $3,221 - 148$ (3,073)
4. $24,195 + 8,206 + 14,321$ (46,722)
5. 396×6 (2,376)
6. $200,000 + 300 + 70 + 7$ (200,377)
7. $8 \times \$15.75$ ($126.00)
8. $26,271 + 39,393$ (65,664)
9. $\$308.27 - \$256.94$ ($51.33)
10. $25 + 47 + 38 + 21$ (131)

Extra Credit *Statistics*

Give each group of students a deck of playing cards with the following instructions:

Remove the jokers from the deck. Shuffle. Deal four cards face up. How many spades are turned up? Record the results with tally marks on a chart having a column for each suit. Put the cards back in the deck. Repeat the process 20 times. Have students write a description of their results. Ask what predictions they could make about results if the activity were repeated 20 more times.

Multiplying by Multiples of 10

pages 57-58

Objective

To review multiplying multiples of ten

Materials

Mental Math

Ask students to add three numbers to each series.

1. 2, 4, 6, . . . (8, 10, 12)
2. 5, 10, 15, . . . (20, 25, 30)
3. 4, 8, 12, . . . (16, 20, 24)
4. 7, 14, 21, . . . (28, 35, 42)
5. 3, 6, 9, . . . (12, 15, 18)
6. 10, 20, 30, . . . (40, 50, 60)

Skill Review

Have students write the number for:

1. 2 tens (20)
2. 7 tens (70)
3. 4 tens (40)
4. 8 tens (80)
5. 10 tens (100)
6. 12 tens (120)
7. 15 tens (150)
8. 20 tens (200)
9. 30 tens (300)
10. 100 tens (1,000)
11. 200 tens (2,000)
12. 250 tens (2,500)

Multiplying by Multiples of 10

Opal is using a typewriter to type her article for the school newspaper. Her editor limited her to 4,000 characters for the entire article. She set the margins to allow for a line width of 80 characters. So far she has typed 46 lines. Is her article too long?

We want to find the total number of characters in Opal's article.

We know each line has __80__ characters.

Opal has typed __46__ lines.

To find the total number of characters in Opal's article, we multiply the number of lines by the number of characters in each line.

We multiply __80__ by __46__.

Multiply by the digit in the ones place.	Multiply by the digit in the tens place.
46 × 80 ——— 0	46 × 80 ——— 3,680

Opal's article has __3,680__ characters. It is __less__ than the limit of 4,000 characters.

Getting Started

Multiply. Check by estimation.

1. 52
   × 20
   ————
   1,040

2. 38
   × 60
   ————
   2,280

3. $1.45
   × 30
   ————
   $43.50

4. 186
   × 70
   ————
   13,020

Copy and multiply.

5. 2,365 × 40
   94,600

6. $68.86 × 50
   $3,443

7. 21,725 × 90
   1,955,250

8. 85,648 × 80
   6,851,840

57

MCP All rights reserved

Teaching the Lesson

Introducing the Problem Read the problem aloud and have a student read the information sentences. Read the plan sentences aloud (multiply 80 by 46) and put the problem on the board. Explain that the problem illustrates a multiplication shortcut. Have a student multiply the ones (0) and put a zero in the ones place to indicate no ones. Have a student multiply the tens, and explain that they will start in the tens column to write the product because they are multiplying by tens. Have a student read and complete the solution sentence. (report has 3,680 characters; less than the limit)

Developing the Skill Write out one problem in full to show students how the multiples of ten shortcut works:

```
    567
  ×  40
  ——————
    000
+ 2268
  ——————
 22,680
```

Explain that it is not necessary to multiply by zero across the top number. To save time, they can simply put a zero in the ones column to hold that place while they complete the multiplication in one step. Have students do these problems on paper while you do them on the board:

1. 65
   × 20
   ————
   1,300

2. 347
   × 40
   ————
   13,880

3. 824
   × 60
   ————
   49,440

Practice

Multiply. Check by estimation.

1. 67 × 50 3,350	2. 98 × 30 2,940	3. 67 × 80 5,360	4. 32 × 20 640
5. 615 × 90 55,350	6. 723 × 70 50,610	7. $9.03 × 40 $361.20	8. 363 × 60 21,780
9. $36.25 × 40 $1,450.00	10. 8,275 × 60 496,500	11. 5,926 × 90 533,340	12. 2,658 × 20 53,160

Copy and Do

13. 13,258 × 30
397,740
14. $512.75 × 50
$25,637.50
15. 24,023 × 70
1,681,610
16. 85,658 × 80
6,852,640

17. 48 × 80
3,840
18. 70 × 385
26,950
19. 20 × $12.97
$259.40
20. 3,968 × 60
238,080

21. 5,796 × 20
115,920
22. $623.49 × 90
$56,114.10
23. 16,350 × 50
817,500
24. 72,056 × 40
2,882,240

Apply

Solve these problems.

25. How many minutes are there in one day?
1,440 minutes

26. How many seconds are there in one half-hour?
1,800 seconds

27. Nancy uses her computer 20 times each month. How many times does Nancy use her computer in one year?
240 times

28. A can contains 80 pounds of cleaning compound. Bill used 46 pounds. How much compound is left in the can?
34 pounds

EXCURSION

Using each digit only once, form two numbers from the digits 1, 2, 3, 4, 5, 6, 7, 8 and 9, so that one number is twice as large as the other.

13,458   6,729

58

Correcting Common Errors

Some students may write the incorrect number of zeros when the product of the nonzero digits ends in zero. Have students multiply by the digit in the tens place first and then write the zero to show that the product is a number of tens and there are no ones.

56
× 50
2800

Enrichment

Explain that on a computer, each binary digit is called a **bit.** Computers vary. Some are 8-bit, meaning that it takes 8 bits to make one **byte.** There are 16-bit and even 32-bit computers. Bytes are grouped together into **K.** Each K is 1,024 bytes. Ask students to calculate:

1. the number of bits in an 8-bit, 4K computer. (8 × 4 × 1,024 = 32,768)
2. the number of bits in a 16-bit, 8K computer. (16 × 8 × 1,024 = 131,072)

Practice

Have students complete the practice problems. Remind them to mark the ones place with a zero when they multiply.

Excursion

This is a good time for students to practice the strategy of guess and check. Encourage them to record each guess in a table, to eliminate any time wasted in repetition of numbers.

Extra Credit   *Applications*

Remind students of the process and purpose of making flow charts. Circles are used for **Stop** and **Start,** rectangles are used for each step, and diamonds are used when a decision must be made. Discuss and develop flow charts for simple tasks such as tying a shoe, sharpening a pencil or making popcorn. Have students make a poster flow chart for a specific task they do at home. Have them display the flow charts and ask other students to follow them. Invite a computer programer to discuss the use of flow charts in designing computer programs. Some students can make a flow chart for a program they use in the classroom computer.

2-digit Multipliers

pages 59-60

Objective

To review multiplication by 2-digit factors

Materials

*overhead projector
6-digit place value charts

Mental Math

Ask students to supply the next problem in each series:

1. $2 \times 2 = 4$, $2 \times 3 = 6$, $2 \times 4 = 8$
   $(2 \times 5 = 10)$
2. $5 \times 0 = 0$, $5 \times 1 = 5$, $5 \times 2 = 10$
   $(5 \times 3 = 15)$
3. $10 \times 4 = 40$, $10 \times 5 = 50$,
   $10 \times 6 = 60$ $(10 \times 7 = 70)$
4. $3 \times 2 = 6$, $3 \times 4 = 12$, $3 \times 6 = 18$
   $(3 \times 8 = 24)$
5. $1 \times 2 = 2$, $2 \times 2 = 4$, $3 \times 2 = 6$
   $(4 \times 2 = 8)$

Skill Review

Have students copy and complete these 1-digit multiplication problems.

1. $35 \times 6 = (210)$
2. $581 \times 9 = (5,229)$
3. $402 \times 3 = (1,206)$
4. $97 \times 5 = (485)$
5. $822 \times 7 = (5,754)$
6. $83 \times 4 = (332)$

Multiplying by a 2-digit Factor

In June, 1965, Ed White was the first American astronaut to walk in space. His Gemini space capsule made a complete trip around the globe every 89 minutes. How many minutes, altogether, did Ed White's ship spend orbiting the earth?

62 orbits

We want to find the total time Gemini was in orbit.

We know Gemini made __62__ orbits.

Each orbit took __89__ minutes.

To find the total time in orbit, we multiply the length of time for one orbit by the number of orbits made.

We multiply __62__ by __89__.

Multiply by the digit in the ones place.	Multiply by the digit in the tens place.	Add the products.

$$\begin{array}{r} 62 \\ \times\, 89 \\ \hline 558 \end{array} \leftarrow 9 \times 62$$

$$\begin{array}{r} 62 \\ \times\, 89 \\ \hline 558 \\ 4960 \end{array} \leftarrow 80 \times 62$$

$$\begin{array}{r} 62 \\ \times\, 89 \\ \hline 558 \\ 4\,960 \\ \hline 5,518 \end{array} \begin{array}{l} \leftarrow 9 \times 62 \\ \leftarrow 80 \times 62 \\ \leftarrow 89 \times 62 \end{array}$$

Gemini was in orbit for __5,518__ minutes.

Getting Started

Multiply. Check by estimation.

1. $\begin{array}{r} 45 \\ \times\, 17 \\ \hline 765 \end{array}$ 2. $\begin{array}{r} 38 \\ \times\, 45 \\ \hline 1,710 \end{array}$ 3. $\begin{array}{r} \$65.89 \\ \times\quad 74 \\ \hline \$4,875.86 \end{array}$

Copy and multiply.

4. $\$7.86 \times 37$ 5. $2,056 \times 53$ 6. 475×28
   $\$290.82$ $108,968$ $13,300$

MCP All rights reserved

59

Teaching the Lesson

Introducing the Problem Read the problem aloud. Ask a student to find the number of orbits and read the information sentences. (Gemini made 62 orbits, each took 89 minutes) Read the plan sentences. Use the overhead projector and work the problem on the board. Explain that they will multiply by ones first and then by tens. Put a zero in the ones column of the answer, explaining that because you are multiplying by tens, the answer will be in tens. Show students that they have two products: 9×62 and 80×62. Explain that the product they want is the sum of the two they have calculated. Add and have a student read the solution sentence. (in orbit 5,518 minutes)

Developing the Skill Show students how to work 2-digit multiplication in two steps. Write this example on the board:

$$\begin{array}{cccc} 34 & 34 & 34 & 238 \\ \times\, 67 = & \times\quad 7 & \times\, 60 & +\, 2,040 \\ \hline & 238 & 2,040 & 2,278 \end{array}$$

Point out that the same problem can be worked writing the products one over the other to begin with:

$$\begin{array}{r} 34 \\ \times\, 67 \\ \hline 238 \\ +\, 2040 \\ \hline 2,278 \end{array}$$

Ask them to do problems 1 and 2 in the first way, 3 and 4 in the second.

1. 46×29 (1,334) 2. 468×26 (12,168) 3. $4,057 \times 95$ (385,415) 4. $\$6.50 \times 43$ ($279.50)

Practice

Multiply. Check by estimation.

1.	34 × 27 918	**2.**	18 × 56 1,008	**3.**	97 × 86 8,342	**4.**	47 × 39 1,833
5.	167 × 43 7,181	**6.**	$8.15 × 67 $546.05	**7.**	$23.18 × 54 $1,251.72	**8.**	3,795 × 76 288,420
9.	$86.24 × 28 $2,414.72	**10.**	4,708 × 52 244,816	**11.**	$20.08 × 35 $702.80	**12.**	9,870 × 49 483,630

Copy and Do

13. 32 × 58
1,856

14. 67 × 88
5,896

15. 139 × 47
6,533

16. $3.85 × 15
$57.75

17. 3,228 × 39
125,892

18. $67.75 × 72
$4,878.00

19. 36 × 8,476
305,136

20. $30.19 × 68
$2,052.92

21. $6.46 × 75
$484.50

22. 9,465 × 39
369,135

23. 85 × 74
6,290

24. 538 × 69
37,122

25. 49 × 87
4,263

26. 33 × 4,096
135,168

27. $53.42 × 54
$2,884.68

28. 8,328 × 58
483,024

Apply

Solve these problems.

29. Ed White's capsule reached a height of 282 miles. Its lowest orbit was 121 miles below this height. What was the height of the capsule's lowest orbit?
161 miles

30. An electrician in the space program earns $24.83 per hour. How much does the electrician earn in one week, working 38 hours?
$943.54

31. There were 27 meeting rooms reserved for a space seminar. Each room contained 134 chairs. How many chairs were in use for the seminar?
3,618 chairs

32. Mrs. Davis works 35 hours each week for the space program. She gets 3 weeks vacation annually. How many hours does Mrs. Davis work each year?
1,715 hours

60

Correcting Common Errors

Some students may multiply incorrectly because they confuse the renamed numbers used when multiplying by ones with those used when multiplying by tens. After multiplying by ones, have students erase or cross out the renamed numbers that they have written.

Enrichment

Show students this expanded multiplication: 15 × 12 =

10 + 5
× 10 + 2

Explain that they can solve the problem by multiplying along the arrows: 10 × 10, 10 × 5, 2 × 10 and 2 × 5. If they add these products, they will get the answer. (100 + 50 + 20 + 10 = 180) Have them do these problems by the cross-product method:

1. 58 × 82 (4,756)
2. 39 × 51 (1,989)
3. 83 × 17 (1,411)

Practice

Have students complete the practice problems. Point out the importance of keeping columns straight as they multiply and add.

Mixed Practice

1. 9 + 7 + 6 + 3 (25)
2. 50,000 + 8,000 + 20 + 1 (58,021)
3. 62,851 × 9 (565,659)
4. 87 × 78 (6,786)
5. 8,000 − 1,658 (6,342)
6. 29 × 8,476 (245,804)
7. $9.06 × 70 ($634.20)
8. $25.93 + $108.98 + $651.27 ($786.18)
9. $2,183.92 + $17.56 + $959.38 ($3,160.86)
10. 495 × 38 (18,810)

Extra Credit *Applications*

Explain to students that ratios are often used in recipes. Bring in a frozen juice can and have a student read the directions. Point out that the usual directions, one can of juice to three cans of water is a ratio. Have students complete a ratio table for making juice from 2, 3 and 4 cans.

cans of juice	1	(2)	(3)	(4)
cans of water	3	(6)	(9)	(12)

Ask students to look for simple recipes and bring them to class. Have them work in pairs to make a ratio table showing 2, 3 and 4 times the basic recipe, for all the ingredients.

3-digit Multipliers

pages 61-62

Objective

To multiply by 3-digit factors

Materials

9-digit place value charts

Mental Math

Have students round to the nearest ten and add, estimating the sum.

1. 12 + 34 (40)
2. 59 + 17 (80)
3. 55 + 14 (70)
4. 88 + 12 (100)
5. 24 + 38 (60)
6. 71 + 36 (110)

Skill Review

Have students complete these 2-digit multiplication problems.

1.	45	2.	132
	×38		×42
	(1710)		(5544)
3.	272	4.	56
	×34		×92
	(9248)		(5152)
5.	423	6.	812
	×62		×56
	(26,226)		(45,472)

Multiplying by a 3-digit Factor

Mrs. Mayer delivers meat for the Angus Meat Company. She must travel on the toll road for part of her daily route. She enters the turnpike at Exit 10 and leaves at Exit 8. On the return trip she reverses the route. If Mrs. Mayer worked 234 days last year, how many turnpike miles did she drive?

We want to find the total number of turnpike miles Mrs. Mayer drove on her route last year.

We know she drove __62__ turnpike miles one way. We need to double that distance to get her total daily mileage.

We multiply __62__ by __2__.
To find the total turnpike miles, we multiply the number of miles driven in one day by the number of days this route was taken.

We multiply __124__ by __234__.

EXIT 10 TO EXIT 9 ...30 MILES

EXIT 9 TO EXIT 8 ...32 MILES

Multiply by ones.	Multiply by tens.	Multiply by hundreds.	Add the products.
124 ×234 ――― 496 ↑ 4 × 124	124 ×234 ――― 496 3 720 ↑ 30 × 124	124 ×234 ――― 496 3 720 24 800 ↑ 200 × 124	124 ×234 ――― 496 ← 4 × 124 3 720 ← 30 × 124 24 800 ← 200 × 124 29,016 ← 234 × 124

Mrs. Mayer drove __29,016__ turnpike miles last year.

Getting Started

Multiply. Check by estimation.

1.	587	2.	$709	3.	648
	× 265		× 826		× 354
	155,555		$585,634		229,392

Copy and multiply.

4. 783 × 612
   479,196

5. 891 × 323
   287,793

6. $5.18 × 427
   $2,211.86

MCP All rights reserved

61

Teaching the Lesson

Introducing the Problem Have a student read the problem aloud. Ask another to read and complete the information sentences. Read the plan sentences aloud (multiply 62 by 2) and (multiply 124 by 234). Explain that there are four steps when multiplying by a 3-digit number. Direct their attention to the multiplication steps in the model. Put the problem on the board and have one student work each step while the others complete it in their books. Ask a student to read the solution sentence. (29,016 turnpike miles)

Developing the Skill Work this problem on the board:
485 × 273 =

485	485	485	1,455
×3	×70	×200	33,950
1455	33,950	97,000	+97,000
			132,405

Explain that this is one way of doing the four steps of 3-digit multiplication. Point out that they can save time and space by putting the products of each separate multiplication in a column:

$$\begin{array}{r} 485 \\ \times\ 273 \\ \hline 1455 \\ 33950 \\ +\ 97000 \\ \hline 132,405 \end{array}$$

Have students try these problems using either method:

1. 735 × 462 (339,570)
2. 903 × 853 (770,259)
3. $4.57 × 614 ($2,805.98)

Practice

Multiply. Check by estimation.

1.	795 × 243 193,185	2.	654 × 575 376,050	3.	$818 × 375 $306,750	4.	518 × 221 114,478
5.	407 × 476 193,732	6.	$5.39 × 681 $3,670.59	7.	438 × 159 69,642	8.	713 × 390 278,070
9.	683 × 725 495,175	10.	909 × 367 333,603	11.	$816 × 793 $647,088	12.	666 × 635 422,910

Copy and Do

13. 527 × 382
201,314
14. $7.82 × 356
$2,783.92
15. 428 × 847
362,516
16. 120 × 789
94,680
17. 923 × $4.85
$4,476.55
18. 615 × 238
146,370
19. 916 × 746
683,336
20. 306 × 473
144,738
21. 226 × 739
167,014
22. 656 × 531
348,336
23. $7.62 × 489
$3,726.18
24. 199 × 886
176,314

Apply

Solve these problems.

25. The school cafeteria serves 326 meals each day. If there are 182 school days, how many meals are served in one school year?
59,332 meals

26. Today, the cafeteria paid $163 for milk and $40.95 for fruit. How much did the cafeteria spend on milk and fruit altogether?
$203.95

27. Six cafeteria helpers each work 12 hours a week. If each helper earns $4.87 per hour, what is the payroll for cafeteria helpers each week?
$350.64

28. On Tuesday, the cafeteria took in $891.50. If 285 hot meals were served for $1.15 each, how much money was earned from cold meal sales?
$563.75

62

Correcting Common Errors

Some students may multiply incorrectly with three digits because they cannot keep their work organized and the digits aligned correctly. Correct by having them do their work on grid paper using the lines and squares to help them keep the columns aligned properly.

Enrichment

Remind students that in a computer an individual character is called a bit (binary digit). On an 8-bit computer, every 8 bits is called a byte. Every 1,024 bytes is a K. Ask the group to calculate the amount of unused space in an 8K computer if 4K of the available space is taken up by a program to run the computer.
($8 \times 8 = 64$, $1024 \times 64 = 65,536$; $8 \times 4 = 32$, $1024 \times 32 = 32,768$; $65,536 - 32,768 = 32,768$ bits left over)

Practice

Have students complete the problems on the page. Emphasize the importance of straight columns as they copy, multiply or add.

Extra Credit *Applications*

Reading and interpretating a menu is an activity that can combine many mathematical skills. Have students bring in menus from various restaurants. Have them develop an activity card using information from each menu. Activities may include calculating the price of a list of menu items; ordering an item from each section of the menu, such as appetizer, salad, main course, dessert and beverage; calculating the total price of the meal; or calculating the exact price of meals that have a special discount such as two for the price of one, etc. Remind students to include a 15% gratuity in the total price of each meal. Save the menus and attached activity cards to be used for later independent practice.

Multiplying with Zeros

pages 63-64

Objective

To review multiplying 3-digit numbers by 3-digit numbers with zeros

Materials

*overhead projector

Mental Math

Ask students to give the correct operation sign:

1. 20 ( ) 1 = 20 (×)
2. 200 ( ) 100 = 100 (−)
3. 9 ( ) 9 = 81 (×)
4. 150 ( ) 50 = 200 (+)
5. 10 ( ) 10 = 100 (×)
6. 35 ( ) 5 = 30 (−)
7. 42 ( ) 7 = 35 (−)

Skill Review

Have students multiply each of these numbers by 368.

1. 423 (155,664)
2. $623 ($229,264)
3. 749 (275,632)
4. 59 (21,712)

Multiplying with Zeros

The Lincoln School Drama Club uses the proceeds from its plays to fund future productions. The latest play was attended by 79 students and 307 adults. How much did the drama club earn from the adult sales?

We are looking for the amount of money collected from adult ticket sales.

We know an adult ticket costs __$5.25__.

The play was attended by __307__ adults.

To find the total amount collected from the adult tickets, we multiply the cost of one ticket by the number of adult tickets sold.

We multiply __$5.25__ by __307__.

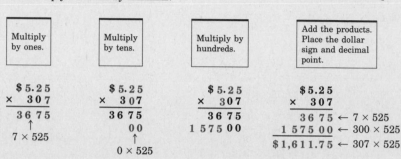

Multiply by ones.	Multiply by tens.	Multiply by hundreds.	Add the products. Place the dollar sign and decimal point.

$$\begin{array}{r}\$5.25 \\ \times\ 307 \\ \hline 3675 \\ \uparrow \\ 7\times 525 \end{array}$$

$$\begin{array}{r}\$5.25 \\ \times\ 307 \\ \hline 3675 \\ 00 \\ \uparrow \\ 0\times 525 \end{array}$$

$$\begin{array}{r}\$5.25 \\ \times\ 307 \\ \hline 3675 \\ 157500 \end{array}$$

$$\begin{array}{r}\$5.25 \\ \times\ 307 \\ \hline 3675 \leftarrow 7\times 525 \\ 157500 \leftarrow 300\times 525 \\ \$1,611.75 \leftarrow 307\times 525 \end{array}$$

The drama club earned __$1,611.75__ from adult ticket sales.

Getting Started

Multiply. Check by estimation.

1. 756
× 408
308,448

2. $4.85
× 609
$2,953.65

3. $807
× 501
$404,307

Copy and multiply.

4. 567 × 703
398,601

5. $9.46 × 506
$4,786.76

6. 148 × 209
30,932

MCP All rights reserved

63

Teaching the Lesson

Introducing the Problem Read the problem aloud. Have a student read and complete the information sentences. Ask a student to identify the extra information provided in the problem, but not needed to solve the problem. (79 students attended) Read the plan sentences. Use the overhead projector or the board as you work the problem in four stages. Have students follow the multiplication steps in the model. Put in the dollar sign and decimal point. Have a student read the solution sentence. (club earned $1,611.75)

Developing the Skill Remind students how to multiply when one factor was a multiple of 10. The problem 43 × 20, for example, can be done in one step even though the factor 20 has two digits, because one of those digits is zero. Explain that any time they multiply by a number with a zero in it, they eliminate one step of the multiplication. Point out, however, that it is important to hold the place of the zero. When zero is in the tens place in the factor, zeros in the tens and ones columns will help them remember to start writing the hundred's product in the correct column. Work this example with them: 634 × 302. (191,468)

Practice

Multiply. Check by estimation.

1. $736
    × 103
    $75,808

2. $9.76
    × 406
    $3,962.56

3. $1.08
    × 504
    $544.32

4. 479
    × 210
    100,590

5. 653
    × 356
    232,468

6. $5.22
    × 720
    $3,758.40

7. 378
    × 902
    340,956

8. 123
    × 818
    100,614

Copy and Do

9. $4.81 × 206
   $990.86

10. 759 × 307
    233,013

11. 509 × 824
    419,416

12. 285 × 616
    175,560

13. $3.07 × 805
    $2,471.35

14. $297 × 536
    $159,192

15. 905 × 483
    437,115

16. 610 × 199
    121,390

17. 507 × 658
    333,606

18. 489 × 409
    200,001

19. $4.06 × 405
    $1,644.30

20. 708 × 509
    360,372

Apply

Solve these problems. Use the data from page 63 where necessary.

21. How much did the Lincoln School Drama Club make from the sale of student tickets?
    $296.25

22. What was the total amount of money collected by the drama club for the school play?
    $1,908.00

23. This year, the make-up crew used 103 grease pencils, costing $1.98 each, and 19 cans of hair spray, costing $1.09 each. How much did the crew spend on pencils alone?
    $203.94

24. Satin costume fabric costs $4.63 a yard, and cotton costs $2.89 a yard. The costume crew needs 210 yards of fabric. How much money would be saved by making the costumes out of cotton, rather than silk?
    $365.40

EXCURSION

Imagine placing three colored balls (one red, one green and one blue) into three colored boxes (one red, one green and one blue) so that no ball is in a box of the same color. If the blue ball is not in the red box, which ball is in the green box?

blue

64

Correcting Common Errors

When the multiplier has a zero in the tens place, some students may forget that they are multiplying by hundreds when multiplying by the digit in the hundreds place.

INCORRECT	CORRECT
257	257
× 906	× 906
1 542	1 542
23 130	231 300
24,672	232,842

Have students write zeros in the ones and tens places of the partial product for hundreds before multiplying by the digit in the hundreds place.

Enrichment

G.H. Hardy (in *Mathematician's Apology*) discovered that 8,712 and 9,801 are multiples of their reversals (2,178 and 1,089 respectively). Have students prove that this is true. (2,178 × 4 = 8,712; 1,089 × 9 = 9,801) See if they can find another curious thing about these two numbers. If they start with 1,089 and create a new number by increasing the first 2 digits by 1, and decreasing the last 2 by 1, the pattern will eventually create 9,801. (1,809, 2,178, 3,267,-4,356-5,445-6,534-7,623-8,712, 9,801)

Practice

Have students complete all the problems on the page.

Excursion

Let students try their own solution methods before suggesting they use a chart, like this example:

	Red Box	Blue Box	Green Box
Red Box	X		
Blue Box		X	
Green Box			X

Tell them to put an X in each square that is not a possible outcome; for example, RR, BB and GG, etc. As students continue, they will find that the Green Ball is in the Red Box, so it cannot be in the Blue Box.

Extra Credit *Numeration*

Students are often intrigued by large numbers. Tell them a particularly interesting number is a googol, a one followed by a hundred 0's. Have students research the names of other large numbers such as billions, trillions, quadrillions, quintillions, sextillions, septillions, octillions, nonillions and decillions. Have students look through the newspaper, dictionary, encyclopedia or other reference materials to find uses for such large numbers. Compile a class report listing the various uses.

Problem Solving Restating Problems

pages 65-66

Objective

To solve problems by rewording them

Materials

Mental Math

Have students substitute 3 for the **a** and solve:

1. 2 + a (5)
2. a − 2 (1)
3. a × a (9)
4. a ÷ a (1)
5. 20 × a (60)
6. a + a + a + a (12)
7. 12 ÷ a (4)

Restating the Problem in Your Own Words

As I was going to St. Ives I met a group of seven wives. Every wife had seven sacks; every sack had seven cats; every cat had seven kits. Kits, cats, sacks and wives; how many were going to St. Ives?

★ **SEE**

We want to know the total number of kits, cats, sacks and wives which were going to St. Ives.

There were ___7___ wives with ___7___ sacks.

Every sack had ___7___ cats.

Every cat had ___7___ kits.

★ **PLAN**

Since the wording of this rhyme is confusing, we restate the problem in our own words. We also start to count the number of each as we reword the problem.

★ **DO**

There were ___7___ wives. Each had ___7___ sacks.

(There were ___49___ sacks altogether.)

Each sack contained ___7___ cats.

(There were ___49___ × 7, or ___343___ cats.)

Each cat had ___7___ kittens.

(There were ___343___ × 7, or ___2,401___ kittens.)

To find the total number of wives, sacks, cats and kits we add the number of each.

___7___ + ___49___ + ___343___ + ___2,401___ = ___2,800___

There were a total of ___2,800___ wives, sacks, cats and kits going to St. Ives.

★ **CHECK**

2,401 ÷ 7 = ___343___ cats   ___343___ ÷ 7 = ___49___ sacks   ___49___ ÷ 7 = ___7___ wives

MCP All rights reserved

65

Teaching the Lesson

Read the problems aloud. Explain that many problems are easier to solve if they can say the problem again, using their own words. Point out that this is a way of finding out if they really understand what the problem is asking. Have a student read the SEE section of the text. Read the PLAN section of the text aloud, pointing out that the problem will be easier when it has been restated. Have a student read the DO section, and ask students to provide the numbers called for. Point out that to find the total number, they must add. Have one student put the addition on the board. (7 + 49 + 343 + 2,401 = 2,800) Read the solution sentence aloud. (total of 2,800 going to St. Ives) Show the class that they can check by working the problem backwards from the number of kittens to the number of cats; (2,401 ÷ 7 = 343) from the number of cats to the number of sacks; (343 ÷ 7 = 49) from the number of sacks to the number of wives. (49 ÷ 7 = 7)

Apply

Solve these problems.

1. A student had $10.00 and spent all but $2.00. How much money did the student have left?

   $2.00

2. Old MacDonald had some chicks. At the auction he bought twice as many chicks as he had originally. Now he has 27 chicks. How many chicks did he have originally?

   9 chicks

3. Five snips cost 5 million snipes, three snaps cost 300 snipes, and two snops cost 20 thousand snipes. What would it cost to purchase one snip, two snaps and three snops?

   1,030,200 snipes

4. The combined cost of a baseball card and bubble gum is $1.05. The card costs 5 cents more than the gum. How much does each item cost?

   50¢ for gum   55¢ for card

5. Ivan purchased several items whose total cost was $1.96. All the items were the same price. As many items were bought as the number of total cents in the cost of each item. How many items were bought?

   14 items at 14¢ each

6. Five and one half million dollars worth of diamonds were lost in a lake. $200,000 worth were recovered. What is the value of the diamonds still to be recovered?

   $5,300,000

7. Read Exercise 2 again. Rewrite the problem so that the correct answer is 3 chicks.

   Answers may vary.

8. Read Exercise 4 again. What if the card cost 15¢ more than the gum? Now how much does each cost?

   45¢ for the gum, 60¢ for the card

9. Eeny, Meeny, and Moe each multiply the same 3-digit number by a 2-digit number. Eeny gets a 7-digit answer, Meeny gets a 2-digit answer, and Moe gets a 5-digit answer. Whose answers are incorrect and how do you know?

   Eeny's and Meeny's

10. Harvey says, "I am thinking of two numbers. Their product is 0 and their sum is 15. What are the two numbers?" Answer Harvey's question and explain why your answer is correct.

    15 and 0

66

Extra Credit *Biography*

Leonardo Fibonacci, of Pisa, Italy, was the first great mathematician of medieval Christian Europe, and one of the leading European mathematicians of the Middle Ages. His books on arithmetic, algebra and geometry, written around 1200, introduced the modern Hindu-Arabic system of numerals using ten symbols. Fibonacci introduced trigonometry, and is best remembered for his Fibonacci Sequence. This is a mathematical sequence wherein each term is the sum of the two terms immediately preceding it. Beginning with 1, it continues 1, 2, 3, 5, 8, 13, 21, 34, 55, etc. This sequence is useful in such an unlikely application as the Golden Section, a spiral shape valued in art and architecture. Fibonacci ironically had the nickname Bighellone, meaning dunce; yet not for 300 years would Europe see another mathematician of such outstanding ability.

Solution Notes

1. Help students restate this problem.
2. Have students give the number of chicks the name, C. MacDonald had C chicks, bought twice as many, $2 \times C$. Then he had $C + (2 \times C)$ or $(3 \times C)$ chickens. $3 \times C = 27$, $C = 9$.
3. Have students reduce:

   5 snips = 5,000,000 snipes
   1 snip = 1,000,000 snipes
   3 snaps = 300 snipes
   1 snap = 100 snipes
   2 snops = 20,000 snipes
   1 snop = 10,000 snipes
   1 snip + 2 snaps + 3 snops = $1,000,000 + (2 \times 100) + (3 \times 10,000) = 1,030,200$ snipes

4. Have students call the cost of the gum, G. Ask how much the card costs, compared to G. (G + 5¢) Together they total $1.05, so G + G + 5¢ = $1.05. Two G's must equal $1. Each G is 50¢ and the card (G + 5), 55¢.
5. Give the price and the number of items a letter name, n. Show that n multiplied by itself equals $1.96 or $n \times n = \$1.96$. Make a few guesses to 14 ($1.96).
6. Ask students to restate the question at the end. Now have students subtract: 5½ million = $5,500,000, $5,500,000 − $200,000 = $5,300,000 worth of diamonds.

Higher-Order Thinking Skills

7. Synthesis: One answer is he now has 9 chicks; another is to change "twice as many" to "8 times as many."
8. Analysis: Add 10¢ to the old answer for the card and subtract 10¢ from the old answer for the gum.
9. Analysis: The greatest number of digits is 5 because $99 \times 999 = 98,901$. The least number is 4 because $10 \times 100 = 1,000$. Only Moe's answer is within the limits of 4 or 5 digits.
10. Analysis and Evaluation: If the product of 2 numbers is 0, then at least one number is 0. Since the sum is 15, the other number is 15.

Calculators and Inventory

pages 67-68

Objective

To use a calculator to multiply large numbers

Materials

calculator

Mental Math

Have students multiply each by 10:

1. 3 (30)
2. 7 (70)
3. 0 (0)
4. 10 (100)
5. 23 (230)

Have them multiply each by 20:

6. 5 (5 × 2 × 10 = 100)
7. 2 (40)
8. 6 (120)

Skill Review

Review addition, subtraction, multiplication and estimating skills by having students first estimate and then complete these problems:

1. 475 + 16,834 (17,300; 17,309)
2. 81,067 − 47,850 (33,000; 33,217)
3. 776 × 826 (640,000; 640,976)

MCP All rights reserved

Calculators and Inventory

Stan manages the inventory at the Running Supply Store. One cost he must keep track of, is the amount of money he has invested in any item he has in stock. Help Stan find the total cost of his inventory of running shorts and tops.

We need to find the total amount of money the store has invested in shorts and tops.

We know that one pair of shorts costs $22.48 and the store has 39 pairs of shorts in stock.

The cost of one running top is $16.27 and there are 165 of them in stock.

To find the total inventory cost of either item, we multiply the cost of one, by the number of that item in stock.

We multiply $22.48 by 39 , and $16.27 by 165 .

Enter these codes on your calculator. Write your answer on the screens.

Item	Cost of One		Number of Items		Inventory Costs
Running Shorts	22.48	×	39	=	876.72
Running Tops	16.27	×	165	=	2,684.55

Inventory Cost for Running Shorts		Inventory Cost for Running Tops		Total Inventory Cost
876.72	+	2,684.55	=	3,561.27

The total inventory cost of these two items is $3,561.27 .

67

Teaching the Lesson

Introducing the Problem Have a student read the problem aloud. Read the information sentences. (pair of shorts costs $22.48; store has 39 pairs; cost of running top is $16.27; there are 165 in stock) Ask a student to read and complete the plan sentences. Direct their attention to the calculator codes in their texts. Explain that when they enter money amounts, they will enter a decimal point between the dollars and cents. Have students enter the first problem (22.48 × 39 = 876.72) and have a student give the answer. Ask them to work the second problem in the same way. (16.27 × 165 = 2684.55) Be sure they clear each problem before they go on. Ask a student to do the addition and give the final answer, reading the solution sentence. (Cost of these items is $3,561.27.)

Developing the Skill Remind students that calculators will not show dollar signs or zeros to the far right of the decimal point. Explain, too, that when they work with money, they must remember to put the decimal point between the dollars and cents. Show them that the answer will list the decimal point if they put it in to begin with. Have students complete this problem on their calculators: $45 × 178 = (8010) Put the calculator's answer on the board and show students how to put the number in proper form: $8,010.

Practice

Enter these codes on your calculator. Write the answers on the screens.

1. 48 $\times$ 15 $=$ (720)
2. 139 $\times$ 48 $=$ (6,672)
3. 56.48 $\times$ 12 $=$ (677.76)
4. 75.46 $\times$ 75 $=$ (5,659.5)
5. 25.29 $\times$ 42 $=$ (1,062.18)
6. 13.29 $\times$ 98 $=$ (1,302.42)
7. 36.58 $\times$ 146 $=$ (5,340.68)
8. 59.99 $\times$ 11 $=$ (659.89)

Use a calculator to find each product. Estimate to see if your answer seems reasonable.

9. $326
   $\times$ 59
   $19,234

10. $175.26
    $\times$ 38
    $6,659.88

11. $12,278
    $\times$ 12
    $147,336

12. $3,215.25
    $\times$ 8
    $25,722.00

Apply

Use your calculator to solve these problems.

13. Find the total cost of 26 pairs of running shoes at $39.85 each, and 17 pairs of running shoes at $49.98 each.
    $1,885.76

14. Lucia works 3 hours after school at the Running Supply Store. She earns $2.68 an hour. She worked 21 days in February, and 22 days in March. How much did Lucia earn?
    $345.72

Use your calculator to complete these inventory cost sheets for The Good Earth Grocery Store.

15.
Item	Cost	Number	Inventory Amount
Clothes softener	$1.59	48	$ 76.32
Dish soap	$0.89	129	$114.81
Laundry soap	$2.15	23	$ 49.45
Bar soap	$0.89	107	$ 95.23

16.
Item	Cost	Number	Inventory Amount
Leashes	$3.18	12	$ 38.16
Dog treats	$0.79	116	$ 91.64
Puppy bones	$1.59	215	$341.85
Dog food	$2.83	96	$271.68

68

Correcting Common Errors

Some students may have trouble entering long numbers on the calculator without making a mistake. Have them check each entry by putting the number on the calculator and then writing down the number that appears on the the display screen.

Enrichment

Give students this magic multiplication square devised by Martin Gardner:

12	1	18
9	6	4
2	36	3

Have them use calculators to show that if they multiply three factors in a row (including diagonals) the product will always be the same. (216) See if they can make a magic multiplication square of their own. (Answers will vary.)

Practice

Have students complete the practice problems. Remind them to put dollar signs and decimal points in their answers and to add zeros to the far side of each decimal.

Extra Credit *Probability*

Have students guess what number will appear with each roll of a single die. Working in pairs, have students roll a die 100 times. After rolling, they should record on a table if their guess was right or wrong, and indicate what number appeared. Have students then answer the following questions:

1. How many times were your guesses correct?
2. How many times was each number 1 through 6 rolled?
3. What is ⅙ of 100?
4. Compare this number with the number of times you rolled each number. Do you have close to a 1 out of 6 chance for rolling a 6?
5. How many times did you predict correctly what the roll would be? (Answers will vary.)

Chapter Test

page 69

Item	Objective
1-6	Recall basic multiplication facts (See pages 45-46)
7	Multiply 2-digit by 1-digit factors (See pages 53-54)
8-9	Multiply up to 6-digits by 1-digit factor (See pages 55-56)
10	Multiply money by 1-digit factor (See pages 55-56)
11-14	Multiply two 2-digit factors (See pages 57-58)
15-18	Multiply up to 5-digits by 2-digit number; estimate product of two numbers (See pages 51-52, 59-60)
19-22	Multiply two 3-digit numbers; estimate product of two numbers (See pages 51-52, 63-64)
23-31	Identify least common multiple (See pages 47-48)
32-40	Identify even or odd numbers (See page 48)

Multiply. Check by estimation.

1. 7
   × 3
   ‾‾‾
   21

2. 9
   × 6
   ‾‾‾
   54

3. 5
   × 0
   ‾‾‾
   0

4. 8
   × 7
   ‾‾‾
   56

5. 9
   × 7
   ‾‾‾
   63

6. 6
   × 4
   ‾‾‾
   24

7. 37
   × 6
   ‾‾‾‾
   222

8. 259
   ×   7
   ‾‾‾‾‾
   1,813

9. 1,384
   ×   4
   ‾‾‾‾‾‾
   5,536

10. $16.97
    ×   8
    ‾‾‾‾‾‾‾
    $135.76

11. 62
    × 25
    ‾‾‾‾
    1,550

12. 40
    × 80
    ‾‾‾‾
    3,200

13. 57
    × 29
    ‾‾‾‾
    1,653

14. 87
    × 36
    ‾‾‾‾
    3,132

15. 186
    × 72
    ‾‾‾‾‾
    13,392

16. 1,309
    ×   84
    ‾‾‾‾‾‾
    109,956

17. $39.65
    ×   90
    ‾‾‾‾‾‾‾
    $3,568.50

18. 2,431
    ×   56
    ‾‾‾‾‾‾
    136,136

19. 628
    × 247
    ‾‾‾‾‾
    155,116

20. 825
    × 409
    ‾‾‾‾‾
    337,425

21. $7.15
    ×   326
    ‾‾‾‾‾‾
    $2,330.90

22. 618
    × 510
    ‾‾‾‾‾
    315,180

Write the least common multiple of each pair of numbers.

23. 6 and 8 __24__

24. 12 and 15 __60__

25. 2 and 9 __18__

26. 7 and 14 __14__

27. 4 and 9 __36__

28. 5 and 7 __35__

29. 6 and 9 __18__

30. 14 and 21 __42__

31. 15 and 16 __240__

Write even or odd for each number.

32. 27 __odd__

33. 34 __even__

34. 158 __even__

35. 167 __odd__

36. 900 __even__

37. 702 __even__

38. 758 __even__

39. 489 __odd__

40. 205 __odd__

MCP All rights reserved

69

Circle the letter of the correct answer.

1 What is the place value of the 6 in 427,165?
- a ones
- b tens
- c hundreds (circled)
- d NG

2 What is the place value of the 9 in 493,274?
- a thousands
- b ten thousands (circled)
- c hundred thousands
- d NG

3 709 ◯ 790
- a < (circled)
- b >
- c =

4 12,739 ◯ 12,740
- a < (circled)
- b >
- c =

5 $6.75
  + 3.19
- a $9.84
- b $9.94 (circled)
- c $10.94
- d NG

6 27,096
  + 14,375
- a 31,361
- b 31,371
- c 41,371
- d NG (circled)

7 Estimate the sum.
  3,621
  + 975
- a 4,600
- b 5,000 (circled)
- c 6,000
- d NG

8 $9.27 − $4.88
- a $4.39 (circled)
- b $5.39
- c $5.61
- d NG

9 80,096
  − 24,798
- a 55,298 (circled)
- b 56,298
- c 64,702
- d NG

10 Estimate the difference.
  67,963
  − 13,750
- a 60,000 (circled)
- b 70,000
- c 80,000
- d NG

11 27 × 5
- a 105
- b 135 (circled)
- c 1,035
- d NG

12 1,429
  × 9
- a 12,816
- b 11,861
- c 12,861 (circled)
- d NG

13 23
  × 48
- a 1,004
- b 1,104 (circled)
- c 1,204
- d NG

☐ score

70

Cumulative Review

Alternate Cumulative Review

Circle the letter of the correct answer.

1 Give the place value of the 5 in 807,953.
- a ones
- b tens (circled)
- c hundreds
- d NG

2 Give the place value of the 7 in 374,192.
- a thousands
- b ten thousands (circled)
- c hundred thousands
- d NG

3 16,273 ◯ 16,274
- a < (circled)
- b >
- c =

4 806 ◯ 860
- a < (circled)
- b >
- c =

5 $2.38
  +7.54
- a $8.92
- b $9.92 (circled)
- c $8.93
- d NG

6 4,532
  + 864
- a 4,396
- b 5,396 (circled)
- c 5,296
- d NG

7 Estimate the sum.
  6,413
  + 764
- a 6,500
- b 8,000
- c 7,000 (circled)

8 $8.62
  − 3.78
- a $4.84 (circled)
- b $5.84
- c $5.16
- d NG

9 73,006
  − 13,389
- a 60,383
- b 60,617
- c 59,617 (circled)
- d NG

10 Estimate the difference after rounding to the nearest thousand.
  58,500
  − 23,723
- a 34,000
- b 35,000 (circled)
- c 36,000
- d NG

11 45
  ×7
- a 315 (circled)
- b 285
- c 1,315
- d NG

12 1,539
  ×8
- a 8,312
- b 11,312
- c 12,312 (circled)
- d NG

70

1-digit Division

Objective

To review division facts and properties

Materials

100-fact multiplication test 3 × 5 cards

Mental Math

Have students multiply:

1. 3 × 4 × 10 (120)
2. 5 × 3 × 10 (150)
3. 2 × 2 × 10 (40)
4. 1 × 8 × 10 (80)
5. 7 × 0 × 10 (0)
6. 5 × 5 × 10 (250)
7. 4 × 5 × 10 (200)

Skill Review

Review multiplication facts with the 100 fact, 3-minute timed test. Go over with the class any facts that seem to be difficult.

Reviewing Division Facts and Properties

The **quotient** in a division fact is the same as a missing factor in the related multiplication fact. If you remember the multiplication facts and how to make **fact families,** you will know the division facts.

Since we know $9 \times 4 = 36$, we also know $36 \div 9 = 4$.

We can write two multiplication and two division equations for the numbers 4, 9 and 36.

$9 \times n = 36$
$n = ?$

$n \times 4 = 36$
$n = ?$

The four equations form a **fact family.** The fact family for 4, 9 and 36 can also be written in vertical form.

$9 \times 4 = \underline{36}$ $36 \div 4 = \underline{9}$

$\underline{4} \times 9 = 36$ $36 \div 9 = \underline{4}$

$$\begin{array}{cc} 9 & 4 \\ \times 4 & \times 9 \\ \hline 36 & 36 \end{array}$$

$$9\overline{)36} \qquad 4\overline{)36}$$

Division has several basic properties that help you remember the division facts.

✔ If the **divisor** is 1, the quotient is the same as the **dividend.**

$$1\overline{)5}^{\,5} \qquad 9 \div 1 = \underline{9}$$

✔ If the dividend is zero, the quotient is zero.

$$2\overline{)0}^{\,0} \qquad 0 \div 7 = \underline{0}$$

✔ If the divisor and the dividend are the same number, the quotient is 1.

$$8\overline{)8}^{\,1} \qquad 6 \div 6 = \underline{1}$$

✔ NEVER divide by zero.

Getting Started

Divide.

1. $12 \div 6 = \underline{2}$ 2. $0 \div 7 = \underline{0}$ 3. $6 \div 6 = \underline{1}$

4. $7\overline{)49}^{\,7}$ 5. $1\overline{)9}^{\,9}$ 6. $6\overline{)54}^{\,9}$ 7. $3\overline{)0}^{\,0}$ 8. $8\overline{)32}^{\,4}$ 9. $5\overline{)5}^{\,1}$

MCP All rights reserved

71

Teaching the Lesson

Introducing the Problem Read the text aloud. Have a student put the two related multiplication facts on the board and have another write the related division facts. Ask a student to label the multiplication (factor, factor, product) while you label the division. (dividend, divisor, quotient) Explain that these four problems form a fact family and write the four facts in the alternative form shown in their texts. Continue reading the text aloud and provide additional examples of the properties presented.

Developing the Skill Put a 4 × 6 array of x's on the board. Show students that it can represent multiplication (4 × 6, 6 × 4) or division (24 ÷ 6 or 24 ÷ 4). Explain that the array is a good way of showing how multiplication and division are related and why they form fact families. Have students draw an array and write a complete fact family for the problem: 7 × 9. (7 × 9 = 63; 9 × 7 = 63; 63 ÷ 7 = 9; 63 ÷ 9 = 7) Remind students of the two ways to write division problems, using ÷ and $\overline{)}$.

Practice

Divide.

4 $1\overline{)4}$	7 $9\overline{)63}$	1 $8\overline{)8}$	0 $3\overline{)0}$	9 $5\overline{)45}$	0 $4\overline{)0}$	1 $9\overline{)9}$	6 $8\overline{)48}$	1 $5\overline{)5}$
2 $8\overline{)16}$	0 $7\overline{)0}$	6 $5\overline{)30}$	2 $9\overline{)18}$	0 $2\overline{)0}$	7 $1\overline{)7}$	1 $1\overline{)1}$	4 $3\overline{)12}$	7 $6\overline{)42}$
3 $4\overline{)12}$	2 $7\overline{)14}$	8 $3\overline{)24}$	3 $1\overline{)3}$	7 $2\overline{)14}$	6 $3\overline{)18}$	5 $1\overline{)5}$	5 $9\overline{)45}$	3 $2\overline{)6}$
2 $3\overline{)6}$	9 $8\overline{)72}$	5 $3\overline{)15}$	8 $5\overline{)40}$	4 $9\overline{)36}$	3 $9\overline{)27}$	2 $2\overline{)4}$	0 $8\overline{)0}$	3 $6\overline{)18}$
7 $4\overline{)28}$	2 $1\overline{)2}$	9 $2\overline{)18}$	5 $4\overline{)20}$	6 $6\overline{)36}$	5 $2\overline{)10}$	8 $9\overline{)72}$	6 $7\overline{)42}$	9 $7\overline{)63}$
1 $7\overline{)7}$	7 $3\overline{)21}$	2 $4\overline{)8}$	1 $4\overline{)4}$	2 $5\overline{)10}$	5 $8\overline{)40}$	4 $4\overline{)16}$	3 $3\overline{)9}$	5 $7\overline{)35}$
8 $2\overline{)16}$	4 $5\overline{)20}$	0 $1\overline{)0}$	7 $5\overline{)35}$	8 $7\overline{)56}$	9 $4\overline{)36}$	6 $4\overline{)24}$	1 $6\overline{)6}$	6 $1\overline{)6}$
4 $7\overline{)28}$	0 $9\overline{)0}$	4 $8\overline{)32}$	6 $9\overline{)54}$	9 $1\overline{)9}$	8 $6\overline{)48}$	0 $6\overline{)0}$	2 $6\overline{)12}$	9 $3\overline{)27}$
3 $7\overline{)21}$	8 $1\overline{)8}$	0 $5\overline{)0}$	5 $5\overline{)25}$	9 $6\overline{)54}$	8 $8\overline{)64}$	4 $6\overline{)24}$	5 $6\overline{)30}$	1 $2\overline{)2}$
1 $3\overline{)3}$	3 $5\overline{)15}$	7 $8\overline{)56}$	9 $9\overline{)81}$	6 $2\overline{)12}$	8 $4\overline{)32}$	3 $8\overline{)24}$	7 $7\overline{)49}$	4 $2\overline{)8}$

72

Correcting Common Errors

Some students may not have mastered their division facts. Have them work with partners to use a set of flash cards. Have them take turns quizzing each other to practice the facts.

Enrichment

Have students take a sheet of construction paper and fold it in half. Show them how to cut slits one inch wide in the paper from the fold to an inch from the edge.
Now have them cut individual one-inch strips of a contrasting colored paper. Show them how to weave the strips through the slits to make an array of colored squares.

Practice

Have students complete the practice problems remembering the related multiplication problem if they have trouble with a division fact.

Mixed Practice

1. $658,397 + 193,708$ $(852,105)$
2. 600×70 $(42,000)$
3. $93 + 58 + 63 + 29$ (243)
4. $85,658 \times 70$ $(5,996,060)$
5. $\$100.00 - \$43.72$ $(\$56.28)$
6. 48×39 $(1,872)$
7. $507,916 - 217,847$ $(290,069)$
8. $6 \times \$217.81$ $(\$1,306.86)$
9. $\$315.20 + \$12.78 + \$156.35$ $(\$484.33)$
10. $12,095 - 8,168$ $(3,927)$

Extra Credit *Applications*

Have students bring in newspaper grocery ads. After scanning the ads, have students make a list of what they estimate they could buy with $10.00. (Remind them to round off the prices to the nearest tens or hundreds when they are estimating). After estimating, have them list the actual items and prices and calculate the total cost. How close did their estimate come to the cost? Have students work in pairs and reverse the process. One student would scan the ads, make a list of groceries and calculate their total cost. The other student would use the ad to estimate the list's total cost and then check to see how close the estimate was.

Greatest Common Factor

pages 73-74

Objective

To find the greatest common factor

Materials

3 × 5 cards

Mental Math

Have students provide the missing operation:

1. 4 ( ) 2 = 2 (÷ or −)
2. 5 ( ) 3 = 8 (+)
3. 15 ( ) 3 = 5 (÷)
4. 24 ( ) 2 = 48 (×)
5. 10 ( ) 2 = 5 (÷)
6. 42 ( ) 6 = 7 (÷)
7. 8 ( ) 8 = 0 (−)

Skill Review

Have students provide the other three facts in the fact family:

1. 12 ÷ 4 = 3 (12 ÷ 3 = 4; 3 × 4 = 12, 4 × 3 = 12)
2. 27 ÷ 3 = 9
3. 45 ÷ 9 = 5
4. 81 ÷ 9 = 9
5. 4 ÷ 1 = 4

Finding the Greatest Common Factor

Every number has at least 2 factors: 1 and the number itself. Numbers such as 18 and 24 have several factors in common. What is their **greatest common factor?**

We are looking for the **greatest common factor** of 18 and 24.

We need to list all the factors of each number, from the least to the greatest.

The factors of 18 are 1 , 2 , 3 , 6 , 9 and 18 .

The factors of 24 are 1 , 2 , 3 , 4 , 6 , 8 , 12 and 24 .

The factors that are common to both 18 and 24 are 1 , 2 , 3 and 6 .

Their greatest common factor is 6 .

✔ The letters **GCF** are often used for the term greatest common factor.

The GCF of 18 and 24 is 6 .

Factors:
3 × 6 = 18
2 × 9 = 18
1 × 18 = 18

4 × 6 = 24
3 × 8 = 24
2 × 12 = 24
1 × 24 = 24

Getting Started

Write the factors for each number.

1. 6 — 1, 2, 3, 6
2. 8 — 1, 2, 4, 8
3. 10 — 1, 2, 5, 10
4. 16 — 1, 2, 4, 8, 16
5. 18 — 1, 2, 3, 6, 9, 18
6. 9 — 1, 3, 9

Write the common factors for each pair of numbers and circle the GCF.

7. 6 and 8 — 1, ②
8. 8 and 16 — 1, 2, 4, ⑧
9. 10 and 18 — 1, ②
10. 8 and 36 — 1, 2, ④
11. 20 and 35 — 1, ⑤
12. 21 and 49 — 1, ⑦
13. 18 and 12 — 1, 2, 3, ⑥
14. 2 and 6 — 1, ②

MCP All rights reserved

73

Teaching the Lesson

Introducing the Problem Read the text aloud and draw student's attention to the chart. Remind them that a factor is one part of a multiplication problem. Ask a student to read the factors of 18 while you write them on the board. (1, 2, 3, 6, 9, 18) Have another read the factors of 24. (1, 2, 3, 4, 6, 8, 12, 24) Ask a student to find the numbers common to both sets of factors and circle them. (1, 2, 3, 6) Explain that the **greatest common factor** (GCF) means the largest number common to both sets of factors. Ask a student to tell which of the common factors is greatest. (6) Read the solution sentence aloud. (GCF of 18 and 24 is 6)

Developing the Skill Make two columns on the board, one headed with the number 30, the other with 45. Have students write as many multiplication problems as they can with 30 or 45 as the product under each.

30: 5 × 6, 2 × 15, 3 × 10, 1 × 30 . . .
45: 5 × 9, 3 × 15, 1 × 45 . . .

Ask the class to find the greatest common factor. (15) Have students find all the problems with 42 and 36 as products and see who can find the greatest common factor. (42: 1, 2, 3, 6, 7, 14, 21) (36: 1, 2, 3, 4, 6, 9, 12, 18) (GCF = 6)

Practice

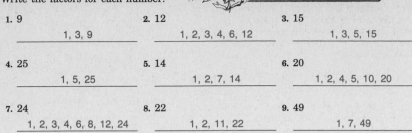

Write the factors for each number.

1. 9

1, 3, 9

2. 12

1, 2, 3, 4, 6, 12

3. 15

1, 3, 5, 15

4. 25

1, 5, 25

5. 14

1, 2, 7, 14

6. 20

1, 2, 4, 5, 10, 20

7. 24

1, 2, 3, 4, 6, 8, 12, 24

8. 22

1, 2, 11, 22

9. 49

1, 7, 49

Write the common factors for each pair of numbers and circle the GCF.

10. 6 and 9

1, ③

11. 9 and 12

1, ③

12. 15 and 25

1, ⑤

13. 28 and 49

1, ⑦

14. 32 and 40

1, 2, 4, ⑧

15. 18 and 22

1, ②

16. 32 and 72

1, 2, 4, ⑧

17. 9 and 81

1, 3, ⑨

18. 6 and 12

1, 2, 3, ⑥

19. 15 and 30

1, 3, 5, ⑮

20. 7 and 11

①

21. 20 and 50

1, 2, 5, ⑩

EXCURSION

Division is another method for finding the greatest common factor, or GCF. To find the GCF of 18 and 24 using division, we ask: what is the largest number that will divide evenly into both 18 and 24?

Think:

$18 \div 1 = 18$
$18 \div 2 = 9$ and
$18 \div 3 = 6$

$24 \div 1 = 24$
$24 \div 2 = 12$
$24 \div 3 = 8$
$24 \div 4 = 6$

The greatest common divisor for both 18 and 24 is __6__.

The GCF for 18 and 24 is __6__.

Write the largest number that will divide evenly into both numbers.

1. 4 and 12

GCF = __4__

2. 22 and 55

GCF = __11__

3. 12 and 16

GCF __4__

4. 42 and 12

GCF = __6__

74

Correcting Common Errors

If students have trouble finding the greatest common factor of two numbers, have them work with partners. Each partner takes one of the two numbers and writes all the pairs of numbers that have the number as a product. They use these pairs to make a list of factors for each number. Once the lists have been made, they can compare them to find and write the common factors and the greatest common factor.

Enrichment

Explain that the way some foods are packaged presents a problem for whoever does the family shopping. For example, if they have three people in their family and donuts come in a package of 10, it is not possible to share the package evenly. Ask students to bring in a list of examples of packages that cannot be divided evenly among those in their families.

Practice

Have students complete the practice problems. Suggest they use extra paper, if necessary, to find all the factors.

Excursion

Tell students to study the division charts for 18 and 24 before they start the excursion problems. Encourage them to make similar charts for the numbers they will be working with.

Extra Credit   *Statistics*

Divide the class into four groups. Have each group prepare a chart which includes the following information on each student:

their name, age, height, heartbeats per minute and their color of eyes.

Using the data they have gathered, have each group report to the class the following statistics:

number of students in their group, their average age, their average height, their average heartbeats/minute and the percentages of each eye color.

The activity can be extended by finding total class averages, by comparing the data for boys and girls and by creating graphs based on the data.

Factoring for Primes

pages 75-76

Objective

To find the prime factors of a composite number

Materials

*multiplication and division flashcards

Mental Math

Have students identify the larger number:

1. 81 ÷ 9 or 3 × 4 (12)
2. 6 × 6 or 10 × 5 (50)
4. 100 ÷ 10 or 4 × 2 (10)
5. 49 ÷ 7 or 3 × 2 (7)
6. 15 ÷ 3 or 45 ÷ 9 (same, 5)
7. 20 ÷ 5 or 20 ÷ 4 (5)

Skill Review

Use mixed multiplication and division flashcards to quiz students. Ask them to answer the problem on the card and then give one fact from the same fact family.

Factoring for Primes

A **prime** is any whole number that has exactly two factors: itself and 1. Primes can be multiplied together to make **composite numbers**. What set of prime numbers, when multiplied, equals 64?

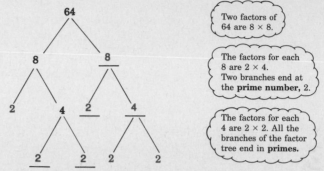

Prime Numbers: 1 through 40

$2 = 1 \times 2$ $11 = 1 \times 11$ $23 = 1 \times 23$
$3 = 1 \times 3$ $13 = 1 \times 13$ $29 = 1 \times 29$
$5 = 1 \times 5$ $17 = 1 \times 17$ $31 = 1 \times 31$
$7 = 1 \times 7$ $19 = 1 \times 19$ $37 = 1 \times 37$

We are looking for the __prime__ numbers that can be multiplied to equal the composite number __64__.

To find the **prime factors**, we use a **factor tree**.

```
            64
          /    \
         8      8
        / \    / \
       2   4  2   4
          / \    / \
         2   2  2   2
```

> Two factors of 64 are 8 × 8.

> The factors for each 8 are 2 × 4. Two branches end at the **prime number, 2**.

> The factors for each 4 are 2 × 2. All the branches of the factor tree end in **primes**.

The branches of the factor tree end with the primes __2__, __2__, __2__, __2__, __2__ and __2__.

✔ We call the set of prime factors for a composite number the **product of primes**.

The product of primes for 64 is

__2__ × __2__ × __2__ × __2__ × __2__ × __2__.

Getting Started

MCP All rights reserved

Use a factor tree to find the product of primes for each composite number.

1. 28 = __2 × 2 × 7__
2. 36 = __2 × 2 × 3 × 3__
3. 33 = __3 × 11__
4. 35 = __5 × 7__
5. 69 = __3 × 23__
6. 75 = __3 × 5 × 5__

75

Teaching the Lesson

Introducing the Problem Read the text and have students examine the chart. Write these words on the board: **prime, composite numbers, prime factors** and **factor tree.** Explain that a prime number has only two factors, itself and one, and that prime numbers multiplied yield a **composite number.** Explain that every number can be reduced to a set of **prime factors.** Read the information sentences. Reproduce the factor tree on the board and show students how to find pairs of factors. Have a student fill in the missing factors. (8; 2,4; 2,2) Point to all the prime factors of 64. Read and complete the final sentences with the class.

Developing the Skill Write **27** on the board and ask a student to start a factor tree. Ask another to reduce each branch until they have only prime factors. Have a student list the prime factors (3, 3, 3) and ask another to multiply the prime factors. Ask if the product of primes equals the number they started with. (yes, 27) Tell them not to reduce 3 to factors 1 and 3. To show that one is a trivial factor, ask them the difference between 3 × 3 and 3 × 3 × 1. (no difference) Have students make a factor tree of 16. Ask a volunteer to put it on the board.

```
     27
    /  \
   3    9
       / \
      3   3
```

Practice

Use a factor tree to find the product of primes for each composite number.

1. 16 = __2 × 2 × 2 × 2__ 2. 24 = __2 × 2 × 2 × 3__

3. 30 = __2 × 3 × 5__ 4. 32 = __2 × 2 × 2 × 2 × 2__

5. 45 = __3 × 3 × 5__ 6. 48 = __2 × 2 × 2 × 2 × 3__

7. 60 = __2 × 2 × 3 × 5__ 8. 72 = __2 × 2 × 2 × 3 × 3__

9. 6 = __2 × 3__ 10. 18 = __2 × 3 × 3__

11. 26 = __2 × 13__ 12. 42 = __2 × 3 × 7__

13. 15 = __3 × 5__ 14. 54 = __2 × 3 × 3 × 3__

15. 77 = __7 × 11__ 16. 65 = __5 × 13__

17. 20 = __2 × 2 × 5__ 18. 56 = __2 × 2 × 2 × 7__

EXCURSION

Here is another method for finding the **greatest common factor (GCF)** of two numbers. It is called **prime factoring.** First write each number as a product of primes. Then choose the primes which are common to both numbers, and multiply the common primes together. Ex: 27 = 3 × 3 × 3 and 36 = 2 × 2 × 3 × 3. The common primes are 3 × 3. Since 3 × 3 = 9, the GCF for 27 and 36 is __9__. Write the product of primes and GCF for each set of numbers.

1. 20 and 48 __2 × 2 × 5__   2. 54 and 48 __2 × 3 × 3 × 3__   3. 70 and 105 __2 × 5 × 7__
   __2 × 2 × 2 × 2 × 3__   __2 × 2 × 2 × 2 × 3__   __3 × 5 × 7__
   GCF = 2 × 2 = 4   GCF = 2 × 3 = 6   GCF = 5 × 7 = 35

4. 45 and 75 __3 × 3 × 5__   5. 72 and 120 __2 × 2 × 2 × 3 × 3__   6. 28 and 42 __2 × 2 × 7__
   __3 × 5 × 5__   __2 × 2 × 2 × 3 × 5__   __2 × 3 × 7__
   GCF = 3 × 5 = 15   GCF = 2 × 2 × 2 × 3 = 24   GCF = 2 × 7 = 14

76

Correcting Common Errors

Some students may have difficulty identifying prime numbers. Give each student one-inch graph paper. Have them write the numbers 2 through 50, one number in each square. Have them circle 2 and then cross out all the other multiples of 2. Have them follow the same procedure for 3, 5, and 7. They can then circle all the remaining numbers and make a list of the primes that are less than 50: 2, 3, 5, 7, 11, 13, 17, 19, 23, 29, 31, 37, 41, 43, and 47.

Enrichment

Show students this three-dimensional factor framework:

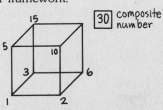

Point out that each number is a prime factor of the composite number. Give them plastic straws and straight pins, and paper and pencil for labels, so that they can make a factor framework for a different composite number.

Practice

Have students complete the practice problems. Explain that the composite number is the whole number they are given, and that the product of primes will be all the primes found in a factor tree, multiplied together.

Excursion

This is another way to find the GCF and more practice in prime factorization.

Extra Credit *Sets*

Duplicate the following example and problems for students to solve.
Taft School has a student council made up of 6 students, one from each grade level. A committee of three was formed to set up a bake sale. A is the set of student council members. B is the set of bake sale committee members.

   Set A = [Linda, Sam, Dwayne, Susan, Joe, Anne]
   Set B = [Anne, Dwayne, Joe]

We say Set B is a subset of Set A because all the members of B are in A.
For each of the following, indicate which applies: A is a subset of B (A ⊂ B), B is a subset of A (B ⊂ A), A is not a subset of B (A ⊄ B).

1. A = [30,60,90]   B = (10,20,30,40,50,60,70,80]
2. A = [red, yellow, green, blue]   B = [red]
3. A = [hot dog, hamburger, peanut butter, spaghetti, cheese]
   B = [all different kinds of sandwiches]
4. A = [all the girls in your class who wear glasses]
   B = [all the girls in your class]
   (1. A ⊄ B; 2. B ⊂ A; 3. A ⊄ B; 4. A ⊂ B)

Quotients with Remainders

pages 77-78

Objective

To review division of 1-digit quotients with remainders

Materials

*overhead projector
*39 counters

Mental Math

Ask students to add:

1. $(2 \times 4) + (3 \times 1)$ (11)
2. $(5 \times 1) + (6 \times 0)$ (5)
3. $(15 \div 3) + (4 \times 3)$ (17)
4. $(10 \div 2) + (10 \div 2)$ (10)
5. $(49 \div 7) + (3 \times 1)$ (10)
6. $(40 \div 10) + (4 \div 2)$ (6)

Skill Review

Ask students to give two factors for each of these numbers. If a number has more than one set of factors (excluding the factor 1) ask another student to give a second set of factors:

1. 24 $(12 \times 2, 8 \times 3, 6 \times 4)$
2. 32 $(16 \times 2, 8 \times 4)$
3. 10 (5×2)
4. 20 $(10 \times 2, 5 \times 4)$
5. 49 (7×7)
6. 45 $(15 \times 3, 9 \times 5)$

Dividing, 1-digit Quotients with Remainders

Quan had trouble setting up enough chairs for the school play, because of a large post in the middle of the room. He finally arranged the chairs in 9 equal rows and 1 shorter row. How many chairs were in the equal rows? How many were in the shorter row?

We want to find the number of chairs in each of the equal rows.
We also want to know how many chairs were in the shorter row.

We know Quan used __75__ chairs.

There were __9__ equal rows.
To find out the number of chairs in each equal row, we divide the total number of chairs by the number of equal rows. We divide __75__ by __9__.
The remainder will tell us how many chairs are in the shorter row.

```
        quotient  remainder
              ↓      ↓
divisor      8 R3
        → 9)75  ← dividend
          72   ← 9 × 8 = 72
           3   ← Subtract. The
                 remainder must be
                 less than the
                 divisor.
```

We check division problems using multiplication and addition if necessary.

$(9 \times 8) + 3 =$ __75__

Quan set up __8__ chairs in each of the equal rows,

and __3__ chairs in the shorter row.

Getting Started

Divide and check.

1. 4)26   6 R2
2. 2)19   9 R1
3. 3)18   6
4. 5)27   5 R2

Copy and divide.

5. $85 \div 9$ 9 R4
6. $56 \div 7$ 8
7. $63 \div 8$ 7 R7
8. $55 \div 6$ 9 R1

77

MCP All rights reserved

Teaching the Lesson

Introducing the Problem Have one student read the problem aloud and another read the information sentences. Read the plan sentences aloud. Put the division on the board as it appears in the model. Ask students how many nines in 75. (8) Explain that 8 is the quotient. Ask students to multiply 9×8. Explain that because there is a difference of three between the dividend and the product of the divisor and quotient, the problem will have a remainder. (3) Show students that the problem means that 75 chairs can be divided into 9 rows of 8 chairs in each row, with one row of the three remaining chairs.

Developing the Skill Write **48 ÷ 7** on the board using a division bracket. Ask how many sevens are in 48. (6) Write the quotient on the board and explain that they multiply quotient by divisor and write the product beneath the dividend. Have a student do this and subtract. $(48 - 42 = 6)$ Ask if the difference is bigger than the divisor. Ask a student to read the quotient. (6 R6) Work another problem, $55 \div 9$, with the class.

77

Practice

Divide.

1. 7)37 5 R2
2. 5)45 9
3. 2)15 7 R1
4. 3)22 7 R1

5. 9)82 9 R1
6. 6)57 9 R3
7. 8)26 3 R2
8. 4)30 7 R2

9. 6)14 2 R2
10. 7)27 3 R6
11. 3)18 6
12. 5)28 5 R3

13. 9)70 7 R7
14. 8)36 4 R4
15. 7)58 8 R2
16. 4)18 4 R2

Copy and Do

17. 48 ÷ 7
   6 R6
18. 40 ÷ 8
   5
19. 19 ÷ 3
   6 R1
20. 18 ÷ 4
   4 R2

21. 45 ÷ 6
   7 R3
22. 39 ÷ 9
   4 R3
23. 11 ÷ 5
   2 R1
24. 27 ÷ 7
   3 R6

25. 25 ÷ 3
   8 R1
26. 50 ÷ 7
   7 R1
27. 41 ÷ 6
   6 R5
28. 80 ÷ 9
   8 R8

Apply

Solve these problems.

29. The drama teacher invited 21 students to a cast party. If all the students come in cars that carry 6 passengers, how many cars will be needed?
4 cars

30. Each act in the play was cast with 5 different actors. There were 3 acts. How many actors were in the play?
15 actors

31. The Jones family attended the play. They spent $24 for tickets. If each ticket costs $4, how many people in the Jones family attended the play?
6 people

32. 75 people attended the play altogether. There were 26 children in the audience. How many adults attended?
49 adults

78

Correcting Common Errors

Some students may write the remainder as part of the quotient. Have them use counters to model the problem, dividing 30 counters into 5 equal groups to find that there are 6 counters in each group; the 2 counters that are left over, or remaining, are shown as the remainder.

```
INCORRECT
    62
  5)32
    30
  ---
     2
```

Enrichment

Explain that as addition can check subtraction, multiplication can check division. When there is a remainder in division, they will add it to the product of the quotient and divisor. Show students that when the problem involves division and subtraction, the check will be multiplication and addition. Ask students to show a check problem for the practice problems they did in this lesson.

Practice

Have students complete the practice problems. Remind them to write the remainder with an R, after the quotient.

Extra Credit *Numeration*

Many ancient cultures, including the Chinese and the Roman, had finger symbols for numbers. There are still tribes of people who remember finger symbols. In New Guinea, for example, people use the right hand to point to fingers of the left hand (little finger = 1 through thumb = 5), then the numbers 6 through 13 are obtained by pointing to the left wrist, forearm, elbow, bicep, collarbone, shoulder, ear and eye, in that order. The numbers 14 through 27 are possible by reversing these movements and doing them with the left hand pointing to the right side. Have students try these symbols. Explain that people in this tribe do not count past 27! As an extension, have students go to the library and find out how deaf people use sign language to express numbers.

2-digit Quotients

pages 79-80

Objective

To review division with 2-digit quotients

Materials

Mental Math

Have students add:

1. 2 threes and 1 three (9)
2. 4 fives and 2 fives (30)
3. 6 sevens and 1 seven (49)
4. 4 nines and 4 nines (72)
5. 2 sixes and 5 sixes (42)

Skill Review

Ask students to do the first step in each of these problems mentally, telling the greatest possible quotient. Ask them to ignore the remainder for this exercise.

1. 57 ÷ 9 (6)   6. 79 ÷ 9 (8)
2. 35 ÷ 8 (4)   7. 64 ÷ 7 (9)
3. 26 ÷ 6 (4)   8. 67 ÷ 8 (8)
4. 17 ÷ 5 (3)   9. 36 ÷ 7 (5)
5. 43 ÷ 7 (6)   10. 58 ÷ 9 (6)

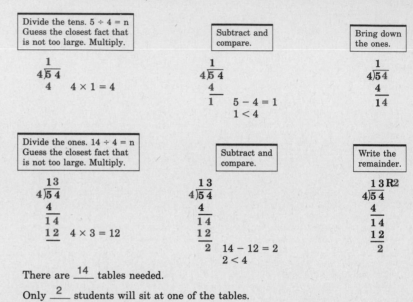

Dividing, 2-digit Quotients

Mr. Porter is getting his science classroom ready for the new quarter. His largest class will have 54 students. How many tables will he need for his classroom?

We want to find the number of tables needed in Mr. Porter's classroom.

We know there will be __54__ students in his largest class.

Each table seats only __4__ students.
To find the number of tables needed, we divide the total number of students by the number of seats available at each table.

We divide __54__ by __4__.

Divide the tens. 5 ÷ 4 = n Guess the closest fact that is not too large. Multiply.	Subtract and compare.	Bring down the ones.
1 4)5 4 4 4 × 1 = 4	1 4)5 4 4 1 5 − 4 = 1 1 < 4	1 4)5 4 4 14

Divide the ones. 14 ÷ 4 = n Guess the closest fact that is not too large. Multiply.	Subtract and compare.	Write the remainder.
13 4)5 4 4 14 12 4 × 3 = 12	13 4)5 4 4 14 12 2 14 − 12 = 2 2 < 4	13 R2 4)5 4 4 14 12 2

There are __14__ tables needed.

Only __2__ students will sit at one of the tables.

Getting Started

Divide and check.

13 R1
1. 4)53

11
2. 6)66

Copy and divide.

3. 24 ÷ 4
   6

4. 70 ÷ 9
   7 R7

79

MCP All rights reserved

Teaching the Lesson

Introducing the Problem Read the problem aloud. Ask a student to examine the illustration and fill in the information sentences. Put the problem on the board and work it in stages while students follow in their texts. Have a student read the solution sentence. (14 tables needed) Explain that the remainder means that there will be 2 extra students and the teacher will need another table. (15)

Developing the Skill Put this series of steps on the board: **divide, multiply, subtract, compare, bring down.** Explain that they will follow these steps in multi-digit division. Point out that in multiplication they multiply by ones and then by tens, in division they divide into tens and then into ones. When they bring down ones, they are really adding ones to the remaining tens just as they remember extra ones and add them to tens in multiplication. Help students use the five steps to do these problems:

1. 57 ÷ 4 (14 R1)
2. 85 ÷ 5 (17)
3. 79 ÷ 3 (26 R1)

Practice

Divide and check.

1. $15\text{ R}3$ $4\overline{)63}$
2. 45 $2\overline{)90}$
3. $12\text{ R}3$ $6\overline{)75}$
4. $28\text{ R}2$ $3\overline{)86}$

5. 15 $5\overline{)75}$
6. 12 $7\overline{)84}$
7. $10\text{ R}5$ $9\overline{)95}$
8. $12\text{ R}1$ $8\overline{)97}$

9. $21\text{ R}1$ $3\overline{)64}$
10. $28\text{ R}1$ $2\overline{)57}$
11. 11 $5\overline{)55}$
12. $13\text{ R}2$ $7\overline{)93}$

Copy and Do

13. $59 \div 3$
    $19\text{ R}2$
14. $36 \div 2$
    18
15. $83 \div 5$
    $16\text{ R}3$
16. $92 \div 7$
    $13\text{ R}1$

17. $27 \div 4$
    $6\text{ R}3$
18. $73 \div 6$
    $12\text{ R}1$
19. $99 \div 9$
    11
20. $94 \div 8$
    $11\text{ R}6$

21. $36 \div 5$
    $7\text{ R}1$
22. $57 \div 3$
    19
23. $47 \div 4$
    $11\text{ R}3$
24. $32 \div 2$
    16

25. $45 \div 2$
    $22\text{ R}1$
26. $79 \div 6$
    $13\text{ R}1$
27. $87 \div 3$
    29
28. $90 \div 4$
    $22\text{ R}2$

Apply

Solve these problems.

29. Nona is filling 5 beakers with the same amount of water, to observe evaporation. She has 75 ounces of water. How many ounces should Nona put into each beaker?
    15 ounces

30. Each of the 54 science students bought a notebook that cost $1.53. How much did the whole class pay for notebooks?
    $82.62

31. There are 4 groups of science students experimenting with batteries and bulbs. The materials for this activity cost the lab $64. What was the supply cost per group?
    $16

32. Only 44 of the science students signed up to go on a field trip. Each chaperone for the trip will be in charge of 3 students. How many chaperones are needed?
    15 chaperones

80

Correcting Common Errors

Some students may write a remainder that is larger than the divisor. Have them discuss why they always should compare the remainder with the divisor and how, if the remainder is larger than the divisor, then there is another "divisor" and they should increase the quotient by one.

Enrichment

Students have been told that division is repeated subtraction just as multiplication is repeated addition. Have them work these problems by repeated subtraction. Explain that the number of times they can subtract the divisor will be the quotient, and anything left when they can no longer subtract is the remainder. Have them check their subtraction by division:

1. $78 \div 4$ (19 R2)
2. $59 \div 3$ (19 R2)
3. $95 \div 4$ (23 R3)
4. $61 \div 3$ (20 R1)
5. $95 \div 7$ (13 R4)

Practice

Have students complete the problems on the page. Remind them to bring up any remainder and write it next to the quotient.

Mixed Practice

1. $95,090 - 81,478$ (13,612)
2. $108,721 + 9,336$ (118,057)
3. $54 \div 8$ (6 R6)
4. $\$75.45 \times 4$ ($301.80)
5. $68 \div 3$ (22 R2)
6. $47,158 - 13,644$ (33,514)
7. $\$323.17 + \$651.95 + \$1,295.48$ ($2,270.60)
8. $27 \div 3$ (9)
9. 32×258 (8,256)
10. $1,798 \times 12$ (21,576)

Extra Credit *Numeration*

Explain to students that a perfect number in mathematics is any number whose factors, other than the number itself, add up to the given number. For example, 6 is a perfect number since the factors of 6, 1, 2 and 3 when added, equal 6.

Have the students find out which one of the following numbers is perfect by listing all the factors of each number and then adding them: 9, 12, 15, 28 or 30. (28)

3-digit Quotients

pages 81-82

Objective

To divide with 3-digit quotients

Materials

Mental Math

Have students give the value for n:

1. $15 \div n = 3$ (5)
2. $24 \div 7 = 3$ Rn (3)
3. $6 \times n = 54$ (9)
4. $82 \div n = 9$ R1 (9)
5. $10 \times n = 150$ (15)
6. $9 \div 4 = 2$ Rn (1)
7. $n \times n = 64$ (8)

Skill Review

Have students work these problems on paper.

1. $37 \div 3$ (12 R1)
2. $52 \div 4$ (13)
3. $96 \div 7$ (13 R5)
4. $83 \div 5$ (16 R3)
5. $27 \div 2$ (13 R1)
6. $58 \div 3$ (19 R1)
7. $91 \div 5$ (18 R1)

MCP All rights reserved

Dividing, 3-digit Quotients

At the end of each month the Mighty Mowers divide their profits. The leftover profit is added to the next month's income. In June, the Mighty Mowers earned $370. How much did each person receive? How much profit was left to start July?

We want to find out how much money each person received in June, and how much was left over for July.

We know the Mighty Mowers earned ___$370___ in June.

The money was divided evenly among ___3___ people. To find their individual earnings, we divide the group's June income by the number of workers in their group.

We divide ___$370___ by ___3___.

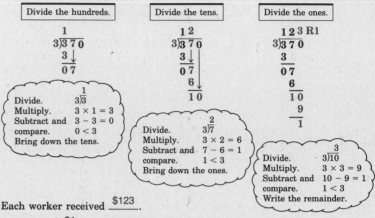

Each worker received ___$123___.

There was ___$1___ left over for July.

Getting Started

Divide and check.

1. 127
   5)635

2. 182 R1
   4)729

Copy and divide.

3. $850 \div 7$ 121 R3

4. $423 \div 6$ 70 R3

81

Teaching the Lesson

Introducing the Problem Read the problem aloud. Ask a student to read and complete the information sentences. Tell students to look at the problem worked in three steps in their books. Work through the problem on the board as they follow in their texts. Explain that they will begin with hundreds, finding the number of threes in 3 hundred. Continue dividing into tens and ones. Explain that in each case they will divide, multiply, subtract and bring down the number in the next place. Ask a student to read the answer and ask another to complete the solution sentence.

Developing the Skill List the steps on the board: **divide, multiply, subtract, compare** and **bring down.** Work this problem with the class: $492 \div 3$. (164) Ask students to work these examples. Have them refer to the steps listed on the board so they see that none are missed. Emphasize the importance of comparing each difference with the divisor to be sure the quotient is complete.

1. $576 \div 4$ (144)
2. $750 \div 6$ (125)
3. $545 \div 2$ (272 R1)

Practice

Divide.

1. 6)725 — 120 R5
2. 8)944 — 118
3. 3)756 — 252
4. 4)639 — 159 R3

5. 7)826 — 118
6. 9)996 — 110 R6
7. 5)785 — 157
8. 2)837 — 418 R1

9. 4)956 — 239
10. 8)890 — 111 R2
11. 2)509 — 254 R1
12. 5)623 — 124 R3

13. 9)999 — 111
14. 7)853 — 121 R6
15. 3)727 — 242 R1
16. 6)815 — 135 R5

Copy and Do

17. $654 \div 3$
    218
18. $945 \div 2$
    472 R1
19. $715 \div 6$
    119 R1
20. $858 \div 7$
    122 R4

21. $856 \div 5$
    171 R1
22. $848 \div 4$
    212
23. $991 \div 9$
    110 R1
24. $975 \div 8$
    121 R7

Apply

Solve these problems.

25. The Mighty Mowers, together, worked 462 hours in one summer. If they all worked the same number of hours, how much did each person work?
    154 hours

26. Pablo earned $52 in two weeks. How much money did he have left after he spent $38 on clothes?
    $14

27. Anita and Larry each mowed lawns 6 hours on Saturday. How much did they earn for the Mighty Mowers?
    $48

28. The Mighty Mowers earned $347 in August. How much did each person receive? How much money was left over?
    $115 each $2 left

82

Correcting Common Errors

Some students will place the digits incorrectly in the quotient. Have them divide by writing the partial quotients as shown in the example at the right.

```
          122 R2
            2
           20
          100
      6)734
      - 600
        134
      - 120
         14
       -  12
          2
```

Enrichment

Have students answer the following:

1. There are 5,280 feet in a mile and 3 feet in a yard. How many yards in a mile? (1,760)
2. There are 365 days in a year and 7 days in a week. How many weeks in a year? (52 R1)
3. The speed of sound in dry air is 1,090 feet per second, how many yards per second? (363 R1)

Practice

Have students complete the problems on the page.

Extra Credit *Biography*

Emmy Noether's story represents the lack of recognition women of her era faced in a man's world. At Emmy's death, Einstein wrote that she had been the most significant genius since the start of higher education for women. She was born in Erlangen, Germany, in 1882, the daughter of a university professor. Her family encouraged her to pursue her studies. At the University of Erlangen, she was one of two women students in a class of 1,000. After receiving her doctorate, the only work she could find was to lecture under colleague David Hilbert's name without pay. At the age of 50, for political reasons, Emmy and other German mathematicians and scientists were forced to leave the country. She settled in Pennsylvania, became a professor at Bryn Mawr, a women's college, and had a successful career as an educator. Emmy's best work came late in life, making her early death, at age 53, especially tragic.

Partial Dividends

pages 83-84

Objective

To divide a 3-digit number by a 1-digit number

Materials

Mental Math

Ask students to calculate the following if n = 4:

1. $4 \times n$ (16)
2. $15 - n$ (11)
3. $20 \div n$ (5)
4. $n \div 2$ (2)
5. $n \times 10$ (40)
6. $40 \div n$ (10)
7. $(3 \times n) + (2 \times n)$ (20)

Skill Review

Have students complete these problems on paper.

1. $57 \div 8$ (7 R1)
2. $27 \div 4$ (6 R3)
3. $89 \div 7$ (12 R5)
4. $57 \div 3$ (19)
5. $385 \div 3$ (128 R1)
6. $671 \div 5$ (134 R1)
7. $994 \div 4$ (248 R2)

Dividing, Deciding Where to Start

The human body continues to burn calories 24 hours a day, no matter how inactive a person is. How many calories are used by someone sleeping for 1 hour?

Activity	Calories Used
Walk 1 hour	about 250
Sit 4 hours	about 340
Sleep 8 hours	about 520

We are looking for the number of calories used while sleeping for 1 hour.

A person sleeping for 8 hours uses about __520__ calories. To find the hourly rate of calories used while sleeping, we divide the total calories burned by the number of hours slept.

We divide __520__ by __8__.

Decide where to start. 8 < 5
There are not enough hundreds.
Rename the hundreds as tens and start with 52 tens.

Divide the tens.

$$
\begin{array}{r}
6 \\
8\overline{)520} \\
48 \\
\hline
40
\end{array}
$$

Divide the ones.

$$
\begin{array}{r}
65 \\
8\overline{)520} \\
48 \\
\hline
40 \\
40 \\
\hline
\end{array}
$$

A human being burns about __65__ calories while sleeping for 1 hour.

Getting Started

Divide and check.

1. $6\overline{)348}$ — 58
2. $4\overline{)216}$ — 54
3. $7\overline{)248}$ — 35 R3
4. $9\overline{)624}$ — 69 R3

Copy and divide.

5. $435 \div 5$ — 87
6. $343 \div 7$ — 49
7. $856 \div 9$ — 95 R1
8. $183 \div 2$ — 91 R1

MCP All rights reserved

83

Teaching the Lesson

Introducing the Problem Read the problem aloud and have students look over the calorie chart. Have students read the information sentences and the plan sentences. Ask a student to work the problem on the board as others follow the model problem. Explain that they will have to consider tens, since there are too few hundreds. Point to the tens, explaining that with 5 hundreds and 2 tens they have 52 tens all together. Have the student divide 52 by 8. (6) Explain that once they have decided where to begin, the division will be the same: divide, multiply, subtract, compare, bring down. Have the students complete the problem. (65) Read the solution sentence aloud.

Developing the Skill Put these problems on the board and ask students how they would begin each: $4\overline{)856}$ $4\overline{)312}$ Point out that in the first problem, four can be divided directly into hundreds because there are 8 hundreds and 8 > 4. Explain that in the second problem, however, four can not be divided directly into hundreds because 3 < 4. Show students that in the case where the first digit of the dividend is smaller than the divisor, they must consider the first two digits of the dividend in order to divide. Complete the division of the second problem on the board. (78) Have students work these problems independently: $583 \div 7$ (83 R2) and $208 \div 9$. (23 R1)

83

Practice

Divide and check.

1. 112 R2 — 6)674
2. 16 R1 — 8)129
3. 99 — 4)396
4. 232 R2 — 3)698

5. 56 R2 — 7)394
6. 84 — 6)504
7. 368 — 2)736
8. 47 R4 — 9)427

9. 58 R4 — 8)468
10. 38 R1 — 4)153
11. 167 — 5)835
12. 36 R1 — 3)109

Copy and Do

13. 268 ÷ 4
    67
14. 371 ÷ 9
    41 R2
15. 814 ÷ 3
    271 R1
16. 917 ÷ 7
    131

17. 427 ÷ 8
    53 R3
18. 812 ÷ 5
    162 R2
19. 906 ÷ 7
    129 R3
20. 159 ÷ 2
    79 R1

21. 613 ÷ 5
    122 R3
22. 875 ÷ 9
    97 R2
23. 675 ÷ 3
    225
24. 428 ÷ 8
    53 R4

Apply

Solve these problems. Use the chart on page 81 as needed.

25. Willie swam 285 meters in 3 minutes. How far did he swim in 1 minute?
95 meters

26. Alicia walked 4,560 meters in the marathon. Wanda walked 2,315 meters farther than Alicia. How far did Wanda walk?
6,875 meters

27. The team of 5 archers shot 250 arrows in 2 rounds each. How many arrows were shot by each archer in each round?
25 arrows

28. Each student competed in the spring physical fitness test. Rob did 325 situps in 5 minutes. How many did he do in 2 minutes?
130 situps

29. How many calories are used by a person sitting for 1 hour?
85 calories

30. How many calories does a person burn by walking for 3 hours?
750 calories

84

Correcting Common Errors

Watch for students who have difficulty deciding where to place the first digit of the quotient. Have them multiply the divisor by 1, by 10, by 100, by 1,000, until their answer is greater than the dividend. This tells them whether the quotient is in the ones, the tens, or the hundreds.

Enrichment

Duplicate the following table. Ask students to calculate the monthly cost of operating each appliance:

Appliance	6 Months	1 Month
dishwasher	$36.42	($6.07)
refrigerator	$17.29	($2.88)
television	$6.55	($1.09)
water heater	$179.00	($29.83)
iron	$2.35	($.39)
hair dryer	$.42	($.07)
radio	$1.32	($.22)

Practice

Have students complete the problems on the page. Explain that they will have to decide whether to begin dividing with hundreds or tens.

Mixed Practice

1. 63 ÷ 8 (7 R7)
2. $200.58 − $165.47 ($35.11)
3. 707 × 240 (169,680)
4. 378,912 + 19,518 (398,430)
5. 8,912 × 3 (26,736)
6. 73,502 − 61,491 (12,011)
7. 195 ÷ 3 (65)
8. 361 + 1,952 + 457 + 48 (2,818)
9. 48 ÷ 6 (8)
10. 95 × 1,487 (141,265)

Extra Credit   *Logic*

Duplicate the following for students to solve:
Lucy, Bill and Jill, 3 contestants on a game show, were asked 1 question in each of 5 categories: math, space exploration, history, animals and cooking. Each player got 3 answers correct, but no one category question was answered correctly by all three. We know that:
  Bill did not know what a fraction was.
  Jill had never heard of Neil Armstrong.
  Lucy was the only one who knew when the War of 1812 began.
Which categories did each player answer correctly? (Bill-space exploration, animals, cooking; Lucy-history, math, space exploration; Jill-math, animals, cooking.)

Quotients With Zeros

pages 85-86

Objective

To divide 3-digit numbers by 1-digit numbers when the quotient has a zero

Materials

Mental Math

Ask students to divide:

1. 49 ÷ 8 (6 R1)
2. 35 ÷ 7 (5)
3. 25 ÷ 8 (3 R1)
4. 31 ÷ 3 (10 R1)
5. 54 ÷ 9 (6)
6. 71 ÷ 8 (8 R7)
7. 60 ÷ 7 (8 R4)

Skill Review

Ask students to complete these problems on the board:

1. (131) 6)786
2. (65) 7)455
3. (43 R3) 8)347
4. (25 R3) 5)128

Dividing, Zeros in the Quotient

Nadia and 3 friends spent Saturday afternoon sightseeing. They had lunch and decided to split the bill evenly. What was each person's share of the restaurant check?

We want to find what each person owed for lunch.

The total bill was __$8.36__.

There were __4__ people.
To determine the amount each person paid for lunch, we divide the total bill by the number of people splitting the cost.

We divide __$8.36__ by __4__.

Divide the dollars.	Divide the dimes.	Bring down the pennies and divide. Place the dollar sign and decimal point.
2 4)$8.36 8 0	2 0 4)$8.36 8 3	$2.09 4)$8.36 8 36 36 0

4 > 3. There are not enough dimes. Put a zero in the quotient, and rename the dimes as pennies.

Each person owed __$2.09__ for lunch.

Getting Started

Divide and check.

1. $1.02 7)$7.14
2. 480 2)960
3. 200 4)800
4. 105 R3 8)843

Copy and divide.

5. 920 ÷ 9 102 R2
6. 530 ÷ 5 106
7. $9.15 ÷ 3 $3.05
8. 654 ÷ 6 109

85

MCP All rights reserved

Teaching the Lesson

Introducing the Problem Read the problem aloud. Ask a student to read the information sentences. Write the plan sentence and the problem on the board and ask students to follow in their texts as you work it. Remind students to give special attention to the placement of zero in the quotient. Put the dollar sign and decimal point in and ask a student to read the answer. Have another read the solution sentence. (Each owed $2.09.)

Developing the Skill Explain that in these problems it is very important to remember to put a zero in the quotient any time the digit in ones column is too small for division; and the number in the adjoining column must be brought down to complete a problem. Put **342 ÷ 5 = 068** or **68 R2** on the board to show students that if this occurs in the first digits of the division, the zero can be written in, but is insignificant. When the zero occurs in the middle of a problem, however, it is essential to put it in the quotient to hold that place. Work this problem on the board with the students:

(307 R1)
2)615

Practice

Divide and check.

102	$1.05	307	100
1. 8)816	2. 9)$9.45	3. 3)921	4. 6)600
90	$4.03	205	108
5. 5)450	6. 2)$8.06	7. 4)820	8. 7)756
228 R3	104 R7	$1.10	108 R3
9. 4)915	10. 8)839	11. 9)$9.90	12. 6)651
205 R2	105	27 R2	$3.07
13. 3)617	14. 7)735	15. 5)137	16. 2)$6.14

Copy and Do

17. $8.08 ÷ 8
    $1.01

18. 437 ÷ 2
    218 R1

19. 529 ÷ 5
    105 R4

20. 613 ÷ 6
    102 R1

21. 903 ÷ 9
    100 R3

22. $9.27 ÷ 3
    $3.09

23. 821 ÷ 4
    205 R1

24. 767 ÷ 7
    109 R4

Apply

Solve these problems.

25. Marge ordered a hamburger for $1.46, french fries for $0.75 and orange juice for $1.15. How much was her bill?
    $3.36

26. Earle spent $6.24 when he took his two brothers out for lunch. They all ordered the same thing. How much was each lunch?
    $2.08

27. Gene paid $6.36 for 6 gallons of milk. How much did each gallon cost?
    $1.06

28. Betty's lunch cost $3.87 and Juan's lunch cost $4.15. How much change did Betty get from a $10 bill, if she bought both lunches?
    $1.98

86

Correcting Common Errors

Some students may forget to write a necessary zero in the quotient. Have them practice with partners where both show and discuss every step taken to find the quotient.

$$
\begin{array}{r}
106\,\text{R}4 \\
5)\overline{534} \\
-5 \quad \leftarrow 1 \times 5 \\
\hline
03 \\
-0 \quad \leftarrow 0 \times 5 \\
\hline
34 \\
-30 \leftarrow 6 \times 5 \\
\hline
4
\end{array}
$$

Enrichment

1. Ask students to read their car odometer today and again in a week. Ask them to figure out how far, on the average, the car was driven each day of the week. Have students write out a plan for solving the problem and do the calculations. (subtract today's reading from that of a week from today, and divide mileage by 7)

Practice

Have students complete the practice problems. Remind them to put in each required zero.

Extra Credit *Statistics*

Give students 1/2-inch graph paper. Have them write consecutive numbers across the bottom and up the side forming a coordinate graph. Have them draw a simple line picture on the graph paper. Instruct them to put a dot on the picture wherever two lines of the graph paper meet, and list the coordinates for that dot. Remind them that the first number of the coordinates indicates the number across the bottom and the second coordinate is read up the side. Provide each student with a second sheet of graph paper. Have them exchange their graph drawing with coordinates listed with another student who will plot the coordinates and connect the dots. If correctly done, they will recreate the same picture as the original.

Dividing Larger Numbers

pages 87-88

Objective

To divide up to 6 digits, by a 1-digit number

Materials

Mental Math

Have students multiply:

1. 3×100 (300)
2. 15×10 (150)
3. $1,000 \times 10$ (10,000)
4. 42×100 (4,200)
5. $8 \times 1,000,000$ (8,000,000)
6. $12 \times 10,000$ (120,000)
7. 40×40 (1,600)

Skill Review

Have one student work these problems on the board while the others do them at their desks:

1. $4)\overline{438}$ (109 R2)
2. $6)\overline{673}$ (112 R1)
3. $7)\overline{345}$ (49 R2)

Dividing Larger Numbers

Miss Lopez wrote a newspaper article about the Air Show held last weekend. She reported that the attendance this year was 3 times greater than last year's. How many people were at last year's Air Show?

We want to find the number of people who attended the Air Show last year.
We know the number of people attending this year was ___14,115___.

There were ___3___ times more people this year. To determine last year's attendance, we divide the number of people attending this year, by the number of times greater the attendance was, compared to last year.

We divide ___14,115___ by ___3___.

```
       4,705
   3)14,115        Divide,
      12            multiply,
       2 1          subtract,
       2 1          compare and
         1 5        bring down.
         1 5
            0
```

Last year, only ___4,705___ people attended the Air Show.

Getting Started

Divide and check.

1. $7)\overline{4,265}$ 609 R2
2. $8)\overline{\$40.56}$ \$5.07
3. $3)\overline{92,765}$ 30,921 R2

Copy and divide.

4. $157,623 \div 6$ 26,270 R3
5. $636,720 \div 9$ 70,746 R6
6. $\$847.35 \div 5$ \$169.47

MCP All rights reserved

87

Teaching the Lesson

Introducing the Problem Ask a student to read the problem and the information sentences aloud. Write the problem on the board as it appears in the model. Include the five basic steps: **divide, multiply, subtract, compare** and **bring down.** Explain that dividing a 5-digit dividend is no different than dividing a 3-digit dividend. Point out that there will be more steps, but that the repetition of the five basic steps will be the same. Work the problem on the board while students follow in their texts. Have a student read the solution sentence. (last year, only 4,705 people)

Developing the Skill Put this problem and the list of five steps on the board by the problem:

divide
multiply
subtract $5)\overline{6,785}$ (1,357)
compare
bring down

Ask different students to come up and divide thousands, then hundreds, then tens and ones as the class works at their desks. Remind them of the importance of placing a zero in the quotient if the divisor cannot be divided into a single digit in the dividend. Illustrate the problem on the board when they are finished: $452,654 \div 3$. (150,884 R2)

87

Divide and check.

    1,824
1. 3)5,472

    1,173 R5
2. 7)8,216

    $12.59
3. 5)$62.95

    1,382
4. 9)12,438

    12,535 R4
5. 6)75,214

    9,008
6. 8)72,064

    9,867 R1
7. 2)19,735

    $34.87
8. 4)$139.48

    7,156 R4
9. 7)50,096

    14,089 R3
10. 8)112,715

    42,500
11. 6)255,000

    $105.08
12. 3)$315.24

Copy and Do

13. 4,248 ÷ 4
    1,062

14. 6,793 ÷ 8
    849 R1

15. $7,476 ÷ 6
    $1,246

16. 9,318 ÷ 7
    1,331 R1

17. $3,009 ÷ 3
    $1,003

18. 16,250 ÷ 5
    3,250

19. $753.26 ÷ 2
    $376.63

20. 82,571 ÷ 9
    9,174 R5

21. 117,359 ÷ 6
    19,559 R5

22. 259,371 ÷ 4
    64,842 R3

23. $1,429.35 ÷ 5
    $285.87

24. 490,560 ÷ 7
    70,080

Apply

Solve these problems.

25. The deep sea angler can swim at an ocean depth of 26,955 feet. This is 9 times deeper than the oar fish can swim. At what depth is the oar fish usually found?
2,995 feet

26. If a blue whale weighs 305,750 pounds and a grey whale weighs 89,380 pounds, how much heavier is the blue whale?
216,370 pounds

Correcting Common Errors

Some students may fail to keep their digits aligned properly and in the correct places. Encourage them to work their problems on grid paper using the squares to guide their placement of the digits.

Enrichment

1. Explain that students can check their division by rounding the numbers and estimating an answer; for example 4,789 ÷ 6 is almost 4,800 ÷ 6 = 800.

2. Ask them to estimate answers for the practice problems on page 88 and then check to see how close the actual answer is to the estimate. Explain that if the two numbers are far apart, they should look for computational error.

Practice

Have students complete the practice problems. Urge them to write each digit in the quotient directly over the appropriate digit in the dividend.

Mixed Practice

1. 957,121 − 606,357 (350,764)
2. 4,214 ÷ 7 (602)
3. 621,916 × 8 (4,975,328)
4. $54.27 ÷ 9 ($6.03)
5. 82,216 − 28,018 (54,198)
6. $2,107.48 + $3,568.29 ($5,675.77)
7. 18,250 ÷ 6 (3,041 R4)
8. 82,027 × 40 (3,281,080)
9. 39 + 195 + 206 + 17 (457)
10. 76 × $95.27 ($7,240.52)

Extra Credit *Numeration*

Present the following sequence to the students and tell them this sequence was first introduced by Leonardo of Pisa (nicknamed Fibonacci) around the year 1202. It is especially noteworthy because of its relationship to many natural objects. Have them discover the pattern for finding consecutive terms in the following:

1, 1, 2, 3, 5, 8, 13, 21, . . .

Have them list the next five terms of the sequence.
Have the students research more about the significance of the Fibonacci sequence. Then have them find pictures in magazines to display on a bulletin board of objects in which the Fibonacci sequence seems to have a natural occurrence. (pinecones, sunflowers, etc.)

Dividing the Short Way

Objective

To find quotients using short division

Materials

Mental Math

Ask students to round to the nearest ten and add:

1. 23 + 45 (70)
2. 52 + 81 (130)
3. 17 + 21 (40)
4. 120 + 35 (160)
5. 49 + 51 (100)
6. 92 + 94 (180)
7. 42 + 89 (130)

Skill Review

Have students work these problems on paper:

1. (2,114)
   4)8,456
2. (1,860 R5)
   9)16,745
3. ($93.57)
   5)$467.85

Dividing the Short Way

Roosevelt High School is proud of its basketball team. Every home game this year was a sellout. The total season attendance for these games was 10,950. How many fans came to each game?

Roosevelt High School

Home Games	
Macon	December 20
Fairfield	January 3
Roberts	January 10
Pittsfield	January 17
Lincoln	January 24
Danville	January 31

We are looking for the attendance at each home game.

The total attendance for the year was __10,950__.

Roosevelt played __6__ home games.

To find the number of fans who attended each home game, we divide the season attendance by the number of home games.

We divide __10,950__ by __6__.

We can use a shortcut method.

Divide the thousands. Rename the remainder as hundreds.	Divide the hundreds. Rename the remainder as tens.	Divide the tens. Rename the remainder as ones.	Divide the ones. Write the remainder if there is one.
1 6)10,950	1,8 6)10,950	1,82 6)10,950	1,825 6)10,950

The attendance for each home game was __1,825__.

Getting Started

Divide and check.

955 R2 1. 6)5,732	$3.64 2. 9)$32.76	3,846 3. 4)15,384	10,755 R1 4. 7)75,286

Copy and divide.

5. $623.84 ÷ 2
   $311.92
6. 139,257 ÷ 8
   17,407 R1
7. 457,382 ÷ 3
   152,460 R2
8. 926,034 ÷ 5
   185,206 R4

MCP All rights reserved

89

Teaching the Lesson

Introducing the Problem Read the problem aloud. Ask a student to read and fill in the information and plan sentences. Ask students to look at the problem as it is worked in the model. Put the problem on the board and explain that as you divide, you are going to do the multiplication and subtraction in your head. You may want to write each remainder in as a small number within the dividend.

$$\begin{array}{r} 1,825 \\ 6)\overline{10,_49_15_30} \end{array}$$

Point out that they continue to do all the steps required, but that many are done in their heads and only the quotient appears on paper. Have a student read the solution sentence.

Developing the Skill Most students will need to keep track of the remainders within the problem. Have them work these problems on one line, doing the multiplication and subtraction in their heads. Tell them to write each remainder next to the following digit in the dividend.

1. (8 9)
   4)3 5₃6
2. (1, 3 0 9 R2)
   6)7,₁8 5 6
3. ($2 3 5. 7 1)
   2)$4 7₁1.₁4 2
4. (1 4 5,0 0 0)
   3)4₁3₁5,0 0 0

89

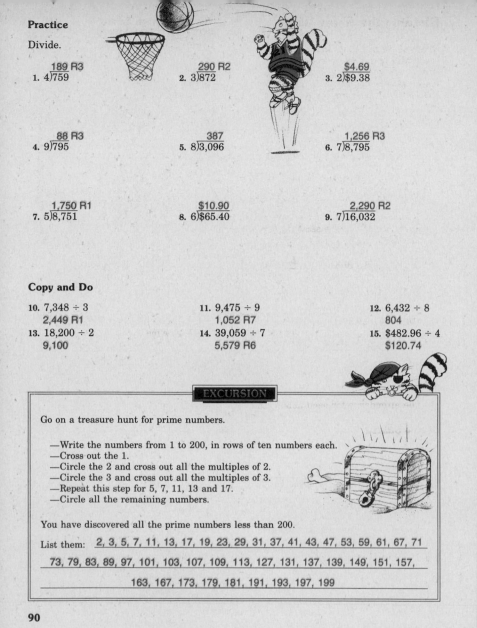

Practice

Divide.

1. 4)759 → 189 R3

2. 3)872 → 290 R2

3. 2)$9.38 → $4.69

4. 9)795 → 88 R3

5. 8)3,096 → 387

6. 7)8,795 → 1,256 R3

7. 5)8,751 → 1,750 R1

8. 6)$65.40 → $10.90

9. 7)16,032 → 2,290 R2

Copy and Do

10. 7,348 ÷ 3
    2,449 R1

11. 9,475 ÷ 9
    1,052 R7

12. 6,432 ÷ 8
    804

13. 18,200 ÷ 2
    9,100

14. 39,059 ÷ 7
    5,579 R6

15. $482.96 ÷ 4
    $120.74

EXCURSION

Go on a treasure hunt for prime numbers.

—Write the numbers from 1 to 200, in rows of ten numbers each.
—Cross out the 1.
—Circle the 2 and cross out all the multiples of 2.
—Circle the 3 and cross out all the multiples of 3.
—Repeat this step for 5, 7, 11, 13 and 17.
—Circle all the remaining numbers.

You have discovered all the prime numbers less than 200.

List them: 2, 3, 5, 7, 11, 13, 17, 19, 23, 29, 31, 37, 41, 43, 47, 53, 59, 61, 67, 71

73, 79, 83, 89, 97, 101, 103, 107, 109, 113, 127, 131, 137, 139, 149, 151, 157,

163, 167, 173, 179, 181, 191, 193, 197, 199

90

Correcting Common Errors

Some students may not be able to do the multiplication and subtraction mentally when doing division the short way. Have these students practice by doing the difficult computations on another piece of paper.

Enrichment

Explain that calculators express remainders as tenths, the digit after the decimal point. Point out that tenths can be rounded like any other number. Have students do these problems on calculators and round the answer to ones.

1. 72,993 ÷ 4 (18,248)
2. 954,781 ÷ 6 (159,130)
3. 6,308 ÷ 8 (789)
4. 55,133 ÷ 3 (18,378)
5. 4,804 ÷ 5 (961)

Practice

Have students complete the practice problems. Suggest that they stop writing in the remainders whenever they can remember the numbers without seeing them on paper.

Excursion

The **Sieve of Eratosthenes** is a fun way to find primes. Ask students to notice which multiple of each new number is first to be crossed out. With 7 we find the first multiple of 7 which has not already been crossed out is 7 × 7 = 49. Ask why this should be the case. Ask how many primes exist. (There is an infinite number.)

Extra Credit *Counting Strategies*

Explain that many types of counting boards have been devised. Show students an abacus and explain that the rows represent different place values, starting with units at the right and going through tens, hundreds and so on. Some have a bar in the middle, with the beads above the bar representing fives. Others are just open rods to which beads can be added and subtracted. If you do not have any open rod type which is often found in kindergarten classrooms, have students draw the arrangements on paper. Tell them to illustrate a way to use the abacus to add and subtract. For example, draw this on the board:

Explain that it represents the number 325. Tell them to copy the drawing and then add 147. Encourage them to see that they will have to trade 10 unit beads for a ten. Have them continue for other addition and subtraction problems.

Finding Averages

Objective

To find the average of a set of numbers

Materials

50 counters
*overhead projector

Mental Math

Ask students to tell whether each is correct or incorrect and give correct answers.

1. $25 \div 4 = 7$ R1 (incorrect, 6 R1)
2. $32 \div 8 = 4$ R2 (incorrect, 4)
3. $55 \div 9 = 6$ R1 (correct)
4. $80 \div 9 = 8$ R8 (correct)
5. $63 \div 7 = 8$ (incorrect, 9)
6. $15 \div 2 = 7$ R1 (correct)

Skill Review

Ask students to do this column addition on paper:

1. $5 + 6 + 3 = (14)$
2. $12 + 15 + 9 = (36)$
3. $9 + 15 + 22 = (46)$
4. $20 + 35 + 19 = (74)$
5. $48 + 52 + 39 = (139)$
6. $35 + 15 + 42 = (92)$
7. $121 + 182 + 53 = (356)$

Finding the Average

Robin is a new member of the bowling league, and her teammates are very happy with her last three bowling scores. What is Robin's average score?

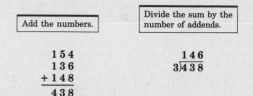

We want to find Robin's average bowling score.

We know Robin bowled ___3___ games.

The scores of her games were ___154___ , ___136___

and ___148___ .

To find her average, we add the scores and divide the sum by the number of addends.

Add the numbers.	Divide the sum by the number of addends.
154	146
136	3)438
+ 148	
438	

Robin's average score for the three games is ___146___ .

✔ Notice the sum of the average scores is the same as the sum of the real scores.

Real Scores	Average Scores
154	146
136	146
+ 148	+ 146
438	438

Getting Started

Find the average for each set of numbers.

1. 627 550	2. 2,347 1,672	3. 95 56
512	968	38
310	1,701	21
751		49
		77

MCP All rights reserved

91

Teaching the Lesson

Introducing the Problem Read the problem aloud and ask a student to read and complete the information sentences. Explain that an **average** number is a number that represents a set of numbers. Point out that in this case, the average score will tell about how well Robin bowled without repeating each score. Have students look at the problem in the model, pointing out the scores are added and then divided by the number of scores. Ask a student to read the solution sentence aloud. (average score for three games, 146)

Developing the Skill Arrange 12 counters on the overhead projector in groups of 5, 4 and 3. Ask students to find the average number of counters in each pile. Tell the class to describe the size of the groups without enumerating all of them. (that there are about four counters in each pile.) To show that this is true, rearrange the groups into fours. Write on the board: **$5 + 4 + 3 = 12$. $12 \div 3 = 4$.** Explain that when they are dealing with larger numbers, it is not possible to make piles of counters and rearrange them in order to find the average distribution. Have students find the average of these sets of numbers:

1. 9, 5, 6, 7, 3 (6)
2. 15, 34, 21, 22 (23)
3. 472, 696, 386 (518)

Practice

Find the average for each set of numbers.

1. 67, 85
76

2. 34, 26, 58, 17, 28, 35
33

3. 138, 249, 435
274

4. 651, 486, 715, 811, 912
715

5. 3,248, 6,914, 4,124
4,762

6. 838, 472, 596, 850
689

Apply

Solve these problems.

7. Rex paid $5.55 to bowl 3 games. What was the average amount he paid for each game?
$1.85

8. If the bowling alley snack bar sold 918 bags of pretzels in 6 months, how many bags of pretzels should the owner expect to sell this month?
153 bags

9. After two weeks on the bowling team, Tavia's scores were 129, 186, 147 and 150. What was her bowling average?
153

10. Art bought a bowling shirt for $11.89, in one store; one for $17.55 in another store; and one for $8.21 in a third store. What was the average cost of his shirts?
$12.55

11. Mr. Hope drives the team car pool for bowling. His car can travel 432 miles on 12 gallons of gas. What is his average gas mileage?
36 miles per gallon

12. Mr. Hope had to wait for the team an average of 25 minutes, each day they bowled. If the team bowled twice a week, how many minutes did Mr. Hope spend waiting each week?
50 minutes

Use the graph to complete problems 13 through 15.

13. What was the average number of spares made by team members in the Bowlathon?
20 spares

14. Which bowlers scored higher than the average?
Rex and Tavia

15. What is the average number of spares made by the three top spare makers?
22 spares

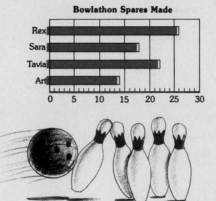

Bowlathon Spares Made

Correcting Common Errors

To help students understand that the average is a number that could represent each number in a group, have them work with partners and a set of counters. For each exercise, have them make piles of counters for the given numbers. Then have them re-arrange the counters until each pile has the same number. This number is the average.

1. 4, 9, 10, 5 (7)
2. 21, 13, 11 (15)
3. 17, 12, 14, 9 (13)
4. 6, 11, 8, 4, 6 (7)

Enrichment

Explain that on the stock market, shares of stock are bought and sold in large numbers each day. Some are bought at one price, some at another, but at the end of the day an average price is computed. Have students calculate the average price per share of Consolidated School Products if 200 were sold for $56 per share and 500 for $58 per share. ($57)

Practice

Have students complete the practice problems. Explain that in some problems, the addition may already have been done.

Extra Credit   *Numeration*

Explain that the Chinese have a method of using a thin brush to write their numbers and letters. Use the overhead projector to show the class these symbols for the numbers one through ten, plus 100 and 1,000.

Chinese Number Symbols

一 1
二 2
三 3
四 4
五 5
六 6
七 7
八 8
九 9
十 10
囗 100
千 1,000

Tell students that by using these symbols, the Chinese could form all the numbers they needed. If they put the symbol of a larger number over a smaller one, that meant to add the smaller to the larger. If they put a smaller symbol over a larger one, it means multiply the smaller by the larger.

十 13
三

三 30
十

五 50
十

五 53
十
三

Have students copy the first ten symbols with a brush and black paint or fine-line markers. Then give them several 2-digit numbers to translate into Chinese symbols.

Problem Solving Patterns

pages 93-94

Objective

To solve problems by finding patterns in shapes or numbers

Materials

Mental Math

Have students provide the next two numbers in each series:

1. 10, 20, 15, 25 . . . (20, 30)
2. 1, 4, 9, 16 . . . (25, 36)
3. 2, 6, 4, 8 . . . (6, 10)
4. 100, 90, 80, 70 . . . (60, 50)
5. 1, 2, 4, 7 . . . (11, 16)
6. 0, 3, 8, 15 . . . (24, 35)
7. 1, 3, 5, 7, 9 . . . (11, 13)

Looking for a Pattern

The staircase shown here is made of blocks and has five steps. How many blocks would be needed to build a staircase with ten steps?

★ SEE

We want to know the number of blocks we would need for a staircase with ten steps.

It takes __15__ blocks to build a staircase with 5 steps.

★ PLAN

Since the blocks in the picture appear to form a pattern, it is likely that a pattern with numbers will help us to solve this problem.
Making a table and recording information will be helpful in finding the pattern.

★ DO

How many blocks are in a 1-step staircase? __1__

How many blocks must be added to make a 2-step-staircase? __2__

There are a total of __3__ blocks in a 2-step-staircase.

Number of Steps	1	2	3	4	5	6	7	8	9	10
Number of Blocks	1	3	6	10	15	21	28	36	45	55

It takes __55__ blocks to build a ten-step staircase.

★ CHECK

We can check our solution by drawing a ten-step staircase and adding the number of blocks used for each step.

$1 + 2 + 3 + 4 + 5 + 6 + 7 + 8 + 9 + 10 =$ __55__

MCP All rights reserved

93

Teaching the Lesson

Read the problem aloud. Remind students of the SEE, PLAN, DO, CHECK procedure for solving problems. Ask a student to read the SEE section. Read the PLAN aloud, explaining that the pattern in the numbers may become more obvious if they arrange them in a table. Ask a student to read the DO section in the text, while the others examine the table. Draw the table on the board and ask students what they notice about the way the number of blocks increases. One way to do this is to add another column to the table, showing the difference between one step and the next:

number of steps	1	2	3	4	5	6 . . .
number of blocks	1	3	6	10	15	21 . . .
difference		2	3	4	5	6 . . .

Now ask students to provide the missing numbers. (8 steps, 36 blocks; 9 steps, 45 blocks; 10 steps, 55 blocks)
Explain that to check the problem, they can actually draw a 10-step staircase and count the blocks. Have a student put the drawing on the board. When it is complete, number each block to 55.

Apply

Look for a pattern to help solve these problems.

1. Study this pattern carefully.

Draw a sketch of the rectangle in the twelfth position and in the thirty-seventh position.

3. Bacteria double in number every hour. Study the following table:

Hours	1	2	3	4	5
Bacteria	2	4	8	16	32

How many bacteria will there be during the tenth hour?
1,024 bacteria

5. A patio, in the general shape of the picture, is to be made from square tiles. If the middle row will contain 15 tiles, how many tiles are needed to complete this patio?
113 tiles

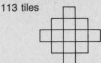

7. Read Exercise 2 again. What if the wall requires 5 bricks for the bottom row? How many bricks are needed now? 30 whole bricks or 27 whole bricks and 6 half bricks

9. A pattern is started below.

Write two different questions about the pattern for your classmates to answer.
Questions will vary.

2. A brick wall is constructed using only full bricks and half bricks. How many bricks are needed to build the whole wall?

13 whole bricks or 12 whole bricks and 2 half bricks

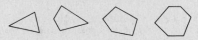

4. Study the pattern below and construct a possible next figure.

Any 7-sided figure

6. Four-sided polygons have two possible diagonals, and five-sided polygons have five possible diagonals. Six-sided polygons have 9 possible diagonals. How many possible diagonals are in a seven-sided polygon?
14 possible diagonals

8. Read Exercise 2 again. Draw another picture and rewrite the problem so that the answer is 24 bricks.
Answers will vary.

10. At a math-club party, Eric Matick said, "I will give a free prize to anyone who can tell me the greatest quotient possible, with no remainder, when you divide a 4-digit number by a 2-digit number." How can you win the prize?
999

94

Solution Notes

1. The 9 figures should be repeated.
2. Encourage the student to establish the pattern beginning at the bottom of the wall. Only the missing bricks should be counted.
3. Extend the table begun in the text remembering the numbers of bacteria double every hour.
5. Sketch patios with middle rows of 7 and 9 tiles and the shape remains the same. Construct a table and look for a pattern in the numbers.

middle 1 3 5   7   9 . . .
tiles   1 5 13 25 41 . . .

The number of tiles is increasing by multiples of 4. Have them complete the increases up to the 15-tile patio, and then add to get the total number of tiles.

6. Construct a table of sides, diagonals and differences:

sides   4 5 6 7
diagonals 2 5 9 ____

The differences are increasing by one, so the next number of diagonals will be 9 + 5 or 14. Have students draw a septagon to show this is correct.

Higher-Order Thinking Skills

7. Analysis: This is simply requiring 1 more brick per row, or 6 more bricks, whether or not the row is complete.
8. Synthesis: By changing the number of rows or the number of bricks in each row or the number of bricks already shown in the drawing, the number of possibilities are many.
9. Synthesis: Encourage questions about the number of sides and vertices as well as the number of squares.
10. Synthesis: The greatest quotient would be the greatest 4-digit dividend and the least 2-digit divisor, or 9,999 ÷ 10 with no remainder. The dividend must be 9,990 and, the quotient is 999.

Extra Credit *Logic*

After students have had experience in making flow charts for simple tasks, extend the activity. Tell students to think of a common, but multi-stepped, complicated task that they have had to do recently. Have them construct a flow chart for that task, leaving two of the steps blank. Have them exchange charts with a partner to have them fill in the missing steps in the chart.

Chapter Test

page 95

Item	Objective
1-5	Recall basic division facts (See pages 71-72)
6-8	Basic facts to find 1-digit quotients, remainders (See pages 77-78)
9-11	Divide 2-digit by 1-digit number, quotient with or without remainder (See pages 79-80)
12-14	Divide 3-digit number by 1-digit number with or without remainder (See pages 81-86)
15-21	Divide 4- and 5-digit numbers by 1-digit number with or without remainder (See pages 87-90)
22-23	Find prime factors for composite number (See pages 75-76)
24-25	Find greatest common factor (See pages 73-74)
26-28	Find averages (See pages 91-92)

Divide and check.

1. $7\overline{)7}$ → 1   2. $3\overline{)12}$ → 4   3. $7\overline{)56}$ → 8   4. $8\overline{)0}$ → 0   5. $1\overline{)6}$ → 6

6. $3\overline{)19}$ → 6 R1   7. $8\overline{)36}$ → 4 R4   8. $6\overline{)45}$ → 7 R3   9. $3\overline{)67}$ → 22 R1

10. $7\overline{)91}$ → 13   11. $2\overline{)85}$ → 42 R1   12. $8\overline{)256}$ → 32   13. $6\overline{)\$7.38}$ → \$1.23

14. $4\overline{)426}$ → 106 R2   15. $7\overline{)3,496}$ → 499 R3   16. $8\overline{)12,075}$ → 1,509 R3   17. $6\overline{)90,168}$ → 15,028

18. $3\overline{)618}$ → 206   19. $5\overline{)\$85.25}$ → \$17.05   20. $2\overline{)10,603}$ → 5,301 R1   21. $4\overline{)9,898}$ → 2,474 R2

Write the product of primes for each composite number.

22. 27 = ___$3 \times 3 \times 3$___   23. 60 = ___$2 \times 2 \times 3 \times 5$___

Write the greatest common factor for each pair of numbers.

24. 6 and 15 ___3___   25. 36 and 50 ___2___

Find the average for each set of numbers.

26. 86, 58   72   27. 127, 249, 311   229   28. 9, 6, 18, 12, 25   14

MCP All rights reserved

95

Circle the letter of the correct answer.

1 What is the place value of the 3 in 503,291?
a tens
b hundreds
c thousands (circled)
d NG

2 8,235 ◯ 8,325
a < (circled)
b >
c =

3 529 + 487
a 906
b 916
c 1,016 (circled)
d NG

4 $124.95 + 93.27
a $218.22 (circled)
b $227.22
c $228.22
d NG

5 Estimate the sum. 6,753 + 5,215
a 10,000
b 11,000
c 12,000 (circled)
d NG

6 7,096 − 4,398
a 3,402
b 3,798
c 3,708
d NG (circled)

7 $547.83 − 78.49
a $468.34
b $469.34 (circled)
c $531.46
d NG

8 Estimate the difference. 8,643 − 7,500
a 1,400
b 1,500
c 1,600
d NG (circled)

9 38 × 7
a 264
b 266 (circled)
c 2,156
d NG

10 3,209 × 4
a 12,836 (circled)
b 12,876
c 128,036
d NG

11 37 × 54
a 323
b 1,798
c 1,898
d NG (circled)

12 5)83
a 16
b 16 R3 (circled)
c 17
d NG

13 4)4,204
a 151
b 1,051 (circled)
c 1,501
d NG

☐ score

96

Cumulative Review

page 96

Item	Objective
1	Identify place value in a number less than 1,000,000 (See pages 11-12)
2	Compare and order numbers through thousands (See pages 9-10)
3	Add two numbers with sums less than 1,000, one regrouping (See pages 23-24)
4	Add two numbers up to 5-digits (See pages 27-28)
5	Estimate sums by rounding to the nearest 1,000 and adding (See pages 29-30)
6	Subtract up to 4-digit numbers, zeros in the minuend (See pages 33-34)
7	Subtract two numbers up to 6-digits (See pages 35-36)
8	Estimate differences by rounding to the nearest 100 and subtracting (See pages 37-38)
9	Multiply a 2-digit by a 1-digit factor (See pages 53-54)
10	Multiply up to a 6-digit by 1-digit factor (See pages 55-56)
11	Multiply two 2-digit factors (See pages 57-58)
12	Divide a 2-digit by 1-digit number, quotient with remainder (See pages 79-80)
13	Divide up to 6-digits, by 1-digit number, quotient with zero (See pages 87-88)

Alternate Cumulative Review

Circle the letter of the correct answer.

1 Give the place value of the 4 in 614,852.
a tens
b hundreds
c thousands (circled)
d NG

2 9,457 ◯ 9,547
a < (circled)
b >
c =

3 348 + 561
a 809
b 919
c 909 (circled)
d NG

4 $235.86 + 81.47
a $317.33 (circled)
b $326.33
c $327.33
d NG

5 Estimate the sum by rounding to the nearest thousand.
7,901 + 5,501
a 12,000
b 13,000
c 14,000 (circled)
d NG

6 8,075 − 4,279
a 2,796
b 3,896
c 4,796
d NG (circled)

7 $356.92 − 67.48
a $288.44
b $289.44 (circled)
c $311.56
d NG

8 Estimate the difference by rounding to the nearest hundred.
9,721 − 7,600
a 2,000
b 2,200
c 2,300
d NG (circled)

9 24 ×8
a 102
b 192 (circled)
c 1,632
d NG

10 4,608 ×3
a 13,824 (circled)
b 13,854
c 138,024
d NG

11 56 × 38
a 2,126
b 2,028
c 2,128 (circled)
d NG

12 4)75
a 18
b 18 R3 (circled)
c 183
d NG

96

Dividing by Multiples of Ten

pages 97-98

Objective

To divide 2- or 3-digit numbers by multiples of 10

Materials

100 facts division test

Mental Math

Have students add:

1. 23 + 7 (30)
2. 45 + 9 (54)
3. 17 + 20 (37)
4. 55 + 13 (68)
5. 29 + 6 (35)
6. 14 + 24 (38)
7. 49 + 15 (64)

Skill Review

Prepare a page of 100 basic division problems. Ask students to work through the page as quickly as possible. See how many can finish in three minutes. Have students check each other's work and review with the class any facts frequently missed.

Dividing by Multiples of 10

Fran is recording the results of her timed science experiment. How many minutes and seconds did her experiment take?

We want to find the number of minutes and seconds Fran's experiment took.

We know Fran's experiment took __500__ seconds.

There are __60__ seconds in 1 minute.
To find the minutes spent on her experiment, we divide the total seconds by the number of seconds in 1 minute. The remainder will represent the number of seconds.

We divide __500__ by __60__.

First, decide where to start.

$$60\overline{)500}$$ 60 > 5   Not enough hundreds
Rename the 5 hundreds as 50 tens.

60 > 50   Not enough tens
Rename the 50 tens as 500 ones.

60 < 500   Start with 500 ones.

Divide.

```
        8  ← minutes
60)500
   480
    20  ← seconds
```

Check.

```
   60  ← divisor
 ×  8  ← quotient
  480
+  20  ← remainder
  500  ← dividend
```

The experiment took __8__ minutes and __20__ seconds.

Getting Started

Divide and check.

1. $30\overline{)120}$ → 4

2. $20\overline{)45}$ → 2 R5

Copy and divide.

3. 421 ÷ 50   8 R21

4. 86 ÷ 70   1 R16

MCP All rights reserved

97

Teaching the Lesson

Introducing the Problem   Read the problem aloud. Have students read and complete the information sentences. Read the plan sentences aloud having students supply the answers. Work through the steps of the model with students. Tell students to estimate an answer by thinking that the number of sixties in 500 will be the same as the number of sixes in 50, or about 8. Have a student work the problem on the board, using 8 as the quotient. Have another student label the answer. (8 minutes, 20 seconds) Show students that to check the answer, they will multiply and add. Have students complete the solution sentence.

Developing the Skill   Explain that each time they divide by a multiple of ten, they will find it easier to approximate an answer before they try any quotient. Explain that the placement of the first digit in the quotient is important, and depends on where they were able to actually begin dividing. Put this example on the board:

$$60\overline{)454} \quad (7\ R34)$$

Ask if there are sixties in 4, in 45 or in 454. (454) Explain that because the division has to include hundreds, tens and ones, the quotient will be written above ones. Point out that they can approximate the answer. There are as many sixties in 454 as there are sixes in 45, or about 7. Have a student work the problem on the board.

Practice

Divide and check.

1. 7)420   6

2. 80)560   7

3. 30)180   6

4. 50)400   8

5. 60)425   7 R5

6. 90)634   7 R4

7. 40)212   5 R12

8. 20)142   7 R2

9. 30)212   7 R2

10. 50)$150 $3

11. 80)719   8 R79

12. 70)650   9 R20

13. 20)105   5 R5

14. 90)736   8 R16

15. 40)45   1 R5

16. 60)490   8 R10

Copy and Do

17. 536 ÷ 60
    8 R56

18. 248 ÷ 50
    4 R48

19. 177 ÷ 20
    8 R17

20. 735 ÷ 90
    8 R15

21. 109 ÷ 40
    2 R29

22. $560 ÷ 70
    $8

23. 136 ÷ 30
    4 R16

24. 700 ÷ 80
    8 R60

25. 512 ÷ 60
    8 R32

26. 126 ÷ 90
    1 R36

27. 360 ÷ 60
    6

28. 216 ÷ 70
    3 R6

Apply

Solve these problems.

29. In April, Dino spent 30 hours delivering 500 directories for the phone company. He earned $120. How much did Dino earn each hour he worked?
    $4

30. It takes 480 minutes to travel from San Francisco to San Diego. How many hours does it take to travel between the two cities?
    8 hours

31. Mrs. Gomez bought a car that averages 30 miles to each gallon of gas. She drove 270 miles. How many gallons of gas did she use?
    9 gallons

32. If a tablet of writing paper contains 80 sheets and costs $1.15, what would you expect to pay for a total of 560 sheets of paper?
    $8.05

98

Correcting Common Errors

Watch for students who forget to write the remainder in their answer. Encourage them to check their answers by multiplying the quotient times the divisor to see that they must add the remainder in order to obtain the dividend.

Enrichment

Have students work the following problems: 40 ÷ 8 (5), 400 ÷ 8 (50), 4,000 ÷ 8 (500). Ask them to identify the pattern. Have students create 3 division problems that develop a pattern and exchange with a partner to work.

Practice

Have students complete the problems on the page. Remind them to approximate the quotient before they begin dividing.

Extra Credit *Sets*

Remind students how to construct a Venn diagram and dictate the following: Washington High School has many student activities, including the Chess Club and the Math Club. The members of the Chess Club are Bob, Sue, Frank, Jim, Ted and Ellen. The members of the Math Club are Pete, Andy, Ellen, Michelle, Jim, Carol and Bob.
Construct the Venn diagram, indicating the universal set and the elements which belong in subsets A, B and C.

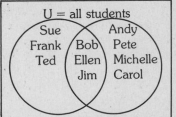

1-digit Quotients

pages 99-100

Objective

To divide a 2- or 3-
digit number by a 2-digit number

Materials

Mental Math

Have students identify the digit in the
hundreds place:

1. 672 (6)
2. 34,390 (3)
3. 52 (none)
4. 1,339,592 (5)
5. 552,947 (9)
6. 400,051 (0)
7. 1,830 (8)
8. 5,449,830 (8)

Skill Review

Review division by multiples of 10.
Ask students to work these problems
on the board while the others work
them at their seats:

1. $\frac{(7)}{40\overline{)280}}$ 2. $\frac{(9\,R36)}{60\overline{)576}}$
3. $\frac{(8\,R25)}{50\overline{)425}}$ 4. $\frac{(6\,R28)}{90\overline{)568}}$

Dividing, 1-digit Quotients

Kwan wants to use the store's credit
plan to buy a television that costs
$289. About how much will he have to
pay each week?

We want to find Kwan's approximate
weekly payment.

The television costs $289 .

Kwan has 32 weeks to pay.

To determine Kwan's weekly payment,
we divide the total cost by the number
of weeks in the store's payment plan.

We divide $289 by 32 .

Decide where to start.

$$32\overline{)\$289}$$

32 > 2   Not enough hundreds, rename as tens.
32 > 28   Not enough tens, rename as ones.
Start with 289 ones.

Divide.
Round the divisor
to the nearest 10.
Estimate how many
30's are in 289.

$$\begin{array}{r} \$9\,R1 \\ 32\overline{)\$289} \\ 288 \\ \hline 1 \end{array}$$

Check.

$$\begin{array}{r} 32 \leftarrow \text{divisor} \\ \times\ 9 \leftarrow \text{quotient} \\ \hline 288 \\ +\ \ 1 \leftarrow \text{remainder} \\ \hline 289 \leftarrow \text{dividend} \end{array}$$

Kwan will pay about $9 each week.

Getting Started

Divide and check.

1. $\overset{7\,R5}{13\overline{)96}}$ 2. $\overset{8}{22\overline{)176}}$ 3. $\overset{2\,R16}{49\overline{)114}}$ 4. $\overset{3\,R8}{54\overline{)170}}$

Copy and divide.

5. 260 ÷ 27
   9 R17

6. 208 ÷ 45
   4 R28

7. 242 ÷ 29
   8 R10

8. 465 ÷ 78
   5 R75

MCP All rights reserved

99

Teaching the Lesson

Introducing the Problem   Read the problem aloud and
then have students read and complete the information sentences. Read the plan sentences aloud and have students
supply answers. Ask students to look at the problem worked
in their texts. Have a student explain where the division will
begin. (the number of thirty-twos in 289) Ask students to
round the divisor and dividend to the nearest ten (30, 290)
and estimate the number of thirties in 290. (9) Remind
them that the number of thirties in 290 is the same as the
number of threes in 29. Have a student do the division on
the board. (9 R1) Point out the multiplication and addition
check, and have students complete the solution sentence.

Developing the Skill   Write these steps on the board:

1. **Decide where to start the division.**
2. **Round divisor and dividend.**
3. **Simplify the problem.**

4. **Estimate a quotient.**
5. **Divide.**

Write this example on the board:

$$52\overline{)364}^{(7)}$$

Show students that they will have to start with 364 ones.
They will round divisor and dividend to 50 and 360. They
will simplify, remembering that 360 ÷ 50 is the same as
36 ÷ 5, or about 7. The estimate will be 7 and they can
proceed to divide. Have students do these problems using
the five steps:

521 ÷ 73 (7 R10)   567 ÷ 87 (6 R45)

99

Practice

Divide and check.

1. $\overset{8 \text{ R4}}{43\overline{)348}}$ 2. $\overset{6 \text{ R6}}{32\overline{)198}}$ 3. $\overset{3 \text{ R2}}{46\overline{)140}}$ 4. $\overset{6}{49\overline{)294}}$

5. $\overset{8 \text{ R18}}{53\overline{)442}}$ 6. $\overset{5 \text{ R2}}{87\overline{)437}}$ 7. $\overset{2 \text{ R1}}{51\overline{)103}}$ 8. $\overset{9 \text{ R1}}{73\overline{)658}}$

9. $\overset{6 \text{ R37}}{88\overline{)565}}$ 10. $\overset{\$7}{46\overline{)\$322}}$ 11. $\overset{9 \text{ R18}}{92\overline{)846}}$ 12. $\overset{8 \text{ R39}}{67\overline{)575}}$

Copy and Do

13. $232 \div 43$
    5 R17
14. $516 \div 94$
    5 R46
15. $\$128 \div 32$
    $4
16. $210 \div 48$
    4 R18

17. $616 \div 83$
    7 R35
18. $561 \div 58$
    9 R39
19. $438 \div 72$
    6 R6
20. $534 \div 62$
    8 R38

21. $752 \div 91$
    8 R24
22. $682 \div 75$
    9 R7
23. $432 \div 64$
    6 R48
24. $\$165 \div 15$
    $11

Apply

Solve these problems.

25. It took Megan 54 weeks to save $275 towards her airfare to Hawaii. About how much did Megan save each week?
$5

26. Mr. Rinoldi made car payments for 39 months. If each payment was $226, how much did Mr. Rinoldi pay for his car?
$8,814

EXCURSION

Twin primes are any two prime numbers which differ by 2.
For example, 11 and 13 are twin primes because $13 - 11 = 2$.
Write three other sets of twin primes less than 100.

    3 and 5, 5 and 7, 17 and 19, 29 and 31, 41 and 43, 59 and 61, 71 and 73

100

Some students may have difficulty deciding where to place the first digit in the quotient. Have them multiply the divisor by 1, 10, and 100 to help them decide.

$$1 \times 59 = 59$$
$$59\overline{)482} \rightarrow$$
$$10 \times 59 = 590$$
$$100 \times 59 = 5,900$$

Enrichment

Ask students to calculate the following: In a city of 36,000 people, there are 90 doctors. On the average, how many people does each doctor care for? (400) In a poor country, 360,000 people depend on 90 doctors. How many people does each of these doctors care for? (4,000) During great migrations or famine, as many as 3,600,000 may depend on only 90 doctors. How many people must each handle? (40,000)

Practice

Have students complete the problems on the page. Remind them to round and estimate before they begin to divide.

Excursion

This should be a timed exercise since there are an infinite number of twin primes. The Sieve of Eratosthenes is the quickest way to search for twin primes.

Extra Credit   *Logic*

Duplicate the following for students to solve:
The teacher returned to class to find four boys fighting and asked them who started the fight.

Paul said it was Larry. Larry said John did it. Mike said, "It wasn't me." John said, "Larry's a liar."

The rest of the class then told the teacher that 1 boy was lying and 3 were being truthful. The teacher thought briefly, and then took the guilty boy to the office. Who started the fight? (Larry)

Estimating Quotients

pages 101-102

Objective

To estimate when dividing a 2- or 3-digit dividend by a 2-digit divisor

Materials

Mental Math

Ask students to give the total:

1. 25¢ + 5¢ + 5¢ = (35¢)
2. $1 + 50¢ + 10¢ = ($1.60)
3. 10¢ + 1¢ + 25¢ + 25¢ = (61¢)
4. 50¢ + 10¢ + 10¢ = (70¢)
5. $5 + $5 + $1 + 50¢ = ($11.50)
6. $10 + 25¢ + 50¢ = ($10.75)
7. 25¢ + 25¢ + 25¢ = (75¢)

Skill Review

Have students round divisor and dividend to the nearest ten and do the division:

1. 477 ÷ 52 (480 ÷ 50) (9 R9)
2. 256 ÷ 41 (260 ÷ 40) (6 R10)
3. 640 ÷ 68 (640 ÷ 70) (9 R28)
4. 804 ÷ 90 (800 ÷ 90) (8 R84)
5. 623 ÷ 72 (620 ÷ 70) (8 R47)
6. 180 ÷ 26 (180 ÷ 30) (6 R24)
7. 296 ÷ 39 (300 ÷ 40) (7 R23)

Estimating, 1-digit Quotients

Mark worked the division problem 176 ÷ 24 at the board. Mark's classmates disagreed with his answer. What did Mark do wrong?

We are looking for the correct quotient for the problem 176 ÷ 24.

When Mark rounded 24 to __20__ and estimated the quotient, he got __8__. He estimated there are __8__ 24's in 176. But when he tried __8__, his product was larger than 176. He must try a smaller quotient.

Sometimes, the first quotient we try gives a product larger than the dividend. Then a __smaller__ number must be tried.

How many 24's in 176?

$$24\overline{)176} \quad \text{(Try 8.)}$$
$$192 \quad \text{(Too big)}$$

Try again!

$$24\overline{)176} \quad 7\ R8 \quad \text{(Try 7.)}$$
$$168 \quad \text{(It works.)}$$
$$8$$

The correct quotient for the problem 176 ÷ 24 is __7 R8__.

Getting Started

Divide and check.

1. $38\overline{)228}$ → 6
2. $59\overline{)435}$ → 7 R22
3. $17\overline{)99}$ → 5 R14

4. $48\overline{)346}$ → 7 R10
5. $39\overline{)238}$ → 6 R4
6. $23\overline{)138}$ → 6

Copy and divide.

7. 232 ÷ 25 9 R7
8. 265 ÷ 37 7 R6
9. 814 ÷ 95 8 R54
10. 217 ÷ 35 6 R7
11. 547 ÷ 61 8 R59
12. 483 ÷ 53 9 R6

MCP All rights reserved

101

Teaching the Lesson

Introducing the Problem Read the problem aloud. Have students examine the model problem, and then ask a student to read and complete the information sentences. Read the plan sentences and ask students to supply the answer. Tell students to look at the problem worked twice in the model. Explain that they can get a quotient that is too large (quotient/divisor product is larger than the dividend) or too small. (difference between quotient/divisor product is larger than divisor) Show that in the first problem the quotient was too big, and subtraction was impossible. In the second problem the quotient was reduced by one and the problem completed. Have students read and complete the solution sentence.

Developing the Skill Show students these two examples; one in which the estimated quotient is too big, the other in which it is too small:

$43\overline{)241} \rightarrow 40\overline{)240}$ Estimate the quotient is 6.
$$43\overline{)241}^{\ 6} \\ -258$$

$15\overline{)149} \rightarrow 20\overline{)150}$ Estimate the quotient is 7.
$$15\overline{)149}^{\ 7} \\ -105 \\ \overline{44 > 15}$$

Explain that if the first estimate is incorrect, they should correct the quotient in the appropriate direction and start again.

Divide and check.

1. 52)436   8 R20

2. 38)216   5 R26

3. 58)412   7 R6

4. 16)$144 $9

5. 64)486   7 R38

6. 85)396   4 R56

7. 39)106   2 R28

8. 73)680   9 R23

9. 94)658   7

10. 23)112   4 R20

11. 48)288   6

12. 62)509   8 R13

Copy and Do

13. 86 ÷ 12
    7 R2

14. 247 ÷ 34
    7 R9

15. 315 ÷ 76
    4 R11

16. 612 ÷ 89
    6 R78

17. 295 ÷ 43
    6 R37

18. $416 ÷ 52
    $8

19. 185 ÷ 96
    1 R89

20. 150 ÷ 27
    5 R15

Apply

Solve these problems.

21. In July, Wally's Campground supplied 527 gallons of drinking water to its campers from a tank which can hold 85 gallons. How many times was the tank filled that month?
    7 times

22. The Brittingham College alumni band concert is a popular fund raiser. This year, 846 concert tickets were sold for $12 each. How much money was collected for the benefit of the college?
    $10,152

23. One tree produced 175 avocados. The avocados are packaged in boxes of 24. How many boxes are needed?
    8 boxes

24. Rose bought a schnauzer for $250. Her parents agreed to pay the down payment of $42. Rose paid the rest in equal payments for 26 weeks. What did Rose pay each week?
    $8

102

Correcting Common Errors

Some students may have difficulty estimating quotients. Have them tell whether the following quotients are too large or too small; then have them divide correctly.

```
        7
  23)142    (too large; 6 R4)
   − 161
```

```
        9
  41)359    (too large, 8 R31)
   − 369
```

```
        6
  25)179    (too small, 7 R4)
   − 150
```

Enrichment

Remind students that area can be calculated by multiplying length by width. These figures represent dimensions of the rooms in a house. Ask that they calculate the area of each room (in square feet) and then find the area of an average room in the house.

Living Room: 20 ft × 15 ft (300 sq ft)
Kitchen: 12 ft × 17 ft (204 sq ft)
Bedroom: 12 ft × 12 ft (144 sq ft)
Bedroom: 13 ft × 14 ft (182 sq ft)
Bathroom: 8 ft × 10 ft (80 sq ft)
Average: (182 sq ft)

Practice

Have students complete the problems. Suggest they use extra paper for the first quotient.

Mixed Practice

1. 321 × 27 (8,667)
2. 143 ÷ 20 (7 R3)
3. 9 + 4 + 7 + 8 (28)
4. 4,376 × 8 (35,008)
5. $258.90 − $69.08 ($189.82)
6. 380 ÷ 47 (8 R4)
7. 900 × 700 (630,000)
8. 6,541 ÷ 7 (934 R3)
9. 5 × 3,275 (16,375)
10. 28,156 + 17,494 (45,650)

Extra Credit   *Numeration*

Show students this diagram of a medieval counting board:

−X−   (thousands)
 •   (five hundreds)
───   (hundreds)
       (fifties)
•••• (tens)
 •   (fives)
─•─   (ones)

The number shown is 546. Tell the class that the counting board works much like an abacus. A pebble or counter on the line stood for a single unit of the given place value. Point out that the X on the thousands line was to help them remember which place they were in just as the comma we put between thousands and hundreds helps us read large numbers. Have students show on paper what the counters for the number 153 would look like. Then have them show the position of the counters after 462 has been added. Have them try a variety of problems on paper or on a simple model made out of cardboard and counters.

2-digit Quotients

pages 103-104

Objective

To divide a 3- or 4-digit dividend by a 2-digit divisor

Materials

Mental Math

Ask students to identify the larger quantity:

1. 3×3 or $10 \div 1$ $(10 \div 1 = 10)$
2. 12×2 or 5×5 $(5 \times 5 = 25)$
3. $15 + 5$ or 3×7 $(3 \times 7 = 21)$
4. $100 \div 10$ or 4×3 $(4 \times 3 = 12)$
5. 7×7 or $100 \div 2$ $(100 \div 2 = 50)$
6. 4×0 or $0 \div 4$ $(4 \times 0 = 0, 0 \div 4 = 0,$ same)

Skill Review

Have students work these problems. Remind them to revise the quotient if necessary.

1. (7)   2. (7 R13)
   37)259   19)146
3. (8 R26)   4. (5 R1)
   65)546   29)146

Dividing, 2-digit Quotients

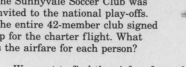

The Sunnyvale Soccer Club was invited to the national play-offs. The entire 42-member club signed up for the charter flight. What is the airfare for each person?

We want to find the airfare for each club member.

The charter air flight costs $3,486 .

There were __42__ members on the flight.

We find the per-person cost by dividing the total cost of the charter flight by the number of passengers.

We divide $3,486 by __42__.

Decide where to start.

42)3 48 6

$42 > 3$ Not enough thousands
$42 > 34$ Not enough hundreds
Start with 348 tens.

Divide the tens.
How many 40's in 348?
About 8

```
        8
42 )$3 48 6
    3 36
      12
```

Divide the ones.
How many 40's in 126?
About 3

```
       $83
42 )$3,486
    3 36
      126
      126
        0
```

Each person pays __$83__ .

Getting Started

Divide and check.

1. 23 ; 38)874
2. $83 ; 32)$2,656
3. 24 ; 68)1,632

4. 23 ; 67)1,541
5. 43 R29 ; 58)2,523
6. 33 R9 ; 94)3,111

Copy and divide.

7. $1,345 \div 15$ **89 R10**
8. $5,470 \div 82$ **66 R58**
9. $2,706 \div 33$ **82**
10. $143 \div 15$ **9 R8**
11. $\$1,505 \div 43$ **$35**
12. $392 \div 24$ **16 R8**

103

MCP All rights reserved

Teaching the Lesson

Introducing the Problem Read the problem aloud. Ask a student to find the required facts in the illustration and then fill in the information sentences. Read the plan sentences and have students supply answers. Write the division steps on the board: **divide, multiply, subtract, compare** and **bring down.** Work through each step of the model. Have the answer read, and then have students complete the solution sentence.

Developing the Skill Explain that these problems will not differ from the division they have already done. In each case they will decide where to start by comparing the divisor to the first digits of the dividend. Then they will follow the basic steps, revising the quotient and starting again if necessary. Point out that when the quotient has two digits, they will have to estimate a quotient twice. This means that there are two times when they may guess incorrectly and have to revise the quotient. Suggest that students use paper when

doing this division to try out quotients they have estimated. Work this problem with the class:

```
       12                 13
37)  481            37)  481
   - 37               - 37
     111                111
   - 74               - 111
     37 Whoops          0 Correct
```

103

Divide and check.

1. 31)899 — 29

2. 46)908 — 19 R34

3. 23)529 — 23

4. 56)730 — 13 R2

5. 65)5,790 — 89 R5

6. 23)563 — 24 R11

7. 71)1,988 — 28

8. 83)1,411 — 17

9. 79)1,659 — 21

Copy and Do

10. 154 ÷ 22 7

11. 493 ÷ 29 17

12. 648 ÷ 38 17 R2

13. 2,401 ÷ 49 49

14. 2,108 ÷ 62 34

15. 1,890 ÷ 51 37 R3

16. 1,270 ÷ 67 18 R64

17. 7,052 ÷ 82 86

18. 3,591 ÷ 63 57

EXCURSION

Think of a number. Multiply it by 2. Add 6. Subtract 3. Add 13. Divide this sum by 2. Subtract the original number. The answer is 8. Try it again with another number. Why does this work?

See TE notes.

Correcting Common Errors

Some students may forget to bring down the ones digit in order to obtain ones in the quotient. Have them do the division showing the partial products, subtracting until the answer is less than the divisor.

```
        16 R4
         6
        10
    47)756
    − 470  ← 10 × 47
       286
    − 282  ← 6 × 47
         4
```

Enrichment

Have students use calculators to solve this problem: A summer camp has decided to build a bunkhouse of 2,650 square feet. It will have a hallway, 5 ft × 50 ft, and rooms that are each 10 ft × 12 ft. How many rooms will there be? (20 rooms) If the cost is $35 per square foot, how much will the building cost? ($92,750)

Practice

Have students work the problems on the page. Remind them to bring remainders up.

Excursion

Suggest that some letter be used to represent the original number. Then write out the various steps in the procedure and simplify each time.

$$\left[(2 \times n + 6 - 3 + 13) \times \frac{1}{2} - n\right]$$

$$\left[(2n + 16) \times \frac{1}{2}\right] - n$$

$$\left[n + 8\right] - n = 8$$

Extra Credit *Measurement*

Working in small groups, have students plan a city playground. Provide them with ½-inch graph paper. Tell them the scale for the drawing is ½ in. = 1 foot. All equipment, sidewalks and benches, etc. and areas on the playground must be drawn to scale. Tell them to include swings, slides, a water area, tennis courts and a picnic area, plus any other equipment they choose.

Estimating Quotients

pages 105-106

Objective

To estimate 2-digit quotients with up to 4-digit dividends and 2-digit divisors

Materials

Mental Math

Ask students to round these numbers to the nearest 10 and the nearest 100.

1. 338 (340, 300)
2. 1,289 (1,290, 1,300)
3. 552 (550, 600)
4. 92 (90, 100)
5. 4,384 (4,380, 4,400)
6. 45 (50, 0)
7. 625 (630, 600)

Skill Review

Have students review 2-digit division, working these problems on paper.

1.   (38)
   27)1,026
2.   (56 R45)
   55)3,125
3.   (29 R50)
   87)2,573
4.   (75 R18)
   63)4,743

Finding 2-digit Quotients

Roberta Chen kept track of the gasoline used and miles driven on her family's vacation. Her family drove 1,512 miles. How many miles to the gallon did they average?

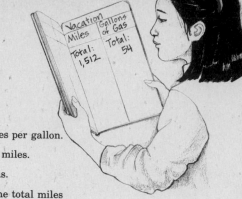

We need to find the average miles per gallon.

The Chen family drove __1,512__ miles.

They used __54__ gallons of gas.

To find the average, we divide the total miles driven by the number of gallons used on the trip.

We divide __1,512__ by __54__.

Decide where to start.

$$54\overline{)1{,}51\,2}$$

$54 > 1$ Not enough thousands
$54 > 15$ Not enough hundreds
Start with 151 tens.

Divide the tens. How many 50's in 151? Try 3. $3 \times 54 = 162$ 3 is too big.

$$\begin{array}{r} 3 \\ 54\overline{)1{,}51\,2} \\ 1\,62 \end{array}$$

Try again! Try 2. $2 \times 54 = 108$ 2 works. Subtract and bring down the ones. Continue dividing.

$$\begin{array}{r} 2\,8 \\ 54\overline{)1{,}51\,2} \\ 1\,08 \\ \hline 4\,3\,2 \\ 4\,3\,2 \\ \hline 0 \end{array}$$

The Chen family averaged __28__ miles per gallon.

Getting Started

Divide and check.

1. 13)371   **28 R7**
2. 28)1,988   **71**
3. 37)1,752   **47 R13**

Copy and divide.

4. 3,278 ÷ 36   **91 R2**
5. 3,273 ÷ 52   **62 R49**
6. 6,412 ÷ 75   **85 R37**

MCP All rights reserved

105

Teaching the Lesson

Introducing the Problem   Read the problem aloud and point to the illustration indicating mileage and gas consumption. Have students read and complete the information and plan sentences. Work through each step of the model problem with students. Have a student work the problem on the board, starting with a quotient of 2 tens. Have one student read the final quotient. Then have students complete the solution sentence.

Developing the Skill   Remind students of the steps they go through in the division problem. Explain that these problems will not differ. Show these two examples on the board, having them round to get started:

$$45\overline{)3{,}165} \;\rightarrow\; 50\overline{)3{,}200}^{\,(64)}$$

Have a student work the division through to arrive at the exact quotient. (70 R15) Have a student check their division by multiplication on the board.

Practice

Divide and check.

1. $12\overline{)348}$ **29**

2. $64\overline{)2,432}$ **38**

3. $38\overline{)2,095}$ **55 R5**

4. $51\overline{)3,425}$ **67 R8**

5. $72\overline{)3,721}$ **51 R49**

6. $24\overline{)1,468}$ **61 R4**

7. $39\overline{)2,408}$ **61 R29**

8. $93\overline{)9,225}$ **99 R18**

9. $86\overline{)3,250}$ **37 R68**

Copy and Do

10. $4,247 \div 45$ **94 R17**

11. $5,219 \div 63$ **82 R53**

12. $2,176 \div 37$ **58 R30**

13. $1,290 \div 21$ **61 R9**

14. $7,056 \div 75$ **94 R6**

15. $4,238 \div 58$ **73 R4**

16. $6,453 \div 84$ **76 R69**

17. $1,916 \div 28$ **68 R12**

18. $7,391 \div 93$ **79 R44**

Apply

Solve these problems.

19. How many days are in 864 hours?
    36 days

20. Ken has collected 336 colored eggs for the Jaycee's annual Easter egg hunt. He will put them in 1-dozen cartons to prevent breakage. How many cartons does Ken need?
    28 cartons

21. Mr. Murray paid $1,274 for a stereo system. He paid for the system in equal installments over 26 weeks. What were Mr. Murray's weekly payments?
    $49

22. Wimona's car gets 32 miles to a gallon of gas. If gas costs $0.96 per gallon, how much does it cost her to drive 1,504 miles?
    $45.12

106

Correcting Common Errors

Some students, when they fail to notice that their first estimate is too little, divide again and place a 1 as the second digit in the quotient.

INCORRECT

$$
\begin{array}{r}
313 \\
23\overline{)989} \\
-69 \\
\hline
29 \\
-23 \\
\hline
69 \\
-69 \\
\hline
0
\end{array}
$$

CORRECT

$$
\begin{array}{r}
43 \\
23\overline{)989} \\
-92 \\
\hline
69 \\
-69 \\
\hline
0
\end{array}
$$

Make sure they always compare after they subtract in the 4-step process of: Divide; Multiply; Subtract; Compare.

Enrichment

Ask students to recall Mrs. Chen and the gas mileage. Ask them to figure out how Mrs. Chen knew how many gallons of gas she had used. Remind them that you can not see into a gas tank and that the gauge indicating the amount of gas in the tank is an approximate measure showing only full and empty. (The usual method is to start the trip with a full tank, fill the tank again at the end of the trip, and add up the number of gallons bought.)

Practice

Have students complete the practice problems. Suggest that they check all problems by multiplication and addition.

Mixed Practice

1. $1,989 \div 34$ (58 R17)
2. $52,070 - 48,764$ (3,306)
3. $12,256 + 3,451 + 25,195$ (40,902)
4. $9 \times \$15.07$ ($135.63)
5. $4,722 \div 3$ (1,574)
6. $27 + 85 + 91 + 76$ (279)
7. $95,817 - 14,121$ (81,696)
8. $20 \times 24,024$ (480,480)
9. $3,878 \div 40$ (96 R38)
10. 324×791 (256,284)

Extra Credit   *Applications*

Have students collect schedules from a commercial bus line for this project. Have students study the schedules and practice reading them. Identify route numbers, departures, arrivals and fares. Have students work in pairs and take turns being a ticket seller or driver for the bus company and a traveling customer. Their job is to answer questions from the customer about the schedule. For example: What is the cheapest fare to Chicago? What is the earliest bus to any city on Tuesday? When does it arrive, and how long will it take to get there? As an extension, have students report on other types of transportation that use schedules of this kind.

Dividing Larger Numbers

pages 107-108

Objective

To divide dividends through 5 digits by 2-digit divisors

Materials

Mental Math

Have students calculate:

1. $5 + 4 - 2 + 10 = (17)$
2. $12 - 4 + 5 - 3 = (10)$
3. $5 + 15 - 4 + 2 = (18)$
4. $7 + 0 - 3 + 13 = (17)$
5. $20 - 1 + 3 - 7 = (15)$
6. $14 + 7 - 9 + 2 = (14)$
7. $3 + 3 + 3 - 7 = (2)$

Skill Review

Have students work these problems on paper, then have volunteers do them on the board. Remind them of the steps: decide where to begin, divide, multiply, subtract, compare, bring down.

1. (25) 34)850
2. (86) 64)5,504
3. (63 R77) 93)5,936

Dividing Larger Numbers

Lime Delight is a popular new soft drink bottled by The Natural Soda Company. It is shipped to market in wooden cases of 24 each. How many cases are filled each day?

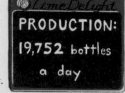

We need to find the number of cases filled each day.

The Natural Soda Company bottles __19,752__ sodas each day.

There are __24__ bottles in each case.

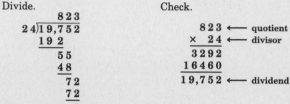

To find the number of cases, we divide the daily production by the number of bottles in each case.

We divide __19,752__ by __24__.

Decide where to start.

24)19,752

24 > 1   Not enough ten thousands
24 > 19   Not enough thousands
Start with 197 hundreds.

Divide.

```
      823
24)19,752
   19 2
      55
      48
      72
      72
       0
```

Check.

```
      823  ← quotient
    ×  24  ← divisor
    3292
  16460
  19,752  ← dividend
```

The Natural Soda Company fills __823__ cases of Lime Delight each day.

Getting Started

Divide and check.

1. 256
   16)4,096

2. 274
   37)10,138

3. 628 R16
   58)36,440

Copy and divide.

4. $12,740 \div 79$ 161 R21

5. $23,098 \div 44$ 524 R42

6. $78,813 \div 81$ 973

107

MCP All rights reserved

Teaching the Lesson

Introducing the Problem   Have a student read the problem aloud. Ask another to examine the illustration and read the information sentences. Read the plan sentences and put the problem on the board. Tell students to start by dividing 24 into 197 hundreds. When that is determined, the steps are as before: divide, multiply, subtract, compare, bring down. Explain that the problem illustrated shows the correct quotient, but remind students that they will estimate each quotient and revise it if necessary. Point out the multiplication check, and ask a student to read the solution sentence. (fills 823 cases each day)

Developing the Skill   Put the steps for division on the board: **decide where to start, divide, multiply, subtract, compare** and **bring down.** Remind students that when they are estimating a quotient, it helps to round the divisor and dividend. Suggest that one way to make a good estimate the first time is to round the divisor up and the dividend down, no matter what the numbers are. Explain that this is counter to the usual procedure for rounding numbers. Work this problem with the class to show that dividing larger numbers is the same as division they have already done:

(457)
56)25,592

Practice

Divide and check.

1. $21\overline{)6,615}$ **315**

2. $67\overline{)10,318}$ **154**

3. $48\overline{)29,376}$ **612**

4. $68\overline{)37,148}$ **546 R20**

5. $82\overline{)50,456}$ **615 R26**

6. $93\overline{)76,680}$ **824 R48**

7. $45,752 \div 93$ **491 R89**

8. $56,443 \div 67$ **842 R29**

9. $49,747 \div 84$ **592 R19**

Copy and Do

10. $4,370 \div 38$ **115**

11. $14,504 \div 56$ **259**

12. $33,396 \div 46$ **726**

13. $31,683 \div 65$ **487 R28**

14. $29,658 \div 36$ **823 R30**

15. $54,069 \div 84$ **643 R57**

16. $62,700 \div 76$ **825**

17. $47,571 \div 57$ **834 R33**

18. $44,431 \div 92$ **482 R87**

19. $37,596 \div 43$ **874 R14**

20. $68,316 \div 86$ **794 R32**

21. $67,861 \div 79$ **859**

Apply

Solve these problems.

22. The Holden Novelty Company produces 17,010 drinking straws each day. The straws are packaged in boxes of 54. How many boxes are packaged each day?
315 boxes

23. The Bee Clean Solvents Company sells $1,706 worth of its product each day. The cost of doing business is $1,238 each day. How much is left over for profit?
$468

24. The Fast File Company files 567 cards each 8-hour day. How many cards can the Fast File Company file in 3 days?
1,701 cards

25. The Yellow Pencil Company sells pencils in cases of 36 for $1.75 per case. If 32,256 pencils are sold daily, how much money does the Yellow Pencil Company make each day?
$1,568

108

Correcting Common Errors

Watch for students who do not align their digits properly. Have them do their work on grid paper, using the squares to help them keep the digits aligned properly.

Enrichment

Put the following on the board:

$$12,345,679$$
$$\underline{\times 45}$$
$$(555,555,555)$$

Explain that the magic number (12,345,679) multiplied by 9 yields 111,111,111; by (2 × 9) or 18 yields 222,222,222; by (3 × 9), that is 27, gives 333,333,333 and so on. Have students find the reason this is true. (because 111,111,111 ÷ 9 = 12,345,679.)

Practice

Have students complete the practice problems. Suggest they show all their work.

Extra Credit   *Numeration*

Show students that the numeration system of the Aztecs did not use place value. They used these symbols:

    1   20   400   8,000

Point out that each unit was 20 times the previous unit. They modified the symbol for 400 to mean:

   100   200   300   400

Ask students to write the Aztec symbols for 732 and 1,300.

    (732)   (1,300)

Quotients With Zeros

pages 109-110

Objective

To divide up to 5-digit dividends to get quotients with zeros

Materials

Mental Math

Ask students to identify the next two answers in each series:

1. $2 \times 1, 2 + 2, 3 \times 2, \ldots$
   (2, 4, 6, 8, 10)
2. $6 \div 6, 10 \div 5, 3 \times 1, \ldots$
   (1, 2, 3, 4, 5)
3. $100 \div 10, 3 \times 3, 4 + 4, \ldots$
   (10, 9, 8, 7, 6)
4. $2 + 1, 12 \div 2, 45 \div 5, \ldots$
   (3, 6, 9, 12, 15)
5. $5 + 5, 4 \times 5, 15 \times 2, \ldots$
   (10, 20, 30, 40, 50)

Skill Review

Review division by 2-digit numbers by having students work these problems on paper. Ask volunteers to work them on the board when the class has finished:

1. (246)
    47)11,562
2. (683 R30)
    58)39,644

Dividing, Quotients with Zeros

Richard has been saving all the money he earned doing his paper route for a year. How much savings did Richard average each week?

We are asked to find Richard's average weekly savings.

Richard has saved __$315.64__ in one year.

There are __52__ weeks in one year.

To find Richard's weekly savings, we divide the total he saved by the number of weeks in a year.

We divide __$315.64__ by __52__.

```
        6
52 )$315.64
    312
     36
```
52 > 3
52 > 31
52 < 315
Start with 315 ones.
Divide, multiply, subtract and bring down.

```
        60
52 )$315.64
    312
     36
```
52 > 36
$36 \div 52 = 0$ with a remainder of 36.
Put 0 in the quotient.

```
      $6.07
52 )$315.64
    312
     364
     364
       0
```
Bring down the next digit and divide again. Place the dollar sign and decimal point in alignment with the dividend.

Check.
```
   $6.07
 ×    52
   1214
  30350
$315.64
```

Richard's average weekly savings were __$6.07__.

Getting Started

Divide and check.

1. $2.06
    26)$53.56
2. $4.80
    46)$220.80
3. 408 R31
    83)33,895

Copy and divide.

4. $45,000 \div 64$ 703 R8
5. $26,609 \div 38$ 700 R9
6. $65,088 \div 92$ 707 R44

109

Teaching the Lesson

Introducing the Problem Have a student read the problem aloud, and read and complete the information sentences. Read the plan sentence aloud and put the problem on the board. Ask a student to show the class where to start dividing. Remind students to divide, multiply, subtract and bring down the next digit. Finish the problem and put in the dollar sign and decimal point. Have a student read the solution sentence. (weekly savings were $6.07)

Developing the Skill Explain that the special challenge of the problems in this lesson is that sometimes when they bring down a digit, it is still not possible to divide. Give them this example:

```
        $3.01
  24)$72.24
    −72
      0 2
     − 0
       24
      −24
        0
```

Show that although you brought down the 2, it is not possible to divide 24 into 2. Because there are no 24's in 2, they will put a zero in the quotient to show that division in that place was not possible. Ask a student to complete the division.

Have students work this problem: $37,596 \div 53 =$ (709 R19).

109

Practice

Divide and check.

1. $\begin{array}{r} \$1.06 \\ 15\overline{)\$15.90} \end{array}$

2. $\begin{array}{r} \$4.06 \\ 29\overline{)\$117.74} \end{array}$

3. $\begin{array}{r} 406 \\ 65\overline{)26,390} \end{array}$

4. $\begin{array}{r} 460 \text{ R6} \\ 58\overline{)26,686} \end{array}$

5. $\begin{array}{r} \$7.06 \\ 72\overline{)\$508.32} \end{array}$

6. $\begin{array}{r} 905 \text{ R45} \\ 86\overline{)77,875} \end{array}$

7. $24,146 \div 59$
409 R15

8. $\$800.40 \div 87$
$9.20

9. $48,058 \div 68$
706 R50

Copy and Do

10. $4,715 \div 23$ 205

11. $\$216.77 \div 53$ $4.09

12. $23,829 \div 47$ 507

13. $38,955 \div 64$ 608 R43

14. $52,490 \div 87$ 603 R29

15. $\$608.00 \div 76$ $8.00

16. $33,615 \div 48$ 700 R15

17. $\$391.68 \div 96$ $4.08

18. $22,563 \div 28$ 805 R23

19. $\$553.88 \div 61$ $9.08

20. $27,265 \div 58$ 470 R5

21. $\$713.78 \div 89$ $8.02

Apply

Solve these problems.

22. Courtney subscribes to a weekly sports magazine for $108.16 a year. How much is she paying for each single copy?
$2.08

23. Ryan's new bike costs $146.88. If Ryan pays for the bike in 36 weeks, what are his weekly payments?
$4.08

EXCURSION

Try this number puzzle and see why it is called Double Vision. Write down any three-digit number and multiply it by 11. Then multiply that product by 91. What do you notice about the answer? Try it again with a new number. Can you figure out why this happens?

See TE notes.

110

Correcting Common Errors

Some students may forget to write one or more zeros in the quotient when required. Have them work with partners to do the division on grid paper. They should take turns deciding where the first digit of the quotient goes, and then both discuss each step that follows in the division algorithm. Use practice problems such as these.

1. $\begin{array}{r} (600 \text{ R49}) \\ 68\overline{)40,849} \end{array}$

2. $\begin{array}{r} (530 \text{ R22}) \\ 29\overline{)15,392} \end{array}$

Enrichment

Remind students how to do division on calculators. Explain that remainders are expressed as decimals. Show them that to find a whole number remainder they will take the whole number quotient, multiply by the divisor and subtract that product from the dividend. Demonstrate with this problem: $12,285 \div 84 = 146.25$; $146 \times 84 = 12,264$; $12,285 - 12,264 = 21$; and so $12,285 \div 84 = 146$ R21. Have them work these problems with calculators, expressing the answer with a remainder.

1. $49,871 \div 57$ (874 R53)
2. $14,503 \div 84$ (172 R55)

Practice

Have students complete the practice problems. Remind them that it is important to put a zero in the quotient each time they bring down a digit from the dividend, but find they cannot divide.

Excursion

The resulting number is a repeated 3-digit series. Encourage students to use a letter of the alphabet to represent his number in order to see what is happening. Point out that the problem works because of the mathematical principle, not the number chosen.

$$(n \times 11) \times 91 = n \times (11 \times 91) = n \times 1001$$

Ask if this would work for a four-digit number. What would happen to a two-digit number? (For a 4-digit number we would multiply by 10001. A search for factors of 10001 gives 73 and 137. So a 4-digit number should be multiplied by 73 and then 137.)

Extra Credit *Geometry*

Make a classroom mailbox out of a set of packing boxes. Boxes used for shipping bottles are especially good. Label the boxes with letters and numbers, and assign each student a set of coordinates. For example, Amy—B, 4; Steve—D, 3 and so on.

	A	B	C	D	E	F	G
1							
2							
3							
4							

Encourage students to learn their coordinates by using the mailboxes to return homework assignments and other class work. Change the assigned coordinates from time to time.

Problem Solving
Guess and Check

pages 111-112

Objective

To solve problems by estimating an answer

Materials

Mental Math

Have students estimate the quotient:

1. $329 \div 80 = (\approx 4)$
2. $253 \div 51 = (\approx 5)$
3. $181 \div 31 = (\approx 6)$
4. $209 \div 69 = (\approx 3)$
5. $99 \div 10 = (\approx 10)$
6. $545 \div 60 = (\approx 9)$
7. $729 \div 81 = (\approx 9)$

Guessing and Checking

Complete the division example by replacing the question marks with digits that will make the problem work.

★ SEE

We need to find the missing digits in this division problem.
We know: $2 \times 2 = 54$.
The 4 in the hundred's place was brought down.
When a number was subtracted from 4,

the result was ___6___.

The 3 in the ___ones___ place was brought down.

The remainder is ___19___.

★ PLAN

Using our knowledge of the division process, we make an educated guess to decide which digits are missing. As we replace each question mark, we use the information we get to help us decide the next digit.

★ DO

```
        24 22
  27 ⟌65413
     54
     11 4
     108
       61
       54
        7 3
        54
        19
```

- $2 \times 27 = 54$, so the missing digit in the divisor is 7.
- $14 - 8 = 6$, so we place an 8 below the 4.
- 27×4 ends in an 8, so we enter 4 in the quotient and multiply.
- $108 + 6 = 114$, so we enter 114 as the minuend.
- $54 + 11 = 65$, so 6 and 5 are the first two digits in the dividend.
Continue to find clues such as those shown here to complete the problem.

MCP All rights reserved

★ CHECK

To check division we can use multiplication and addition.

$27 \times \underline{2,422} = \underline{65,394} + \underline{19} = \underline{65,413}$

111

Teaching the Lesson

Read the problem aloud. Remind students of the SEE, PLAN, DO, CHECK method for solving problems. Explain that in this lesson they will estimate answers and try them to see how close their estimate is. Have a student read the SEE section of the text. Read the PLAN aloud. Put the problem on the board as it appears in the DO section of the text. Have a student fill in the numbers as others suggest possible answers. Help students find more clues and complete the problem together. Have a student read the dividend, divisor and quotient. (65,413 ÷ 27 = 2,422 R19) Point out that the check for division is multiplication. Have a student do this check on the board. (2,422 × 27 = 65,394; 65,394 + 19 = 65,413)

Apply

1. In a collection of quarters and nickels, there are 2 more nickels than quarters. How many nickels are there if the collection is worth $3.40?
13 nickels

2. Fill in each blank with a single digit to make this equation true.

   _9_63_,4_08_ × 7 = 6,743,_8_56

3. 2, 4, 6 is a set of 3 consecutive even numbers. 11, 13, 15 is a set of 3 consecutive odd numbers. Find a set of 3 consecutive even numbers whose sum is 216. Find a set of 4 consecutive odd numbers whose sum is 216.
70, 72, 74   51, 53, 55, 57

4. Solve this cryptarithm. Each letter stands for a unique digit.

HOCUS	92,836
+ POCUS	+ 12,836
PRESTO	105,672

5. What whole number between 10 and 100 is twice the product of its digits?
36

6. The same two numbers are added and subtracted. Each letter represents a different digit. Find all the digits.

XYZ	XYZ	945	945
+ AB	− AB	+ 78	− 78
CDEF	BGA	1,023	867

7. Using exactly four 4's, addition, subtraction, multiplication, division and parentheses, write an equation to equal each of the numbers from 0 to 9.
Answers will vary.

8. Find each missing digit if the remainder is the greatest possible remainder and explain how you did it.

   $$\square\square \overline{)161}\ \ \square\ R26$$

   See Solution Notes.

9. When you divide a 5-digit number by a 2-digit number, what is the greatest number of digits possible in the whole number part of the quotient?
See Solution Notes.

10. Write a problem that can be solved using Guessing and Checking. Choose 2 numbers. Give the sum and the product of the numbers to your classmates and ask them to find the numbers.
Problems will vary.

112

1. Suggest that students start with calculated guesses:

quarters	nickels	total
9 ($2.25)	11 ($.55)	$2.80
10 ($2.50)	12 ($.60)	$3.10
11 ($2.75)	13 ($.65)	$3.40

2. Have students make the problem a division problem.

3. Suggest students start by dividing 216 by 3. This gives the middle number 72. The series must be 70, 72, 74. Have them divide by 4 to find the middle of the series of odd numbers, 54. The series must be 51, 53, 55, 57.

4. Let students work in pairs. Point out that the last four digits of each addend are identical. P is repeated from addend to sum and must be a 1. This will help them see that H must be 9 and R = 0. Show that 0 must be less than 5, because nothing is carried over to the addition of H + P, and 0 is even because when S and S are added, they give 0. So 0 is either 2 or 4. Continue until students have a solution. (92,836 + 12,836 = 105,672)

5. Assign one group the numbers 10-20; another, 21-30; and so on. Have them search their own group for a number matching the requirements. [36 = 2 × (3 × 6)]

6. Let students work together following the pattern they used in Problem 4 to unravel information about single digits. Lead them off, noting that XYZ is large enough that when a 2-digit number is added, the sum goes to 4 digits. Explain that makes X = 9. For the same reason, AB is probably more than 50. (XYZ = 945, AB = 78)

7. Let students solve this in various ways. Examples might include: 44 − 44 = 0, 44 ÷ 44 = 1, (4 × 4) − (4 + 4) = 8, and so on. (Answers will vary.)

Higher-Order Thinking Skills

8. Analysis: If the remainder is the greatest possible, then the divisor is 1 more, or 27. Divide 161 by 27 and the quotient is 5 with a remainder of 26.

9. Synthesis: There will be one less digit than in the dividend, or 4 digits.

10. Synthesis

Extra Credit   *Numeration*

Put the following crypt-arithmetic problems on the board. Have students work in pairs to solve the codes and discover what numbers each of the letters represents. You may want to warn them the problems become progressively harder.

3A7	6C5	3E6	A5A
−1BA	+D2D	×2F	×3B
212	111C	9968	908

(A = 5   (C = 9   (E = 5   136B
B = 4)   D = 4)   F = 8)   1A5B8
                              (A = 4
| 70M4 | A9A9 | B = 2)
| − 835 | + B0B |
| 6PP9 | BABA |

(M = 6   (A is any digit,
P = 2)   B is one more than A)

When they have finished, have them make up problems for each other, making sure that they give enough information so that the problems can be solved.

Calculators and Averages

Objective

To use the division key on calculators

Materials

calculators

Mental Math

Ask students to estimate the quotient:

1. 240 ÷ 60 (4)
2. 300 ÷ 50 (6)
3. 400 ÷ 80 (5)
4. 155 ÷ 31 (5)
5. 820 ÷ 90 (9)
6. 141 ÷ 70 (2)
7. 103 ÷ 10 (10)

Skill Review

Remind students that to find the average of a set of numbers, they will add the numbers and then divide the sum by how many numbers are in the set. Ask them to find the average of these sets:

1. 23, 41, 35 (33)
2. 15, 18, 11, 20 (16)
3. 9, 6, 7, 3, 9, 4, 4 (6)
4. 32, 40, 28, 44 (36)
5. 8, 9, 9, 8, 1 (7)

Calculators and Averages

Ricky kept track of the high and low temperatures for his city during a twelve-day period. What were the average high and low temperatures during this time?

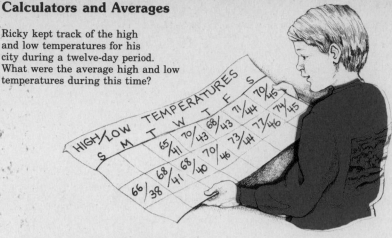

We want to find the average of a set of numbers. We add the numbers and divide by how many there are. To find the average high temperature, we add all the highs and divide by __12__. Complete the code to find the average high temperature.

65 [+] 70 [+] 68 [+] 71 [+] 70 [+] 66 [+] 68 [+] 68 [+] 70 [+] 73 [+] 77 [+]
74 [÷] 12 [=] (__70__)

The average 12-day high for Ricky's city was __70__ degrees.

Complete the following code to find the average low temperature.

41 [+] 43 [+] 43 [+] 44 [+] 45 [+] 38 [+] 41 [+] 40 [+] 46 [+] 44 [+] 46 [+]
45 [÷] 12 [=] (__43__)

The average 12-day low for Ricky's city was __43__ degrees.

Use a calculator to find the average of each set of numbers.

1. 128, 246, 342, 263, 519, 470 328
2. 648, 236, 489, 714, 563 530
3. 715, 689, 814, 753, 449, 518, 622, 304 608

MCP All rights reserved

113

Teaching the Lesson

Introducing the Problem Have one student read the problem aloud and another, the plan sentences. Direct their attention to the calculator codes written in their books. Explain that this shows the addition of the 12 high temperatures, and the division by 12 to find the average high. Have students follow the codes with their calculators and ask a student to give the answer. (70) Have students write the daily low temperatures in the calculator code in their texts and work out the average following the code. (43)

Developing the Skill Explain that the two steps required to find an average, adding and then dividing, can be done consecutively on the calculator. Remind them that in the sample problems, they entered each number, separating them by the addition operation. After they entered the last number, the total appeared. At that point they could touch the division key and enter the number of numbers in the set and do not have to clear the total and reenter to divide. Point out that the average is frequently a number not in the original set of numbers. Have them find averages for these sets on their calculators.

1. 126, 129, 215, 186, 225, 135, 209 (175)
2. 53, 86, 91, 55, 38, 49 (62)

Practice

Complete these codes. Write the answers on the screens.

1. 21 [+] 25 [+] 14 [+] 12 [÷] 4 [=] (18)

2. 72 [+] 46 [+] 98 [+] 76 [+] 90 [+] 84 [+] 48 [+] 88 [+] 28 [÷] 9 [=] (70)

3. 183 [+] 256 [+] 157 [+] 354 [+] 458 [+] 258 [+] 126 [÷] 7 [=] (256)

4. 98 [+] 87 [+] 29 [+] 46 [+] 24 [+] 63 [+] 86 [+] 39 [÷] 8 [=] (59)

5. 75 [+] 82 [+] 756 [+] 409 [+] 97 [+] 842 [+] 84 [÷] 7 [=] (335)

6. 76 [+] 94 [+] 88 [+] 96 [+] 75 [+] 92 [+] 96 [+] 82 [+] 86 [+] 85 [÷] 10 [=]

(87)

Use a calculator to find the average of each set of numbers.

7. 36, 84, 87, 159, 79 89

8. 34, 62, 39, 54, 31 44

9. 25, 36, 24, 58, 63, 57, 52 45

10. 62, 85, 56, 45, 12, 56, 48 52

11. 269, 247, 354, 267, 355, 344 306

12. 654, 956, 547, 562, 603, 428 625

13. 24, 69, 58, 12, 29, 31, 25, 20, 47 35

14. 90, 76, 76, 85, 58, 64, 64, 95 76

Apply

Use the table to answer these questions.

Dow-Jones Average

	Monday	Tuesday	Wednesday	Thursday	Friday
High	9334	9305	9183	9363	9390
Low	9208	9122	9099	9143	9228

15. On which day is the Dow-Jones high average the highest?
Friday

16. How many points did the low increase from Tuesday to Thursday?
21 points

17. On which day is the Dow-Jones low average the highest?
Friday

18. What is the high average for the week?
9315

19. How many points did the high increase from Wednesday to Friday?
207 points

20. What is the low average for the week?
9160

114

Correcting Common Errors

When students divide using a calculator, they may forget that the dividend is entered before the divisor. Have them practice on the following problems. First, they should write the key strokes in the code; then they should use the code to divide.

1. 21)131,418   131418 [÷] 21 [=]
(6,258)

2. 17)8,330   8330 [÷] 17 [=]
(490)

3. 82)61,910   61910 [÷] 82 [=]
(755)

Enrichment

Have students keep track of the number of students buying lunch in your school each day for a week. Then have them find the average number of students buying lunch each day. Similarly, have them keep track of the number of students riding a particular school bus each day for a week, and calculate the average number of daily riders at the end.

Practice

Have students complete the practice problems. Explain that commas cannot be entered on a calculator and are not necessary.

Mixed Practice

1. 3,921 − 1,208 (2,713)
2. $189.51 × 2 ($379.02)
3. 47,751 ÷ 77 (620 R11)
4. 28 × 351 (9,828)
5. 8,395 + 27,655 + 2,943 (38,993)
6. 865,128 + 39,408 (904,536)
7. 20,773 ÷ 8 (2,596 R5)
8. 22,010 − 14,195 (7,815)
9. 27,791 ÷ 90 (308 R71)
10. 27 × 195 (5,265)

Extra Credit *Measurement*

Divide students into groups. Tell them they are to research and report on two topics: the weight and length of 5 dinosaurs; and the length and weight of 3 of the largest animals now alive on earth. Have students make bar graphs showing their data. When reports are given, have groups compare results to see if they came up with the same information, or chose different representative animals.

114

Chapter Test

page 115

Item	Objective
1-2	Divide 2- or 3-digit number by multiple of 10, quotient with or without remainder (See pages 97-98)
3-9	Divide 2- or 3-digit number by 2-digit number, quotient with or without remainder (See pages 101-102)
10-16	Divide 4-digit number by 2-digit number to get 2-digit quotient with or without remainder (See pages 103-104)
17-25	Divide 4- or 5-digit number by 2-digit number to get 3-digit quotient with or without remainder (See pages 107-110)

Divide.

1. $60\overline{)300}$ — 5

2. $40\overline{)264}$ — 6 R24

3. $12\overline{)98}$ — 8 R2

4. $18\overline{)73}$ — 4 R1

5. $38\overline{)308}$ — 8 R4

6. $34\overline{)275}$ — 8 R3

7. $63\overline{)489}$ — 7 R48

8. $79\overline{)700}$ — 8 R68

9. $23\overline{)966}$ — 42

10. $36\overline{)1,728}$ — 48

11. $35\overline{)1,680}$ — 48

12. $28\overline{)1,876}$ — 67

13. $68\overline{)1,632}$ — 24

14. $42\overline{)3,250}$ — 77 R16

15. $82\overline{)7,298}$ — 89

16. $56\overline{)5,568}$ — 99 R24

17. $14\overline{)4,872}$ — 348

18. $26\overline{)\$110.50}$ — $4.25

19. $56\overline{)6,048}$ — 108

20. $58\overline{)27,190}$ — 468 R46

21. $96\overline{)77,595}$ — 808 R27

22. $65\overline{)\$589.55}$ — $9.07

23. $27\overline{)11,029}$ — 408 R13

24. $67\overline{)\$573.52}$ — $8.56

25. $58\overline{)36,482}$ — 629

MCP All rights reserved

115

115

Circle the letter of the correct answer.

1 What is the place value of the 0 in 402,568?
- **a** hundred thousands
- **ⓑ** ten thousands
- **c** thousands
- **d** NG

2 4,309 ◯ 4,039
- **a** <
- **ⓑ** >
- **c** =

3 676
   + 528
- **a** 1,194
- **b** 1,104
- **c** 1,294
- **ⓓ** NG

4 $309.56
   + 651.76
- **a** $950.32
- **ⓑ** $961.32
- **c** $1,061.32
- **d** NG

5 8,005
   − 6,309
- **a** 706
- **ⓑ** 1,696
- **c** 2,304
- **d** NG

6 $915.38
   − 274.59
- **ⓐ** $640.79
- **b** $641.79
- **c** $761.21
- **d** NG

7 43 × 8
- **a** 324
- **ⓑ** 344
- **c** 3,224
- **d** NG

8 5,307
   ×   5
- **a** 16,535
- **ⓑ** 26,535
- **c** 265,035

9 28
   × 36
- **a** 252
- **b** 768
- **c** 1,208
- **ⓓ** NG

10 6,006 ÷ 6
- **a** 11
- **b** 101
- **ⓒ** 1,001
- **d** NG

11 3)21,709
- **a** 7,236
- **ⓑ** 7,236 R1
- **c** 7,237
- **d** NG

12 Find the average.
22, 16, 23, 15
- **a** 16
- **ⓑ** 19
- **c** 23
- **d** NG

13 56)450
- **a** 11
- **ⓑ** 8 R2
- **c** 9
- **d** NG

☐ score

116

Cumulative Review

page 116

Item	Objective
1	Identify place value in a number less than 1,000,000 (See pages 11-12)
2	Compare and order numbers through thousands (See pages 9-10)
3	Add two numbers with sums less than 1,000, one regrouping (See pages 23-24)
4	Add two numbers up to 5-digits (See pages 27-28)
5	Subtract two 4-digit numbers, zeros in the minuend (See pages 29-30)
6	Subtract two numbers up to 6-digits (See pages 31-32)
7	Multiply a 2-digit by 1-digit factor (See pages 53-54)
8	Multiply up to a 6-digit by 1-digit factor (See pages 55-56)
9	Multiply two 2-digit factors (See pages 57-58)
10-11	Divide up to 6-digits by 1-digit number (See pages 87-88)
12	Find the average (See pages 91-92)
13	Divide a 2- or 3-digit by 2-digit number (See pages 101-102)

Alternate Cumulative Review

Circle the letter of the correct answer.

1 Give the place value of the 0 in 608,692.
- **a** hundred thousands
- **ⓑ** ten thousands
- **c** thousands
- **d** NG

2 2,407 ◯ 2,047
- **a** <
- **ⓑ** >
- **c** =

3 657
   +248
- **a** 805
- **b** 895
- **c** 995
- **ⓓ** NG

4 $806.94
   + 134.68
- **a** $930.62
- **ⓑ** $941.62
- **c** $1,041.62
- **d** NG

5 7,003
   −2,439
- **ⓐ** 4,564
- **b** 4,574
- **c** 5,436
- **d** NG

6 $827.85
   − 46.96
- **a** $781.89
- **ⓑ** $780.89
- **c** $780.99
- **d** NG

7 82
   ×9
- **a** 728
- **ⓑ** 738
- **c** 7,218
- **d** NG

8 4,206
   ×7
- **ⓐ** 29,442
- **b** 29,512
- **c** 294,042
- **d** NG

9 24
   ×84
- **a** 1,916
- **b** 2,116
- **c** 2,006
- **ⓓ** NG

10 7)7,854
- **a** 122
- **b** 1,122 R1
- **ⓒ** 1,122
- **d** NG

11 4)32,903
- **a** 8,225
- **ⓑ** 8,225 R3
- **c** 8,226
- **d** NG

12 Find the average.
34, 13, 18, 27
- **a** 21
- **ⓑ** 23
- **c** 24
- **d** NG

13 47)330
- **a** 7
- **ⓑ** 7 R1
- **c** 7 R2
- **d** NG

116

Time

pages 117-118

Objective

To compare and convert units of time

Materials

Mental Math

Dictate the following:

1. 2 × (2 + 3) (10)
2. 4 × (5 − 1) (16)
3. (9 ÷ 3) × 10 (30)
4. (18 ÷ 2) × 3 (27)
5. (4 × 2) ÷ 2 (4)
6. 20 ÷ (2 + 2) (5)
7. (6 ÷ 2) × (1 × 2) (6)

Skill Review

Have students complete this chart:

1. 1 minute = ____ seconds (60)
2. 1 hour = ____ minutes (60)
3. 1 day = ____ hours (24)
4. 1 week = ____ days (7)
5. one month = ____ days (28, 29, 30 or 31)
6. one year = ____ days (365) or ____ weeks (52) or ____ months (12)

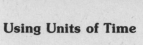

6 MEASUREMENT

Using Units of Time

Thirty days have September, April, June and November. All others have 31 days except February, which has 28 (29 in leap year). How many minutes are in February during the leap year of 1996?

We are looking for the number of minutes in February, 1996.

There are __29__ days in February, 1996.

There are __24__ hours in a day and __60__ minutes in an hour.

To find the number of minutes in this month, we multiply the number of days in February by the number of hours in a day and by the number of minutes in an hour. We multiply __29__ by __24__ by __60__.

Time Equivalents
1 minute = 60 seconds
1 hour = 60 minutes
1 day = 24 hours
1 week = 7 days
1 year = 52 weeks
1 year = 12 months
1 year = 365 days
1 leap year = 366 days

```
  29      Days in February, 1996        696    Hours in February, 1996
× 24      Hours in one day            × 60     Minutes in one hour
 116                                 41,760    Minutes in February, 1996
 580
 696      Hours in February, 1996
```

There are __41,760__ minutes in February, 1996.

✔ To rename larger units as smaller units, we multiply.
To rename smaller units as larger units, we divide.

Getting Started

Use the table of time equivalents to help complete these.

1. 5 weeks = __35__ days
2. 5 hours 15 minutes = __315__ minutes

Complete these sentences.

3. To change hours to minutes, __multiply__ by 60.

4. To change hours to days, __divide__ by 24.

117

MCP All rights reserved

Teaching the Lesson

Introducing the Problem Read the problem aloud. Have a student read and complete the information sentences, referring to the conversion chart if necessary. Ask students to read the plan sentences and explain how to multiply three numbers. (Multiply the first two. Multiply that product by the third.) Have students follow in their texts while you work the problem on the board. Have a student read the solution sentence (41,760 minutes in February, 1988) and the rule sentences.

Developing the Skill Explain that knowing whether to multiply or divide depends on whether students are looking for a larger or smaller number than the answer. If looking for the number of minutes in 2 hours, the answer is going to be a larger number than the number they are given. Show the multiplication on the board. (120 minutes) If looking for the number of weeks in 140 days, the answer will be smaller than the number given, and so they will divide. Work the division on the board. (20 weeks) Show students that another way to analyze the problems is to pay special attention to the units. Explain, for example, that minutes multiplied by seconds per minute will give an answer in seconds.

Practice

Use the table of time equivalents to help complete these.

1. 6 years = __312__ weeks

2. 4 minutes = __240__ seconds

3. 133 days = __19__ weeks

4. 144 months = __12__ years

5. 1 day = __86,400__ seconds

6. 6 days 4 hours = __148__ hours

7. 15 minutes 10 seconds = __910__ seconds

8. 100 hours = __4__ days __4__ hours

9. 5 years 3 months = __63__ months

10. 24 hours = __1,440__ minutes

11. 950 seconds = __15__ minutes __50__ seconds

12. 2,000 days = __285__ weeks __5__ days

13. 4 hours 15 minutes = __255__ minutes

14. 107 weeks = __2__ years __3__ weeks

15. 4 days = __345,600__ seconds

16. 1 week 3 days = __14,400__ minutes

Complete these sentences.

17. To change minutes to seconds, multiply by __60__.

18. To change weeks to years, divide by __52__.

19. To change months to years, __divide__ by 12.

20. To change minutes to hours __divide__ by 60.

Apply

Solve these problems.

21. Daphne was 12 years old on January 1, 1990. How old was she in years and days on July 1, 1992?
14 years 181 days

22. How many days are in the last 4 months of this year?
122 days

23. Miss Lopez edits 4 maps each hour at the Travel Atlas Company. She works 6 hours each day for 5 days a week. How many maps can she edit in 1 year?
6,240 maps

24. Morris works at the Freedom Book Store from 9:00 AM to 3:00 PM, Monday through Thursday. If Morris makes $4.25 per hour, what is his weekly pay?
$102

118

Some students may convert units of time incorrectly because they multiply when they should divide or vice versa. For each problem, have them write whether they are going from larger to smaller units, meaning there will be more and you multiply, or from smaller units to larger units, meaning there will be fewer and you divide.

Enrichment

Tell students they will be able to tell the day of the week for any date in the years 1900 through 2000, with this perpetual calendar. Write the months and days of the week and their code numbers on the board. They should subtract 1 from the date if it falls before March 1, in a leap year.

Jan-1	Apr-0	July-0	Oct-1
Feb-4	May-2	Aug-3	Nov-4
Mar-4	June-5	Sept-6	Dec-6

Mon-2	Wed-4	Fri-6	Sun-1
Tues-3	Thurs-5	Sat-0	

Have them start with a year and:

1. Divide 4 into the last two digits and disregard the remainder.
2. Add the quotient to the original two digits.
3. Add the number for the month.
4. Add the date.
5. Divide 7 into the last number and look up the remainder in the code for days.

Practice

Have students complete the practice problems. For reference, put these statements on the board:

1. **To rename larger units as smaller units, multiply.**
2. **To rename smaller units as larger units, divide.**

Mixed Practice

1. 227,195 + 481,658 (708,853)
2. 30,940 − 14,863 (16,077)
3. 1,907 ÷ 48 (39 R35)
4. 6,937 × 90 (624,330)
5. 2,459 ÷ 60 (40 R59)
6. 307 × 258 (79,206)
7. $795.48 + $396.47 ($1,191.95)
8. $71.56 ÷ 4 ($17.89)
9. 937 × 7 (6,559)
10. $70.00 − $38.36 ($31.64)

Extra Credit *Geometry*

This activity will introduce students to the Mobius strip. Have students cut strips of paper 1 inch wide and about 12 inches long. Have tape available. Ask a student to show that the strip of paper has two sides. Demonstrate by drawing a line across one side and showing that you have to lift the pencil, turn the paper over, and resume drawing to make a mark on the other side. Ask students to take their strip, give it a half twist, and then tape the two ends together in a loop.

Now have each student take a pencil and draw a line along the strip. Show students that they can cover the entire strip without lifting the pencil; the paper has only one side. Explain that this configuration is called a Mobius strip.

118

Time Zones

pages 119-120

Objective

To compare U.S. time zones

Materials

*map of the U.S. with time zones marked

Mental Math

Have students tell how many:

1. minutes in half an hour. (30)
2. days in two weeks. (14)
3. hours in a day and a half. (36)
4. months in half a year. (6)
5. seconds in a quarter of a minute. (15)

Skill Review

Ask students, if it is 10:00 AM, what time will it be in:

1. 4 hours (2 PM)
2. 1½ hours (11:30 AM)
3. 12 hours (10 PM)
4. 6½ hours (4:30 PM)
5. 24 hours (10 AM, the next day)
6. 15 hours (1 AM)

Understanding Time Zones

Erica lives in Chicago and her brother attends college in Honolulu. Erica's brother is expecting a call from her at noon local time. What time should Erica place the call?

We want to find out the time in Chicago when it is noon in Honolulu.

Erica lives in the __Central__ time zone. Her brother

lives in the __Alaska-Hawaii__ time zone.

To find what time Erica should call her brother, we must find the difference in hours between their time zones and add that to the time he is expecting her call.

There is __4__ hours difference in their times.

To find Erica's time at noon in Honolulu,

we add __4__ hours to 12:00.

Erica should call her brother at __4:00__ PM.

Getting Started

Write the correct time.

1. 4 hours and 15 minutes after 2:45 AM
7:00 AM

2. If it is 12:00 midnight, how many hours and minutes ago was it 8:27 AM?
15 hours 33 minutes

3. If it is 7:30 PM in New York City, what time is it in San Francisco?
4:30 PM

Use the time zone chart and this clock to write the correct times in problems 5 and 6.

4. A bus left Los Angeles at 8:00 AM Pacific time. It arrived in Phoenix 7 hours later. Phoenix is in the Mountain time zone. What time was it in Phoenix when the bus arrived?
4:00 PM

MCP All rights reserved

5. It is __3:15__ Pacific time.

6. It is __5:15__ Central time.

119

Teaching the Lesson

Introducing the Problem Have a student read the problem aloud. Ask students where the sun comes up in the morning. (in the East) Point out that during the day, the sun moves across the sky, setting in the west. The further west you live, the later the sun will seem to rise. Explain that to have noon coincide with the sun's high point everywhere, the earth is divided into zones. Point out that the time zones are arranged from east to west in one–hour increments. Read the information and plan sentences aloud. Ask a student to do the addition and read the solution sentence. (should call brother at 4:00 PM)

Developing the Skill Post the U.S. map and point to each time zone. Have one student start at 2 PM in the Eastern zone and explain what time it would be in each of the others. (1 PM; 12 noon; 11 AM; 10 AM; 9 AM) Explain that to decide whether to add or subtract hours to find the time in another zone, they have to determine whether the zone is to

the east or west of the zone they start in. To find the time in a more westerly zone, they will subtract; in a more easterly zone, add. Ask a student to come to the map and show what time it would be in Atlanta, Georgia, if it is 11:45 AM in Seattle, Washington. (2:45 PM)

Practice

Write the correct time.

1. When it is 12:00 noon in Honolulu, what time is it in Denver?
   _3 PM_

2. 2 hours and 45 minutes before 6:00 AM _3:15 AM_

3. 4 hours and 7 minutes before 1:00 PM _8:53 AM_

4. 5 hours and 27 minutes after 11:25 PM _4:52 AM_

5. If it is 5:15 AM, how many hours and minutes ago was it 4:45 PM
   12 hours and 30 minutes

6. Ed left Chicago at 4:00 AM and arrived in Florida 27 hours later. In Eastern time, what time did Ed arrive? _8:00 AM_

Use the time zone chart and this clock on Pacific time to write the correct times.

7. It is _3:25 PM_ Mountain time.

8. It is _5:25 PM_ Eastern time.

9. It is _12:25 PM_ Alaska-Hawaii time.

Use the time zone chart and this clock on Central time to write the correct times.

10. It is _9:36 PM_ Pacific time.

11. It is _10:36 PM_ Mountain time.

12. It is _12:36 PM_ Eastern time.

Apply

Use the time zone chart to solve.

13. The flight time from Boston to San Francisco is 5 hours and 15 minutes. If a plane leaves Boston at 6:05 PM, what time will it arrive in San Francisco?
    8:20 PM

14. A plane left Los Angeles at 8:30 AM and arrived in Denver at 11:00 AM. The plane left Denver at 11:30 AM and arrived in New York City at 6:00 PM. What was the flight time of the plane?
    6 hours

120

Correcting Common Errors

Some students may not remember if the time is earlier to the east or west. To give them a reference, have them draw a chart with the time zones labeled. They fill in 12 noon for their time zone and then fill in the other zones accordingly. They can refer to this chart as they solve the problems.

Enrichment

Explain that the time zones only roughly equal out the variations in sunrise and sunset in different parts of the world. Point out that from one side of a time zone to the other there will be an hour's difference in the time of sunrise. Ask students to look at the map and determine whether it will be light sooner or later in Philadelphia, Pennsylvania, than in Gary, Indiana. (sooner)

Practice

Have students complete the practice problems. Remind them to label answers with the correct unit of time.

Extra Credit *Geometry*

Have each student make a Mobius band. Remind them to put a one-half twist in the paper strip and connect the ends with tape. Ask them to draw a line down the center of the strip. They will remember that the Mobius strip with one half-twist has only one side and, incidently, only one edge. Now have students use scissors to cut the loop along the line they have drawn. Ask them to guess in advance what the result will be. Now have them cut and hold up the finished product. (one larger loop) Give students more paper and have them make another Mobius strip, at least one inch wide. Tell them to trisect this loop, dividing its width into three parts and cutting it. Have them predict what will happen and then try it. (The result will be two interlocking loops.) To extend the activity, suggest that students try cutting Mobius strips with differing numbers of half-twists.

Customary Length

Objective

To measure lengths from the nearest inch, through nearest eighth-inch

Materials

12-inch rulers marked in eighths
several pieces of tagboard

Mental Math

Have students identify the number for n:

1. $(3 \times 4) + n = 22$ (10)
2. $(15 \div 3) + 5 = n$ (10)
3. $(7 \times n) \div 21 = 1$ (3)
4. $(2 \times 3) \times n = n$ (0)
5. $n \times n \times n = 8$ (2)
6. $(16 \div n) + n = 8$ (4)

Skill Review

Review the rules for rounding numbers. Have students round these numbers to the nearest ten:

1. 52 (50)	4. 122 (120)
2. 69 (70)	5. 288 (290)
3. 84 (80)	6. 1,250 (1,250)

Have them round these to the nearest hundred:

1. 338 (300)	4. 1,399 (1,400)
2. 792 (800)	5. 1,781 (1,800)
3. 101 (100)	6. 6,003 (6,000)

Measuring Length, Inches

Jayne is learning how to make keys. She has to measure each in inches, the customary unit of length. What is the length of this key to the nearest inch? to the nearest half-inch? to the nearest quarter-inch? to the nearest eighth-inch?

We want to find the measurement of the key.

To approximate measurements, we look at the small lines between the inches.

If a measure is less than halfway between the lines, we round ___down___. If the measure is exactly or more than halfway between the lines, we round ___up___.

The length of the key is ___3___ inches to the nearest inch, or

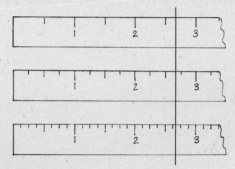

$2\frac{1}{2}$ inches to the nearest half-inch,

$2\frac{3}{4}$ inches to the nearest quarter-inch,

$2\frac{5}{8}$ inches to the nearest eighth-inch.

Getting Started

Use a ruler to complete these problems.

1. Measure the width of this page to the nearest half-inch, quarter-inch and eighth-inch. _____ inches _____ inches _____ inches
   Answers will vary.
2. Draw a pencil $5\frac{3}{4}$ inches long.

3. Draw a pen $4\frac{1}{8}$ inches long.

MCP All rights reserved

121

Teaching the Lesson

Introducing the Problem Have a student read the problem aloud and complete the information sentences. Direct students to the three rulers illustrated in their texts. Explain that the actual length can be read in different ways depending on how the reading is to be used. Point out that the first ruler shows the length rounded to the nearest half-inch, the second to the nearest quarter-inch and the third to the nearest eighth-inch.

Developing the Skill Draw an enlarged ruler on the board, exaggerating the half-, quarter- and eighth-inch markings. Point to various spots on the ruler and ask students to read the lengths to the nearest half-inch, then to the nearest quarter- and eighth-inch. Explain that the kind of reading they make when measuring will depend on the use of the information. If they are measuring beams for the roof of a house they will measure to the nearest inch, but if they are making a doll's dress they may need to round to the nearest eighth-inch. Remind students to carefully line up the zero marking when they measure length. Show students that some rulers have zero at the end of the ruler and others have a space before the markings actually begin.

Use a ruler to complete these problems.

1. Measure to the nearest eighth-inch.

___2___ inches

2. Measure to the nearest half-inch.

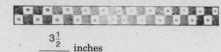

___$3\frac{1}{2}$___ inches

3. Measure to the nearest inch.

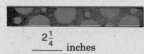

___2___ inches

4. Measure to the nearest quarter-inch.

___$2\frac{1}{4}$___ inches

5. Measure to the nearest inch, half-inch, quarter-inch and eighth-inch.

___7___ inches ___$6\frac{1}{2}$___ inches ___$6\frac{3}{4}$___ inches ___$6\frac{6}{8}$___ inches

6. Draw a key $7\frac{3}{8}$ inches long.

7. Draw a string $4\frac{7}{8}$ inches long.

8. Draw a ribbon $5\frac{1}{2}$ inches long.

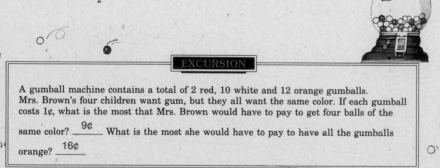

EXCURSION

A gumball machine contains a total of 2 red, 10 white and 12 orange gumballs. Mrs. Brown's four children want gum, but they all want the same color. If each gumball costs 1¢, what is the most that Mrs. Brown would have to pay to get four balls of the same color? ___9¢___ What is the most she would have to pay to have all the gumballs orange? ___16¢___

122

Correcting Common Errors

Some students may have difficulty measuring to the nearest unit because they cannot read the ruler to name the units that the measure is between. For each measure, have them first count and write the two measures the end of the object is between and then circle the one to which it is closer.

Enrichment

Explain that a carpenter's tape measure is like an ordinary ruler, though much longer. Show students that the zero point is at the tip and the reading is made along the tape. Point out that when they measure an enclosed space, the length of the case, which is marked on each tape measure, is added to the tape reading.

Have students measure several enclosed dimensions in the room with a tape measure to practice using this special feature.

Practice

Have students complete the practice problems. Suggest that they circle the significant fraction in each problem, for example, nearest eighth-inch, before they measure.

Excursion

Suggest that students think of the worst possible situation, since that would require the greatest amount of money.
For example, if they first drew 2 red, 3 white and 3 orange, then on the next try either a white or an orange ball would give four of one color. (9¢)
If they drew 2 red, 10 white and 4 orange they would get four orange balls. (16¢)

Extra Credit   *Logic*

Duplicate the following or write on the board:

Jim and his younger brother Joe were helping their dad build a backyard barbecue when their father realized he did not have enough bricks to finish. The boys volunteered to go to the brickyard and bring back what was needed. After paying for the bricks, each costing 75¢, the boys started back.

Part way home, Joe realized Jim was carrying more bricks than he. Wanting to be treated equally, he demanded Jim give him two bricks so they would have an equal number. This was fine for a while, but then Joe began to tire. He had to give Jim back his two bricks and two more of his own. That meant that Jim now had twice as many bricks as Joe.

Considering all this, how much did the boys have to pay for the load of bricks? (Jim started out with 14 bricks and Joe with 10 so the total cost had to be $18.00.)

Add and Subtract Customary Units

pages 123-124

Objective

To add and subtract customary units of length

Materials

*yardstick

Mental Math

Have students tell which is longer:

1. 30 minutes or 1 hour (1 hour)
2. 6 hours or half a day (half a day)
3. 90 seconds or 1 minute (90 seconds)
4. two hours or 120 minutes (same)
5. 5 weeks or 1 month (5 weeks)
6. 2 years or 36 months (36 months)
7. 1 year or 62 weeks (62 weeks)

Skill Review

Put this chart on the board and have students complete it.

1 foot = ___ inches (12)
1 yard = ___ feet (3)
1 yard = ___ inches (36)
1 mile = ___ feet (5,280)
1 mile = ___ yards (1,760)

Adding and Subtracting Customary Units

1 foot (ft) = 12 inches (in.)
1 yard (yd) = 3 feet
1 mile (mi) = 1,760 yards

During Parent-student Activity Day, customary units of length were used to measure. Mr. Herzog and Tammy both competed in the long-jump event. How much farther did Mr. Herzog jump?

We want to find how much farther Mr. Herzog jumped than his daughter.

Mr. Herzog jumped __6__ feet __4__ inches.

Tammy jumped __4__ feet __9__ inches.

To find the difference, we subtract the length of Tammy's jump from the length of her father's jump.

We subtract __4 feet 9 inches__ from __6 feet 4 inches__.

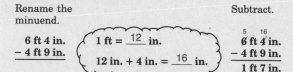

Rename the minuend.

6 ft 4 in.
− 4 ft 9 in.

1 ft = __12__ in.

12 in. + 4 in. = __16__ in.

Subtract.

    5 16
6 ft 4 in.
− 4 ft 9 in.
────────────
1 ft 7 in.

Change the difference to inches.

1 ft 7 in. =
(1 × 12 in.) + 7 in. =
__19__ in.

Mr. Herzog jumped __1__ foot __7__ inches or __19__ inches farther than Tammy.

✔ When adding or subtracting customary units, simplify the sum or difference by renaming, if necessary. 11 ft 13 in. = 12 ft 1 in., 14 ft = 4 yds 2 ft.

Getting Started

Rename these measurements.

1. 1 yd = __36__ in.
2. 6 ft 8 in. = __80__ in.
3. 500 ft = __166__ yd __2__ ft
4. 1 mi = __5,280__ ft

Add or subtract.

5. 8 ft 3 in.
  + 4 ft 11 in.
  ─────────────
   13 ft 2 in.

6. 6 yd 1 ft
  − 4 yd 2 ft
  ───────────
    1 yd 2 ft

7. 9 ft
  − 6 ft 6 in.
  ───────────
    2 ft 6 in.

8. 4 yd 2 ft 9 in.
  + 5 yd 1 ft 5 in.
  ─────────────────
  10 yd 1 ft 2 in.

Copy and add or subtract.

9. 5 ft 4 in. + 6 ft 9 in.
   12 ft 1 in.

10. 7 yd 16 in. − 2 ft 11 in.
    6 yd 1 ft 5 in.

MCP All rights reserved

123

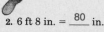

Teaching the Lesson

Introducing the Problem   Have a student read the problem and the information sentences aloud. Have a student read and complete the plan sentences. Direct students' attention to the problem in the model. Ask students why the subtraction cannot be done with the problem in this form. (can't subtract 9 from 4) Work through the problem with students renaming one foot in the minuend. Have a student do this problem on the board. Have a student read the solution sentence aloud. (jumped 1 ft 7 in. farther)

Developing the Skill   Explain to students that while there are 10 ones in 10 and 10 tens in 100, there are 12 inches in 1 foot and 36 inches in 1 yard. Have students practice with this problem: 1 yd 2 ft 7 in. + 2 ft 8 in. (2 yd 2 ft 3 in.)

Practice

Rename these measurements.

1. 49 in. = __4__ ft __1__ in.

2. 10 ft 7 in. = __127__ in.

3. 3 mi = __15,840__ ft

4. 84 in. = __7__ ft

5. 16 yd = __576__ in.

6. 6 mi 660 yd = __11,220__ yd

7. 144 in. = __4__ yd

8. 8 yd 1 ft = __300__ in.

9. 2 mi 220 yd = __11,220__ ft

10. 5 yd 2 ft 5 in. = __209__ in.

Add or subtract.

11. 5 ft 6 in.
    + 2 ft 3 in.
    7 ft 9 in.

12. 8 ft 6 in.
    − 5 ft 2 in.
    3 ft 4 in.

13. 11 ft 9 in.
    − 6 ft 10 in.
    4 ft 11 in.

14. 5 yd 2 ft
    + 4 yd 2 ft
    10 yd 1 ft

Copy and Do

15. 5 yd 2 ft − 3 yd 2 ft
    2 yd

16. 9 ft 6 in. − 8 ft 8 in.
    10 in.

17. 2 yd 2 ft 8 in. + 3 yd 1 ft 2 in.
    6 yd 10 in.

18. 5 yd 2 ft − 3 yd 9 in.
    2 yd 1 ft 3 in.

19. 3 yd 1 ft 5 in. + 2 ft 8 in.
    4 yd 1 ft 1 in.

20. 3 ft 9 in. + 2 ft 8 in. + 7 ft 11 in.
    14 ft 4 in.

Apply

Solve these problems.

21. A mixed relay team ran 1 mile 220 yards, 880 yards, 880 yards, 880 yards and 440 yards. How many miles and yards did the team run?
    2 miles 1,540 yards

22. The school record for sailing a paper airplane is 30 feet 9 inches. Paul sailed his airplane 7 yards 2 feet 6 inches. How far short of the record was his flight?
    2 yards 1 foot 3 inches

23. At activity day, Carl long-jumped 14 feet 3 inches. Alice long-jumped 15 feet 9 inches. How much farther did Alice jump?
    1 foot 6 inches

24. Mr. Cook needs some jump rope for gym class. Rope costs $1.89 for each foot. How much does a rope 4 yards 2 feet long cost?
    $26.46

124

Correcting Common Errors

Some students may add and subtract customary units incorrectly because they rename as in whole numbers; that is, they use tens instead of the proper conversion unit. After these students have written their problem, have them write the conversion fact that will be needed. Then they can rename and solve the problem.

Enrichment

Have students lay out a walking course around the school or playground with a tape measure and compass. Explain that they are to give directions that someone else can follow from start to finish, using only measured distances and compass directions. Give them this example:

Start at the school entrance. Go 25 feet north, 10 feet east . . .

Practice

Have students complete the practice problems. If necessary put a conversion chart on the board for reference.

Mixed Practice

1. $25.98 × 16 ($415.68)
2. 84,197 + 6,303 + 491 (90,991)
3. 3 × 212,639 (637,917)
4. $106.26 ÷ 21 ($5.06)
5. 21,295 − 11,376 (9,919)
6. 398 + 291 + 2,470 (3,159)
7. 12,836 ÷ 40 (320 R36)
8. 700 × 500 (350,000)
9. $3,095.81 − $1,273.60 ($1,822.21)
10. 39,105 ÷ 5 (7,821)

Extra Credit *Geometry*

Give students several sheets of one-inch graph paper and a sheet of quarter-inch graph paper. Draw a similar square grid on the board and a simple line pattern within it. Ask students to transfer the pattern from the board to the one-inch graph paper by following the way the pattern crosses the grid on the board.

Now have each student draw a simple pattern on the quarter-inch graph paper. Then tell them to enlarge the pattern by copying it onto one-inch graph paper. Enlarging is called geometric transformation. As an extension, students may want to take a cartoon, draw a grid over it and then transfer it to a larger grid drawn on poster board.

Perimeter

pages 125-126

Objective

To find perimeter

Materials

Mental Math

Ask students to provide products for the next two problems in each series:

1. 2×4, 3×4, 4×4 (20, 24)
2. 5×1, 5×2, 5×3 (20, 25)
3. 7×4, 7×5, 7×6 (49, 56)
4. 6×9, 7×9, 8×9 (81, 90)
5. 2×2, 2×3, 2×4 (10, 12)
6. 5×7, 6×7, 7×7 (56, 63)
7. 8×2, 9×2, 10×2 (22, 24)

Skill Review

Have students review column addition with these problems:

1. $23 + 23 + 14$ (60)
2. $120 + 40 + 120 + 40$ (320)
3. $15 + 15 + 15 + 15$ (60)
4. $12 + 12 + 21 + 21$ (66)
5. $19 + 10 + 21 + 10 + 29 + 31$ (120)
6. $13 + 9 + 13 + 9$ (44)
7. $72 + 78 + 52$ (202)

Finding Perimeter

The **perimeter** of a figure is the distance around the figure. The city recreation department is preparing to accept bids for a new fence around the tennis court. What is the perimeter of the tennis court?

We need to find the total distance around the tennis court.

The tennis court has ___4___ sides. The lengths are

__78__, __78__, __36__ and __36__ feet.

To find the perimeter, we add the lengths of the sides. We add __78__, __78__, __36__ and __36__.

```
  7 8
  7 8
  3 6
+ 3 6
-----
  228
```

The perimeter of the tennis court is __228__ feet.

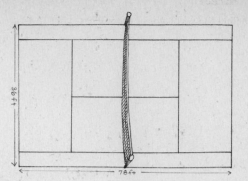

Getting Started

Find the perimeter of each figure.

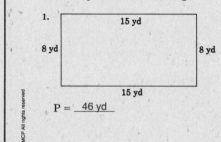

1.

15 yd
8 yd   8 yd
15 yd

P = __46 yd__

2.

12 ft
12 ft
22 ft   16 ft
10 ft
28 ft

P = __100 ft__

MCP All rights reserved

125

Teaching the Lesson

Introducing the Problem Read the problem aloud and remind students that the perimeter is the distance around the outside of a figure. Explain that this can be calculated by adding the lengths of all the sides of the figure. Have students read the information sentences and the plan sentences. Ask a student to do the column addition on the board, and read the solution sentence aloud.

Developing the Skill Explain that finding the perimeter is a matter of adding the lengths of all the sides of a figure. Point out that sometimes not all the lengths are given. Draw on the board a rectangle with only two sides marked, the length, 9 ft and width, 4 ft.

Explain that while the lengths of two sides are shown, the other two sides are unmarked. Ask if anyone can guess the lengths of the unmarked sides. (9 ft, 4 ft) Although they have not had the geometry necessary to prove it, most students will know that if the figure has right angles, the lengths of the mystery sides can be derived from the known lengths. Have students calculate the perimeter of the figure. (26 ft)

Find the perimeter of each figure.

1.

2 yd

P = __12 yd__

2.

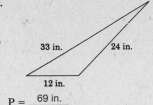

33 in.   24 in.

12 in.

P = __69 in.__

3.

48 ft

P = __144 ft__

4.

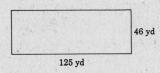

46 yd

125 yd

P = __342 yd__

5.

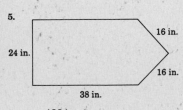

16 in.

24 in.

16 in.

38 in.

P = __132 in.__

6.

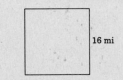

16 mi

P = __64 mi__

Apply

Draw a picture and solve.

7. A parking lot has 4 sides, each measuring 75 feet. What is the perimeter of the parking lot?
300 feet

8. A yard has 2 sides 80 feet long and 2 sides 115 feet long. If fencing cost $8.55 for each foot, how much will it cost to fence in the yard?
$3,334.50

9. A park has 3 equal sides. If its perimeter is 189 feet, what is the length of each side?
63 feet

10. The length of a picture frame is 6 inches. The width is twice as long. What is the perimeter of the picture frame?
36 inches

126

Correcting Common Errors

When students find the perimeter of a rectangle, they may forget to add two lengths and two widths. Have them write the number of sides, write a measure for each side, and then add.

Enrichment

Ask students to design an imaginary house and draw a floor plan. They will need rulers or yardsticks and large paper. Explain that the scale will be one inch to one foot, so that a room intended to be 15 feet by 12 feet will measure 15 inches by 12 inches on their drawing. Ask them to label the outer dimensions as well as the dimensions of interior features.

Practice

Have students complete the practice problems. Explain that if the sides of a rectangle or square look similar, they can assume they are equal.

Extra Credit   *Probability*

Have students play the following probability game with one die. Pairs of students are given a single die. They agree on a number, larger than 20, as a goal. One player rolls the die and records the number. Then the partner is allowed to turn the die a quarter-turn in any direction to bring up a new number which is added to the first number. The play goes to the first player who adds another quarter-turn and a new number to the running total. The object of the game is to reach the agreed number or force the opponent to go over that number. See if students can develop any strategies for winning. Ask if the first player or the second seems more likely to win. (the second)

Area

pages 127-128

Objective

To find the area of a rectangle

Materials

one-inch graph paper
ruler
*one-inch-squared transparency
*overhead projector

Mental Math

Ask students to rename:

1. 24 inches = ____ feet (2)
2. 9 feet = ____ yards (3)
3. 120 seconds = ____ minutes (2)
4. 30 minutes = ____ hour (1/2)
5. 18 inches = ____ feet (1 1/2)
6. 2 hours = ____ minutes (120)

Skill Review

Give each student a piece of one-inch graph paper. Ask them to draw several figures on the paper and then exchange with a partner. Remind them that area is the number of square units within the figure. Ask them to count to find the area of the figures on the paper they receive. Have them label the number of square inches on each figure.

Finding Area

The **area** of a figure is the number of square units it takes to cover it. Sandy is crocheting a blanket using a granny square design. What is the area of Sandy's blanket?

We want to find the area of Sandy's blanket in square units.

The blanket is __9__ units wide and

__8__ units long.

We can find the number of square units by using a formula.

There are __8__ rows of squares.

There are __9__ squares in each row.

To find the total number of squares, we multiply the number of rows by the number of squares in each.

__8__ × __9__ = __72__ squares

✔ If we multiply the length of a rectangle by its width, we will get its area in square units.
The formula is: **A = L × W.**

There are __72__ square units in Sandy's blanket.

Getting Started

Find the area.

1.
16 ft
8 ft

A = ___128 sq ft___

2.
12 yd

A = ___144 sq yd___

3.
8 in.
8 in.
10 in.
6 in.

A = ___128 sq in.___

4. A rectangle has a length of 146 feet and a width of 89 feet.

A = ___12,994 sq ft___

5. A rectangle has a length of 245 inches and a width of 136 inches.

A = ___33,320 sq in.___

6. A square is 85 yards on each side.

A = ___7,225 sq yd___

MCP All rights reserved

127

Teaching the Lesson

Introducing the Problem Read the problem aloud. Ask students to look at the blanket illustrated and have a student read the information sentences. Remind students that the area can be figured by counting the squares, but explain that it can be computed by multiplying the length times the width. Read the plan sentences aloud while students follow in their texts. Have a student read the last sentences and put the formula on the board: **area = length × width.** Ask another student to read the solution sentence. (There are 72 square units.)

Developing the Skill Give each student inch-square graph paper and ask them to outline a rectangle that is 6 squares by 8 squares. Demonstrate with the overhead projector. Have half the class multiply 6 × 8 to find the area, have the other half count the squares. Repeat this for a rectangle that is 11 by 8. Explain that rectangular shapes are not usually drawn on graph paper since it is easy to count the number of square units within. The formula A = L × W, allows them to calculate the area of any rectangle. Have each student measure the length and width of the top of their desk, to the closest inch, and multiply to find the area. Show students how to find the area of an irregular figure such as an L-shaped room, by breaking it into two rectangles, figuring each area and then adding to get the total.

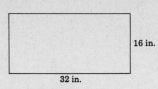

Practice

Practice

Find the area.

1.

16 in.

32 in.

A = 512 sq in.

2.

42 ft

56 ft

A = 2,352 sq ft

3.

39 yd

A = 1,521 sq yd

4.

10 in.

10 in.

8 in.

12 in.

A = 316 sq in.

Apply

Solve these problems.

5. Carpet tiles cost $4.08 each. How much will it cost to cover a rectangular floor that uses 246 tiles?
$1,003.68

6. A square floor is 4 yards on each side. A can of varnish covers 8 square yards. How many cans of varnish will be needed to cover the floor once?
2 cans

7. The width of a rectangular ceiling is 18 feet. The length is 3 feet less than the width. What is the area of the ceiling?
270 square feet

8. The area of a rectangular wall is 192 square feet. The height of the wall is 12 feet. What is the width?
16 feet

Use the ad to complete problems 9 and 10.

Paint	$ 7.80 per gallon
Brushes	$ 3.59 each
Rollers	$ 1.89 each
Ladders	$11.85 each

9. Lori used 4 gallons of paint to cover 4,992 square feet of walls. What was the cost of her paint if she paid $2.03 in tax?
$33.23

10. Lori bought a ladder, 3 brushes and a roller. The tax was $1.68. She gave the clerk $30. How much change did she receive?
$3.81

128

Practice

Have students complete the practice problems. Remind them that the formula, $A = L \times W$, only works for rectangles. Remind students to express each area in square units.

Mixed Practice

1. $1,000.00 − $565.75 ($434.25)
2. 907 × 388 (351,916)
3. 83,127 ÷ 56 (1,484 R23)
4. $512.75 × 50 ($25,637.50)
5. 3,127 + 48,951 + 2,146 (54,224)
6. 4,871 ÷ 8 (608 R7)
7. 19 + 35 + 176 + 8 (238)
8. $178.00 ÷ 50 ($3.56)
9. 1,573 − 895 (678)
10. 5,276 × 4 (21,104)

Correcting Common Errors

Some students may have difficulty seeing the difference between perimeter and area. Have them work with partners and different rectangles drawn on grid paper. Have them count the number of units a little bug would have to walk to go around the edge of the rectangle, the perimeter. Then have them count the number of squares the bug would need to completely cover the rectangle, the area.

Enrichment

Ask students to work in pairs to calculate the amount of wall space in the classroom. Point out that they will have to subtract the area of each window, door and chalkboard.

Extra Credit   *Geometry*

Give students paper, paints, scissors and a paper punch to make 3 symmetrical patterns. Have them put blots of paint on paper and then fold the paper while the paint is wet, making a symmetrical pattern about the fold line.

Have them take another sheet of paper, fold it in half, and then punch out a pattern with the paper punch. Ask students to open these sheets to see that the pattern is symmetrical about the fold line. Then have students fold a third sheet of paper and use scissors to cut out a pattern. Ask a student to demonstrate that the patterns are symmetrical. Explain that this kind of symmetry is called reflectional symmetry or mirror symmetry. Have a mirror available for students to hold along the fold lines to show that what they see in the mirror represents the whole pattern.

128

Volume

pages 129-130

Objective

To find the area of a rectangular solid

Materials

*set of inch cubes

Mental Math

Have students identify the correct unit:

1. 2 ___ = 120 minutes (hours)
2. 6 nickels = 30 ___ (pennies)
3. 10,560 feet = 2 ___ (miles)
4. 480 ___ = 8 minutes (seconds)
5. 5,000 pennies = 50 ___ (dollars)
6. 3 ___ = 36 inches (feet)
7. 3 years = 36 ___ (months)

Skill Review

Remind students that to find the area of a rectangular figure they multiply length by width. Write the formula on the board: **A = L × W**. Ask them to find the following areas:

length	width	area
42 in.	37 in.	(1,554 sq in.)
12 ft	19 ft	(228 sq ft)
1 ft	1 ft	(1 sq ft)
10 in.	10 in.	(100 sq in.)
12 in.	12 in.	(144 sq in.)
35 mi	25 mi	(875 sq mi)

Finding Volume

The **volume** of a container is the number of cubic units it takes to fill the container. Jose's new hobby is raising tropical fish. What is the volume of Jose's aquarium?

We want to find the aquarium's volume in cubic units.

The aquarium is ___8___ units high,

___6___ units long and ___4___ units wide.

We can find the volume by using a formula.

There are ___4___ times ___6___, or ___24___ blocks, on the bottom layer. There are

___8___ layers.

To find the total number of cubes, we multiply the number of rows, by the number of cubes in each, and again by the number of layers.

___4___ × ___6___ × ___8___ = ___192___ cubes.

If we multiply the length of a rectangular prism by its width, and again by its height, we will get its volume in cubic units.
The formula is: **V = L × W × H.**

There are ___192___ cubic units in Jose's aquarium.

Getting Started

Find the volume.

1.

V = ___60 cu units___

2.

V = ___40 cu units___

3.

V = ___30 cu units___

Complete the table.

4.	Length	3 yd	2 ft	27 in.	6 yd	4 ft
	Width	6 yd	6 ft	9 in.	2 yd	12 ft
	Height	8 yd	1 ft	15 in.	5 yd	25 ft
	Volume	144 cu yd	12 cu ft	3,645 cu in.	60 cu yd	1,200 cu ft

MCP All rights reserved

129

Teaching the Lesson

Introducing the Problem Read the problem aloud and remind students that the volume of a 3-dimensional object is the number of cubic units that will fit within it. Remind students that the formula for area (A = L × W) means that the area is L rows of W units in each row. Explain that the formula for volume results from multiplying the area of one face by the height of the solid. Read the information and plan sentences. Read the formula and have a student write it in words on the board. (Volume equals length times width times height.) Have a student read the solution sentence. (192 cubic units)

Developing the Skill Use the cubes to make a rectangular solid 3 cubes wide, 4 cubes long and 3 cubes high. Ask one student to count the area of the top of the solid. (12 cubes) Ask another to explain how many twelves are in the entire solid. (3 layers of 12 cubes each) Explain that the volume can be calculated without counting by multiplying to find the area of one face (3 × 4) and then multiplying by the other dimension (×3 = 36). Show students that it does not matter which face they start with. Have them calculate the area of one end (3 × 3) and multiply by the length. (×4 = 36) Remind students that multiplication is commutative.

Find the volume.

1.

2.

3.

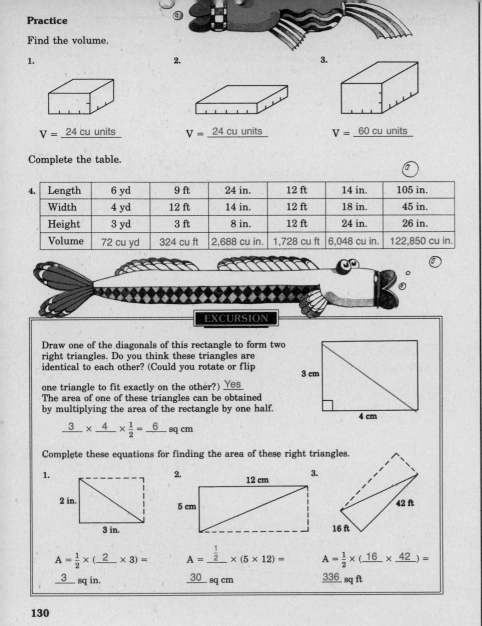

$V = \underline{24 \text{ cu units}}$

$V = \underline{24 \text{ cu units}}$

$V = \underline{60 \text{ cu units}}$

Complete the table.

4.	Length	6 yd	9 ft	24 in.	12 ft	14 in.	105 in.
	Width	4 yd	12 ft	14 in.	12 ft	18 in.	45 in.
	Height	3 yd	3 ft	8 in.	12 ft	24 in.	26 in.
	Volume	72 cu yd	324 cu ft	2,688 cu in.	1,728 cu ft	6,048 cu in.	122,850 cu in.

EXCURSION

Draw one of the diagonals of this rectangle to form two right triangles. Do you think these triangles are identical to each other? (Could you rotate or flip one triangle to fit exactly on the other?) __Yes__
The area of one of these triangles can be obtained by multiplying the area of the rectangle by one half.

3 cm

4 cm

$\underline{3} \times \underline{4} \times \frac{1}{2} = \underline{6}$ sq cm

Complete these equations for finding the area of these right triangles.

1.

2 in.

3 in.

2.

12 cm

5 cm

3.

42 ft

16 ft

$A = \frac{1}{2} \times (\underline{2} \times 3) = $

$\underline{3}$ sq in.

$A = \frac{1}{2} \times (5 \times 12) = $

$\underline{30}$ sq cm

$A = \frac{1}{2} \times (\underline{16} \times \underline{42}) = $

$\underline{336}$ sq ft

130

Correcting Common Errors

Some students may have difficulty understanding the relationship between multiplication and finding the volume of solid figures. Have them work with partners and small cubes to build rectangular prisms of varying sizes. Have them count the number of cubes in each and record it as the volume. Then have them discuss how they can use multiplication to find the number of cubes in one layer and then multiply by the number of layers to get the total number of cubes. Have them find the product of the 3 dimensions and compare it with the volume they recorded earlier to see that they are equal, or $V = L \times W \times H$.

Enrichment

Bring in a number of empty containers such as cereal boxes, ice cream cartons and cardboard boxes. Ask students to measure the dimensions of each container to the closest inch and multiply to find the volume.

Practice

Have students complete the practice problems. Explain that the table shows a series of rectangular solids, each with different dimensions. Point out that they are to read down each column to find the dimensions for one solid and then write its volume in the space below.

Excursion

Have students notice that the area of the triangle depends on the measure of the legs of the triangle and not the hypotenuse. It is helpful to draw the corresponding rectangle on each triangle to see which measures should be used.

Extra Credit *Probability*

Give each student a small cube made of paper or wood and ask them to number the sides 1 through 6 so that it looks like a die. Hand out commercially prepared dice and let students compare the one they made with the real die. Ask if they are the same. (probably not) Ask students to figure out the total number of ways that the six numbers can be arranged on the six sides of the dice. Let them discuss the problem with other students and compare their original dice. (There are 30 possible arrangements.) On modern dice, the opposite sides of each die equal 7. Ask students to find the total number of ways the numbers can be arranged and still meet this requirement. (There are 2 ways.) Show students these two patterns and tell them that the one on the left is the kind of die used in the Western world, the one on the left is used in Japan for the game Mah-Jongg.

Customary Capacity

pages 131-132

Objective

To rename customary units of weight and capacity

Materials

containers: ounce, cup, pint, quart and gallon weights: ounce and pound

Mental Math

Have students substitute 5 for n:

1. 3 × n (15)
2. (2 + n) × (n − 2) (21)
3. n × n (25)
4. (n × n) × 2 (50)
5. 21 − n (16)
6. (n × 0) + n (5)

Skill Review

Give each student a copy of this chart and have them fill in the blanks. Then go over the chart with the class.

    ——— fluid ounces = 1 cup (8)
    ——— cups = 1 pint (2)
    ——— pints = 1 quart (2)
    ——— cups = 1 quart (4)
    ——— quarts = 1 gallon (4)
    ——— fl oz = 1 quart (32)
    ——— ounces = 1 pound (16)

Customary Units, Weight and Capacity

Martin Elliot drinks 12 pints of milk each week. Martin's mother buys milk in gallon containers. How many gallons does Mrs. Elliot buy for Martin each week?

Table of Equivalent Measures	
1 cup (c) = 8 fluid ounces (fl oz)	1 quart (qt) = 2 pt
1 pint (pt) = 2 c	1 qt = 32 fl oz
1 pt = 16 fl oz	1 gallon (gal) = 4 qt
1 pound (lb) = 16 ounces (oz)	
1 ton (T) = 2,000 lb	

We want to find the number of gallons of milk Mrs. Elliot must buy each week.

There are __2__ pints in a quart and __4__ quarts in a gallon.
We find the number of pints in a gallon

by multiplying __2__ by __4__.
We find the number of gallons Mrs. Elliot needs by dividing the number of pints Martin drinks, by the

number of pints in a gallon. We divide __12__ by __8__.

$$\begin{array}{r} 1\text{ R}4 \\ 8\overline{)12} \end{array}$$ 12 pt = 1 gal 4 pt

Since 12 pints is more than 1 gallon, Mrs. Elliot

must buy __2__ gallons for Martin each week.

Getting Started

Rename these measurements.

1. 6 qt = __12__ pt

2. 1 qt = __32__ oz

3. 55 oz = __3__ lb __7__ oz

4. 5 gal = __20__ qt

5. 3 qt 4 pt = __20__ c

6. 2 gal 2 qt = __20__ pt

Complete these sentences.

7. To change quarts to ounces, __multiply__ by 32.

8. To change pounds and ounces to ounces, multiply the pounds by __16__ and __add__ the ounces.

Add or subtract. Simplify your answer.

9.	10.	11.	12.
3 pt 2 c + 2 pt 3 c —————— 7 pt 1 c	4 gal 3 qt − 2 gal 5 qt —————— 1 gal 2 qt	3 qt − 2 qt 5 oz —————— 27 oz	15 lb 11 oz + 9 lb 15 oz —————— 25 lb 10 oz

MCP All rights reserved

131

Teaching the Lesson

Introducing the Problem Have a student read the problem aloud. Ask the class to study the chart and have a student read the information sentences. Read the plan sentences aloud. Ask a student to work the division on the board and label the answer. (1 gal, 4 pt) Have another student interpret the answer and read the solution sentence. (must buy 2 gallons)

Developing the Skill Illustrate different standard units of volume and weight by showing the class a fluid ounce, cup, pint, quart, gallon, ounce and pound. Explain that although volume and weight can each be measured in ounces, the fluid ounce is always volume. Remind students that volume refers to the space that an object occupies and weight refers to its mass. Explain that they will multiply when converting larger units to smaller, and divide when converting smaller units to larger. Explain that when they add and subtract units of volume and weight they may have to rename units. Write these examples on the board:

3 gal 2 qt	5 pt 9 oz	4 pt 25 oz
+ 2 gal 3 qt	− 1 pt 12 oz =	− 1 pt 12 oz
——————	——————	——————
5 gal 5 qt = 6 gal 1 qt		3 pt 13 oz

Rename these measurements.

1. 12 pt = ___6___ qt

2. 1 T = ___32,000___ oz

3. 59 oz = ___3___ lb ___11___ oz

4. 5 qt 3 pt = ___26___ c

5. 64 oz = ___2___ qt

6. 1 qt = ___32___ oz

7. 2 gal 1 qt = ___9___ qt

8. 80 oz = ___5___ lb

9. 73 lb 12 oz = ___1,180___ oz

10. 4 qt 5 pt 1 c = ___216___ oz

11. 23 pt = ___2___ gal ___3___ qt ___1___ pt

12. 3 T 250 lb = ___6,250___ lb

Complete these sentences.

13. To change gallons to pints,
    multiply by ___8___ .

14. To change tons to pounds,
    multiply by ___2,000___ .

15. To change quarts and pints
    to pints, multiply the quarts
    by ___2___ and ___add___ the pints.

16. To change ounces to gallons,
    ___divide___ by 128.

Add or subtract. Simplify your answer.

17. 2 qt 1 pt
   + 3 qt 2 pt
   ‾‾‾‾‾‾‾‾‾‾
     6 qt 1 pt

18. 5 gal 3 qt
   − 2 gal 1 qt
   ‾‾‾‾‾‾‾‾‾‾‾
     3 gal 2 qt

19. 1 pt 9 oz
   + 5 pt 7 oz
   ‾‾‾‾‾‾‾‾‾‾
     7 pt

20. 6 qt 3 pt
   − 2 qt 5 pt
   ‾‾‾‾‾‾‾‾‾‾
     3 qt

21. 9 lb 8 oz
   − 3 lb 14 oz
   ‾‾‾‾‾‾‾‾‾‾‾
     5 lb 10 oz

22. 8 qt 24 oz
   + 5 qt 19 oz
   ‾‾‾‾‾‾‾‾‾‾‾
    14 qt 11 oz

23. 5 T 700 lb
   + 2 T 500 lb
   ‾‾‾‾‾‾‾‾‾‾‾
     7 T 1,200 lb

24. 3 gal
   − 1 gal 3 qt
   ‾‾‾‾‾‾‾‾‾‾‾
     1 gal 1 qt

Apply

Solve these problems.

25. Amy weighed nine pounds seven
    ounces at birth. Ricky's birth
    weight was eight pounds eleven
    ounces. How much more did Amy
    weigh?
    12 ounces

26. Happy Juice was on sale in the
    3-quart 8-ounce size for $7.28. The
    sale price for Super Juice in the
    2-quart 9-ounce size was $5.84.
    Which brand is more expensive per
    ounce?
    Super Juice

Correcting Common Errors

Some students may not simplify their
answer when they are adding customary units. Have them work with partners to write the conversion unit and
then write each of the following in
simplest form.
1. 2 qt 5 c (3 qt 1 c)
2. 4 gal 9 qt (6 gal 1 qt)
3. 4 lb 16 oz (5 lb)
4. 52 c (3 gal 1 qt)

Enrichment

Bring in an assortment of containers
and a quantity of puffed rice. Tell students to invent a system of volumetric
measurements from these objects.
Suggest that they name each unit and
then use the puffed rice to figure out
the number of smaller units to be
found in the next larger unit. Be sure
that there is a variety of containers so
that students can try many combinations. They will find that some do not
make convenient sets.

Practice

Have students complete the practice problems. Remind
them to label each answer with the proper units and to reduce units to the simplest answer.

Extra Credit *Biography*

Sophie Germain was born in 1776 to wealthy French parents who later felt her interest in mathematics was un-
healthy. They tried to discourage her studies but Sophie
persisted and lead the way for women to study mathematics. Sophie could not enter the Polytechnic Academy because she was a woman. So, she copied lecture notes from
friends, and wrote a final paper under the name (Mr.) Le-
Blanc. Her professor, Lagrange, was so impressed by the
paper that he insisted on meeting its author. When he found
out she was a woman, he was surprised but not disap-
pointed and encouraged her to continue her studies. The
high point of Sophie's career came when she submitted a
paper to the French Academy, that stated a law for vibrating
elastic surfaces. This paper, bearing her own name, won the
grand prize. Sophie Germain died at age 55.

Metric Length

pages 133-134

Objective

To measure length to the nearest centimeter and millimeter

Materials

inch rulers
centimeter rulers with millimeter markings
several pieces of tagboard

Mental Math

Have students identify the larger unit and give the equivalence of the smaller to the larger:

1. day, year (yr; 365 days = yr)
2. foot, inch (ft; 12 in. = ft)
3. ounce, pound (lb; 16 oz = lb)
4. cup, ounce (c; 8 oz = c)
5. year, mile (not possible; year = time, mile = distance)

Skill Review

Give each student a 12-inch ruler and have them measure numbered pieces of tagboard in different sizes. Have students list the length and width of each piece, to the closest inch, on a separate piece of paper.

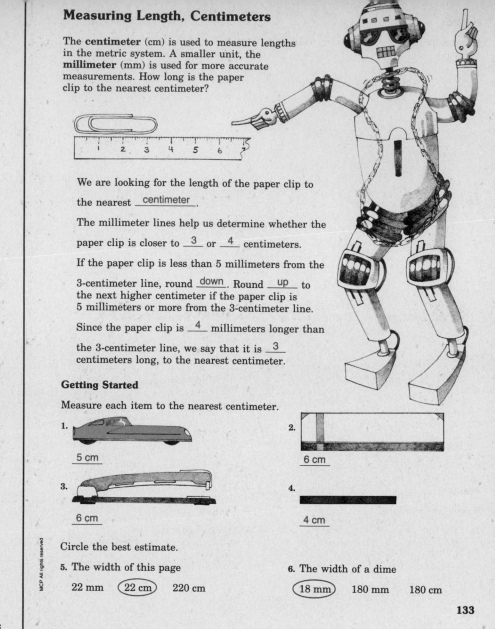

Measuring Length, Centimeters

The **centimeter** (cm) is used to measure lengths in the metric system. A smaller unit, the **millimeter** (mm) is used for more accurate measurements. How long is the paper clip to the nearest centimeter?

We are looking for the length of the paper clip to the nearest _centimeter_.

The millimeter lines help us determine whether the paper clip is closer to _3_ or _4_ centimeters.

If the paper clip is less than 5 millimeters from the 3-centimeter line, round _down_. Round _up_ to the next higher centimeter if the paper clip is 5 millimeters or more from the 3-centimeter line.

Since the paper clip is _4_ millimeters longer than the 3-centimeter line, we say that it is _3_ centimeters long, to the nearest centimeter.

Getting Started

Measure each item to the nearest centimeter.

1. 5 cm
2. 6 cm
3. 6 cm
4. 4 cm

Circle the best estimate.

5. The width of this page

22 mm   (22 cm)   220 cm

6. The width of a dime

(18 mm)   180 mm   180 cm

MCP All rights reserved

133

Teaching the Lesson

Introducing the Problem Have a student read the problem aloud and have students examine the illustration. Explain that length can be measured in inches, using the customary system of measurement, or in centimeters, using the metric system. Point out that in this lesson they will use centimeters and millimeters. Have a student read the information sentences. Remind students that rounding to read length on a ruler follows the same rules as rounding to the nearest ten or hundred. Have a student read the solution sentence. (4 mm longer; 3 cm long)

Developing the Skill Give each student a centimeter ruler and draw an enlarged 5-centimeter ruler on the board. Explain that they will read this ruler in centimeters (large markings) and the smaller millimeters (smaller markings). Ask a student to count the number of millimeters in a centimeter. (10) Point out that the metric system is easy to remember because all the units convert by a factor of ten. Put these conversions and abbreviations on the board:
10 mm = 1 cm, 10 cm = 1 dm, 10 dm = 1 m
Have students measure the pieces of tagboard and write the length and width of each to the nearest cm on another piece of paper.

133

Practice

Measure each item to the nearest centimeter.

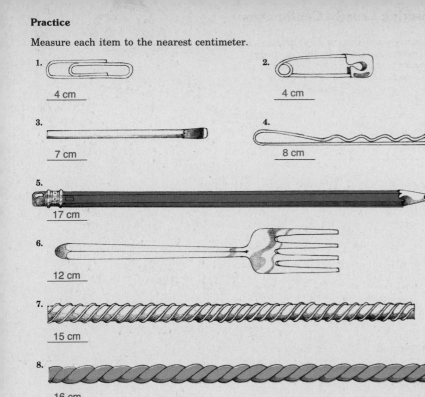

1. 4 cm

2. 4 cm

3. 7 cm

4. 8 cm

5. 17 cm

6. 12 cm

7. 15 cm

8. 16 cm

Circle the best estimate.

9. The width of a fingernail

(10 mm)   100 mm   10 cm

10. The height of a chair

45 mm   (45 cm)   450 cm

Apply

Solve these problems.

11. Find the perimeter of a picture frame that is 150 millimeters long and 125 millimeters wide.
550 millimeters

12. The area of a rectangle is 108 square centimeters. If the length of the rectangle is 12 centimeters, what is the width?
9 centimeters

134

Correcting Common Errors

Some students measure incorrectly because they do not properly line up the end of their ruler or the mark for 0 with the end of the object. Have these students work in pairs measuring objects such as the following:

1. their pencil to the nearest centimeter
2. the width of their desk to the nearest centimeter
3. the length of a fingernail to the nearest millimeter

Enrichment

Have students measure the circumference of:

1. their wrist to the nearest cm.
2. a finger to the nearest mm.
3. their foot to the nearest cm.
4. a pencil to the nearest mm.

Have string and scissors ready for students who ask for them. Have students compare methods for measuring circumference.

Practice

Have students complete the practice problems. Remind them to line up the zero end of the ruler each time they measure a length.

Extra Credit *Applications*

Explain to students that a statistician is a person who gathers and interprets information and then makes predictions. One way of making a prediction is to use **median** and **mode**. The median is the number in the middle when the numbers are arranged in order from the smallest to the largest. The mode is the number that occurs most often. For example:

Median: 17 19 23 28 32   23
Mode: 3 6 2 3 9 5 3 8   3

Have students ask the attendance officer in the school district or in their own school to supply a set of figures that shows the number of students absent each day for a four-week period. Working in pairs, have them find the median and the mode for each week, for the first two weeks, for each day of the week, the last two weeks and all four weeks. Then using the medians and modes, have them predict the number of absences for the next two weeks. Check with the attendance officer again in two weeks for the official figures to see how correct their predictions were.

134

More Metric Length

pages 135-136

Objectives

To choose the appropriate metric unit of length

To rename metric units of length

To calculate the perimeter, area, and volume of figures

Materials

meterstick

Mental Math

Have students substitute 3 for n:

1. $10 + 12 + n = $ (25)
2. $n + n + n + 15 = $ (24)
3. $10 + 10 + (n \times 0) = $ (20)
4. $50 + 100 + n + n = $ (156)
5. $(10 \times n) + (10 \times n) = $ (60)
6. $(n \times n) + (n \times n) + (n \times n) = $ (27)
7. $25 + n + 25 = $ (53)

Skill Review

Give each student a paper with 4 lines of different lengths on it. Have them measure the lines and round each length to the nearest centimeter and then to the nearest millimeter.

Measuring Length, Meters and Kilometers

Kathryn is training for the spring marathon. For practice, she ran in a 5-kilometer race. How many meters did she run?

> 1 meter (m) = 100 cm
> 1 kilometer (km) = 1,000 m

We are looking for the number of meters Kathryn ran.

One kilometer equals __1,000__ meters. Kathryn ran __5__ kilometers.

To find the total meters Kathryn ran, we multiply the number of meters in a kilometer by the number of kilometers she ran.

We multiply __1,000__ by __5__.

$1,000 \times 5 = $ __5,000__

Kathryn ran __5,000__ meters.

Getting Started

Circle the best estimate.

1. A person can walk ___?___ in 10 minutes.
   1 cm   1 m   (1 km)

2. The United States is about ___?___ wide.
   4,000 cm   4,000 m   (4,000 km)

3. A pair of scissors is about ___?___ long.
   (20 cm)   20 m   20 km

Rename these measurements.

4. 6 kilometers = __6,000__ meters   5. 10,000 meters = __10__ kilometers

Find the perimeter and the area of each figure.

6.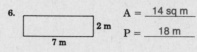
   A = __14 sq m__
   P = __18 m__

7.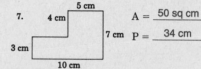
   A = __50 sq cm__
   P = __34 cm__

Find the volume of boxes having these measurements.

8. length = 15 cm
   width = 20 cm
   height = 10 cm   V = __3,000 cu cm__

9. length = 6 m
   width = 9 m
   height = 5 m   V = __270 cu m__

MCP All rights reserved

135

Teaching the Lesson

Introducing the Problem Have a student read the problem aloud. Ask the class to look at the chart of equivalents and notice that a meter is 100 centimeters and a kilometer, 1,000 meters. Read the information sentences aloud. Have a student explain whether the number of meters will be more or less than the number of kilometers. (more) Have a student read the plan sentences and the solution sentence aloud. (Kathryn ran 5,000 meters.)

Developing the Skill Have a student list customary units of length on the board: inch, foot, yard, mile. Explain that metric units can also be used to measure length and are preferable in many instances because they are easy to convert. List the metric units: **millimeter, centimeter, meter, kilometer.** Have students complete this conversion chart:

_____ millimeters = 1 centimeter (10)
_____ centimeters = 1 meter (100)
_____ meters = 1 kilometer (1,000)

Point out that because metric units differ by multiples of 10 they can be converted by adding or subtracting zeros. Ask students to explain how to multiply by 10 (add a zero), by 100 (add two zeros) and how to divide by 100. (subtract two zeros)

Circle the best estimate.

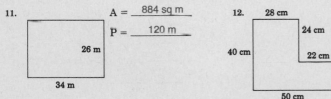

1. This page is about _____?_____ long.
   (28 cm)   28 m   28 km

2. The distance from Chicago to Los Angeles is about _____?_____
   2,800 cm   2,800 m   (2,800 km)

3. The distance around a running track is about _____?_____.
   400 cm   (400 m)   400 km

4. The English Channel is about _____?_____ long.
   560 cm   560 m   (560 km)

5. A necktie is about _____?_____ long.
   (60 cm)   60 m   60 km

6. A staple is about _____?_____ long.
   (1 cm)   1 m   1 km

Rename these measurements.

7. 2,000 meters = __2__ kilometers

8. 200 meters = _20,000_ centimeters

9. 3,000 centimeters = __30__ meters

10. 1 kilometer = _100,000_ centimeters

Find the perimeter and the area of each figure.

11.   A = _884 sq m_
      P = _120 m_
      26 m
      34 m

12.   28 cm   A = _1,472 sq cm_
      24 cm   P = _180 cm_
      40 cm
      22 cm
      16 cm
      50 cm

Find the volume of boxes having these measurements.

13. length = 5 m
    width = 9 m   V = _180 cu m_
    height = 4 m

14. length = 18 cm
    width = 18 cm   V = _5,832 cu cm_
    height = 18 cm

136

Correcting Common Errors

Some students may have difficulty choosing the appropriate unit of measure. Have them find and list items in the classroom that measure a centimeter, a decimeter, and a meter. Have them use these as models as they estimate the measures of other objects in the classroom. This provides students with everyday-life models to use for comparisons and estimates.

Enrichment

Have students estimate each of these lengths in an appropriate metric unit. Then ask them to measure each exactly. Explain that some cannot be measured with a meterstick. They are to use research materials for these.

1. height of a standard desk (about 73 cm)
2. height of a mature oak tree (Answers will depend on source.)
3. height of classroom door (about 2 meters)
4. distance from New York to Chicago (1,350 km)

Practice

Have students complete the practice problems. Remind them that centimeters could be used where inches are appropriate; meters, for feet or yards, and kilometers for miles.

Mixed Practice

1. 400 × 50 (20,000)
2. 60,150 − 28,395 (31,755)
3. 685,127 + 965,178 (1,650,305)
4. 28,549 ÷ 31 (920 R29)
5. 9 × 82,246 (740,214)
6. $411.21 ÷ 9 ($45.69)
7. 777 × 28 (21,756)
8. 2,158 ÷ 60 (35 R58)
9. $2,751.38 + $421.95 + $1,568.39 ($4,741.72)
10. 15,070 − 8,962 (6,108)

Extra Credit   *Applications*

Show the class a road map and explain that the letters and numbers along the edges of a map help locate towns or particular streets. Point out how the map key coincides with these indicators. Ask each student to make a map of the classroom, drawing in each desk, etc. Tell them to write the alphabet, evenly spaced, across the top and the numbers 1–10 down the left side. When the maps are finished, have students use the numbers and letters to locate particular student desks in the room. Ask them to put a key next to the map. For example: A-1, Jennifer; A-2, Tracy; and so on.

More Metric Capacity

pages 137-138

Objective

To choose appropriate metric units of capacity and weight

To rename metric units of capacity and weight

Materials

*cubic centimeter (milliliter)
*cubic decimeter (liter)
*gram/kilogram balance

Mental Math

Have students divide.

1. 25 ÷ 4 (6 R1)
2. 54 ÷ 6 (9)
3. 35 ÷ 8 (4 R3)
4. 100 ÷ 10 (10)
5. 75 ÷ 9 (8 R3)
6. 48 ÷ 7 (6 R6)

Skill Review

Remind students that to find the volume of a rectangular solid, they multiply width by length by height. Ask them to find the volume of:

	length	width	height	volume
1.	10 in.	6 in.	2 in.	(120 cu in.)
2.	4 cm	2 cm	2 cm	(16 cu cm)
3.	9 m	6 m	3 m	(162 cu m)
4.	11 m	8 m	1 m	(88 cu m)

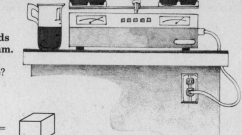

Metric Units, Weight and Capacity

In the metric system, there is a simple relationship between volume, capacity and weight. **One cubic centimeter holds 1 milliliter of water and weighs 1 gram.** What does a container of water weigh if it measures 20 centimeters on each edge?

1 cu cm = 1 mL = 1 g

1 liter (L) = 1,000 milliliters (mL)   1 kilogram (kg) = 1,000 grams (g)

1 metric ton = 1,000 kg

Since 1 cubic centimeter holds 1 milliliter of water, 8,000 cubic centimeters will hold __8,000__ milliliters or __8__ liters of water.

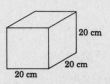

Since 1 milliliter of water weighs 1 gram, 8,000 milliliters of water weigh __8,000__ grams. The weight of the container is __8,000__ grams or __8__ kilograms.

Getting Started

Circle the answer that seems most reasonable.

1. A small puppy
   (450 g)   450 kg   450 T

2. A compact auto
   1,500 g   (1,500 kg)   1,500 T

3. A bathtub
   320 mL   (320 L)

4. A bottle of milk
   2 mL   (2 L)

Complete these equations.

5. 6,000 grams = __6__ kilograms

6. 3 liters = __3,000__ milliliters

Solve this problem.

7. How many milliliters of water will a container hold that is 4 centimeters long, 9 centimeters wide and 7 centimeters in height?
   252 milliliters

MCP All rights reserved

137

Teaching the Lesson

Introducing the Problem Have a student read the problem aloud. Explain that volume can also be called capacity, and that milliliters and liters are the metric units for capacity. Point out that the metric units for mass include the gram and the kilogram. Demonstrate with the cubic centimeter the relationship between units of length, capacity and mass. Have a student read the information and plan sentences. Explain that in these sentences the volume of the box has been calculated and that, because the gram is defined as one cu cm (mL) of water, the box weighs 8,000 gm or 8 kg.

Developing the Skill Explain the difference between mass and weight: mass is the amount of material in an object and weight is what that mass represents in the earth's gravitational field. Point out that because we usually speak of mass on Earth, the terms mass and weight are often used interchangeably. Fill the milliliter and liter with water and let students handle them to see what a gram and kilogram feel like.

Practice

Circle the answer that seems most reasonable.

1. A container holds about ___?___ of milk.

   4 mL (4 L)

2. This book

   1 g (1 kg) 1 T

3. A can of soup

   (150 g) 150 kg 150 T

4. A basketball

   (150 g) 150 kg 150 T

5. A comb

   (60 g) 60 kg 60 T

6. An eyedropper

   (1 mL) 1 L

Complete these equations.

7. 3 kilograms = ___3,000___ grams

8. 6,000 kilograms = ___6___ metric tons

9. 8,000 milliliters = ___8___ liters

10. 15 liters = ___15,000___ milliliters

11. 11,000 grams = ___11___ kilograms

12. 1 metric ton = ___1,000,000___ grams

Apply

Solve these problems.

13. If a dairy produces 24,000 milliliters of chocolate milk each minute, how many 2-liter bottles can be filled each minute?
    12 bottles

14. A container is 15 centimeters long, 12 centimeters wide and 6 centimeters in height. How many milliliters of water will it hold? How many grams does the water weigh?
    1,080 mL   1,080 g

15. Which container would hold more: a tin that measures 10 by 8 by 8 centimeters or a bottle that contains 1 liter?
    bottle

16. How many milliliters of water do you need to fill a container that measures 7 by 8 by 9 centimeters?
    504 mL

138

Correcting Common Errors

Some students will have difficulty choosing the appropriate unit of capacity. Have them work in groups to find the capacity of containers using an eyedropper and liter measures and record their measurements. Rotate the containers among the groups and have students compare their findings. For students who have difficulty choosing the appropriate unit of weight, have them weigh 1 liter of water (1 kilogram) and 1 milliliter of water (1 gram). They can then experiment with other amounts and weights of water.

Enrichment

Ask students to bring in an assortment of rocks. Show them one way to find the volume of an irregular object. Have them fill a container with water. Explain that when they put the rock in, water will spill out. Point out that it is possible to measure the water before and after the rock is put in and then calculate the volume of water each rock displaced.

Practice

Have students complete the practice problems. Suggest that they refer to the table of capacity and weight when renaming units.

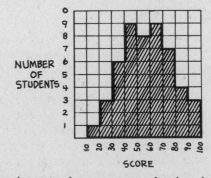

Extra Credit *Statistics*

Write **histogram** on the board and tell the class that a histogram is a bar graph with no space left between bars. Present the following example of a histogram, showing the number of students who received particular grades on a spelling text:

Explain that the unit of measurement for the observations is listed along the horizontal axis and the number of observations made at each level is listed along the vertical axis. Have students create their own histogram showing class size in your school. The number of classrooms in each category will be listed on the vertical axis and the number of children in a classroom along the horizontal axis. Display the graphs when students have finished.

Problem Solving Pictures, Diagrams

pages 139-140

Objective

To use pictures and diagrams to solve problems

Materials

Mental Math

Have students add:

1. 23 + 40 = (63)
2. 51 + 32 = (83)
3. 62 + 7 = (69)
4. 58 + 9 = (67)
5. 82 + 12 = (94)
6. 36 + 36 = (72)
7. 48 + 24 = (72)
8. 49 + 51 = (100)
9. 32 + 14 + 11 = (57)
10. 15 + 15 + 15 = (45)

Drawing a Picture or Diagram

The desks in our classroom are in straight rows with the same number of desks in each row. Unless someone is absent, each desk is filled. Fred sits in the second row from the front and the fourth row from the back. He is the third student from the left end of the room, and the fourth student from the right end. How many students are in the class?

★ **SEE**

We want to know how many students are in the class. There is a student at each desk.

The number of desks equals the number of __students__. There are the same number of desks in each row.

Fred's desk is in the __second__ row from the front.

His desk is in the __fourth__ row from the back.

His desk is the __third__ from the left side of the room.

His desk is the __fourth__ from the right side of the room.

★ **PLAN**

We can understand all of this information by drawing a picture.

★ **DO**

There are __30__ students in the class.

★ **CHECK**

Compare your drawing with the clues in the problem. Is Fred's desk in the right place in relation to the

four sides of the classroom? __Yes__

Draw in the missing desks so that there are straight rows and the number of students in each row is the same.

MCP All rights reserved

139

Teaching the Lesson

Read the problem aloud. Ask students if they can visualize where Fred sits. (probably not) Remind them of the SEE-PLAN-DO-CHECK method of working problems. Explain that this problem can be solved by drawing the room, following the instructions given in the text. Have one student read the SEE section of the model. Read the PLAN section aloud, and explain that while they cannot visualize the room, they can draw a picture of it. Ask the class to look at the drawing in their texts. Use the overhead projector to show that Fred can be located two rows from the front, four from the back, third from the left and fourth from the right. Have each student make a picture including all the desks in the class, putting an X through Fred's. Ask a student to count the number of desks in the picture. (30) Have another multiply the number of desks in one row times the number of rows. (5 × 6 = 30) Ask a student to read the CHECK section of the problem aloud while the others check their drawings.

139

Apply

Draw a picture or diagram to help solve each problem.

1. There are six flags equally spaced around the track. It takes Susan 20 seconds to run from the first to the second flag. If she continues at the same rate, how long will it take Susan to run the complete track?
120 seconds or 2 minutes

2. The school driveway is 90 meters long. The fifth grade decided to plant trees along each side of it. The trees are to be evenly spaced 5 meters apart. How many trees will be needed?
38 trees

3. Mrs. Nolanski fenced in her square vegetable garden. There were 15 fenceposts on each side. How many fenceposts did she use?
56 fence posts

4. Farmer Anderson has 9 pigs in a pigpen. Draw a plan for him to use four straight lines to put each pig in its own individual pen.
See Solution Notes.

5. How much will it cost to cut a log into 8 pieces, if cutting it into four pieces costs $0.75?
$1.75

6. Timothy is on a ladder leaning against a wall that he is painting. He starts on the middle rung, goes up 5 rungs, down 7 rungs, up 4 rungs and up 9 more rungs to reach the top bar. How many rungs are on the ladder?
23 rungs

7. Samuel's father wants to build a fence around his patio. The fence will be in the shape of a rectangle 60 feet long and 48 feet wide. The posts will be 6 feet apart. How many posts will be needed?
36 posts

8. A frog is at the bottom of a 20-foot well. Each day he jumps 5 feet but during the night he slides down 2 feet. How many days will it take him to jump out of the well?
6 days

9. Aunt Sarah has a rectangular-shaped vegetable patch that is 48 feet long and 16 feet wide. Uncle Samuel has a square-shaped vegetable patch. If his patch has the same perimeter as Aunt Sarah's patch, how long is one side of his patch?
32 feet

10. Cousin Caroline has 64 feet of fence including a gate. She wants to enclose a rectangular space in her yard for a flower garden. She wants to enclose the greatest area possible with her fence. What should be the dimensions of her garden?
16 ft by 16 ft

11. Percy has a picture of his pet poodle. He decides to have it enlarged by doubling both the length and the width. How does this affect the area?
4 times as large

12. Betty is making a box for her bows. She decides to make it larger by doubling all three of its dimensions. How does this affect the volume?
8 times as large

140

Extra Credit   *Applications*

Collect several mail-order catalogs. Allow the students to study them, noting how they are organized and the procedure used to order from them. Give the students a spending limit of $100, including tax, shipping and other charges. Let them select some items to order and help them to complete an order form.

Solution Notes

1. Have students draw an oval track with six flags evenly spaced, label 20 seconds between each flag, and add or multiply. (100 sec or 1 min 40 sec)

2. Ask where the first trees will be. (at one end of drive) Suggest that they draw each tree as a circle along the drive and keep track of the distance. (38 trees)

3. The number of posts is not just 15×4, because those at the corners are shared by two sides. Have them draw the garden. Point out that there are actually $(15 - 1) \times 4$ posts.

4. The four lines required do not include the pen itself. The four straight lines divide it into nine compartments.

5. Suggest students draw the log and count the number of lines (cuts) to make four pieces. (3) Explain that each cut must have cost $.25. Now have them count the number of cuts required to make 4 pieces into 8 (4 more), multiply by $.25 ($1), and add to get the total cost. ($1 + .75 = $1.75)

6. Have students draw a ladder and show upward and downward movement with arrows. Remind them to count the center rung. (23 rungs)

7. Remind them that there will be posts shared at each corner.

8. Some students may be able to solve this without a drawing, noticing that the total movement up each day is 3 feet, except on the last day when he will go the entire 5 feet out. (5 days at 3 feet + 1 day at 5 feet.)

Higher-Order Thinking Skills

9. Synthesis: Find the perimeter of Aunt Sarah's patch. (128 ft) Since a square has 4 equal sides, divide 128 by 4 to find the length of one side.

10. Analysis: The answer can be found by finding the areas of different rectangles, all of which have a perimeter of 64 ft.

11. Synthesis

12. Synthesis

140

Chapter Test

page 141

Item	Objective
1-8	Rename units of customary and metric measures (See pages 117-118, 123-124, 131-132, 135-138)
9	Find area of rectangles (See pages 127-128)
10	Find volume of rectangular solids (See pages 129-130)
11-12	Answer questions about time (See pages 117-120)
13-14	Find perimeter of simple figures (See pages 125-126)
15-16	Add, subtract customary units of length (See pages 123-124)
17-18	Choose appropriate units of length (See pages 133-136)

Rename these measurements.

1. 5 hours 15 minutes = ___315___ minutes

2. 3 hours = ___10,800___ seconds

3. 5 feet 9 inches = ___69___ inches

4. 79 feet = ___26___ yards ___1___ feet

5. 39 ounces = ___2___ pounds ___7___ ounces

6. 3 gallons = ___12___ quarts

7. 3 kilometers = ___3,000___ meters

8. 5,000 milliliters = ___5___ liters

Solve these problems.

9. Find the area of a square that is 16 feet on each side.
256 square feet

10. Find the volume of a box that is 24 inches long, 16 inches wide and 9 inches high.
3,456 cubic inches

Complete these sentences.

11. There are ___31___ days in July.

12. When it is 4:00 PM in Boston, it is ___1:00 PM___ in Seattle.

Find the perimeter.

13.
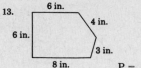
6 in.
6 in.
4 in.
3 in.
8 in.
P = ___27 in.___

14.

8 cm
P = ___48 cm___

Add or subtract.

15.   6 ft 9 in.
    + 3 ft 8 in.
    ----
    10 ft 5 in.

16.   8 yd 2 ft
    − 5 yd 3 ft
    ----
    2 yd 2 ft

Circle the best estimate.

17. A desk is about ___?___ high.
75 mm   (75 cm)   75 m

18. A pencil can be most accurately measured in ___?___.
(cm)   m   km

MCP All rights reserved

141

Circle the letter of the correct answer.

1 What is the place value of the 7 in 326,475?

- a ones
- (b) tens
- c hundreds
- d NG

2 13,605 ◯ 13,506

- (a) >
- b <
- c =

3 596
  + 437

- a 933
- b 1,023
- (c) 1,033
- d NG

4 $637.15
  + 209.18

- a $836.33
- (b) $846.33
- c $946.33
- d NG

5 7,462
  − 6,847

- a 625
- b 1,425
- c 1,625
- (d) NG

6 $923.06
  − 218.39

- a $604.67
- (b) $704.67
- c $715.33
- d NG

7 408 × 9

- (a) 3,672
- b 3,762
- c 36,072
- d NG

8 39
  × 28

- a 390
- (b) 1,092
- c 1,292
- d NG

9 What is the GCF of 21 and 36?

- a 7
- b 9
- (c) 3
- d NG

10 Find the average of 36, 39 and 42.

- a 36
- (b) 39
- c 42
- d NG

11 46)2,900

- a 63
- (b) 63 R2
- c 63 R46
- d NG

12 47)$349.21

- (a) $7.43
- b $74.30
- c $743
- d NG

13 Find the area.

16 ft
21 ft

- a 74 ft
- b 336 ft
- (c) 336 sq ft
- d NG

☐ score

142

Cumulative Review

Item	Objective
1	Identify place value in a number less than 1,000,000 (See pages 11-12)
2	Compare and order numbers through hundred thousands (See pages 21-22)
3	Add two numbers, sums less than 1,000, one regrouping (See pages 23-24)
4	Add two numbers up to 5-digits (See pages 27-28)
5	Subtract two 4-digit numbers (See pages 33-34)
6	Subtract two numbers up to 6-digits, zeros in the minuend (See pages 35-36)
7	Multiply up to a 6-digit by 1-digit factor (See pages 55-56)
8	Multiply two 2-digit factors (See pages 57-58)
9	Find the greatest common factor (See pages 95-96)
10	Find the average (See pages 91-92)
11	Divide a 4-digit by 2-digit number, quotient with remainder (See pages 103-106)
12	Divide a 5-digit by 2-digit number (See pages 107-108)
13	Find the area of rectangles (See pages 127-128)

142

Alternate Cumulative Review

Circle the letter of the correct answer.

1 Give the place value of the 6 in 497,165.

- a ones
- (b) tens
- c hundreds
- d NG

2 18,708 ◯ 18,807

- (a) <
- b >
- c =

3 648
  + 347

- a 985
- (b) 995
- c 1,095
- d NG

4 $579.67
  + 319.05

- a $888.72
- b $898.62
- (c) $898.72
- d NG

5 9,372
  − 8,625

- a 737
- b 746
- c 1,747
- (d) NG

6 $841.03
  − 438.59

- a $403.44
- (b) $402.44
- c $412.44
- d NG

7 703
  ×8

- (a) 5,624
- b 5,704
- c 56,024
- d NG

8 49
  ×72

- a 3,518
- (b) 3,528
- c 3,428
- d NG

9 What is the GCF of 12 and 42?

- (a) 6
- b 12
- c 3
- d NG

10 Find the average. 44, 37, 54

- a 44
- (b) 45
- c 48
- d NG

11 37)2,702

- a 73
- (b) 73 R1
- c 73 R37
- d NG

12 48)$456.96

- (a) $9.52
- b $9.51 R4
- c $9.52
- d NG

Fractions

pages 143-144

Objective

To use fractions to describe part of a whole

Materials

sheets of paper
ruler marked in eighths

Mental Math

Have students multiply:

1. $5 \times 3 \times 2 =$ (30)
2. $8 \times 2 \times 1 =$ (16)
3. $12 \times 2 \times 2 =$ (48)
4. $2 \times 5 \times 5 =$ (50)
5. $4 \times 9 \times 2 =$ (72)
6. $4 \times 4 \times 0 =$ (0)
7. $3 \times 3 \times 3 =$ (27)

Skill Review

Draw a ruler marked in eighths, on the board. Ask the class to find the following points on their rulers and demonstrate the position of each fraction on the board: ½, 1¾, ⅞, 3⅜, 9⅛, 5¼, 5½, 4⅝. Have students indicate points on the board ruler and ask others to identify each point.

7

FRACTIONS

Writing Fractions

Fractions are used to show a part of a region or a part of a set. What part of the flag is red? What part of the set is pennants?

We want to find what part of the flag is red.

The flag is divided into 4 equal parts. 3 parts are colored red. We use a fraction to show what part is red.

number of red parts	3	**numerator**
total number of equal parts	4	**denominator**

Three fourths of the flag is red.

We want to find what part of the set is pennants.

There are 3 objects in the set. 2 of the objects are pennants. We use a fraction to show what part of the total set is pennants.

number of pennants	2	**numerator**
total number of objects	3	**denominator**

Two thirds of the set is pennants.

✔ When writing a fraction to name parts of a region or parts of a set, the **numerator** always represents the portion of the region or set we are naming in the fraction. The **denominator** always represents the total number of parts or objects in the set.

Getting Started

Write the word-name for each fraction.

1. $\frac{1}{3}$ one third
2. $\frac{2}{5}$ two fifths
3. $\frac{2}{9}$ two ninths

Write the fraction.

4. three fourths $\frac{3}{4}$
5. five eighths $\frac{5}{8}$
6. five sixths $\frac{5}{6}$
7. one fourth $\frac{1}{4}$

Write the fraction for each red part.

8. 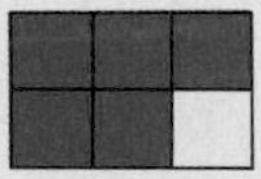 $\frac{5}{6}$

9. 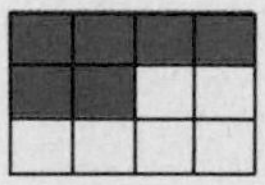 $\frac{6}{12}$

Write a fraction to answer the question.

10. What part of the apples is red?

$\frac{5}{5}$

MCP All rights reserved

Teaching the Lesson

Introducing the Problem Have a student read the problem aloud and describe the illustration. Have one student read the first set of information sentences. Write: **numerator** and **denominator** on the board. Explain that the denominator identifies the size of each fractional part or denomination, and the numerator tells how many of that part are being described or the number. Write the fraction **¾** on the board making sure to write the numerator directly **over** the denominator. Have students point to numerator and denominator and explain the meaning of the fraction. (3 red parts out of a total of 4) Ask another student to complete the information sentences. Have a student write the fraction that describes this part of the set on the board. (⅔)

Developing the Skill Draw a circle on the board and divide it into fifths. Ask a student to describe one piece of the circle as a fraction. (⅕) Ask another to shade ⅖ of the circle. Explain that the circle has been divided into five equal parts, each one is a fifth. Put a number line on the board and ask a student to divide it into sixths. Have others shade 2⁄6 of the line, then ⅚ of the line. Draw a set of 10 objects on the board. Shade three and ask a student to write a fraction expressing the unshaded area. (7⁄10) Have another student change the shaded fraction to 5⁄10.

Practice

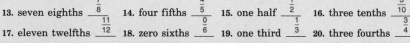

Write the word-name for each fraction.

1. $\frac{2}{3}$ ___two thirds___ 2. $\frac{1}{5}$ ___one fifth___ 3. $\frac{5}{8}$ ___five eighths___ 4. $\frac{7}{9}$ ___seven ninths___

5. $\frac{7}{10}$ ___seven tenths___ 6. $\frac{5}{12}$ ___five twelfths___ 7. $\frac{2}{8}$ ___two eighths___ 8. $\frac{0}{3}$ ___zero thirds___

9. $\frac{1}{4}$ ___one fourth___ 10. $\frac{7}{8}$ ___seven eighths___ 11. $\frac{1}{10}$ ___one tenth___ 12. $\frac{5}{6}$ ___five sixths___

Write the fraction.

13. seven eighths ___$\frac{7}{8}$___ 14. four fifths ___$\frac{4}{5}$___ 15. one half ___$\frac{1}{2}$___ 16. three tenths ___$\frac{3}{10}$___

17. eleven twelfths ___$\frac{11}{12}$___ 18. zero sixths ___$\frac{0}{6}$___ 19. one third ___$\frac{1}{3}$___ 20. three fourths ___$\frac{3}{4}$___

Write the fraction for each red part.

21. $\frac{2}{8}$ 22. $\frac{3}{8}$ 23. $\frac{5}{12}$ 24. $\frac{1}{5}$

25. $\frac{1}{2}$ 26. 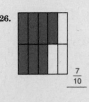 $\frac{7}{10}$ 27. $\frac{2}{6}$ 28. $\frac{5}{12}$

Write a fraction to answer each question.

29. What part of the cars is red?

 $\frac{5}{5}$

30. What part of the glasses is red?

 $\frac{3}{5}$

31. What part of all the figures is boxes?

 $\frac{4}{6}$

32. What part of all the numbers is greater than 10?

1 3 11 2 6 15 $\frac{2}{6}$

Shade the objects each fraction represents.

33. $\frac{2}{3}$

34. $\frac{7}{8}$

144

Correcting Common Errors

Watch for students who confuse the numerator and denominator when writing a fraction. Have them work with partners and the following fractions: ⅓, ¾, ⅖, and ⅞. Have students take turns identifying the numerator and denominator and drawing a model to illustrate the fraction.

Enrichment

Ask members of the group to count the number of students in the class. Now ask them to express each of these numbers as a fraction of the total class: (Answers will vary.)

1. the number of students with blond hair.
2. the number of students with brown eyes.
3. the number of students wearing blue.
4. the number of students who have at least one brother.
5. the number of students with brown hair and brown eyes.

Practice

Have students complete the practice problems. Write these words on the board for reference: **half, third, fourth, fifth, sixth, seventh, eighth, ninth, tenth.**

Extra Credit *Applications*

Tell students it is often important to know how to figure the number of hours in a particular time span. When they get a job that pays an hourly wage, they will want to be able to calculate their wages. Demonstrate and practice with the class how to figure work hours accurately. Ask how many hours they worked if they punched in at 8:00 and punched out at 5:00, or worked from 7:15 until 3:45. Have students calculate how many hours a week they would work if they worked this same schedule 3, 5 and 6 days a week. Have students research the meanings of flex-time, comp time and paid vacations.

144

Equivalent Fractions

pages 145-146

Objective

To recognize equivalent fractions

Materials

*overhead transparencies with equivalent fractional parts
*overhead projector

Mental Math

Ask students to divide each of these sums by 2:

1. 24 + 4 (14)
2. 12 + 18 (15)
3. 10 + 10 + 6 (13)
4. 20 + 20 + 10 (25)
5. 26 + 22 (24)
6. 16 + 32 (24)
7. 50 + 30 (40)

Skill Review

Use circles divided like pies to illustrate each of these fractions on the board: ⅓, ⅖, ¼, ¹⁄₁₀, ¾ and ⅔.
Ask students to identify each fraction.

Finding Equivalent Fractions

Craig has a recipe that calls for $\frac{2}{4}$ of a cup of milk. How many times should Craig fill his measuring cup to measure the right amount?

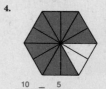

We want to find a way Craig can measure the correct amount with his cup.

His cup measures $\frac{1}{2}$ of a cup and he

needs to measure $\frac{2}{4}$ of a cup of milk.

We need to compare $\frac{1}{2}$ and $\frac{2}{4}$.

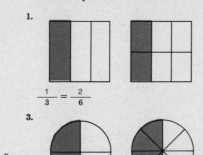

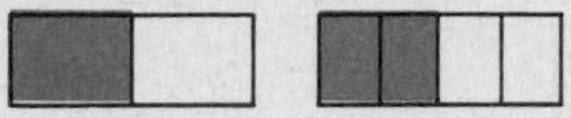

$\frac{1}{2}$ and $\frac{2}{4}$ measure the same amount.

✔ They are **equivalent fractions** because both fractions represent the same amount.

We write: $\frac{1}{2} = \frac{2}{4}$.

Craig can fill his measuring cup $\frac{1}{2}$ time

because $\frac{1}{2}$ of a cup is equal to $\frac{2}{4}$ of a cup.

Getting Started

Write the equivalent fractions for the red parts.

1.
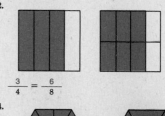
$$\frac{1}{3} = \frac{2}{6}$$

2.
$$\frac{3}{4} = \frac{6}{8}$$

3.

$$\frac{2}{4} = \frac{4}{8}$$

4. 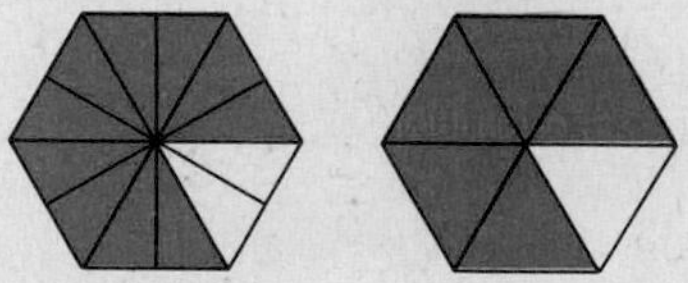
$$\frac{10}{12} = \frac{5}{6}$$

MCP All rights reserved

145

Teaching the Lesson

Introducing the Problem   Read the problem aloud and ask a student to read and complete the information sentences. Explain that they have to compare the two measures and have them complete the plan sentence in their texts. Direct their attention to the cups illustrated in their books. Ask a student to compare the amounts. (They are the same.) Have another read the solution sentence. (½ and ²⁄₄ measure the same amount.) Explain that ½ and ²⁄₄ are equivalent fractions, meaning they represent the same amount. Read the final sentence to the class.

Developing the Skill   Make a set of overhead transparencies showing circles divided into halves, thirds, fourths, fifths, sixths, eighths, ninths and tenths. Use the overhead projector to show the class equivalent fractions. Start by showing students that fourths can be laid directly over halves. Ask a student to identify the number of fourths in each half. (2) Write ²⁄₄ = ½ on the board. Put up circles for thirds and sixths. Ask a student to count the number of sixths in a third (2) and the number of sixths in two thirds (4). Write ²⁄₆ = ⅓ and ⁴⁄₆ = ⅔ on the board. Continue, comparing fourths and eighths, fifths and tenths, halves and eighths, and thirds and ninths.

145

Write the equivalent fractions for the red parts.

1.
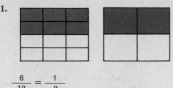

$$\frac{6}{12} = \frac{1}{2}$$

2.

$$\frac{2}{3} = \frac{4}{6}$$

3.
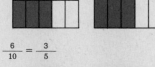

$$\frac{6}{10} = \frac{3}{5}$$

4.

$$\frac{1}{2} = \frac{5}{10}$$

5.
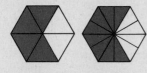

$$\frac{4}{6} = \frac{8}{12}$$

6.
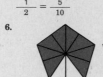

$$\frac{8}{10} = \frac{4}{5}$$

7.
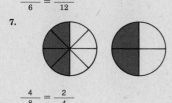

$$\frac{4}{8} = \frac{2}{4}$$

8.

$$\frac{6}{9} = \frac{12}{18}$$

EXCURSION

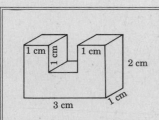

Find the surface area of this 3-dimensional figure by finding the area of each of its faces. You will have to imagine the faces which are not visible to you, such as the back face, the bottom face, etc.

22 square centimeters

146

Correcting Common Errors

Have students who have trouble with equivalent fractions work with partners. The first partner draws a model for the first fraction in the exercise. The second partner divides the model into the number of parts indicated by the denominator of the second fraction and writes the numerator by counting the number of parts in the shaded section of the model.

1. $\frac{1}{2} = \frac{\square}{6}$ (3)
2. $\frac{3}{4} = \frac{\square}{8}$ (6)
3. $\frac{3}{4} = \frac{\square}{12}$ (9)

Enrichment

Ask students to double this recipe and then reduce each measurement to the simplest, equivalent fraction.

Cookies
$\frac{2}{3}$ c shortening ($\frac{4}{3} = 1\frac{1}{3}$)
$\frac{3}{4}$ c sugar ($\frac{6}{4} = 1\frac{1}{2}$)
1 eggs (2)
1 t vanilla (2)
$1\frac{1}{2}$ c flour ($2\frac{2}{2} = 3$)
$1\frac{1}{2}$ t baking powder ($2\frac{2}{2} = 3$)
$\frac{1}{4}$ t salt ($\frac{2}{4} = \frac{1}{2}$)
4 t milk (8)
Mix. Bake at 375° for 12 minutes.

Practice

Have students complete all the problems. Remind them that to write a fraction for the shaded areas, they will put the number of shaded parts over the total number of parts.

Excursion

Suggest that the faces be named, such as the front, back, right side, left side, bottom, tops or sides in the U-shape. The front and back faces will need to be partitioned into squares or rectangles in order to find their areas.

Extra Credit *Applications*

Discuss with students the problems astronauts have had dealing with weightlessness in space. Provide students with a spring scale. Ask them to weigh a number of ordinary objects and list these as Earth weight. Then have them calculate what each object would weigh on the moon, where the pull of gravity is $\frac{1}{6}$ that of the Earth's.

Find Equivalent Fractions

pages 147-148

Objective

To use multiplication to find equivalent
  fractions

Materials

set of equivalent fraction
  manipulatives

Mental Math

Have students order these fractions
from smallest to largest:

1. ¼, ¾, ²⁄₄ (¼, ²⁄₄, ¾)
2. ³⁄₈, ¼, ⅝ (¼, ³⁄₈, ⅝)
3. ⅘, ¹⁄₁₀, ⅗ (¹⁄₁₀, ⅗, ⅘)
4. ²⁄₈, ½, ⅛ (⅛, ²⁄₈, ½)

Skill Review

Draw 3 parallel lines on the board:
one divided in half, one in fourths and
one in sixths. Explain that each line
represents a whole divided into fractional parts. Have students identify
pairs of equivalent fractions by comparing points on the lines.

Multiplying to Find Equivalent Fractions

Chang said $\frac{3}{4}$ of the cars were red, but
Raul thought $\frac{9}{12}$ of them were red. The
teacher said both boys were correct.
Why are they both right?

They are both right because $\frac{3}{4}$ and $\frac{9}{12}$ are
equivalent fractions.

To understand this, we need to consider
the **identity element of multiplication.**
Whenever the same non-zero number
appears in both the numerator and
denominator, the fraction is equal to 1.

Thus, $\frac{2}{2} = 1$, $\frac{3}{3} = 1$, $\frac{4}{4} = 1$ and $\frac{7}{7} = \boxed{1}$.

✔ The number 1 is the identity element of
multiplication. This means that whenever we multiply
a number by 1, we get the same number.

To prove that $\frac{3}{4}$ and $\frac{9}{12}$ are equivalent fractions, we
need to show how $\frac{3}{4}$ has been multiplied by 1 to get $\frac{9}{12}$.

$$\frac{3}{4} \times \frac{\boxed{3}}{\boxed{3}} = \frac{3 \times \boxed{3}}{4 \times \boxed{3}} = \frac{9}{12}$$

✔ Equivalent fractions can be found by multiplying
both the numerator and denominator by the same
non-zero number.

Getting Started

Write the missing factors.

1. $\frac{5}{6} \times \frac{\boxed{4}}{\boxed{4}} = \frac{20}{24}$ 2. $\frac{1}{5} \times \frac{\boxed{3}}{\boxed{3}} = \frac{3}{15}$ 3. $\frac{3}{4} \times \frac{\boxed{2}}{\boxed{2}} = \frac{6}{8}$ 4. $\frac{2}{7} \times \frac{\boxed{3}}{\boxed{3}} = \frac{6}{21}$

Write the equivalent fraction.

5. $\frac{2}{3} = \frac{6}{9}$ 6. $\frac{3}{7} = \frac{6}{14}$ 7. $\frac{2}{5} = \frac{6}{15}$ 8. $\frac{3}{8} = \frac{15}{40}$

Are these fractions equivalent?

9. $\frac{1}{2}$ $\frac{4}{8}$ __Yes__   10. $\frac{2}{9}$ $\frac{5}{27}$ __No__   11. $\frac{2}{3}$ $\frac{4}{12}$ __No__   12. $\frac{2}{4}$ $\frac{8}{16}$ __Yes__

MCP All rights reserved

147

Teaching the Lesson

Introducing the Problem Have a student read the
problem aloud and describe the illustration. Explain the
identity element in multiplication: a number multiplied by
one equals itself. For fractions this means a fraction multiplied by a fraction equaling one, will equal the original fraction. Explain that any fraction in which numerator and denominator are the same, equals one. Continue to read
aloud and put the next steps on the board: $\frac{3}{4} \times \frac{n}{n} = \frac{3}{4}$,
$\frac{3}{4} \times \frac{3}{3} = \frac{9}{12}$, $\frac{3}{4} = \frac{9}{12}$. Remind students that the product
of two fractions has the product of numerators in the nu-
merator, and of denominators in the denominator. Read the
final sentence.

Developing the Skill Explain that finding equivalent
fractions usually involves looking for a missing factor. Write
on board: $\frac{1}{5} \times \frac{n}{n} = \frac{2}{10}$. Point out that there is some number, n, which when multiplied by 1 gives 2, when multiplied
by 5 gives 10. Ask a student to identify the number n. (2)
Repeat for $\frac{2}{3}$ and $\frac{6}{9}$. (3) Explain that sometimes they have
to find the missing factor in order to find an equivalent fraction. Put on the board: $\frac{1}{2} = \frac{?}{8}$. Show the class that to
change halves to eighths they must multiply both numerator
and denominator by 4: $\frac{1}{2} = \frac{4}{8}$.

147

Write the missing factors.

1. $\frac{3}{4} \times \frac{\boxed{2}}{\boxed{2}} = \frac{6}{8}$

2. $\frac{1}{2} \times \frac{\boxed{6}}{\boxed{6}} = \frac{6}{12}$

3. $\frac{2}{5} \times \frac{\boxed{4}}{\boxed{4}} = \frac{8}{20}$

4. $\frac{5}{7} \times \frac{\boxed{5}}{\boxed{5}} = \frac{25}{35}$

5. $\frac{1}{4} \times \frac{\boxed{4}}{\boxed{4}} = \frac{4}{16}$

6. $\frac{5}{6} \times \frac{\boxed{6}}{\boxed{6}} = \frac{30}{36}$

7. $\frac{6}{15} \times \frac{\boxed{4}}{\boxed{4}} = \frac{24}{60}$

8. $\frac{3}{8} \times \frac{\boxed{8}}{\boxed{8}} = \frac{24}{64}$

9. $\frac{2}{3} \times \frac{\boxed{5}}{\boxed{5}} = \frac{10}{15}$

10. $\frac{1}{6} \times \frac{\boxed{7}}{\boxed{7}} = \frac{7}{42}$

11. $\frac{3}{10} \times \frac{\boxed{5}}{\boxed{5}} = \frac{15}{50}$

12. $\frac{4}{9} \times \frac{\boxed{7}}{\boxed{7}} = \frac{28}{63}$

13. $\frac{2}{9} \times \frac{\boxed{3}}{\boxed{3}} = \frac{6}{27}$

14. $\frac{3}{11} \times \frac{\boxed{4}}{\boxed{4}} = \frac{12}{44}$

15. $\frac{7}{8} \times \frac{\boxed{7}}{\boxed{7}} = \frac{49}{56}$

16. $\frac{3}{14} \times \frac{\boxed{3}}{\boxed{3}} = \frac{9}{42}$

Write the equivalent fraction.

17. $\frac{7}{8} = \frac{14}{16}$

18. $\frac{3}{5} = \frac{15}{25}$

19. $\frac{2}{3} = \frac{8}{12}$

20. $\frac{7}{8} = \frac{21}{24}$

21. $\frac{3}{4} = \frac{15}{20}$

22. $\frac{7}{9} = \frac{35}{45}$

23. $\frac{3}{8} = \frac{24}{64}$

24. $\frac{3}{10} = \frac{30}{100}$

25. $\frac{5}{6} = \frac{30}{36}$

26. $\frac{5}{12} = \frac{25}{60}$

27. $\frac{7}{15} = \frac{14}{30}$

28. $\frac{9}{16} = \frac{36}{64}$

29. $\frac{1}{3} = \frac{4}{12}$

30. $\frac{2}{5} = \frac{6}{15}$

31. $\frac{5}{12} = \frac{15}{36}$

32. $\frac{4}{9} = \frac{8}{18}$

33. $\frac{1}{2} = \frac{30}{60}$

34. $\frac{4}{5} = \frac{36}{45}$

35. $\frac{1}{4} = \frac{16}{64}$

36. $\frac{3}{7} = \frac{24}{56}$

Are these fractions equivalent?

37. $\frac{2}{3}$ $\frac{6}{9}$ Yes

38. $\frac{1}{3}$ $\frac{8}{12}$ No

39. $\frac{7}{8}$ $\frac{14}{16}$ Yes

40. $\frac{1}{2}$ $\frac{9}{20}$ No

41. $\frac{1}{4}$ $\frac{6}{24}$ Yes

42. $\frac{3}{5}$ $\frac{15}{25}$ Yes

43. $\frac{5}{6}$ $\frac{30}{42}$ No

44. $\frac{5}{6}$ $\frac{30}{36}$ Yes

45. $\frac{1}{2}$ $\frac{14}{24}$ No

46. $\frac{2}{3}$ $\frac{12}{18}$ Yes

47. $\frac{7}{10}$ $\frac{49}{70}$ Yes

48. $\frac{5}{9}$ $\frac{35}{64}$ No

49. $\frac{2}{7}$ $\frac{21}{49}$ No

50. $\frac{3}{8}$ $\frac{27}{72}$ Yes

51. $\frac{2}{9}$ $\frac{18}{81}$ Yes

52. $\frac{1}{11}$ $\frac{11}{121}$ Yes

148

Correcting Common Errors

Some students may not multiply the numerator by the same number used to multiply the denominator. When students are working with a problem such as $\frac{4}{5} = \frac{\square}{10}$, have them write the factors so they multiply the numerator by the correct number.

$$\frac{4 \times 2}{5 \times 2} = \frac{8}{10}$$

Enrichment

Have students work as a group to make a set of fraction manipulatives out of tagboard. Show them how to use a compass to make a circle. Explain the use of a protractor to divide a circle into parts. Put the following table on the board:

fraction	protractor reading
halves	180°
thirds	120°
fourths	90°
fifths	72°
sixths	60°
eighths	45°
tenths	36°

Practice

Have students complete the practice problems. Explain that in some problems they will find a missing factor.

Mixed Practice

1. $65,208 - 24,195$ (41,013)
2. $\$319.03 \div 61$ ($5.23)
3. $\$614.59 \times 50$ ($30,729.50)
4. 62×45 (2,790)
5. $\frac{5}{8} = \frac{}{24}$ (15)
6. $476 + 1,290 + 3,809$ (5,575)
7. $6,205 \div 30$ (206 R25)
8. $\$127.93 - \$106.56$ ($21.37)
9. $1,760 \times 8$ (14,080)
10. $9,457 \div 9$ (1,050 R7)

Extra Credit *Numeration*

Have students make their own version of a question-and-answer TV board game similar to Jeopardy. Use a large piece of poster board. On it, have students make 25 pockets for the questions. These can be made by attaching envelopes in 5 columns of 5 envelopes each. Across the top of each column have students write 10, 20, 30, 40 and 50 for the different point values. Next, have students choose 5 categories of problems, such as: properties, division, multiplication, fractions and geometry, and write them above each column. Tell groups to make up 5 questions for each category, with the 10-point question the easiest and the 50-point question the most difficult. Write the questions and answers on small slips of paper to place in the pockets. Divide the students into 2 groups or have students play with a partner. Have one student be the moderator. Players may select any question to answer, accumulating points if he is correct. Another player may be allowed to answer any question missed by another player.

Simplifying Fractions

pages 149-150

Objective

To reduce fractions to lowest terms

Materials

Mental Math

Have students find the equivalent:

1. half an hour = ____ minutes (30)
2. half a cup = ____ ounces (4)
3. half a pound = ____ ounces (8)
4. half a year = ____ months (6)
5. half a minute = ____ seconds (30)
6. half a dollar = ____ cents (50)
7. half a gallon = ____ quarts (2)

Skill Review

Have students find the missing factor in each.

1. $\frac{5}{10} = \frac{}{20}$ (10)
2. $\frac{3}{4} = \frac{}{20}$ (15)
3. $\frac{5}{8} = \frac{}{64}$ (40)
4. $\frac{6}{10} = \frac{}{100}$ (60)
5. $\frac{2}{7} = \frac{}{49}$ (14)
6. $\frac{3}{5} = \frac{}{25}$ (15)
7. $\frac{6}{9} = \frac{}{72}$ (48)

Simplifying Fractions

Mrs. Phillips has a full bus load of children this morning. If 32 boys are riding the bus today, what fraction of the children on the bus are boys?

We want to find what fraction of the bus load is boys.

The bus holds __48__ children.

There are __32__ boys on the bus.

✔ Remember, the numerator of a fraction represents a portion of the total set. The denominator represents the total number of objects in the set.

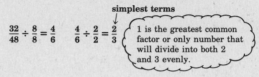

$$\frac{32}{48} = \frac{\text{the number of boys on the bus}}{\text{the total number of children on the bus}}$$

The numerator and denominator of a fraction are called the **terms** of the fraction. The terms in this fraction can be **simplified.** To simplify a fraction, divide each term by a single number that will divide evenly into both the numerator and the denominator. We call this divisor a **common factor.** A fraction is in simplest terms if the greatest common factor of the terms is 1.

$$\frac{32}{48} \div \frac{8}{8} = \frac{4}{6} \qquad \frac{4}{6} \div \frac{2}{2} = \frac{2}{3}$$

simplest terms

> 1 is the greatest common factor or only number that will divide into both 2 and 3 evenly.

The fraction of children on the bus that is boys is $\frac{2}{3}$.

Getting Started

Write each fraction in simplest terms.

1. $\frac{4}{8} \div \frac{4}{4} = \frac{\boxed{1}}{\boxed{2}}$
2. $\frac{6}{9} \div \frac{3}{3} = \frac{\boxed{2}}{\boxed{3}}$
3. $\frac{8}{12} \div \frac{4}{4} = \frac{\boxed{2}}{\boxed{3}}$
4. $\frac{5}{15} \div \frac{5}{5} = \frac{\boxed{1}}{\boxed{3}}$

Write each fraction in simplest terms.

5. $\frac{4}{20} = \frac{1}{5}$
6. $\frac{6}{12} = \frac{1}{2}$
7. $\frac{10}{25} = \frac{2}{5}$
8. $\frac{9}{27} = \frac{1}{3}$

149

MCP All rights reserved

Teaching the Lesson

Introducing the Problem Read the problem aloud. While students survey the illustration, have one read the information sentences aloud. Read the plan sentences and put the fraction **32/48** on the board. Explain that the numerator represents the number of boys on the bus, the denominator, the total number of children. Explain that this fraction is difficult to visualize, but that it can be simplified. Remind students that as fractions can be multiplied by one and not change, they can be divided by one and remain the same. Ask a student to explain what happens when any number is divided by one. (nothing, number remains the same) Explain that a fraction divided by a fraction equaling one will result in an equivalent, but simpler fraction. Put the example shown in the model on the board. (**32/48** can be reduced to **2/3**)

Developing the Skill Explain that as long as both numerator and denominator can be divided by a common divisor, a fraction is not in its lowest terms. Put this fraction on the board and ask students to identify at least one common divisor: **24/72**. Have students reduce the fraction to ⅓ and then identify what the largest common divisor would have been. (24)

Practice

Write each fraction in simplest terms.

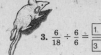

1. $\frac{2}{6} \div \frac{2}{2} = \boxed{\frac{1}{3}}$

2. $\frac{21}{24} \div \frac{3}{3} = \boxed{\frac{7}{8}}$

3. $\frac{6}{18} \div \frac{6}{6} = \boxed{\frac{1}{3}}$

4. $\frac{16}{20} \div \frac{4}{4} = \boxed{\frac{4}{5}}$

5. $\frac{12}{16} \div \frac{4}{4} = \boxed{\frac{3}{4}}$

6. $\frac{20}{32} \div \frac{4}{4} = \boxed{\frac{5}{8}}$

7. $\frac{4}{10} \div \frac{2}{2} = \boxed{\frac{2}{5}}$

8. $\frac{25}{35} \div \frac{5}{5} = \boxed{\frac{5}{7}}$

9. $\frac{6}{9} \div \frac{3}{3} = \boxed{\frac{2}{3}}$

10. $\frac{16}{40} \div \frac{8}{8} = \boxed{\frac{2}{5}}$

11. $\frac{8}{12} \div \frac{4}{4} = \boxed{\frac{2}{3}}$

12. $\frac{27}{63} \div \frac{9}{9} = \boxed{\frac{3}{7}}$

Write each fraction in simplest terms.

13. $\frac{4}{20} = \frac{1}{5}$

14. $\frac{4}{16} = \frac{1}{4}$

15. $\frac{15}{25} = \frac{3}{5}$

16. $\frac{3}{12} = \frac{1}{4}$

17. $\frac{10}{15} = \frac{2}{3}$

18. $\frac{4}{8} = \frac{1}{2}$

19. $\frac{6}{12} = \frac{1}{2}$

20. $\frac{21}{28} = \frac{3}{4}$

21. $\frac{6}{9} = \frac{2}{3}$

22. $\frac{32}{40} = \frac{4}{5}$

23. $\frac{9}{12} = \frac{3}{4}$

24. $\frac{6}{18} = \frac{1}{3}$

25. $\frac{24}{48} = \frac{1}{2}$

26. $\frac{14}{16} = \frac{7}{8}$

27. $\frac{15}{60} = \frac{1}{4}$

28. $\frac{27}{36} = \frac{3}{4}$

29. $\frac{96}{100} = \frac{24}{25}$

30. $\frac{72}{81} = \frac{8}{9}$

31. $\frac{96}{144} = \frac{2}{3}$

32. $\frac{20}{100} = \frac{1}{5}$

Apply

Solve these problems.

33. Mrs. Phillips drove 16 boys and 20 girls to a ball game. What fraction of the children were girls?
$\frac{5}{9}$

34. The baseball team has 18 players. 15 of the players are right-handed. What fraction of the team is not right-handed?
$\frac{1}{6}$

150

Correcting Common Errors

Some students may not write the fraction in simplest terms because they do not divide by the largest possible divisor. Have students work in pairs with fractions not in lowest terms. For each denominator, have them make a list of all the numbers by which it is divisible. Then have them identify the largest number that is also a divisor of the numerator. They then divide by this number to write the fraction in simplest terms.

Enrichment

Tell students that the digits 0 through 9 can be arranged as two fractions, that added will equal 1. Have them find one such arrangement. (There are many possibilities. Among them: $^{35}/_{70} + {}^{148}/_{296} = \frac{1}{2} + \frac{1}{2}$; $^{38}/_{76} + {}^{145}/_{290} = \frac{1}{2} + \frac{1}{2}$.)

Practice

Have students complete the practice problems. Remind them that in reducing a fraction to simplest terms, they must divide both numerator and denominator by the same number.

Extra Credit *Applications*

Ask students to pretend they are on a city planning commission and have the job of planning a new city block. Ask them to draw the buildings on the street, showing an overhead view, using a pre-selected scale of measurement. Have them vary the size and the shape of each building. Tell them to mark the dimensions for each building. Ask them to compute the amount of land each building needs (area) and the distance around each building (perimeter). Display their city planning.

Comparing Fractions

pages 151-152

Objective

To compare fractions with a number line or equivalent fractions

Materials

number lines

Mental Math

Ask students to calculate:

1. ⅓ of 12 (4)
2. ⅕ of 10 (2)
3. ½ of 4 (2)
4. ¼ of 8 (2)
5. ¼ of 100 (25)
6. ⅕ of 20 (4)

Skill Review

Have students find equivalent fractions:

1. ½ = /10 (5)
2. ⅜ = /24 (9)
3. 6/10 = /100 (60)
4. ⅗ = /40 (24)
5. 6/7 = /49 (42)

Have students reduce these fractions to simplest terms:

1. 12/24 (½)
2. 3/30 (1/10)
3. 5/25 (⅕)
4. 12/36 (⅓)
5. 24/36 (⅔)

Comparing Fractions

Martina and Joan are members of the track team. During practice, Martina ran $\frac{2}{3}$ of a mile and Joan ran $\frac{3}{4}$ of a mile. Who ran farther?

We want to find which of the two distances is greater.

Martina ran $\frac{2}{3}$ of a mile and Joan ran $\frac{3}{4}$ of a mile.

A number line can be used to compare these fractions.

$\frac{0}{4}$ $\frac{1}{4}$ $\frac{2}{4}$ $\frac{3}{4}$ $\frac{4}{4}$ or 1 mile

$\frac{0}{3}$ $\frac{1}{3}$ $\frac{2}{3}$ $\frac{3}{3}$ or 1 mile

Since $\frac{3}{4}$ is closer to 1 mile than $\frac{2}{3}$, we write $\frac{3}{4} > \frac{2}{3}$.

Joan ran farther.

Fractions can also be compared by changing them to equivalent fractions with a common denominator and comparing the numerators. The greater fraction is the one with the greater numerator.

$\frac{3}{4} = \frac{9}{12}$ and $\frac{2}{3} = \frac{8}{12}$

$\frac{9}{12} > \frac{8}{12}$ because $9 > 8$.

Since $\frac{9}{12}$ is greater than $\frac{8}{12}$, $\frac{3}{4}$ is greater than $\frac{2}{3}$.

$\frac{3}{4} > \frac{2}{3}$

Getting Started

Use a number line to compare the fractions. Write > or < in each circle.

1. $\frac{1}{4} > \frac{1}{5}$ (number lines 0 to 1)
2. $\frac{3}{5} < \frac{2}{3}$ (number lines 0 to 1)

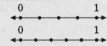

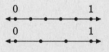

Write > or < in each circle.

3. $\frac{3}{4} > \frac{5}{8}$
4. $\frac{1}{2} > \frac{1}{3}$
5. $\frac{4}{5} > \frac{3}{4}$
6. $\frac{2}{3} > \frac{5}{8}$

Write the fractions in order from least to greatest.

7. $\frac{1}{2}, \frac{2}{8}, \frac{4}{12}$ $\frac{2}{8}, \frac{4}{12}, \frac{1}{2}$
8. $\frac{3}{4}, \frac{5}{8}, \frac{4}{7}$ $\frac{4}{7}, \frac{5}{8}, \frac{3}{4}$

MCP All rights reserved

151

Teaching the Lesson

Introducing the Problem Have a student read the problem and information sentences. Ask students to study the lines in their texts. Point out that one is divided into fourths, the other into thirds. Ask which is farther, ¾ or ⅔. (¾) Have a student write the inequality on the board. (¾ > ⅔) Explain that fractions can also be compared by finding a common denominator. Read the next section of the problem and ask a student to convert ¾ and ⅔ to twelfths on the board. (¾ = 9/12, ⅔ = 8/12) Ask which is larger. (9/12 is greater than 8/12, so ¾ > ⅔)

Developing the Skill Although number lines can be used to compare small fractions, explain that the usual method is to find a common denominator. Point out that the common denominator may be the denominator of one of the fractions being compared: for example, ⅔ and 7/9 can be compared if ⅔ is changed to 6/9. Sometimes the common denominator will be the product of the denominators of the fractions being compared: for example, ⅓ and ⅖ can be changed to 5/15 and 6/15. Sometimes the smallest common denominator will be a number both can be converted to: for example, 3/12 and ⅛ can be compared when 3/12 = 6/24 and ⅛ = 3/24.

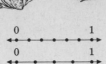

Practice

Use a number line to compare the fractions.
Write > or < in each circle.

1. $\frac{3}{4}$ ⊘ $\frac{5}{6}$

2. $\frac{3}{6}$ ⊘ $\frac{3}{4}$

3. $\frac{1}{2}$ ⊘ $\frac{4}{10}$

4. $\frac{2}{3}$ ⊘ $\frac{5}{8}$

Write > or < in the circle.

5. $\frac{5}{8}$ ⊘ $\frac{3}{4}$ 6. $\frac{2}{3}$ ⊘ $\frac{4}{5}$ 7. $\frac{1}{3}$ ⊘ $\frac{3}{8}$ 8. $\frac{3}{4}$ ⊘ $\frac{8}{10}$

9. $\frac{2}{5}$ ⊘ $\frac{4}{15}$ 10. $\frac{5}{6}$ ⊘ $\frac{1}{2}$ 11. $\frac{11}{12}$ ⊘ $\frac{7}{8}$ 12. $\frac{1}{3}$ ⊘ $\frac{3}{8}$

13. $\frac{2}{3}$ ⊘ $\frac{9}{15}$ 14. $\frac{5}{6}$ ⊘ $\frac{3}{4}$ 15. $\frac{5}{9}$ ⊘ $\frac{6}{12}$ 16. $\frac{2}{5}$ ⊘ $\frac{4}{6}$

17. $\frac{3}{12}$ ⊘ $\frac{4}{15}$ 18. $\frac{9}{10}$ ⊘ $\frac{89}{100}$ 19. $\frac{5}{12}$ ⊘ $\frac{6}{10}$ 20. $\frac{7}{20}$ ⊘ $\frac{15}{50}$

Write the fractions in order from least to greatest.

21. $\frac{3}{4}, \frac{2}{3}, \frac{3}{5}, \frac{3}{5}, \frac{2}{3}, \frac{3}{4}$

22. $\frac{5}{6}, \frac{3}{4}, \frac{3}{8}, \frac{3}{8}, \frac{3}{4}, \frac{5}{6}$

23. $\frac{2}{3}, \frac{5}{9}, \frac{7}{12}, \frac{5}{9}, \frac{7}{12}, \frac{2}{3}$

Apply

Solve these problems.

24. If Susan spent $\frac{2}{3}$ of an hour at
the drug store and Jim spent $\frac{7}{12}$
of an hour at the mall, who spent
more time shopping?
Susan

25. While Ellen ran $\frac{3}{4}$ miles in 9
minutes, Josh ran $\frac{5}{9}$ miles in the
same time. Who ran the farthest?
Ellen

26. Of the fractions $\frac{3}{4}, \frac{2}{3}, \frac{7}{8}, \frac{5}{6}, \frac{4}{5}$ and $\frac{6}{7}$,
which is the largest? Which is the
smallest?
largest $\frac{7}{8}$, smallest $\frac{2}{3}$

27. Arrange the fractions in question
26 from the least to the greatest.
Name a fraction larger than any in
this series.
$\frac{2}{3}, \frac{3}{4}, \frac{4}{5}, \frac{5}{6}, \frac{6}{7}, \frac{7}{8}, \frac{8}{9}$

152

Correcting Common Errors

When comparing fractions, some students may compare just the numerators or just the denominators. Have
them work with partners and two fractions such as ⅚ and ⁴⁄₉. Have the students write a set of equivalent fractions
for each fraction until they find one in
each set with the same denominator.
When they compare these, they can
see that ¹⁵⁄₁₈ > ⁸⁄₁₈, therefore ⅚ > ⁴⁄₉.

Enrichment

Give students graph paper and ask
them to draw an equilateral triangle
with a base of 32 squares. Have them
divide the triangle in such a way that
they can show fourths, sixteenths,
thirty-seconds and sixty-fourths.

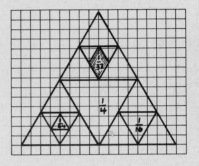

Practice

Have students complete the problems on the page.

Mixed Practice

1. 80,270 − 38,381 (41,889)
2. 259,879 + 430,307 (690,186)
3. 3,467 ÷ 43 (80 R27)
4. $229.35 × 5 ($1,146.75)
5. Simplify: $\frac{12}{16}$ $\left(\frac{3}{4}\right)$
6. 713 × 490 (349,370)
7. 198 + 4,358 + 21 (4,577)
8. 7,543 ÷ 60 (125 R43)
9. $\frac{3}{5} = \frac{}{20}$ (12)
10. $180.88 ÷ 7 ($25.84)

Extra Credit *Everyday Math*

Students can practice both mathematics and conservation by
conducting a recycling drive. Have them follow these steps:

1. Find out what recycling centers are in the area and
   choose the material they will collect.
2. Decide how the money earned from the collection will be
   spent. Establish a goal.
3. Find out the price per pound for the material. Estimate
   how much material must be collected to reach their goal.
4. Design posters and flyer advertising their drive.
5. Design a central collection area that includes a scale,
   containers and a record chart.
6. Weigh materials and keep records of pounds you collect.
   (Be sure to subtract the weight of the containers).
7. Calculate the value of the material by multiplying the
   price per pound by the number of pounds collected.
8. Evaluate the collection drive. Did they reach their goal?
   How close were their estimates?

152

Mixed Numbers

pages 153-154

Objective

To learn to change mixed numbers to fractions

Materials

Mental Math

Have students identify n:

1. $\frac{1}{2} = \frac{n}{6}$ (3)
2. $\frac{2}{5} = \frac{n}{10}$ (4)
3. $\frac{3}{6} = \frac{n}{2}$ (1)
4. $\frac{4}{8} = \frac{n}{16}$ (8)
5. $\frac{2}{20} = \frac{n}{10}$ (1)
6. $\frac{4}{100} = \frac{n}{25}$ (1)
7. $\frac{4}{6} = \frac{n}{3}$ (2)

Skill Review

Have students compare these fraction pairs:

1. $\frac{3}{5}$, $\frac{5}{10}$ $(\frac{3}{5} > \frac{5}{10})$
2. $\frac{1}{4}$, $\frac{3}{8}$ $(\frac{1}{4} < \frac{3}{8})$
3. $\frac{7}{10}$, $\frac{3}{4}$ $(\frac{7}{10} < \frac{3}{4})$
4. $\frac{1}{3}$, $\frac{1}{2}$ $(\frac{1}{3} < \frac{1}{2})$
5. $\frac{1}{6}$, $\frac{2}{12}$ $(\frac{1}{6} = \frac{2}{12})$
6. $\frac{4}{5}$, $\frac{8}{9}$ $(\frac{4}{5} < \frac{8}{9})$
7. $\frac{2}{7}$, $\frac{2}{5}$ $(\frac{2}{7} < \frac{2}{5})$

Understanding Mixed Numbers

Irwin is building a model airplane to scale. How many quarter inches long is the propeller of Irwin's airplane?

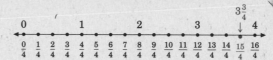

We want to find how long Irwin's propeller is to the nearest $\frac{1}{4}$ of an inch. The propeller is exactly three fourths of an inch longer than __3__ inches.

We write this measurement as a **mixed number**,

whole number ⟶ $3\frac{3}{4}$ ⟵ fraction

We use a number line to help us understand this mixed number and rename it as a fraction.

$3\frac{3}{4} = \frac{15}{4}$. The propeller is $\boxed{\frac{15}{4}}$ inches long.

We can also use a shortcut to rename a mixed number as a fraction.

Multiply the denominator by the whole number.	Add the numerator.	Write the sum over the denominator.
$3\frac{3}{4}$ $3 \times 4 = \underline{12}$	$3\frac{3}{4}$ $12 + 3 = \underline{15}$	$\frac{15}{4}$

Any fraction whose numerator is larger than the denominator is an **improper fraction**.

Getting Started

Write each mixed number as an improper fraction.

1. $4\frac{1}{2} = \frac{9}{2}$
2. $1\frac{7}{8} = \frac{15}{8}$
3. $5\frac{2}{3} = \frac{17}{3}$
4. $6\frac{7}{8} = \frac{55}{8}$
5. $7\frac{3}{10} = \frac{73}{10}$
6. $9\frac{1}{3} = \frac{28}{3}$
7. $3\frac{1}{12} = \frac{37}{12}$
8. $6\frac{4}{7} = \frac{46}{7}$
9. $8\frac{4}{5} = \frac{44}{5}$
10. $3\frac{5}{16} = \frac{53}{16}$

MCP All rights reserved

153

Teaching the Lesson

Introducing the Problem Ask a student to read the problem and information sentences aloud. Explain that this measurement is made up of a whole number (3) and a fraction (¾). Write **3¾** on the board and read it aloud. Read the next sentences aloud. Ask students to examine the number line in their texts, explaining that whole numbers can be written as fractions. Ask a student to read the fraction written below 1 (⁴⁄₄), 2 (⁸⁄₄) and 3 (¹²⁄₄). Tell students that if the numerator is larger than the denominator, the fraction represents a mixed number. Demonstrate renaming a mixed number as a fraction. (3¾ = ¹⁵⁄₄) Ask a student to read the solution sentence. (¹⁵⁄₄ inches long) Explain that a mixed number can be renamed by multiplying the whole number times the denominator, and adding the numerator of the original fraction. Read the definition of improper fractions.

Developing the Skill Give each student a worksheet with four circles each divided in half, with 7 halves shaded and the equivalence 3½ = ⁷⁄₂. Explain that the shaded area represents a mixed number. It can be written as a mixed number or as an improper fraction. Have students write both on the paper. Give them the mixed number 2⅔. Ask them to illustrate it with shaded rectangles and rewrite it as an improper fraction. (⁸⁄₃)

Practice

Write each mixed number as an improper fraction.

1. $1\frac{3}{4} = \frac{7}{4}$ 2. $3\frac{1}{2} = \frac{7}{2}$ 3. $5\frac{1}{8} = \frac{41}{8}$ 4. $4\frac{3}{5} = \frac{23}{5}$ 5. $6\frac{3}{8} = \frac{51}{8}$

6. $5\frac{2}{3} = \frac{17}{3}$ 7. $2\frac{3}{8} = \frac{19}{8}$ 8. $8\frac{3}{5} = \frac{43}{5}$ 9. $6\frac{7}{10} = \frac{67}{10}$ 10. $4\frac{5}{6} = \frac{29}{6}$

11. $4\frac{5}{12} = \frac{53}{12}$ 12. $3\frac{7}{9} = \frac{34}{9}$ 13. $6\frac{1}{4} = \frac{25}{4}$ 14. $9\frac{4}{5} = \frac{49}{5}$ 15. $7\frac{9}{10} = \frac{79}{10}$

16. $8\frac{5}{8} = \frac{69}{8}$ 17. $4\frac{3}{7} = \frac{31}{7}$ 18. $6\frac{1}{9} = \frac{55}{9}$ 19. $5\frac{7}{12} = \frac{67}{12}$ 20. $8\frac{9}{16} = \frac{137}{16}$

Apply

Solve these problems.

21. It took Patti $3\frac{1}{4}$ hours to ride the train to her cousin's home. How many quarter-hours did it take?
13 quarter-hours

22. There are $5\frac{1}{3}$ pints of juice in the restaurant's cooler. How many people can be served $\frac{1}{3}$ of a pint of juice?
16 people

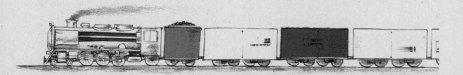

EXCURSION

Simplify these fractions by first writing both the numerator and denominator as products of primes. Then cross out common factors in the numerator and denominator. Multiply the remaining factors in the numerator and denominator to get the simplified fraction. The first one has been done for you.

1. $\frac{84}{90} = \frac{2 \times 2 \times 3 \times 7}{2 \times 3 \times 3 \times 5} = \frac{2 \times 7}{3 \times 5} = \frac{14}{15}$

2. $\frac{16}{80} = \frac{2 \times 2 \times 2 \times 2}{2 \times 2 \times 2 \times 2 \times 5} = \frac{1}{5}$

3. $\frac{72}{90} = \frac{2 \times 2 \times 2 \times 3 \times 3}{2 \times 3 \times 3 \times 5} = \frac{2 \times 2}{5} = \frac{4}{5}$

4. $\frac{9}{51} = \frac{3 \times 3}{3 \times 17} = \frac{3}{17}$

5. $\frac{36}{42} = \frac{2 \times 2 \times 3 \times 3}{2 \times 3 \times 7} = \frac{2 \times 3}{7} = \frac{6}{7}$

6. $\frac{57}{70} = \frac{3 \times 19}{2 \times 5 \times 7} = \frac{57}{70}$

7. $\frac{33}{121} = \frac{3 \times 11}{11 \times 11} = \frac{3}{11}$

8. $\frac{24}{45} = \frac{2 \times 2 \times 2 \times 3}{3 \times 3 \times 5} = \frac{2 \times 2 \times 2}{3 \times 5} = \frac{8}{15}$

154

Correcting Common Errors

Some students may have difficulty writing mixed numbers as improper fractions. For a mixed number such as $3\frac{3}{4}$, have them write it as the sum of a whole number and fraction, then write the whole number as a fraction with the same denominator.

$$3 + \frac{3}{4} = \frac{12}{4} + \frac{3}{4} = \frac{15}{4}$$

Enrichment

Have students use their own birthdate to calculate the dates in the year on which they become another quarter, half and three-quarters of a year older. For example, if a student's tenth birthday was May 25: the student will be $10\frac{1}{4}$ on August 25, $10\frac{1}{2}$ on November 25, $10\frac{3}{4}$ on February 25 and 11 on the next May 25.

Practice

Have students complete the practice problems. Suggest they use extra paper for multiplying and adding as they rename mixed numbers as fractions.

Excursion

The cancellation of common factors in the numerator and denominator is equivalent to dividing the numerator and denominator by the same factor. In the second problem, all numerator factors cancel leaving one, not zero.

Extra Credit *Applications*

Discuss the concept of radius. Have students draw a circle on a map to locate towns within a 100-mile radius of their school. Using car advertisements that give estimated gas mileage, have students estimate the amount of gas different cars would need to make a trip to any city within the 100-mile radius. Have students make a chart listing city, mileage, gallons of gasoline estimated and car make. Discuss the difference in gas mileage for different cars. Finally, have students find the cost/gallon of gas, and figure the cost of a trip to each of the cities listed.

154

Mixed Number in Quotients

pages 155-156

Objective

To divide, expressing the quotient as a whole number and fraction

Materials

Mental Math

Have students round each to the nearest 10:

1. 34 (30)
2. 4,581 (4,580)
3. 56,800 (56,800)
4. 19 (20)
5. 3 (0)
6. 2,235 (2,240)
7. 511 (510)

Skill Review

Have students convert these improper fractions to whole or mixed numbers.

1. 23/4 (5¾)
2. 15/2 (7½)
3. 9/3 (3)
4. 7/5 (1⅖)
5. 81/9 (9)
6. 34/7 (4⁶/₇)
7. 30/4 (7½)

Writing Quotients as Mixed Numbers

Crystal runs the packaging line at the Bubbly Soap Works. Each hour 327 bottles of liquid detergent are packed into cases. How many cases does Crystal pack each hour?

We need to find the number of cases Crystal packs each hour.

Each case holds __12__ bottles, and Crystal can pack __327__ bottles in an hour.

To find the number of cases she packs in an hour, we divide the bottles packed per hour by the number in each case. We divide __327__ by __12__.

$$\begin{array}{r} 27\ R3 \\ 12\overline{)327} \\ 24 \\ \hline 87 \\ 84 \\ \hline 3 \end{array}$$

The quotient's remainder can be written as a fraction

$\dfrac{3}{12}$ ← remainder
← divisor

We rewrite the quotient as the mixed number, $27\frac{3}{12}$.

We can simplify the fraction by dividing both the numerator and denominator by the greatest common factor, __3__.

Crystal packs __$27\frac{1}{4}$__ cases of Bubbly Soap each hour.

Getting Started

Divide. Write each quotient as a mixed number. Simplify if necessary.

1. $4\overline{)218}$ $\quad 54\frac{1}{2}$
2. $9\overline{)321}$ $\quad 35\frac{2}{3}$
3. $14\overline{)395}$ $\quad 28\frac{3}{14}$

4. $25\overline{)960}$ $\quad 38\frac{2}{5}$
5. $46\overline{)2,921}$ $\quad 63\frac{1}{2}$
6. $21\overline{)16,933}$ $\quad 806\frac{1}{3}$

Copy and divide.

7. $593 \div 12$ $\quad 49\frac{5}{12}$
8. $87,813 \div 51$ $\quad 1721\frac{14}{17}$
9. $3,021 \div 67$ $\quad 45\frac{6}{67}$

MCP All rights reserved

155

Teaching the Lesson

Introducing the Problem Read the problem aloud and have a student read the information sentences. Ask a student to explain how the problem can be worked (by division) and read the plan sentences. Ask a student to work the problem on the board while the others follow in their texts. Explain that the remainder, 3, can be expressed as a part of the divisor. Write the quotient on the board: **27³/₁₂.** Show students that the fraction indicates that Crystal can fill 27 and ³/₁₂ or 27¼ cases. Explain that this fractional remainder is easier to work with than the R3 way of expressing the same number.

Developing the Skill Have students come to the board and complete these problems:

$$15\overline{)873} \quad (58\ R3) \qquad 36\overline{)16,864} \quad (468\ R16)$$

Explain that these answers would be easier to work with if each is rewritten as a mixed number. Show students how to write each fraction with the whole number remainder as numerator and divisor as denominator. (58³/₁₅ and 468¹⁶/₃₆) Explain that this fraction can be reduced like any other. (58⅕ and 468⁴/₉)

Practice

Divide. Write each quotient as a mixed number. Simplify if necessary.

1. $3\overline{)58}$ $19\frac{1}{3}$

2. $6\overline{)93}$ $15\frac{1}{2}$

3. $4\overline{)130}$ $32\frac{1}{2}$

4. $9\overline{)4,169}$ $463\frac{2}{9}$

5. $18\overline{)654}$ $36\frac{1}{3}$

6. $35\overline{)1,230}$ $35\frac{1}{7}$

7. $28\overline{)2,360}$ $84\frac{2}{7}$

8. $48\overline{)2,696}$ $56\frac{1}{6}$

9. $85\overline{)36,225}$ $426\frac{3}{17}$

Copy and Do

10. $1,400 \div 26$ $53\frac{11}{13}$

11. $3,111 \div 34$ $91\frac{1}{2}$

12. $3,069 \div 45$ $68\frac{1}{5}$

13. $10,575 \div 29$ $364\frac{19}{29}$

14. $13,878 \div 15$ $925\frac{1}{5}$

15. $14,670 \div 27$ $543\frac{1}{3}$

16. $30,640 \div 48$ $638\frac{1}{3}$

17. $32,388 \div 64$ $506\frac{1}{16}$

18. $62,050 \div 75$ $827\frac{1}{3}$

Apply

Solve these problems. Simplify if necessary.

19. A sidewalk along French Street is 500 inches wide. How many feet wide is the sidewalk?
$41\frac{2}{3}$ feet

20. A car gets 371 miles on 14 gallons of gas. How many miles does the car get for each gallon of gas?
$26\frac{1}{2}$ miles

21. Yoko weighs 1,380 ounces. How many pounds does Yoko weigh?
$86\frac{1}{4}$ pounds

22. Wayne is making juice bars. Each bar weighs 8 ounces. If juice costs $1.65 a pint, how much will it cost to make 12 juice bars?
$9.90

23. A farmer is preparing to ship 950 pounds of potatoes. He ships them in 50 pound sacks. How many sacks does he need for today's shipment?
19 sacks

24. A cement block weighs 65 pounds. If a crane can lift 1,040 pounds at a time, how many blocks can the crane lift?
16 blocks

156

Correcting Common Errors

When dividing, some students may continue to write the remainder as a whole number. Discuss with them how the remainder can be shown as a fractional part of the divisor. Then have them work with partners to practice with problems such as these.
1. $308 \div 8$ $(38\frac{1}{2})$
2. $14,586 \div 36$ $(405\frac{1}{6})$

Enrichment

Give students this list of fractional remainders and divisors. Have them find the whole number remainder.

fractional remainder	divisor	whole remainder
$\frac{1}{2}$	24	(12)
$\frac{5}{8}$	16	(10)
$\frac{2}{3}$	12	(8)
$\frac{7}{8}$	24	(21)
$\frac{4}{9}$	27	(12)
$\frac{5}{7}$	21	(15)

Practice

Have students complete the practice problems. Have them reduce the remainders to simplest form.

Extra Credit *Geometry*

Have students use geoboards and work with a partner. Explain that one of each two students will make a shape on the geoboard without letting the partner see and then describe it by means of the coordinates. For example, the triangle shown could be described: C,1 to A,4 to D,4 to C,1.

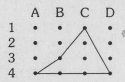

The second student in each pair will follow the coordinate directions to reproduce the shape on his geoboard. Ask students to compare shapes in the end to see whether the directions given and received were followed. Have students exchange roles and repeat the exercise.

156

Improper Fractions

pages 157–158

Objective

To rename improper fractions as mixed or whole numbers

Materials

Mental Math

Have students supply the next term in each series:

1. $\frac{1}{4}$, $\frac{2}{4}$, $\frac{3}{4}$ ($\frac{4}{4}$ or 1)
2. $\frac{2}{6}$, $\frac{3}{6}$, $\frac{4}{6}$ ($\frac{5}{6}$)
3. $\frac{3}{8}$, $\frac{1}{2}$, $\frac{5}{8}$ ($\frac{6}{8}$ or $\frac{3}{4}$)
4. $\frac{1}{9}$, $\frac{2}{9}$, $\frac{1}{3}$ ($\frac{4}{9}$)
5. $\frac{2}{5}$, $\frac{3}{5}$, $\frac{4}{5}$ ($\frac{5}{5}$ or 1)
6. 1, $1\frac{1}{2}$, 2 ($2\frac{1}{2}$)
7. $\frac{5}{3}$, $\frac{7}{3}$, $\frac{9}{3}$ ($\frac{11}{3}$)

Skill Review

Ask students to work these division problems, expressing the remainders as fractions.

1. $341 \div 6$ ($56\frac{5}{6}$)
2. $503 \div 9$ ($55\frac{8}{9}$)
3. $7,326 \div 4$ ($1,831\frac{1}{2}$)
4. $782 \div 13$ ($60\frac{2}{13}$)
5. $3,280 \div 5$ (656)
6. $21,836 \div 7$ ($3,119\frac{3}{7}$)

Renaming Improper Fractions

Cleve uses his computer to play math games. Each game takes $\frac{1}{4}$ of an hour. How long has Cleve been playing the computer games today?

We are looking for how long Cleve has been playing games on the computer today.

Each game takes $\frac{1}{4}$ of an hour.

Cleve has played 11 games.

To find his total computer game time, we multiply the time it takes for one game by the number of games.

He has played for 11 quarters of an hour.

We write the fraction $\frac{11}{4}$ hours to show how long Cleve has played.

$\frac{11}{4}$ is called an **improper fraction** because the numerator, 11, is larger than the denominator, 4.

$\frac{11}{4}$ can also represent division. We can read the fraction as **eleven divided by four.**

✔ To simplify an improper fraction, rename it as a whole or mixed number by dividing the denominator into the numerator. Write any remainder as a simplified fraction.

$$\frac{11}{4} \rightarrow 4\overline{)11} \quad \begin{array}{c} 2\text{ R3} \to 2\frac{3}{4} \\ \underline{8} \\ 3 \end{array}$$

Cleve has played computer games for $\frac{11}{4}$ or $2\frac{3}{4}$ hours.

Getting Started

Rename each improper fraction as a whole or mixed number.

1. $\frac{7}{6} = 1\frac{1}{6}$
2. $\frac{5}{5} = 1$
3. $\frac{9}{5} = 1\frac{4}{5}$
4. $\frac{8}{6} = 1\frac{1}{3}$
5. $\frac{16}{12} = 1\frac{1}{3}$
6. $\frac{15}{10} = 1\frac{1}{2}$
7. $\frac{3}{2} = 1\frac{1}{2}$
8. $\frac{11}{3} = 3\frac{2}{3}$
9. $\frac{12}{4} = 3$
10. $\frac{12}{8} = 1\frac{1}{2}$

157

MCP All rights reserved

Teaching the Lesson

Introducing the Problem Read the problem aloud. Ask a student to refer to the illustration and then read the information sentences. Explain that Cleve has played 11 quarter hours and write the fraction on the board: $\mathbf{11/4}$. Ask students if this is a proper or improper fraction. (improper) Show students that the fraction can be reduced to a mixed number by dividing 11 into groups of 4. Do the division on the board:

$$4\overline{)11} \quad 2\text{ R3 or } 2\frac{3}{4}$$

Have a student read the solution sentence.

Developing the Skill Remind students that any fraction that has a numerator larger than the denominator is called an improper fraction. Ask a student to explain why this is so. (Because the denominator shows the fractional unit; if the numerator is larger, it means that the number is more than one whole.) Explain that to change an improper fraction to a mixed number, they will divide the numerator into groups the size of the denominator. Write this on the board:

$$\frac{14}{8} = 8\overline{)14} \quad 1\frac{6}{8} \text{ or } 1\frac{3}{4}$$

Remind students to reduce fractional remainders to lowest terms.

157

Rename each improper fraction as a whole or mixed number.

1. $\frac{6}{5}$ = $1\frac{1}{5}$ 2. $\frac{12}{3}$ = 4 3. $\frac{7}{4}$ = $1\frac{3}{4}$ 4. $\frac{10}{8}$ = $1\frac{1}{4}$ 5. $\frac{12}{5}$ = $2\frac{2}{5}$

6. $\frac{18}{6}$ = 3 7. $\frac{20}{12}$ = $1\frac{2}{3}$ 8. $\frac{16}{10}$ = $1\frac{3}{5}$ 9. $\frac{24}{16}$ = $1\frac{1}{2}$ 10. $\frac{21}{7}$ = 3

11. $\frac{44}{8}$ = $5\frac{1}{2}$ 12. $\frac{25}{15}$ = $1\frac{2}{3}$ 13. $\frac{20}{6}$ = $3\frac{1}{3}$ 14. $\frac{18}{4}$ = $4\frac{1}{2}$ 15. $\frac{21}{9}$ = $2\frac{1}{3}$

16. $\frac{40}{16}$ = $2\frac{1}{2}$ 17. $\frac{63}{18}$ = $3\frac{1}{2}$ 18. $\frac{70}{20}$ = $3\frac{1}{2}$ 19. $\frac{105}{35}$ = 3 20. $\frac{145}{10}$ = $14\frac{1}{2}$

Apply

Solve these problems.

21. Mr. Seldon rode his horse around a $\frac{1}{2}$ mile track a total of 7 times. How many miles did Mr. Seldon ride?

$3\frac{1}{2}$ miles

22. Monica practices the piano for $\frac{25}{3}$ hours each month. Julia practices the violin $\frac{33}{4}$ hours each month. Who practices their instrument longer each month?
Monica

EXCURSION

When simplifying a fraction, test to see if 3 divides evenly into both the numerator and denominator. A number has 3 as a factor if the sum of its digits has 3 as its factor. For example, 1,551 is divisible by 3 because 1 + 5 + 5 + 1 = 12 and 12 is divisible by 3. Write the sums of the digits for each number. Write **yes** if the number is divisible by 3. Write **no** if it does not have 3 as a factor.

1. 151 7 no   2. 243,171 18 yes   3. 7,015,206 21 yes

4. 1,731 12 yes   5. 111,222,444 21 yes   6. 9,201,555 27 yes

7. 222 6 yes   8. 987,654,321 45 yes   9. 687,490,100 35 no

10. If 3 is a factor of Tom's number and 3 is a factor of Jim's number, will 3 be a factor of the product of their numbers? yes

11. Will 3 be a factor of the sum of their numbers? yes

When students write a fraction as a mixed number, they may write the whole-number part and forget the fraction part. Have students work in pairs rewriting problems as shown here: $1\frac{1}{8} = \frac{8}{8} + \frac{3}{8} = 1 + \frac{3}{8}$, or $1\frac{3}{8}$.

Enrichment

Give students this problem: Velcro costs $1.29 per foot. A lion costume requires $2\frac{1}{3}$ yards of Velcro. How much will the Velcro cost? ($9.03)

Practice

Have students complete the practice problems. Remind them to reduce fractions to simplest terms.

Mixed Practice

1. $1.57 × 27 ($42.39)
2. 617 ÷ 3 (205 R2)
3. 95,471 − 82,656 (12,815)
4. Simplify: $\frac{30}{9}$ $\left(3\frac{1}{3}\right)$
5. 796 × 308 (245,168)
6. $\frac{4}{7} = \frac{}{28}$ (16)
7. $194.58 ÷ 46 ($4.23)
8. $756.21 + $10,295.84 ($11,052.05)
9. $302.07 − $156.48 ($145.59)
10. Simplify: $\frac{42}{48}$ $\left(\frac{7}{8}\right)$

Extra Credit   *Applications*

Ask students to bring in their favorite cookie recipe. Have them figure the amount of each ingredient they would need if they tripled the recipe. Then ask how much of each ingredient they would need if they cut the recipe in half and then in thirds. Have a cook from the school cafeteria discuss cooking methods used for large meals, and share a recipe used in school lunches.

Problem Solving
Identify Subgoals

pages 159-160

Objective

To solve problems by identifying sub-goals

Materials

Mental Math

Have students rename these improper fractions:

1. $\frac{3}{2}$ $(1\frac{1}{2})$
2. $\frac{5}{3}$ $(1\frac{2}{3})$
3. $\frac{8}{4}$ (2)
4. $\frac{10}{4}$ $(2\frac{2}{4}$ or $2\frac{1}{2})$
5. $\frac{7}{5}$ $(1\frac{2}{5})$
6. $\frac{4}{4}$ (1)
7. $\frac{9}{7}$ $(1\frac{2}{7})$

Identifying a Subgoal

The Terrific T-Shirt Shop is having a sale. In the morning T-shirts are on sale for $4.00 each. The shop sells $240 worth of shirts in the morning. After lunch, the price is dropped to $3.00 and the shop sells twice as many shirts. How much money did the shop take in on T-shirts that day?

★ SEE

We want to know how much money the shop took in on the day of the sale.

In the morning the shirts cost $4.00 each.

The store took in $240 in the morning.

In the afternoon the price of a shirt is $3.00.

In the afternoon the shop sold 2 times as many shirts as in the morning.

★ PLAN

We need to answer several questions before we can reach a solution to the problem. This is known as **identifying a subgoal.**

We find the number of shirts sold in the morning by dividing the money from the morning by the cost of a T-shirt.

$$\begin{array}{r}60\\ \$4\overline{)\$240}\end{array}$$

We double this number to get the number of shirts sold in the afternoon.

We find the amount of money made from the afternoon sales by multiplying the number of shirts sold by the cost of one.

We add the morning and the afternoon money to find the total.

★ DO

$60 \times 2 = 120$ $120 \times \$3 = \$360$ $\$240 + \$360 = \$600$

The Terrific T-Shirt Shop took in $600 the day of the sale.

★ CHECK

$\$240 \div \$4 = 60$ $60 \times 2 = 120$

$120 \times \$3 = \$360$ $\$240 + \$360 = \$600$

MCP All rights reserved

159

Teaching the Lesson

Have a student read the problem aloud. Explain that you will use the SEE-PLAN-DO-CHECK method to work this problem. Ask a student to read the SEE section in the text. Read the next sentence aloud, explaining that this problem must be worked in stages. Write **identify a subgoal** on the board and point out that the subgoal must be worked first. Have a student read the first DO section and work the problem on the board. ($240 ÷ 4 = 60; 60 shirts sold) Have another student read and complete the second DO section. Explain how to find the afternoon total (120 × $3 = $360) and add it to the morning total. ($240 + $360 = $600) Have a student read the solution sentence. Explain that to check this problem they will repeat each of the calculations to see that there are no errors. List the stages on the board and have students complete each problem.

$240 \div 4 = (60)$
$(60) \times 2 = (120)$
$(120) \times 3 = (\$360)$
$(\$360) + 240 = (\$600)$

Apply

Identify a subgoal to help solve these problems.

1. A ballot box that is 1 foot long, 7 inches wide and 5 inches high, is taped along the length of each edge. If tape costs 10 cents per foot, what is the cost of the tape used?
$0.80

2. A used car cost $800, but it needed four new tires and painting. Each new tire's original cost was $60, but they were on sale for one-third off. A new paint job costs $129. Mr. Sands had $500 to pay down on the car and will have to borrow the rest. How much will he have to borrow to pay for the car, the tires and the paint job?
$589

3. Frosted doughnuts sell for $2.85 per dozen and doughnut holes for $0.60 per dozen. If you buy 2 dozen frosted doughnuts and 6 dozen doughnut holes, what would be the fewest number of coins in change you could receive from a ten-dollar bill?
3 coins

4. What is the ones digit of the product when seven is used as a factor one hundred times?
1

5. Woody Weed has a rectangular lawn 48 by 75 feet. The Green Pair Company will weed and feed the lawn for one season for 1¢ per square foot. The Jolly Onion Company will do the same thing for 10¢ per square yard. Assuming both do good work, which company offers the better buy?
Green Pair Company

6. Carrie Consumer buys butter in pound boxes. Each box has 4 bars that weigh $\frac{1}{4}$ pound each. Carrie and her family use an average of $\frac{1}{8}$ pound of butter each week. Explain how to compute only with whole numbers to tell how much butter they use in 48 weeks.
Answers will vary.

7. How do the numerator and denominator of a fraction compare when the fraction is
   a. close to 1?
   b. close to $\frac{1}{2}$?
   c. close to 0?
   See Solution Notes.

160

Extra Credit *Statistics*

Demonstrate a pie graph by using a paper plate divided into sections. Have students construct a pie graph showing how they spent all their time for the preceding 24-hour day. Ask students how they would translate time allocations into fractional pieces of the pie. Display their graphs and compare them. Have students note similarities and differences and explain how these charts might be used to help maximize their time. Ask students to suggest ways that a chart like this could help a business or factory worker.

Solution Notes

1. Help students see that the subgoal is to find the total length of the edges. Ask how many edges a box has. (12) Write this formula on the board. **(4 × L) + (4 × W) + (4 × H) = T.**
   Have students find the total length, convert length to feet and multiply to find total cost. (4 ft + 28 in. + 20 in. = 4 ft + 48 in. = 8 ft; 8 × 10¢ = 80¢)

2. Have students find cost of tires and add cost of car, tires and paint job. ($60 − $20 = $40, $40 × 4 = $160, $800 + $160 + $129 = $1,089) Ask them to solve for amount needed. ($1,089 − $500 = $589)

3. Have students calculate the total cost of donuts and donut holes. ($2.85 × 2) + ($.60 × 6) = $9.30 Now have them find the minimum coins in change. ($10.00 − 9.30 = $.70; 50¢ + 10¢ + 10¢ = 3 coins)

4. Have students multiply 7 × 7, 7 × 7 × 7, etc. to eight 7's recording only the ones digit of each product. (9, 3, 1, 7, 9, 3, 1, 7, . . .) Suggest they make up a chart of
   7's: 2 3 4 5 6 7 8 9 . . . 100
   ones: 9 3 1 7 9 3 7 1 . . . 1
   Have them predict to 100 factors of seven. (1 in ones digit)

Higher-Order Thinking Skills

5. Analysis and Evaluation: Students should recognize that it is not necessary to find the total area. Just compare the costs of one square yard, i.e., 9¢ vs 10¢.

6. Analysis: Answers should be similar to this procedure: 8 eighths make 1 whole; so they use a whole pound every 8 weeks. Since there are 6 eighths in forty-eight, they use 6 pounds.

7. Synthesis: Sample answers include:
   a. They are almost equal.
   b. The denominator is about double the numerator.
   c. The denominator is much greater than the numerator.

160

Calculators and Unit Prices

pages 161-162

Objective

To use calculators to find unit prices

Materials

calculators

Mental Math

Have students work these problems:

1. $14 - 5 + 3 = (12)$
2. $20 + 12 - 5 = (27)$
3. $15 - 8 + 5 = (12)$
4. $4 + 15 + 9 = (28)$
5. $6 - 6 + 14 - 3 = (11)$
6. $13 + 21 - 7 = (27)$
7. $25 + 15 - 8 = (32)$

Skill Review

Review function keys with the class. Then have students work the following problems on their calculators.

1. $1,483 + 4,992 = (6,475)$
2. $32,773 - 9,820 = (22,953)$
3. $563 \times 23 = (12,949)$
4. $9,345 + 1,005 = (10,350)$
5. $882 \div 9 = (98)$
6. $5,224 \div 4 = (1,306)$
7. $9,554 \div 17 = (562)$

Calculators and Unit Prices

Mrs. Nordquist is shopping for the best buy in dog food. She uses her calculator to find the cost of one pound of dog food for each brand. Which brand is the best buy?

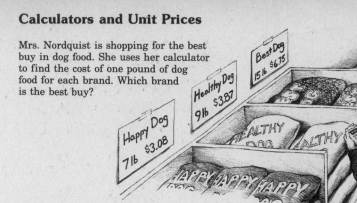

When we find the price of one pound of dog food we are finding the **unit price**.

✔ To find the unit price, we divide the price by the number of units of measurement in the bag. The lower the unit price, the better the buy for the shopper.

Complete this code.

Happy Dog   3.08 $\div$ 7 $=$ (0.44)

0.44 means $0.44 or __44__ ¢.

The unit price of Happy Dog is __44¢__ .

Complete these codes.

Healthy Dog $3.87 $\div$ __9__ $=$ (0.43)
Best Dog $6.75 $\div$ __15__ $=$ (0.45)

The unit price of Healthy Dog is __43¢__ .

The unit price of Best Dog is __45¢__ .

The best buy is the brand __Healthy Dog__ .

The symbol @ is frequently used before the unit price.

Use a calculator to find the total cost of each purchase.

5 lb @ $0.36 a pound __$1.80__   10 gal @ $0.96 a gallon __$9.60__

7 oz @ $4.52 an ounce __$31.64__   75 lb @ $1.45 a pound __$108.75__

MCP All rights reserved

161

Teaching the Lesson

Introducing the Problem   Have a student read the problem aloud. Explain that this is a problem they will encounter frequently in a grocery or drugstore. Define the unit price as the cost of an item per unit of weight or volume. Have a student read the next section of the text explaining how to find the unit price. Have the class use calculators to find the price per pound of Happy Dog by following the calculator code in their books. ($.44/pound) Ask a student to write out the codes for Healthy Dog and Best Dog on the board while others work the problems with their calculators. ($3.87 ÷ 9 = $.043 and $6.75 ÷ 15 = $.45) Read the unit prices for Healthy Dog (43¢) and Best Dog (45¢). Ask a student to read the solution sentence. (best buy Healthy Dog)

Developing the Skill   Explain again that the unit price is found by dividing the total cost of an item by the number of units of weight or volume in the item. The unit price will be the cost per unit of weight or volume. Point out that some items are sold by weight, some by volume. For example, milk is sold by volume (gallons) but cheese, by weight. (pounds) Ask students to find the cost per ounce of each of these cereals and to determine which is least expensive: Raisin Bran, $1.99, 14 oz (14¢/oz, most expensive) Rice Pops, $1.38, 13 oz (11¢/oz, least expensive) Corn Flakes, $2.29, 17 oz (13¢/oz).

Practice

Find the unit price.

1. 6 pounds of hamburger, $11.34 _$1.89_   2. 16 pounds of apples, $7.84 _49¢_

3. 5 kilograms of potatoes, $4.95 _99¢_   4. 8 liters of oil, $16.48 _$2.06_

5. 25 ounces of soap, $4.25 _17¢_   6. 96 feet of lumber, $218.88 _$2.28_

7. 32 liters of gasoline, $15.68 _49¢_   8. 56 grams of vitamins, $36.40 _65¢_

9. 9 tons of coal, $211.95 _$23.55_   10. 28 meters of trim, $97.72 _$3.49_

Use a calculator to find the total cost of each purchase.

11. 15 oz @ $0.47 an ounce _$7.05_   12. 46 T @ $14.50 a ton _$667_

13. 25 yd @ $1.99 a yard _$49.75_   14. 12 qt @ $1.01 a quart _$12.12_

15. 256 mi @ $0.18 a mi _$46.08_   16. 360 pt @ $0.26 a pint _$93.60_

Apply

Use a calculator to solve these problems. Use estimation to be sure the answer seems correct.

17. Midway Electric had two brands of video tapes on sale. One brand was selling at 6 tapes for $28.50 and the other was 8 tapes for $37.52. Which brand was the best buy?
8 for $37.52

18. Grass seed can be purchased in three sizes: 15 pounds for $18.75, 18 pounds for $23.76 or 25 pounds for $32.25. Which size is the best buy?
15 pounds for $18.75

19. The West Side Market is selling 24 bottles of cola for $13.68. The East End Market is selling 36 bottles of the same cola brand for $20.52. Which has the better buy?
They are the same.

20. Ben's Butcher Shop ran this advertisement. Which is the best meat buy?
 T-Bone 3 pounds for $11.37
 Porterhouse 5 pounds for $17.45
 New York 2 pounds for $ 7.18
 Porterhouse

21. China plates that usually sell at 8 plates for $98.80 are sold at a fire sale for $6.79 each. How much is saved on each plate?
$5.56

22. Soap that usually sells for $2.15 a pound is on sale at 3 pounds for $5.85. How much is saved when 6 pounds of soap is bought on sale?
$1.20

162

Correcting Common Errors

If students have difficulty using their calculators to find the unit price of an item, have them first write the key strokes, or calculator code, and then use the code to enter data into their calculators.

Enrichment

Ask students to find unit prices and compare the cost of these cheeses:
Brie is $4.29 per pound.
Camembert is $1.59 for 4 ounces.
Swiss is $2.59 for 8 ounces.
American cheese is $5.09 for a
 2-pound box.
(cost per ounce: Brie (27¢) Camembert (40¢) Swiss (32¢) American (16¢))

Practice

Have students use calculators to complete the practice problems. You may want them to put the unit of weight or volume in parentheses.

Extra Credit   *Probability*

Give each student paper with a set of parallel lines equally spaced, the length of a toothpick apart.
Have students drop a toothpick on the paper and record the number of times the pick falls on a line. Have them try 25 drops then repeat the 25 drops ten times. Now have students cut a bit off the toothpick and repeat the trials. Have students tell if it was more likely to fall on a line when it was longer or when it was shorter. (longer) You may want to explain that the problem is called **Bouffon's Needle** and that an exact probability that the stick will hit a line has been calculated: probability = (2 × length of the stick) divided by (3.14 × the distance between the lines).

Chapter Test

page 163

Item	Objective
1-4	Find equivalent fractions by multiplying (See pages 147-148)
5-12	Reduce fractions to lowest terms (See pages 149-150)
13-16	Compare and order fractions (See pages 151-152)
17-24	Change mixed numbers to fractions (See pages 153-154)
25-32	Divide by a whole number, quotient as mixed number (See pages 155-156)
33-40	Change improper fractions to whole or mixed numbers (See pages 157-158)

Write the equivalent fraction.

1. $\frac{2}{3} = \frac{8}{12}$ 2. $\frac{3}{8} = \frac{6}{16}$ 3. $\frac{4}{5} = \frac{16}{20}$ 4. $\frac{5}{6} = \frac{50}{60}$

Write each fraction in simplest terms.

5. $\frac{5}{10} = \frac{1}{2}$ 6. $\frac{8}{12} = \frac{2}{3}$ 7. $\frac{4}{20} = \frac{1}{5}$ 8. $\frac{9}{27} = \frac{1}{3}$

9. $\frac{24}{30} = \frac{4}{5}$ 10. $\frac{16}{18} = \frac{8}{9}$ 11. $\frac{35}{49} = \frac{5}{7}$ 12. $\frac{32}{40} = \frac{4}{5}$

Write < or > in the circle.

13. $\frac{5}{8} \bigcirc< \frac{2}{3}$ 14. $\frac{5}{12} \bigcirc< \frac{9}{16}$ 15. $\frac{1}{2} \bigcirc< \frac{4}{7}$ 16. $\frac{3}{8} \bigcirc> \frac{1}{3}$

Write each mixed number as an improper fraction.

17. $6\frac{2}{3} = \frac{20}{3}$ 18. $5\frac{3}{8} = \frac{43}{8}$ 19. $5\frac{4}{7} = \frac{39}{7}$ 20. $8\frac{5}{12} = \frac{101}{12}$

21. $3\frac{4}{9} = \frac{31}{9}$ 22. $4\frac{5}{11} = \frac{49}{11}$ 23. $7\frac{2}{5} = \frac{37}{5}$ 24. $9\frac{5}{8} = \frac{77}{8}$

Write each quotient as a mixed number. Simplify if necessary.

25. $5\overline{)27}$ $5\frac{2}{5}$ 26. $8\overline{)188}$ $23\frac{1}{2}$ 27. $35\overline{)308}$ $8\frac{4}{5}$ 28. $16\overline{)740}$ $46\frac{1}{4}$

29. $15\overline{)607}$ $40\frac{7}{15}$ 30. $12\overline{)461}$ $38\frac{5}{12}$ 31. $41\overline{)856}$ $20\frac{36}{41}$ 32. $14\overline{)295}$ $21\frac{1}{14}$

Rename each improper fraction as a whole or mixed number.

33. $\frac{9}{6} = 1\frac{1}{2}$ 34. $\frac{15}{7} = 2\frac{1}{7}$ 35. $\frac{36}{4} = 9$ 36. $\frac{63}{12} = 5\frac{1}{4}$

37. $\frac{56}{7} = 8$ 38. $\frac{95}{7} = 13\frac{4}{7}$ 39. $\frac{49}{8} = 6\frac{1}{8}$ 40. $\frac{54}{7} = 7\frac{5}{7}$

MCP All rights reserved

Circle the letter of the correct answer.

1 7,326 ◯ 7,236
    a <
    ⓑ >
    c =

2 259
  + 186
    a 335
    b 444
    ⓒ 445
    d NG

3 13,296
  + 8,474
    a 2,177
    b 21,760
    ⓒ 21,770
    d NG

4 5,036
  − 2,984
    ⓐ 2,052
    b 2,952
    c 3,952
    d NG

5 $436.18
  − 82.86
    a $343.32
    b $352.32
    c $454.72
    ⓓ NG

6 $6.15
  × 8
    a $48.02
    b $48.20
    ⓒ $49.20
    d NG

7 27 × 56
    a 297
    ⓑ 1,512
    c 11,592
    d NG

8 Find the average.
28, 16, 20, 24
    a 20
    ⓑ 22
    c 24
    d NG

9 6)60,326
    a 154 R2
    b 1,054 R2
    ⓒ 10,054 R2
    d NG

10 4,518 ÷ 36
    a 12 R18
    ⓑ 125 R18
    c 126 R18
    d NG

11 Find the perimeter.
5 cm, 4 cm, 6 cm
    ⓐ 15 cm
    b 120 cm
    c 120 sq cm
    d NG

12 6 ft 3 in.
  + 2 ft 10 in.
    a 8 ft 3 in.
    ⓑ 9 ft 1 in.
    c 9 ft 3 in.
    d NG

13 Find the equivalent fraction.
$\frac{3}{5} = \frac{?}{15}$
    a 3
    b 5
    ⓒ 9
    d NG

☐ score

164

Cumulative Review

page 164

Item	Objective
1	Compare and order numbers through thousands (See pages 9-10)
2	Add two numbers with sums less than 1,000, one regrouping (See pages 23-24)
3	Add two numbers up to 5-digits (See pages 27-28)
4	Subtract two 4-digit numbers, zero in the minuend (See pages 33-34)
5	Subtract two numbers up to 6-digits (See pages 35-36)
6	Multiply money by 1-digit factor (See pages 55-56)
7	Multiply two 2-digit factors (See pages 57-58)
8	Find the average (See pages 91-92)
9	Divide a 5-digit by 2-digit number, quotient with zero (See pages 109-110)
10	Divide a 4-digit by 2-digit number (See pages 107-108)
11	Find the perimeter of triangles (See pages 125-126)
12	Add and subtract customary units of length (See pages 123-124)
13	Find equivalent fractions by multiplying (See pages 147-148)

Alternate Cumulative Review

Circle the letter of the correct answer.

1 4,653 ◯ 4,563
  a <
  ⓑ >
  c =

2 475
  + 391
  a 766
  b 865
  ⓒ 866
  d NG

3 18,378
  + 9,562
  a 2,794
  b 27,930
  ⓒ 27,940
  d NG

4 6,029
  − 3,587
  ⓐ 2,442
  b 2,542
  c 3,562
  d NG

5 $549.27
  − 75.83
  a $473.34
  b $474.44
  c $534.64
  ⓓ NG

6 $4.26
  × 5
  a $2.13
  b $20.30
  ⓒ $21.30
  d NG

7 94
  × 38
  a 1,034
  ⓑ 3,572
  c 2,572
  d NG

8 Find the average.
17, 29, 26, 32
  a 24
  ⓑ 26
  c 28
  d NG

9 80)8,537
  a 16 R57
  ⓑ 106 R57
  c 1,006 R57
  d NG

10 29)6857
  a 23 R18
  ⓑ 236 R13
  c 237 R13
  d NG

11 Find the perimeter of a triangle 5 cm by 6 cm by 8 cm.
  a 240 sq cm
  b 240 cm
  ⓒ 19 cm
  d NG

12 7 ft 9 in.
  + 3 ft 6 in.
  a 10 ft 3 in.
  ⓑ 11 ft 3 in.
  c 11 ft 5 in.
  d NG

164

Adding Fractions

Objective

To add fractions with like denominators

Materials

Scissors
circles divided into eighths

Mental Math

Have students identify n:

1. $\frac{1}{2} = \frac{n}{4}$ (2)
2. $\frac{1}{3} = \frac{n}{9}$ (3)
3. $\frac{1}{2} = \frac{4}{n}$ (8)
4. $\frac{5}{10} = \frac{1}{n}$ (2)
5. $\frac{4}{5} = \frac{n}{10}$ (8)
6. $\frac{5}{5} = \frac{7}{n}$ (7)

Skill Review

Draw a circle on the board and divide it into fourths. Shade one fourth and stripe another fourth.

Have students write a fraction for the shaded area $\frac{1}{4}$, the striped area $\frac{1}{4}$, the clear area $\frac{2}{4}$ or $\frac{1}{2}$ and the entire circle $\frac{4}{4}$. Repeat this activity with circles divided into fifths and sixths.

Adding Fractions

Elmwood School's theme for this year's All-American Week is patriotism. Jaime is decorating some of the windows in his fifth grade classroom. He will put stars on 3 more windows. What fractional part of the classroom windows will be covered with stars?

We are looking for a fraction that shows the part of all the windows that will be covered with stars.

We know there are $\underline{8}$ windows in the classroom. Jaime has covered 1 window with stars and will put stars on $\underline{3}$ more windows.

The fractional part of windows already decorated is $\underline{\frac{1}{8}}$.

The fraction representing the additional windows Jaime plans to cover with stars is $\underline{\frac{3}{8}}$.

To find the fraction for the total number of decorated windows, we add the fraction for the window completed to the fractional part Jaime plans to do.

We add the fractions $\underline{\frac{1}{8}}$ and $\underline{\frac{3}{8}}$.

✔ To add fractions with common denominators, add the numerators and write the sum over the denominator. Simplify if necessary.

$$\frac{1}{8} + \frac{3}{8} = \frac{4}{8} = \frac{1}{2}$$

$$\begin{array}{r} \frac{1}{8} \\ + \frac{3}{8} \\ \hline \frac{4}{8} = \frac{1}{2} \end{array}$$

Jaime will cover $\underline{\frac{2}{?}}$ of the windows with stars.

Getting Started

Add. Simplify if necessary.

1. $\begin{array}{r} \frac{5}{8} \\ + \frac{1}{8} \\ \hline \frac{3}{4} \end{array}$
2. $\begin{array}{r} \frac{1}{2} \\ + \frac{1}{2} \\ \hline 1 \end{array}$
3. $\begin{array}{r} \frac{5}{9} \\ + \frac{1}{9} \\ \hline \frac{2}{3} \end{array}$
4. $\begin{array}{r} \frac{5}{6} \\ + \frac{3}{6} \\ \hline 1\frac{1}{3} \end{array}$

Copy and add.

5. $\frac{3}{12} + \frac{4}{12}$ $\frac{7}{12}$
6. $\frac{2}{3} + \frac{2}{3}$ $1\frac{1}{3}$
7. $\frac{3}{5} + \frac{2}{5}$ 1

MCP All rights reserved

165

Teaching the Lesson

Introducing the Problem Read the problem aloud, reminding students that a fraction can describe part of a set. Have students read the information sentences. Read the plan sentences aloud and put $\frac{1}{8} + \frac{3}{8} = \frac{4}{8} = \frac{1}{2}$ on the board. Have a student read the solution sentence. (will cover $\frac{1}{2}$) Explain that when fractions have like denominators, they simply add numerators. Write the problem in vertical form on the board and remind students to simplify the sum or rename an improper fraction as a mixed number.

Developing the Skill Put this addition on the board:

$$\frac{2}{9} + \frac{4}{9} = \frac{6}{9} = \frac{2}{3}$$

Explain that because these fractions have like denominators, students will add numerators. Point out that denominators describe the size of the fractional unit, the numerator describes the number of pieces. When they add, they add only the number of pieces; the size of the pieces will not change. Remind them to reduce a fraction in which numerator and denominator have a common factor. Remind students to reduce any sum that is an improper fraction. Have a student work $\frac{5}{8} + \frac{7}{8}$ on the board and rename the answer. ($\frac{12}{8} = 1\frac{4}{8} = 1\frac{1}{2}$)

Add. Simplify if necessary.

1. $\frac{7}{12}$
    $+\frac{1}{12}$
    $\frac{2}{3}$

2. $\frac{3}{4}$
    $+\frac{2}{4}$
    $1\frac{1}{4}$

3. $\frac{7}{8}$
    $+\frac{3}{8}$
    $1\frac{1}{4}$

4. $\frac{7}{16}$
    $+\frac{7}{16}$
    $\frac{7}{8}$

5. $\frac{9}{12}$
    $+\frac{7}{12}$
    $1\frac{1}{3}$

6. $\frac{4}{7}$
    $+\frac{3}{7}$
    1

7. $\frac{5}{10}$
    $+\frac{7}{10}$
    $1\frac{1}{5}$

8. $\frac{5}{9}$
    $+\frac{6}{9}$
    $1\frac{2}{9}$

9. $\frac{5}{8}$
    $+\frac{7}{8}$
    $1\frac{1}{2}$

10. $\frac{13}{16}$
    $+\frac{7}{16}$
    $1\frac{1}{4}$

11. $\frac{3}{10}$
    $+\frac{5}{10}$
    $\frac{4}{5}$

12. $\frac{1}{6}$
    $+\frac{3}{6}$
    $\frac{2}{3}$

13. $\frac{5}{7}$
    $+\frac{6}{7}$
    $1\frac{4}{7}$

14. $\frac{1}{6}$
    $+\frac{5}{6}$
    1

15. $\frac{8}{15}$
    $+\frac{12}{15}$
    $1\frac{1}{3}$

16. $\frac{3}{8}$
    $+\frac{7}{8}$
    $1\frac{1}{4}$

17. $\frac{2}{5}$
    $+\frac{3}{5}$
    1

18. $\frac{3}{12}$
    $+\frac{3}{12}$
    $\frac{1}{2}$

19. $\frac{8}{9}$
    $+\frac{4}{9}$
    $1\frac{1}{3}$

20. $\frac{9}{10}$
    $+\frac{7}{10}$
    $1\frac{3}{5}$

Copy and Do

21. $\frac{5}{8} + \frac{3}{8}$ 1
22. $\frac{3}{7} + \frac{2}{7}$ $\frac{5}{7}$
23. $\frac{5}{9} + \frac{3}{9}$ $\frac{8}{9}$
24. $\frac{7}{12} + \frac{3}{12}$ $\frac{5}{6}$
25. $\frac{3}{5} + \frac{4}{5}$ $1\frac{2}{5}$
26. $\frac{1}{4} + \frac{2}{4}$ $\frac{3}{4}$
27. $\frac{5}{6} + \frac{2}{6}$ $1\frac{1}{6}$
28. $\frac{3}{16} + \frac{5}{16}$ $\frac{1}{2}$

Apply

Solve these problems. Simplify if necessary.

29. Katie and Dale worked together on a poster for All-American Week. Katie painted $\frac{5}{12}$ of the poster red and Dale painted $\frac{3}{12}$ of it blue. They left the rest of the white poster board unpainted. What fractional part of the poster did Katie and Dale paint?
$\frac{2}{3}$

30. Sun Lin made a quilt for her sister's cradle using left-over fabric. She used $\frac{7}{8}$ of a yard of blue calico, $\frac{5}{8}$ of a yard of rose calico and $\frac{3}{8}$ of a yard of white cloth. How many yards of material did Sun Lin use for her quilt?
$1\frac{7}{8}$ yards

166

Correcting Common Errors

Watch for students who add the numerators and the denominators to find the sum.

INCORRECT	CORRECT
$\frac{3}{7} + \frac{2}{7} = \frac{5}{14}$	$\frac{3}{7} + \frac{2}{7} = \frac{5}{7}$

Have students work in pairs to model addition problems. They should use a circle to model each fraction and then count to find the number of fractional parts shaded in both circles.

Enrichment

Put this number line on the board and have students copy it.

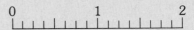

Have students use the number line to add these fractions.

1. $\frac{3}{8} + \frac{7}{8} = (1\frac{1}{4})$
2. $\frac{1}{8} + \frac{1}{8} + \frac{1}{8} = (\frac{3}{8})$
3. $\frac{5}{8} + \frac{7}{8} = (1\frac{1}{2})$
4. $\frac{3}{8} + \frac{3}{8} = (\frac{6}{8} = \frac{3}{4})$
5. $\frac{2}{8} + \frac{2}{8} + \frac{7}{8} = (1\frac{3}{8})$

Practice

Have students complete the problems on the page.

Extra Credit *Numeration*

Have the students study the arrays of dots in the diagram above. The number of dots in each picture is called a <u>triangular</u> number since they fit into an array in the shape of a triangle.

Have students draw the arrays for the next five triangular numbers and continue the sequence of triangular numbers: (15, 21, 28, 36, 45)

After students have finished, ask them to see the pattern for finding the next five triangular numbers without drawing the triangular arrays. (55, 66, 78, 91, 105; to find the 10th number add 10 to the previous number, to find the 11th number add 11 to the 10th, then add 12, etc., . . .)

166

Subtracting Fractions

pages 167-168

Objective

To subtract fractions with like denominators

Materials

circles divided into eighths
scissors

Mental Math

Have students tell:

1. how many tens in 32? (3)
2. how many fives in 42? (8)
3. how many elevens in 56? (5)
4. how many threes in 29? (9)
5. how many fours in 42? (10)
6. how many sevens in 36? (5)
7. how many twos in 26? (13)

Skill Review

Have students copy and add these fractions:

1. $\frac{2}{3} + \frac{4}{3} = (2)$
2. $\frac{4}{5} + \frac{3}{5} = (1\frac{2}{5})$
3. $\frac{8}{9} + \frac{4}{9} = (1\frac{1}{3})$
4. $\frac{6}{7} + \frac{3}{7} = (1\frac{2}{7})$
5. $\frac{1}{8} + \frac{6}{8} = (\frac{7}{8})$
6. $\frac{2}{5} + \frac{3}{5} + \frac{3}{5} = (1\frac{3}{5})$
7. $\frac{3}{9} + \frac{4}{9} + \frac{1}{9} = (\frac{8}{9})$

Subtracting Fractions

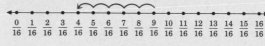

Neil and Todd explored two different trails near their campsite on Bear Mountain. Neil hiked to Bear View and Todd hiked to Vista Point. How much farther did Neil have to hike to his destination?

We want to find how much farther Neil had to walk.

Neil hiked $\frac{9}{16}$ of a mile and Todd hiked $\frac{5}{16}$ of a mile.

To find the difference in distance, we need to subtract Todd's distance from the distance hiked by Neil.

We subtract $\frac{5}{16}$ from $\frac{9}{16}$.

We can use a number line to help us subtract.

| 0/16 | 1/16 | 2/16 | 3/16 | 4/16 | 5/16 | 6/16 | 7/16 | 8/16 | 9/16 | 10/16 | 11/16 | 12/16 | 13/16 | 14/16 | 15/16 | 16/16 |

$$\frac{9}{16} - \frac{5}{16} = \frac{4}{16} = \frac{1}{4}$$

Neil hiked $\frac{1}{4}$ of a mile farther than Todd.

✔ To subtract fractions with common denominators, subtract the numerators.
Write the difference over the denominator.
Simplify if necessary.

$$\frac{9}{16}$$
$$-\frac{5}{16}$$
$$\frac{4}{16} = \frac{1}{4}$$

✔ If the difference is an improper fraction, simplify by renaming it as a whole or mixed number.

Getting Started

Subtract. Simplify if necessary.

1. $\frac{15}{9}$ $-\frac{4}{9}$ $1\frac{2}{9}$

2. $\frac{21}{12}$ $-\frac{9}{12}$ 1

3. $\frac{9}{8}$ $-\frac{9}{8}$ 0

4. $\frac{12}{5}$ $-\frac{4}{5}$ $1\frac{3}{5}$

Copy and subtract.

5. $\frac{7}{8} - \frac{1}{8}$ $\frac{3}{4}$

6. $\frac{9}{4} - \frac{3}{4}$ $1\frac{1}{2}$

7. $\frac{4}{15} - \frac{3}{15}$ $\frac{1}{15}$

MCP All rights reserved

167

Teaching the Lesson

Introducing the Problem Have a student read the problem, information sentences and plan sentences aloud. Ask students to look at the number line in their texts. Have them start at 0 and move 9/16 to the right. Explain that to subtract they will move 5/16 to the left. Have a student read the answer. (4/16) Have another student write the subtraction on the board as it appears in their texts. (9/16 − 5/16 = 4/16 = 1/4) Show students that just as they could add numerators when the denominators were the same, they can subtract numerators when denominators are equal. Ask a student to read the solution sentence. (hiked 4/16 of a mile farther) Write the subtraction in vertical form on the board and remind students to simplify if necessary.

Developing the Skill Put a number line marked in sixteenths on the board. Draw two line segments above the line, one showing 9/16 and 5/16 long.
Have a student explain how this illustrates the difference between 9/16 and 5/16. Remind them that the denominator shows the size of the fractional unit and is not involved in any computation. Have students work this example on the board: 9/16 − 3/16 = (6/16 = 3/8) and illustrate it on the line.

Practice

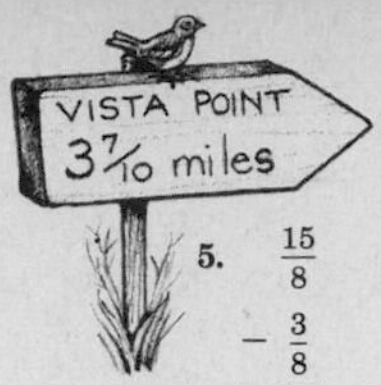
VISTA POINT
3 7/10 miles

Subtract. Simplify if necessary.

1. $\frac{5}{7} - \frac{3}{7}$ $\frac{2}{7}$
2. $\frac{8}{9} - \frac{2}{9}$ $\frac{2}{3}$
3. $\frac{11}{4} - \frac{3}{4}$ 2
4. $\frac{7}{2} - \frac{1}{2}$ 3
5. $\frac{15}{8} - \frac{3}{8}$ $1\frac{1}{2}$
6. $\frac{9}{16} - \frac{5}{16}$ $\frac{1}{4}$
7. $\frac{9}{10} - \frac{4}{10}$ $\frac{1}{2}$
8. $\frac{9}{15} - \frac{3}{15}$ $\frac{2}{5}$
9. $\frac{12}{5} - \frac{3}{5}$ $1\frac{4}{5}$
10. $\frac{10}{6} - \frac{1}{6}$ $1\frac{1}{2}$
11. $\frac{7}{12} - \frac{3}{12}$ $\frac{1}{3}$
12. $\frac{17}{4} - \frac{2}{4}$ $3\frac{3}{4}$
13. $\frac{13}{9} - \frac{2}{9}$ $1\frac{2}{9}$
14. $\frac{23}{10} - \frac{16}{10}$ $\frac{7}{10}$
15. $\frac{15}{16} - \frac{7}{16}$ $\frac{1}{2}$
16. $\frac{17}{6} - \frac{11}{6}$ 1
17. $\frac{25}{4} - \frac{15}{4}$ $2\frac{1}{2}$
18. $\frac{27}{10} - \frac{15}{10}$ $1\frac{1}{5}$
19. $\frac{17}{3} - \frac{11}{3}$ 2
20. $\frac{37}{15} - \frac{25}{15}$ $\frac{4}{5}$

Copy and Do

21. $\frac{7}{8} - \frac{4}{8}$ $\frac{3}{8}$
22. $\frac{13}{16} - \frac{9}{16}$ $\frac{1}{4}$
23. $\frac{7}{5} - \frac{1}{5}$ $1\frac{1}{5}$
24. $\frac{2}{3} - \frac{1}{3}$ $\frac{1}{3}$
25. $\frac{5}{4} - \frac{1}{4}$ 1
26. $\frac{5}{6} - \frac{1}{6}$ $\frac{2}{3}$
27. $\frac{4}{3} - \frac{2}{3}$ $\frac{2}{3}$
28. $\frac{9}{12} - \frac{1}{12}$ $\frac{2}{3}$

Apply

Use the graph to solve problems 29 and 30. Simplify if necessary.

29. How much farther did Mike run than Bess? $\frac{3}{8}$ of a mile

30. How many total miles did all three children run? $2\frac{1}{2}$ miles

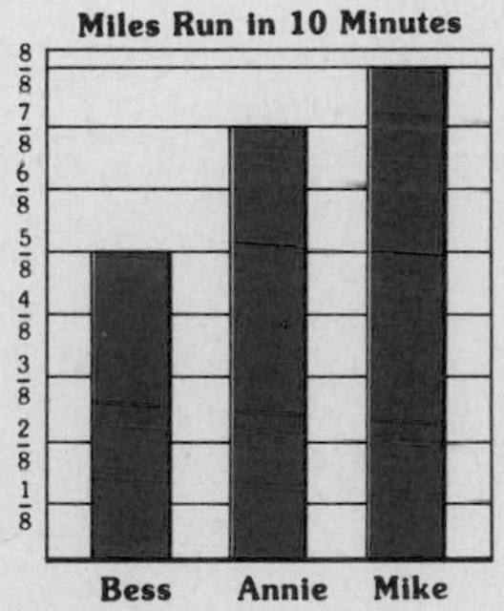
Miles Run in 10 Minutes
8/8
7/8
6/8
5/8
4/8
3/8
2/8
1/8
Bess
Annie
Mike

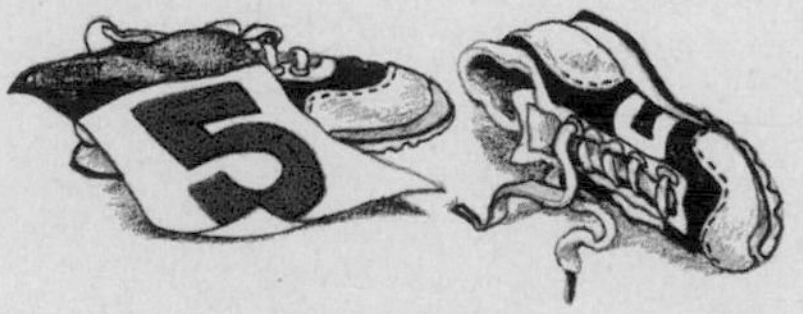
5

168

Correcting Common Errors

When subtracting fractions, some students may use the procedure for adding instead. Have students work in pairs to model subtraction problems, such as 5/6 − 3/6. Have them divide a rectangle into 6 parts and color 5 of them. Then have them cross out 2 of the parts to show subtraction and count to find that 2/6 is left. Although 1/3 is no more correct than 2/6, students can be encouraged to simplify after they understand subtraction.

Enrichment

Have students solve this problem: Classes at Eastwood School had pizza on the last day. One very large pizza was ordered for each class and cut into 32 pieces. Some students did not have any, so each class had pizza left.

green room − 3 pieces
brown room − 8 pieces
yellow room − 4 pieces
red room − 1 piece

The teachers are thinking of having a party after school with the left-over pizza. What fractional part of a pizza is left? (1/2 pizza)

Practice

Have students complete the problems on the page. Remind them to reduce fractions to simplest terms.

Mixed Practice

1. 35 + 88 + 90 + 48 (261)
2. $\frac{5}{7} + \frac{1}{7}$ $\left(\frac{6}{7}\right)$
3. 302,108 − 4,179 (297,929)
4. 24,138 ÷ 40 (603 R18)
5. $\frac{3}{7} = \frac{\quad}{14}$ (6)
6. $3,036.58 × 3 ($9,109.74)
7. 41,097 ÷ 73 (562 R71)
8. 805 × 906 (729,330)
9. $\frac{17}{5} - \frac{10}{5}$ $\left(1\frac{2}{5}\right)$
10. 56 × 37 (2,072)

Extra Credit *Statistics*

Put the following table of information on the board and have students draw a histogram on graph paper to show the data.

Average weight of children

0 − ½ yr	**8 kg**
½ − 1 yr	**9 kg**
1 − 4 yr	**13 kg**
4 − 7 yr	**20 kg**
7 − 10 yr	**28 kg**

Be sure that students make the width of their histogram columns proportional to the number of years represented.

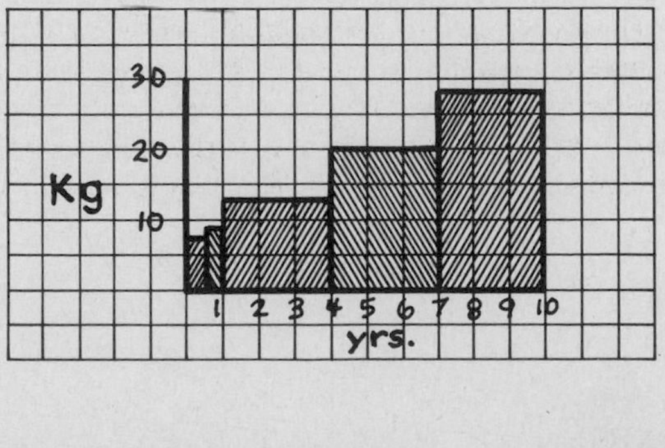
30
20
10
Kg
1 2 3 4 5 6 7 8 9 10
yrs.

Common Multiples

pages 169-170

Objective

To find common multiples

Materials

large-squared graph paper

Mental Math

Have students give the other three problems in each fact family:

1. $54 \div 9 = 6$ ($54 \div 6 = 9$, $9 \times 6 = 54$, $6 \times 9 = 54$)
2. $5 + 4 = 9$ ($4 + 5 = 9$, $9 - 4 = 5$, $9 - 5 = 4$)
3. $25 \div 5 = 5$
4. $14 - 7 = 7$
5. $30 \div 6 = 5$
6. $3 \times 7 = 21$

Skill Review

Have students complete this table:

x	1	2	3	4	5	6	7	8	9
1	1	2	3						
2	2	4	6						
3	3	6	9	. . .					
4			.						
5			.						
6			.						
7									
8									
9									

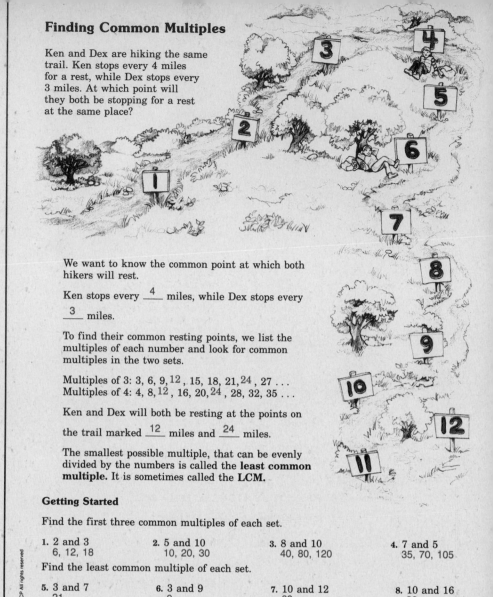

Finding Common Multiples

Ken and Dex are hiking the same trail. Ken stops every 4 miles for a rest, while Dex stops every 3 miles. At which point will they both be stopping for a rest at the same place?

We want to know the common point at which both hikers will rest.

Ken stops every __4__ miles, while Dex stops every __3__ miles.

To find their common resting points, we list the multiples of each number and look for common multiples in the two sets.

Multiples of 3: 3, 6, 9, 12, 15, 18, 21, 24, 27 . . .
Multiples of 4: 4, 8, 12, 16, 20, 24, 28, 32, 35 . . .

Ken and Dex will both be resting at the points on the trail marked __12__ miles and __24__ miles.

The smallest possible multiple, that can be evenly divided by the numbers is called the **least common multiple**. It is sometimes called the **LCM**.

Getting Started

Find the first three common multiples of each set.

1. 2 and 3
6, 12, 18

2. 5 and 10
10, 20, 30

3. 8 and 10
40, 80, 120

4. 7 and 5
35, 70, 105

Find the least common multiple of each set.

5. 3 and 7
21

6. 3 and 9
9

7. 10 and 12
60

8. 10 and 16
80

MCP All rights reserved

169

Teaching the Lesson

Introducing the Problem Read the problem aloud and have a student read the information sentences. Read the plan sentence and direct their attention to multiples of 3 and 4 listed in their texts. Put the multiples on the board and ask a student to circle multiples common to both lists. (12 and 24) Read the solution sentence. (will both be resting at 12- and 24-mile points) Explain that in these two sets of numbers, 12 is the smallest multiple the sets have in common and for that reason is called the **least common multiple.** This is sometimes abbreviated **LCM.**

Developing the Skill Explain that common multiples are also dividends. Each of the original numbers can divide a common multiple evenly. Put these sets on the board:

multiples of 5: 5, 10, 15, 20, 25, 30, 35, . . .
multiples of 6: 6, 12, 18, 24, 30, 36, . . .

Point out that the least common multiple of 5 and 6 is 30, and that 30 can be divided evenly by both 5 and 6. Ask students to find the least common multiple for 4 and 7. (LCM = 28)
Ask students how many sevens are in 28? (4) How many fours in 28? (7)

Practice

Find the first three common multiples of each set.

1. 5 and 3
15, 30, 45

2. 7 and 14
14, 28, 42

3. 4 and 10
20, 40, 60

4. 6 and 9
18, 36, 54

5. 8 and 12
24, 48, 72

6. 2 and 5
10, 20, 30

7. 4 and 8
8, 16, 24

8. 3 and 12
12, 24, 36

9. 6 and 15
30, 60, 90

10. 8 and 9
72, 144, 216

11. 4 and 6
12, 24, 36

12. 5 and 20
20, 40, 60

Find the least common multiple of each set.

13. 4 and 9
36

14. 3 and 12
12

15. 6 and 18
18

16. 7 and 8
56

17. 10 and 15
30

18. 12 and 15
60

19. 8 and 12
24

20. 6 and 7
42

21. 9 and 15
45

22. 6 and 4
12

23. 9 and 21
63

24. 10 and 25
50

Apply

Solve these problems.

25. Mr. Phelps is buying bolts and washers. He needs to have the same number of each. Bolts are sold in packages of 8. Washers are sold in packages of 20. How many packages of each should he buy?
5 packages of bolts
2 packages of washers

26. Tom, Alice and Nancy are hiking the same trail. Tom rests every 5 kilometers, Alice rests every 4 kilometers and Nancy rests every 3 kilometers. At what point is the first rest stop where all three hikers stop together?
60-kilometer point

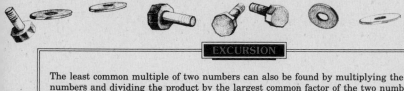

EXCURSION

The least common multiple of two numbers can also be found by multiplying the numbers and dividing the product by the largest common factor of the two numbers.

The least common multiple of 4 and 16 is $4 \times 16 \div 4$. LCM = 16

The least common multiple of 8 and 12 is $8 \times 12 \div \underline{4}$. LCM = 24

The least common multiple of 4 and 5 is $4 \times 5 \div \underline{1}$. LCM = 20

Find the least common multiple of each set.

1. 15 and 25
LCM = _75_

2. 12 and 40
LCM = _120_

3. 24 and 30
LCM = _120_

4. 15 and 16
LCM = _240_

170

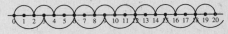

Correcting Common Errors

Some students may have trouble understanding common multiples. Have them work with partners to show multiples on a number line. For example, have one partner draw arcs above the line to show multiples of 2. The other partner draws arcs below the line to show multiples of 3. The points where the arcs above and below the line meet are common multiples.

The first four common multiples of 2 and 3 are 0, 6, 12, and 18.

Enrichment

A good shortcut to finding the least common multiple is to multiply the two numbers in the set. Students recognize that the product of the two is bound to be a common multiple. In order to insure it is the least common multiple, they can try dividing by the common factors 2, 3 or 5. Have them use this shortcut to find the LCM of these number pairs.

1. 5 and 8 (40)   3. 2 and 5 (10)
2. 3 and 7 (21)   4. 7 and 8 (56)

Practice

Have students complete the page. Explain that to find the common multiples they may need long lists of multiples.

Excursion

Encourage students to list the multiples to arrive at the LCM if the method shown in the excursion confuses them.

Extra Credit   *Measurement*

Tell students to draw Pirate Treasure Maps for treasure they have hidden around the school grounds. Have them include a starting point; the directions North, South, East and West; and as many landmarks (trees, equipment, bushes etc.) as possible and a scale. The exact location of the treasure should not be shown, but clues for finding it are to be given. Students may want to actually hide a "treasure." An example of a clue would be: Travel 5 feet west of the main school door. After the maps are drawn, have students exchange with a partner and try to find their hidden treasure.

Adding Uncommon Denominators

pages 171-172

Objective

To add fractions with unlike denominators

Materials

Mental Math

Have students subtract:

1. $24 - 10 = (14)$
2. $35 - 17 = (18)$
3. $55 - 13 = (42)$
4. $27 - 8 = (19)$
5. $38 - 18 = (20)$
6. $52 - 47 = (5)$
7. $99 - 38 = (61)$

Skill Review

Dictate these number pairs and a possible LCM. Ask if the multiple given is the least common multiple:

1. 3,4 LCM = 12 (true)
2. 4,8 LCM = 32 (false, 8)
3. 5,10 LCM = 20 (false, 10)
4. 5,6 LCM = 30 (true)
5. 7,4 LCM = 28 (true)
6. 4,6 LCM = 24 (false, 12)
7. 2,6 LCM = 6 (true)

Adding Fractions with Unlike Denominators

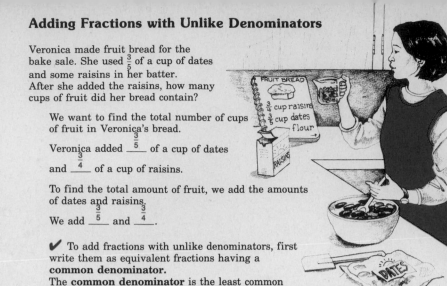

Veronica made fruit bread for the bake sale. She used $\frac{3}{5}$ of a cup of dates and some raisins in her batter. After she added the raisins, how many cups of fruit did her bread contain?

We want to find the total number of cups of fruit in Veronica's bread.

Veronica added $\frac{3}{5}$ of a cup of dates

and $\frac{3}{4}$ of a cup of raisins.

To find the total amount of fruit, we add the amounts of dates and raisins.

We add $\frac{3}{5}$ and $\frac{3}{4}$.

✔ To add fractions with unlike denominators, first write them as equivalent fractions having a **common denominator.**
The **common denominator** is the least common multiple of the denominators.

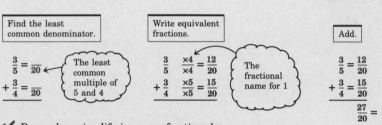

Find the least common denominator.	Write equivalent fractions.	Add.

$$\frac{3}{5} = \frac{}{20}$$
$$+\frac{3}{4} = \frac{}{20}$$

The least common multiple of 5 and 4

$$\frac{3}{5} \quad \frac{\times 4}{\times 4} = \frac{12}{20}$$
$$+\frac{3}{4} \quad \frac{\times 5}{\times 5} = \frac{15}{20}$$

The fractional name for 1

$$\frac{3}{5} = \frac{12}{20}$$
$$+\frac{3}{4} = \frac{15}{20}$$
$$\frac{27}{20} = 1\frac{7}{20}$$

✔ Remember, simplify improper fractions by dividing the denominator into the numerator. Write any remainders as simplified fractions.

Veronica put $1\frac{7}{20}$ cups of fruit in her bread.

Getting Started

Add. Simplify if necessary.

1. $\frac{3}{5}$
$+\frac{1}{3}$
$\overline{\frac{14}{15}}$

2. $\frac{1}{2}$
$+\frac{3}{4}$
$\overline{1\frac{1}{4}}$

3. $\frac{5}{6}$
$+\frac{3}{8}$
$\overline{1\frac{5}{24}}$

Copy and add.

4. $\frac{3}{7} + \frac{4}{5}$ $1\frac{8}{35}$

5. $\frac{7}{10} + \frac{40}{100}$ $1\frac{1}{10}$

MCP All rights reserved

171

Teaching the Lesson

Introducing the Problem Read the problem aloud and have a student read the information sentences. Read the next sentences and point out that these fractions do not have the same denominator. Ask a student to explain why that is important. (Because it is not possible to add fractions unless they are expressed in similar units.) Put the example on the board and have students follow in their texts while you change fifths to twentieths and fourths to twentieths. ($^{12}\!/_{20}$ and $^{15}\!/_{20}$) Point out that when fractions are in equal units, they can be added by adding numerators. Have a student do the addition on the board and read the solution sentence. ($^{27}\!/_{20} = 1^{7}\!/_{20}$)

Developing the Skill

Remind students that they have worked with equivalent fractions before. In this lesson they will have to change each fraction to an equivalent fraction before they can add. To determine what the new denominator should be, they will look for the LCM of the given denominators. Although any common multiple of the denominators will give a correct answer, the smaller the common multiple, the easier it will be to change from the original fractions to the equivalents. Write ⅔ + ½ = on the board. Ask what the LCM is for 3 and 2. (6) Have a student work the problem on the board. (1⅙)

171

Practice

Add. Simplify if necessary.

1. $\frac{1}{5}$
  $+\frac{1}{3}$
  —————
  $\frac{8}{15}$

2. $\frac{3}{4}$
  $+\frac{5}{8}$
  —————
  $1\frac{3}{8}$

3. $\frac{3}{8}$
  $+\frac{1}{2}$
  —————
  $\frac{7}{8}$

4. $\frac{5}{6}$
  $+\frac{5}{9}$
  —————
  $1\frac{7}{18}$

5. $\frac{7}{10}$
  $+\frac{1}{5}$
  —————
  $\frac{9}{10}$

6. $\frac{2}{3}$
  $+\frac{7}{8}$
  —————
  $1\frac{13}{24}$

7. $\frac{9}{10}$
  $+\frac{1}{2}$
  —————
  $1\frac{2}{5}$

8. $\frac{11}{4}$
  $+\frac{4}{6}$
  —————
  $3\frac{5}{12}$

9. $\frac{9}{16}$
  $+\frac{5}{8}$
  —————
  $1\frac{3}{16}$

10. $\frac{15}{12}$
  $+\frac{3}{8}$
  —————
  $1\frac{5}{8}$

11. $\frac{15}{16}$
  $+\frac{1}{6}$
  —————
  $1\frac{5}{48}$

12. $\frac{9}{15}$
  $+\frac{7}{10}$
  —————
  $1\frac{3}{10}$

13. $\frac{25}{30}$
  $+\frac{6}{10}$
  —————
  $1\frac{13}{30}$

14. $\frac{3}{6}$
  $+\frac{7}{12}$
  —————
  $1\frac{1}{12}$

15. $\frac{8}{9}$
  $+\frac{3}{7}$
  —————
  $1\frac{20}{63}$

16. $\frac{5}{8}$
  $+\frac{8}{9}$
  —————
  $1\frac{37}{72}$

Copy and Do

17. $\frac{4}{5}+\frac{7}{10}$ $1\frac{1}{2}$

18. $\frac{7}{8}+\frac{1}{4}$ $1\frac{1}{8}$

19. $\frac{2}{3}+\frac{5}{9}$ $1\frac{2}{9}$

20. $\frac{5}{6}+\frac{7}{9}$ $1\frac{11}{18}$

21. $\frac{7}{8}+\frac{1}{6}$ $1\frac{1}{24}$

22. $\frac{3}{6}+\frac{3}{4}$ $1\frac{1}{4}$

23. $\frac{5}{16}+\frac{3}{4}$ $1\frac{1}{16}$

24. $\frac{9}{6}+\frac{2}{4}$ 2

25. $\frac{7}{10}+\frac{13}{15}$ $1\frac{17}{30}$

26. $\frac{7}{3}+\frac{9}{4}$ $4\frac{7}{12}$

27. $\frac{3}{9}+\frac{7}{12}$ $\frac{11}{12}$

28. $\frac{6}{7}+\frac{1}{3}$ $1\frac{4}{21}$

29. $\frac{18}{100}+\frac{5}{10}$ $\frac{17}{25}$

30. $\frac{15}{8}+\frac{7}{12}$ $2\frac{11}{24}$

31. $\frac{17}{21}+\frac{5}{6}$ $1\frac{9}{14}$

32. $\frac{14}{6}+\frac{21}{9}$ $4\frac{2}{3}$

Apply

Solve these problems. Simplify if necessary.

33. Ruth practices her piano $\frac{3}{4}$ of an hour each day and Bert practices his violin $\frac{2}{3}$ of an hour each day. How long do Ruth and Bert together practice each day?
    $1\frac{5}{12}$ hours

34. Leon used $\frac{2}{3}$ of a quart of blue paint, $\frac{1}{4}$ of a quart of red paint and $\frac{1}{2}$ of a quart of yellow paint on his soap box derby car. How much paint did Leon use?
    $1\frac{5}{12}$ quarts

172

Correcting Common Errors

When adding fractions, some students may find a common denominator but forget to change the numerators. Have them make diagrams to show the equivalent fractions and then perform the operations correctly.

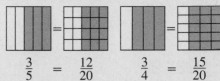

$$\frac{3}{5} = \frac{12}{20} \qquad \frac{3}{4} = \frac{15}{20}$$

Enrichment

Ask students to use mathematical common sense in doing these problems. Suggest they consider the problem carefully before finding a denominator common to all the addends.

1. ½ + ⅓ + ⅙ = (1)
2. ¼ + ⅛ + ½ + ⅛ = (1)
3. ¾ + ¹⁄₁₆ + ⅜ + ³⁄₁₆ = (1⅜)

Practice

Have students complete the practice problems. Remind students to reduce improper fractions. Explain that if they do not find the least common multiple, they can complete the problem and reduce the answer at the end.

Extra Credit *Sets*

Present the following to students:
In Mrs. Smith's fifth–grade class, Susan, Frank and José play the piano and all three are taking tennis lessons. Using Set A to equal the piano players and Set B to equal the tennis players, use brackets to list the elements of each set.

          Set A = [Susan, Frank, José]
          Set B = [Susan, Frank, José]

Because the elements of Set A are the same as the elements of Set B, these are equal sets. (Set A = Set B) For each of the following problems, indicate if the sets are equal (=) or not equal (≠):

a) Set A = [3, 6, 9, 12, 15], Set B = [12, 9, 15, 3, 6] (=)
b) Set C = [j, t, l, i, s, m], Set D = [s, j, i, t, n, l] (≠)
c) Set E = all boys with freckles, Set F = all girls with freckles (≠)
d) Set G is the set of even numbers up to 10.
   Set H is the set of numbers divisible by 2 up to 10. (=)
e) Set I is the set of vowels. Set J is the set of letters in your first name. (≠)

Subtracting Uncommon Denominators

pages 173-174

Objective

To subtract fractions with unlike denominators

Materials

Mental Math

Have students find the value for n:

1. $(2 \times n) \div 3 = 4$ (6)
2. $n \div (3 \times 3) = 4$ (36)
3. $15 \div 2 = 7 \text{ Rn}$ (1)
4. $(42 \div n) + 6 = 12$ (7)
5. $(7 + 3) \times n = 40$ (4)
6. $(21 \div 3) + 3 = n$ (10)
7. $(n \div 10) + 1 = 6$ (50)

Skill Review

Have students review subtracting fractions with like denominators:

1. $7/8 - 1/8$ ($6/8 = 3/4$)
2. $9/4 - 3/4$ ($6/4 = 1\frac{1}{2}$)
3. $3/3 - 1/3$ ($2/3$)
4. $9/5 - 4/5$ ($5/5 = 1$)

Have them review working with unlike fractions:

1. $3/4 + 1/2$ ($3/4 + 2/4 = 5/4 = 1\frac{1}{4}$)
2. $2/3 + 3/2$ ($4/6 + 9/6 = 13/6 = 2\frac{1}{6}$)

Subtracting with Unlike Denominators

The average height for a 10-year-old American child is $4\frac{1}{2}$ feet. Cindy kept track of her height for 4 months during one year. How much more did Cindy grow in October than in November?

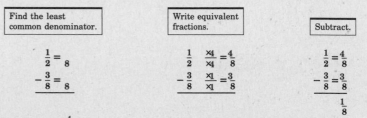

We need to find how much more Cindy grew in October than in November.

In October, Cindy grew $\frac{1}{2}$ of an inch.

She grew $\frac{3}{8}$ of an inch in November.

To find her difference in growth, we subtract her growth in November from her growth in October. To subtract fractions with unlike denominators, first write them as equivalent fractions having **common denominators.**

Find the least common denominator.	Write equivalent fractions.	Subtract.
$\begin{array}{r}\frac{1}{2}=\\[4pt]-\frac{3}{8}=\end{array}\ \ \dfrac{}{8}$	$\begin{array}{r}\frac{1}{2}\ \frac{\times 4}{\times 4}=\frac{4}{8}\\[4pt]-\frac{3}{8}\ \frac{\times 1}{\times 1}=\frac{3}{8}\end{array}$	$\begin{array}{r}\frac{1}{2}=\frac{4}{8}\\[4pt]-\frac{3}{8}=\frac{3}{8}\\\hline \frac{1}{8}\end{array}$

Cindy grew $\frac{1}{8}$ of an inch more in October than she did in November.

Getting Started

Subtract. Simplify if necessary.

1. $\begin{array}{r}\frac{5}{9}\\-\frac{1}{3}\\\hline\frac{2}{9}\end{array}$
2. $\begin{array}{r}\frac{5}{6}\\-\frac{1}{4}\\\hline\frac{7}{12}\end{array}$
3. $\begin{array}{r}\frac{4}{5}\\-\frac{3}{10}\\\hline\frac{1}{2}\end{array}$
4. $\begin{array}{r}\frac{13}{4}\\-\frac{2}{3}\\\hline2\frac{7}{12}\end{array}$

Copy and subtract.

5. $\frac{11}{6} - \frac{4}{9}$ $1\frac{7}{18}$
6. $\frac{60}{100} - \frac{2}{10}$ $\frac{2}{5}$
7. $\frac{12}{9} - \frac{13}{45}$ $1\frac{2}{45}$
8. $\frac{2}{4} - \frac{1}{3}$ $\frac{1}{6}$

173

MCP All rights reserved

Teaching the Lesson

Introducing the Problem Read the problem aloud. Have a student read the information sentences. Read the plan sentences and direct the students' attention to the problem worked in stages in their texts. Explain that as in addition of unlike fractions, they must find a common denominator before they can subtract. Ask a student to explain why this is so. (Because only like fractions can be added or subtracted. If they have unequal denominators, the sizes of the fractional pieces are not the same.) Ask students to find the LCM of 2 and 8 (8), rename the fractions in eighths ($1/2 = 4/8$; $3/8 = 3/8$), and work the subtraction on the board. ($4/8 - 3/8 = 1/8$) Read the solution sentence aloud.

Developing the Skill Remind students that the denominator refers to the size of each fractional part. In order to add or subtract these parts, they must all be of equal size. Write this problem on the board: $3/8 - 1/5 =$. Ask if eighths and fifths are the same size. (no) Have students identify the least common multiple. (40) Have students rename each fraction and subtract.
$3/8 \times 5/5 = 15/40$ and $1/5 \times 8/8 = 8/40$ so $15/40 - 8/40 = 7/40$

173

Practice

Subtract. Simplify if necessary.

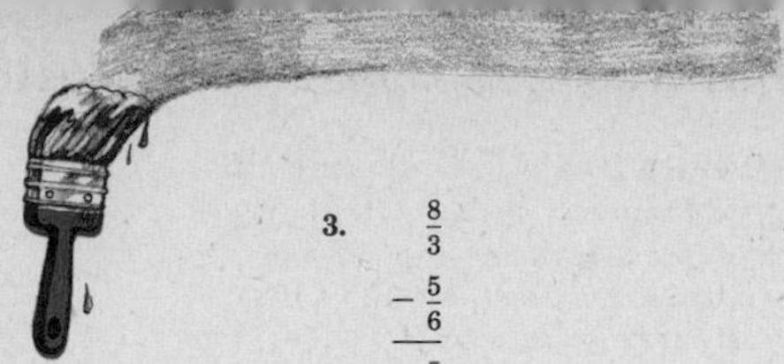

1. $\frac{3}{4}$
$-\frac{1}{2}$
———
$\frac{1}{4}$

2. $\frac{7}{9}$
$-\frac{1}{3}$
———
$\frac{4}{9}$

3. $\frac{8}{3}$
$-\frac{5}{6}$
———
$1\frac{5}{6}$

4. $\frac{5}{8}$
$-\frac{1}{4}$
———
$\frac{3}{8}$

5. $\frac{1}{3}$
$-\frac{1}{5}$
———
$\frac{2}{15}$

6. $\frac{5}{6}$
$-\frac{3}{8}$
———
$\frac{11}{24}$

7. $\frac{2}{3}$
$-\frac{3}{5}$
———
$\frac{1}{15}$

8. $\frac{7}{8}$
$-\frac{1}{3}$
———
$\frac{13}{24}$

9. $\frac{5}{8}$
$-\frac{2}{5}$
———
$\frac{9}{40}$

10. $\frac{18}{5}$
$-\frac{6}{4}$
———
$2\frac{1}{10}$

11. $\frac{85}{100}$
$-\frac{5}{10}$
———
$\frac{7}{20}$

12. $\frac{3}{2}$
$-\frac{2}{3}$
———
$\frac{5}{6}$

Copy and Do

13. $\frac{7}{12} - \frac{1}{4}$ $\frac{1}{3}$

14. $\frac{21}{15} - \frac{6}{5}$ $\frac{1}{5}$

15. $\frac{87}{100} - \frac{3}{4}$ $\frac{3}{25}$

16. $\frac{9}{16} - \frac{3}{8}$ $\frac{3}{16}$

17. $\frac{2}{3} - \frac{1}{4}$ $\frac{5}{12}$

18. $\frac{9}{10} - \frac{2}{3}$ $\frac{7}{30}$

19. $\frac{5}{8} - \frac{2}{6}$ $\frac{7}{24}$

20. $\frac{4}{5} - \frac{3}{4}$ $\frac{1}{20}$

21. $\frac{3}{4} - \frac{1}{5}$ $\frac{11}{20}$

22. $\frac{2}{3} - \frac{3}{8}$ $\frac{7}{24}$

23. $\frac{3}{4} - \frac{2}{3}$ $\frac{1}{12}$

24. $\frac{9}{8} - \frac{5}{6}$ $\frac{7}{24}$

25. $\frac{9}{10} - \frac{5}{6}$ $\frac{1}{15}$

26. $\frac{11}{6} - \frac{8}{9}$ $\frac{17}{18}$

27. $\frac{13}{9} - \frac{25}{36}$ $\frac{3}{4}$

28. $\frac{12}{10} - \frac{9}{15}$ $\frac{3}{5}$

Apply

Solve these problems. Simplify if necessary.

29. Ronnie had $\frac{3}{4}$ of a gallon of house paint. He used $\frac{1}{3}$ of a gallon on the doors. How much paint did Ronnie have left?
$\frac{5}{12}$ of a gallon

30. The Malinowski's started their trip to visit Aunt Stella with $\frac{7}{8}$ of a tank of gas. They returned home with $\frac{1}{6}$ of a tank. What part of a tank of gas did the Malinowski's use on their trip?
$\frac{17}{24}$ of a tank

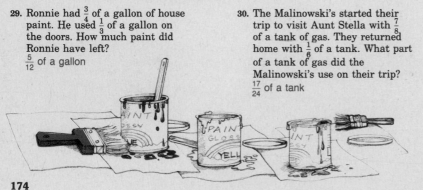

Correcting Common Errors

Some students may have difficulty when one of the two denominators is not the common denominator. Have them work with partners to list multiples of both denominators in pairs, such as 3 and 5 or 8 and 12, until they find a common multiple, 15 and 24 respectively. Then have them use these numbers to work problems such as the following.

⅔ − ½ (⁷/₁₅) and ⅞ − ⁵/₁₂ (¹¹/₂₄)

Enrichment

Ask students to find a common denominator and work these problems:

1. ⅖ + ¾ − ½ = (¹³/₂₀)
2. ⁴/₉ − ⅓ + ⅚ = (¹⁷/₁₈)

Practice

Have students complete the practice problems. Remind students to reduce each difference to simplest terms.

Extra Credit *Creative Drill*

Have the class design a quilt to illustrate concepts of a Social Studies unit. Each student can be responsible for designing one square. For example, a unit on the American Revolution might have quilt squares showing the Liberty Bell, 1776, Betsy Ross sewing the first flag, etc. Have students decide how large the quilt and each square will be. Next, calculate how many yards of material will be needed after students have decided upon their design and the materials they will need. They may wish to use several different types and colors of materials. Point out that material comes in different widths, so they need to calculate the area of a yard of material by multiplying its width by its length. Have students research the cost of fabric and calculate the total cost of the quilt. Make sure they include the cost of thread, trim and other materials.

Adding Mixed Numbers

pages 175-176

Objective

To add two mixed numbers

Materials

Mental Math

Have students round each number to the nearest hundred:

1. 351 (400)
2. 4,591 (4,600)
3. 87 (100)
4. 502 (500)
5. 87,218 (87,200)
6. 513,550 (513,600)

Skill Review

Have students rewrite these numbers as improper fractions:

1. $1\frac{1}{3}$ ($\frac{4}{3}$)
2. $3\frac{5}{9}$ ($\frac{32}{9}$)
3. $2\frac{1}{2}$ ($\frac{5}{2}$)
4. $5\frac{3}{4}$ ($\frac{23}{4}$)

Have them rewrite these as mixed numbers:

5. $\frac{31}{7}$ ($4\frac{3}{7}$)
6. $\frac{19}{2}$ ($9\frac{1}{2}$)
7. $\frac{32}{3}$ ($10\frac{2}{3}$)
8. $\frac{22}{4}$ ($5\frac{1}{2}$)

Adding Mixed Numbers

Runners can improve their stamina by gradually increasing their running distance. Ryan keeps a log of his jogging distances. How far did Ryan jog on Friday and Sunday?

We are looking for how far Ryan ran on Friday and Sunday.

Ryan jogged $3\frac{2}{5}$ miles on Friday and $4\frac{1}{10}$ miles on Sunday.

To find the total number of miles jogged, we add the mileage for both days. We add $3\frac{2}{5}$ and $4\frac{1}{10}$.

✔ Remember, to add fractions with unlike denominators, first write them as equivalent fractions having **common denominators.**

Write equivalent fractions.	Add the fractions.	Add the whole numbers. Simplify.
$3\frac{2}{5} = 3\frac{4}{10}$ $+\ 4\frac{1}{10} = 4\frac{1}{10}$	$3\frac{2}{5} = 3\frac{4}{10}$ $+\ 4\frac{1}{10} = 4\frac{1}{10}$ $\frac{5}{10}$	$3\frac{2}{5} = 3\frac{4}{10}$ $+\ 4\frac{1}{10} = 4\frac{1}{10}$ $7\frac{5}{10} = 7\frac{1}{2}$

Ryan jogged $7\frac{1}{2}$ miles on Friday and Sunday.

Getting Started

Add. Simplify if necessary.

1. $5\frac{3}{8}$
   $+\ 2\frac{1}{8}$
   $7\frac{1}{2}$

2. $7\frac{10}{15}$
   $+\ 6\frac{4}{15}$
   $13\frac{14}{15}$

3. $9\frac{1}{2}$
   $+\ 8\frac{1}{4}$
   $17\frac{3}{4}$

4. $6\frac{1}{4}$
   $+\ 9\frac{1}{3}$
   $15\frac{7}{12}$

Copy and add.

5. $5\frac{3}{7} + 4\frac{3}{7}$
   $9\frac{6}{7}$

6. $6\frac{2}{8} + 5\frac{2}{12}$
   $11\frac{5}{12}$

7. $9\frac{1}{2} + 7\frac{1}{3}$
   $16\frac{5}{6}$

8. $4\frac{1}{4} + 1\frac{1}{5}$
   $5\frac{9}{20}$

175

MCP All rights reserved

Teaching the Lesson

Introducing the Problem Have a student read the problem aloud. Ask the class to look at the illustration and read the information sentences. Read the plan sentences. Put the addition, in vertical form, on the board and have students follow in their texts. Have individual students change the fractions to a common denominator ($\frac{2}{5} = \frac{4}{10}$; $\frac{1}{10} = \frac{1}{10}$), add the fractions and reduce the sum to lowest terms ($\frac{5}{10} = \frac{1}{2}$) and add whole numbers. (7) Read the answer and the solution sentence aloud. (jogged $7\frac{1}{2}$ miles)

Developing the Skill Ask a student to explain the steps to follow when mixed numbers are added. (Change fractions to common denominator, if necessary; add fractions; reduce fraction to lowest terms; add whole numbers; simplify the answer.) Explain that in some cases the added fractions will give an improper fraction as the sum. In this case, the fraction must be changed to a mixed number and added to the whole number sum. Work this example on the board:

$$2\frac{5}{6} = \quad 2\frac{5}{6}$$
$$+\ 5\frac{2}{3} = \quad +\ 5\frac{4}{6}$$
$$7\frac{9}{6} = 7 + 1\frac{3}{6} = 8\frac{1}{2}$$

175

Add. Simplify if necessary.

1. $3\frac{5}{9}$
$+ 8\frac{2}{9}$
$11\frac{7}{9}$

2. $6\frac{2}{5}$
$+ 9\frac{1}{5}$
$15\frac{3}{5}$

3. $7\frac{1}{4}$
$+ 8\frac{1}{8}$
$15\frac{3}{8}$

4. $9\frac{5}{9}$
$+ 7\frac{1}{3}$
$16\frac{8}{9}$

5. $7\frac{5}{8}$
$+ 6\frac{1}{6}$
$13\frac{19}{24}$

6. $7\frac{1}{3}$
$+ 9\frac{2}{5}$
$16\frac{11}{15}$

7. $6\frac{7}{10}$
$+ 4\frac{1}{5}$
$10\frac{9}{10}$

8. $7\frac{1}{4}$
$+ 8\frac{1}{6}$
$15\frac{5}{12}$

9. $6\frac{1}{8}$
$+ 5\frac{2}{3}$
$11\frac{19}{24}$

10. $2\frac{2}{5}$
$+ 5\frac{1}{4}$
$7\frac{13}{20}$

11. $4\frac{1}{3}$
$+ 9\frac{1}{6}$
$13\frac{1}{2}$

12. $7\frac{2}{7}$
$+ 8\frac{3}{5}$
$15\frac{31}{35}$

Copy and Do

13. $6\frac{1}{3} + 6\frac{1}{2}$ $12\frac{5}{6}$

14. $4\frac{3}{8} + 9\frac{1}{6}$ $13\frac{13}{24}$

15. $9\frac{2}{3} + 6\frac{1}{4}$ $15\frac{11}{12}$

16. $1\frac{2}{3} + 6\frac{1}{5}$ $7\frac{13}{15}$

17. $7\frac{1}{9} + 6\frac{2}{3}$ $13\frac{7}{9}$

18. $8\frac{7}{10} + 8\frac{1}{5}$ $16\frac{9}{10}$

19. $4\frac{3}{4} + 2\frac{1}{6}$ $6\frac{11}{12}$

20. $6\frac{1}{2} + 9\frac{3}{10}$
$15\frac{4}{5}$

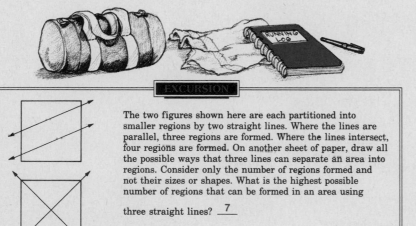

EXCURSION

The two figures shown here are each partitioned into smaller regions by two straight lines. Where the lines are parallel, three regions are formed. Where the lines intersect, four regions are formed. On another sheet of paper, draw all the possible ways that three lines can separate an area into regions. Consider only the number of regions formed and not their sizes or shapes. What is the highest possible number of regions that can be formed in an area using three straight lines? __7__

Some students may add the fractions but forget to add the whole numbers. Have these students work in pairs to solve the problem $\frac{7}{3} + \frac{27}{5}$. $(7\frac{11}{15})$ Next, have them rewrite $\frac{7}{3}$ and $\frac{27}{5}$ as mixed numbers and add,

$$2\frac{1}{3} + 5\frac{2}{5} = 2\frac{5}{15} + 5\frac{6}{15}, \text{ or } 7\frac{11}{15}$$

and then compare their answers to see that they are the same. Have them repeat the procedures for other problems such as $\frac{7}{2} + \frac{22}{3}$ $(10\frac{5}{6})$.

Enrichment

Show students a shortcut for adding fractions with unlike denominators. In the shortcut, each numerator is multiplied by the opposite denominator and then added. For example, in the problem $\frac{3}{5} + \frac{1}{3}$:

$$\frac{3}{5} \times \frac{1}{3} = \frac{(3 \times 3) + (1 \times 5)}{15} =$$
$$\frac{9 + 5}{15} = \frac{14}{15}$$

Have students cross multiply:

1. $\frac{3}{4} + \frac{2}{7} = (\frac{29}{28} = 1\frac{1}{28})$
2. $\frac{3}{5} + \frac{1}{2} = (\frac{11}{10} = 1\frac{1}{10})$
3. $\frac{5}{6} + \frac{3}{4} = (\frac{38}{24} = 1\frac{7}{12})$

Practice

Have students complete the practice problems. Put these steps on the board for reference: **find common denominator, add fractions, add whole numbers, simplify answer.**

Excursion

Point out how parallel and intersecting lines form different numbers of regions. Have students complete the problem by trial and error. Remind them to use straight lines only, and count every region regardless of size.

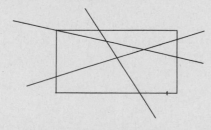

Extra Credit *Logic*

Duplicate the following:

Professor Smartie's computer has been stolen. The suspects are the mathematicians, Smith, Williams and Jones. They all say they are innocent but you know one of them always lies. You give each of them this problem:

$$[(25 \times 103) - 2] \times 3 = ?$$

They respond:

Smith: The answer is the same as $(50 \times 60) + (1,573 \times 3)$.
Jones: The answer is the same as the square root ($\sqrt{}$) of $20,912,329 + [(11 \times 13) \times 22]$.
Williams: The answer is the same as $14,099 - (9 \times 709)$.
You arrest the liar. Who is it? (Williams)

Adding Mixed Numbers

pages 177-178

Objective

To add three mixed numbers

Materials

Mental Math

Have students identify any common multiple for these numbers: (Answers may vary.)

1. 2 and 5 (10)
2. 3 and 5 (15)
3. 3 and 8 (24)
4. 2 and 4 (4, 8)
5. 4 and 6 (12 or 24)
6. 6 and 9 (18, 36 or 54)
7. 4 and 5 (20)

Skill Review

Have students find the least common multiple for these sets of numbers:

1. 2, 4, 5 (20)
2. 3, 4, 5 (60)
3. 2, 4, 8 (8)
4. 3, 6, 9 (18)
5. 2, 4, 7 (28)
6. 6, 8, 9 (72)

Renaming Mixed Numbers in Sums

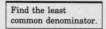

WORK SCHEDULE
Juanita
Monday $2\frac{1}{2}$ hrs.
Tuesday $3\frac{3}{4}$ hrs.
Friday $3\frac{2}{3}$ hrs.

Many students work after school, but have to save time for homework. Juanita works part time three days a week, but never works more than 11 hours in any week. How many hours did Juanita work this week?

We want to find the number of hours Juanita worked this week.

She worked $2\frac{1}{2}$ hours on Monday, $3\frac{3}{4}$ hours on Tuesday and $3\frac{2}{3}$ hours on Friday.

To find the total hours, we add her hours for all 3 days.

We add $2\frac{1}{2}$, $3\frac{3}{4}$ and $3\frac{2}{3}$.

✔ The fractions in a set of mixed numbers must have a **common denominator** before they can be added.

Find the least common denominator.	Write equivalent fractions.	Add. Simplify the mixed number.
$2\frac{1}{2} = 2\frac{}{12}$ $3\frac{3}{4} = 3\frac{}{12}$ $+\,3\frac{2}{3} \quad 3\frac{}{12}$ *12 is the least common multiple of 2, 4 and 3.*	$2\frac{1}{2} = 2\frac{6}{12}$ $3\frac{3}{4} = 3\frac{9}{12}$ $+\,3\frac{2}{3} = 3\frac{8}{12}$	$2\frac{1}{2} = 2\frac{6}{12}$ $3\frac{3}{4} = 3\frac{9}{12}$ $+\,3\frac{2}{3} = 3\frac{8}{12}$ $\qquad 8\frac{23}{12} = 9\frac{11}{12}$

✔ When an **improper fraction** appears in the mixed number, simplify the mixed number by dividing the fraction's denominator into the numerator. Add this renamed fraction to the original whole number.

$$8\frac{23}{12} = 8 + 1\frac{11}{12} = 9\frac{11}{12}$$

Juanita worked $9\frac{11}{12}$ hours.

Getting Started

Simplify these mixed numbers.

1. $5\frac{7}{4} = 6\frac{3}{4}$ 2. $6\frac{9}{3} = 9$

Add. Simplify if necessary.

3. $\quad 4\frac{2}{3}$
   $\quad 5\frac{1}{3}$
   $+\,4\frac{2}{3}$
   $\overline{\quad 14\frac{2}{3}}$

4. $\quad 7\frac{1}{8}$
   $\quad 4\frac{1}{2}$
   $+\,6\frac{1}{4}$
   $\overline{\quad 17\frac{7}{8}}$

Copy and add.

5. $2\frac{1}{7} + 4 + 2\frac{13}{14}$
   $9\frac{1}{14}$

MCP All rights reserved

177

Teaching the Lesson

Introducing the Problem   Have a student read the problem aloud and complete the information sentences. Ask a student to identify the unnecessary number in the problem. (11 hours) Read the plan sentences aloud and put the problem on the board in vertical form. Have individual students identify the common multiple for 2, 4 and 3 (12), rename each fraction as twelfths ($\frac{6}{12}$, $\frac{9}{12}$, $\frac{8}{12}$) and add whole numbers and fractions. Show the class how to change $8\frac{23}{12}$ to $9\frac{11}{12}$. ($\frac{23}{12} = 1\frac{11}{12}$, $8 + 1\frac{11}{12} = 9\frac{11}{12}$) Read the next section of the text aloud, explaining that any improper fraction in the sum must be changed to a mixed number and added to the whole number sum. Have a student read the solution sentence. (worked $9\frac{11}{12}$ hours)

Developing the Skill   Explain that the steps in adding three mixed numbers will be the same as when adding two: find a common denominator, add fractions, add whole numbers, reduce the answer to simplest terms. Point out that when three fractions are added, it is more likely that their sum will be an improper fraction. Explain that it is not necessary to find the least common denominator. Encourage students to look for the smallest common denominator, but remind them that the answer can always be reduced in the end.

Practice

Simplify these mixed numbers.

1. $2\frac{7}{2} = \underline{5\frac{1}{2}}$
2. $5\frac{14}{10} = \underline{6\frac{2}{5}}$
3. $6\frac{9}{6} = \underline{7\frac{1}{2}}$
4. $5\frac{12}{8} = \underline{6\frac{1}{2}}$
5. $1\frac{16}{10} = \underline{2\frac{3}{5}}$
6. $2\frac{18}{4} = \underline{6\frac{1}{2}}$
7. $10\frac{25}{15} = \underline{11\frac{2}{3}}$
8. $2\frac{40}{16} = \underline{4\frac{1}{2}}$

Add. Simplify if necessary.

9.
$$\begin{array}{r} 7\frac{5}{6} \\ 4\frac{2}{3} \\ + 6\frac{1}{3} \\ \hline 18\frac{5}{6} \end{array}$$

10.
$$\begin{array}{r} 8\frac{1}{5} \\ 6\frac{4}{5} \\ + 7\frac{5}{10} \\ \hline 22\frac{1}{2} \end{array}$$

11.
$$\begin{array}{r} 2\frac{3}{4} \\ 7\frac{5}{8} \\ + 6\frac{1}{2} \\ \hline 16\frac{7}{8} \end{array}$$

12.
$$\begin{array}{r} 9\frac{7}{8} \\ 2\frac{3}{4} \\ + 5\frac{2}{3} \\ \hline 18\frac{7}{24} \end{array}$$

13.
$$\begin{array}{r} 4\frac{1}{2} \\ 5\frac{2}{3} \\ + 6\frac{1}{6} \\ \hline 16\frac{1}{3} \end{array}$$

14.
$$\begin{array}{r} 7\frac{1}{5} \\ 6 \\ + 8\frac{3}{4} \\ \hline 21\frac{19}{20} \end{array}$$

15.
$$\begin{array}{r} 9\frac{2}{3} \\ 7\frac{7}{15} \\ + 6\frac{4}{5} \\ \hline 23\frac{14}{15} \end{array}$$

16.
$$\begin{array}{r} 6\frac{1}{2} \\ 7\frac{2}{3} \\ + 8\frac{5}{8} \\ \hline 22\frac{19}{24} \end{array}$$

Copy and Do

17. $9\frac{5}{8} + 8\frac{3}{4} + 6\frac{1}{3}$ $24\frac{17}{24}$
18. $2\frac{5}{7} + 1\frac{2}{3} + 9\frac{7}{21}$ $13\frac{5}{7}$
19. $1\frac{7}{10} + 9\frac{3}{5} + 4\frac{1}{4}$ $15\frac{11}{20}$

20. $8 + 2\frac{2}{3} + 5\frac{5}{8}$ $16\frac{7}{24}$
21. $8\frac{4}{5} + 5\frac{7}{8} + 2\frac{3}{10}$ $16\frac{39}{40}$
22. $5\frac{1}{2} + 6\frac{2}{3} + 5\frac{5}{6}$ 18

Apply

Solve these problems. Simplify if necessary.

23. Find the perimeter of the triangle.

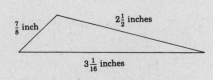

$\frac{7}{8}$ inch $\quad$ $2\frac{1}{2}$ inches $\quad$ $3\frac{1}{16}$ inches

$6\frac{7}{16}$ inches

24. Marissa rode her unicycle $3\frac{1}{2}$ miles on Monday. On Tuesday she rode $2\frac{2}{3}$ miles farther than she did on Monday. How far did Marissa ride on Monday and Tuesday? $9\frac{2}{3}$ miles

178

Correcting Common Errors

Students may have difficulty keeping their work organized because there are many different steps. Have them work with partners where the first student finds the common denominator and the equivalent fractions and the partner adds and writes the sum in simplest terms. Then they trade roles.
1. $1\frac{2}{3} + 3\frac{5}{6} + 1\frac{1}{3}$ ($6\frac{5}{6}$)
2. $3\frac{7}{10} + 1\frac{1}{3} + 1\frac{1}{2}$ ($6\frac{8}{15}$)

Enrichment

Put this shortcut for adding unlike fractions with numerators of 1 on the board:

$$sum = \frac{sum\ of\ denominators}{product\ of\ denominators}$$

For example:

$$\frac{1}{3} + \frac{1}{4} = \frac{3+4}{3 \times 4} = \frac{7}{12}$$

Have students use this method to do the following addition:

1. $\frac{1}{5} + \frac{1}{7}$ ($\frac{12}{35}$)
2. $\frac{1}{8} + \frac{1}{2}$ ($\frac{10}{16} = \frac{5}{8}$)
3. $\frac{1}{10} + \frac{1}{2}$ ($\frac{12}{20} = \frac{3}{5}$)
4. $\frac{1}{20} + \frac{1}{7}$ ($\frac{27}{140}$)
5. $\frac{1}{8} + \frac{1}{12}$ ($\frac{20}{96} = \frac{5}{24}$)

Practice

Have students complete the problems on the page. Remind them to simplify each answer.

Mixed Practice

1. $\frac{15}{7} - \frac{1}{2}$ $\left(1\frac{9}{14}\right)$
2. $4 \times 5{,}869$ (23,476)
3. Simplify: $\frac{32}{6}$ $\left(5\frac{1}{3}\right)$
4. $395\frac{1}{3} + 12\frac{1}{2}$ $\left(407\frac{5}{6}\right)$
5. $657{,}108 + 247{,}392$ (904,500)
6. $20{,}542 \div 32$ (641 R30)
7. $\frac{7}{12} = \frac{}{36}$ (21)
8. $\$300.00 - \$147.22$ ($152.78)
9. $6\frac{2}{3} + 17\frac{3}{4} + 8\frac{1}{6}$ $\left(32\frac{7}{12}\right)$
10. 800×600 (480,000)

Extra Credit *Measurement*

Have students list the alphabet on the board and assign each letter a weight in $\frac{1}{4}$-pound increments; for example: $A = \frac{1}{4}$ lb, $B = \frac{1}{2}$ lb, $C = \frac{3}{4}$ lb, etc. Have students calculate the weight of their names in pounds. The outcomes should be shared and compared to see whose name weighs the most or least. Then have students calculate the weight of their family members' names, the name of the school, the total class name weight, etc. As an extension, have them create weight addition and subtraction problems, adding words together, to exchange with a partner.

Subtracting Mixed Numbers

pages 179-180

Objective

To subtract mixed numbers

Materials

circles divided into fourths and rectangles divided into tenths

Mental Math

Have students identify the lowest common denominator for each pair:

1. $\frac{1}{2}$ and $\frac{2}{3}$ (sixths)
2. $\frac{2}{5}$ and $\frac{1}{10}$ (tenths)
3. $\frac{3}{4}$ and $\frac{1}{3}$ (twelfths)
4. $\frac{1}{5}$ and $\frac{3}{4}$ (twentieths)
5. $\frac{1}{6}$ and $\frac{1}{5}$ (thirtieths)
6. $\frac{4}{5}$ and $\frac{2}{3}$ (fifteenths)
7. $\frac{1}{3}$ and $\frac{2}{9}$ (ninths)

Skill Review

Have students review subtracting fractions:

1. $\frac{2}{3} - \frac{1}{3}$ ($\frac{1}{3}$)
2. $\frac{2}{3} - \frac{1}{5}$ ($\frac{7}{15}$)
3. $\frac{7}{4} - \frac{3}{4}$ ($\frac{4}{4} = 1$)
4. $\frac{2}{5} - \frac{1}{10}$ ($\frac{3}{10}$)
5. $\frac{5}{6} - \frac{1}{6}$ ($\frac{4}{6} = \frac{2}{3}$)
6. $\frac{7}{8} - \frac{2}{8}$ ($\frac{5}{8}$)
7. $\frac{1}{6} - \frac{1}{12}$ ($\frac{1}{12}$)

Subtracting Mixed Numbers

Bruce bought $5\frac{5}{6}$ yards of denim to make some clothes. He needs $2\frac{1}{3}$ yards to make one jacket. How many yards of denim will Bruce have left?

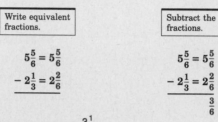

We want to find how many yards of denim Bruce will have left.

He bought $\underline{5\frac{5}{6}}$ yards and the pattern calls for $\underline{2\frac{1}{3}}$ yards.

To find the yards left, we subtract the number of yards he will use from the number of yards he bought.

We subtract $\underline{2\frac{1}{3}}$ from $\underline{5\frac{5}{6}}$.

✔ The fractions in a set of mixed numbers must have **common denominators** before they can be subtracted.

Write equivalent fractions.	Subtract the fractions.	Subtract the whole numbers. Simplify.
$5\frac{5}{6} = 5\frac{5}{6}$ $-\ 2\frac{1}{3} = 2\frac{2}{6}$	$5\frac{5}{6} = 5\frac{5}{6}$ $-\ 2\frac{1}{3} = 2\frac{2}{6}$ $\frac{3}{6}$	$5\frac{5}{6} = 5\frac{5}{6}$ $-\ 2\frac{1}{3} = 2\frac{2}{6}$ $3\frac{3}{6} = 3\frac{1}{2}$

Bruce will have $\underline{3\frac{1}{2}}$ yards of denim left.

Getting Started

Subtract. Simplify if necessary.

1. $4\frac{5}{9} - 1\frac{3}{9}$ $3\frac{2}{9}$
2. $16\frac{7}{8} - 9\frac{3}{8}$ $7\frac{1}{2}$
3. $8\frac{5}{6} - 3\frac{1}{4}$ $5\frac{7}{12}$
4. $16\frac{3}{4} - 9\frac{2}{3}$ $7\frac{1}{12}$

Copy and subtract.

5. $10\frac{3}{7} - 3\frac{2}{14}$ $7\frac{2}{7}$
6. $15\frac{2}{5} - 8\frac{1}{15}$ $7\frac{1}{3}$
7. $5\frac{2}{3} - 3\frac{4}{8}$ $2\frac{1}{6}$
8. $9\frac{4}{5} - 4\frac{2}{6}$ $5\frac{7}{15}$

MCP All rights reserved

Teaching the Lesson

Introducing the Problem Read the problem aloud. Have a student read and complete the information sentences. Read the plan sentences and have students look at the problem worked in the model. Remind students that before they can add or subtract mixed numbers, the fractions must have common denominators. Write the problem on the board. Have one student change the fractions to a common denominator. ($\frac{5}{6}$ and $\frac{2}{6}$) Ask another to come to the board and subtract fractions. ($\frac{3}{6}$) Have a third subtract whole numbers and simplify the answer. ($3\frac{3}{6} = 3\frac{1}{2}$) Read the solution sentence. (will have $3\frac{1}{2}$ yd left)

Developing the Skill Explain that subtracting mixed numbers will follow a pattern. Point out the importance of subtracting fractions before whole numbers and ask a student to explain why. (in case the fractional minuend is smaller than the fraction subtrahend) List the steps on the board: **change fractions to a common denominator; subtract fractions; subtract whole numbers; simplify the answer.** Remind students that while it is convenient to find the lowest common denominator, it is not essential because the answer can be reduced to lowest terms in the end.

Practice

Subtract. Simplify fractions.

1. $7\frac{9}{16}$
$-3\frac{5}{16}$
$\overline{\quad 4\frac{1}{4}\quad}$

2. $8\frac{3}{4}$
$-2\frac{1}{4}$
$\overline{\quad 6\frac{1}{2}\quad}$

3. $11\frac{7}{9}$
$-3\frac{4}{9}$
$\overline{\quad 8\frac{1}{3}\quad}$

4. $5\frac{7}{8}$
$-2\frac{1}{4}$
$\overline{\quad 3\frac{5}{8}\quad}$

5. $9\frac{4}{5}$
$-7\frac{3}{10}$
$\overline{\quad 2\frac{1}{2}\quad}$

6. $11\frac{2}{3}$
$-6\frac{1}{6}$
$\overline{\quad 5\frac{1}{2}\quad}$

7. $10\frac{4}{5}$
$-7\frac{1}{3}$
$\overline{\quad 3\frac{7}{15}\quad}$

8. $13\frac{2}{3}$
$-6\frac{1}{4}$
$\overline{\quad 7\frac{5}{12}\quad}$

9. $6\frac{5}{8}$
$-3\frac{1}{5}$
$\overline{\quad 3\frac{17}{40}\quad}$

10. $12\frac{4}{5}$
$-6\frac{1}{2}$
$\overline{\quad 6\frac{3}{10}\quad}$

11. $18\frac{2}{3}$
$-9\frac{1}{2}$
$\overline{\quad 9\frac{1}{6}\quad}$

12. $12\frac{7}{8}$
$-7\frac{1}{6}$
$\overline{\quad 5\frac{17}{24}\quad}$

Copy and Do

13. $3\frac{5}{7} - 2\frac{1}{7}$ $1\frac{4}{7}$

14. $9\frac{2}{3} - 2\frac{1}{9}$ $7\frac{5}{9}$

15. $8\frac{1}{2} - 6\frac{1}{8}$ $2\frac{3}{8}$

16. $18\frac{3}{4} - 9\frac{1}{5}$ $9\frac{11}{20}$

17. $13\frac{5}{6} - 4\frac{3}{8}$ $9\frac{11}{24}$

18. $13\frac{46}{100} - 5\frac{3}{20}$ $8\frac{31}{100}$

19. $13\frac{9}{10} - 8\frac{5}{6}$ $5\frac{1}{15}$

20. $16\frac{3}{4} - 7\frac{2}{3}$ $9\frac{1}{12}$

21. $12\frac{7}{8} - 8\frac{5}{6}$ $4\frac{1}{24}$

22. $11\frac{9}{16} - 6\frac{3}{8}$ $5\frac{3}{16}$

23. $5\frac{5}{6} - 3\frac{5}{9}$ $2\frac{5}{18}$

24. $12\frac{9}{10} - 8\frac{7}{15}$ $4\frac{13}{30}$

Apply

Solve these problems. Simplify if necessary.

25. Mr. Roberts felt tired on the second day of his trip. Although he drove $6\frac{3}{4}$ hours on Monday, he drove only $4\frac{1}{3}$ hours on Tuesday. How much longer did Mr. Roberts drive on Monday?
$2\frac{5}{12}$ hours

26. Gerri worked $3\frac{2}{3}$ hours on Monday and $4\frac{1}{2}$ hours on Tuesday. She knows she must work a total of $10\frac{1}{2}$ hours to earn enough money to pay for a set of school pictures. How many more hours does Gerri need to work?
$2\frac{1}{3}$ hours

180

Correcting Common Errors

Some students may not find a common denominator and simply subtract the numerators, writing the "answer" over the larger denominator. Have these students work with partners. Give each pair a page with circles divided into fourths and rectangles divided into tenths. Have them use these diagrams to do the following problems by shading the minuend, crossing out the subtrahend, and writing the difference.
1. $4\frac{3}{4} - 1\frac{1}{2}$ $(3\frac{1}{4})$
2. $3\frac{7}{10} - 2\frac{2}{5}$ $(1\frac{3}{10})$

Enrichment

Put this shortcut for subtracting unlike fractions with numerators of 1 on the board:

difference =
$$\frac{\text{difference of denominators}}{\text{product of denominators}}$$

For example:

$$\frac{1}{2} - \frac{1}{8} = \frac{8 - 2}{8 \times 2} = \frac{6}{16} = \frac{3}{8}$$

Have them use this method to do the following subtraction:

1. $\frac{1}{3} - \frac{1}{4} =$ $(\frac{1}{12})$
2. $\frac{1}{2} - \frac{1}{8} =$ $(\frac{6}{16} = \frac{3}{8})$
3. $\frac{1}{4} - \frac{1}{10} =$ $(\frac{6}{40} = \frac{3}{20})$
4. $\frac{1}{5} - \frac{1}{6} =$ $(\frac{1}{30})$

Practice

Have students complete the page. Remind them to reduce answers to simplest terms and check their work.

Extra Credit *Statistics*

Explain that the midrange of a set of numbers is the number in the numerical middle of the set, halfway between the smallest and largest numbers. Give students this set of numbers as an example: 3, 4, 5, 6, 7. Ask a student to identify the midrange. (5) Write the set and the following on the board: **midrange = 5.** Have students find the midrange of each of these sets of numbers:

1. 21, 23, 25, 27, 29, 31, 33   (midrange = 27)
2. 50, 55, 60   (midrange = 55)
3. 101, 111, 121, 131   (midrange = 116)

Have students write a formula that would help them find the midrange of any set of numbers. (midrange = smallest number + largest number ÷ 2)

180

Subtracting Fractions

pages 181-182

Objective

To subtract a fraction from a whole number

Materials

Mental Math

Have students add, simplifying the answer if necessary.

1. $\frac{1}{5} + \frac{2}{5} = (\frac{3}{5})$
2. $\frac{2}{3} + \frac{1}{3} = (1)$
3. $\frac{2}{9} + \frac{4}{9} = (\frac{2}{3})$
4. $\frac{3}{4} + \frac{3}{4} + \frac{3}{4} = (2\frac{1}{4})$
5. $\frac{2}{5} + \frac{3}{5} + \frac{6}{5} = (2\frac{1}{5})$
6. $\frac{4}{9} + \frac{3}{9} = (\frac{7}{9})$
7. $\frac{1}{4} + \frac{3}{4} + \frac{3}{4} = (1\frac{3}{4})$

Skill Review

Have students change these mixed numbers to improper fractions:

1. $1\frac{2}{3}$ $(\frac{5}{3})$
2. $1\frac{4}{5}$ $(\frac{9}{5})$
3. $1\frac{2}{6}$ $(\frac{8}{6})$
4. $1\frac{1}{3}$ $(\frac{4}{3})$
5. $1\frac{7}{9}$ $(\frac{16}{9})$
6. $1\frac{4}{7}$ $(\frac{11}{7})$
7. $1\frac{3}{5}$ $(\frac{8}{5})$

Subtracting from a Whole Number

The winners of the athletic club's annual swim-a-thon were posted. Diane was the top swimmer this year. How much farther did Diane swim than Cheryl?

We want to find how many more miles Diane swam than Cheryl.

Diane swam ___3___ miles and Cheryl swam ___$1\frac{7}{8}$___ miles.

To find out how many more miles Diane swam, we subtract Cheryl's distance from Diane's.

We subtract ___$1\frac{7}{8}$___ from ___3___.

✔ Remember, the whole number 1 can be renamed as a fraction whose numerator and denominators are the same.
$$1 = \frac{8}{8}$$

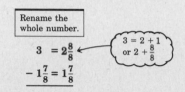

Rename the whole number.	Subtract the mixed numbers.
$3 = 2\frac{8}{8}$ ← $3 = 2 + 1$ or $2 + \frac{8}{8}$	$3 = 2\frac{8}{8}$
$-1\frac{7}{8} = 1\frac{7}{8}$	$-1\frac{7}{8} = 1\frac{7}{8}$
	$1\frac{1}{8}$

Diane swam ___$1\frac{1}{8}$___ miles farther than Cheryl.

Getting Started

Rename each whole number as a mixed number.

1. $8 = 7\frac{5}{5}$ 2. $4 = 3\frac{6}{6}$ 3. $7 = 6\frac{3}{3}$ 4. $12 = 11\frac{10}{10}$

Subtract. Simplify if necessary.

5. 5
    $-2\frac{1}{2}$
    $\overline{2\frac{1}{2}}$

6. 7
    $-3\frac{3}{4}$
    $\overline{3\frac{1}{4}}$

7. 5
    $-2\frac{2}{3}$
    $\overline{2\frac{1}{3}}$

8. 10
    $-1\frac{3}{8}$
    $\overline{8\frac{5}{8}}$

Copy and subtract.

9. $9 - 2\frac{3}{4}$
   $6\frac{1}{4}$

10. $7 - 3\frac{1}{5}$
    $3\frac{4}{5}$

11. $17 - 9\frac{4}{12}$
    $7\frac{2}{3}$

12. $12 - 8\frac{8}{16}$
    $3\frac{1}{2}$ **181**

MCP All rights reserved

Teaching the Lesson

Introducing the Problem Read the problem aloud. Ask a student to read and complete the information sentences. Read the plan sentences aloud and explain that in order to subtract a mixed number from a whole number, there will have to be renaming. Draw three circles on the board and divide the last one into eighths. Explain that in order to subtract $1\frac{7}{8}$ from 3 students can think of the 3 as 2 and $\frac{8}{8}$. Write the problem on the board as it appears in their texts. Ask a student to subtract the mixed numbers. Have another read the solution sentence. (Diane swam $1\frac{1}{8}$ miles farther.)

Developing the Skill Use another problem to illustrate the method for subtracting mixed numbers from whole numbers. Have a student draw 5 squares on the board. Ask a student to illustrate taking $3\frac{1}{2}$ squares away. Have the student divide a square in half in order to take one half away. Point out that this is like changing 5 into the sum of 4 and $\frac{2}{2}$. Write $4\frac{2}{2} - 3\frac{1}{2} = 1\frac{1}{2}$ in vertical form on the board. Tell students that when they rename they will always use the denominator of the fraction in the mixed number.

Practice

Rename each whole number as a mixed number.

1. $6 = 5\frac{8}{8}$ 2. $4 = 3\frac{9}{9}$ 3. $8 = 7\frac{7}{7}$ 4. $5 = 4\frac{12}{12}$

Subtract. Simplify if necessary.

5. 9
   $-3\frac{1}{3}$
   $\overline{5\frac{2}{3}}$

6. 10
   $-3\frac{1}{5}$
   $\overline{6\frac{4}{5}}$

7. 12
   $-7\frac{3}{8}$
   $\overline{4\frac{5}{8}}$

8. 16
   $-9\frac{3}{5}$
   $\overline{16\frac{2}{5}}$

9. 11
   $-5\frac{5}{7}$
   $\overline{5\frac{2}{7}}$

10. 16
    $-7\frac{5}{10}$
    $\overline{8\frac{1}{2}}$

11. 16
    $-8\frac{5}{12}$
    $\overline{7\frac{7}{12}}$

12. 15
    $-9\frac{1}{2}$
    $\overline{5\frac{1}{2}}$

Copy and Do

13. $8 - 2\frac{3}{5}$
    $5\frac{2}{5}$

14. $8 - 7\frac{5}{9}$
    $\frac{4}{9}$

15. $15 - 7\frac{7}{8}$
    $7\frac{1}{8}$

16. $9 - 8\frac{3}{4}$
    $\frac{1}{4}$

17. $7 - 5\frac{7}{12}$
    $1\frac{5}{12}$

18. $16 - 8\frac{15}{16}$
    $7\frac{1}{16}$

19. $13 - 5\frac{3}{10}$
    $7\frac{7}{10}$

20. $10 - 4\frac{9}{15}$
    $5\frac{2}{5}$

Apply

Solve these problems. Simplify if necessary.

21. Rosalie estimated that it would take 12 days to thoroughly clean every room, window, drawer and closet in her house. She finished in $9\frac{3}{4}$ days. How early did Rosalie finish her work?

    $2\frac{1}{4}$ days

22. Devin gave $\frac{2}{3}$ of his stamp collection to Belva and $\frac{1}{5}$ of his collection to Rosita. What fraction of his collection does Devin have left?

    $\frac{2}{15}$

EXCURSION

Imagine this scene at the zoo.
In one area there are peacocks and camels. All together there are 30 eyes and 46 feet.

How many of each animal are there? __8__ camels __7__ peacocks
Suppose there were 528 eyes and 752 feet, then how many of each animal would there

be? __112__ camels __152__ peacocks

182

Correcting Common Errors

Some students may have difficulty writing a whole number as a mixed number. Have them work with partners to address the whole number 6. Have them practice writing the number, and others, with the denominators 1 through 9 in the following manner.

$6 = 5 + \frac{1}{1} = 5 + \frac{2}{2} = 5 + \frac{3}{3} =$ etc.

Enrichment

Give students paper and scissors, but no rulers. Have students divide sheets of paper into fractional parts: halves, thirds, fourths, fifths, sixths, sevenths, eighths, ninths, tenths and twelfths. Let them work in small groups to exchange ideas. Explain that they can cut the paper any way they like, but in the end they must have pieces of equal size. Have them label the pieces and keep each set in an envelope.

Practice

Have students complete the problems on the page. Remind them to rename using the denominator of the mixed number fraction.

Excursion

Since every animal has two eyes there must be 15 animals in the cage. Trial and error calculations can yield the answer here since the numbers are not large. Have them build on this pattern to work with the larger numbers.

Extra Credit *Statistics*

Explain that the mode is a term used in statistics to describe the observation which occurs most often in a sample. The table shows weekly allowances:

Rob	$1.00
Sharon	$1.25
Liz	$1.00
Stuart	$1.50
Marybeth	$1.00

The mode of the allowances is $1, because that is the number that appears most often in the sample. Have students survey the class to find out how many siblings each class member has. Put the results of the survey on the board: the names of the students followed by the number of siblings, brothers + sisters. Have students identify the mode of the survey. (Number will vary.) Have students devise their own survey topic, complete it and report to the class.

Subtracting Mixed Numbers

pages 183-184

Objective

To subtract two mixed numbers

Materials

Mental Math

Have students identify the better estimate:

1. $355 \div 7 = 40$ or 50 (50)
2. $218 \div 10 = 20$ or 30 (20)
3. $145 \div 2 = 50$ or 70 (70)
4. $246 \div 5 = 40$ or 50 (50)
5. $482 \div 60 = 8$ or 9 (8)
6. $370 \div 90 = 4$ or 5 (4)
7. $189 \div 90 = 1$ or 2 (2)

Skill Review

Have students change each mixed number to a whole number and an improper number:

1. $3\frac{2}{3} = (2\frac{5}{3})$
2. $5 = (4 + \frac{3}{3}$ or $\frac{4}{4}$, etc.$)$
3. $6\frac{1}{5} = (5\frac{6}{5})$
4. $10\frac{1}{2} = (9\frac{3}{2})$
5. $7\frac{2}{7} = (6\frac{9}{7})$
6. $8\frac{1}{4} = (7\frac{5}{4})$
7. $21\frac{3}{4} = (20\frac{7}{4})$

MCP All rights reserved

Subtracting Mixed Numbers with Renaming

A prize is awarded at the carnival to the person who comes closest to correctly guessing the weight of this jar. The jar of beans weighs $6\frac{1}{4}$ pounds. How close is Marty's estimate?

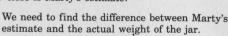

$4\frac{2}{3}$ pounds?

GUESS THE WEIGHT ‼

We need to find the difference between Marty's estimate and the actual weight of the jar.

The jar of beans weighs $6\frac{1}{4}$ pounds.

Marty estimated $4\frac{2}{3}$ pounds.
To find how close Marty's estimate was, we subtract it from the actual weight.

Write equivalent fractions.	Rename mixed number if needed.	Subtract.
$6\frac{1}{4} = 6\frac{3}{12}$ $-4\frac{2}{3} = 4\frac{8}{12}$	$6\frac{1}{4} = 6\frac{3}{12} = 5\frac{15}{12}$ $\left(6\frac{3}{12} = 5 + \frac{12}{12} + \frac{3}{12}\right)$ $-4\frac{2}{3} = 4\frac{8}{12} = 4\frac{8}{12}$	$6\frac{1}{4} = 6\frac{3}{12} = 5\frac{15}{12}$ $-4\frac{2}{3} = 4\frac{8}{12} = 4\frac{8}{12}$ $\overline{1\frac{7}{12}}$

✔ Remember, the whole number 1 can be renamed as a fraction having the same numerator and denominator.
$1 = \frac{12}{12}$
Thus, the 6 in the mixed number $6\frac{3}{12}$ can be renamed as $5\frac{12}{12}$. When we add $5\frac{12}{12}$ to $\frac{3}{12}$ we get a new mixed number with an improper fraction, $5\frac{15}{12}$.

Marty's estimate is $1\frac{7}{12}$ pounds less than the actual weight of the jar.

Getting Started

Rename as mixed numbers with improper fractions.

1. $5\frac{2}{3} = 4\frac{5}{3}$
2. $7\frac{3}{10} = 6\frac{13}{10}$
3. $9\frac{1}{5} = 8\frac{6}{5}$
4. $4\frac{4}{8} = 3\frac{12}{8}$

Subtract. Simplify if necessary.

5. $8\frac{1}{3}$
 $-4\frac{5}{6}$
 $\overline{3\frac{1}{2}}$

6. $11\frac{1}{8}$
 $-6\frac{3}{8}$
 $\overline{4\frac{3}{4}}$

Copy and subtract.

7. $16\frac{1}{5} - 9\frac{2}{4}$
 $6\frac{7}{10}$

8. $11\frac{3}{7} - 4\frac{13}{14}$
 $6\frac{1}{2}$

Teaching the Lesson

Introducing the Problem Read the problem aloud and ask a student to read the information sentences. Read the plan sentence and put the problem on the board in vertical form. Have students change the fractions to a common denominator ($\frac{3}{12}$ and $\frac{8}{12}$) and subtract fractions. Write on the board: $6\frac{3}{12} = 5 + 1 + \frac{3}{12} = 5\frac{15}{12}$. Have a student substitute $5\frac{15}{12}$ for the minuend and subtract both fractions and whole numbers. ($1\frac{7}{12}$) Read the next sentences to remind students of how they renamed $6\frac{3}{12}$. Have a student read the solution sentence. (estimate $1\frac{7}{12}$ pounds less than actual)

Developing the Skill Draw four rectangles on the board, shading $3\frac{1}{2}$. Have a student take $1\frac{3}{4}$ of the shaded rectangles away. While the student will be able to erase one whole rectangle, it is not possible to subtract $\frac{3}{4}$ from $\frac{1}{2}$. Suggest that the student divide one of the whole rectangles into fourths and then erase $\frac{3}{4}$. The result will be 1 whole, $\frac{1}{2}$ and $\frac{1}{4}$ rectangles. Simplify that answer to $1\frac{3}{4}$. Now write the subtraction on the board in vertical form. Show the renaming in this way: $3\frac{1}{2} = 2 + 1 + \frac{1}{2} = 2\frac{3}{2}$, $2\frac{3}{2} = 2\frac{6}{4}$.

Practice

Rename as mixed numbers with improper fractions.

1. $6\frac{1}{4} = 5\frac{5}{4}$
2. $7\frac{2}{3} = 6\frac{5}{3}$
3. $11\frac{3}{5} = 10\frac{8}{5}$
4. $3\frac{7}{9} = 2\frac{16}{9}$
5. $17\frac{5}{8} = 16\frac{13}{8}$
6. $5\frac{1}{2} = 4\frac{3}{2}$
7. $6\frac{7}{10} = 5\frac{17}{10}$
8. $7\frac{7}{12} = 6\frac{19}{12}$

Subtract. Simplify if necessary.

9. $5\frac{1}{6}$ $-4\frac{5}{6}$ $\overline{\frac{1}{3}}$

10. $8\frac{3}{8}$ $-7\frac{5}{8}$ $\overline{\frac{3}{4}}$

11. $9\frac{2}{3}$ $-7\frac{5}{6}$ $\overline{1\frac{5}{6}}$

12. $14\frac{1}{5}$ $-9\frac{9}{10}$ $\overline{4\frac{3}{10}}$

13. $14\frac{1}{4}$ $-6\frac{1}{3}$ $\overline{7\frac{11}{12}}$

14. $10\frac{1}{5}$ $-6\frac{3}{4}$ $\overline{3\frac{9}{20}}$

15. $15\frac{3}{8}$ $-6\frac{5}{6}$ $\overline{8\frac{13}{24}}$

16. $7\frac{2}{15}$ $-5\frac{7}{10}$ $\overline{1\frac{13}{30}}$

17. $16\frac{1}{2}$ $-9\frac{3}{5}$ $\overline{6\frac{9}{10}}$

18. $17\frac{1}{8}$ $-8\frac{7}{12}$ $\overline{8\frac{13}{24}}$

19. $13\frac{5}{12}$ $-6\frac{7}{9}$ $\overline{6\frac{23}{36}}$

20. $16\frac{3}{8}$ $-9\frac{1}{2}$ $\overline{6\frac{7}{8}}$

Copy and Do

21. $12\frac{1}{3} - 7\frac{3}{5}$ $4\frac{11}{15}$
22. $9\frac{3}{8} - 7\frac{3}{4}$ $1\frac{5}{8}$
23. $18\frac{1}{5} - 9\frac{1}{6}$ $9\frac{1}{30}$
24. $13\frac{3}{4} - 7\frac{5}{6}$ $5\frac{11}{12}$

25. $10\frac{1}{2} - 5\frac{2}{3}$ $4\frac{5}{6}$
26. $15\frac{1}{3} - 6\frac{3}{4}$ $8\frac{7}{12}$
27. $9\frac{1}{2} - 1\frac{3}{5}$ $7\frac{9}{10}$
28. $16\frac{4}{9} - 8\frac{1}{2}$ $7\frac{17}{18}$

Apply

Solve these problems. Simplify if necessary.

29. A recent Olympic record for pole vaulting is $19\frac{17}{24}$ feet. The earliest recorded vault was $10\frac{5}{6}$ feet in the year 1896, by William Hoyt of the U.S.A. How far from the current record was Hoyt's vault?
$8\frac{7}{8}$ feet

30. Rita worked on the party decorations for $2\frac{1}{2}$ hours, but Walt worked $1\frac{3}{4}$ longer. How long did Walt work on the decorations?
$4\frac{1}{4}$ hours

31. If Pete guessed that the jar at the carnival weighed $5\frac{3}{8}$ pounds, how far off was his estimate?
$\frac{7}{8}$ of a pound

32. Last Sunday, Jamie spent $5\frac{1}{3}$ hours on homework. She spent $1\frac{1}{2}$ hours on math, $2\frac{1}{2}$ hours reading and the rest of the time on spelling. How many hours did Jamie spend on spelling homework?
$1\frac{1}{3}$ hours

184

Correcting Common Errors

Once students have found a common denominator and renamed, they may have difficulty renaming a mixed number as a mixed number with an improper fraction part. Have them work with partners. Give each pair a variety of mixed numbers, such as $7\frac{5}{8}$, which they rewrite in the following way:

$$7\frac{5}{8} = 6 + \frac{8}{8} + \frac{5}{8} = 6\frac{13}{8}.$$

Enrichment

Tell students to subtract twice:

1. $6\frac{1}{2} - 1\frac{2}{3} - 1\frac{1}{6} = (3\frac{4}{6} = 3\frac{2}{3})$
2. $8\frac{1}{3} - 4\frac{3}{4} - 1\frac{1}{2} = (2\frac{1}{12})$
3. $25\frac{1}{2} - 10\frac{2}{5} - 3\frac{3}{10} = (11\frac{8}{10} = 11\frac{4}{5})$
4. $16\frac{1}{9} - 4\frac{2}{3} - 1\frac{2}{3} = (9\frac{7}{9})$

Practice

Have students complete the problems on the page. Remind them of the steps in mixed number subtraction.

Mixed Practice

1. $\frac{1}{5} + \frac{3}{10} + \frac{3}{4}$ $\left(1\frac{1}{4}\right)$
2. $12\frac{5}{9} + 14\frac{5}{6}$ $\left(27\frac{7}{18}\right)$
3. $165 + 496 + 2,375$ $(3,036)$
4. $42,091 \div 64$ $(657\ R43)$
5. 281×434 $(121,954)$
6. $8,020 - 4,312$ $(3,708)$
7. $7 - 5\frac{1}{8}$ $\left(1\frac{7}{8}\right)$
8. $\$372.65 \div 5$ $(\$74.53)$
9. $17,461 \times 40$ $(698,440)$
10. $\frac{12}{7} - \frac{2}{3}$ $\left(1\frac{1}{21}\right)$

Extra Credit *Applications*

Have students research the discovery of sonar and its use to calculate the depths of the ocean floor. Ask students to use the formula: time × speed of sound in water = ocean depth to solve the following problems:

1. If a ping takes 4 seconds to make a round trip from the sonar to the ocean floor and back to the ship, what is the depth of the ocean?
2. If a ping takes eight seconds to make a round trip, what is the depth of the ocean?
3. If a ping takes 16 seconds to make a round trip, what is the depth of the ocean at that point?

(The speed of sound in water is 1,500 meters/second. To calculate the depth, multiply by half the round-trip time.)

Add or Subtract Fractions

pages 185-186

Objective

To add and subtract mixed numbers

Materials

checklist of steps for adding and
subtracting mixed numbers

Mental Math

Have students identify the next number in each series:

1. ¼, ½, ¾ (1)
2. ⅛, ¼, ⅜ (⁴⁄₈ or ½)
3. ⅕, ⅖, ⅗ (⅘)
4. ⅙, ⅓, ½ (⁴⁄₆ or ⅔)
5. 1½, 2, 2½ (3)
6. 5, 5⅓, 5⅔ (6)
7. 3, 3½, 4 (4½)

Skill Review

Have students practice addition and
subtraction of fractions:

1. ⅔ + ⅔ = (1⅓)
2. ¾ + ⅖ = (²³⁄₂₀ = 1³⁄₂₀)
3. ⅕ + ⅔ = (¹³⁄₁₅)
4. ⅘ − ½ = (³⁄₁₀)
5. ⅞ − ⅛ = (⁶⁄₈ = ¾)
6. ¼ − ⅐ = (³⁄₂₈)
7. ⅔ + ⅙ = (⅚)

Adding and Subtracting Mixed Numbers

Tracy needs to mail a letter at the post office
before she goes to the library. How much
farther is Tracy's trip to the library past the
post office, than her trip directly home?

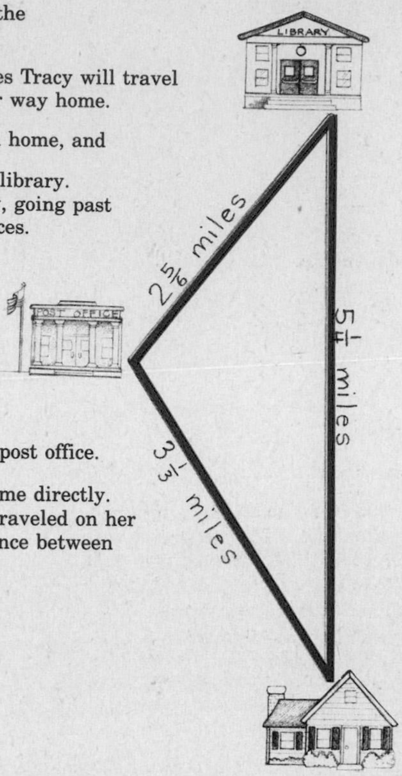

We want to find how many more miles Tracy will travel
on her way to the library than on her way home.

It is $3\frac{1}{3}$ miles to the post office from home, and
$2\frac{5}{6}$ miles from the post office to the library.
To find Tracy's distance to the library, going past
the post office, we add the two distances.

We add $3\frac{1}{3}$ and $2\frac{5}{6}$.

$$3\frac{1}{3} = 3\frac{2}{6}$$
$$+ 2\frac{5}{6} = 2\frac{5}{6}$$
$$5\frac{7}{6} = 6\frac{1}{6}$$

It is $6\frac{1}{6}$ miles to the library via the post office.

It is $5\frac{1}{4}$ miles from the library to home directly.
To find how many more miles Tracy traveled on her
trip to the library, we find the difference between
the lengths of her two trips.

We subtract $5\frac{1}{4}$ from $6\frac{1}{6}$.

$$6\frac{1}{6} = 6\frac{2}{12} = 5\frac{14}{12}$$
$$- 5\frac{1}{4} = 5\frac{3}{12} = 5\frac{3}{12}$$
$$\frac{11}{12}$$

Tracy's trip was $\frac{11}{12}$ of a mile farther going to the
library past the post office.

Getting Started

Add or subtract. Simplify if necessary.

1. $20\frac{1}{5}$
    $- \ 7\frac{7}{15}$
    $\overline{12\frac{11}{15}}$

2. $8\frac{3}{4}$
    $+ 7\frac{2}{9}$
    $\overline{15\frac{35}{36}}$

Copy and add or subtract.

3. $\left(3\frac{1}{2} + 2\frac{5}{8}\right) - 2\frac{1}{2}$ $3\frac{5}{8}$

4. $\left(8\frac{1}{10} - 3\frac{2}{5}\right) + 6\frac{1}{2}$ $11\frac{1}{5}$

MCP All rights reserved

185

Teaching the Lesson

Introducing the Problem Read the problem aloud and
ask a student to read the information sentences. Explain that
to find the distance to the library in a route going past the
post office, they will have to add 3⅓ and 2⅚. Ask a student to write the problem on the board in vertical form and
find a common denominator. Add the fractions and have a
student add whole numbers and simplify the answer.
(5⁷⁄₆ = 6⅙) Have a student read the first solution sentence
(6⅙ mi to library via post office) and read the next information sentence. Explain that to find the difference in the two
routes, they will have to subtract 5¼ from 6⅙. Have students write the subtraction on the board in vertical form,
find a common denominator and subtract fractions, renaming the minuend first. Read the solution sentence aloud.
(trip was ¹¹⁄₁₂ mi farther)

Developing the Skill Explain that the model problem in
this lesson involved both addition and subtraction of mixed
numbers. List these steps on the board: **find a common
denominator and convert fractions, rename the minuend if necessary, add or subtract fractions, add or
subtract whole numbers, simplify the answer and
rename or reduce the fraction if necessary.**

185

Practice

Add or subtract. Simplify if necessary.

1. $3\frac{2}{3}$
     $-2\frac{1}{2}$
     ———
     $1\frac{1}{6}$

2. $7\frac{3}{8}$
     $+4\frac{5}{6}$
     ———
     $12\frac{5}{24}$

3. $9\frac{1}{4}$
     $+7\frac{1}{6}$
     ———
     $16\frac{5}{12}$

4. $14\frac{1}{2}$
     $-6\frac{3}{8}$
     ———
     $8\frac{1}{8}$

5. $13\frac{7}{8}$
     $+5\frac{1}{3}$
     ———
     $19\frac{5}{24}$

6. $19\frac{1}{10}$
     $-12\frac{5}{15}$
     ———
     $6\frac{23}{30}$

7. $13\frac{2}{3}$
     $-7\frac{7}{8}$
     ———
     $5\frac{19}{24}$

8. $8\frac{1}{8}$
     $+4\frac{3}{10}$
     ———
     $12\frac{17}{40}$

Copy and Do

9. $\left(2\frac{1}{2}+3\frac{1}{4}\right)-1\frac{2}{3}$ $4\frac{1}{12}$

10. $\left(7\frac{3}{8}-1\frac{1}{4}\right)+5\frac{1}{3}$ $11\frac{11}{24}$

11. $21\frac{1}{4}-\left(4\frac{2}{3}+5\frac{1}{2}\right)$ $11\frac{1}{12}$

12. $\left(17\frac{1}{8}-11\frac{5}{6}\right)+10\frac{7}{12}$ $15\frac{7}{8}$

13. $13\frac{2}{3}+\left(10\frac{1}{4}-4\frac{5}{6}\right)$ $19\frac{1}{12}$

14. $19\frac{2}{3}-\left(6\frac{1}{4}-3\frac{5}{8}\right)$ $17\frac{1}{24}$

Apply

Solve these problems. Simplify if necessary.

15. The record snowfall in Portland, Maine for a 24-hour period is $15\frac{5}{16}$ inches. If $3\frac{1}{4}$ inches of snow falls between 7 AM and noon on Monday, then $5\frac{1}{2}$ more inches accumulate by midnight and $7\frac{1}{3}$ additional inches are on the ground as of 6:59 AM on Tuesday, by how much will this snowfall exceed the record? $\frac{37}{48}$ of an inch

16. Margo bought stock in the Tops are Top Clothing Company for $19\frac{1}{4}$ on Friday. The stock moved up $1\frac{1}{8}$ on Monday, $2\frac{1}{2}$ on Tuesday and dropped $1\frac{3}{4}$ on Wednesday. What was Margo's stock worth after Wednesday? $21\frac{1}{8}$

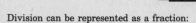
EXCURSION

Division can be represented as a fraction:

$\left(\dfrac{\text{dividend}}{\text{divisor}}=\text{quotient}\rightarrow\dfrac{30}{6}=5\right)$

Write the quotients. Then write each division equation as a fraction.

1. $42\div7=\underline{\ \ 6\ \ }$ $\dfrac{42}{7}=6$

2. $4\overline{)32}$ (quotient 8) $\dfrac{32}{4}=8$

3. $15\div3=\underline{\ \ 5\ \ }$ $\dfrac{15}{3}=5$

4. $6\overline{)12}$ (quotient 2) $\dfrac{12}{6}=2$

5. $54\div6=\underline{\ \ 9\ \ }$ $\dfrac{54}{6}=9$

6. $9\overline{)63}$ (quotient 7) $\dfrac{63}{9}=7$

186

Correcting Common Errors

When adding and subtracting mixed numbers, students may perform the opposite operation because they did not read the problem carefully. As they work each problem in a mixed set, have them first circle the symbol for the operation to make them more aware of what they are to do.

Enrichment

Give students a cookbook and ask them to find a recipe for cookies they like. Have them triple the recipe. Point out that each measurement must be added three times. Encourage students to try the recipe at home.

Practice

Have students complete the page. Remind them of the steps for working with mixed numbers and the importance of reducing the answer to lowest terms.

Excursion

Remind students to place the divisor in place of a denominator, and the dividend in place of a numerator, to write the fraction. Demonstrate how different $^{30}/_6$ is from $^6/_{30}$.

Extra Credit *Creative Drill*

Gather necessary supplies, and tell students they will be making Soap Crayons for the kindergarten play group, using the following recipe. The recipe makes 3 crayons. However, since the group has 18 students, the recipe will have to be increased if each student is to receive a crayon.

   ¾ Ivory Snow detergent
   10 drops food coloring
   ⅛ cup water

Mix water and soap together, stirring until the mixture is a soapy paste without lumps. Add food coloring and mix thoroughly. Press soap into plastic ice cube trays. Put trays in a dry, warm place overnight. Pop out crayons when dry. Ask students by how much they should increase the recipe (multiplying each amount by 6) and allow them to make the crayons.

Problem Solving Select Notation

pages 187-188

Objective

To choose the appropriate notation in a problem

Materials

Mental Math

Ask students to double each number and subtract 5:

1. 12 (19)
2. 5 (5)
3. 7 (9)
4. 20 (35)
5. 100 (195)
6. 25 (45)
7. 1,000 (1,995)

Selecting Appropriate Notation

Andy has an eight-cup container of sugar. He also has an empty five-cup container and an empty three-cup container. None of the containers has any markings. How can Andy measure exactly four cups of sugar using only these three containers?

★ SEE

We want to know how Andy can measure exactly four cups of sugar. He has a 5-cup and a 3-cup container that are empty. He has an 8-cup container that is filled with sugar

★ PLAN

Since the solution to this problem requires showing how Andy can get exactly four cups of sugar, we will need to record how he transfers sugar from container to container. We can do this by using three numbers to show the amount of sugar in each container. The first number will represent the amount of sugar in the 8-cup container. The second number will represent the amount of sugar in the 5-cup container. The third number will

represent the amount of sugar in the __3__-cup container.

★ DO

8, 0, 0   There are 8 cups of sugar in the __8__-cup container.

3, 5, 0   Andy transfers __5__ cups of sugar into the 5-cup container.

3, 2, __3__   He transfers 3 cups of sugar from the __5__-cup to the __3__-cup container.

6, 2, __0__   He transfers __3__ cups of sugar from the __3__-cup to the 8-cup container.

6, 0, __2__   He transfers __2__ cups of sugar from the __5__-cup to the 3-cup container.

1, __5__, 2   He transfers 5 cups of sugar from the 8-cup to the __5__-cup container.

1, 4, 3   He transfers 1 cup of sugar from the __5__-cup to the 3-cup container.

Andy now has __4__ cups of sugar in the __5__-cup container.

★ CHECK

We can check our work by reviewing each step.

MCP All rights reserved

187

Teaching the Lesson

Ask a student to read the problem aloud. Remind them of the SEE-PLAN-DO-CHECK problem solving method. Ask one student to read the SEE section. Ask another to read the PLAN section of the text. Continue reading the DO section of the problem yourself and explain that at each step the trio of numbers will represent the amount of sugar in each of the three containers. You may want students to label the columns in their texts. (8-c, 5-c, 3-c) Have students read the next section of text as you list and explain each configuration of numbers on the board.

8-cup	5-cup	3-cup
8	0	0
3	5	0
3	2	3
6	2	0
6	0	2
1	5	2
1	4	3

Have students check their calculations by reviewing each step.

1. You have two pails: one that will hold 4 quarts of water and one that will hold 9 quarts. There are no markings on either pail to indicate smaller quantities. How can you measure out six quarts of water using only these two pails?
See Solution Notes.

2. How can you cook an egg for exactly 15 minutes, if all you have is a 7-minute hourglass and an 11-minute hourglass?
See Solution Notes.

3. Joe and Sam like to trade. They agree that six peanuts are worth two suckers, and ten suckers are worth five apples. How many peanuts should Joe give Sam in trade for three apples?
18 peanuts

4. You have a 7-gallon pail and a 5-gallon pail. How can you measure exactly four gallons of water using only these two pails?
See Solution Notes.

5. All students in the class like milkshakes. Sixteen like vanilla, 16 like chocolate and 20 like strawberry. Five like both chocolate and strawberry, four like both strawberry and vanilla and two like both vanilla and chocolate. Three students like all three. How many are in the class?
35 students

6. Palmer, Smith and West are a teacher, a doctor and a lawyer, but not necessarily in that order. Their first names are Anne, Frank and Ed. Smith is neither a teacher nor a doctor. West is not the doctor and Anne is not the teacher. Ed is older than Smith and West. Give the full name and occupation of each person.
(Ed Palmer–doctor, Anne Smith–lawyer, Frank West–teacher)

7. The Basset Hound Musicians practiced $1\frac{3}{4}$ hours on Friday and $2\frac{2}{3}$ hours on Saturday. Do not use pencil and paper to compute. Was the total time that they practiced more or less than 4 hours? Explain how you know.
See Solution Notes.

8. Adelle added two fractions with unlike denominators. She used a denominator of one of the fractions as a common denominator for both of the fractions. What had to be true about the two denominators so that she could do this?
See Solution Notes.

9. If the sum of 2 like fractions is equal to 1, what is true about the sum of the numerators?
See Solution Notes.

10. If the sum of any 2 fractions is less than 1, what is true about the fractions?
See Solution Notes.

188

Extra Credit *Applications*

Give students practice in figuring shopping discounts. Have them bring in advertisements that show both the regular and sale prices of various items. Have them chart 10 items showing: original price, sale price and amount of discount. Then have students answer questions such as the following, using their charts:

1. Which item was the best buy?
2. Which item was the worst buy?
3. How much would be saved by buying all 10 items?

Solution Notes

1. Suggest that students use number pairs as in the sample problem. The 4 qt is listed first in each pair: 4, 0; 0, 4; 4, 4; 0,8; 4, 8; 3, 9; 0, 3; 4, 3; 0, 7; 4, 7; 2, 9; 2, 0; 0, 2; 4, 2; 0, 6.

2. Start both timers together. Start egg when 7-min timer is complete. (4 min) Then restart 11-min timer.

3. Have students lay out the ratio of peanuts to suckers to apples. (10:5, simplified 2:1) Show that if the ratio of peanuts to apples is 6:1, the price of 3 apples is 18 peanuts.

4. Have students use number pairs. The 7 gal is listed first in each pair: 7, 0; 2, 5; 2, 0; 0, 2; 7, 2; 4, 5.

5. From the total who like vanilla (V), chocolate (C) and strawberry (S) must be subtracted those who like two kinds and so appear on two lists (VC, CS, VS) and also twice the number who like all three kinds because they appear on all three lists (VCS): number of students = V + C + S − VC − CS − VS − (2 × VCS) = 52 − 11 − 6 = 35.

6. Students must find the first name of each person as well as the occupation, and chart each.

Higher-Order Thinking Skills

7. Synthesis: It was more than 4 hours. The sum of the whole-number parts is 3 and since each of the fractions is greater than ½, their sum is greater than 1.

8. Analysis: One denominator had to be a multiple of the other denominator.

9. Analysis: The sum of the numerators equals the common denominator.

10. Analysis: Both fractions are less than 1, and at least one fraction is less than ½.

188

Chapter Test
page 189

Item	Objective
1-2	Add fractions with like denominators (See pages 165-166)
3-4	Subtract fractions with like denominators (See pages 167-168)
5-6	Add fractions with unlike denominators (See pages 171-172)
7-8	Subtract fractions with unlike denominators (See pages 173-174)
9-12	Add two mixed numbers (See pages 175-176)
13-16	Subtract two mixed numbers (See pages 179-180)
17-20	Subtract mixed numbers with renaming (See pages 181-184)
21-24	Rename whole numbers as mixed numbers (See pages 181-184)
25-28	Simplify mixed numbers (See pages 177-178)

Add or subtract. Simplify if necessary.

1. $\frac{2}{5}$
$+ \frac{1}{5}$
$\frac{3}{5}$

2. $\frac{3}{8}$
$+ \frac{1}{8}$
$\frac{1}{2}$

3. $\frac{7}{8}$
$- \frac{1}{8}$
$\frac{3}{4}$

4. $\frac{9}{4}$
$- \frac{3}{4}$
$1\frac{1}{2}$

5. $\frac{8}{4}$
$+ \frac{1}{3}$
$2\frac{1}{3}$

6. $\frac{1}{2}$
$+ \frac{3}{5}$
$1\frac{1}{10}$

7. $\frac{7}{10}$
$- \frac{1}{2}$
$\frac{1}{5}$

8. $\frac{7}{8}$
$- \frac{1}{6}$
$\frac{17}{24}$

9. $4\frac{3}{5}$
$+ 6\frac{7}{10}$
$11\frac{3}{10}$

10. $8\frac{1}{2}$
$+ 9\frac{2}{3}$
$18\frac{1}{6}$

11. $6\frac{3}{8}$
$+ 5\frac{5}{6}$
$12\frac{5}{24}$

12. $6\frac{9}{10}$
$+ 8\frac{7}{15}$
$15\frac{11}{30}$

13. $9\frac{2}{3}$
$- 6\frac{1}{2}$
$3\frac{1}{6}$

14. $12\frac{7}{8}$
$- 5\frac{1}{4}$
$7\frac{5}{8}$

15. $13\frac{9}{10}$
$- 4\frac{3}{5}$
$9\frac{3}{10}$

16. $14\frac{7}{16}$
$- 8\frac{5}{16}$
$6\frac{1}{8}$

17. 8
$- 6\frac{3}{4}$
$1\frac{1}{4}$

18. $10\frac{1}{6}$
$- 8\frac{2}{3}$
$1\frac{1}{2}$

19. $17\frac{2}{5}$
$- 8\frac{3}{4}$
$8\frac{13}{20}$

20. $16\frac{3}{10}$
$- 7\frac{5}{6}$
$8\frac{7}{15}$

Rename as mixed numbers.

21. $2 = 1\frac{12}{12}$

22. $10\frac{3}{4} = 9\frac{7}{4}$

23. $3 = 2\frac{5}{5}$

24. $5\frac{3}{5} = 4\frac{8}{5}$

Simplify these mixed numbers.

25. $11\frac{12}{10} = 12\frac{1}{5}$

26. $1\frac{4}{16} = 1\frac{1}{4}$

27. $10\frac{43}{30} = 11\frac{13}{30}$

28. $10\frac{63}{81} = 10\frac{7}{9}$

MCP All rights reserved

189

Circle the letter of the correct answer.

1
563
+ 739

a 1,202
b 1,292
(c) 1,302
d NG

2
15,763
+ 9,839

a 24,602
(b) 25,602
c 27,602
d NG

3
6,248
− 951

(a) 5,297
b 5,397
c 6,717
d NG

4
$708.15
− 429.38

a $221.23
(b) $278.77
c $288.77
d NG

5
$9.06
× 7

(a) $63.42
b $64.14
c $630.42
d NG

6
75
× 36

a 675
b 2,570
c 2,900
(d) NG

7 4)48,084

a 1,212
b 1,221
(c) 12,021
d NG

8 49)11,768

a 24 R8
(b) 240 R8
c 240
d NG

9 Find the area.

9 in.

6 in.

a 30 in.
b 30 sq in.
(c) 54 sq in.
d NG

10
7 gal 3 qt
+ 4 gal 2 qt

a 11 gal
b 11 gal 1 qt
(c) 12 gal 1 qt
d NG

11 Simplify.
$\frac{5}{25}$

(a) $\frac{1}{5}$
b $\frac{1}{3}$
c $\frac{5}{25}$
d NG

12 Simplify.
$\frac{20}{6}$

a $\frac{1}{3}$
b $3\frac{1}{6}$
(c) $3\frac{1}{3}$
d NG

☐ score

190

Cumulative Review

page 190

Item	Objective
1	Add two numbers with sums less than 1,000, one regrouping (See pages 23-24)
2	Add two numbers up to 5-digits (See pages 27-28)
3	Subtract two numbers up to 4-digits (See pages 33-34)
4	Subtract two numbers up to 6-digits, zeros in minuend (See pages 35-36)
5	Multiply money by 1-digit factor (See pages 55-56)
6	Multiply two 2-digit factors (See pages 57-58)
7	Divide up to 6-digits by 1-digit number (See pages 87-88)
8	Divide a 5-digit by 2-digit number, quotient with zero (See pages 109-110)
9	Find the area of rectangles (See pages 127-128)
10	Add customary units of capacity (See pages 131-132)
11	Reduce fractions to lowest terms (See pages 149-150)
12	Change improper fractions to mixed number (See pages 157-158)

Alternate Cumulative Review

Circle the letter of the correct answer.

1
563
+ 292

a 845
b 755
(c) 855
d NG

2
25,695
+ 6,327

a 31,022
(b) 32,022
c 32,922
d NG

3
7,486
− 793

(a) 6,693
b 6,793
c 7,313
d NG

4
$609.84
−537.96

a $72.88
(b) $71.88
c $171.88
d NG

5
$5.09
×5

a $25.95
(b) $25.45
c $250.45
d NG

6
19
× 87

a 953
b 1,593
c 1,650
(d) NG

7 3)28,674

a 2,891 R1
b 9,558 R1
(c) 9,558
d NG

8 67)24,799

a 37 R9
(b) 370 R9
c 370 R19
d NG

9 Find the area of a rectangle 6 in. by 8 in.

a 28 in.
b 28 sq in.
(c) 48 sq in.
d NG

10
11 gallons 6 quarts
+ 7 gallons 3 quarts

a 19 gallons 1 quart
b 19 gallons 5 quarts
(c) 20 gallons 1 quart
d NG

11 Simplify.
$\frac{6}{30}$

a $\frac{2}{10}$
b $\frac{1}{6}$
(c) $\frac{1}{5}$
d NG

12 Simplify.
$\frac{59}{8}$

(a) $7\frac{3}{8}$
b $7\frac{4}{8}$
c $6\frac{3}{8}$
d NG

190

Fractions

Objective

To review finding fractions of a number

Materials

*12 counters
*overhead projector

Mental Math

Have students reduce each fraction to lowest terms:

1. ⁴⁄₆ (²⁄₃)
2. ⁵⁄₁₀ (½)
3. ⅕ (in lowest terms)
4. ⁶⁄₈ (¾)
5. ²⁄₈ (¼)
6. ⁸⁄₁₀ (⁴⁄₅)

Skill Review

Remind students how to find a fraction of a whole number. Ask a student to find one third of nine apples. (3 apples; ⅓ × 9 = 3) Have them find these fractions:

1. ⅕ of 10 (2)
2. ½ of 12 (6)
3. ½ of 5 (2½)
4. ⅓ of 12 (4)
5. ¼ of 8 (2)
6. ¼ of 12 (3)
7. ⅕ of 20 (4)

Finding Fractional Parts of Whole Numbers

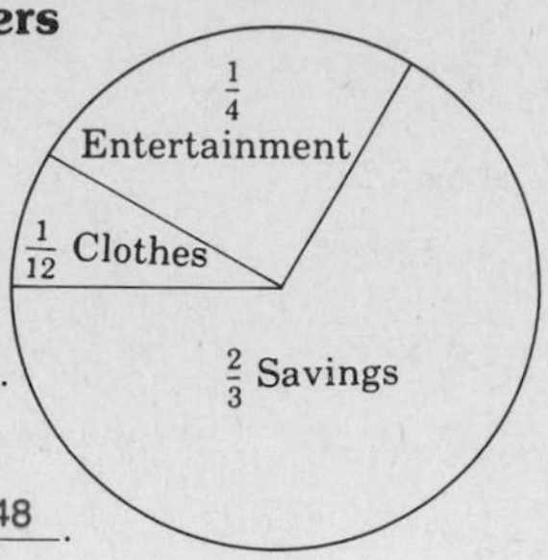

Ysidra tries to save as much money as she can for her college expenses. Ysidra earns \$48 each week tutoring history students at the campus learning center. How much does she save each week?

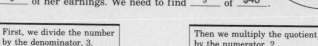

We want to find the amount Ysidra saves each week.

We know Ysidra earns ___\$48___ each week. She saves ___²⁄₃___ of her earnings. We need to find ___²⁄₃___ of ___\$48___.

First, we divide the number by the denominator, 3.	Then we multiply the quotient by the numerator, 2.

$\frac{1}{3}$ of 48 $\frac{16}{3)\overline{48}}$ $\frac{2}{3}$ of 48 $2 × 16 = \underline{32}$

We can draw a picture to help us understand this.

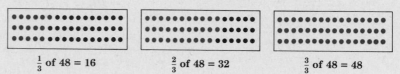

$\frac{1}{3}$ of 48 = 16 $\frac{2}{3}$ of 48 = 32 $\frac{3}{3}$ of 48 = 48

✔ To find a fraction of a number, divide the number by the denominator and multiply that result by the numerator.

Ysidra saves ___\$32___ each week.

Getting Started

Write the number for each fractional part.

1. $\frac{1}{8}$ of 16 = ___2___   2. $\frac{1}{10}$ of \$100 = ___\$10___   3. $\frac{1}{12}$ of 96 = ___8___

Copy and solve.

4. $\frac{3}{4}$ of 24
   18

5. $\frac{5}{6}$ of 96
   80

6. $\frac{9}{16}$ of \$288
   \$162

191

MCP All rights reserved

Teaching the Lesson

Introducing the Problem Read the problem aloud, and have a student read and complete the information sentences. Remind students that to find a fraction of a number, they must multiply the fraction by the number, in this case, ²⁄₃ × \$48. Explain that when they multiply by a fraction, they divide by the denominator then multiply by the numerator. They find the number of fractional units in the number when they divide by the denominator, and find the total number of these parts when they multiply by the numerator. Work the problem on the board while students follow in their texts. Draw the dot array on the board and have a student circle thirds. Have another count the number of dots in two thirds. (32) Read the solution sentence aloud. (saves \$32 each week)

Developing the Skill Place 12 counters on the overhead projector. Ask a student to find ¼ of the counters. (3) Separate the counters into four groups. Write on the board: **12 ÷ 4 = 3, 3 × 1 = 3** and **¼ × 12 = 3**. Have another student find ²⁄₄ of the counters. (6) Write on the board: **²⁄₄ × 12 = (12 ÷ 4) × 2 = 3 × 2 = 6**. Ask a student to calculate ¾ of 12 without using the counters. Have the class find ³⁄₅ of 25. (15)

Practice

Write the number for each fractional part.

1. $\frac{1}{3}$ of 21 = __7__
2. $\frac{1}{2}$ of 24 = __12__
3. $\frac{4}{7}$ of $84 = __$48__
4. $\frac{5}{6}$ of 36 = __30__
5. $\frac{3}{4}$ of 36 = __27__
6. $\frac{3}{8}$ of 64 = __24__
7. $\frac{4}{5}$ of $35 = __$28__
8. $\frac{2}{3}$ of 21 = __14__
9. $\frac{1}{12}$ of 24 = __2__
10. $\frac{1}{7}$ of $49 = __$7__
11. $\frac{3}{10}$ of 40 = __12__
12. $\frac{7}{8}$ of 56 = __49__

Copy and Do

13. $\frac{2}{3}$ of 42 28
14. $\frac{1}{8}$ of 80 10
15. $\frac{3}{7}$ of 84 36
16. $\frac{4}{5}$ of 75 60

17. $\frac{1}{12}$ of $48 $4
18. $\frac{1}{16}$ of 608 38
19. $\frac{1}{2}$ of 806 403
20. $\frac{3}{8}$ of $496 $186

21. $\frac{3}{4}$ of 948 711
22. $\frac{3}{5}$ of $1,080 $648
23. $\frac{3}{16}$ of 1,792 336
24. $\frac{7}{15}$ of 1,905 889

Apply

Solve these problems.

25. Winston bought $\frac{1}{2}$ dozen macaroni and cheese dinners. If he eats one dinner each day, how many days will his supply of macaroni and cheese dinners last?
6 days

26. It took Dean $\frac{3}{5}$ of an hour to walk home from basketball practice. How many minutes did it take?
36 minutes

27. Jessica bought a package of 36 paper napkins for her party. She used $\frac{2}{3}$ of the napkins. How many were left in the package?
12 napkins

28. Tina has to sell 144 tickets to the student and faculty volleyball game. On Monday, she sold $\frac{3}{8}$ of the tickets. On Tuesday, she sold $\frac{1}{6}$ of the original number of tickets. How many did Tina have left to sell on Wednesday?
66 tickets

Use the ad to solve problems 29 and 30.

29. What is the sale price of a coat that usually sells for $87?
$29

30. A pair of shoes costs $72 and a jacket costs $116. How much is saved if Paul buys the shoes and jacket on sale?
$123

SALE
COATS $\frac{2}{3}$ off
SHOES $\frac{1}{2}$ off
JACKETS $\frac{3}{4}$ off

192

Correcting Common Errors

Some students may forget to multiply by the numerator when finding the fraction of a number. Have them re-write a problem, such as ⅔ of 24, with the whole number written as a fraction. Then they can multiply the numerators and denominators as they do when multiplying fractions.

⅔ of 24 = ⅔ × ²⁴/₁ = ⁴⁸/₃, or 16

Enrichment

Show students that they can simplify the multiplication of fractions by removing common factors from numerator and denominator. This is usually called cancelling, and is equivalent to dividing by 1. Use this example:

$$\frac{5}{\overset{}{\underset{1}{\cancel{6}}}} \times \frac{\overset{2}{\cancel{12}}}{1} = \frac{10}{3} = 3\tfrac{1}{3}$$

Explain that a 6 has been taken from both numerator and denominator. Have students use this method to do these problems:

1. ⅜ × 12 = (⁹/₂ = 4½)
2. ³/₁₀ × 20 = (⁶/₁ = 6)
3. ¹/₁₂ × 9 = (¾)

Practice

Have students complete all the problems. Remind them of the two steps in finding a fraction of a number: divide by the denominator, then multiply by the numerator.

Mixed Practice

1. $71 - 43\frac{9}{10}$ $\left(27\frac{1}{10}\right)$
2. $17.95 + $21.76 + $108.95 ($148.66)
3. $68,603 \div 76$ (902 R51)
4. $95 \times 1,906$ (181,070)
5. $15\frac{3}{7} + 21\frac{2}{3}$ $\left(37\frac{2}{21}\right)$
6. $8 \times 43,901$ (351,208)
7. $\frac{9}{10} = \frac{}{40}$ (36)
8. 300×800 (240,000)
9. $650.01 - $438.28 ($211.73)
10. $16\frac{1}{5} - 9\frac{3}{4}$ $\left(6\frac{9}{20}\right)$

Extra Credit *Statistics*

Remind students that the mode of a set of numbers is that number that appears most often in the set or sample. Explain that some sets of numbers will have no mode, which means that none of the numbers appear more often than the others. Other sets will be bimodal (have two modes) or multi-modal (have many modes). Have students record the average daily temperature for a week and identify whether that set of numbers is unimodal (one mode), bi-modal, multi-modal or has no mode. Extend the activity to other data-collecting projects.

Multiplying Fractions

pages 193-194

Objective

To multiply fractions

Materials

*12 counters
*overhead projector

Mental Math

Have students identify the related division problem for each:

1. 6 × 9 = 54 (54 ÷ 6 = 9 or 54 ÷ 9 = 6)
2. 7 × 4 = 28 (28 ÷ 4 = 7 or 28 ÷ 7 = 4)
3. 8 × 3 = 24 (24 ÷ 8 = 3 or 24 ÷ 3 = 8)
4. 5 × 5 = 25 (25 ÷ 5 = 5)
5. 8 × 9 = 72 (72 ÷ 8 = 9 or 72 ÷ 9 = 8)
6. 3 × 4 = 12 (12 ÷ 3 = 4 or 12 ÷ 4 = 3)

Skill Review

Have students find the fraction of each whole number:

1. ⅔ of 24 (16)
2. ¾ of 16 (12)
3. ⅓ of 21 (7)
4. ⅚ of 12 (10)
5. ⅜ of 8 (3)
6. 7⁄10 of 20 (14)

Multiplying Fractions

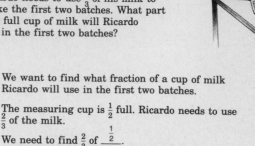

Ricardo has all the ingredients ready to bake three batches of corn muffins. Ricardo needs to use $\frac{2}{3}$ of his milk to make the first two batches. What part of a full cup of milk will Ricardo use in the first two batches?

We want to find what fraction of a cup of milk Ricardo will use in the first two batches.

The measuring cup is $\frac{1}{2}$ full. Ricardo needs to use $\frac{2}{3}$ of the milk.

We need to find $\frac{2}{3}$ of $\underline{\frac{1}{2}}$.

We can draw a picture to help us understand the problem.

Total Milk Available

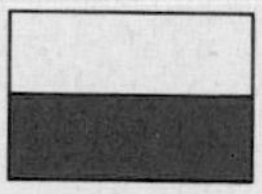

$\frac{1}{2}$ $\frac{1}{2}$

Milk Allotted for Each Batch

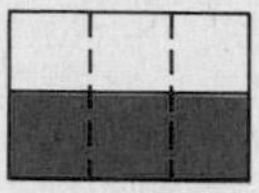

$\frac{1}{6}$ $\frac{1}{6}$ $\frac{1}{6}$

We can also multiply to find $\frac{2}{3}$ of $\frac{1}{2}$.

Multiply the numerators to find the part used.

$\frac{2}{3} \times \frac{1}{2} = 2$

Multiply the denominators to find how many parts in all. Simplify.

$\frac{2}{3} \times \frac{1}{2} = \frac{2}{6} = \frac{1}{3}$

Ricardo will use $\underline{\frac{1}{3}}$ of a cup of milk for two batches.

Getting Started

Multiply. Simplify if necessary.

1. $\frac{3}{4} \times \frac{5}{8} = \underline{\frac{15}{32}}$
2. $\frac{1}{5} \times \frac{3}{4} = \underline{\frac{3}{20}}$
3. $\frac{7}{3} \times \frac{2}{5} = \underline{\frac{14}{15}}$
4. $\frac{6}{10} \times \frac{2}{3} = \underline{\frac{2}{5}}$
5. $\frac{7}{8} \times \frac{4}{5} = \underline{\frac{7}{10}}$
6. $\frac{2}{3} \times \frac{9}{10} = \underline{\frac{3}{5}}$
7. $\frac{2}{5} \times \frac{5}{2} = \underline{1}$
8. $\frac{7}{2} \times \frac{6}{7} = \underline{3}$

Copy and multiply.

9. $\frac{1}{3} \times \frac{2}{5}$ $\frac{2}{15}$
10. $\frac{5}{9} \times \frac{7}{9}$ $\frac{35}{81}$
11. $\frac{9}{15} \times \frac{5}{3}$ 1
12. $\frac{9}{4} \times \frac{2}{6}$ $\frac{3}{4}$

MCP All rights reserved

193

Teaching the Lesson

Introducing the Problem Have a student read the problem aloud. Have another read and complete the information sentences. Have students look at the illustration in their texts. Explain that it shows one half and then shows the half divided into thirds. Ask a student how many pieces are in the whole now. (6) Have another tell the fraction that describes two of those pieces. (2⁄6 or ⅓) Explain that finding ⅔ of ½ is the same as multiplying ⅔ × ½. Have a student write the problem as multiplication on the board and complete the solution sentence. (2⁄6 = ⅓)

Developing the Skill Using the overhead projector and counters, illustrate these problems: ¾ of 12 (9) ⅔ of 9 (6) ½ of 12. (6) Now show ¾ of 12 and then ⅓ of that. (3) Show students that they can multiply ¾ × ⅓ × 12⁄1 = 36⁄12 and get the same answer, 3. Ask a student to illustrate ⅖ of ½ on the board using a rectangle divided into tenths. (3⁄10) Put the multiplication on the board: **⅖ × ½ = 2⁄10.** Have students work these problems, multiplying numerators and denominators.

1. ⅜ of 5⁄2 (15⁄16)
2. ⅖ of ⅞ (14⁄40 = 7⁄20)
3. ⅘ of ¾ (⅗)
4. ⅛ of ½ (1⁄16)

Practice

Multiply. Simplify if necessary.

1. $\frac{3}{4} \times \frac{2}{5} = \frac{3}{10}$ 2. $\frac{1}{8} \times \frac{3}{8} = \frac{3}{64}$ 3. $\frac{6}{5} \times \frac{2}{3} = \frac{4}{5}$ 4. $\frac{4}{5} \times \frac{5}{8} = \frac{1}{2}$

5. $\frac{8}{9} \times \frac{3}{4} = \frac{2}{3}$ 6. $\frac{7}{8} \times \frac{8}{7} = 1$ 7. $\frac{3}{12} \times \frac{6}{10} = \frac{3}{20}$ 8. $\frac{3}{7} \times \frac{7}{15} = \frac{1}{5}$

9. $\frac{9}{10} \times \frac{5}{3} = 1\frac{1}{2}$ 10. $\frac{6}{10} \times \frac{5}{12} = \frac{1}{4}$ 11. $\frac{5}{16} \times \frac{8}{10} = \frac{1}{4}$ 12. $\frac{2}{3} \times \frac{9}{16} = \frac{3}{8}$

Copy and Do

13. $\frac{8}{5} \times \frac{5}{4}$ 2   14. $\frac{7}{3} \times \frac{9}{14}$ $1\frac{1}{2}$ 15. $\frac{4}{9} \times \frac{12}{16}$ $\frac{1}{3}$ 16. $\frac{7}{12} \times \frac{8}{21}$ $\frac{2}{9}$

17. $\frac{10}{4} \times \frac{8}{15}$ $1\frac{1}{3}$ 18. $\frac{9}{16} \times \frac{1}{3}$ $\frac{3}{16}$ 19. $\frac{3}{3} \times \frac{9}{10}$ $\frac{9}{10}$ 20. $\frac{5}{6} \times \frac{12}{5}$ 2

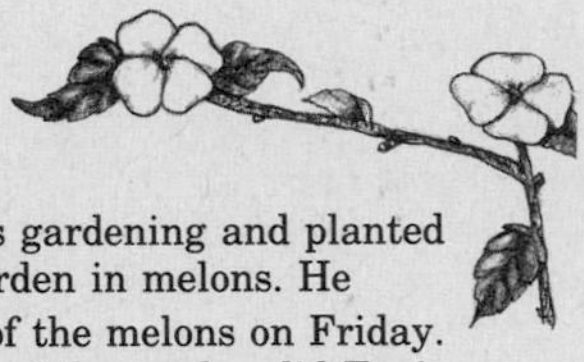

Apply

Solve these problems. Simplify if necessary.

21. Dorothy is redecorating by painting $\frac{1}{4}$ of her room pink. She plans to cover $\frac{2}{3}$ of the pink wall with mirrors. What part of her room is covered with mirrors?
$\frac{1}{6}$

22. Ernie likes gardening and planted $\frac{3}{4}$ of his garden in melons. He planted $\frac{3}{5}$ of the melons on Friday. What part of the garden did Ernie plant on Friday?
$\frac{9}{20}$

23. The planning commission has determined that Parkville is $\frac{3}{16}$ park land. About $\frac{4}{9}$ of the park land is used for recreation. What part of Parkville is used for recreation?
$\frac{1}{12}$

24. Shasta lives $\frac{7}{8}$ of a mile from school. She walks $\frac{2}{3}$ of the way with Joan. How far does Shasta walk alone?
$\frac{7}{24}$ of a mile

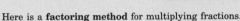

EXCURSION

Here is a **factoring method** for multiplying fractions.

First, write the prime factors for each numerator and denominator.

Cross out primes which are common in the set of numerators and denominators.

Multiply the remaining primes to get the product.

$\frac{9}{14} \times \frac{21}{6} = \frac{3 \times 3}{2 \times 7} \times \frac{3 \times 7}{2 \times 3}$

$\frac{3 \times 3}{2 \times \cancel{7}} \times \frac{\cancel{3} \times \cancel{7}}{2 \times \cancel{3}}$

$\frac{3 \times 3}{2 \times 2} = \frac{9}{4} = 2\frac{1}{4}$

Multiply. Use the **factoring method**.

1. $\frac{12}{13} \times \frac{5}{18} = \frac{10}{39}$ 2. $\frac{7}{12} \times \frac{18}{21} = \frac{1}{2}$ 3. $\frac{6}{7} \times \frac{5}{3} = 1\frac{3}{7}$

4. $\frac{72}{49} \times \frac{21}{16} = 1\frac{13}{14}$ 5. $\frac{121}{45} \times \frac{15}{33} = 1\frac{2}{9}$ 6. $\frac{3}{7} \times \frac{5}{14} \times \frac{49}{30} = \frac{1}{4}$

Correcting Common Errors

Some students may have difficulty understanding the concept of multiplying fractions. Have them work with partners to model problems, such as ¼ of ⅘, by drawing a rectangle. First, they divide the rectangle horizontally into fifths and shade 4 of them to represent ⅘. Then they divide the rectangle vertically into fourths and shade 1 of them to represent ¼. Then, to find the product, they count the numbers of parts in the whole, the denominator, and the number of parts that are shaded twice, the numerator, 4/20 or, in simplest form, ⅕.

Enrichment

Show students how to find ¾ of any number. Have them find ¼ of the number by dividing by 4. Have them subtract the fourth from the original number. Point out that this gives the remaining ¾. Use this example: ¾ × 136 = 136 − (136 ÷ 4) = 136 − 34 = 102. Have them find ¾ of:

1. 2,152 (1,614)
2. 500 (375)
3. 5,432 (4,074)

Practice

Have students complete the page. If some have worked with cancelling common factors, suggest they try that method for simplifying the problem before multiplication.

Excursion

The two middle steps of the example can be eliminated as soon as the student masters the order of the steps. The factoring can be placed above and below the original numerators and denominators without recopying.

Extra Credit *Statistics*

Explain that there are many terms in statistics to describe the position of one number in a set of numbers, and including midrange and mode of a set. Explain that there is also a **median** for every set of numbers. Show students that if the set has an odd number of elements, the median is the number in the middle when the numbers are arranged from smallest to largest. Emphasize that this is, in spite of the value of the numbers. For example, in the set 1, 15, 16, 17, 18, the median is 16. Show them that if the set has an even number of elements, the median is the number halfway between the two center elements when the numbers are arranged from smallest to largest. For example in the set 24, 27, 28, 30, 34, 35, the median is 29. Have students find the median class size in the school. Ask them to find out how many students are in each class, list the class and size in order from smallest to largest and then find the median. (Answers will vary.)

194

Multiply Fractions or Mixed Numbers

pages 195-196

Objective

To multiply fractions

Materials

Mental Math

Have students provide the missing numerator:

1. /4 = ¹⁶/8 (8)
2. /5 = ⁴/4 (5)
3. /3 = ¹⁸/9 (6)
4. /2 = ⁵/10 (1)
5. /6 = ½ (3)
6. /7 = ⁶/2 (21)
7. /8 = ⁶/16 (3)

Skill Review

Have students multiply these fractions:

1. ²/3 × ³/4 (⁶/12 = ½)
2. ¾ × ⁷/9 (²¹/36 = ⁷/12)
3. ³/5 × ⁹/10 (²⁷/50)
4. ⁴/5 × ¼ (⅕)
5. ¾ × ³/5 (⁹/20)
6. ⁵/6 × ²/3 (¹⁰/18 = ⁵/9)
7. ⁵/7 × ¹¹/14 (⁵⁵/98)

Multiplying Fractions and Mixed Numbers

Yong is applying for a part time job at Sam's Sandwich Shop. The waiter's position pays $4 per hour. How much can Yong make each week as a waiter?

Wanted Part Time	Hours per Week
Cook	12
Waiter	$8\frac{1}{4}$
Hostess	$6\frac{2}{3}$

We want to know the weekly amount Yong can earn as a waiter.

The waiter's position pays __$4__ per hour and is available for __$8\frac{1}{4}$__ hours a week.

To find the weekly earnings for this position, we multiply the hourly rate by the total working hours per week. We multiply __$4__ by __$8\frac{1}{4}$__.

Rename the factors as fractions.	Multiply numerators and denominators.	Simplify the product as a whole or mixed number.
$4 \times 8\frac{1}{4}$ $\frac{4}{1} \times \frac{33}{4}$	$\frac{4}{1} \times \frac{33}{4} = \frac{132}{4}$	$\frac{4}{1} \times \frac{33}{4} = \frac{132}{4} = 33$

✔ Remember to rename a whole number as a fraction, we write the whole number in the numerator and 1 in the denominator. $4 = \frac{4}{1}$

Yong can make __$33__ each week as a waiter.

Getting Started

Multiply. Simplify if necessary.

1. $\frac{2}{3} \times 3\frac{1}{3} =$ __$2\frac{2}{9}$__

2. $7 \times 1\frac{1}{2} =$ __$10\frac{1}{2}$__

3. $2\frac{3}{4} \times \frac{1}{2} =$ __$1\frac{3}{8}$__

4. $5\frac{1}{3} \times \frac{3}{4} =$ __4__

Copy and multiply.

5. $4\frac{1}{2} \times \frac{5}{9}$ $2\frac{1}{2}$

6. $\frac{3}{5} \times 6\frac{1}{3}$ $3\frac{4}{5}$

7. $\frac{2}{9} \times 7$ $1\frac{5}{9}$

8. $8 \times \frac{3}{16}$ $1\frac{1}{2}$

9. $3\frac{5}{7} \times 3$ $11\frac{1}{7}$

10. $\frac{1}{5} \times 9\frac{1}{2}$ $1\frac{9}{10}$

MCP All rights reserved

195

Teaching the Lesson

Introducing the Problem Have a student read the problem aloud. Have another student read and complete the information sentences. Ask the class to look at the problem worked in their texts. Show them that the first step in multiplying by a mixed number is to change the number to an improper fraction. (8¼ = ³³/4) Explain that 4 can be expressed as an improper fraction. (⁴/1) Remind students that when multiplying fractions they multiply numerators and then denominators. (⁴/1 × ³³/4 = ¹³²/4) Simplify the product on the board, changing the improper fraction to a whole number. (33) Have a student read the solution sentence aloud.

Developing the Skill Explain the steps in multiplying a whole number by a mixed number. Show them how to write a whole number as an improper fraction by putting it over a denominator of one. Explain that to change a mixed number to an improper fraction, they multiply the whole number by the denominator, add the numerator, and write the fraction as that sum over the original denominator. Show that to multiply any fractions, improper or not, they multiply numerators and multiply denominators. Put this problem on the board:

$$5 \times 4\frac{1}{3} = ⁵/1 \times ¹³/3 = ⁶⁵/3 = 21²/3$$

195

Practice

Multiply. Simplify if necessary.

1. $\frac{3}{4} \times 2\frac{1}{2} =$ ___ $1\frac{7}{8}$

2. $1\frac{2}{3} \times \$6 =$ ___ \$10

3. $\frac{3}{8} \times 1\frac{1}{3} =$ ___ $\frac{1}{2}$

4. $5\frac{1}{3} \times 15 =$ ___ 80

5. $4\frac{2}{3} \times \frac{1}{4} =$ ___ $1\frac{1}{6}$

6. $\frac{5}{12} \times 1\frac{1}{5} =$ ___ $\frac{1}{2}$

7. $6\frac{1}{3} \times 9 =$ ___ 57

8. $1\frac{1}{2} \times \frac{4}{5} =$ ___ $1\frac{1}{5}$

9. $3\frac{1}{3} \times \frac{2}{5} =$ ___ $1\frac{1}{3}$

10. $\$10 \times 4\frac{1}{5} =$ ___ \$42

11. $2\frac{1}{6} \times 3 =$ ___ $6\frac{1}{2}$

12. $9\frac{1}{2} \times \frac{2}{3} =$ ___ $6\frac{1}{3}$

13. $5\frac{1}{8} \times 4 =$ ___ $20\frac{1}{2}$

14. $\frac{5}{7} \times 1\frac{3}{4} =$ ___ $1\frac{1}{4}$

15. $\$12 \times 5\frac{1}{3} =$ ___ \$64

16. $\frac{5}{8} \times \$16 =$ ___ \$10

Copy and Do

17. $1\frac{1}{5} \times \frac{5}{6}$ 1

18. $15 \times 2\frac{1}{3}$ 35

19. $8\frac{1}{2} \times \$20$ \$170

20. $\frac{4}{5} \times 12$ $9\frac{3}{5}$

21. $3\frac{1}{8} \times \frac{2}{5}$ $1\frac{1}{4}$

22. $\frac{5}{7} \times \frac{1}{10}$ $\frac{1}{14}$

23. $1\frac{2}{3} \times 8$ $13\frac{1}{3}$

24. $3\frac{3}{5} \times \$25$ \$90

25. $2\frac{1}{12} \times \frac{3}{10}$ $\frac{5}{8}$

26. $48 \times \frac{5}{8}$ 30

27. $18 \times 2\frac{1}{9}$ 38

28. $6\frac{1}{4} \times \frac{1}{10}$ $\frac{5}{8}$

Apply

Use the recipe for griddle cakes to solve problems 29 through 32.

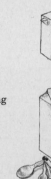

29. How much baking powder and baking soda is needed for 4 servings?
$\frac{1}{3}$ of a teaspoon of powder
$\frac{3}{4}$ of a teaspoon of soda

30. How much milk is needed for 8 servings?
5 cups

31. How much more sugar than baking soda is used for 4 servings?
$1\frac{11}{12}$ teaspoons

32. How much flour is needed for 10 servings?
$1\frac{1}{4}$ cups

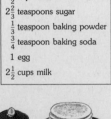

GRIDDLE CAKES
4 servings
$\frac{1}{2}$ cup flour
$2\frac{2}{3}$ teaspoons sugar
$\frac{1}{3}$ teaspoon baking powder
$\frac{3}{4}$ teaspoon baking soda
1 egg
$2\frac{1}{2}$ cups milk

Correcting Common Errors

Some students may multiply a fraction times a mixed number without changing the mixed number to an improper fraction, using the whole number as a separate part of the problem.

INCORRECT
¾ × 3⅕ = 3³⁄₂₀

Remind students to change each mixed number to an improper fraction first, before they begin to multiply.

Enrichment

Explain that when students multiply improper fractions, taking common factors out of numerators and denominators can simplify the problem considerably. (This is often called cancelling.)

Have students use this technique to do these problems:

1. ⅔ × ²¹⁄₁₀ = (²⁄₃ × ²¹⁄₁₀ = ⁷⁄₅ = 1⅖)

2. 8 × 1¾ = (8 × ⁷⁄₄ = 14)

Practice

Have students complete all the problems. Remind them to rename any whole numbers as fractions by putting them over a denominator of 1. Have them rename any mixed numbers as improper fractions.

Mixed Practice

1. $\$256.80 \div 8$ (\$32.10)

2. $625,403 - 198,648$ (426,755)

3. $25\frac{3}{5} + 14\frac{7}{10} + 12\frac{1}{4}$ $\left(52\frac{11}{20}\right)$

4. 208×380 (79,040)

5. $117 - 109\frac{3}{7}$ $\left(7\frac{4}{7}\right)$

6. 95×47 (4,465)

7. $24 + 38 + 46 + 34$ (142)

8. $26,200 \div 40$ (655)

9. Simplify: $\frac{48}{9}$ $\left(5\frac{1}{3}\right)$

10. $17\frac{1}{3} - \left(3\frac{1}{4} - 2\frac{3}{8}\right)$ $\left(16\frac{11}{24}\right)$

Extra Credit *Sets*

Duplicate the following:
Three students in Mr. Brown's class, Sally, Ed and Bill, were always getting into trouble. It was not always at the same time, but when there was trouble, Mr. Brown had to consider each of them as possibilities. One day Mr. Brown discovered the class gerbils missing from their cage. Help Mr. Brown discover all the possible combinations of who let the gerbils out. Start with the Universal Set A. (known trouble-makers) (8 subsets are possible: [Sally], [Ed], [Bill], [Sally, Ed] [Sally, Bill] [Ed, Bill] [Sally, Ed, Bill] [Empty set, none of them did it.]

Multiplying Mixed Numbers

pages 197-198

Objective

To multiply two mixed numbers

Materials

check lists for multiplying mixed numbers

Mental Math

Have students identify the larger number:

1. ³⁄₂ or 1¼ (³⁄₂)
2. ⁵⁄₄ or 2 (2)
3. ⁷⁄₂ or 4 (4)
4. ⁶⁄₃ or 1⅓ (⁶⁄₃)
5. ⁸⁄₅ or 2½ (2½)
6. ⁶⁄₅ or 2 (2)

Skill Review

Review multiplying a fraction and a mixed number by having students work these problems on the board:

1. 2½ × ⅕ = (⁵⁄₂ × ⅕ = ½)
2. ⅔ × 4⅛ = (⅔ × ³³⁄₈ = ¹¹⁄₄ = 2¾)
3. 7 × 3⅓ = (⁷⁄₁ × ¹⁰⁄₃ = ⁷⁰⁄₃ = 23⅓)
4. ⅞ × 5⅓ = (⅞ × ¹⁶⁄₃ = ¹⁴⁄₃ = 4⅔)

Multiplying Mixed Numbers

Mrs. Reynolds is buying wall-to-wall carpeting for her dining room. Carpeting is sold by the square yard. How many square yards of carpeting will Mrs. Reynolds need?

We want to know the number of square yards of carpeting needed.

To know this we need to find the area of Mrs. Reynolds' dining room.

The length is $3\frac{1}{3}$ yards and the width is $2\frac{1}{4}$ yards.

To find the area, we multiply the length of the room by the width.

We multiply $3\frac{1}{3}$ by $2\frac{1}{4}$.

Rename the factors as fractions.	Multiply numerators and denominators.	Simplify the product.
$2\frac{1}{4} \times 3\frac{1}{3}$ $\frac{9}{4} \times \frac{10}{3}$	$\frac{9}{4} \times \frac{10}{3} = \frac{90}{12}$	$\frac{9}{4} \times \frac{10}{3} = \frac{90}{12} = \frac{15}{2} = 7\frac{1}{2}$

Mrs. Reynolds will need $7\frac{1}{2}$ square yards of carpeting.

✔ Remember, to rename a mixed number as an improper fraction, we write the numerator as the product of the denominator and whole number plus the numerator.

$$2\frac{1}{4} = \frac{4 \times 2 + 1}{4} = \frac{9}{4}$$

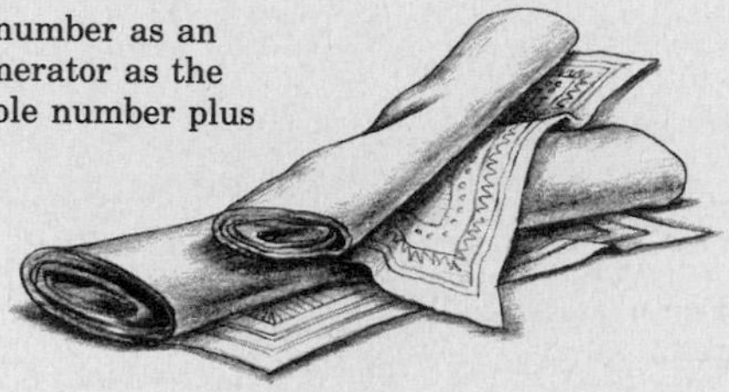

Getting Started

Multiply. Simplify if necessary.

1. $2\frac{1}{5} \times 3\frac{1}{2} = \underline{7\frac{7}{10}}$
2. $1\frac{1}{8} \times 3\frac{1}{9} = \underline{3\frac{1}{2}}$
3. $1\frac{1}{3} \times 2\frac{1}{2} = \underline{3\frac{1}{3}}$
4. $2\frac{3}{8} \times 1\frac{1}{3} = \underline{3\frac{1}{6}}$

Copy and multiply.

5. $1\frac{1}{6} \times 1\frac{1}{8}$ $1\frac{5}{16}$
6. $2\frac{1}{2} \times 3\frac{3}{4}$ $9\frac{3}{8}$
7. $5\frac{3}{7} \times 2\frac{1}{5}$ $11\frac{33}{35}$
8. $2\frac{1}{3} \times 1\frac{3}{5}$ $3\frac{11}{15}$
9. $3\frac{1}{3} \times 1\frac{7}{10}$ $5\frac{2}{3}$
10. $3\frac{2}{3} \times 4\frac{2}{12}$ $15\frac{5}{18}$

MCP All rights reserved

197

Teaching the Lesson

Introducing the Problem Read the problem aloud and have a student read the information sentences. Direct their attention to the problem worked in their texts. Explain that the first step is to rename each number as an improper fraction. Remind students that to change a mixed number to an improper fraction, they must multiply the whole number by the denominator, add the numerator, and put the sum over the original denominator. Write the improper fractions on the board and have students multiply numerators and denominators and simplify the answer. (¹⁵⁄₂ = 7½) Read the solution sentence aloud.

Developing the Skill Explain that multiplying two mixed numbers is as easy as multiplying a mixed number by a whole number or a fraction. Point out that they will change each mixed number to a fraction by multiplying the whole number part by the denominator, adding the numerator and putting the sum over the original denominator. Have students practice changing these mixed numbers to improper fractions: 4½ (⁹⁄₂), 5⅔ (¹⁷⁄₃), 7⅕ (³⁶⁄₅) and 10⅔ (³²⁄₃). Have students review reducing answers to simplest terms. Ask students to come to the board and reduce these: ⁴⁵⁄₃ (15), ³²⁄₅ (6⅖), ²⁰⁄₆ (3⅓) and ⁵⁷⁄₈ (7⅛).

197

Practice

Multiply. Simplify if necessary.

1. $2\frac{1}{3} \times 1\frac{1}{2} = $ ___ $3\frac{1}{2}$

2. $1\frac{1}{5} \times 1\frac{1}{6} = $ ___ $1\frac{2}{5}$

3. $4\frac{1}{2} \times 1\frac{5}{9} = $ ___ 7

4. $3\frac{1}{7} \times 1\frac{3}{11} = $ ___ 4

5. $7\frac{1}{2} \times 1\frac{3}{5} = $ ___ 12

6. $1\frac{1}{5} \times 1\frac{3}{4} = $ ___ $2\frac{1}{10}$

7. $4\frac{1}{3} \times 1\frac{1}{3} = $ ___ $5\frac{7}{9}$

8. $1\frac{4}{5} \times 3\frac{1}{3} = $ ___ 6

9. $1\frac{1}{3} \times 2\frac{1}{5} = $ ___ $2\frac{14}{15}$

10. $2\frac{1}{2} \times 2\frac{1}{2} = $ ___ $6\frac{1}{4}$

Copy and Do

11. $2\frac{1}{4} \times 2\frac{2}{5}$ $5\frac{2}{5}$ 12. $1\frac{3}{4} \times 1\frac{1}{7}$ 2 13. $2\frac{2}{5} \times 5\frac{5}{6}$ 14 14. $3\frac{2}{3} \times 2\frac{1}{4}$ $8\frac{1}{4}$

15. $2\frac{3}{4} \times 1\frac{5}{11}$ 4 16. $2\frac{1}{2} \times 2\frac{3}{4}$ $6\frac{7}{8}$ 17. $1\frac{1}{4} \times 3\frac{3}{5}$ $4\frac{1}{2}$ 18. $2\frac{4}{5} \times 1\frac{3}{7}$ 4

19. $4\frac{2}{3} \times 7\frac{1}{2}$ 35 20. $5\frac{5}{12} \times 4\frac{2}{5}$ $23\frac{5}{6}$ 21. $9\frac{1}{7} \times 2\frac{5}{8}$ 24 22. $15\frac{1}{3} \times 17\frac{1}{4}$
                                                                $264\frac{1}{2}$

Apply

Solve these problems.

23. A bottle of Fruity Grape Juice will fill $3\frac{1}{3}$ four-ounce glasses. How many four-ounce glasses will $1\frac{1}{2}$ bottles fill?
5 glasses

24. Elmer devotes more time to his studies than to his hobbies. He spent $3\frac{3}{4}$ hours on homework and $1\frac{3}{5}$ hours labeling his shell collection. How much longer did Elmer spend on homework?
$2\frac{3}{20}$ hours

Use the rectangle to answer problems 25 through 28.

25. Find the perimeter of the rectangle.
$10\frac{7}{10}$ yards

26. Find the area of the rectangle.
6 square yards

27. Rename the dimensions of the rectangle in feet.
$11\frac{1}{4}$ feet, $4\frac{4}{5}$ feet

28. It costs $1.25 per foot to buy molding for the walls. How much will it cost to buy molding for a room with the same dimensions as the rectangle?
$40.13

$1\frac{3}{5}$ yards

$3\frac{3}{4}$ yards

198

Correcting Common Errors

Students may have difficulty remembering all the steps in the proper order when they are multiplying mixed numbers. Give each student the following check list, like pilots use before they take off, and remind them to refer to it as they work problems.
- change whole numbers and mixed numbers to improper fractions.
- multiply the numerators.
- multiply the denominators.
- remove any common factors from the numerator and denominator of the product.
- If necessary, change the product from an improper fraction to a mixed number.

Enrichment

Demonstrate how to round a mixed number before multiplying:
$21\frac{3}{4} \times 15 = ?$
$22 \times 15 = 330$ but this is ($\frac{1}{4} \times 15$) or $\frac{15}{4}$ too much
$330 - \frac{15}{4} = 326\frac{1}{4}$
The product of $21\frac{3}{4}$ and 15 is $326\frac{1}{4}$. Have students round up and subtract to solve these:

1. $12\frac{7}{8} \times 35 = (450\frac{5}{8})$
2. $5\frac{5}{6} \times 24 = (140)$

Practice

Have students complete the page. Remind them to reduce answers to simplest terms.

Mixed Practice

1. $183 - 152\frac{5}{9}$ $\left(30\frac{4}{9}\right)$
2. $983,421 + 4,688$ $(988,109)$
3. $\left(7\frac{3}{8} - 1\frac{1}{4}\right) + 8\frac{2}{3}$ $\left(14\frac{19}{24}\right)$
4. 6.50×96 (624.00)
5. $9,783 - 647$ $(9,136)$
6. $\frac{5}{6} + \frac{1}{3} + \frac{4}{9}$ $\left(1\frac{11}{18}\right)$
7. 90×54.76 $(4,928.40)$
8. $24.32 \div 38$ $(.64)$
9. Simplify: $\frac{64}{7}$ $\left(9\frac{1}{7}\right)$
10. $53,721 \div 60$ $(895 \text{ R}21)$

Extra Credit   *Biography*

Through history, the field of mathematics has grown more complex, and it has become more important to organize and simplify information. In 1614, the Scottish mathematician, John Napier, discovered the logarithm to aid astronomers in their calculations. Logarithms are numbers, usually grouped in a table, that reduce complicated multiplication and division to simpler addition and subtraction problems. Napier simplified the finding of squared and cubed roots. He devised a multiplication table with movable parts, nicknamed Napier's Bones, because it consisted of long, ivory rods which were marked with numbers. Napier also influenced the introduction of decimal notation for fractions. For Napier, mathematics was only a hobby. A fervent Protestant, he devoted his life to taking part in religious controversies of the time.

198

Writing Reciprocals

pages 199-200

Objective

To find the reciprocal of a fraction or mixed number

Materials

Mental Math

Have students work the following problems:

1. $(2 \times 3) \times \frac{1}{2} = (3)$
2. $(1 \times 8) \times \frac{1}{4} = (2)$
3. $(3 \times 5) \times \frac{1}{3} = (5)$
4. $(4 \times 3) \times \frac{1}{2} = (6)$
5. $(5 \times 2) \times \frac{1}{5} = (2)$
6. $(3 \times 6) \times \frac{2}{3} = (12)$
7. $(5 \times 4) \times \frac{1}{2} = (10)$

Skill Review

Have students work these problems:

1. $\frac{2}{3} \times 1\frac{2}{3} = (\frac{10}{3} = 3\frac{1}{3})$
2. $1\frac{1}{5} \times \frac{5}{6} = (\frac{30}{30} = 1)$
3. $\frac{3}{4} \times \frac{2}{5} = (\frac{6}{20} = \frac{3}{10})$
4. $\frac{4}{5} \times 1\frac{1}{10} = (\frac{44}{50} = \frac{22}{25})$
5. $2\frac{1}{2} \times \frac{1}{10} = (\frac{5}{20} = \frac{1}{4})$
6. $\frac{1}{6} \times \times\frac{1}{7} = (\frac{1}{42})$
7. $\frac{5}{6} \times \frac{4}{7} = (\frac{20}{42} = \frac{10}{21})$

Writing Reciprocals

When the product of two fractions is 1, the fractions are called **reciprocals**. What are the reciprocals of $\frac{4}{5}$, of 7 and of $4\frac{1}{3}$?

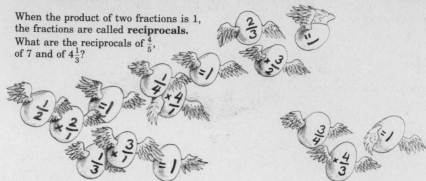

To find the reciprocal of a fraction, invert it, or exchange the positions of the numerator and denominator.

Fraction	Reciprocal	Check. Multiply the fraction and its reciprocal.
$\frac{4}{5}$	$\frac{5}{4}$ or $1\frac{1}{4}$	$\frac{4}{5} \times \frac{5}{4} = \frac{4 \times 5}{5 \times 4} = \frac{20}{20} = 1$

✔ To find the reciprocal of a whole or mixed number, first rename it as a fraction, then invert the fraction.

Number	Reciprocal	Check.
$7 = \frac{7}{1}$	$\frac{1}{7}$	$\frac{7}{1} \times \frac{1}{7} = \frac{7}{7} = 1$
$4\frac{1}{3} = \frac{13}{3}$	$\frac{3}{13}$	$\frac{13}{3} \times \frac{3}{13} = \frac{39}{39} = 1$

Getting Started

Write the reciprocal.

1. $\frac{3}{8}$ $\frac{8}{3}$ 2. $\frac{7}{3}$ $\frac{3}{7}$ 3. $1\frac{5}{6}$ $\frac{6}{11}$ 4. $8\frac{1}{8}$ 5. $2\frac{4}{5}$ $\frac{5}{14}$

Circle each pair of reciprocals.

6. $\left(\frac{4}{5}, 1\frac{1}{4}\right)$ 7. $\left(\frac{1}{12}, 12\right)$ 8. $2\frac{1}{3}, \frac{7}{3}$ 9. $\left(3\frac{1}{2}, \frac{2}{7}\right)$ 10. $\left(4\frac{3}{8}, \frac{8}{35}\right)$

MCP All rights reserved

199

Teaching the Lesson

Introducing the Problem Read the problem aloud. Explain that the definition of a reciprocal includes the operation of multiplication. Have students look at the first section of the problem worked in their texts. Write **⁴⁄₅** on the board. Write the reciprocal, **⁵⁄₄** next to the fraction. Explain that the reciprocal could be written as a mixed number, 1¼, but that you will use the improper fraction in this lesson. Multiply the fractions for the class (⁴⁄₅ × ⁵⁄₄ = ²⁰⁄₂₀) and show students that 20 twentieths is the same as one whole (1). Direct their attention to the next section in their texts. Explain that the reciprocal of a whole number can be written after the number, as an improper fraction. (7 = ⁷⁄₁, reciprocal = ¹⁄₇) Have a student write the improper fraction, the reciprocal and the product on the board. (⁷⁄₁ × ¹⁄₇ = ⁷⁄₇ = 1) Ask another student to change the number 4⅓ to an improper fraction, write its reciprocal and multiply the two. (¹³⁄₃, ³⁄₁₃, ³⁹⁄₃₉ = 1)

Developing the Skill Explain again the definition of a reciprocal: the number which when multiplied by the original will give 1. Have students give the reciprocals for these numbers: 2 (½); ½ (²⁄₁); ⅘ (⁵⁄₄); 1½ (⅔); ⅝ (⁸⁄₅); ⁴⁄₁ (¼); 2⅔ (³⁄₈) and 4⅕ (⁵⁄₂₁).

199

Practice

Write the reciprocal.

1. $\frac{3}{5}$ $\frac{5}{3}$ 2. $\frac{1}{9}$ $\frac{9}{1}$ 3. $4\frac{1}{4}$ 4. $1\frac{1}{2}$ $\frac{2}{3}$ 5. $3\frac{4}{5}$ $\frac{5}{19}$

6. $\frac{8}{7}$ $\frac{7}{8}$ 7. $5\frac{1}{3}$ $\frac{3}{16}$ 8. $\frac{2}{7}$ $\frac{7}{2}$ 9. $10\frac{1}{10}$ 10. $3\frac{5}{12}$ $\frac{12}{41}$

Circle each pair of reciprocals.

11. $\frac{3}{8}, \frac{8}{2}$ 12. $\boxed{\frac{3}{4}, \frac{4}{3}}$ 13. $\boxed{3\frac{1}{5}, \frac{5}{16}}$ 14. $6\frac{1}{2}, \frac{13}{2}$ 15. $\boxed{4\frac{1}{3}, \frac{3}{13}}$

16. $\boxed{2\frac{1}{4}, \frac{4}{9}}$ 17. $4\frac{3}{8}, \frac{35}{8}$ 18. $6\frac{2}{3}, \frac{6}{20}$ 19. $\boxed{9, \frac{1}{9}}$ 20. $7\frac{1}{2}, \frac{15}{2}$

21. $\frac{7}{5}, \frac{12}{7}$ 22. $\frac{7}{12}, 1\frac{5}{12}$ 23. $\frac{9}{10}, \frac{90}{100}$ 24. $\frac{5}{8}, 1\frac{3}{8}$ 25. $\boxed{\frac{4}{15}, 3\frac{3}{4}}$

EXCURSION

The **Fundamental Theorem of Counting** can help us determine the total number of ways a problem can be solved. The theorem states we must first determine what steps are necessary to solve the problem. Then multiply the number of choices in each step.

For example: How many 3-digit area codes are possible if no code starts with zero?

Step 1: How many different digits can be used in the first place? __9__

Step 2: How many can be used in the second place? __10__

Step 3: How many can be used in the third place? __10__

Then we multiply: __9__ × __10__ × __10__ = __900__

We can form __900__ different 3-digit area codes.

Apply the Fundamental Theorem to solve these problems.

1. How many license plates are possible if each one has three numbers and three letters of the alphabet?
   17,576,000 license plates

2. How many ways can you choose a president, vice-president and secretary from a class of 25 fifth graders? (No person can hold more than one office at a time.)
   13,800 ways

3. An auto dealer offers 15 exterior colors, 10 interior fabrics and 12 accessory packages on its latest model luxury car. How many different combinations are possible for the customer to choose from?
   1,800 combinations

200

Correcting Common Errors

When writing the reciprocal of a mixed number, students may write only the reciprocal of the fraction part. Remind them to change the mixed number to an improper fraction before they attempt to write the reciprocal. They can check their work by multiplying the original number times its reciprocal to see if they get 1 as the product.

Enrichment

Have students identify the number n:

1. $\frac{2}{n} \times \frac{n}{2} = \frac{6}{6} = 1$ ($n = 3$)
2. $\frac{5}{n} \times \frac{n}{5} = \frac{35}{35} = 1$ ($n = 7$)
3. $\frac{n}{8} \times \frac{8}{n} = \frac{80}{80} = 1$ ($n = 10$)

Practice

Have students complete the problems on the page. Explain that mixed numbers must be changed to improper fractions before their reciprocals can be determined.

Excursion

Emphasize that it is first necessary to determine the STEPS and how many ways to do each one. In number 2, since no person can hold more than one office, this is equivalent to drawing without replacement. So on the second draw, there is one less person available.

Extra Credit *Logic*

Duplicate for students to complete the analogies. Have them first note the example.

Examples: 12 is to 4 as 21 is to 7.
           6 is to 66 as 2 is to 22.

1. 2, 4 is to 6, 8 as 39, 41 is to ____ , ____ (43, 45)
2. 5 is to 125 as ____ is to 729. (9)
3. An addend is to a sum as a factor is to a ____ . (product)
4. ¾ is to ²²⁵/₃₀₀ as ____ is to ¹⁶⁰/₂₄₀. (⅔)
5. ⅞ is to .875 as ¹⁴/₃₂ is to ____. (.4375)
6. 12 is to 144 as a dozen is to a ____. (gross)
7. ¼ is to 2 as ⅛ is to ____. (1)
8. ⅓ is to ⅑ as ½ is to ____. (¼)
9. 100 is to 10,000 as 15 is to ____. (225)
10. 1, 2, 3, 4, 6, 12 are to 12 as 1, 2, 3, 6 and 18 are to ____ (18)

Dividing Fractions

pages 201-202

Objective

To divide two fractions or a mixed number

Materials

Mental Math

Have students multiply:

1. $4 \times 7 = (28)$
2. $\frac{1}{4} \times \frac{1}{2} = (\frac{1}{8})$
3. $8 \times 10 = (80)$
4. $52 \times 0 = (0)$
5. $\frac{2}{3} \times 1 = (\frac{2}{3})$
6. $\frac{2}{5} \times \frac{3}{1} = (\frac{6}{5} = 1\frac{1}{5})$
7. $\frac{1}{2} \times \frac{2}{1} = (\frac{2}{2} = 1)$

Skill Review

Have students work problems on the board:

1. $\frac{2}{3} \times 9 = (6)$
2. $3\frac{1}{3} \times 5 = (\frac{50}{3} = 16\frac{2}{3})$
3. $4\frac{1}{2} \times 8\frac{1}{2} = (\frac{153}{4} = 38\frac{1}{4})$
4. $\frac{1}{4} \times 8 = (2)$
5. $5\frac{1}{4} \times 2 = (\frac{21}{2} = 10\frac{1}{2})$
6. $1\frac{5}{6} \times \frac{3}{8} = (\frac{11}{16})$
7. $\frac{1}{5} \times 5 = (1)$

Dividing Fractions

Eve is serving fruit punch at the school graduation party. Each glass holds $\frac{2}{3}$ of a pint of liquid. Eve is anxious to empty her punch bowl so that she can join the fun. How many full glasses must she pour?

We want to know how many full glasses Eve must serve to empty her punch bowl.

We know there are __8__ pints of fruit punch and each glass will hold __$\frac{2}{3}$__ of a pint.

To find how many glasses of fruit punch Eve must serve, we divide the total pints of fruit punch by the capacity of one glass.

We divide __8__ by __$\frac{2}{3}$__.

✔ To divide when either the dividend or divisor is a fraction, multiply by the reciprocal of the divisor.

$8 \div \frac{2}{3}$ is the same as $8 \times \frac{3}{2} = \frac{24}{2} = 12$.

We can use a picture to help us understand this.

We have divided 8 by $\frac{2}{3}$. What is the number of $\frac{2}{3}$'s in 8? __12__

Eve should pour __12__ glasses of punch.

✔ Remember, whole numbers can be renamed as fractions.

$$\frac{5}{6} \div 30 = \frac{5}{6} \div \frac{30}{1} = \frac{5}{6} \times \frac{1}{30} = \frac{5}{180} = \frac{1}{36}$$

Getting Started

Complete each division problem. Simplify if necessary.

1. $\frac{3}{4} \div \frac{1}{2} = \frac{3}{4} \times \frac{2}{1} = \underline{1\frac{1}{2}}$

2. $\frac{5}{8} \div \frac{3}{8} = \frac{5}{8} \times \frac{8}{3} = \underline{1\frac{2}{3}}$

Divide. Simplify if necessary.

3. $\frac{3}{7} \div \frac{5}{8}$ $\frac{24}{35}$

4. $\frac{5}{8} \div 10$ $\frac{1}{16}$

Copy and divide.

5. $10 \div \frac{1}{2}$ 20

6. $\frac{2}{3} \div \frac{1}{4}$ $2\frac{2}{3}$

MCP All rights reserved

201

Teaching the Lesson

Introducing the Problem Have students read the problem aloud and then read the information sentences. Read the sample problem, pointing out that to divide a number by a fraction, students will multiply by the reciprocal of the divisor. Put the following on the board: $8 \div \frac{2}{3} = \frac{8}{1} \times \frac{3}{2} = \frac{24}{2} = 12$. Direct their attention to the picture in their texts. Have them count the number of two thirds in 8 wholes. (12)

Developing the Skill The concept of reciprocals and division of fractions is very difficult. Remind students of the reciprocal nature of multiplication and division: if $18 \div 3 = 6$ then $6 \times 3 = 18$. Explain that if $1 \div \frac{1}{2} = 2$, then $1 = \frac{1}{2} \times 2$; if $1 \div \frac{2}{3} = \frac{3}{2}$ and $1 = \frac{2}{3} \times \frac{3}{2}$. These fraction pairs, $\frac{1}{2}$ and $\frac{2}{1}$, $\frac{2}{3}$ and $\frac{3}{2}$, are reciprocals. Write on the board: $3 \div \frac{1}{4} = (3 \times 1) \div \frac{1}{4} = 3 \times (1 \div \frac{1}{4})$. Explain that you have used the associative property of multiplication to regroup terms. Now write $= 3 \times \frac{4}{1} = 12$. Show students that you substituted $\frac{4}{1}$ for the expression $(1 \div \frac{1}{4})$, just as above you showed that $1 \div \frac{1}{2} = \frac{2}{1}$. Explain again that to divide a number by a fraction, students will multiply the number by the fraction's reciprocal. Have a student work this problem on the board: $9 \div \frac{3}{4} = 9 \times (1 \div \frac{3}{4}) = 9 \times \frac{4}{3} = \frac{36}{3} = 12$.

201

Practice

Complete each division problem. Simplify if necessary.

1. $\frac{2}{7} \div \frac{5}{6} = \frac{2}{7} \times \frac{6}{5} = \underline{\frac{12}{35}}$

2. $\frac{5}{8} \div \frac{5}{6} = \frac{5}{8} \times \frac{6}{5} = \underline{\frac{3}{4}}$

3. $\frac{2}{3} \div 12 = \frac{2}{3} \times \frac{1}{12} = \underline{\frac{1}{18}}$

4. $\frac{5}{6} \div \frac{5}{6} = \frac{5}{6} \times \frac{6}{5} = \underline{1}$

5. $\frac{2}{3} \div \frac{5}{6} = \frac{2}{3} \times \frac{6}{5} = \underline{\frac{4}{5}}$

6. $15 \div \frac{3}{5} = 15 \times \frac{5}{3} = \underline{25}$

Divide. Simplify if necessary.

7. $9 \div \frac{9}{10}$ 10

8. $\frac{2}{3} \div \frac{2}{5}$ $1\frac{2}{3}$

9. $\frac{1}{2} \div \frac{2}{3}$ $\frac{3}{4}$

10. $\frac{3}{4} \div 8$ $\frac{3}{32}$

11. $\frac{5}{8} \div \frac{1}{4}$ $2\frac{1}{2}$

12. $\frac{3}{11} \div \frac{6}{7}$ $\frac{7}{22}$

13. $\frac{5}{9} \div \frac{2}{3}$ $\frac{5}{6}$

14. $15 \div \frac{3}{4}$ 20

Copy and Do

15. $\frac{4}{5} \div \frac{3}{10}$ $2\frac{2}{3}$

16. $\frac{5}{8} \div 15$ $\frac{1}{24}$

17. $12 \div \frac{2}{3}$ 18

18. $\frac{1}{8} \div \frac{1}{4}$ $\frac{1}{2}$

19. $\frac{1}{4} \div \frac{1}{8}$ 2

20. $\frac{5}{6} \div \frac{5}{9}$ $1\frac{1}{2}$

21. $\frac{4}{7} \div \frac{5}{14}$ $1\frac{3}{5}$

22. $\frac{7}{12} \div \frac{1}{6}$ $3\frac{1}{2}$

23. $16 \div \frac{4}{5}$ 20

24. $\frac{5}{10} \div \frac{2}{3}$ $\frac{3}{4}$

25. $18 \div \frac{5}{6}$ $21\frac{3}{5}$

26. $\frac{7}{9} \div \frac{14}{15}$ $\frac{5}{6}$

Apply

Solve these problems. Draw a picture to help you if necessary.

27. Mei Ling has just received unexpected guests and has only $\frac{3}{4}$ of a pound of nuts for 4 people. What part of a pound will that be for each person?
$\frac{3}{16}$ of a pound

28. Alan walks for exercise, at the rate of $\frac{2}{3}$ of a mile each 15 minutes. How far can Alan walk in 1 hour?
$2\frac{2}{3}$ miles

29. A bag of dinner rolls contains 6 rolls and weighs $\frac{2}{3}$ pounds. What is the weight of 1 roll in pounds?
$\frac{1}{9}$ of a pound

30. The cafeteria is offering applesauce as an extra dessert today. They have 48 cups of applesauce. Each serving is $\frac{2}{3}$ of a cup. How many servings can be made?
72 servings

202

Correcting Common Errors

When doing a division problem, students may forget to write the reciprocal of the divisor when they multiply. As they work each problem, have them first circle the divisor to remind themselves that they must write its reciprocal before computing.

Enrichment

Explain that as in multiplication, students can reduce the fractions they are dividing by removing common factors from the numerator and denominator. Put this example on the board:

$\frac{2}{3} \div \frac{1}{3} = \frac{2}{3} \div \frac{1}{3} = \frac{2}{1} \times \frac{1}{1} = \frac{2}{1} = 2$

Have students remove any common factors before multiplying:

1. $\frac{4}{7} \div \frac{2}{7} =$ (2)
2. $\frac{4}{5} \div \frac{8}{5} =$ ($\frac{1}{2}$)
3. $\frac{5}{9} \div \frac{7}{9} =$ ($\frac{5}{7}$)

Practice

Have students complete the problems. Put these examples of reciprocals on the board:

The reciprocal of ½ is 2.
The reciprocal of 3 is ⅓.
The reciprocal of ¾ is ⁴⁄₃.

Remind students that to divide by a fraction, they will multiply by the reciprocal of the divisor.

Extra Credit *Estimation*

Provide students with a pan balance and a small container of each of the following: salt, rice, sand, mineral oil, water and sand. Give the students a duplicated copy of the instructions and chart given below.

Instructions:

1. Estimate the order from heaviest to lightest of each of the small containers. Using the numerals 1-6 record the results on the chart given.
2. Estimate the mass or weight of each of the items in grams. Record the results.
3. Measure the mass or weight of each of the items. Remember to subtract the weight of each container. Record the results.

Item	Estimated Order	Estimated Mass in grams	Actual Mass in grams
Salt			
Rice			

Dividing Mixed Numbers

pages 203-204

Objective

To divide one mixed number by another

Materials

Mental Math

Have students subtract:

1. $1.50 − $0.25 = ($1.25)
2. $.75 − $0.50 = ($.25)
3. $10.00 − $5.00 = ($5.00)
4. $7.00 − $3.50 = ($3.50)
5. $2.50 − $1.25 = ($1.25)
6. $5.00 − $2.75 = ($2.25)
7. $4.25 − $1.75 = ($2.50)

Skill Review

Have students work these problems on paper. Remind them that when they divide by a fraction, they multiply by the reciprocal.

1. $4 \div \frac{2}{3} = (6)$
2. $7 \div \frac{1}{2} = (14)$
3. $10 \div \frac{2}{5} = (25)$
4. $13 \div \frac{3}{4} = (17\frac{1}{3})$
5. $5 \div \frac{7}{8} = (5\frac{5}{7})$
6. $\frac{1}{2} \div \frac{3}{4} = (\frac{2}{3})$
7. $\frac{3}{5} \div \frac{4}{5} = (\frac{3}{4})$

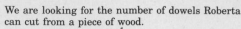

Dividing Mixed Numbers

Roberta is preparing miniature cornhusk dolls for the school craft show. She is using small wooden dowels to make the arms. Each one measures $1\frac{1}{8}$ inches in length. How many dowels can she cut from a piece of wood $5\frac{1}{4}$ inches long?

We are looking for the number of dowels Roberta can cut from a piece of wood.

We know the wood is $\underline{5\frac{1}{4}}$ inches long.

She needs to cut dowels that are $\underline{1\frac{1}{8}}$ inches long. To find the possible number of dowels that can be cut, we divide the length of the wood by the length of one dowel.

We divide $\underline{5\frac{1}{4}}$ by $\underline{1\frac{1}{8}}$.

Rename the mixed numbers as fractions.	Multiply the dividend by the reciprocal of the divisor. Simplify.	Check. Multiply the divisor by the quotient.
$5\frac{1}{4} \div 1\frac{1}{8}$ $\frac{21}{4} \div \frac{9}{8}$	$\frac{21}{4} \times \frac{8}{9} = \frac{168}{36} = 4\frac{24}{36} = 4\frac{2}{3}$	$1\frac{1}{8} \times 4\frac{2}{3}$ $\frac{9}{8} \times \frac{14}{3} = \frac{126}{24} = 5\frac{1}{4}$ ↑ dividend

Roberta will cut $\underline{4}$ dowels $1\frac{1}{8}$ inches long.

She will have $\underline{\frac{2}{3}}$ of a dowel left over.

✔ Remember, whole numbers can be renamed as fractions.

$$7 \div 2\frac{1}{4} = \frac{7}{1} \times \frac{4}{9} = \frac{28}{9} = 3\frac{1}{9} \quad \text{or} \quad 3\frac{4}{10} \div 2 = \frac{34}{10} \times \frac{1}{2} = \frac{34}{20} = 1\frac{7}{10}$$

Getting Started

Divide and check.

1. $\frac{5}{9} \div 1\frac{1}{2}$ $\frac{10}{27}$ 2. $2\frac{1}{3} \div \frac{3}{5}$ $3\frac{8}{9}$

Copy and divide.

3. $2\frac{1}{5} \div 1\frac{1}{3}$ $1\frac{13}{20}$ 4. $3 \div 4\frac{1}{5}$ $\frac{5}{7}$ 5. $6\frac{5}{8} \div 4$ $1\frac{21}{32}$ 6. $10\frac{6}{9} \div 3\frac{1}{3}$ $3\frac{1}{5}$

MCP All rights reserved

203

Teaching the Lesson

Introducing the Problem Read the problem aloud and ask a student to read the information sentences. Have the class look at the problem worked in their texts. Show that each mixed number must be renamed as an improper fraction. (²¹/₄, ⁹/₈) Remind them that to divide ²¹/₄ by ⁹/₈, they will multiply by the reciprocal. (²¹/₄ × ⁸/₉) Have one student come to the board and do the multiplication. (¹⁶⁸/₃₆) Ask another to rename it as a mixed number and simplify. (4²/₃) Show students that this problem can be checked, multiplying divisor by quotient, to give the dividend. (⁹/₈ × ¹⁴/₃ = ¹²⁶/₂₄ = 5¹/₄) Have a student read and interpret the solution sentences. (will cut 4 dowels, will have ¹/₃ of an inch left over) Remind students that whole numbers, like mixed numbers, can be renamed as fractions.

Developing the Skill Review the reason that dividing by a fraction is the same as multiplying by the fraction's reciprocal. Put this problem on the board: ⁴/₃ ÷ ¹/₂. Rewrite this: ⁴/₃ × (1 ÷ ¹/₂). Show the class that 1 ÷ ¹/₂ = ²/₁ and rewrite again: ⁴/₃ × ²/₁. Have a student do the multiplication on the board. (⁸/₃ = 2²/₃) Ask another student to check the problem, multiplying divisor (¹/₂) by quotient (⁸/₃), to get the dividend. (⁸/₆ = ⁴/₃)

203

Practice

Divide and check.

1. $7 \div 2\frac{1}{3}$ 3
2. $1\frac{5}{8} \div 13$ $\frac{1}{8}$
3. $9 \div 1\frac{4}{5}$ 5
4. $6 \div 1\frac{2}{3}$ $3\frac{3}{5}$
5. $2\frac{3}{4} \div 1\frac{1}{8}$ $2\frac{4}{9}$
6. $4\frac{1}{5} \div 2\frac{3}{5}$ $1\frac{8}{13}$
7. $2\frac{5}{8} \div 5\frac{1}{4}$ $\frac{1}{2}$
8. $1\frac{1}{7} \div 1\frac{1}{3}$ $\frac{6}{7}$
9. $5\frac{1}{3} \div \frac{8}{9}$ 6
10. $7 \div 1\frac{3}{4}$ 4
11. $4\frac{1}{2} \div 2\frac{7}{10}$ $1\frac{2}{3}$
12. $3\frac{1}{5} \div 3\frac{1}{10}$ $1\frac{1}{31}$
13. $6\frac{2}{3} \div 5$ $1\frac{1}{3}$
14. $9 \div 3\frac{2}{3}$ $2\frac{5}{11}$
15. $5\frac{1}{4} \div 2\frac{1}{3}$ $2\frac{1}{4}$
16. $4\frac{1}{8} \div 2\frac{1}{4}$ $1\frac{5}{6}$
17. $8\frac{1}{3} \div 6\frac{1}{2}$ $1\frac{11}{39}$
18. $7\frac{1}{5} \div 3\frac{3}{4}$ $1\frac{23}{25}$

Copy and Do

19. $12 \div 2\frac{2}{3}$ $4\frac{1}{2}$
20. $1\frac{3}{4} \div 2\frac{1}{2}$ $\frac{7}{10}$
21. $5\frac{1}{2} \div 9$ $\frac{11}{18}$
22. $4\frac{1}{8} \div 1\frac{4}{7}$ $2\frac{5}{8}$
23. $1\frac{3}{5} \div 1\frac{1}{15}$ $1\frac{1}{2}$
24. $3\frac{2}{3} \div 2\frac{1}{6}$ $1\frac{9}{13}$
25. $1\frac{3}{16} \div 1\frac{1}{2}$ $\frac{19}{24}$
26. $1\frac{3}{4} \div 2\frac{5}{6}$ $\frac{21}{34}$
27. $21 \div 3\frac{1}{2}$ 6
28. $\frac{9}{10} \div 2\frac{2}{5}$ $\frac{3}{8}$
29. $1\frac{5}{9} \div 1\frac{3}{4}$ $\frac{8}{9}$
30. $2\frac{2}{5} \div 1\frac{1}{3}$ $1\frac{4}{5}$

Apply

Solve these problems.

31. Naomi's favorite blouse pattern requires $1\frac{2}{3}$ yards of material. How many blouses can she make from 10 yards?
6 blouses

32. It took Mr. and Mrs. Williams $4\frac{1}{2}$ hours to drive their son to camp. They took turns driving. If Mr. Williams drove $1\frac{1}{2}$ hours, what part of the way did Mr. Williams drive?
$\frac{1}{3}$

33. After avoiding sweets and exercising regularly, Jerry lost $7\frac{1}{5}$ pounds in 6 weeks. What was Jerry's average weekly loss?
$1\frac{1}{5}$ pounds

34. Mr. and Mrs. Brightwater are planning to build a patio sidewalk using a single row of $\frac{2}{3}$ of a foot square blocks. How many blocks will be needed to build a walk $10\frac{2}{3}$ feet long?
16 blocks

204

Correcting Common Errors

Once students have written the mixed numbers as improper fractions and written the reciprocal of the divisor, they may treat the problem as if it were addition and find a common denominator before multiplying. Discuss with them how this is an unnecessary step making the process more complicated than it need be.

Enrichment

Show students a shortcut to divide a number by a mixed number ending in ½. Use the example 9 ÷ 2½. Tell them to multiply dividend and divisor by 2, and then divide: 18 ÷ 5 = 3⅗. This works because dividend and divisor are in the same ratio when doubled as they were before, so the quotient remains the same. Have students work these using the shortcut.

1. 14 ÷ 4½ (28 ÷ 9 = 3⅑)
2. 20 ÷ 5½ (40 ÷ 11 = 3⁷⁄₁₁)
3. 21 ÷ 3½ (42 ÷ 7 = 6)

Practice

Have students complete all the problems. Remind them to reduce all answers to simplest terms and to check their work by multiplying.

Extra Credit   *Sets*

Duplicate the following:

Your ship is sinking! The five lifeboats on board will carry 10 passengers each. The first mate says, "We have 67 people on board! 17 of us will die!" You look at his list and see that some people are counted more than once. But can the lifeboats save everyone?

Make a Venn Diagram, to show the following information: All persons on board are either passengers, crew members or members of a guest band. There are 26 passengers, 21 crew members and 20 in the band. However, 4 crew members are on leave as passengers who are playing in the band. Two of the passengers are also vacationing crew members. Five of the passengers and 3 of the crew have also joined the band. What was the fate of the people aboard the sinking ship? (There are a total of 49 people, so all will survive.)

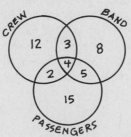

204

Review Fractions

pages 205-206

Objective

To review all basic operations with fractions

Materials

Mental Math

Have students find:

1. ½ of 24 (12)
2. ⅓ of 12 (4)
3. ⅕ of 50 (10)
4. ⅓ of 36 (12)
5. ½ of 100 (50)
6. ⅙ of 6 (1)
7. ⅐ of 14 (2)

Skill Review

Review the four basic operations by having students complete these problems on the board:

1. ½ + 2¾ = (3¼)
2. ⅔ + ⅗ = (1⁴⁄₁₅)
3. 6¼ − 2⅓ = (3¹¹⁄₁₂)
4. 3½ − 1¾ = (1¾)
5. 3⅔ × 1¼ = (4⁷⁄₁₂)
6. ⁵⁄₉ × 6 = (3⅓)
7. 5¼ ÷ 5⅓ = (⁶³⁄₆₄)
8. 10 ÷ 3½ = (2⁶⁄₇)

Reviewing Fraction Operations

Clay participated in Midview City's annual triathlon. He ran $\frac{2}{15}$ of the way and biked $\frac{5}{6}$ of it, but still had enough strength to complete the swimming portion of the event. How many miles did Clay swim?

MIDVIEW CITY ANNUAL 140 MILE TRIATHLON

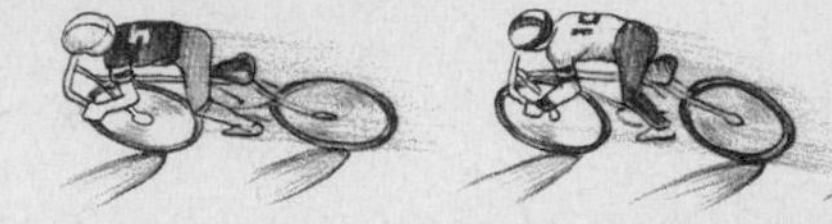

We need to find how many miles Clay swam.

The triathlon is __140__ miles long.

Clay ran __$\frac{2}{15}$__ of the way and biked __$\frac{5}{6}$__ of the way.

One way to find the miles he swam is to add the fractions and subtract from 1.

Then multiply this fraction by the total miles in the triathlon.

We add __$\frac{2}{15}$__ and __$\frac{5}{6}$__. We subtract this sum from __1__.

We multiply this fraction by __140__.

Add the fractions.	Subtract the sum from 1.	Multiply the fraction by 140.
$\frac{2}{15} = \frac{4}{30}$ $+ \frac{5}{6} = \frac{25}{30}$ $\frac{29}{30}$	$1 = \frac{30}{30}$ $- \frac{29}{30} = \frac{29}{30}$ $\frac{1}{30}$	$\frac{1}{30} \times 140 = \frac{140}{30} = 4\frac{2}{3}$

Clay swam __$4\frac{2}{3}$__ miles.

Getting Started

Solve.

1. $3\frac{1}{2} + 4\frac{2}{3} =$ __$8\frac{1}{6}$__
2. $5\frac{2}{3} - 1\frac{3}{4} =$ __$3\frac{11}{12}$__
3. $7\frac{1}{2} \times 3\frac{1}{3} =$ __25__
4. $6\frac{4}{5} \div 1\frac{3}{10} =$ __$5\frac{3}{13}$__

Copy and do.

5. $6\frac{1}{7} + 4\frac{1}{3}$ $10\frac{10}{21}$
6. $9\frac{3}{7} - 1\frac{1}{3}$ $8\frac{2}{21}$
7. $2\frac{3}{5} \times \frac{4}{6}$ $1\frac{11}{15}$
8. $2\frac{5}{8} \div \frac{1}{2}$ $5\frac{1}{4}$

MCP All rights reserved

205

Teaching the Lesson

Introducing the Problem Read the problem aloud and have a student read the information sentences. Read the plan sentences. Point out that when they know the fraction of the distance Clay swam, students can figure out the number of miles by multiplying the fraction by the total distance. (140) Ask students to look at the steps in their texts and work through each step with them. Have a student read the solution sentence. (swam 4⅔ mi)

Developing the Skill

Review the steps involved in the basic operations. Remind students to find a common denominator before they add. The least common denominator is often the product of the given denominators. In subtraction, they will also find a common denominator before subtracting, but they may have to rename one in the minuend as a fraction and add it to the fractional part of the minuend first. In multiplication, students will change any mixed numbers to improper fractions before they multiply. In division, they will not only change mixed numbers to improper fractions, but also change the operation to multiplication as they invert the divisor. In each type of problem, the answer is reduced to simplest terms.

Practice

Solve.

1. $1\frac{2}{3} \times 1\frac{4}{5} = $ ___3___
2. $3\frac{1}{8} + 2\frac{1}{3} = $ $5\frac{11}{24}$
3. $3\frac{1}{5} \div 2\frac{1}{2} = $ $1\frac{7}{25}$
4. $9\frac{1}{3} - 6\frac{3}{4} = $ $2\frac{7}{12}$

Copy and Do

5. $10 - \frac{2}{3}$ $9\frac{1}{3}$
6. $3\frac{2}{3} \times 12$ 44
7. $9\frac{1}{4} + 8\frac{3}{4}$ 18
8. $4\frac{1}{2} \times \frac{2}{9}$ 1

9. $1\frac{1}{2} \div 1\frac{1}{8}$ $1\frac{1}{3}$
10. $15\frac{1}{2} - 12\frac{3}{5}$ $2\frac{9}{10}$
11. $2\frac{1}{7} \div \frac{5}{6}$ $2\frac{4}{7}$
12. $7\frac{5}{12} + 6\frac{3}{8}$ $13\frac{19}{24}$

13. $4\frac{5}{16} + 3\frac{1}{2}$ $7\frac{13}{16}$
14. $3\frac{1}{5} \times 6\frac{1}{4}$ 20
15. $5\frac{5}{6} \div 1\frac{1}{4}$ $4\frac{2}{3}$
16. $9\frac{1}{7} - 8\frac{2}{3}$ $\frac{10}{21}$

Apply

Use the rectangle to answer problems 17 through 19.

17. Find the perimeter.
$11\frac{7}{15}$ yards
18. Find the area. 8 square yards

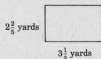

19. Carpeting costs $15.50 per square yard. What will it cost to carpet a room with the dimensions of the rectangle?
$124

$2\frac{2}{5}$ yards

$3\frac{1}{3}$ yards

Use the graph of Mr. Bate's budget to answer problems 20 through 22.

20. What fraction represents OTHER?
$\frac{1}{4}$
21. What fractional part more does Mr. Bate spend on rent than food?
$\frac{1}{12}$
22. Mr. Bate earns $1,320 each month. How much does he spend on travel?
$220

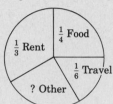

Use the recipe for trail mix to answer problems 23 through 25.

23. Penny has 9 cups of raisins. How many servings of trail mix can Penny make?
12 servings
24. How many total cups of raisins and nuts are needed for 2 servings of trail mix?
$2\frac{7}{10}$ cups
25. How many cups of wheat squares are needed for $2\frac{1}{4}$ servings? $3\frac{3}{4}$ cups

TRAIL MIX—1 serving
$1\frac{2}{3}$ cups wheat squares
$\frac{3}{4}$ cup raisins
$\frac{3}{5}$ cup nuts

206

Correcting Common Errors

Students may confuse the procedures for the basic operations with fractions when working with a mixed set of exercises. Have them work with partners, circling all the addition problems in a set. They discuss and use the proper procedure for all the addition problems, crossing off each one as they work it. Then they follow this same procedure for all the subtraction problems, then all the multiplication problems, and finally all the division problems.

Enrichment

Have students halve each ingredient in this recipe for oatmeal raisin cookies:

1 c flour (½ c)
½ t soda (¼ t)
½ t salt (¼ t)
1 t cinnamon (½ t)
½ c shortening (¼ c)
½ c brown sugar (¼ c)
¼ c sugar (⅛ c)
1 egg (½ or usually the whole)
2 T milk (1 T)
2 c oatmeal (1 c)
¾ c raisins (⅜ c)

To make the recipe for the class, multiply amounts by 2½ and bake at 350° for 10 to 12 minutes.

Practice

Have students complete the problems on the page. Remind them to check the operational sign in each problem.

Mixed Practice

1. $\frac{3}{5} + \frac{7}{10} + \frac{1}{2}$ $\left(1\frac{4}{5}\right)$
2. $80,962 - 21,448$ $(59,514)$
3. $15 \div \frac{3}{5}$ (25)
4. $\frac{5}{9} = \frac{}{45}$ (25)
5. $18 - 11\frac{3}{8}$ $\left(6\frac{5}{8}\right)$
6. $$7.82 \times 56$ $($437.92)$
7. $\frac{6}{7} \times \frac{2}{15}$ $\left(\frac{4}{35}\right)$
8. $3,733 \div 57$ $(65 \text{ R}28)$
9. $92,187 + 48,098$ $(140,285)$
10. $2\frac{2}{5} \times 4\frac{1}{8}$ $\left(9\frac{9}{10}\right)$

Extra Credit *Sets*

Duplicate the following:

You have been given the honor of representing Earth at the Galactic Peace Conference. You know that you will be meeting with the delegates from the three most powerful groups in the Milky Way: the 47 members of the Denebian Empire, the 56 members from the Polaris Pact and the 57 members of the Federation of Unified Planets.

As you arrive, you find that war is about to begin because there are only 110 seats available in the meeting room and there seem to be 160 delegates. Using the following data, can you resolve the conflict? Try making a Venn Diagram.

10 planets are members of both the Denebian Empire and the Polaris Pact. 17 planets belong to both the Polaris Pact and the Federation. 11 planets are joined with both the Federation and the Empire. 7 planets belong to all three groups. (All 108 delegates will be peacefully seated.)

Problem Solving Using a Formula

pages 207-208

Objective

To solve problems by using a formula

Materials

Mental Math

Have students identify n:

1. $\frac{24}{4} = \frac{n}{1}$ (6)
2. $3\frac{1}{2} = \frac{n}{2}$ (7)
3. $n\frac{2}{3} = \frac{32}{3}$ (10)
4. $\frac{21}{n} = 7$ (3)
5. $5\frac{n}{4} = \frac{21}{4}$ (1)
6. $\frac{3}{3} = \frac{7}{n}$ (7)
7. $\frac{15}{3} = \frac{30}{n}$ (6)

Using a Formula, Writing an Open Sentence

A plane flight from New York to Miami takes 4 hours. If the total distance in the air is 2,140 miles, what is the average speed of the plane?

★ SEE

We want to know the rate of speed of the plane.

The flight from New York to Miami takes __4__ hours.

The distance the plane travels is __2,140__.

We can use the formula for finding distance to help us solve this problem.
The formula is: **Rate × Time = Distance**

The TIME of the trip is __4__.

The DISTANCE the plane travels is __2,140__ miles.

★ PLAN

We can use this information and a formula, to write an **open sentence.** We need to fill in the numbers we know.

$$\text{Rate} \times \text{Time} = \text{Distance}$$

$$\underline{\quad ? \quad} \times 4 = 2{,}140$$

Since we are missing a factor in this problem, we need to divide to find the rate. **Distance ÷ Time = Rate**

★ DO

$$
\begin{array}{r}
535 \\
4\overline{)2{,}140} \\
\underline{20} \\
14 \\
\underline{12} \\
20 \\
\underline{20} \\
\end{array}
$$

The rate the plane travels is __535__ miles per hour.

★ CHECK

We can check our work by using the original formula.

$$\text{Rate} \times \text{Time} = \text{Distance}$$

$$535 \times 4 = \underline{2{,}140}$$

MCP All rights reserved

207

Teaching the Lesson

Read the problem aloud. Remind students that the strategy for solving problems involves four steps: SEE, PLAN, DO, CHECK. Ask one student to read the SEE section of the text. Explain that the rule relating rate, time and distance is expressed: **Rate × Time = Distance.** This is called a formula. (Some students will also see that: Rate = Time ÷ Distance) Have a student read the PLAN section of the text. Show the class that of the elements in the formula, they know rate and distance. Write the open sentence on the board, explaining that it is open because there is one piece of information missing, the Rate. (__ × 4 = 2,140) Ask a student to explain how the rate can be calculated. (divide distance by time) Have another do the calculation on the board while others follow in the DO section in their books. (535 miles per hour) Show them they can check their work by inserting the rate in the formula to see if it works. (535 × 4 = 2,140)

Explain that many problems can be solved by finding the formula that relates the elements of the problem, writing an open sentence that incorporates the elements already known and then solving for the unknown value.

207

Apply

Use a formula or open sentence to help solve these problems.

1. The first successful gas-powered car was a three-wheeler, built in 1886 by Carl Benz. If the car could travel 54 miles in six hours, how fast was the car traveling?
   9 miles per hour

2. Miss Prentiss won a bicycle race by traveling 168 miles in 8 hours. What was Miss Prentiss' average speed?
   21 miles per hour

3. The Queen Ann ocean liner travels at an average rate of 32 miles per hour. How far would the Queen Ann travel in a 24-hour day?
   768 miles

4. A train travels at an average rate of 80 miles per hour. How long would it take the train to travel between two cities that are 560 miles apart?
   Hint: Distance ÷ Rate = Time.
   7 hours

5. Miss Muffet's pet spider can travel at an average rate of 55 yards per hour. How many hours would it take the spider to travel 495 yards?
   9 hours

6. The first flight across the Atlantic Ocean took 33 hours and covered a distance of 3,610 miles. What was the plane's approximate rate of speed?
   Between 109 and 110 miles per hour

7. Superwoman can circle the earth five times in a one-hour period. If one trip around the earth is 25,000 miles, how fast can Superwoman travel?
   125,000 miles per hour

8. At 7:00 in the morning Mr. Rash took his dog for a walk around the block. Mr. Rash and his dog returned at 7:30, one half-hour later. The two walked at an average rate of 4 miles per hour. How far did they walk?
   2 miles

9. Anita wants to make a circular tablecloth for a table. The radius of the circular top of the table is 4 ft. She wants the tablecloth to hang down 3 ft all around. Use $A = \frac{22}{7} \times r \times r$ to find the area of the fabric that Anita needs.
   154 square feet

10. Ernie multiplied two fractions and wrote the following:
    $$\frac{3}{5} \times \frac{7}{8} = \frac{21}{40}$$
    Did it matter in what order Ernie multiplied the numerators and the denominators? Explain why or why not.
    See Solution Notes.

11. If each of two fractions is less than 1, how does their product compare to 1?
    See Solution Notes.

12. If each of two fractions is less than 1, how does their product compare to each fraction?
    See Solution Notes.

208

Solution Notes

1. Remind students that the formula is: Rate × Time = Distance or Rate = Distance ÷ Time. Have them substitute values and write the open sentence. (Rate = $\frac{54}{6}$ = 9 miles per hour)
2. Rate = Distance ÷ Time. (168 ÷ 8 = 21 miles per hour)
3. They have to solve for the distance. Distance = Rate × Time. (32 × 24 = 768 miles)
4. (Time = 560 ÷ 80 = 7 hours)
5. (Time = Distance ÷ Rate, 495 ÷ 55 = 9 hours)
6. (Rate = 3,610 ÷ 33 = between 109 and 110 miles per hour.)
7. They multiply to find the total distance before they divide to find the rate. (25,000 × 5 = 125,000 miles) (Rate = 125,000 ÷ 1 = 125,000 miles per hour)
8. (Distance = 4 × ½ = 2 miles)

Higher-Order Thinking Skills

9. Analysis: Students should recognize that the radius of the tablecloth is 4 + 3, or 7 feet.
10. Synthesis: It does not matter because of the order property that states a × b = b × a.
11. Analysis: It is less than 1.
12. Analysis: It is less than each fraction.

Extra Credit   *Numeration*

Make a chart of 10 columns and at least 5 rows. Across the columns, fill in each box with a whole number and operation, such as × 4, or ÷ 2. Duplicate the chart or draw on the board. Tell students they will be timed. Ask them to pick a number 1 through 10 and to work the problems across the row without paper and pencil, doing what each square tells them to do. Have them keep track of their times and number of correct answers. The student working the most problems correctly, in the shortest amount of time wins. Repeat the activity using fractions and decimals.

Calculators and Sales Prices

pages 209-210

Objective

To use a calculator to find the sale price

Materials

calculators

Mental Math

Have students divide, expressing each remainder as a fraction.

1. $25 \div 4 =$ ($6\frac{1}{4}$)
2. $14 \div 3 =$ ($4\frac{2}{3}$)
3. $32 \div 5 =$ ($6\frac{2}{5}$)
4. $41 \div 8 =$ ($5\frac{1}{8}$)
5. $36 \div 8 =$ ($4\frac{1}{2}$)
6. $29 \div 9 =$ ($3\frac{2}{9}$)
7. $54 \div 6 =$ (9)

Skill Review

Review the use of the function keys: +, −, ×, −, =, C and CE . Have students work the following problems with calculators:

1. 241 + 392 = (633)
2. 570 − 127 = (443)
3. 23 × 40 = (920)
4. 786 ÷ 3 = (262)
5. \$12.59 + 14.89 = (\$27.48)
6. \$24.00 − 13.50 = (\$10.50)
7. \$15.25 × 6 = (\$91.50)

Calculators and Sale Price

Robin always takes her calculator with her shopping and uses it to help find the sale prices. What will Robin pay for the radio if she buys it on sale?

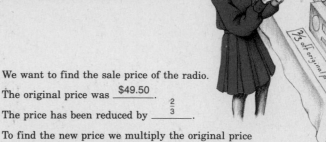

We want to find the sale price of the radio.

The original price was \$49.50.

The price has been reduced by $\frac{2}{3}$.

To find the new price we multiply the original price by the fraction it is reduced, and subtract that number from the original price.

We multiply \$49.50 by 2 and divide by 3.

Then we subtract that result from \$49.50.

Complete the codes.

Amount Off

$\frac{2}{3}$ of \$49.50   49 [·] 5 [×] 2 [÷] 3 [=] [33]

Sale Price

\$49.50 − \$33.00   49 [·] 5 [−] 33 [=] [16.5]

Robin will pay \$16.50 for the radio.

Robin's sister, Ann, uses another method to find the sale price. She knows that if the sale price is $\frac{2}{3}$ off the original price, the sale price must be $\frac{1}{3}$ of the original price.

Complete the code to show how Ann thinks.

$\frac{1}{3}$ of \$49.50   49.5 [÷] 3 [=] [16.5]

Use Ann's method to find the sale price of a stereo costing \$275.25 and being reduced by $\frac{2}{3}$ of the original price.

275.25 [÷] 3 [=] [91.75]

The sale price of the stereo is \$91.75.

MCP All rights reserved

Teaching the Lesson

Introducing the Problem Have a student read the problem aloud. Read the information sentences. Ask a student to read the plan sentence and have the class follow in their books. Explain that to calculate \$49.50 × ⅔, they will multiply \$49.50 by 2, then divide it by 3. Have them complete these operations. Now have them find the sale price by subtracting. (49.5 − 33 = 16.5) Ask a student to write the labeled answer on the board and read the solution sentence. (will pay \$16.50) Point out the second method for finding the sale price. Read the plan sentences and explain that instead of taking ⅔ and subtracting, they will simply find ⅓ of the original price because ⅔ from the original price is the same as ⅓ of that price. Have students follow the calculator codes indicated in their texts and solve the second problem. (275.25 ÷ 3 = 91.75) Read the second solution sentence. (Sale price is \$91.75.)

Developing the Skill Ask a student to explain the two ways to find the price of a \$39.96 item if everything in the store is ⅓ off. (Find ⅓ of \$39.96, then subtract that amount from \$39.96 to get the sale price. Or find ⅔ of the original price to get the sale price.) Have students do the problem with calculators using whichever method they prefer. (\$26.64)

Practice

Use Ann's method to find the sale price.

1. $429, $\frac{1}{3}$ off $286

2. $625, $\frac{2}{5}$ off $375

3. $720, $\frac{3}{4}$ off $180

4. $9.30, $\frac{1}{6}$ off $7.75

5. $952.40, $\frac{5}{8}$ off $357.15

6. $2,025, $\frac{2}{3}$ off $675

Use Robin's method to find the sale price.

7. $640, $\frac{3}{4}$ off $160

8. $984, $\frac{7}{8}$ off $123

9. $2,082, $\frac{5}{6}$ off $347

10. $1,674, $\frac{2}{3}$ off $558

11. $5,224, $\frac{3}{8}$ off $3,265

12. $182.95, $\frac{3}{5}$ off $73.18

Apply

Solve these problems.

13. Ron saw an ad that gave $\frac{2}{3}$ off all games and books. If games originally sold for $12 and books sold for $9 what were the sale prices?
$4 $3

14. Elaine went to a clothing sale that advertised $\frac{1}{5}$ off. She bought a skirt that originally sold for $56 and a sweater that originally sold for $32.50. How much did Elaine spend on the two items?
$70.80

Use the ad to solve problems 15 and 16.

KIRBY'S STORE
⅓ off all items under $100
½ off all items over $100
an additional ⅒ off the sale price if you pay cash

15. Kerry bought a pair of shoes that originally sold for $75. If Kerry paid cash, how much did the shoes cost?
$45

16. Nancy bought a coat that originally sold for $145. If Nancy paid cash, how much did the coat cost?
$65.25

210

Correcting Common Errors

Some students will forget to subtract to find the sale price when they are using Ann's method. Before students enter any number into their calculators, have them first write the two sets of calculator codes, with a blank in the second code until they find the first answer.

Enrichment

Explain that there is a rack of sportswear in a shop that has been reduced by ½ and is now marked "⅓ off the already marked down price". Have them use calculators to find the new sale prices.

1. sweatshirt, originally $36 (now $12)
2. sweatpants, originally $30 (now $10)
3. jogging suit, originally $48 (now $16)

Practice

Have students complete all the problems. Remind them that to multiply by a fraction on the calculator, they multiply by the numerator and divide by the denominator.

Extra Credit   *Numeration*

Show students the Mayan system of counting. Explain that the Mayans had symbols for one, a dot and five, a line. When combined, these symbols were used for numbers up to 20.

3	7	12	19

These symbols were repeated using different place values. After single units, the next place value was twenties, the next was 18 times twenties (or 360s), and the next place value was 20 times that place (or 7,200s). In addition they used this symbol for zero:

The place values were written vertically, with units on the bottom. Show students this number representing 7,305:

(1 7200)
(0 360s)
(5 20s)
(5   1s)

Have them write the symbol for 793:

(2 360s)
(2 30s)
(13 1s)

Chapter Test

page 211

Item	Objective
1-16	Find fraction of a number (See pages 191-192)
17-32	Multiply fractions and mixed numbers (See pages 193-198)
33-44	Find reciprocals of fractions and mixed numbers (See pages 199-200)
45-52	Divide mixed numbers and fractions (See pages 201-204)

Write the number for each fractional part.

1. $\frac{2}{3}$ of 9 = __6__   2. $\frac{1}{8}$ of \$96 = __\$12__   3. $\frac{3}{5}$ of 35 = __21__   4. $\frac{1}{10}$ of 640 = __64__

5. $\frac{1}{4}$ of \$128 = __\$32__   6. $\frac{3}{4}$ of 72 = __54__   7. $\frac{2}{5}$ of \$125 = __\$50__   8. $\frac{7}{8}$ of 160 = __140__

9. $\frac{2}{7}$ of 217 = __62__   10. $\frac{4}{5}$ of \$195 = __\$156__   11. $\frac{5}{6}$ of \$252 = __\$210__   12. $\frac{4}{7}$ of 483 = __276__

13. $\frac{3}{10}$ of 820 = __246__   14. $\frac{4}{9}$ of \$603 = __\$268__   15. $\frac{9}{9}$ of 504 = __504__   16. $\frac{3}{7}$ of \$406 = __\$174__

Multiply. Simplify if necessary.

17. $\frac{3}{4} \times \frac{5}{6}$ = __$\frac{5}{8}$__   18. $\frac{2}{3} \times \frac{1}{4}$ = __$\frac{1}{6}$__   19. $\frac{5}{8} \times \frac{7}{10}$ = __$\frac{7}{16}$__   20. $\frac{3}{5} \times \frac{10}{21}$ = __$\frac{2}{7}$__

21. $7\frac{1}{2} \times 8$ = __60__   22. $4\frac{1}{2} \times 2\frac{2}{3}$ = __12__   23. $6\frac{1}{2} \times \frac{8}{9}$ = __$5\frac{7}{9}$__   24. $2\frac{1}{7} \times 4\frac{1}{5}$ = __9__

25. $4\frac{1}{3} \times \frac{3}{8}$ = __$1\frac{5}{8}$__   26. $5\frac{3}{4} \times \frac{1}{2}$ = __$2\frac{7}{8}$__   27. $\frac{3}{7} \times 3\frac{3}{4}$ = __$1\frac{17}{28}$__   28. $\frac{7}{9} \times 2\frac{1}{4}$ = __$1\frac{3}{4}$__

29. $8\frac{1}{10} \times 2\frac{1}{3}$ = __$18\frac{9}{10}$__   30. $3\frac{1}{2} \times 4\frac{4}{5}$ = __$16\frac{4}{5}$__   31. $7\frac{1}{6} \times 8\frac{1}{4}$ = __$59\frac{1}{8}$__   32. $10\frac{1}{3} \times 6\frac{2}{3}$ = __$68\frac{8}{9}$__

Write the reciprocal.

33. $\frac{1}{7}$ $\frac{7}{1}$ 34. 9 $\frac{1}{9}$ 35. $\frac{4}{6}$ $\frac{6}{4}$

36. $5\frac{1}{6}$ $\frac{6}{31}$ 37. $\frac{2}{16}$ $\frac{16}{2}$ 38. $2\frac{4}{7}$ $\frac{7}{18}$

39. 10 $\frac{1}{10}$ 40. $9\frac{2}{5}$ $\frac{5}{47}$ 41. $\frac{5}{3}$ $\frac{3}{5}$

42. $5\frac{1}{3}$ $\frac{3}{16}$ 43. $\frac{1}{8}$ $\frac{8}{1}$ 44. $10\frac{1}{4}$ $\frac{4}{41}$

Divide. Simplify if necessary.

45. $\frac{1}{2} \div \frac{1}{3}$ $1\frac{1}{2}$ 46. $\frac{2}{3} \div \frac{5}{6}$ $\frac{4}{5}$

47. $\frac{3}{5} \div \frac{9}{10}$ $\frac{2}{3}$ 48. $\frac{4}{5} \div \frac{2}{9}$ $3\frac{3}{5}$

49. $8 \div 1\frac{1}{5}$ $6\frac{2}{3}$ 50. $4\frac{2}{3} \div 7$ $\frac{2}{3}$

51. $3\frac{1}{3} \div 2\frac{1}{2}$ $1\frac{1}{3}$ 52. $6\frac{1}{4} \div 2\frac{1}{2}$ $2\frac{1}{2}$

MCP All rights reserved

211

211

Circle the letter of the correct answer.

1 $421.36
   + 89.57

a $500.93
b $510.93
c $511.93
d NG

2 7,901
   − 837

a 6,974
b 7,064
c 7,136
d NG

3 43,215
   − 11,941

a 31,274
b 31,374
c 32,734
d NG

4 $4.25
   × 9

a $36.25
b $37.25
c $38.25
d NG

5 28 × 74

a 308
b 2,052
c 2,072
d NG

6 6)7,206

a 131
b 1,301
c 10,301
d NG

7 63)6,630

a 15 R15
b 105 R15
c 150 R15
d NG

8 Find the perimeter.

7 cm   7 cm
   7 cm

a 21 cm
b 21 sq cm
c 29 sq cm
d NG

9 5 ft 9 in.
   + 3 ft 8 in.

a 9 ft 7 in.
b 9 ft 5 in.
c 9 ft 3 in.
d NG

10 $6\frac{1}{4}$
    $+ 7\frac{5}{8}$

a $13\frac{1}{4}$
b $13\frac{7}{8}$
c $14\frac{1}{8}$
d NG

11 $9\frac{1}{3}$
    $- 4\frac{2}{3}$

a $4\frac{1}{3}$
b $4\frac{2}{3}$
c $5\frac{1}{3}$
d NG

12 $7\frac{1}{5}$
    $- 6\frac{2}{3}$

a $\frac{8}{15}$
b $1\frac{7}{15}$
c $1\frac{8}{15}$
d NG

☐ score

212

Cumulative Review

page 212

Item	Objective
1	Add two numbers up to 5-digits (See pages 27-28)
2	Subtract two numbers up to 4-digits, zeros in minuend (See pages 33-34)
3	Subtract two 5-digit numbers (See pages 35-36)
4	Multiply money by 1-digit factor (See pages 55-56)
5	Multiply two 2-digit factors (See pages 57-58)
6	Divide up to 6-digits by 1-digit number, quotient with zero (See pages 87-88)
7	Divide a 4-digit by 2-digit number, quotient with zero (See pages 109-110)
8	Find the perimeter of triangles (See pages 125-126)
9	Add customary units of length (See pages 123-124)
10	Add two mixed numbers (See pages 175-176)
11	Subtract two mixed numbers (See pages 179-180)
12	Subtract two mixed numbers, rename minuend (See pages 183-184)

Alternate Cumulative Review

Circle the letter of the correct answer.

1 $324.69
   + 95.27

a $418.96
b $419.96
c $420.96
d NG

2 8,702
   − 619

a 8,093
b 8,083
c 8,183
d NG

3 54,326
   − 11,842

a 42,484
b 42,584
c 43,524
d NG

4 $7.35
   × 8

a $56.80
b $57.80
c $58.80
d NG

5 42
   × 76

a 3,292
b 3,192
c 3,182
d NG

6 5)9,035

a 187
b 1,801
c 1,907
d NG

7 41)8460

a 26 R14
b 206 R14
c 260 R14
d NG

8 Find the perimeter of a triangle 9 cm by 9 cm by 9 cm.

a 27 cm
b 27 sq cm
c 81 sq cm
d NG

9 9 ft 9 in.
   + 4 ft 9 in.

a 14 ft 6 in.
b 14 ft 7 in.
c 14 ft 8 in.
d NG

10 $7\frac{1}{4}$
    $+ 8\frac{1}{8}$

a $15\frac{1}{8}$
b $15\frac{2}{8}$
c $15\frac{3}{8}$
d NG

11 9
    $- 7\frac{7}{20}$

a $1\frac{3}{20}$
b $1\frac{13}{20}$
c $2\frac{13}{20}$
d NG

12 $23\frac{7}{8}$
    $- 8\frac{1}{6}$

a $15\frac{16}{24}$
b $15\frac{17}{24}$
c $15\frac{18}{24}$
d NG

212

Tenths

pages 213-214

Objective

To read and write tenths

Materials

*transparency with different tenths shaded
*overhead projector
inch-square graph paper

Mental Math

Have students divide each by 5 and express the remainder as a fraction:

1. 6 × 7 (8⅖)
2. 5 × 6 (6)
3. 9 × 3 (5⅘)
4. 8 × 6 (9⅗)
5. 7 × 2 (2⅘)
6. 4 × 4 (3⅕)
7. 2 × 2 (⅘)

Skill Review

Have students work these problems on paper:

1. ¹⁄₁₀ + ³⁄₁₀ = (⁴⁄₁₀ = ²⁄₅)
2. ⁹⁄₁₀ − ²⁄₁₀ = (⁷⁄₁₀)
3. ¹²⁄₁₀ + ⁵⁄₁₀ = (¹⁷⁄₁₀ = 1⁷⁄₁₀)
4. ³⁄₁₀ × ⁷⁄₁₀ = (²¹⁄₁₀₀)
5. ²⁄₁₀ ÷ ¹⁄₁₀ = (2)
6. 1²⁄₁₀ + 3¹⁄₁₀ = (4³⁄₁₀)

Understanding Tenths

Ramon agreed to help his father by painting one side and the back of their garage. What decimal represents the number of walls Ramon has painted so far?

We want to know how many walls are painted.

Each side of the garage has __10__ equal boards.

Ramon painted __10__ boards on the back and __3__ boards on the side of the garage.

To write the number of walls painted as a decimal, we rename the mixed number $1\frac{3}{10}$. We write $1\frac{3}{10}$ as the decimal **1.3**. We say: **one and three tenths.**

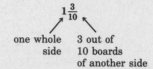

$1\frac{3}{10}$

one whole side   3 out of 10 boards of another side

decimal point

1 . 3

whole number   decimal number

ones	tenths
1	3

Ramon has painted __1.3__ garage walls so far.

✔ Decimal numbers can name parts less than 1. Ramon still has **0.7** of a garage side to paint. We say: **seven tenths.**

0.7
0 ones 7 tenths

✔ Whole numbers can be written as decimal numbers. When he completes both sides, Ramon will have painted **2.0** sides of the garage. We say: **two.**

2.0
2 ones 0 tenths

Getting Started

Write the decimal for the red part.

1.

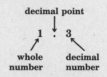

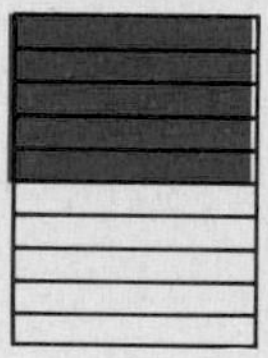

0.5

Write the decimal.

2. $6\frac{6}{10}$ = __6.6__   3. $\frac{4}{10}$ = __0.4__

4. five and six tenths __5.6__

Write the decimal in words.

5. 8.1 __eight and one tenth__

213

MCP All rights reserved

Teaching the Lesson

Introducing the Problem Read the problem aloud and ask a student to read the information sentences. Write **1³⁄₁₀** on the board, explaining that this represents the number of walls painted. Read the plan sentences and show students that 1³⁄₁₀ can be written 1.3. Read the decimal aloud. Explain that the decimal point separates whole numbers from tenths. Have a student read the first solution sentence. (has painted 1.3 walls) Read the next sentence aloud explaining that decimals, like fractions, are used to describe parts less than one. Point out that because Ramon has painted 1.3 walls out of 2, he still has .7 to do. Write **.7** on the board and read it aloud. Read the final sentences and write **2.0** on the board, explaining this represents two wholes and no tenths.

Developing the Skill Use the overhead transparency to illustrate tenths. Point to the first of the divided wholes and ask a student to tell how many tenths are colored. Write the fraction and its decimal equivalent on the board and read the decimal aloud. Repeat for the other tenths shown on your transparency. Explain that decimal tenths are the same as fractional tenths, though they are easier to write. Ask students how many tenths in one whole. (10) Write the following decimals on the board and ask students to read them aloud: **.5, .8, 2.7, 10.1, 1.3.**

Practice

Write the decimal for each red part.

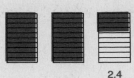

1.

2.

3.

2.4   2.0   3.0

4.

5.

6.

0.4   0.2   1.5

Write the decimal.

7. $2\frac{3}{10} = \underline{2.3}$ 8. $9\frac{9}{10} = \underline{9.9}$ 9. $6\frac{5}{10} = \underline{6.5}$ 10. $8\frac{2}{10} = \underline{8.2}$

11. $7\frac{1}{10} = \underline{7.1}$ 12. $2\frac{7}{10} = \underline{2.7}$ 13. $6\frac{4}{10} = \underline{6.4}$ 14. $9\frac{8}{10} = \underline{9.8}$

15. three and one tenth   16. nine and four tenths   17. nine and five tenths
    3.1   9.4   9.5

18. six tenths   19. eight   20. four and seven tenths
    0.6   8.0   4.7

Write the decimal in words.

21. 7.3   seven and three tenths   22. 8.6   eight and six tenths

23. 0.3   three tenths   24. 5.7   five and seven tenths

25. 8.9   eight and nine tenths   26. 2.5   two and five tenths

27. 9.0   nine   28. 10.1   ten and one tenth

29. 5.2   five and two tenths   30. 9.8   nine and eight tenths

214

Correcting Common Errors

Some students may forget that the decimal point separates the whole-number part from tenths and write five and eight tenths as 0.58. Have these students work with partners taking turns writing the decimal for each of the following on a place-value chart.

three tenths (0.3)
four and three tenths (4.3)
seven tenths (0.7)
two and seven tenths (2.7)
eight tenths (0.8)
nine and eight tenths (9.8)

After writing each decimal, partners should discuss whether the notation is correct and why or why not.

Enrichment

Have students change each of these fractions to tenths and rewrite them as decimals:

1. ½ (= ⁵/₁₀ = .5)
2. ⁶/₂₀ (= ³/₁₀ = .3)
3. ¹⁰/₁₀₀ (= ¹/₁₀ = .1)
4. ³/₆ (= ⁵/₁₀ = .5)
5. ¹²/₈ (= 1⁵/₁₀ = 1.5)
6. ²/₅ (= ⁴/₁₀ = .4)
7. ⁴/₂ (= 2 = 2.0)

Practice

Have students complete the practice problems. Write a decimal in words on the board to show students what the written form looks like.

Mixed Practice

1. $625.98 + $724.93 + $595.47 ($1,946.38)
2. $5\frac{1}{9} + 16\frac{2}{3} \left(21\frac{7}{9}\right)$
3. 13,298 ÷ 65 (204 R38)
4. $125\frac{7}{8} - 114\frac{1}{6} \left(11\frac{17}{24}\right)$
5. 20,565 − 8,270 (12,295)
6. $\frac{1}{6} + \frac{3}{5} + \frac{4}{15} \left(1\frac{1}{30}\right)$
7. $\frac{4}{7} \div \frac{8}{9} \left(\frac{9}{14}\right)$
8. 41,724 × 80 (3,337,920)
9. $2\frac{1}{4} \times 3\frac{2}{5} \left(7\frac{13}{20}\right)$
10. $92.60 ÷ 20 ($4.63)

Extra Credit   *Creative Drill*

Duplicate cross number puzzles like the following or ask the students to make puzzles of their own and exchange.

Across

1. the sum of 21 + 21
3. the product of 7 × 5
5. 64 − 32
6. from the product of 43 × 13 subtract 520
9. twelve 5's + 5
10. (13 × 4) + (4 × 9)

Down

1. the multiplier in 43 × 166
2. 2 × 111
3. (3 × 110) + 3
4. subtract 4 from the product of 7 × 9
7. 5 dozen + 6
8. 54 ÷ 3

214

Hundredths

pages 215-216

Objective

To read and write hundredths

Materials

*transparency showing several different hundredths
*overhead projector
graph paper

Mental Math

Ask students to identify the fractional part of a dollar represented by:

1. one quarter (¼)
2. one penny (¹⁄₁₀₀)
3. two dimes (²⁄₁₀)
4. three quarters (¾)
5. a fifty-cent piece (½)
6. three nickels (³⁄₂₀)

Skill Review

Read these decimals aloud and have students write them:

1. three and four tenths (3.4)
2. nine tenths (.9)
3. four and five tenths (4.5)

Write these fractions on the board and have students rewrite them as decimals:

1. 1⁴⁄₁₀ (1.4) 3. 3¹⁄₁₀ (3.1)
2. ⁷⁄₁₀ (.7)   4. 5⁹⁄₁₀ (5.9)

Understanding Hundredths

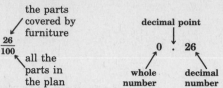

Donna is using graph paper to design a floor plan for her living room. What decimal represents the portion of her living room that will be filled with furniture?

We want to know what part of Donna's floor plan is filled with furniture.

The graph paper is divided into __100__ equal squares.

Donna filled __26__ of these squares with furniture.

To find the decimal number which represents the part that will be filled with furniture, we rename the fraction $\frac{26}{100}$.

We write $\frac{26}{100}$ as the decimal **0.26**.   We say: **twenty-six hundredths.**

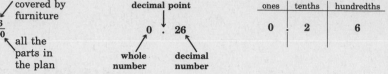

ones	tenths	hundredths
0	2	6

the parts covered by furniture

$\frac{26}{100}$

all the parts in the plan

decimal point

0 . 26

whole number   decimal number

Donna will fill __0.26__ of the room with furniture.

Getting Started

Write the decimal for each red part.

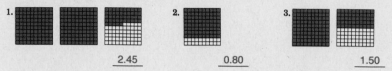

1. 2.45
2. 0.80
3. 1.50

Write the decimal.

4. $5\frac{3}{100}$ = __5.03__   5. $\frac{37}{100}$ = __0.37__   6. $\frac{6}{100}$ = __0.06__   7. $9\frac{5}{100}$ = __9.05__

8. two and twenty-five hundredths
   __2.25__

9. eighty-five hundredths
   __0.85__

Write the decimal in words.

10. 5.03   __five and three hundredths__

11. 0.74   __seventy-four hundredths__

12. 2.25   __two and twenty-five hundredths__

13. 0.86   __eighty-six hundredths__

MCP All rights reserved

215

Teaching the Lesson

Introducing the Problem   Have a student read the problem aloud. Ask another to read and complete the information sentences. Explain that to find the decimal, they will rename the fraction, ²⁶⁄₁₀₀. Write the decimal on the board: **0.26.** Point to each part: whole number, decimal point, tenths and hundredths. Read the decimal aloud. Explain that the new place value in this decimal is hundredths. Have them notice that as they move to the right of the decimal point, the place values get smaller. One hundredth is a tenth the size of one tenth. Ask a student what decimal part the furniture covers. (²⁶⁄₁₀₀, 0.26)

Developing the Skill   Use transparencies to show decimal hundredths: 0.25, 0.60 and 1.12. Ask students to identify the number of hundredths. (25, 60, 112) Have students write these on the board as fractions and decimals. (²⁵⁄₁₀₀ = 0.25, ⁶⁰⁄₁₀₀ = 0.60, 1¹²⁄₁₀₀ = 1.12) Point to the whole number, decimal point, tenths and hundredths. Remind students ¹⁰⁄₁₀₀ = ¹⁄₁₀. Re-emphasize that ¹⁄₁₀₀ is **smaller** than ¹⁄₁₀. Explain that in numbers less than ¹⁰⁄₁₀₀, a zero must be written in the tenths place to show no tenths, for example, ³⁄₁₀₀ = 0.03.

215

Practice

Write the decimal for each red part.

1.
   0.46

2.
   2.21

3.
   0.07

4.
   1.50

5.
   1.01

6.
   0.15

Write the decimal.

7. $\frac{67}{100}$ = __0.67__

8. $\frac{4}{100}$ = __0.04__

9. $3\frac{25}{100}$ = __3.25__

10. $2\frac{1}{100}$ = __2.01__

11. $6\frac{96}{100}$ = __6.96__

12. $3\frac{10}{100}$ = __3.10__

13. $4\frac{2}{100}$ = __4.02__

14. $5\frac{19}{100}$ = __5.19__

15. six and nine hundredths __6.09__

16. fifteen and seventy hundredths __15.70__

17. four hundredths __0.04__

18. nine and ninety-nine hundredths __9.99__

Write the decimal in words.

19. 9.06 __nine and six hundredths__

20. 0.65 __sixty-five hundredths__

21. 3.75 __three and seventy-five hundredths__

22. 7.90 __seven and ninety hundredths__

Apply

Solve these problems.

23. There are 100 centimeters in 1 meter. Write 48 centimeters as a decimal part of a meter.
    0.48

24. Bob shot 100 free throws. He missed 14. What decimal represents the number of free throws Bob made?
    0.86

216

Correcting Common Errors

Some students may omit zero as a place holder and write three and seven hundredths as 3.7. Have them work in pairs to take turns to write the decimals for the following on a place-value chart.

six tenths (0.6)
six hundredths (0.06)
five and six tenths (5.6)
five and six hundredths (5.06)
one tenth (0.1)
one hundredth (0.01)
eight and one tenth (8.1)
eight and one hundredth (8.01)

After writing each decimal, partners should discuss whether the notation is correct and why or why not.

Enrichment

Have students change each of these fractions to hundredths and rewrite them as decimals:

1. ½ ($\frac{50}{100}$ = .50)
2. ⅖ ($\frac{40}{100}$ = .40)
3. ³⁄₂₀ ($\frac{15}{100}$ = .15)
4. ²⁄₂₀₀ ($\frac{1}{100}$ = .01)
5. ³⁄₃ ($\frac{100}{100}$ = 1.00)
6. ⁶⁄₄ ($\frac{150}{100}$ = 1.50)
7. ⁸⁄₅ ($\frac{160}{100}$ = 1.60)

Practice

Have students complete the practice problems. Remind students that the tenths place will have a zero when there are fewer than 10 hundredths. Write on the board:

$\frac{35}{100}$ = .35 = **thirty-five hundredths**

Extra Credit   *Geometry*

Duplicate the following for students to solve: The cities of A, B and C decided they needed a highway to allow people to travel most directly between the three cities. Because the highway budget was limited, they had to build the shortest possible highway to connect the cities. A is directly west of B and C is located south and midway between A and B. What route did they select for this highway? What is the name of the figure formed by the highways?

$$\begin{pmatrix} A\bullet \quad \bullet B \\ \diagdown \diagup \\ \vert \\ \bullet C \end{pmatrix}$$

216

Thousandths

pages 217-218

Objective

To read and write thousandths

Materials

Mental Math

Have students identify the place value of the 7 in each:

1. 732 (hundreds)
2. 17 (ones)
3. 1,273 (tens)
4. 4,755 (hundreds)
5. 24.7 (tenths)
6. 7,590 (thousands)
7. 70.7 (tens and tenths)

Skill Review

Read the following decimals aloud and have students write the numerals.

1. one and four tenths (1.4)
2. five and thirty-two hundredths (5.32)
3. twenty hundredths (0.20)
4. two and five hundredths (2.05)
5. ten and four tenths (10.4)
6. seven and one hundredth (7.01)

Understanding Thousandths

Fred is hiking to High Ridge to go on a rock hunt. What decimal can be used to represent the distance to High Ridge in kilometers?

We are looking for the hiking distance in kilometers.

It is ___465___ meters to High Ridge.

There are ___1,000___ meters in 1 kilometer.

To write the distance we must rename meters as kilometers by dividing the number of meters by 1,000.

Fractions can represent division. Thus,

$1,000\overline{)465}$ can be written as $\frac{465}{1000}$.

We rename $\frac{465}{1000}$ as the decimal **0.465**.

We say: **four hundred sixty-five thousandths.**

$\frac{465}{1000}$ ← meters hiked
← meters in a kilometer

ones	tenths	hundredths	thousandths
0 .	4	6	5

Fred is hiking ___0.465___ of a kilometer to High Ridge.

Getting Started

Write the decimal.

1. $\frac{405}{1000}$ = ___0.405___
2. $\frac{136}{1000}$ = ___0.136___
3. $\frac{75}{1000}$ = ___0.075___
4. $\frac{6}{1000}$ = ___0.006___
5. $6\frac{15}{1000}$ = ___6.015___
6. $7\frac{120}{1000}$ = ___7.120___
7. $12\frac{500}{1000}$ = ___12.500___
8. $16\frac{10}{1000}$ = ___16.010___

9. seven and three thousandths
   7.003
10. eight and one hundred seven thousandths
   8.107

Write the decimal in words.

11. 0.064 ___sixty-four thousandths___

12. 9.245 ___nine and two hundred forty-five thousandths___

MCP All rights reserved

217

Teaching the Lesson

Introducing the Problem Have a student read the problem aloud. Read the information sentences and explain that to find the distance in kilometers, students must divide the distance by the number of meters in a kilometer. Write ⁴⁶⁵/₁₀₀₀ on the board, explaining that this is one way to express the division. Explain that this can be written as a decimal. Put a decimal place value chart on the board for ones through thousandths. Write **0.465** in the chart and point to each place as you name it. Explain that as there are ten hundredths in a tenth, there are ten thousandths in a hundredth. Remind them that each place value move to the right indicates a lesser value. Ask a student to read the decimal for the class.

Developing the Skill Refer again to the place value chart on the board. Explain that as they move from left to right, each place is one tenth the size of the previous one; as they go from right to left, each place is ten times the size of the other. Add familiar places to the chart: tens, hundreds and thousands. Show students that these fit the same pattern. Remind them that to show very small numbers, like three thousandths, they will have to put zeros in the tenths and hundredths places. Write **0.003** on the board and read the decimal aloud. Write these decimals on the board and have students read them aloud: **3.095, 0.007** and **5.850.**

Write the decimal.

1. $\frac{325}{1000}$ = __0.325__   2. $\frac{16}{1000}$ = __0.016__   3. $\frac{150}{1000}$ = __0.150__   4. $\frac{6}{1000}$ = __0.006__

5. $4\frac{3}{1000}$ = __4.003__   6. $5\frac{214}{1000}$ = __5.214__   7. $8\frac{29}{1000}$ = __8.029__   8. $3\frac{1}{1000}$ = __3.001__

9. $87\frac{4}{1000}$ = __87.004__   10. $12\frac{100}{1000}$ = __12.100__   11. $495\frac{495}{1000}$ = __495.495__   12. $21\frac{86}{1000}$ = __21.086__

13. two hundred fifteen thousandths
    __0.215__

14. six and twelve thousandths
    __6.012__

15. nine thousandths
    __0.009__

16. seven and fifty-six thousandths
    __7.056__

17. nine and forty-eight thousandths
    __9.048__

18. seven and two hundred nine thousandths
    __7.209__

19. seventeen and four thousandths
    __17.004__

20. three hundred eleven thousandths
    __0.311__

Write the decimal in words.

21. 0.531   __five hundred thirty-one thousandths__

22. 4.004   __four and four thousandths__

23. 5.230   __five and two hundred thirty thousandths__

24. 2.015   __two and fifteen thousandths__

25. 7.216   __seven and two hundred sixteen thousandths__

26. 66.033   __sixty-six and thirty-three thousandths__

HIGH RIDGE
5.230 km

Apply

Solve these problems.

27. In a poll of 1,000 teenagers, 428 preferred the color blue. What decimal represents the number of teens that did not prefer blue?
0.572

28. Mr. Ellis returned $1,000 he had borrowed from his credit union. He paid $88 in interest. What decimal represents the amount of interest paid by Mr. Ellis?
0.088

218

Correcting Common Errors

Some students may have trouble writing thousandths correctly. Give each student a place-value chart showing ones through thousandths. Have them mark the chart by putting counters or writing Xs in each column to show how many of that unit are in each of the following numbers.

1.300, 3.281, 0.008, 0.103

Enrichment

Have students change each of these fractions to thousandths and rewrite the number as a decimal:

1. $\frac{1}{4}$ ($\frac{250}{1000}$ = 0.250)
2. $\frac{21}{100}$ ($\frac{210}{1000}$ = 0.210)
3. $\frac{3}{10}$ ($\frac{300}{1000}$ = 0.300)
4. $\frac{1}{5}$ ($\frac{200}{1000}$ = 0.200)
5. $1\frac{3}{5}$ ($1\frac{600}{1000}$ = 1.600)
6. $\frac{9}{6}$ ($1\frac{500}{1000}$ = 1.500)

Practice

Have students complete the practice problems. Remind them to put zeros in tenths and hundredths, when necessary, to write thousandths. Write a sample decimal thousandth on the board in words.

Mixed Practice

1. $300.75 − $27.48 ($273.27)
2. $128\frac{4}{5} − 119$ $\left(9\frac{4}{5}\right)$
3. $1\frac{4}{5} \times 3\frac{2}{3}$ $\left(6\frac{3}{5}\right)$
4. 7 × 307,824 (2,154,768)
5. $157\frac{7}{8} + 216\frac{5}{6}$ $\left(374\frac{17}{24}\right)$
6. $\frac{3}{5}$ of 175 (105)
7. 658 × 121 (79,618)
8. $132.65 ÷ 7 ($18.95)
9. 176 + 834 + 721 (1,731)
10. $\frac{3}{4} ÷ 4$ $\left(\frac{3}{16}\right)$

Extra Credit   *Applications*

Ask students to bring a road map to class. Have them list all the uses that numbers have on such a map. Have students find the scale. Using the scale, have them find the distance from their city to the city within their state that is farthest away. Then have them compute the travel time to that city if they travelled at 55 m.p.h. Extend the activity by having students compute the cost of gasoline for the trip, using current gas prices.

Place Value

pages 219-220

Objective

To identify place value from thousands through thousandths

Materials

place value charts showing thousands through thousandths

Mental Math

Have students give the next number in each of these series:

1. 1, 3, 5, 7, . . . (9)
2. ½, 1, ³⁄₂, 2, . . . (⁵⁄₂)
3. 0, 3, 6, 9, . . . (12)
4. 10, 20, 30, 40, . . . (50)
5. .1, .2, .3, .4, . . . (.5)
6. 64, 56, 48, 40, . . . (32)

Skill Review

Review reading and writing decimals by asking students to write these digits on the board:

1. six and seven hundredths (6.07)
2. nine and three tenths (9.3)
3. four and thirty three thousandths (4.033)
4. two hundred forty thousandths (0.240)
5. thirteen and five tenths (13.5)

Understanding Place Value

Janice is the time keeper for the Blue Team in the Road Runner Relay. She must use a very accurate timer. How long has it taken for the Blue Team to finish the first 5 laps?

We want to read the decimal number that tells the Blue Team's time for the first 5 laps.

The timer shows <u>1936.289</u> seconds have passed. We use the place value chart to help us understand this number.

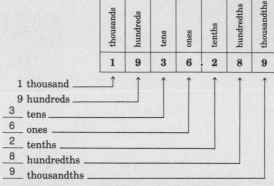

thousands	hundreds	tens	ones	tenths	hundredths	thousandths
1	9	3	6	2	8	9

1 thousand ———
9 hundreds ———
<u>3</u> tens ———
<u>6</u> ones ———
<u>2</u> tenths ———
<u>8</u> hundredths ———
<u>9</u> thousandths ———

The Blue Team took <u>one thousand, nine hundred thirty-six and two hundred eighty-nine thousandths</u> seconds to run the 5 laps.

Getting Started

Write the place value of each red digit.

1. 7.25<u>6</u>   hundredths
2. 23.<u>9</u>2   ones
3. 157.83<u>4</u>   thousandths
4. 16.<u>8</u>40   tenths

5. 2,3<u>6</u>5.381   tens
6. <u>5</u>26.3   hundreds
7. 19.0<u>0</u>3   hundredths
8. 374.<u>2</u>18   tenths

Write the decimal.

9. three hundred ninety-five and one hundred eight thousandths <u>395.108</u>
10. six thousand seven and nineteen thousandths <u>6,007.019</u>

MCP All rights reserved

219

Teaching the Lesson

Introducing the Problem Read the problem aloud and have a student read the information sentences. Direct students' attention to the place value chart in their texts and duplicate the chart on the board. Read the place values aloud as you point to the columns on the board. Read the number aloud.

Developing the Skill Write the following words in a continuous row across the board: **thousands hundreds tens ones tenths hundredths thousandths.** Omit the decimal point and emphasize the symmetry of the units about the ones place. Explain that the decimal point is only a marker. Have students enter these numbers in the appropriate columns as you read them: two hundred forty and thirty-two thousandths; one thousand five and one hundred sixteen thousandths; and one thousand, two hundred eight and four hundred sixty-two thousandths.

(240.032; 1,005.116; 1,208.462) When all have been entered, add commas and decimal points. Show students that when they read decimal numbers, they identify the last decimal place and read the number in terms of that place. Write .33 on the board and point out that the last place is hundredths so the number is read thirty-three hundredths. Write .033 on the board and explain that because the last place is thousandths, it is read thirty-three thousandths.

Write the place value of each red digit.

1. 5.231
   hundredths

2. 16.205
   tens

3. 0.96
   hundredths

4. 751.6
   tens

5. 852.14
   hundredths

6. 396.21
   tenths

7. 47.304
   hundredths

8. 2,158.05
   thousands

9. 3,341.9
   hundreds

10. 7,298.51
    tenths

11. 26.395
    thousandths

12. 765.27
    tens

Write the decimal.

13. five hundred sixteen and six tenths ___516.6___

14. eighty-nine and eight hundred twenty-six thousandths ___89.826___

15. one thousand, three hundred thirty-five and five tenths ___1,335.5___

16. six thousand, two hundred nine and thirty-eight hundredths ___6,209.38___

17. one hundred seventeen and two hundred fifty thousandths ___117.250___

EXCURSION

If our place value system were based on five instead of ten, then we would regroup after every five units and the place value positions would be 1, 5, 25 (five 5's), 125 (five 25's), etc. instead of 1, 10, 100, 1000, etc. We can rewrite our base ten numbers as base five numbers by thinking of them as groups of 125's, 25's, 5's and 1's.

Base 10 Values

$7 = (1 \times 5) + (2 \times 1)$

$69 = (2 \times 25) + (3 \times 5) + (4 \times 1)$

$234 = (1 \times 125) + (4 \times 25) + (1 \times 5) + (4 \times 1)$

Base Five Values

125	25	5	1
		1	2
	2	3	4
1	4	1	4

Write the base five numbers for the base ten counting numbers 1 to 26.

1 2 3 4 10 11 12 13 14 20 21 22 23 24 30

31 32 33 34 40 41 42 43 44 100 101

220

Correcting Common Errors

Some students may have difficulty identifying the place value of a particular digit in a decimal. Have them work with partners to take turns writing the decimal on the place-value chart and identifying the place value of each digit in the decimal.

Enrichment

Remind students of binary numbers in which the place values are twos, fours, eights, sixteens and so on, and the digits are 0 and 1. Explain that there are also binary decimals or bicimals. Their place values are halves (.1), fourths (.01) and eighths (.001). Have students write the bicimal for: ¾ (.11), ⅜ (.011), ⅝ (.101) and ⅝. (1.001)

Practice

Have students complete the practice problems. Write these words across the board: **thousands, hundreds, tens, ones, tenths, hundredths** and **thousandths.**

Excursion

It is helpful to write the place values underneath their positions in order to remember how they are different from base ten. When mentally converting from base ten to base five numerals, have students ask how many fives and how many ones? or in the case of twenty-five and twenty-six, how many 25's? how many 5's and how many 1's?

$$26 \text{ ten} = \frac{1}{25} \ \frac{0}{5} \ \frac{1}{1} \text{ five} = 101 \text{ five}$$

Extra Credit *Creative Drill*

Have a student think of a term or phrase pertaining to mathematics and draw as many dashes on the board as there are letters in it. Have other students take turns asking questions about letters in the word. For example, "Are there any e's in the word?" Fill in correct letters as they are guessed. Continue the procedure until the word or phrase is guessed. The student who makes the class guess the most letters before they get the right word, wins. Have the student who guesses the word give an example or definition of it. Then allow that student to choose the next term.

Comparing Decimals

pages 221-222

Objective

To compare and order decimals

Materials

Mental Math

Have students identify the operation suggested by the following words:

1. plus (add)
2. difference (subtract)
3. all together (add)
4. times (multiply)
5. how much more (subtract)
6. sum (add)
7. product (multiply)

Skill Review

Write **3,565.075** on the board. Have students identify the place value of digits as you point to them at random. Review the use of the symbols < and >. Ask them to compare these numbers:

1. 12, 15, (12 < 15)
2. ½, ⅓ (½ > ⅓)
3. 2,300, 358 (2,300 > 358)
4. 592.5, 592.0 (592.5 > 592.0)

Comparing Decimals

The top three competitors in the county track meet ran faster than 12 seconds in the 100-meter dash. List them in order by their finishing times.

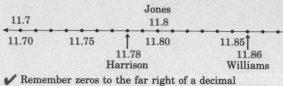

We need to list the three competitors in the order of fastest to slowest.

Williams finished in __11.86__ seconds, Harrison in __11.78__ seconds and Jones in __11.8__ seconds. To compare their finishing times, we find and label __11.86__, __11.78__ and __11.8__ on a number line.

```
                          Jones
11.7                      11.8                         11.9
├──┬──┬──┬──┬──┬──┬──┬──┬──┬──┬──┬──┬──┬──┬──┬──┬──┬──┤
  11.70      11.75      11.80       11.85      11.90
                    ↑                     ↑
                 11.78                 11.86
                Harrison              Williams
```

✔ Remember zeros to the far right of a decimal number do not change its value.

   Thus, **11.8 = 11.80.**

We can also compare these times using place values.

Same number of tens and ones	11.78 has less tenths.	11.80 has less hundredths.	Arranged from greatest to smallest
11.86	11.7 ⊂ 11.8	11.80 ⊂ 11.86	**11.86**
11.86	**11.86**	**11.86**	**11.80**
11.78	**11.78**	**11.80**	**11.78**
11.80	**11.80**		

Since the runner with the shortest time places first,

the order of finish is first place: __Harrison__,

second place: __Jones__ and last: __Williams__.

Getting Started

Compare. Write >, = or < in the circle.

1. 7.215 ⊂ 7.251   2. 9.8 ⊜ 9.800   3. 15.531 ⊃ 15.315

Write in order from least to greatest.

4. 6.21, 6.12, 6.1, 6.15
   __6.1, 6.12, 6.15, 6.21__

5. 48.334, 48.33, 48.343, 48.3
   __48.3, 48.33, 48.334, 48.343__

MCP All rights reserved

221

Teaching the Lesson

Introducing the Problem Have a student read the problem aloud. Ask another to read the information sentences. Direct students' attention to the number line, explaining it shows tenths on top and hundredths underneath. Show them that 11.8 and 11.80 have the same value. Ask students to locate Harrison, Jones and Williams on the line. Ask which runner's time is fastest. (Williams) Put the column of numbers on the board. Point out tens and ones, indicating the numbers are identical. Point to tenths and show that seven tenths is smaller than the other two. Compare the final two numbers, pointing to hundredths, where 0 is smaller than 6. Ask a student to arrange the numbers in order from greatest to smallest on the board. Read the solution sentence. (first, Harrison; second, Jones; last, Williams)

Developing the Skill Explain that to compare decimals, they will look at similar place values, moving from left to right until they find a difference. Point out that this is like comparing whole numbers. In the first place that has a difference, the number with the higher value will be the larger of the two numbers. Write these numbers in a place value chart and help students put them in order, largest to smallest: **322.7, 321.0, 322.64.** (322.7, 322.64, 321.0)

Practice

Compare. Write >, = or < in the circle.

1. 9.315 ⊙ 9.215
2. 5.036 ⊙ 5.306
3. 14.21 ⊙ 14.26
4. 0.024 ⊙ 0.026
5. 9.20 ⊙ 9.200
6. 125 ⊙ 125.6
7. 3.761 ⊙ 3.706
8. 7.003 ⊙ 7.03
9. 5.1 ⊙ 5.100
10. 19.5 ⊙ 19.36
11. 112.06 ⊙ 110.06
12. 48.7 ⊙ 48.763
13. 126.41 ⊙ 126.1
14. 29 ⊙ 29.02
15. 14.374 ⊙ 14.375

Write in order from least to greatest.

16. 9.11, 9.10, 9.01
    <u>9.01, 9.10, 9.11</u>

17. 17.095, 17.19, 17.509
    <u>17.095, 17.19, 17.509</u>

18. 38.271, 38.27, 38.197
    <u>38.197, 38.27, 38.271</u>

Apply

Solve these problems.
Use the table of winning records to answer 19 through 21.

19. Which team has the best record?
    <u>Jefferson</u>

20. Which team has the worst record?
    <u>Anthony</u>

School League Winning Records

Lincoln	0.689
Washington	0.750
King	0.721
Anthony	0.685
Jefferson	0.769

21. Write the decimals in order from least to greatest.
    <u>0.685</u>, <u>0.689</u>, <u>0.721</u>, <u>0.750</u>, <u>0.769</u>

Use the table of metric equivalents to answer 22 and 23.

22. Carol lives 2.65 kilometers from school. Heather lives 2,650 meters from school. Who lives farther from school?
    <u>Both are equally as far.</u>

Metric Equivalents

1 kilometer	= 1,000 meters
1 meter	= 100 centimeters
1 meter	= 1,000 millimeters
1 centimeter	= 10 millimeters

23. Which is larger, 5.96 centimeters or 596 millimeters?
    <u>596 mm</u>

222

Correcting Common Errors

Some students may have difficulty comparing numbers when they are shown side-by-side. Have them rewrite the numbers, one above the other, aligning the decimal points. Then they can compare, one place at a time, from left to right, until they reach the place where the digits differ, at which point they know that the number with the greater digit is the greater number. Remind students that they can annex zeros for missing digits to the right of the decimal point, as when comparing 0.8 and 0.83 (0.83 > 0.80).

Enrichment

Remind students that bicimals are binary decimals with place values ½, ¼, ⅛. Ask students to figure out the next two bicimal place values. (¹⁄₁₆ and ¹⁄₃₂) Have them write these fractions as bicimals:

1. ³⁄₁₆ (0.0011)
2. ⁷⁄₃₂ (0.00111)
3. ⁹⁄₁₆ (0.1001)

Practice

Have students complete the practice problems. Write on the board: **> means more than, < means less than.** Remind students that least means smallest, greatest means largest.

Mixed Practice

1. $37,720 \div 65$ (580 R20)
2. $2\frac{3}{4} \div 1\frac{3}{8}$ (2)
3. $198,176 - 4,094$ (194,082)
4. $3\frac{5}{7} + 2\frac{3}{4}$ $\left(6\frac{13}{28}\right)$
5. $\frac{3}{8} = \frac{}{48}$ (18)
6. $18\frac{1}{3} - 12\frac{5}{7}$ $\left(5\frac{13}{21}\right)$
7. $\frac{3}{4}$ of 1,340 (1,005)
8. $10,392 + 14,076 + 8,208$ (32,676)
9. $\frac{3}{4} + \frac{2}{5} + \frac{7}{10}$ $\left(1\frac{17}{20}\right)$
10. $\$19.78 \times 24$ ($474.72)

Extra Credit *Applications*

Divide students into groups. Tell each group they are to plan a route and compute the mileage to travel around the world, starting with their city. They may use any mode of transportation they choose. Have them choose the route, list cities they would stop over in and find the total mileage. Have groups use a world map to describe their chosen route to the rest of the class. See which group found the shortest route.

Adding Decimals

pages 223-224

Objective

To add decimals

Materials

Mental Math

Have students add:

1. 23 + 51 = (74)
2. 15 + 25 = (40)
3. 44 + 50 = (94)
4. 12 + 85 = (97)
5. 36 + 21 = (57)
6. 34 + 36 = (70)
7. 27 + 14 = (41)

Skill Review

Have students work these problems on paper:

1. $5.98
   + 2.36
   ($8.34)

2. $6.10
   + 15.76
   ($21.86)

3. $456.75
   + 78.25
   ($535.00)

4. $29.40
   + 52.02
   ($81.42)

5. $0.64
   + 1.29
   ($1.93)

6. $5.50
   + .29
   ($5.79)

Adding Decimals

Mrs. Minuez is driving from Bridgetown to Roseville on Route 29. How far will Mrs. Minuez drive?

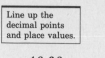

We need to find the total driving distance from Bridgetown to Roseville.

It is __48.68__ kilometers from Bridgetown to

Centerville, and __51.5__ kilometers from

Centerville to Gilman and __37.25__ kilometers from Gilman to Roseville.
To find the total distance, we add the three stages of the journey together.

We add __48.68__ , __51.5__ and __37.25__ .

Line up the decimal points and place values.	Zeros may be placed to the far right without changing the decimal's value.	Add from right to left. Place the decimal point between the ones and the tenths.
48.68 51.5 +37.25	48.68 51.50 +37.25	48.68 51.50 +37.25 137 43

Mrs. Minuez drove __137.43__ kilometers from Bridgetown to Roseville.

✔ When adding a whole number to a decimal number, place a decimal point and zeros after the whole number.

54.72 + 31 should be set up: 54.72
                                +31.00

Getting Started

Add.

1. 4.36
   + 2.59
   6.95

2. 12.9
   + 7.38
   20.28

3. 4.739
   + 1.821
   6.560

4. 11.24
   6.1
   + 9.306
   26.646

Copy and add.

5. 15 + 1.51
   16.51

6. 4.018 + 91.79
   95.808

7. 13 + 0.57 + 2.14
   15.71

223

MCP All rights reserved

Teaching the Lesson

Introducing the Problem Have students read the problem and the information sentences aloud. Explain that to find the total distance, they will add the three distances. Ask students to follow the problem in their texts while you write it on the board. Line up decimal points and place values. Add zeros to the right of the decimal. (51.5 = 51.50) Have a student do the addition on the board and read the answer aloud. (137.43) Read the final sentence aloud, explaining that when whole numbers are added to decimal numbers, zeros should be added to the right of the decimal point. (31 = 31.00)

Developing the Skill Explain that the addition of money is the addition of wholes and hundredths. Write **$43.39** on the board, and point out that 39¢ represents 39 hundredths of a dollar. Explain that adding decimals is like adding money. First they line up place values. They may add zeros to the right of the decimal. Write on the board:

23.4   (23.40)
5.81   (5.81)
13   (13.00)

Ask a student to add zeros until the ragged right-hand edge is gone. Have another student do the addition on the board while the rest work the problem at their seats. (42.21)

Add.

1.	6.81 + 4.75 ————— 11.56	2.	29.7 + 48.6 ————— 78.3	3.	39.21 + 14.7 ————— 53.91	4.	4.372 + 1.985 ————— 6.357
5.	12.762 + 9.36 ————— 22.122	6.	18.4 + 75.329 ————— 93.729	7.	27.8 + 39.2 ————— 67.0	8.	78 + 6.06 ————— 84.06
9.	4.372 2.189 + 8.754 ————— 15.315	10.	9.62 11.8 + 18.375 ————— 39.795	11.	18.28 29 + 56.3 ————— 103.58	12.	45.702 42.37 + 37.9 ————— 125.972
13.	751.06 90.24 + 872.16 ————— 1,713.46	14.	234.31 178.31 + 800.07 ————— 1,212.69	15.	12 0.07 + 123.45 ————— 135.52	16.	0.002 1.713 + 42.04 ————— 43.755

Copy and Do

17. 18.6 + 17.3
35.9

18. 29.65 + 38.29
67.94

19. 12.731 + 18.296
31.027

20. 15.27 + 28.9
44.17

21. 7.593 + 18.2
25.793

22. 49.75 + 85.392
135.142

23. 13.721 + 12.58 + 26.85
53.151

24. 6.475 + 8.21 + 9.323 + 8.4
32.408

25. 12.14 + 61.96 + 5.115
79.215

26. 1.183 + 19.31 + 720 + 8.04
748.533

27. 14.92 + 1.812 + 106.6
123.332

28. 329.8 + 33.01 + 4.92
367.73

29. 86.86 + 423 + 0.001 + 1.7
511.561

30. 289.76 + 22.22 + 4.007
315.987

Apply

Solve these problems.

31. Find the perimeter of a rectangle that is 36.25 centimeters wide and 14.72 centimeters long.
101.94 centimeters

32. One bucket holds 13.735 liters of water. Another bucket holds 4.815 liters more water than the first. How many liters of water will both buckets hold altogether?
32.285 liters

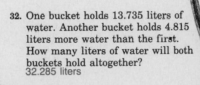

224

Correcting Common Errors

When students are adding decimals, some may add the decimal-parts to the right of the decimal point and the whole-number parts separately.

INCORRECT	CORRECT
24.9 + 43.5 ————— 67.14	24.9 + 43.5 ————— 68.4

Have students work the problems on a place-value chart, renaming from right to left, just as they do when adding whole numbers.

Enrichment

Show students how to convert a fraction to a decimal by dividing. Explain that if they divide the numerator by the denominator, keeping the decimal point in place, the resulting decimal equals the fraction:

$$\frac{1}{5} = 5\overline{)1.0}^{\,.2} \qquad \frac{1}{5} = \,^{.2}$$
$$\phantom{\frac{1}{5} = } \underline{1\,0}$$

Have students find the decimal equivalents for ⅛. (.125) and ¾. (.75)

Practice

Have students do the practice problems. Remind them to line up place values when they copy and add.

Mixed Practice

1. $156 - 98\frac{11}{12}$ $\left(57\frac{1}{12}\right)$
2. $1,700.02 - $1,358.08 ($341.94)
3. $3\frac{1}{8} + 4\frac{5}{6}$ $\left(7\frac{23}{24}\right)$
4. $3\frac{2}{3} \times 4\frac{1}{4}$ $\left(15\frac{2}{3}\right)$
5. $9.53 \times 76 ($724.28)
6. $\frac{2}{7}$ of 420 (120)
7. $1\frac{1}{2} \div \frac{3}{4}$ (2)
8. 5,791 × 60 (347,460)
9. 29.8 + 35.656 (65.456)
10. 30,169 ÷ 6 (5,028 R1)

Extra Credit *Logic*

Duplicate the following for students to solve:
You and two fellow Space Rangers find yourselves forced to crash-land on Em C-P. You must stay in your ship or in a space suit, since the planet's atmosphere is poisonous to humans. You must make the 12-hour walk to the Ranger Base because your radio is out.

Due to Em C-P's gravity, none of you can carry more than 8 hours of oxygen. After much thought, you figure out a way for one of you to get to the Ranger Base, with sufficient oxygen, and bring back help. What solution did you discover? (All three Rangers start out with 8 hours of oxygen, and walk for 2 hours. One transfers two hours of oxygen to you and two to the other Ranger and returns to the ship with the remaining two hours of oxygen. With a full 8 hours of oxygen, you and the other Ranger walk two more hours. Then they transfer two hours of oxygen to you, giving you enough oxygen to get to the Ranger Base, while keeping the necessary 4 hours of oxygen to return to the ship and wait for you to bring back help.)

Subtracting Decimals

pages 225-226

Objective

To subtract decimals

Materials

Mental Math

Have students subtract:

1. 46 − 12 = (34)
2. 19 − 8 = (11)
3. 23 − 10 = (13)
4. 45 − 25 = (20)
5. 56 − 49 = (7)
6. 34 − 17 = (17)
7. 48 − 19 = (29)

Skill Review

Have students work these problems on the board:

1. $9.74
   −6.58
   ($3.16)

2. $25.00
   −17.58
   ($7.42)

3. $4.35
   − .89
   ($3.46)

4. $28.90
   − 19.95
   ($8.95)

5. $.67
   −.09
   ($.58)

6. $52.89
   − 45.59
   ($7.30)

Subtracting Decimals

Hilo has the highest rainfall average in Hawaii and Honolulu has the lowest average. How much more rain does Hilo average each year than Honolulu?

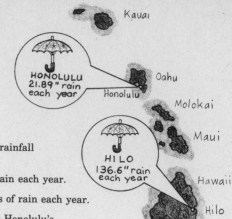

We want to find the difference in rainfall between the two cities.

Hilo averages __136.6__ inches of rain each year.

Honolulu averages __21.89__ inches of rain each year.

To find the difference, we subtract Honolulu's average rainfall from that of Hilo.

We subtract __21.89__ from __136.6__.

Line up the decimal point and place values.	Zeros may be placed to the far right without changing the decimal value.	Subtract from right to left. Place the decimal point between the ones and the tenths.
1 3 6.6 − 2 1.8 9	1 3 6.6 0 − 2 1.8 9	1 3 6.6 0 − 2 1.8 9 1 1 4.7 1

On the average, it rains __114.71__ inches more each year in Hilo than in Honolulu.

Getting Started

Subtract.

1. 9.8
   − 6.4
   3.4

2. 127.34
   − 68.5
   58.84

3. 3.926
   − 1.581
   2.345

4. 5.8
   − 2.785
   3.015

Copy and subtract.

5. 29.372 − 14.785
   14.587

6. 18 − 7.328
   10.672

7. 493.8 − 237.46
   256.34

8. 127.5 − 4.98
   122.52

9. 254.09 − 31.799
   222.291

10. 572.34 − 28.3
    544.04

MCP All rights reserved

225

Teaching the Lesson

Introducing the Problem Have a student read the problem aloud. Read the information sentences and explain that to find the difference, students will have to subtract. Direct their attention to the problem and have them follow in their books while you work the problem on the board. Explain that as in addition of decimals, they will line up place values before they begin. Show them how to add zeros to equalize the number of decimal places. Ask a student to do the subtraction. Read the answer (114.71) and have a student read the solution sentence.

Developing the Skill Explain that the steps in subtracting decimals are like those in adding decimals or whole numbers. First line up like place values. Show them that when place values are in order, the decimal points will also form a column. Next add zeros to the right-hand side of some decimals. Remind them that adding zeros to the right of a decimal does not change its value. Write on the board: .5 = .50 = .500, and underneath write $5/10 = 50/100 = 500/1000$. Point out that when subtracting, renaming will be done as it is with money or with whole numbers. Explain that this is because place values on either side of the decimal point differ from one another by a factor of ten.

Practice

Subtract.

1. $\begin{array}{r} 18.7 \\ -14.9 \\ \hline 3.8 \end{array}$	2. $\begin{array}{r} 26.38 \\ -14.71 \\ \hline 11.67 \end{array}$	3. $\begin{array}{r} 38.421 \\ -16.549 \\ \hline 21.872 \end{array}$	4. $\begin{array}{r} 73.5 \\ -16.68 \\ \hline 56.82 \end{array}$
5. $\begin{array}{r} 15.391 \\ -9.36 \\ \hline 6.031 \end{array}$	6. $\begin{array}{r} 48.21 \\ -12.875 \\ \hline 35.335 \end{array}$	7. $\begin{array}{r} 74.32 \\ -18.7 \\ \hline 55.62 \end{array}$	8. $\begin{array}{r} 89.8 \\ -14.962 \\ \hline 74.838 \end{array}$
9. $\begin{array}{r} 125 \\ -8.75 \\ \hline 116.25 \end{array}$	10. $\begin{array}{r} 3.876 \\ -1.968 \\ \hline 1.908 \end{array}$	11. $\begin{array}{r} 4.003 \\ -2.96 \\ \hline 1.043 \end{array}$	12. $\begin{array}{r} 15.21 \\ -7.857 \\ \hline 7.353 \end{array}$
13. $\begin{array}{r} 987.01 \\ -42.99 \\ \hline 944.02 \end{array}$	14. $\begin{array}{r} 100.78 \\ -1.87 \\ \hline 98.91 \end{array}$	15. $\begin{array}{r} 17.341 \\ -16.279 \\ \hline 1.062 \end{array}$	16. $\begin{array}{r} 87.47 \\ -83.81 \\ \hline 3.66 \end{array}$

Copy and Do

17. $49.75 - 39.87$
9.88

18. $146.01 - 57.376$
88.634

19. $59.327 - 16.9$
42.427

20. $25 - 3.721$
21.279

21. $67.39 - 58.5$
8.89

22. $86.215 - 19.392$
66.823

23. $50.06 - 39.781$
10.279

24. $375.9 - 148.48$
227.42

25. $939.6 - 758.972$
180.628

26. $17.76 - 12.02$
5.74

27. $4.86 - 2.99$
1.87

28. $86.67 - 86.66$
0.01

29. $751.06 - 30.31$
720.75

30. $184.14 - 125.09$
59.05

31. $111.07 - 99.9$
11.17

Apply

Solve these problems.

32. A jar that held 3.348 liters of water now is holding 1.5 liters. How much water has been poured out?
1.848 liters

33. In two hours, the barometer dropped 0.15. The current reading is 29.89. What was the reading before it began to drop two hours ago?
30.04

34. Lin bought a pair of pants for $39.95 and a shirt for $8.45. How much change did he receive from a fifty-dollar bill?
$1.60

35. Roxanne purchased 4.5 kilograms of ground beef yesterday. She froze some of it in 2 packs, one weighing 2.6 kilograms and the other 1.5 kilograms. She made hamburgers out of the remaining beef. How much beef was made into hamburger?
0.4 of a kilogram

226

Correcting Common Errors

When copying decimals to subtract, some students may not line up the decimal points correctly.

INCORRECT	CORRECT
$\begin{array}{r} 93.54 \\ -8.12 \\ \hline 1.234 \end{array}$	$\begin{array}{r} 93.54 \\ -8.12 \\ \hline 85.42 \end{array}$

Have students work the problems on a place-value chart, making sure to line up the decimal points correctly.

Enrichment

Write these equivalents on the board:
$$\frac{1}{8} = .125$$
$$\frac{1}{4} = .25$$
$$\frac{1}{5} = .2$$

Explain that from these they can find other equivalents: $\frac{2}{5} = .2 + .2 = .4$ or $\frac{3}{8} = .125 + .125 + .125 = .375$. Ask students to change these problems to decimal equivalents and then add or subtract:

1. $\frac{1}{2} - \frac{1}{8} = (.500 - .125 = .375)$
2. $\frac{2}{5} + \frac{7}{8} = (.4 + .875 = 1.275)$
3. $\frac{3}{8} + \frac{1}{4} = (.375 + .25 = .400)$

Practice

Have students complete the practice problems. Remind them to line up like place values and add zeros to the right until the columns are even.

Extra Credit   *Creative Drill*

Have students count their heart rate or a partner's, for one minute. Then have them use their calculators to answer the following questions:
How many times does the average 5th grader's heart beat in an hour? How many times does a heart beat in a day? How many times does a heart beat in a year? How many times has your heart beat so far during your lifetime?

226

Add or Subtract Decimals

pages 227-228

Objective

To practice adding and subtracting decimals

Materials

place value charts

Mental Math

Have students identify the missing operation:

1. 12 ( ) 3 = 15 (+)
2. 15 ( ) 12 = 180 (×)
3. 547 ( ) 338 = 209 (−)
4. 38 ( ) 19 = 57 (+)
5. 10 ( ) 2 = 5 (÷)
6. 3 ( ) 2 = 1½ (÷)
7. ⅔ ( ) ⅔ = 1⅓ (+)

Skill Review

Have students copy and do these problems:

1. 23.5 + 9.36 = (32.86)
2. 49.31 + 18.23 = (67.54)
3. 19.03 − 4.6 = (14.43)
4. 3.9 + 1.22 = (5.12)
5. 5 − 3.42 = (1.58)
6. 17.3 − 6 = (11.3)

Adding and Subtracting Decimals

On her business trips to Los Angeles and San Francisco, Mrs. Banks travels around the cities by cab. How much more per mile does it cost her to ride a cab in Los Angeles than San Francisco?

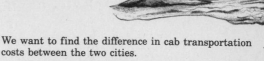

We want to find the difference in cab transportation costs between the two cities.

It costs _60.69¢_ per mile to ride a cab in Los Angeles

and _58.16¢_ per mile to ride in San Francisco.

To find the difference, we subtract the cost per mile of a cab ride in San Francisco from the per-mile cost in Los Angeles.

We subtract _58.16¢_ from _60.69¢_.

Line up the decimal point and place values.	Subtract from right to left. Place the decimal point between the ones and tenths.
60.69¢ − 58.16¢	60.69¢ − 58.16¢ 2.53¢

✔ Use a cent symbol, ¢, when the digits to the left of the decimal point refer to cents.

We read **2.53¢** as **two and fifty-three hundredths cents** and understand that the amount is between 2¢ and 3¢.

It costs _2.53¢_ per mile more to ride a cab in Los Angeles.

Getting Started

Add or subtract.

1.	$37.48 − 16.95 $20.53	2.	7.862 + 1.38 9.242	3.	$217.15 + 622.48 $839.63	4.	19.73 − 8.285 11.445

Copy and add or subtract.

5. 79 − 0.79
78.21

6. $447.23 + $138.15
$585.38

7. 560.19 − 8.7
551.49

8. 103.01 + 0.59
103.60

MCP All rights reserved

227

Teaching the Lesson

Introducing the Problem Read the problem aloud and ask a student to read the information sentences. Explain that to find the difference, they will subtract one cost per mile from the other. Point out the difference between $58.16 and 58.16¢. Show students that the first is 58 dollars and 16 cents; the second, 58¢ and the decimal part of a cent, ¹⁶⁄₁₀₀. Direct students' attention to the subtraction worked in their texts. Have a student do the subtraction on the board, working right to left. Ask a student to read the solution sentence. (costs 2.53¢ per mile more) Have them read the last sentences in the problem, and show on the board that 2.53¢ is between 2¢ and 3¢ on a number line.

Developing the Skill Put these steps on the board:

ADDING AND SUBTRACTING DECIMALS

1. **Line up like place values by putting decimal points in a column.**
2. **Add any necessary zeros to the right of the decimal point.**
3. **Add or subtract, renaming units as with whole numbers.**

Explain that they can work with any decimal or mixed decimal number by following these steps.

227

Practice

Add or subtract.

1.
$$\begin{array}{r} 29.7 \\ + 16.85 \\ \hline 46.55 \end{array}$$

2.
$$\begin{array}{r} \$30.15 \\ - 9.86 \\ \hline \$20.29 \end{array}$$

3.
$$\begin{array}{r} 4.8 \\ - 2.796 \\ \hline 2.004 \end{array}$$

4.
$$\begin{array}{r} 39.751 \\ + 18.56 \\ \hline 58.311 \end{array}$$

5.
$$\begin{array}{r} \$138.50 \\ - 79.97 \\ \hline \$58.53 \end{array}$$

6.
$$\begin{array}{r} 182.47 \\ + 96.5 \\ \hline 278.97 \end{array}$$

7.
$$\begin{array}{r} 45.007 \\ - 12.378 \\ \hline 32.629 \end{array}$$

8.
$$\begin{array}{r} \$126.85 \\ + 589.38 \\ \hline \$716.23 \end{array}$$

9.
$$\begin{array}{r} 67.85 \\ 38.4 \\ + 15.76 \\ \hline 122.01 \end{array}$$

10.
$$\begin{array}{r} 59 \\ - 7.85 \\ \hline 51.15 \end{array}$$

11.
$$\begin{array}{r} \$475.15 \\ - 219.85 \\ \hline \$255.30 \end{array}$$

12.
$$\begin{array}{r} 121.327 \\ 9.8 \\ + 375.67 \\ \hline 506.797 \end{array}$$

Copy and Do

13. 159.46 − 83.75
    75.71
14. 379.2 + 186.38
    565.58
15. $457.56 − $196.88
    $260.68
16. 486.5 − 97.964
    388.536
17. $49.68 + $800.41
    $850.09
18. 752.4 + 379.621
    1,132.021
19. 758.85 − 147.975
    610.875
20. 365 − 29.76
    335.24
21. 189.5 + 79.95 + 265.4
    534.85

Apply

Solve these problems.

22. A molding machine accepts steel cut into lengths of 17.36 centimeters. A piece cut into 17.365 centimeters is rejected. What is the difference in the length of the two pieces?
    0.005 of a centimeter

23. The average cost of T-bone steak was $4.05 a pound in 1985. By 1991, the average price was $5.21 a pound. If the price continues to climb at the same rate, how much will the meat cost per pound in 1997?
    $6.37

Use the graph of snowfall to answer 24 and 25.

24. How much less did it snow in the two months of November and December than in the three months of January, February and March?
    3.7 feet

25. The record snowfall in Skiville in one year is 25 feet. How close to the record is this year's snowfall?
    4.3 feet less

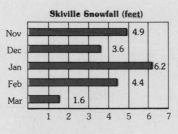

Skiville Snowfall (feet)

Nov 4.9
Dec 3.6
Jan 6.2
Feb 4.4
Mar 1.6

1 2 3 4 5 6 7

228

Correcting Common Errors

Some students may forget to annex zeros when they are required to understand an addition or subtraction problem. Have them align the decimal points and then annex zeros so that there are the same number of places to the right of the decimal point in both numbers in the problem. For example:

$$\begin{array}{r} 44.7 \\ - 23.19 = \end{array} \quad \begin{array}{r} 44.70 \\ - 23.19 \\ \hline 21.51 \end{array}$$

Enrichment

Give students pieces of graph paper that are 10 squares on a side, a total of 100 squares per block. Ask them to shade squares with colored pencils to illustrate these addition problems:

1. 1.3 + .45 = (1.75)
2. .34 + .9 = (1.24)
3. 2.5 + .25 = (2.75)
4. 2.4 + 1.12 = (3.52)

Have them show their decimal visual aids to the rest of the class.

Practice

Have students complete the problems. Suggest they follow the steps as they do each problem.

Mixed Practice

1. $\frac{17}{18} - \frac{5}{6}$ $\left(\frac{1}{9}\right)$

2. 95 + 193 + 765 + 43 (1,096)

3. $\frac{5}{9}$ of 36 (20)

4. 890 × 503 (447,670)

5. 6.7 − 3.95 (2.75)

6. 42,021 − 18,650 (23,371)

7. $250.04 ÷ 38 ($6.58)

8. 17.38 + 12.465 + 3.08 (32.925)

9. $795.41 × 3 ($2,386.23)

10. 18 ÷ $1\frac{1}{2}$ (12)

Extra Credit *Applications*

Have students calculate what their age would be if they lived on the planet Ionium that orbits the sun once every 45 days. Then have them figure how old they would be if Ionium's orbit was every 2,006 days.

Rounding Decimals

pages 229-230

Objective

To round decimals to the nearest whole number, tenth or hundredth

Materials

Mental Math

Have students arrange these in order from smallest to largest:

1. hour, minute, day (minute, hour, day)
2. ounce, gallon, quart (ounce, quart, gallon)
3. centimeter, meter, kilometer (centimeter, meter, kilometer)
4. year, second, month (second, month, year)
5. pound, gram, ounce (gram, ounce, pound)

Skill Review

Ask students to round each of these to the nearest 10, 100 and nearest 1,000:

1. 309 (310, 300, 0)
2. 9,281 (9,280, 9,300, 9,000)
3. 598 (600, 600, 1,000)
4. 423 (420, 400, 0)
5. 12,930 (12,930, 12,900, 13,000)
6. 1,002 (1,000, 1,000, 1,000)

Rounding Decimals

Measurements are never exact. They are only approximate numbers. Rounding decimal numbers, such as these weight measurements, makes them easier to add or subtract. Round each of the pictured measurements to the nearest tenth.

We want to round the decimal numbers, __42.71__ and __32.481__, to the nearest tenth.

To round a decimal, look at the digit to the right of the place you want to round to.

If the digit to the right is **less than 5,** the digit you are rounding to stays the same and you drop all digits to the right.
42.71 ⟶ 42.7

If the digit to the right is **5 or more,** add 1 to the digit you are rounding to and drop all digits to the right.
32.481 ⟶ 32.5

42.71
32.481
Round—↑↑—Look
here.　　here.

42.71 rounded to the nearest tenth is __42.7__.

32.481 rounded to the nearest tenth is __32.5__.

Getting Started

Round to the nearest whole number.

1. 17.8 __18__　　2. 9.63 __10__　　3. 11.05 __11__　　4. 6.591 __7__

Round to the nearest tenth.

5. 26.73 __26.7__　　6. 7.05 __7.1__　　7. 27.391 __27.4__　　8. 14.51 __14.5__

Round to the nearest hundredth.

9. 6.078 __6.08__　　10. 19.999 __20.00__　　11. 16.834 __16.83__　　12. 4.009 __4.01__

MCP All rights reserved

229

Teaching the Lesson

Introducing the Skill Read the problem aloud and ask a student to read the information sentences. Put each number on the board and point to the tenths position. Explain that if the number to the right of tenths is less than five they will drop all the digits to the right to round to the nearest tenth. If the number to the right is five or more, they will increase the digit in the tenths position by one and drop all digits to the right. Have a student round 42.71 to tenths. (42.7) Ask another to round 32.481 to tenths. (32.5) Have students look at the illustration in their texts. Read the solution sentences aloud. (42.71 to 42.7, 32.481 to 32.5)

Developing the Skill Explain that decimals can be rounded to any place value, tenths, hundredths, thousandths and so on. In each case, they will look to the right to decide how to round, just as they look one place to the right when they decide how to round whole numbers. Put this chart on the board and have students complete it:

number	nearest one	nearest tenth	nearest hundredth
3.435	(3	3.4	3.44)
15.993	(16	16.0	16.99)
8.673	(9	8.7	8.67)

Round to the nearest whole numbers.

1. 14.2 _____ 14
2. 6.85 _____ 7
3. 17.061 _____ 17
4. 4.37 _____ 4
5. 89.76 _____ 90
6. 32.4 _____ 32
7. 96.54 _____ 97
8. 128.276 _____ 128

Round to the nearest tenth.

9. 6.25 _____ 6.3
10. 9.387 _____ 9.4
11. 11.006 _____ 11.0
12. 58.715 _____ 58.7
13. 215.87 _____ 215.9
14. 903.99 _____ 904.0
15. 76.508 _____ 76.5
16. 15.75 _____ 15.8

Round to the nearest hundredth.

17. 6.271 _____ 6.27
18. 9.128 _____ 9.13
19. 14.375 _____ 14.38
20. 49.666 _____ 49.67
21. 43.002 _____ 43.00
22. 24.964 _____ 24.96
23. 72.411 _____ 72.41
24. 105.315 _____ 105.32

Apply

Solve these problems.

25. The Willamite meteorite is the largest meteorite ever found in the United States. It measures about 299.72 centimeters in length. Round the length to the nearest centimeter.
300 centimeters

26. The Oroville Dam in California is the tallest dam in the United States. It measures about 230.428 meters in height. Round the height to the nearest meter.
230 meters

EXCURSION

When a number is multiplied by itself several times, a special notation called an **exponent** is used as a shorthand form. In the equation, $3 \times 3 \times 3 \times 3 = 3^4$, 3 is called the **base** and 4 is the **exponent**. The exponent indicates how many times to use the base as a factor. Write the standard product for each of the following exponential expressions. The first one is done for you.

1. $5^4 =$
$5 \times 5 \times 5 \times 5 = 625$

2. $3^4 \times 3^2 =$
$3 \times 3 \times 3 \times 3 \times 3 \times 3 = 729$

3. $1^8 \times 5^2 \times 2^2 =$
$1 \times 1 \times 1 \times 1 \times 1 \times 1 \times 1 \times 1 \times 6 \times 5 \times 2 \times 2 = 100$

4. $2^3 \times 3^2 =$
$2 \times 2 \times 2 \times 3 \times 3 = 72$

5. $10^4 =$
$10 \times 10 \times 10 \times 10 = 10,000$

6. $5^2 \times 5^2 =$
$5 \times 5 \times 5 \times 5 = 625$

230

Correcting Common Errors

Some students may round decimals incorrectly because they forget to drop the digits to the right of the place to which they are rounding. First, have them draw an arrow over the digit in the place to which they are rounding. Once they have decided whether to keep that digit the same or make it one greater, they drop all of the digits to the right of the digit under the arrow.

Enrichment

Explain that most inch rulers are divided into fourths and eighths. Give students one-inch graph paper with the squares subdivided into tenths. Have them cut apart the graph paper, and tape it together to make an inch ruler that is divided into tenths. They may need stiff paper for backing. Have them measure several items in their desk with the new ruler. Ask students when such a ruler would be useful.

Practice

Have students complete the problems on the page. Remind them to look to the right of the place value they want to round to.

Excursion

Have students express the answer to the second problem in a simpler exponential form as 3 to some power. Ask students to give the relationship between the power or exponent of 10 in the fifth problem. Add the number of zeros in the resulting number.

Extra Credit   *Numeration*

Have students research the following questions:
What numbers come after trillions?
(quadrillions, quintillions, sextillions, septillions, octillions, nonillions and decillions)
What is a googol and googolplex?
(Googol is the number 1 followed by 100 zeros; googolplex is the number 1 followed by a googol of zeros.) Have students make a bulletin board display of unusual number words and definitions, adding to it other terms they come across in their research.

Problem Solving
Work Backward

pages 231-232

Objective

To solve problems by working backward

Materials

Mental Math

Ask students how many of each number can be subtracted:

1. How many twos from 14? (7)
2. How many fives from 45? (9)
3. How many tens from 90? (9)
4. How many threes from 24? (8)
5. How many twelves from 24? (2)
6. How many sixes from 36? (6)
7. How many nines from 54? (6)

Working Backwards

Ann spent half of her money on a birthday present for her mother. She then spent half of what was left on two records for herself. On the way home, Ann met Pat who returned the five dollars Ann had lent her. Ann now had $20. How much money did she have at the start?

★ SEE

We want to know how much money Ann had before she went shopping. She spent half of her money on a present for her mother. She spent half of what was left for two records.

She got $5 from a friend. Ann ended up with $20 left.

★ PLAN

Since we know that Ann had twenty dollars in the end, and we know how Ann spent her money, we can work backwards to find out how much she had to start.

★ DO

$20 − $5 = $15	This is the amount of money Ann had before Pat returned $5.00.
$15 × 2 = $30	Since Pat spent half of what was left on records, we can double what she had left to find out what she had before buying the records.
$30 × 2 = $60	Since Pat spent half of her money on a present for her mother, we can double what she had after buying the gift to find the amount she started with.

Pat had $60 at the start.

★ CHECK

We can check our solution by working forward.

$\frac{1}{2}$ of $60 = $30 (The amount Ann spent on the gift)

$60 − $30 = $30 (The amount of money Ann had left after buying the gift)

$\frac{1}{2}$ of $30 = $15 (The amount Ann spent on records)

$30 − $15 = $15 (The amount of money Ann had left after buying the records)

$15 + $5 = $20 (The amount of money Ann had left after the $5.00 was returned)

MCP All rights reserved

231

Teaching the Lesson

Read the problem aloud. Remind students that problems can be solved by the four-step SEE, PLAN, DO, CHECK method. Have a student read the SEE section of the text. Read the PLAN section aloud, explaining that to find what Ann had to begin with, they will have to work backward from what she had in the end. Direct students' attention to the DO section where the problem has been laid out. Have students read aloud the next sections in their texts. Ask a student to read the solution sentence. (had $60 at the start) Explain that some problems can be solved by working them in reverse. Point out that this means not only working backward, but also doing the opposite operation. When an amount has been halved, they will double it; if an amount has been subtracted, they will add it.

Have the class work the CHECK together, going forward through Ann's day to see that she has $20 left if she starts with $60.

Solve these problems.

1. If I multiply my age by three and add 40 I get 85. How old am I?
15 years old

2. Jenny bought a compass for $0.59. Then she bought a notebook that cost four times as much as the compass. She received $2.05 in change. How much money did she give the clerk?
$5.00

3. Mark spent 30 minutes eating dinner, 15 minutes helping with the dishes and 1 hour practicing piano. He then spent one and one half hours on homework, and 30 minutes reading. He went to bed at 9:00. What time did Mark start eating dinner?
5:15

4. The perimeter of a rectangle is 58 inches. One half of the width is 6 inches. What is the length of the rectangle?
17 inches

5. In a Silly-Day contest, George made 100 paper hats in 5 hours. Each hour he made 6 less than he did the previous hour. How many hats did he make during each hour?
32 hats in the first hour
26 in the second   14 in the fourth
20 in the third   8 in the fifth

6. At the Farmer's Market, a farmer sold half of all the watermelons he had plus half of another watermelon. He had 8 watermelons left. How many watermelons did he have to start with?
17 watermelons

7. Puff Dragon's tail is 1.84 meter long. Poof Dragon's tail is 1.57 meter long. Use a pencil only to write whether the difference in the lengths of the tails is greater or less than 1 meter.
Less than 1 meter

8. Puff worked a subtraction problem with decimals and found the correct answer to be 37.6. If he increased each of the two numbers in the subtraction problem by 3.4, what answer would he get?
37.6

9. Poof eats 8.5 apples a day to keep the dragon doctor away. Tell whether this is more or less than 260 apples per month and explain how you got your answer.
See Solution Notes.

232

1. Have students start with 85. Reverse the last operation (add 40) and subtract 40. ($85 - 40 = 45$) Reverse the operation preceeding that (multiply by 3) and divide by 3. ($45 \div 3 = 15$)

2. Have students find the amount of the purchase, $.59 plus ($4 \times$ $.59). The total purchase ($.59 + $2.36) is $2.95. Add the price and the change to find the amount given. ($2.95 + $2.05 = $5.00)

3. Start backward from 9:00 PM: 9:00 − 30 min = 8:30, 8:30 − 1½ hr = 7:00, 7:00 − 1 hr = 6:00, 6:00 − 15 min = 5:45; 5:45 − 30 min = 5:15 PM

4. The perimeter is twice the length plus twice the width. The perimeter is 58, and the width twice 6 inches or 12 inches. Twice the width is 24 inches and the difference between the perimeter and twice the width will be twice the length. (58 − 24 = 34) So the length = 17 inches.

5. This problem involves guessing. They can divide 100 hats into 5 hours, but not evenly because he made 6 more hats in the first hour than in the next, 6 more the second than the third. Have them try initial numbers between 25 and 35. (32, 26, 20, 14, 8)

6. Start with 8 watermelons and add ½ watermelon representing the half sold. (8½) This is half of all he had. Double 8½ to see what he began with. (17 watermelons)

Higher-Order Thinking Skills

7. Analysis: Answers will vary. One is to think in terms of money and recognize that the difference between $1.84 and $1.57 is much less than $1.00.

8. Synthesis: Increasing both subtrahend and minuend by the same amount has no effect on the difference.

9. Evaluation: Because $8.5 \times 31 = 263.5$ and $8.5 \times 30 = 255$, it is less than 260 apples per month for every month except January, March, May, July, August, October, and December.

Extra Credit *Applications*

As an extension of a previous extra credit, tracking a round-the-world trip, have students again refer to their mileage totals. Choose a specific starting day and mode of transportation, and have students figure how long their trips will take, and the exact day they will return. Things they will have to research and consider include: average place speed, lay-over time for refueling, time zones crossed, etc.

Chapter Test

page 233

Item	Objective
1-7	Change mixed numbers and decimal words to equivalent decimal numbers (See pages 213-214)
8-11	Identify place value from thousands through thousandths (See pages 215-220)
12-15	Compare, order decimals (See pages 221-222)
16-19	Add decimals (See pages 223-224)
20-23	Subtract decimals (See pages 225-226)
24-27	Round decimals to nearest tenth (See pages 229-230)
28-31	Round decimals to nearest hundredth (See pages 229-230)

Write the decimal.

1. $7\frac{9}{10}$ = __7.9__   2. $6\frac{5}{100}$ = __6.05__   3. $\frac{8}{1000}$ = __0.008__

4. seventy-four hundredths = __0.74__   5. five and six thousandths __5.006__

6. fourteen thousandths = __0.014__   7. five and seven hundredths __5.07__

Write the place value of each red digit.

8. 29.461   9. 3,485.1   10. 6.009   11. 138.756

   hundredths   tens   hundredths   thousandths

Write <, = or > in the circle.

12. 19.2 (=) 19.20   13. 6.75 (>) 6.7

14. 3.006 (<) 3.018   15. 0.621 (>) 0.612

Add.

16. 742.6
   + 139.24
   __881.84__

17. 16.308
   + 9.75
   __26.058__

18. 421.326
   + 385.775
   __807.101__

19. 7.09
   4.276
   + 8.932
   __20.298__

Subtract.

20. 39.754
   − 15.296
   __24.458__

21. 2.039
   − 0.75
   __1.289__

22. 29
   − 6.75
   __22.25__

23. 126.35
   − 97.482
   __28.868__

Round to the nearest tenth.

24. 17.39 __17.4__   25. 78.556 __78.6__

26. 32.985 __33.0__   27. 8.31 __8.3__

Round to the nearest hundredth.

28. 126.372 __126.37__   29. 829.085 __829.09__

30. 283.192 __283.19__   31. 4.279 __4.28__

MCP All rights reserved

233

233

Circle the letter of the correct answer.

1 12,375
+ 8,196

a 10,461
b 20,461
c 20,571
d NG

2 7,046
− 2,685

a 4,361
b 5,381
c 5,641
d NG

3 $6.25
× 9

a $55.85
b $56.25
c $58.25
d NG

4 39 × 57

a 468
b 2,123
c 2,423
d NG

5 3)30,603

a 121
b 10,201
c 1,201
d NG

6 27)1,300

a 48
b 48 R4
c 48 R6
d NG

7 Find the volume.
Length = 9 cm
Width = 6 cm
Height = 2 cm

a 17 cu cm
b 56 cu cm
c 108 cu cm
d NG

8 6 ft 9 in.
+ 2 ft 6 in.

a 8 ft 3 in.
b 9 ft 3 in.
c 9 ft 5 in.
d NG

9 Simplify.
$\frac{28}{6}$

a $\frac{14}{3}$
b $4\frac{2}{3}$
c $4\frac{3}{4}$
d NG

10 $5\frac{1}{3}$
+ $2\frac{5}{8}$

a $7\frac{3}{4}$
b $8\frac{1}{24}$
c $8\frac{3}{4}$
d NG

11 $9\frac{7}{8}$
− $3\frac{1}{8}$

a $5\frac{3}{4}$
b $7\frac{3}{4}$
c $7\frac{7}{8}$
d NG

12 $11\frac{1}{3}$
− $9\frac{2}{5}$

a $\frac{14}{15}$
b $1\frac{1}{15}$
c $1\frac{14}{15}$
d NG

□ score

234

Item	Objective
1	Add two numbers up to 6-digits (See pages 27-28)
2	Subtract two 4-digit numbers, zero in minuend (See pages 33-34)
3	Multiply money by 1-digit number (See pages 55-56)
4	Multiply two 2-digit factors (See pages 57-58)
5	Divide a 5-digit by 1-digit number, quotient with zeros (See pages 87-88)
6	Divide a 4-digit by 2-digit number (See pages 103-106)
7	Find volume of rectangular solids (See pages 129-130)
8	Add customary units of length (See pages 123-124)
9	Change an improper fraction to a mixed number (See pages 157-158)
10	Add two mixed numbers (See pages 175-176)
11-12	Subtract two mixed numbers (See pages 179-180)

Cumulative Review
page 234

Alternate Cumulative Review

Circle the letter of the correct answer.

1 43,754
+ 7,689

a 51,343
b 51,443
c 50,443
d NG

2 6,052
− 3,998

a 2,054
b 2,154
c 2,164
d NG

3 $7.65
×4

a $3.06
b $30.60
c $31.60
d NG

4 54
×27

a 486
b 1,448
c 1,558
d NG

5 4)43,632

a 1,098
b 10,908
c 1,908
d NG

6 39)1,600

a 41
b 41 R1
c 41 R3
d NG

7 Find the volume of a box 7 cm by 18 cm by 4 cm.

a 29 cu cm
b 126 cu cm
c 504 cu cm
d NG

8 7 ft 8 in.
+ 2 ft 4 in.

a 9 ft 11 in.
b 10 ft
c 10 ft 2 in.
d NG

9 Simplify.
$\frac{44}{6}$

a $7\frac{1}{6}$
b $7\frac{1}{3}$
c $7\frac{2}{3}$
d NG

10 $8\frac{3}{4}$
+ $2\frac{1}{7}$

a $10\frac{25}{28}$
b $10\frac{24}{28}$
c $11\frac{1}{28}$
d NG

11 $13\frac{3}{8}$
− $8\frac{1}{5}$

a $5\frac{3}{40}$
b $5\frac{7}{40}$
c $5\frac{8}{40}$
d NG

12 $11\frac{5}{9}$
− $3\frac{2}{4}$

a $8\frac{3}{36}$
b $8\frac{1}{36}$
c $8\frac{1}{18}$
d NG

Multiplying by a Decimal

pages 235-236

Objective

To multiply a whole number by a decimal

Materials

Mental Math

Have students find the value of n in each equation:

1. 45 ÷ 6 = 7 Rn (3)
2. 30 ÷ 5 = n (6)
3. 29 ÷ 5 = n R4 (5)
4. n ÷ 9 = 7 (63)
5. n ÷ 3 = 2 R1 (7)
6. 18 ÷ n = 9 (2)
7. n ÷ 4 = 4 R2 (18)

Skill Review

Have students add or subtract these decimals. Remind them to add zeros to the right hand side of the decimal number if necessary.

1. 2.23 + 1.005 = (3.235)
2. 4.29 − 3.14 = (1.15)
3. 21.803 − 14.76 = (7.043)
4. 5 + 3.42 = (8.42)
5. 6 − 2.18 = (3.82)
6. 7.09 + 0.624 = (7.714)
7. 32.072 + 45.250 = (77.322)

Multiplying a Whole Number and a Decimal

Rita has 4 gallons of water to carry to her garden. Each gallon weighs 8.33 pounds. What is the total weight of the water?

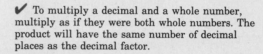

We want to know the total weight of all the water.

Each gallon of water weighs __8.33__ pounds.

Rita will carry __4__ gallons of water.

To find the total weight, we multiply the weight of one gallon by the number of gallons carried.

We multiply __8.33__ by __4__.

$$
\begin{array}{rl}
8.33 & \text{2 decimal places} \\
\times \quad 4 & \text{0 decimal places} \\
\hline
33.32 & \text{2 decimal places}
\end{array}
$$

Four gallons of water will weigh __33.32__ pounds.

✔ To multiply a decimal and a whole number, multiply as if they were both whole numbers. The product will have the same number of decimal places as the decimal factor.

Getting Started

Place the decimal point in these products.

1. 3.45	2. 2.365	3. 1.5	4. 8.05
× 7	× 3	× 93	× 124
2 4 1 5	7 0 9 5	1 3 9 5	9 9 8 2 0

Multiply.

5. 2.7	6. $4.26	7. 148	8. 7.215
× 8	× 24	× 3.6	× 7
21.6	$102.24	532.8	50.505

Copy and multiply.

9. 6 × 5.18
31.08

10. 9.5 × 1,340
12,730.0

11. 20 × 1.271
25.420

12. 8,561 × 1.2
10,273.2

235

MCP All rights reserved

Teaching the Lesson

Introducing the Problem Read the problem aloud. Have a student examine the illustration and read the information sentences. Read the plan sentences (multiply 8.33 by 4) and have students look at the problem worked in their texts. Do the problem on the board and explain that the decimal point must be placed in the product. Show students that when they multiply a whole number by a number with a decimal, the number of decimal places in the product is determined by the number in the decimal factor. In the example, students will notice that there are two decimal places in one factor and therefore two decimal places in the product. Have a student read the answer. (thirty three and thirty-two hundredths) Read the final sentence aloud.

Developing the Skill Show students that counting the decimal places works by changing this decimal problem to fractions:

$3.4 \times 6 = 3\frac{4}{10} \times \frac{6}{1} = \frac{34}{10} \times \frac{6}{1} = \frac{204}{10} = 20\frac{4}{10} = 20.4$

Now work the same problem by multiplying decimal numbers.

Write the following problem on the board. Have students change the decimal to a fraction, multiply and then rewrite the product as a decimal:

$2.12 \times 3 = (2\frac{12}{100} \times \frac{3}{1} = \frac{212}{100} \times \frac{3}{1} = \frac{636}{100} = 6\frac{36}{100} = 6.36)$

Practice

Place the decimal point in these products.

1. 23
    × 0.6
    1 3.8

2. 5.8
    × 7
    4 0.6

3. $1.59
    ×   8
    $1 2.7 2

4. 654
    × 0.5
    3 2 7.0

5. 8.39
    × 26
    2 1 8.1 4

6. 361
    × 4.6
    1,6 6 0.6

7. 6.248
    ×   34
    2 1 2.4 3 2

8. 462
    × 1.84
    8 5 0.0 8

Multiply.

9. 7.3
    × 8
    58.4

10. $6.91
     ×   7
     $48.37

11. 18.6
     ×   5
     93.0

12. 39
     × 1.4
     54.6

13. 862
     × 4.8
     4,137.6

14. 2.76
     × 47
     129.72

15. 1.804
     ×   27
     48.708

16. 64.9
     × 347
     22,520.3

Copy and Do

17. 8 × 6.15
    49.20

18. 13 × 9.5
    123.5

19. 4 × 2.658
    10.632

20. 3.65 × 27
    98.55

21. 47 × 6.4
    300.8

22. 7.5 × 137
    1,027.5

23. 9 × 7.8
    70.2

24. 6.105 × 9
    54.945

25. 8.25 × 49
    404.25

26. 57 × 3.721
    212.097

27. 3,270 × 5.9
    19,293.0

28. 7.125 × 46
    327.75

Apply

Solve these problems.

29. In one year, Americans consumed an average of 22.4 pounds of cheese per person. What is the weight of the cheese eaten by a family of 4 that year?
    89.6 pounds

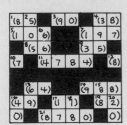

30. Union Pacific's fastest scheduled freight train runs from North Platte to Cheyenne at a speed of 66 miles per hour. The Santa Fe Railroad's fastest freight run is 62.9 miles per hour between Gallup and Winslow. How many miles per hour faster is the Union Pacific run?
    3.1 miles per hour

31. Stay-n-Shop is selling sirloin steak this week for $3.95 a pound. How much will a 2-pound sirloin cost?
    $7.90

32. Mr. Aerts pressed 46 sheets of metal on his shift at the steel mill. How thick is his stack of metal if each sheet is 0.125 centimeters thick?
    5.75 centimeters

236

Correcting Common Errors

Some students may count the decimal places from the left in the product instead of from the right in order to place the decimal point. Have them count the number of decimal places in the factors before they multiply and write this number beside the place for the product with an arrow to remind them of the direction to count.

        61.32
    ×   7
                ← 2

Enrichment

Give students this problem: 36 × 14.1. Tell them to divide one factor in half again and again, dropping any remainder, until they get one as the quotient. Then have them double the other factor as many times as they halved the first. Tell them to list pairs of answers directly next to each other, for example: 36, 14.1; 18, 28.2, etc. Finally ask them to take out any pairs of factors in which the halved factor is even. When they add the remaining doubled factors, the sum will be the product of the original two numbers.

    9   56.4   56.4
    1   451.2   + 451.2
                       507.6

Practice

Have students complete the problems on the page. Remind them that to find the correct number of decimal places.

Extra Credit   *Applications*

Duplicate or write on the board.

¹(8	²⁵)	³(9 0)		⁴(3 8)
⁵(1	o	⁶6)		⁷(1	9 7)
⁸(5	6)		⁹(3 5)
¹⁰(7	¹¹(4	7	8 4)		¹²(8
	¹³(6	4)		¹⁴(9	¹⁵(8 8)
¹⁶(4	9)		¹⁷(1	1)		¹⁹(8
0)		²¹(8	7	8 0)		0)

Across
1. 100 − 15
3. 3,240 ÷ 36
4. 7 + 8 + 9 + 6 + 5 + 3
5. 2,650 ÷ 25

7. 11,820 ÷ 60
8. 8 × 7
9. 315 ÷ 9
11. 52 × 92
12. 12 − 4
13. 8 × 8
14. 14 × 7
16. 7 × 7
17. 121 ÷ 11
19. ½ of 164
21. From 10,272 subtract the year Columbus discovered America

Down
1. 9 × 9
2. 884 − 379
4. 2,765 ÷ 7
6. 3,356 + 3,288
7. 2,408 − 1,059
10. 63 ÷ 9
13. 780 − 711
15. 616 ÷ 7

16. 6 + 7 + 8 + 9 + 10
17. 2 × 4 + 9
18. Reverse the digits in the product of 9 × 9
20. 100 − 80

236

Multiplying Decimals

pages 237-238

Objective

To multiply two decimals

Materials

Mental Math

Have students multiply:

1. $8 \times 10 = (80)$
2. $23 \times 10 = (230)$
3. $14 \times 100 = (1,400)$
4. $9 \times 100 = (900)$
5. $75 \times 1,000 = (75,000)$
6. $160 \times 10 = (1,600)$
7. $1.8 \times 10 = (18)$

Skill Review

Have students tell whether the answer will be in tenths or hundredths and then multiply:

1. $89.2 \times 7 =$ (tenths; 624.4)
2. $2.3 \times 45 =$ (tenths; 103.5)
3. $52 \times .73 =$ (hundredths; 37.96)
4. $36.4 \times 92 =$ (tenths; 3,348.8)
5. $18.02 \times 70 =$ (hundredths; 1,261.40)
6. $41.2 \times 8 =$ (tenths; 329.6)
7. $14 \times 4.9 =$ (tenths; 68.6)

Multiplying Decimals

Debra says she weighs 0.85 as much as Randall. How much does Debra weigh?

We want to know Debra's weight.

Randall weighs ___68.5___ kilograms.

Debra weighs ___0.85___ as much.

To find how much Debra weighs, we multiply Randall's weight by the decimal part of it representing Debra's weight.

We multiply ___68.5___ by ___0.85___.

Multiply like whole numbers.	The product has the same number of decimal places as the sum of the decimal factors.

$$
\begin{array}{r}
68.5 \\
\times 0.85 \\
\hline
3425 \\
5480 \\
\hline
58225
\end{array}
\qquad
\begin{array}{r}
68.5 \\
\times 0.85 \\
\hline
3425 \\
5480 \\
\hline
58.225
\end{array}
$$

1 decimal place
2 decimal places

3 decimal places

Debra weighs ___58.225___ kilograms.

Getting Started

Place the decimal point in these products.

1.	2.	3.	4.
5.6	1.58	92.3	14.25
× 3.2	× 7.3	× 8.51	× 9.4
17.92	11.534	785473	133950

Multiply.

5.	6.	7.	8.
59.1	19.31	8.07	75.2
× 0.7	× 2.6	× 4.9	× 36.5
41.37	50.206	39.543	2,744.80

Copy and multiply.

9. 4.3×7.1	10. 4.32×1.5	11. 3.3×2.72	12. 92.5×2.4
30.53	6.48	8.976	222.00

MCP All rights reserved

237

Teaching the Lesson

Introducing the Problem   Have a student read the problem aloud. Read the information sentences. Remind students that to find a fraction or a decimal part of a number, they multiply by the fraction or decimal. Direct their attention to the problem worked in their texts. Explain that two decimals are multiplied like whole numbers. At the end, decimal places are marked off in the answer. Tell students that the number of decimal places in the product is the sum of the numbers of places in the factors. Show them that in the example, there are a total of 3 decimal places in the factors and so there will be three decimal places in the product. Have a student read the solution sentence. (Debra weighs 58.225 kilograms.)

Developing the Skill   Show students that it works to add the decimal places of the factors to determine the decimal places in the product. Change the decimals in this problem to fractions:

$0.23 \times 0.9 = {}^{23}/_{100} \times {}^{9}/_{10} = {}^{207}/_{1000} = 0.207$

Have students change these decimal numbers to fractions, multiply and rewrite the product as a decimal.

$0.45 \times 0.9 = ({}^{45}/_{100} \times {}^{9}/_{10} = {}^{405}/_{1000} = 0.405)$

$1.23 \times 0.4 = ({}^{123}/_{100} \times {}^{4}/_{10} = {}^{492}/_{1000} = 0.492)$

237

Practice

Place the decimal point in these products.

1. $\begin{array}{r} 7.21 \\ \times\ 8.5 \\ \hline 6\,1285 \end{array}$	2. $\begin{array}{r} 3.98 \\ \times\ 1.6 \\ \hline 6368 \end{array}$	3. $\begin{array}{r} 146.2 \\ \times\ 3.07 \\ \hline 448834 \end{array}$	4. $\begin{array}{r} 19.1 \\ \times\ 24.6 \\ \hline 46986 \end{array}$
5. $\begin{array}{r} 13.24 \\ \times\ \ 4.3 \\ \hline 5\,6932 \end{array}$	6. $\begin{array}{r} 285.6 \\ \times\ 6.24 \\ \hline 1,78\,2144 \end{array}$	7. $\begin{array}{r} 13.85 \\ \times\ \ 0.8 \\ \hline 1\,1080 \end{array}$	8. $\begin{array}{r} 112.5 \\ \times\ 0.43 \\ \hline 48375 \end{array}$

Multiply.

9. $\begin{array}{r} 5.2 \\ \times\ 0.9 \\ \hline 4.68 \end{array}$	10. $\begin{array}{r} 7.28 \\ \times\ 2.1 \\ \hline 15.288 \end{array}$	11. $\begin{array}{r} 57.7 \\ \times\ 4.6 \\ \hline 265.42 \end{array}$	12. $\begin{array}{r} 126.8 \\ \times\ 7.5 \\ \hline 951.00 \end{array}$
13. $\begin{array}{r} 28.2 \\ \times\ 11.1 \\ \hline 313.02 \end{array}$	14. $\begin{array}{r} 52.81 \\ \times\ \ 4.6 \\ \hline 242.926 \end{array}$	15. $\begin{array}{r} 423.2 \\ \times\ 25.91 \\ \hline 10,965.112 \end{array}$	16. $\begin{array}{r} 3.25 \\ \times\ 0.8 \\ \hline 2.600 \end{array}$

Copy and Do

17. 5.3×2.6
13.78

18. 1.18×0.9
1.062

19. 12.3×7.8
95.94

20. 21.36×0.5
10.68

21. 2.73×4.6
12.558

22. 5.1×8.09
41.259

23. 51.3×17.6
902.88

24. 9.53×1.8
17.154

25. 631.5×0.81
511.515

26. 0.46×59.7
27.462

27. 27.3×85.4
2,331.42

28. 426.21×0.8
340.968

Apply

Solve these problems.

29. Between 1951 and 1980 in Dawson, Yukon, the average wind speed was 3.7 kilometers per hour. The highest recorded speed was approximately 1.5 times faster. About how fast was Dawson's highest wind during that period?
5.55 kilometers per hour

30. Mr. Harris' car averages 32.43 miles to a gallon of gas. His tank holds 10.5 gallons. How many miles can Mr. Harris travel on a full tank?
340.515 miles

31. A rectangle is 9.5 inches wide and 15.8 inches long. What is its perimeter?
50.6 inches

32. It takes 8.25 pounds of sand to make a bucket of concrete. How much sand is needed to make 6.5 buckets of concrete?
53.625 pounds

238

Correcting Common Errors

Some students may confuse the form for addition with the form for multiplication and line up the decimal points in the factors and product.

INCORRECT	CORRECT
$\begin{array}{r} 4.7 \\ \times\ 3.5 \\ \hline 164.5 \end{array}$	$\begin{array}{r} 4.7 \\ \times\ 3.5 \\ \hline 16.45 \end{array}$

Correct by having student indicate in writing before they multiply how many decimal places will be in the product.

Enrichment

Have students show that rules for multiplying base-ten numbers work for binary numbers when they multiply the following binary numbers:

1. $1.01 \times 1.1 = (1.111)$ $(1.01 = 1.25, 1.1 = 1.5; 1.25 \times 1.5 = 1.875$ in base ten)
2. $10.01 \times 10.1 = (101.101)$ $(10.01 = 2.25, 10.1 = 2.5; 2.25 \times 2.5 = 5.625$ in base ten)

Practice

Have students complete all the problems. Remind them to add the decimal places of the factors to find the number of places in the product.

Mixed Practice

1. 564×685 (386,340)
2. $\frac{5}{9} \div \frac{1}{3}$ $\left(1\frac{2}{3}\right)$
3. $171,708 + 357,999$ (529,707)
4. $326.08 - 54.976$ (271.104)
5. $1\frac{1}{5} \times 2\frac{1}{6}$ $\left(2\frac{3}{5}\right)$
6. $15.7 \times .52$ (8.164)
7. $\$4,000.58 - \$2,951.93$ ($\$1,048.65$)
8. $127.65 - 93.8$ (33.85)
9. $32,472 \div 72$ (451)
10. $16\frac{2}{3} + 17\frac{5}{6} + 12\frac{1}{9}$ $\left(46\frac{11}{18}\right)$

Extra Credit *Biography*

Cogito, ergo sum. I think, therefore I am. This statement was originated by a 17th-century French mathematician and philosopher, René Descartes. His ideas about God and the physical world earned him the title, Father of Modern Philosophy. Descartes defined the physical world as microscopic, colorless and extended substances that people's minds interpreted as visible, colored, physical objects. Descartes believed he proved the existence of God by saying that the idea of God is perfect, and could only be put into the human mind by the perfect God. Descartes was also a mathematical genius, best remembered for his work in analytical geometry. He combined the study of arithmetic and geometry by using what he called Cartesian coordinates. Descartes' ideas opened new directions of thinking in both mathematics and philosophy.

Multiply Decimals, Zeros in Product

pages 239–240

Objective

To add zeros to the product when multiplying decimals

Materials

Mental Math

Have students simplify:

1. $7/4$ ($1\frac{3}{4}$)
2. $8/10$ ($4/5$)
3. $14/2$ (7)
4. $2/3$ ($2/3$, cannot be reduced)
5. $20/10$ (2)
6. $6/6$ (1)
7. $6/12$ ($1/2$)

Skill Review

Have students multiply:

1. $2.49 \times 3 = (7.47)$
2. $9.1 \times 9.1 = (82.81)$
3. $3.6 \times 5.15 = (18.54)$
4. $14.3 \times 16.3 = (233.09)$
5. $3.45 \times 1.5 = (5.175)$
6. $62.3 \times 9 = (560.7)$

Multiplying, Zeros in the Product

A human hair is about 0.04 as thick as the wire in a paper clip. What is the thickness of a human hair?

We want to know the thickness of a human hair.

The wire in a paper clip is about ___0.1___ of a centimeter thick.

A human hair is about ___0.04___ as thick as this wire.

To find how thick a human hair is, we multiply the thickness of the wire by the decimal part of that wire representing the human hair.

We multiply ___0.1___ by ___0.04___.

Multiply like whole numbers.	The product has the same number of decimal places as the sum of the decimal places in the factors.

$$
\begin{array}{r} 0.1 \\ \times\,0.04 \\ \hline 4 \end{array}
\qquad
\begin{array}{r} 0.1 \\ \times\,0.04 \\ \hline 0.004 \end{array}
\quad
\begin{array}{l} \text{1 decimal place} \\ \text{2 decimal places} \\ \text{3 decimal places} \end{array}
$$

✔ If there are not enough places in the product, annex zeros to the left of the number before placing the decimal point.

A human hair is ___0.004___ of a centimeter thick.

Getting Started

Multiply.

1. $\begin{array}{r} 0.6 \\ \times\,0.2 \\ \hline 0.12 \end{array}$		2. $\begin{array}{r} 0.004 \\ \times\,9 \\ \hline 0.036 \end{array}$		3. $\begin{array}{r} 45 \\ \times\,0.002 \\ \hline 0.090 \end{array}$		4. $\begin{array}{r} 0.03 \\ \times\,1.4 \\ \hline 0.042 \end{array}$	
5. $\begin{array}{r} 8.5 \\ \times\,0.4 \\ \hline 3.40 \end{array}$		6. $\begin{array}{r} 0.1 \\ \times\,0.23 \\ \hline 0.023 \end{array}$		7. $\begin{array}{r} 0.005 \\ \times\,7 \\ \hline 0.035 \end{array}$		8. $\begin{array}{r} 3.4 \\ \times\,9 \\ \hline 30.6 \end{array}$	

Copy and multiply.

9. 0.003×6
0.018

10. 74×0.008
0.592

11. 0.6×0.06
0.036

12. 0.015×3.9
0.0585

MCP All rights reserved

239

Teaching the Lesson

Introducing the Problem Read the problem aloud. Have a student read the information sentences. Remind students that to find a decimal part of another number, they multiply the number by the decimal number. Read the plan sentences. (multiply 0.1 by 0.04) Direct students' attention to the problem worked in their books. Explain that they multiply the numbers as though they were whole numbers and count decimal places as they have done before. Point out that when they count the decimal places and look at the product, they do not find enough places in the product to accommodate the three decimal places required. Show them how to add zeros to the left of the product before they put the decimal point in. Have a student read the answer. (four thousandths) Call attention to the checked sentence explaining that the word annex means add to.

Developing the Skill Have students rewrite this problem using fractions:
$0.2 \times 0.03 = (2/10 \times 3/100 = 6/1000 = 0.006)$
Explain that when they multiply small decimal amounts, the product is even smaller than the factors, just as when they multiply fractions. Point out this means sometimes the product does not have enough decimal places. Put this on the board: **0.003 × 0.3**. Note that zeros have to be added to the left of the product until there are enough decimal places and complete the problem: **0.0009**.

239

Practice

Multiply.

1. 0.3 $\times$ 0.01 0.003	2. 0.03 $\times$ 0.04 0.0012	3. 0.18 $\times$ 0.5 0.090	4. 0.24 $\times$ 1.3 0.312
5. 0.008 $\times$ 9 0.072	6. 6.43 $\times$ 100 643.00	7. 0.05 $\times$ 0.3 0.015	8. 4.75 $\times$ 0.5 2.375

Copy and Do

9. 0.2×0.3
   0.06
10. 7.8×0.02
    0.156
11. 0.06×0.4
    0.024
12. 3.8×0.21
    0.798

13. 0.03×0.45
    0.0135
14. 0.001×28
    0.028
15. 0.123×0.01
    0.00123
16. 4.8×0.03
    0.144

17. 10×0.007
    0.070
18. 5.8×43.8
    254.04
19. 0.003×21
    0.063
20. 0.9×0.09
    0.081

Apply

Use the rectangle to complete problems 21 and 22.

21. The perimeter is __2.2__ meters.

22. The area is __0.24__ square meters.

0.3 meters

0.8 meters

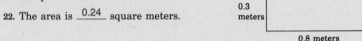

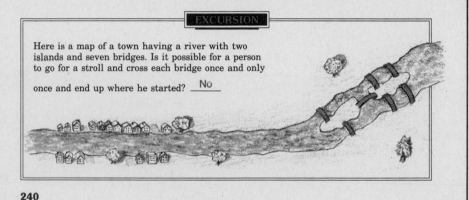

EXCURSION

Here is a map of a town having a river with two islands and seven bridges. Is it possible for a person to go for a stroll and cross each bridge once and only once and end up where he started? __No__

240

Correcting Common Errors

When zeros must be annexed in the product, some students may place them to the right of the digits that are already there instead of to the left.

INCORRECT	CORRECT
0.3	0.3
$\times$ 0.02	$\times$ 0.02
0.600	0.006

Have them rewrite the problem in fraction form to show that the answer is smaller than hundredths or tenths.

$$\tfrac{2}{100} \times \tfrac{3}{10} = \tfrac{6}{1,000}$$

Zeros must be annexed between the decimal point and the 6 to make the 6 as small as it should be.

Enrichment

Have students imagine a balance with the following weights: 1 lb, 8 oz, 4 oz, 2 oz, 1 oz, ½ oz, ¼ oz and ⅛ oz. Have them figure out what combination of weights would balance these objects: a 7¾ oz apple and a 9⅛ oz book.

oz weights	8 4 2 1 ½ ¼ ⅛
apple	(1 1 1 1 1 0)
book	(1 0 0 1 0 0 1)

Some will notice this forms a place value system similar to the binary system.

Practice

Have students complete the problems. Remind them to count the number of decimal places in the factors and add zeros to the left of the product until they can place the decimal point.

Excursion

This is the well known Königsberg bridge problem. The German mathematician, Euler, proved there was no way to accomplish this, as he laid the basis for the mathematical science, topology.

Extra Credit   *Probability*

Have students use one die and a bag containing a red block and a blue block. Tell students that one team will use the even numbers on the die and the red block as their winning combination; the other team will use the odd numbers and the blue block. The students roll the die to determine which team goes first. A student on the first team rolls the die and then draws a block from the bag. If the die and block form a winning combination, the team scores and records one point. Otherwise, a point is put in the "no win" column of the tally sheet. The game continues with the teams alternating plays until each one has rolled the die and drawn a cube twenty times. The winning team is the one which scores the most points. Students should keep track of the scores for twenty-five games and then determine the probability for any given combination occurring.

Multiples of 10

pages 241-242

Objective

To multiply decimals by 10, 100 and 1,000

Materials

Mental Math

Have students add, then multiply:

1. $(2 + 3) \times 4 = (20)$
2. $(10 + 5) \times 2 = (30)$
3. $(5 + 6) \times 4 = (44)$
4. $(8 + 4) \times 3 = (36)$
5. $(9 + 1) \times 6 = (60)$
6. $(3 + 6) \times 9 = (81)$
7. $(7 + 7) \times 2 = (28)$

Skill Review

Have students multiply:

1. $0.3 \times 1.5 = (0.45)$
2. $13.7 \times 4 = (54.8)$
3. $0.29 \times 7 = (2.03)$
4. $7.25 \times 0.8 = (5.8)$
5. $12.4 \times 5.3 = (65.72)$
6. $4.8 \times 5.5 = (26.4)$
7. $0.004 \times 7 = (0.028)$

Multiplying by 10, 100 and 1,000

Adam won the long jump with his final attempt. Find how many centimeters long Adam's jump was.

We want to know the length of Adam's jump expressed in centimeters.

The jump was __3.42__ meters long.

There are __100__ centimeters in 1 meter. To find the number of centimeters in the jump, we multiply the length of the jump in meters by the number of centimeters in one meter.

We multiply __3.42__ by __100__. Complete the following patterns to find a shortcut for multiplying by 10, 100 or 1,000.

	Number of zeros in second factor	Move the decimal point to the right.
$3.42 \times 10 = 34.2$	1	1 place
$3.42 \times 100 = 342$	2	2 places
$3.420 \times 1,000 = 3,420$	3	3 places

✔ Notice, that when there are not enough digits to move the decimal point, zeros are annexed to the right.

Multiplying by 10 moves the decimal __1__ place to the right.

Multiplying by 100 moves the decimal __2__ places to the right.

Multiplying by 1,000 moves the decimal __3__ places to the right.

$3.42 \times 100 = $ __342__

Adam jumped __342__ centimeters in his winning long jump.

Getting Started

Multiply.

1. $5.8 \times 100 = $ __580__

2. $5.75 \times 1,000 = $ __5,750__

Write the missing number.

5. 3,742 meters = __374,200__ centimeters

Write the missing factor.

3. __10__ $\times 325.4 = 3,254$

4. __1,000__ $\times 1.06 = 1,060$

6. To change liters to milliliters, multiply by __1,000__.

MCP All rights reserved

241

Teaching the Lesson

Introducing the Problem Read the problem aloud and have a student read the information sentences. Read the plan sentences (Multiply 3.42 by 100.) and ask students to look at the table in their texts. Explain that there is a short way to multiply decimals by factors of ten. Point out that to multiply by ten, they can simply move the decimal point in the original number one place to the right; to multiply by 100, they move it two places; by 1,000, three places. Have students fill in the table in their texts. Write the problem on the board and have a student fill in the answer. (342) Ask a volunteer to read the solution sentence. (jumped 342 cm)

Developing the Skill Illustrate why the decimal point is moved when multiplying by powers of ten. Write these problems on the board:

$4.5 \times 10 = \frac{45}{10} \times \frac{10}{1} = \frac{450}{10} = 45$ (decimal moved one place to the right)

$2.17 \times 100 = \frac{217}{100} \times \frac{100}{1} = 217$ (decimal moved two places to the right)

Have them illustrate this principle using 15.2×100. $(\frac{152}{10} \times 100 = \frac{15200}{10} = 1520)$

Ask each student to write the rules for multiplying by 10 (Move decimal to right 1 place.), by 100 (Move decimal to right 2 places.) and by 1,000. (Move decimal to right 3 places.)

Practice

Multiply.

1. $6.32 \times 100 =$ __632__

2. $10 \times 7.731 =$ __77.31__

3. $19.21 \times 1{,}000 =$ __19,210__

4. $100 \times 0.241 =$ __24.1__

5. $13.1 \times 1{,}000 =$ __13,100__

6. $100 \times 26 =$ __2,600__

7. $10 \times 0.159 =$ __1.59__

8. $1{,}000 \times 0.001 =$ __1__

9. $10 \times 8.37 =$ __83.7__

10. $14.29 \times 1{,}000 =$ __14,290__

11. $100 \times 2.315 =$ __231.5__

12. $0.39 \times 10 =$ __3.9__

13. $400 \times 100 =$ __40,000__

14. $10 \times 5.675 =$ __56.75__

15. $0.48 \times 1{,}000 =$ __480__

16. $100 \times 13.721 =$ __1,372.1__

Write the missing factor.

17. $9.6 \times$ __10__ $= 96$

18. $1.25 \times$ __1,000__ $= 1{,}250$

19. __10__ $\times 8.245 = 82.45$

20. __100__ $\times 3.75 = 375$

21. $0.321 \times$ __100__ $= 32.1$

22. $14.158 \times$ __100__ $= 1{,}415.8$

Write the missing number.

23. 4.265 kilometers = __4,265__ meters

24. 7.3 liters = __7,300__ milliliters

25. 0.214 kilograms = __214__ grams

26. 14.294 meters = __1,429.4__ centimeters

27. To change meters to centimeters, multiply by __100__ .

28. To change kilometers to meters, multiply by __1,000__ .

EXCURSION

In a right triangle, if a and b are the sides which form the right angle and c is the side opposite the right angle, then $(a \times a) + (b \times b) = (c \times c)$. This is called the **Pythagorean Theorem.** It is usually expressed as $a^2 + b^2 = c^2$. Below, sides a and b of a right triangle are given. Use the Pythagorean Theorem to find the length of the third side.

$a = 5$ mm $b = 12$ mm $c =$ __13__ mm

242

Correcting Common Errors

Watch for students who move the decimal point to the left instead of to the right. Discuss that when you multiply a decimal by 10 or 100 or 1,000, the product will always be larger than the other factor. To make a decimal larger, you move the decimal point to the right. Have students work with partners with problems like the following to see the pattern.

$$10 \times 62 = 620$$
$$100 \times 62 = 6{,}200$$
$$1{,}000 \times 62 = 62{,}000$$

$$10 \times 0.62 = 6.2$$
$$100 \times 0.62 = 62$$
$$1{,}000 \times 0.62 = 620$$

Enrichment

Ask students to use binary numbers to multiply:

1. $7 \times 2 = (111 \times 10 = 1110)$
2. $7 \times 4 = (111 \times 100 = 11100)$
3. $3.5 \times 2 = (11.1 \times 10 = 111)$
4. $3.5 \times 4 = (11.1 \times 100 = 1110)$

Have students generalize the method (As in base ten numbers, when they multiply by the place value 10 (2 in base 10) or 100 (4 in base 10), they move the decimal point the same number of places as there are zeros in the factor.)

Practice

Have students complete the practice problems. Remind students that there are 1,000 meters in a kilometer and 100 centimeters in a meter.

Excursion

Have students work the equation on calculators:

$$\sqrt{a^2 + b^2} = c \text{ or } \sqrt{25 + 144} = \sqrt{(169)}$$
$$(\sqrt{169} = 13)$$

Extra Credit *Applications*

Have students cut 60 two-inch squares of paper and write the numbers from 1 to 20, one number on each square. Have them make two duplicates of each number. Put all the squares in a box. Each student takes a turn drawing three cards from the box. Have students imagine that the numbers are denominators in a fraction problem.

Have students show the three cards that were drawn and tell the lowest common denominator that could be used to work the problem. (for example: 8, 5, 4 the lowest common denominator would be 40.)

Dividing Decimals

pages 243-244

Objective

To divide a decimal by a whole number

Materials

Mental Math

Have students identify these numbers as even, odd, or odd and prime:

1. 4 (even)
2. 7 (odd and prime)
3. 1 (odd and prime)
4. 20 (even)
5. 33 (odd)
6. 50 (even)
7. 49 (odd)

Skill Review

Have students work these problems on the board. Have them pay special attention to placement of the decimal point.

1. $34.5 \times 9 = (310.5)$
2. $5.24 \times 17 = (89.08)$
3. $9.4 \times 59 = (554.6)$
4. $3.28 \times 20 = (65.6)$
5. $7.5 \times 25 = (187.5)$
6. $6.08 \times 52 = (316.16)$

Dividing a Decimal by a Whole Number

It took Cheryl 4 hours to drive from Clinton to San Remo. How many kilometers did she average per hour?

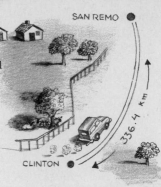

We want to know the kilometers per hour Cheryl drove between the two towns.

She drove __336.4__ kilometers.

The trip took her a total of __4__ hours. To find the kilometers per hour, we divide the number of kilometers in the whole trip by the number of hours it took.

We divide __336.4__ by __4__.

Place the decimal point.	Divide like whole numbers.	Check by multiplication.

$$4\overline{)336\ 4}$$

$$
\begin{array}{r}
84.1 \\
4\overline{)336.4} \\
32 \\
\hline
16 \\
16 \\
\hline
4 \\
4 \\
\hline
0
\end{array}
$$

$$
\begin{array}{r}
84.1 \\
\times\ \ \ \ 4 \\
\hline
336.4
\end{array}
$$

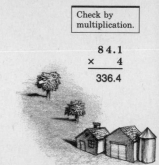

Cheryl averaged __84.1__ kilometers per hour.

Getting Started

Divide and check.

1. $5\overline{)29.35}$ → 5.87
2. $6\overline{)\$6.72}$ → \$1.12
3. $9\overline{)48.123}$ → 5.347

4. $54\overline{)34.668}$ → 0.642
5. $19\overline{)44.46}$ → 2.34
6. $65\overline{)36.40}$ → 0.56

Copy and divide.

7. $\$125.20 \div 5$
  \$25.04

8. $20.360 \div 40$
  0.509

9. $1,914.9 \div 13$
  147.3

MCP All rights reserved

243

Teaching the Lesson

Introducing the Problem Have a student read the problem aloud. Read the information sentences. Explain that to find the rate, kilometers per hour, students will divide the distance by the time. (divide 336.4 by 4) Ask students to look at the problem worked in their texts. Explain that the first step after copying the problem is to place the decimal point above the dividend, where the quotient will be. The next step is to divide as though they were working with whole numbers. Emphasize the importance of keeping columns of numbers straight, tens in the quotient over tens in the dividend and so on. Have a student multiply to check the answer. ($84.1 \times 4 = 336.4$) Ask a volunteer to read the solution sentence. (averaged 84.1 kilometers per hour)

Developing the Skill Work this problem on the board so students can prove to themselves that the placement of the decimal is correct:

$$4.25 \div 5 = {}^{425}/_{100} \div {}^{5}/_{1} = {}^{425}/_{100} \times {}^{1}/_{5} = {}^{425}/_{500} = {}^{85}/_{100} = 0.85$$

and

$$5\overline{)4.25} \to 0.85$$

Have students work this problem using fractions and using the decimal division they have just learned: $15.54 \div 3 = (5.18)$.

Practice

Divide and check.

$$1.\ 3\overline{)2.91} = 0.97$$

$$2.\ 7\overline{)164.5} = 23.5$$

$$3.\ 6\overline{)6.234} = 1.039$$

$$4.\ 11\overline{)\$74.58} = \$6.78$$

$$5.\ 64\overline{)147.84} = 2.31$$

$$6.\ 25\overline{)382.5} = 15.3$$

$$7.\ 72\overline{)155.376} = 2.158$$

$$8.\ 36\overline{)34.632} = 0.962$$

$$9.\ 83\overline{)\$834.98} = \$10.06$$

Copy and Do

10. $143.4 \div 6$
23.9
11. $\$3.84 \div 4$
$0.96
12. $107.95 \div 17$
6.35
13. $\$75.15 \div 45$
$1.67
14. $550.8 \div 36$
15.3
15. $228 \div 38$
6
16. $2,321.16 \div 92$
25.23
17. $30.352 \div 56$
0.542
18. $143.898 \div 87$
1.654

Apply

Solve these problems.

19. If a carton of 24 cans of soup weighs 7.32 kilograms, what is the weight of each can?
0.305 kilograms

20. How many miles can a car travel in 6 hours if it averages 45.6 miles per hour?
273.6 miles

21. Veann's share of her family's garage sale proceeds was $18.56 on Thursday, $16.21 on Friday and $27.36 on Saturday. What was her average daily earnings?
$20.71

22. Mrs. Aguire bought a chair for $426.38. She paid $115.50 as a down payment. She paid the balance in 4 monthly payments. How much was each payment?
$77.72

244

Correcting Common Errors

Some students may forget to place the decimal point in the answer. Have them place the decimal point in the quotient above the decimal point in the dividend *first* before they divide. After they divide, have them check their answer by multiplying.

Enrichment

Have students divide binary numbers as they have multiplied them. Demonstrate with this:

$$10\overline{)101.0}\ \ \text{is the same as}\ \ 2\overline{)5.0}$$

Ask if the rules for dividing decimals apply to dividing binary numbers. (Yes, they seem to.) Have students do these problems in binary division and check them by changing the numbers to base ten and working them again.

1. $1,000.10 \div 10 = (100.01; 8.50 \div 2 = 4.25)$
2. $1,011.01 \div 101 = (10.01; 11.25 \div 5 = 2.25)$

Practice

Have students complete the problems on the page. Remind to place the decimal point carefully.

Mixed Practice

1. $253.8 + 491.764$ (745.564)
2. $22,818 \div 34$ (671 R4)
3. $312.7 - 116.951$ (195.749)
4. $658 + 1,295 + 81,963$ (83,916)
5. $\dfrac{3}{8} \times \dfrac{5}{6}\ \left(\dfrac{5}{16}\right)$
6. 814×470 (382,580)
7. $\dfrac{11}{12} - \dfrac{5}{8}\ \left(\dfrac{7}{24}\right)$
8. $4\dfrac{1}{2} \div 2\dfrac{7}{10}\ \left(1\dfrac{2}{3}\right)$
9. $90 \times \$971.48$ ($87,433.20)
10. 0.07×0.8 (0.056)

Extra Credit *Applications*

Divide students into groups. Make each group responsible for researching the Braille system for numbers 1–10, and devising a set of manipulatives for the class to use incorporating this system. Have each group then create 2-digit addition and subtraction problems using Braille numbers to exchange with another group to solve. Allow them to use their manipulatives, if necessary, and write their answers in Braille. As an extension, have students research and learn the Braille alphabet.

Zeros in Quotients

Objective

To place zeros in quotients, dividing decimals by whole numbers

Materials

graph paper

Mental Math

Ask students to tell which is more:

1. 0.12 or 0.5 (0.5 > 0.12)
2. 0.03 or 0.015 (0.03 > 0.015)
3. 3.2 or 3.04 (3.2 > 3.04)
4. 4.1 or 4.15 (4.15 > 4.1)
5. 0.39 or 0.55 (0.55 > 0.39)
6. 14.3 or 1.52 (14.3 > 1.52)
7. 0.8 or 0.79 (0.8 > 0.79)

Skill Review

Have students divide:

1. $29.16 \div 9 = (3.24)$
2. $35.14 \div 7 = (5.02)$
3. $97.2 \div 6 = (16.2)$
4. $205.4 \div 13 = (15.8)$
5. $411.93 \div 23 = (17.91)$
6. $21.90 \div 30 = (0.73)$
7. $58.48 \div 34 = (1.72)$

Dividing, Zeros in the Quotient

Specimen 1	0.04 mm
Specimen 2	0.05 mm
Specimen 3	0.04 mm
Specimen 4	0.05 mm
Specimen 5	0.05 mm

A scientist is using an electron microscope to measure several skin cells. One of the things she needs to know is the average width of the cells.

We want to know the average width of the skin cells.

The scientist made ___5___ recordings.

The widths were __0.04__, __0.05__, __0.04__, __0.05__ and __0.05__ millimeters.

To find the average width, we add all the widths and divide by the number of recordings.

We add __0.04__, __0.05__, __0.04__, __0.05__ and __0.05__ and divide that sum by ___5___.

Add the recordings.

```
  0.04
  0.05
  0.04
  0.05
+ 0.05
 ─────
  0.23
```

Place the decimal point. Write zeros in place values when the dividend is too small. Divide.

```
    0.0 4
  5)0.2 3
    2 0
    ───
      3
```

Annex a zero in the dividend and divide again.

```
    0.046
  5)0.2 30
    2 0
    ───
      30
      30
      ──
       0
```

The average width of a skin cell is __0.046__ millimeters.

Getting Started

Divide. Annex a zero if necessary.

```
     0.03
1. 7)0.21
```

```
      0.012
2. 4)0.048
```

```
     0.074
3. 5)0.37
```

Copy and divide.

4. $0.003 \div 6$
   0.0005

5. $0.042 \div 14$
   0.003

6. $2.08 \div 52$
   0.04

MCP All rights reserved

245

Teaching the Lesson

Introducing the Problem Have a student read the problem aloud. Read the information sentences. Remind the class that to find the average they add the numbers and divide by the number of addends. (add 0.04, 0.05, 0.04, 0.05 and 0.05; divide by 5) Direct students' attention to the problem worked in their texts. Explain that the first step is to add the recordings. (0.23) To divide, they first place the decimal point in the quotient. Write the problem on the board. Show them that the number 5 can be divided into is 23. Show that the quotient, 4, will be above the hundredths column, leaving a space in the tenths. Point out the importance of putting a zero in the tenths place. Add a zero to the problem on the board and complete the division. (0.046) Have a student read the solution sentence. (average width is 0.046 millimeters)

Developing the Skill Explain that when they divide a decimal, it is important to place the decimal point in the quotient directly above the decimal point in the dividend. Point out that there must be a digit in the quotient above each place value to the right of the decimal point in the dividend. Tell students to fill the places with zeros if necessary. Work this problem on the board: $0.024 \div 6 = (0.004)$

245

Divide. Annex a zero if necessary.

1. 8)0.128 → 0.016

2. 12)0.384 → 0.032

3. 7)0.602 → 0.086

4. 15)0.135 → 0.009

5. 24)8.76 → 0.365

6. 56)19.88 → 0.355

7. 4)0.02 → 0.005

8. 16)0.112 → 0.007

9. 32)0.16 → 0.005

Copy and Do

10. 0.015 ÷ 3
0.005

11. 0.56 ÷ 10
0.056

12. 1.08 ÷ 9
0.12

13. 0.84 ÷ 28
0.03

14. 1.92 ÷ 64
0.03

15. 4.05 ÷ 75
0.054

16. 2.22 ÷ 37
0.06

17. 2.08 ÷ 80
0.026

18. 3.15 ÷ 35
0.09

19. 2.496 ÷ 26
0.096

20. 3.4 ÷ 50
0.068

21. 0.45 ÷ 75
0.006

EXCURSION

Complete the table to find a shortcut for dividing decimals by 10, 100 and 1,000.

Dividends	7.15	265.3	8	5,750.1
Divided by 10	0.715	26.53	0.8	575.01
Divided by 100	0.0715	2.653	0.08	57.501
Divided by 1,000	0.00715	0.2653	0.008	5.7501

To divide a decimal number by 10, 100 or 1,000, count the number of __zeros__ in the divisor to determine how many places the decimal point will be moved to the __left__.

246

Correcting Common Errors

Some students may forget to annex zeros in the quotient when they are required and, therefore, write the quotient incorrectly.

INCORRECT   CORRECT
.62   .062
4)0.248   4)0.248

Have students do their work on grid paper helping them to see that a digit must be in every square between the decimal point and the other digits in the quotient.

Enrichment

Have students use a digital thermometer to take their temperatures. Remind them to change the plastic slip each time they take a new reading. Point out that the temperature showing on the face will increase several times and then start to blink. The blinking number is the temperature they should record. When they have each person's temperature, have them average the readings by adding them and dividing by the number of readings. Ask them to look up the reading that is considered normal (about 98.6 °F), but explain that there is wide variation among people.

Practice

Have students complete all the problems. Remind them to place the decimal point in the quotient first, and to be sure to put some digit in every place to the right of the decimal point.

Excursion

Emphasize that the placement of zero in necessary decimal places will help students avoid mistakes in placement of the decimal point.

Extra Credit   *Logic*

Nine of the fastest runners in Mr. Smalley's fifth grade class challenged each other to a race to see who was the fastest. Each runner wore a number, 1 through 9. Use the following clues to find who came in first, second and third:

The sum of all the numbers who entered the race was three times the sum of the numbers of first, second and third places. Adding the numbers for second and third places, gives a number that is ⅔ of first place. Adding the number for first and second places, gives a number that is twice the third place number. Which runners finished first, second and third? (9, 1, 5)

Dividing by a Decimal

pages 247-248

Objective

To divide a decimal number by a decimal

Materials

graph paper

Mental Math

Remind students that the least common multiple of two numbers is the smallest number that both can be divided into. Have them find the LCM of these pairs:

1. 3 and 4 (12)
2. 2 and 5 (10)
3. 6 and 4 (12)
4. 7 and 2 (14)
5. 4 and 5 (20)
6. 8 and 2 (8)
7. 9 and 3 (9)

Skill Review

Have students divide:

1. $1.015 \div 29 = (0.035)$
2. $25.56 \div 18 = (1.42)$
3. $12.2 \div 4 = (3.05)$
4. $43.74 \div 6 = (7.29)$
5. $160.96 \div 32 = (5.03)$
6. $652.31 \div 43 = (15.17)$
7. $0.884 \div 17 = (0.052)$

Dividing by a Decimal

Mr. Sanduski bought a new sedan. How many miles per gallon can he expect if he drives the average range with a full tank of gas?

Type of Car	Tank Capacity (gallons)	Average Range (miles)	Miles per Gallon
Compact	10.5	327.6	?
Sedan	18.3	452.01	?
Sports	15.6	436.8	?

We want to know the number of miles Mr. Sanduski's car will travel on one gallon of gas.

A sedan holds ___18.3___ gallons of gas.

The range of a sedan on a tank of gas is ___452.01___ miles. To find the miles per gallon, we divide the range by the tank's capacity.

We divide ___452.01___ by ___18.3___.

✔ The divisor must be a whole number. If it is a decimal number, it should be multiplied by a 10, 100 or 1,000 to make it a whole number. Multiply the dividend by the same number.

Multiply the divisor and the dividend by 10.

$$18.3\overline{)452.01}$$

Divide.

$$18.3\overline{)452.01}$$
$$\begin{array}{r} 24.7 \\ \overline{452.01} \\ 366 \\ \overline{86\,0} \\ 73\,2 \\ \overline{12\,81} \\ 12\,81 \\ \overline{0} \end{array}$$

The sedan should average ___24.7___ miles to the gallon.

Getting Started

Divide.

1. $4.8\overline{)43.2}$ → 9
2. $0.6\overline{)3.36}$ → 5.6
3. $1.2\overline{)3.912}$ → 3.26

Copy and divide.

4. $532.8 \div 3.6$
   148
5. $31.08 \div 51.8$
   0.6
6. $133.95 \div 9.4$
   14.25

MCP All rights reserved

247

Teaching the Lesson

Introducing the Problem Read the problem aloud and ask a student to read the information sentences. Read the plan sentences. Explain that to make the divisor a whole number, it must be multiplied by 10 if it has a tenths place, by 100 if it has a hundredths, or by 1,000 if it has a thousandths. Point out that the dividend must be multiplied by the same number if the ratio of divisor to dividend is to remain the same. Write the division on the board and show students that multiplying 18.3 by 10 is the same as moving the decimal one place to the right. Do the same to the dividend, indicating the new position of the decimal point with a caret (∧). Work the problem and put the decimal in the quotient above the caret. Have a student read the solution sentence. (average 24.7 miles to gallon)

Developing the Skill Remind students that fractions express division. The fraction $\frac{7}{4}$ means $7 \div 4$. Point out that if the denominator is multiplied by a number, the numerator must be multiplied by the same number. Multiplying $\frac{7}{4}$ by $\frac{10}{10}$ does not change its value; $\frac{7}{4}$ is the same as $\frac{70}{40}$. Explain that any time they divide by a decimal, they should count the decimal places in the divisor and move the decimal point to the right that number of places in both divisor and dividend. Indicate the new position of the decimal point with a caret. This is the same as multiplying both divisor and dividend by the same power of ten.

247

Practice

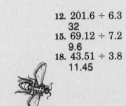

Divide.

1. 0.3)6.96 $\underline{23.2}$

2. 1.2)0.048 $\underline{0.04}$

3. 6.4)230.4 $\underline{36}$

4. 4.3)5.418 $\underline{1.26}$

5. 3.6)21.744 $\underline{6.04}$

6. 2.5)15.875 $\underline{6.35}$

7. 9.5)30.115 $\underline{3.17}$

8. 6.7)20.636 $\underline{3.08}$

9. 7.7)482.02 $\underline{62.6}$

Copy and Do

10. $5.4 \div 1.5$
    3.6
11. $2.6 \div 1.3$
    2
12. $201.6 \div 6.3$
    32
13. $7.596 \div 3.6$
    2.11
14. $12.838 \div 4.9$
    2.62
15. $69.12 \div 7.2$
    9.6
16. $35.316 \div 5.4$
    6.54
17. $1.143 \div 1.8$
    0.635
18. $43.51 \div 3.8$
    11.45

Apply

Solve these problems.

19. Hal worked a total of 18.75 hours last month as an auxiliary policeman. If he worked in shifts of about 2.5 hours each, how many days did Hal work last month?
    7.5 days

20. Paula's average stride is 0.5 of a meter. How many steps will it take for Paula to walk 241.2 meters?
    482.4 steps

EXCURSION

Write a number between each pair whose value is higher than the number on the left, but lower in value than the number on the right.

1. 2.1352, __2.136__, 2.137
2. 0.01, __0.019__, 0.021
3. $5\frac{1}{2}$, __5.52__, 5.545
4. 567.23, __568.0__, 568.95
5. 2.25, __2.30__, 2.33
6. $2\frac{1}{4}$, __$2\frac{7}{24}$__, $2\frac{1}{3}$

Answers may vary.

248

Correcting Common Errors

Some students may move the decimal point in the divisor but forget to move it in the dividend. Have them count the number of places they must move the decimal point in the divisor to make it a whole number, write that number, and then move the decimal point that number of places in the divisor and dividend. Discuss how moving the decimal point the same number of places in both is really multiplying both by the same number, resulting in an equivalent problem.

Enrichment

Have students rename these fractions as decimals and divide:

1. $14\frac{3}{4} \div \frac{1}{2} = (14.75 \div 0.5 = 29.5)$
2. $3\frac{3}{10} \div \frac{8}{10} = (3.3 \div 0.8 = 4.125)$
3. $\frac{7}{25} \div \frac{1}{25} = (0.28 \div 0.04 = 7)$
4. $\frac{99}{100} \div \frac{3}{10} = (0.99 \div 0.3 = 3.3)$
5. $4\frac{8}{100} \div \frac{4}{5} = (4.08 \div 0.8 = 5.1)$

Practice

Have students complete the practice problems. Remind them to mark the new position of the decimal point with a caret and to put the decimal in the quotient directly above the caret.

Excursion

Problems 3 and 6 require the fraction be changed to its decimal form for comparison. Students may find that rewriting numbers in a vertical format makes comparing corresponding place values easier.

eg. 2.1352
    2.136
    2.137

(Answers may vary.)

Extra Credit *Applications*

Duplicate or read the following to students:

Many years ago, a locomotive builder designed a very special engine to pull passenger trains. The builder decided to call it Engine 1089 because of the unusual qualities of that number. The secret is revealed if these steps are followed: Write any 3-digit number without repeating any digit. Reverse the digits and subtract the smaller from the larger. Add the answer to the number arrived at by reversing the digits of the answer. What answer will always result? (1089) Test this secret with several different 3-digit numbers.

Rounding Quotients

pages 249-250

Objective

To round the quotient

Materials

Mental Math

Have students tell whether these objects or distances should be measured in kilometers, meters or centimeters.

1. distance from home to school (km)
2. length of a paperclip (cm)
3. height of a child (cm)
4. length of a driveway (m)
5. length of a sandwich (cm)
6. length of a marathon (km)

Skill Review

Have students divide:

1. $21.36 \div 6 = (3.56)$
2. $17.516 \div 5.8 = (3.02)$
3. $4.32 \div 3 = (1.44)$
4. $46.965 \div 9.3 = (5.05)$

Have them round these to the nearest tenth and nearest whole number:

1. 3.56 (3.6; 4)
2. 23.176 (23.2; 23)
3. 8.95 (9.0; 9)

Rounding Quotients

A jet aircraft flew from San Francisco to Kansas City in 3 hours. What was the average speed of the plane to the nearest tenth of a mile?

We want to know the approximate speed of the airplane to the nearest tenth of a mile.

It is <u>1,506.5</u> miles from San Francisco to Kansas City.

It took the jet <u>3</u> hours to fly that distance.

To find the average speed, we divide the distance between the cities by the length of time it took to make the trip.

Divide until you run out of digits,	Annex a zero in hundredths place and divide again.	Round the quotient to tenths.

```
    5 0 2.1              5 0 2.16
3)1,5 0 6.5          3)1,5 0 6.50
  1 5                  1 5
    0 0 6                0 0 6
        6                    6
      0 5                  0 5
        3                    3
        2                  2 0
                          1 8
                             2
```

$$502.16 \longrightarrow \underline{502.2}$$

✔ Note, that you must divide to one place value beyond the place in which you want to express the quotient.

The average speed of the jet was <u>502.2</u> miles per hour.

Getting Started

Divide. Round the quotient to the nearest whole number.

1. $5\overline{)9.2}$ (2)

2. $3.6\overline{)25.92}$ (7)

Divide. Round the quotient to the nearest tenth.

3. $4\overline{)3.33}$ (0.8)

4. $7.6\overline{)44.08}$ (5.8)

MCP All rights reserved

249

Teaching the Lesson

Introducing the Problem Have a student read the problem aloud and have another read the information sentences. Read the plan sentences and direct students' attention to the division in their texts. Remind them that they divide just as though they were working with whole numbers. Explain that the decimal point in the quotient goes just above that in the dividend. Show them that to complete the division, they have to annex a zero to the right-hand side of the dividend. An important rule of thumb is that a division is always carried one place beyond the value rounded to. Have a student read the solution sentence. (Average speed was 502.2 miles per hour.)

Developing the Skill Put this example on the board:

```
   4.63 = 4.6
3)13.9
  12
   1 9
   1 8
     10
      9
      1
```

Work through the division with the class. Show them how to annex a zero to the right to continue the division through hundredths which is one place beyond the last place in the dividend. Explain that at that point they should round the quotient to tenths. Have them work $9.3 \div 7$. (1.3)

Practice

Divide. Round the quotient to the nearest whole number.

1. $7\overline{)47.6}$ 7

2. $3.5\overline{)23.45}$ 7

3. $7.2\overline{)25.2}$ 4

4. $6.4\overline{)19.968}$ 3

5. $8\overline{)55.2}$ 7

6. $45\overline{)283.5}$ 6

Divide. Round the quotient to the nearest tenth.

7. $9\overline{)6.66}$ 0.7

8. $12\overline{)3.5}$ 0.3

9. $5.4\overline{)14.094}$ 2.6

10. $3.7\overline{)8.732}$ 2.4

11. $1.6\overline{)2.57}$ 1.6

12. $7.6\overline{)41.368}$ 5.4

Apply

Solve these problems.

13. A plumber needs to cut a piece of pipe 2.5 meters long into 3 equal pieces. About how long will each piece be?
    0.8 of a meter

14. A carpenter used a board 3.4 feet long to estimate the length of some formica he needed. He needed a piece of formica 2.7 times the length of the board. What is the length of the needed formica?
    9.18 feet

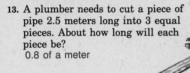

EXCURSION

Circle the correct value for each letter to make the equation true.

I = 6
J = (½) or ⅔
K = (3) or 1
L = (¼) or ¾

$$(I \times J) - (I \div K) = L \times (I - K + 2J)$$

250

Correcting Common Errors

Some students may stop dividing at the place to which they must round, and not have the extra digit in the quotient essential for telling them how to round. Have them draw an arrow above the place to which they must round; then remind them that they need a digit to the right of that place.

Enrichment

Some division of decimals produces repeating numbers. Have students divide:

1. $1.00 \div 3 = (0.33333 \ldots)$
2. $2.00 \div 3 = (0.66666 \ldots)$
3. $1.00 \div 9 = (0.11111 \ldots)$
4. $2.00 \div 9 = (0.22222 \ldots)$

Ask students to find other divisions which will produce repeating decimals. ($3.00 \div 9$; $4.00 \div 9$; $5.00 \div 9$; $6.00 \div 9$; $7.00 \div 9$; $8.00 \div 9$; $7.00 \div 3$; etc.)

Practice

Have students complete the practice problems. Remind them to read the problems carefully, rounding quotients to the nearest whole number or tenth as directed.

Excursion

Encourage students to use the guess and check method for deciding the value of each letter.

Extra Credit   *Probability*

Give each student a pair of dice and ask them to throw the dice 100 times, recording the number of sevens. Have them make a fraction expressing the number of sevens out of the total number of throws. (Answers will vary.) Suggest that they try this experiment at least twice, using the same dice and average the fractions.

Now have them calculate the theoretical probability of throwing 7. (There are 6 ways to throw a seven and 36 ways the dice can land, so the probability is 6/36, 1/6 or 17/100.) Ask students to compare the theoretical probability recorded in their experiments.

Problem Solving
Missing Data

pages 251-252

Objective

To solve problems by finding missing data

Materials

dice
coins
tape measure

Mental Math

Have students identify the missing operation:

1. 23 ( ) 3 = 7⅔ (÷)
2. 49 ( ) 2 = 98 (×)
3. 5 ( ) 3 ( ) 7 = 15 (+); (+)
4. 24 ( ) 15 = 9 (−)
5. 24 ( ) 3 = 72 (×)
6. 8 ( ) 1½ = 5⅓ (÷)
7. 10 ( ) 3 ( ) 3 = 10 (÷); (×)

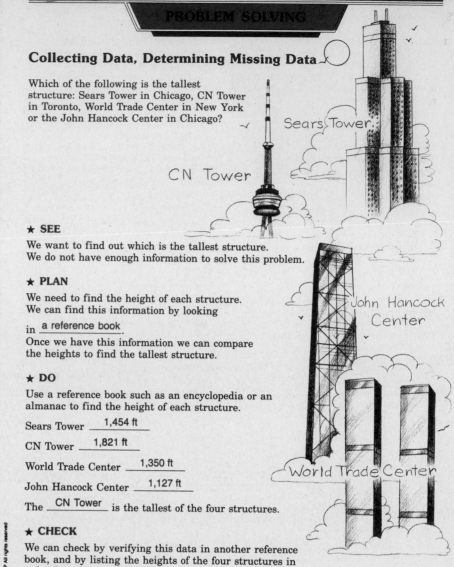

Collecting Data, Determining Missing Data

Which of the following is the tallest structure: Sears Tower in Chicago, CN Tower in Toronto, World Trade Center in New York or the John Hancock Center in Chicago?

★ SEE

We want to find out which is the tallest structure.
We do not have enough information to solve this problem.

★ PLAN

We need to find the height of each structure.
We can find this information by looking

in a reference book .
Once we have this information we can compare the heights to find the tallest structure.

★ DO

Use a reference book such as an encyclopedia or an almanac to find the height of each structure.

Sears Tower ___1,454 ft___

CN Tower ___1,821 ft___

World Trade Center ___1,350 ft___

John Hancock Center ___1,127 ft___

The ___CN Tower___ is the tallest of the four structures.

★ CHECK

We can check by verifying this data in another reference book, and by listing the heights of the four structures in order from largest to smallest.

MCP All rights reserved

251

Teaching the Lesson

Have a student read the problem aloud. Ask the class why it is not possible to solve the problem as it is written. Have a student read the SEE and PLAN sections in the text. Ask students where they could get this kind of information. (almanac, encyclopedia, dictionary, a book of lists or trivia) When students have had time to look up the information required, have them supply the DO section of the problem. (Sears, 1,454 ft; CN, 1,815 ft; World Trade, 1,350 ft; John Hancock, 1,127 ft) Put the heights on the board as students volunteer them and ask one of them to circle the tallest. Read the solution sentence aloud. Ask a student to read the CHECK section. Have students check information from one source against information from another. Ask one student to list the heights in order from largest to smallest.

Apply

Empire State Building

Solve these problems.

1. Roll a single die 50 times and record the outcomes. Perform the experiment a second time and record the outcomes. What number appears most often? What number appears least often?

   Answers will vary but all numbers are equally likely.

2. Roll a pair of dice 30 times and record the number of times each sum appears. Perform the experiment a second time. What sum appears most often? What sum appears least often?

   Answers will vary but expect 7's to appear most often, and 2's and 12's to appear least often.

3. Record the number of pages in your daily newspaper for a week. Explain why some days the papers are larger or smaller.

   Answers will vary.

4. Toss a coin 50 times and record the number of heads and tails. Which side of the coin appears more often?

   Answers will vary but heads and tails are equally likely.

5. Near the front of your classroom textbooks is a copyright date. Find the latest copyright date of each of five books and arrange them in order of newest to oldest.

   Answers will vary.

6. Record the dates of the coins available in your classroom. How many years difference exist between the newest and oldest coin?

   Answers will vary.

7. Jeff and Karen have the same amount of money. Jeff's is all in one-dollar bills. Karen's is all in five-dollar bills. Both of them spend one-half of their money. Who has more money now?

   See Solution Notes.

8. Cindy Loo used a calculator to multiply 35.45×2.18. The display showed only 3 decimal places in the product. Does this mean that she made an error? Why or why not?

   No error

9. Without multiplying, tell which has the greater product. 2.79×1.28 or 27.9×0.128

   See Solution Notes.

10. In Exercise 4, if you tossed the coins 100 times, how would the results differ?

    See Solution Notes.

252

Extra Credit *Geometry*

Draw this "golden rectangle" on the board:

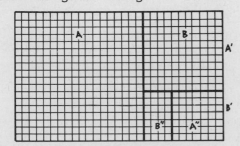

Explain that the relationship between line segments A and B is the same as the relationship between the sum (A + B) and A. That is: A is to B as (A + B) is to A. As the first rectangle is drawn, each succeeding rectangle within it can be divided in the same ratio. Have students draw a golden rectangle on graph paper with the first two numbers, A = 18 and B = 11, and figure out what the ratios will be in the next two divisions. (A' = 11, B' = 7; A'' = 7, B'' = 4)

Solution Notes

1. Have students work in pairs. Let one roll the die and the other record the outcome of each roll with a tally. Add classroom totals to see how close to even the results are.

2. Have students work in pairs again with one keeping a tally of the results. They will find that 2s and 12s appear least often; 6s, 7s and 8s most often. Ask the students to explain why this is so. (Because there are more ways to throw a 6, 7 or 8 than a 2 or 12.)

3. Suggest that students organize the data they collect in a table or chart. Have them compare results of their surveys. See if all papers are larger some days (Sunday, for example) and smaller others. (Monday)

4. Have students work in pairs to toss the coin and tally results. Have each pair determine whether heads or tails are more likely. (They are equally likely, but student results and interpretations will vary.) Add class results and have students decide whether heads or tails are more likely. (These totals will help even out their results.)

5. Have students work in small groups to collect and arrange the books.

6. Give each group a handful of pennies. Have them work together to arrange the coins. Explain that the difference between the oldest and newest coins is called the **range** of the dates.

Higher-Order Thinking Skills

7. Synthesis: If both had x dollars to begin with, then after spending half, they both now have ½x dollars, or an equal amount.

8. Analysis: When one or more of the end digits after the decimal points are zeros, the calculator does not display them.

9. Analysis: Both have the same product; the second pair of factors comes from multiplying and then dividing the first pair by 10. Inverse operations undo each other.

10. Synthesis: Theoretically they would not differ at all. Practically they will differ, but not by much.

252

Calculators and Rates

pages 253-254

Objective

To use a calculator to multiply decimals

Materials

calculator

Mental Math

Have students change each decimal to a fraction as you read them aloud, indicating the "point."

1. 2.1 (2¹⁄₁₀)
2. 13.13 (13¹³⁄₁₀₀)
3. 9.03 (9³⁄₁₀₀)
4. 75.5 (75⁵⁄₁₀)
5. 35.004 (35⁴⁄₁₀₀₀)
6. 7.6 (7⁶⁄₁₀)
7. 0.035 (³⁵⁄₁₀₀₀)

Skill Review

Have students find these products using calculators:

1. 36 × 56 × 82 = (165,312)
2. 145 × 9 × 76 = (99,180)
3. 8 × 24 × 50 = (9,600)
4. 14 × 88 × 7 = (8,624)
5. 36 × 124 × 21 = (93,744)
6. 49 × 49 × 20 = (48,020)

Calculators and Rates

Gene is selling his car by placing a three-line ad in the Daily News. He is going to advertise for 5 days. How much will the ad cost Gene?

Daily News Ad Rate Charge per line, per day (2-line minimum)	
9+ days	$1.98
8 days	$2.20
7 days	$2.51
4 to 6 days	$3.09
1 to 3 days	$4.12

We want to figure the cost of Gene's ad.

He is placing his ad for ___5___ days at a cost of __$3.09__ for each line, each day.

He is writing a ___3___-line ad.

Complete this code to find the cost of the ad.

3 [·] 09 [×] 5 [×] 3 [=] ($46.35)

The ad will cost __$46.35__.

Use a calculator to find the cost of these ads.

6 lines for 6 days __$111.24__   13 lines for 2 days __$107.12__

9 lines for 7 days __$158.13__   4 lines for 8 days __$70.40__

We have been using a calculator to add, subtract, multiply and divide with money. A calculator can be used to do these operations with any decimals.

Complete the following:

6 [·] 48 [×] 12 [·] 9 [=] (83.592)   5 [·] 32 [×] 16 [·] 4 [=] (87.248)

93 [·] 6 [÷] [·] 3 [=] (312)   75 [·] 8 [÷] [·] 2 [=] (379)

17 [·] 9 [+] 36 [·] 72 [=] (54.62)   39 [·] 7 [+] 18 [·] 6 [=] (58.3)

44 [·] 5 [×] 13 [·] 7 [−] 496 [·] 376 [=] (113.274)

73 [·] 9 [×] 8 [·] 4 [−] 63 [·] 49 [×] [·] 2 [=] (111.454)

MCP All rights reserved

253

Teaching the Lesson

Introducing the Problem Read the problem aloud. Ask a student to analyze the information in the illustration and then read the next sentences aloud. Put the calculator code on the board and have students complete the code. (46.35) Have students complete the solution sentence, adding a dollar sign to the answer given by the calculator.

Developing the Skill Explain that multiplying decimals on a calculator is like multiplying whole numbers, except that it is important to remember to enter the decimal point correctly. Remind students that the calculator is only as accurate as the person putting the numbers into it. Point out that one quick way to check that the answer is reasonable, is to count the decimal points. Remind students that when they multiply decimals on paper they count the total decimal places in the factors to find the number in the product. The same should be true when the calculator works the problem. Point out that the only time this check does not work is when the product ends in a zero to the right of the decimal. Working the problem on paper, the zero appears in the product, but calculators drop extra zeros to the right of the decimal. Have students work the problems given and check by counting decimal places.

Use a calculator to complete. Don't forget to use the decimal key when necessary.

1. 49.6 + 39.7 = ___89.3___

2. 85.14 − 57.38 = ___27.76___

3. 4.7 × 3.9 = ___18.33___

4. 393.96 ÷ 14.7 = ___26.8___

5. 39.3 × 16.7 = ___656.31___

6. 0.177 ÷ 5.9 = ___0.03___

7. 268.15 − 199.57 = ___68.58___

8. 615.2 + 189.475 = ___804.675___

9. 476.2 + 89.7 − 112.25 = ___453.65___

10. 126.5 − 96.13 − 7.06 = ___23.31___

11. (9.62 + 4.21) × 0.85 = ___11.7555___

12. (124.3 − 68.8) ÷ 0.5 = ___111___

Apply

Solve these problems.

13. Pat bought a shirt for $10.75 and a belt for $8.35. How much change did Pat receive from a twenty dollar bill?
$0.90

14. Ms. Garcia kept track of how much gas she used in one month. Her records show weekly amounts of 41.36 liters, 36.72 liters, 44.9 liters and 26.81 liters. How much gas did Ms. Garcia use?
149.79 liters

15. Mr. Petit rented a car with 15,748.9 miles on the odometer. He drove the car 212.6 miles on Monday, 307.8 miles on Tuesday and 189.6 miles on Thursday. How many miles were on the odometer when Mr. Petit returned the car?
16,458.9 miles

16. On February 1, Karen had $374.68 in her account. On February 9, she wrote a check for $8.75. On February 28, she wrote a check for $26.18. How much does Karen have left in her account?
$339.75

Use the ad rate on page 253 to solve these problems.

17. Find the cost of a 2-line ad run for 7 days.
$35.14

18. Find the cost of a 4-line ad run for 2 days.
$32.96

Correcting Common Errors

Some students may get incorrect answers when using the calculator because they are careless with the decimal points when entering the numbers. Have them work with partners, one using the calculator and the other pencil and paper to do the same problem. They should compare answers and if they don't match, discuss where and how one of them made an error.

Enrichment

Have students round each decimal to the closest whole number and multiply to estimate each product. Then have them work the problem with their calculators and compare the answers.

1. 2.003 × 7 = (2 × 7 = 14; 14.021)
2. 4.128 × 3 = (4 × 3 = 12; 12.384)
3. 5.026 × 5 = (5 × 5 = 25; 25.13)
4. 6.91 × 4 = (7 × 4 = 28; 27.64)
5. 8.572 × 9 = (9 × 9 = 81; 77.148)

Practice

Have students complete all the problems. Remind them to enter decimal points carefully.

Extra Credit *Applications*

Ask students to bring in empty packages from breakfast, lunch and dinner food items that list the percentages of the recommended daily allowance of vitamins and minerals they need. Let each student select one item for each meal, and calculate the total amounts of vitamins and minerals for their choices for the day. Let some students do some research to find the list of total recommended allowances for vitamins and minerals for their age group. Others can write to a variety of fast food restaurants to request a list of nutritional information for their products. Calculate the nutritional value of a meal and compare it to the RDA list you have found.

Chapter Test

page 255

Item	Objective
1-4	Multiply decimals (See pages 237-238)
5-7	Multiply decimals that need additional zeros written in product (See pages 239-240)
8	Multiply decimals by powers of 10 (See pages 241-242)
9-12	Divide a decimal by whole number (See pages 243-244)
13-16	Divide a decimal by whole number, quotient with zeros (See pages 245-246)
17-20	Divide a decimal by tenths (See pages 247-248)
21-24	Divide a decimal, round quotient to nearest tenth (See pages 249-250)

Multiply.

1. $\begin{array}{r} 4.7 \\ \times\ 1.8 \\ \hline 8.46 \end{array}$

2. $\begin{array}{r} 3.21 \\ \times\ 0.6 \\ \hline 1.926 \end{array}$

3. $\begin{array}{r} 21.3 \\ \times\ 1.9 \\ \hline 40.47 \end{array}$

4. $\begin{array}{r} 6.24 \\ \times\ 0.35 \\ \hline 2.1840 \end{array}$

5. $\begin{array}{r} 0.5 \\ \times\ 0.1 \\ \hline 0.05 \end{array}$

6. $\begin{array}{r} 0.003 \\ \times\ 8 \\ \hline 0.024 \end{array}$

7. $\begin{array}{r} 0.09 \\ \times\ 1.2 \\ \hline 0.108 \end{array}$

8. $\begin{array}{r} 0.007 \\ \times\ 10 \\ \hline 0.07 \end{array}$

Divide.

9. $6\overline{)2.94}$ = 0.49

10. $8\overline{)\$52.64}$ = \$6.58

11. $24\overline{)25.68}$ = 1.07

12. $26\overline{)17.472}$ = 0.672

13. $8\overline{)0.048}$ = 0.006

14. $21\overline{)0.819}$ = 0.039

15. $5\overline{)0.21}$ = 0.042

16. $24\overline{)1.08}$ = 0.045

17. $0.3\overline{)6.66}$ = 22.2

18. $2.4\overline{)3.84}$ = 1.6

19. $1.5\overline{)0.405}$ = 0.27

20. $5.9\overline{)0.354}$ = 0.06

Divide. Round the quotient to the nearest tenth.

21. $6\overline{)3.21}$ = 0.5

22. $8\overline{)1.2}$ = 0.2

23. $1.8\overline{)3.5}$ = 1.9

24. $3.3\overline{)11.11}$ = 3.4

MCP All rights reserved

Circle the letter of the correct answer.

1
36,318
+ 14,273

a 40,591
b 50,591
c 51,591
d NG

2
13,653
− 6,948

a 6,315
b 6,605
c 6,705
d NG

3 48 × 39

a 576
b 1,672
c 1,872
d NG

4 38)8,172

a 215
b 215 R2
c 215 R20
d NG

5 Find the area.

9 in.
6 in.

a 30 in.
b 15 sq in.
c 54 sq in.
d NG

6
7 ft 3 in.
− 2 ft 8 in.

a 4 ft 5 in.
b 4 ft 7 in.
c 5 ft 5 in.
d NG

7 Simplify.
$\frac{42}{10}$

a $\frac{21}{5}$
b $4\frac{2}{5}$
c $4\frac{1}{5}$
d NG

8 $3\frac{1}{2}$
$+ 2\frac{3}{8}$

a $5\frac{1}{8}$
b $5\frac{2}{5}$
c $5\frac{7}{8}$
d NG

9 $15\frac{1}{3} - 8\frac{2}{5}$

a $7\frac{2}{3}$
b $8\frac{1}{5}$
c $8\frac{2}{3}$
d NG

10
14.36
+ 2.9

a 17.26
b 17.2
c 27.26
d NG

11
20.1
− 9.73

a 10.37
b 11.43
c 11.63
d NG

□ score

256

Cumulative Review

page 256

Item	Objective
1	Add two 5-digit numbers (See pages 27-28)
2	Subtract 2 numbers up to 5-digits (See pages 35-36)
3	Multiply two 2-digit factors (See pages 57-58)
4	Divide a 4-digit by 2-digit number (See pages 107-108)
5	Find area of rectangles (See pages 127-128)
6	Subtract customary units of length (See pages 123-124)
7	Change an improper fraction to a mixed number (See pages 157-158)
8	Add two mixed numbers (See pages 175-176)
9	Subtract two mixed numbers, rename minuend (See pages 183-184)
10	Add decimals (See pages 223-224)
11	Subtract decimals (See pages 225-226)

Alternate Cumulative Review

Circle the letter of the correct answer.

1
65,403
+ 25,398

a 80,801
b 90,801
c 90,891
d NG

2
18,782
− 9,876

a 8,906
b 8,916
c 9,906
d NG

3
67
×15

a 1,005
b 1,015
c 1,905
d NG

4 34)9,761

a 287
b 287 R3
c 2,873
d NG

5 Find the area
of a rectangle
5 in. by 16 in.

a 21 sq in.
b 42 sq in.
c 80 sq in.
d NG

6
14 ft 3 in.
− 8 ft 6 in.

a 5 ft 7 in.
b 5 ft 9 in.
c 6 ft 7 in.
d NG

7 Simplify.
$\frac{66}{9}$

a $\frac{22}{3}$
b $7\frac{2}{9}$
c $7\frac{1}{3}$
d NG

8
$5\frac{4}{5}$
$+ 3\frac{4}{15}$

a 9
b $9\frac{1}{15}$
c $9\frac{2}{15}$
d NG

9
$18\frac{1}{4}$
$- 9\frac{5}{6}$

a $8\frac{1}{3}$
b $8\frac{5}{12}$
c $8\frac{1}{2}$
d NG

10
27.83
+ 5.4

a 32.23
b 33.2
c 33.23
d NG

11
36.1
− 8.47

a 27.63
b 27.67
c 27.77
d NG

Points, Lines and Planes

pages 257-258

Objective

To name and draw points, lines, line segments, rays and planes

Materials

*bulletin board
*thumbtacks
*string
*plasticene
straightedge

Mental Math

Have students identify n:

1. n + 10 = 32 (n = 22)
2. ⁿ⁄5 = ²⁄1 (n = 10)
3. n × 6 = 32 − 2 (n = 5)
4. n ÷ 8 = 1⅜ (n = 11)
5. n + 5 − 2 = 3 (n = 0)
6. n × 2.5 = 25 (n = 10)
7. n × 100 = 34 (n = 0.34)

Skill Review

Have students draw and label as many different plane geometric figures on the board as possible. See that they include: square, rectangle, circle, triangle and hexagon. Remind them that the perimeter is the distance around these figures and the area is the space enclosed.

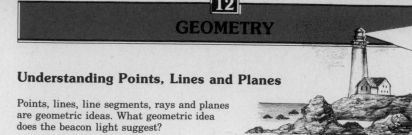

GEOMETRY

Understanding Points, Lines and Planes

Points, lines, line segments, rays and planes are geometric ideas. What geometric idea does the beacon light suggest?

A **point** is a position in space.
We say: **point** A.

A **line segment** is a straight path between two points. It is named by its two endpoints.
We say: **segment** XY. We write: $\overline{XY}$.

A **line** has no endpoints. It extends indefinitely in both directions.
We say: **line** MN. We write: $\overleftrightarrow{MN}$.

A **ray** is part of a line. It has one endpoint and extends indefinitely in one direction.
We say: **ray** RS. We write: $\overrightarrow{RS}$.

A **plane** is a flat surface that extends indefinitely in all directions. It contains points, lines, line segments and rays. A plane is named by any three points in the plane.
We say: **plane** ABC.

The beacon light suggests a ___ray___ because it seems to start at a point and go indefinitely in one direction.

Getting Started

Write the name for each figure.

MCP All rights reserved

1.
R   S
$\overrightarrow{RS}$

2.
    M
L
$\overleftrightarrow{LM}$

Draw and label each figure.

3. Plane PQR
•P •R
•Q

4. $\overleftrightarrow{AB}$

257

Teaching the Lesson

Introducing the Problem Read the problem and definitions aloud. Illustrate each concept on the board as you describe it. Explain that the figures you draw are labeled with capital letters: the point is A; the line segment, XY; the line, MN, with a two-headed arrow over it to show that the line extends beyond anything we can draw on paper; the ray, RS, with a one-directional arrow to show that it starts at a point and extends in only one direction. Point out that the plane is defined by three points and takes its name from those three points, ABC. Have a student read the solution sentence aloud. (beacon suggests a ray)

Developing the Skill Put a single thumbtack in the board and label it A. Put another tack in the board, labeled B, and connect the two points with a string, illustrating the line segment, AB. Put a longer string through points A and B, with students holding the ends. Ask the class to imagine that it extends past the students in each direction. Explain that this is a line that goes through the points AB. Use the same technique to show students a ray. Show that three points define a plane. Put pencils of unequal length into pieces of clay, perpendicular to the table top. Lay a piece of paper on the pencils. Have a volunteer verify that the paper touches all three points. Ask students to imagine that the paper extends in all directions. Show what happens when you add a pencil. (The paper stays in position. There are an infinite number of points in a plane.)

257

Practice

Write the name for each figure.

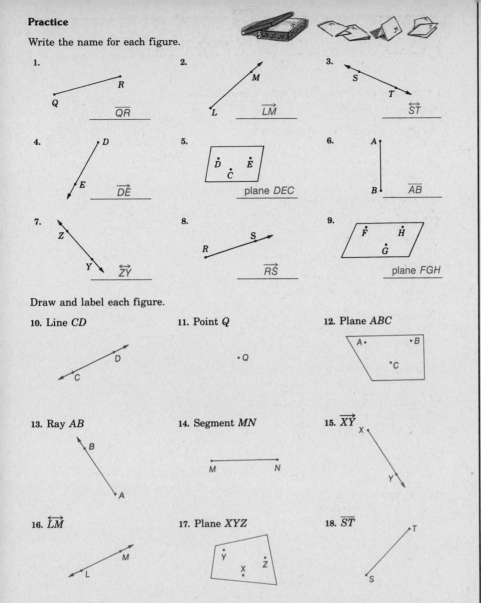

1. $\overline{QR}$

2. $\overrightarrow{LM}$

3. $\overleftrightarrow{ST}$

4. $\overrightarrow{DE}$

5. plane *DEC*

6. $\overline{AB}$

7. $\overrightarrow{ZY}$

8. $\overrightarrow{RS}$

9. plane *FGH*

Draw and label each figure.

10. Line *CD*

11. Point *Q*

12. Plane *ABC*

13. Ray *AB*

14. Segment *MN*

15. $\overrightarrow{XY}$

16. $\overleftrightarrow{LM}$

17. Plane *XYZ*

18. $\overline{ST}$

258

Correcting Common Errors

Some students may confuse the geometric symbols for naming a line and a line segment. Draw line AB on the chalkboard.

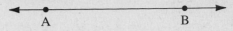

Have students come to the board, discuss and point to the points that are on line AB, those that are on line segment AB, and those that are on line AB but not on line segment AB. Also have them discuss how all the points on line segment AB are on line AB.

Enrichment

Have students think of as many actual examples of points, line segments, lines, rays and planes as they can. (These might include: point, center of the clock face; line segment, width of a desk; line, a street; ray, compass needle pointing north; plane, floor of the school, etc.)

Practice

Have students complete the problems using a straightedge to construct the figures. Remind them that a line is shown with an arrow at each end to suggest that it continues in each direction. A ray is shown with an arrow at one end to suggest that it continues from its origin in that one direction.

Mixed Practice

1. 3.52×6.7 (23.584)
2. $18 \div 3\frac{1}{3}$ $\left(5\frac{2}{5}\right)$
3. $22,075 \times 6$ (132,450)
4. $258.138 - 129.6$ (128.538)
5. 608×395 (240,160)
6. $95.04 \div 18$ (5.28)
7. $\frac{7}{10} = \frac{}{100}$ (70)
8. $8\frac{9}{10} - 3\frac{4}{5}$ $\left(5\frac{1}{10}\right)$
9. $\$808.72 + \$951.28$ ($\$1,760.00$)
10. $6\frac{1}{} \times 1\frac{3}{}$ $\left(10\frac{2}{}\right)$

Extra Credit *Statistics*

Have students take the outside temperature every hour of the school day and record the figures. At the end of the day have students draw a straight-line graph illustrating the fluctuating temperature. (see example below)

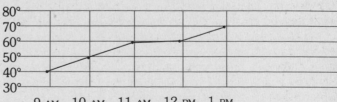

Have students find the median temperature. Ask them to circle and label it on their graph. Extend the activity by repeating the recording for four Mondays in a row. Ask students to identify any trends that emerge.

Angles

pages 259-260

Objective

To identify straight, right, obtuse and acute angles

Materials

*two rulers
straightedge

Mental Math

Have students round to the nearest tenth and the nearest whole number:

1. 103.29 (103.3, 103)
2. 7.92 (7.9, 8)
3. 80.45 (80.5, 80)
4. 1.034 (1.0, 1)
5. 41.200 (41.2, 41)
6. 23.02 (23.0, 23)
7. 99.52 (99.5, 100)

Skill Review

Have students come to the board and illustrate:

1. a point, A
2. a line segment, $\overline{AB}$
3. a line, $\overleftrightarrow{XY}$
4. a ray, $\overrightarrow{RS}$
5. a plane, EFG

Identifying Angles

The clock hands suggest an angle. Is the angle straight, right, obtuse or acute?

An **angle** is formed by two rays with a common endpoint. The common endpoint is called the **vertex.** An angle is usually named by 3 points, the vertex and one on each ray.

We say: **angle** *ABC*. We write: $\angle ABC$.

✔ Notice in naming an angle, the vertex is always named as the center letter.

Angles are measured in **degrees.**
We say: **180 degrees.** We write: **180°.**

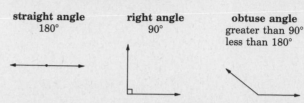

| **straight angle** 180° | **right angle** 90° | **obtuse angle** greater than 90° less than 180° | **acute angle** less than 90° |

The clock hands suggest a ___right___ angle.

Getting Started

Write the name for the angle, its vertex, its rays and identify the type of angle.

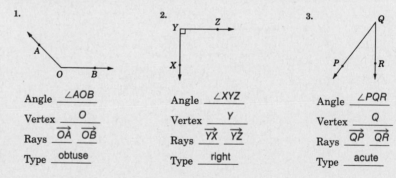

1. Angle ___$\angle AOB$___
   Vertex ___O___
   Rays ___$\overrightarrow{OA}$ $\overrightarrow{OB}$___
   Type ___obtuse___

2. Angle ___$\angle XYZ$___
   Vertex ___Y___
   Rays ___$\overrightarrow{YX}$ $\overrightarrow{YZ}$___
   Type ___right___

3. Angle ___$\angle PQR$___
   Vertex ___Q___
   Rays ___$\overrightarrow{QP}$ $\overrightarrow{QR}$___
   Type ___acute___

MCP All rights reserved

259

Teaching the Lesson

Introducing the Problem Read the problem and the definition of an angle aloud. Hold up two rulers forming an angle. Ask students to imagine each one is a ray. Explain that the point where they meet is the angle's **vertex.** Draw angle ABC on the board. Explain it is made up of the rays BA and BC. In naming an angle, the vertex name is in the middle. Explain that degrees are used to measure angles. Draw a circle on the board and ask students to imagine 360 wedge-shaped pieces in it, each one a degree. Draw straight, right, obtuse and acute angles on the board. Write the number of degrees in each angle, showing students how to write the symbol for degrees. Ask a volunteer to read the solution sentence. (a right angle)

Developing the Skill Refer to the circle you have drawn on the board. Ask a student to tell how many degrees are in the entire circle. (360°) Cut the circle in two and hold up a **straight angle.** Ask how many degrees are in the straight angle. (180°) Divide the straight angle in half. Have a volunteer name the angle formed (right angle) and tell the number of degrees in it. (90°) Explain that an **obtuse angle** is any one that falls between a straight and right angle, and an **acute angle** is smaller than a right angle. Ask students to give examples of right angles. (Most corners are right angles.)

259

Write the name for the angle, its vertex, its rays and identify the type of angle.

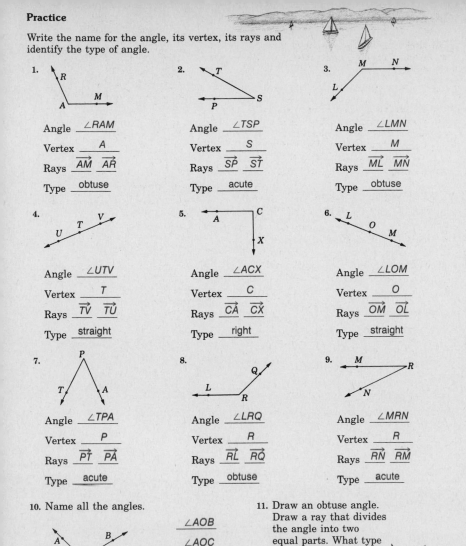

1.

Angle ∠RAM
Vertex A
Rays $\overrightarrow{AM}$ $\overrightarrow{AR}$
Type obtuse

2.

Angle ∠TSP
Vertex S
Rays $\overrightarrow{SP}$ $\overrightarrow{ST}$
Type acute

3.

Angle ∠LMN
Vertex M
Rays $\overrightarrow{ML}$ $\overrightarrow{MN}$
Type obtuse

4.

Angle ∠UTV
Vertex T
Rays $\overrightarrow{TV}$ $\overrightarrow{TU}$
Type straight

5.

Angle ∠ACX
Vertex C
Rays $\overrightarrow{CA}$ $\overrightarrow{CX}$
Type right

6.

Angle ∠LOM
Vertex O
Rays $\overrightarrow{OM}$ $\overrightarrow{OL}$
Type straight

7.

Angle ∠TPA
Vertex P
Rays $\overrightarrow{PT}$ $\overrightarrow{PA}$
Type acute

8.

Angle ∠LRQ
Vertex R
Rays $\overrightarrow{RL}$ $\overrightarrow{RQ}$
Type obtuse

9.

Angle ∠MRN
Vertex R
Rays $\overrightarrow{RN}$ $\overrightarrow{RM}$
Type acute

10. Name all the angles.

∠AOB

∠AOC

∠BOC

11. Draw an obtuse angle. Draw a ray that divides the angle into two equal parts. What type of angles are formed?

acute

260

Correcting Common Errors

Some students may not put the letter for the vertex in the middle when they are naming an angle. Have students work in pairs, drawing two rays with a common endpoint, and labeling the endpoint S. Discuss how point S is the endpoint of both rays and, therefore, the vertex of the angle. Then have students name a point other than the endpoint on each ray and use these points to name the angle.

Enrichment

Have students see if they can find out why a degree was defined as one 360th of a circle. (When it was defined, it was thought that the year had about 360 days, the time it took the earth to go around the sun. In this way, each day would have been about one degree. Of course, this is very close to being true, as the year has 365 days.)

Practice

Have students complete the identifications of the angles and their parts. Remind them that the vertex name is in the center of each angle name. Explain that rays are named with the vertex first and the other point second, with an arrow over both showing the direction of the ray.

Extra Credit *Numeration*

Write on the board several rows of fractions with unlike denominators. Make sure each row contains fractions that could be converted to like denominators. Tell students to copy each row of fractions and draw a yellow circle around the largest quantity and a green circle around the smallest quantity. Have students convert all possible fractions in a row to like denominators.

Measuring Angles

pages 261-262

Objective

To use a protractor to measure and draw an angle

Materials

transparent protractor
straightedge
*overhead projector

Mental Math

Have students multiply and add:

1. $(2 \times 3) + (1 \times 9) = (15)$
2. $(4 \times 5) + (5 \times 2) = (30)$
3. $(8 \times 3) + (6 \times 2) = (36)$
4. $(6 \times 1) + (7 \times 5) = (41)$
5. $(5 \times 3) + (5 \times 3) = (30)$
6. $(6 \times 4) + (3 \times 8) = (48)$
7. $(6 \times 6) + (2 \times 2) = (40)$

Skill Review

Have students draw an example of each of these angles on the board: straight, right, obtuse and acute. Ask other students to label each angle and write its name beside the angle. (for example: $\angle ABC$) Ask students how many degrees are in each type. (180°, 90°, between 180° and 90° and less than 90°)

Measuring Angles

A **protractor** can be used to measure an angle. How many degrees are in the angle formed by the hands of the clock?

The protractor is divided into 180 degrees. Some protractors give the degrees in both directions.

To measure an angle:

1. Extend the rays to make them long enough to go through the grid on the protractor.
2. Place the zero edge along one side of the angle.
3. Place the vertex at the center of the protractor.
4. Read the number of degrees on the same scale as the 0 degree mark.

The hands of the clock form a ___60___ degree angle.

To draw an angle:

1. Place the zero edge along the bottom ray.
2. Place the vertex at the center of the protractor.
3. Mark a point at the degree on the same scale as the 0 degree mark.
4. Use a straight edge to draw the second ray from the vertex through that point.

Getting Started

Estimate the size of each angle. Then use your protractor to find the actual measure. Write the name that identifies the type of angle.

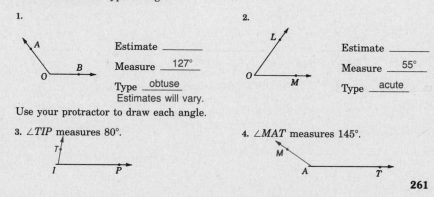

1.

Estimate _____
Measure ___127°___
Type ___obtuse___
Estimates will vary.

2.

Estimate _____
Measure ___55°___
Type ___acute___

Use your protractor to draw each angle.

3. $\angle TIP$ measures 80°.

4. $\angle MAT$ measures 145°.

261

MCP All rights reserved

Teaching the Lesson

Introducing the Problem   Read the problem aloud. Explain that a protractor is a straight angle with an arc over it showing each of the 180 degrees of a half circle. Have students place their protractors over the clock shown in their text. Explain that they should align the vertex of the protractor with the center of the clock. Now have them align one side of the protractor with one hand of the clock. Explain that they can read the size of the angle by finding the point where the second hand crosses the protractor. Ask a volunteer to read their protractor for the rest of the class. (60°) Show students how to follow the directions in the second half of the problem to draw an angle of any size.

Developing the Skill   Place your protractor on the overhead projector pointing out the different scales. Tell students that the bottom ray of the angle corresponds to the zero on the protractor. This can act as an indicator to tell which scale to use. Lay the protractor on a sample angle that opens to the right and show students how to align one side of the protractor with the edge of the angle and read the size by finding the point where the other side crosses the scale. Use an angle which opens to the left to show how to read the other side of the protractor.

Demonstrate on the overhead projector how a protractor can be used to draw an angle of a given size.

Practice

Estimate the size of each angle. Then use your protractor to find the actual measure. Write the name that identifies the type of angle.

1.
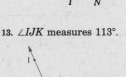
Estimate _____
Measure _76°_
Type _acute_

2.
Estimate _____
Measure _110°_
Type _obtuse_

3.

Estimate _____
Measure _90°_
Type _right_

4.
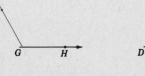
Estimate _____
Measure _41°_
Type _acute_

5.
Estimate _____
Measure _123°_
Type _obtuse_
Estimates will vary.

6.
Estimate _____
Measure _85°_
Type _acute_

Use your protractor to draw each angle.

7. ∠GCO measures 75°.

8. ∠FGH measures 120°.

9. ∠CDE measures 30°.

10. ∠MIN measures 149°.

11. ∠KLM measures 17°.

12. ∠QRS measures 67°.

13. ∠IJK measures 113°.

14. ∠VWX measures 98°.

15. ∠SQT measures 41°.

262

Correcting Common Errors

Some students may read the incorrect scale on their protractor when they are measuring an angle. Before they begin to measure, have them identify the angle by writing acute (less than 90°), right (90°), or obtuse (greater than 90° but less than 180°). Then have them use this label to help them decide which scale on the protractor to use.

Enrichment

Have students use protractors to measure the angle between the ground and the top of the school flagpole or the top of the school at varying distances. Show them how to use a straightedge to sight along a line to the object. Have them record the size of the angles. Ask them to generalize what happens as they increase the distance of the vertex from the height of the object. (angle will decrease)

Practice

Have students complete the practice exercises. Explain that an estimate can be made by imagining how the angle compares to a straight line or to a corner. Remind students of the importance of centering the protractor on the vertex and making sure that the zero on the scale is aligned with the angle to be measured.

Extra Credit   *Creative Drill*

Tell students they can guess each other's birthdays by asking a friend to follow these steps:

1. write their birthday month in numbers, giving the month an ordinal number, ex. January-1, February-2, etc.
2. multiply the month's number by 5
3. add 6 to that answer
4. multiply by 4
5. add 9
6. multiply by 5
7. add the birthday's date to that answer

Now have students take their friend's total and do the secret final operation. To find the birthdate, they must subtract 165 from the total. The last 2 digits of the resulting number will name the date of the birthday and the first number tells the month. (ex. 806 would be August 6)

262

Lines

pages 263-264

Objective

To identify pairs of parallel, intersecting and perpendicular lines

Materials

plastic straws
pins
straightedge

Mental Math

Have students divide and express the remainder as a fraction:

1. $23 \div 4 = (5\frac{3}{4})$
2. $46 \div 9 = (5\frac{1}{9})$
3. $14 \div 7 = (2)$
4. $26 \div 5 = (5\frac{1}{5})$
5. $80 \div 9 = (8\frac{8}{9})$
6. $62 \div 10 = (6\frac{2}{10} = 6\frac{1}{5})$
7. $39 \div 9 = (4\frac{3}{9} = 4\frac{1}{3})$

Skill Review

Have students draw and label examples of each of the following on the board: point, line segment, line, ray, plane, straight angle, right angle, obtuse angle and acute angle.

Identifying Parallel, Intersecting and Perpendicular Lines

Two lines in the same plane are either parallel or they intersect at a point. Do the rungs in the ladder suggest parallel or intersecting lines?

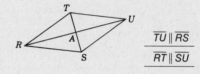

Two lines are **parallel** if they are in the same plane and never meet.
We say: line AB **is parallel to** line CD.
We write: $\overleftrightarrow{AB} \parallel \overleftrightarrow{CD}$.

Two lines **intersect** if they eventually meet or cross each other.
We say: line XY **intersects** line MN at point O.

Two lines are **perpendicular** if they intersect to form right angles.
We say: line RS **is perpendicular to** line TU.
We write: $\overleftrightarrow{RS} \perp \overleftrightarrow{TU}$.

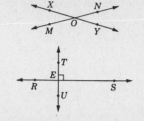

The rungs in the ladder suggest ___parallel___ lines.

Getting Started

Identify each pair of lines by writing the word parallel, intersecting or perpendicular.

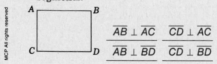

1. ___parallel___
2. ___intersecting___
3. ___perpendicular___
4. ___intersecting___

5. Write the pairs of perpendicular segments.

$\overline{AB} \perp \overline{AC}$ $\overline{CD} \perp \overline{AC}$
$\overline{AB} \perp \overline{BD}$ $\overline{CD} \perp \overline{BD}$

6. Write the pairs of parallel segments.

$\overline{TU} \parallel \overline{RS}$
$\overline{RT} \parallel \overline{SU}$

MCP All rights reserved

263

Teaching the Lesson

Introducing the Problem Read the problem aloud. Ask students to follow in their texts while you read the definitions of parallel, intersecting and perpendicular lines. Illustrate the pairs of lines on the board and show students the symbols for parallel (‖) and perpendicular (⊥). Have a student read the solution sentence. (tracks suggest parallel lines)

Developing the Skill Have each student make a flexible framework of plastic straws to form a square cube. Have them connect the straws at the corners with straight pins. Tell students to use the corner of a book to arrange the straws at right angles initially. Draw a duplicate model on the board to show that the framework can illustrate all three types of lines. There are parallel lines and intersecting lines. The intersecting lines are at right angles. Give students time to talk about the lines in the framework. Have the class think of real examples of parallel, intersecting and perpendicular lines.

Practice

Identify each pair of lines by writing the word parallel, intersecting or perpendicular.

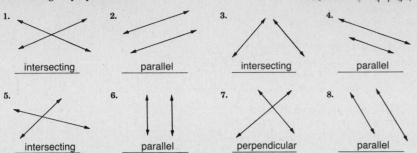

1. intersecting   2. parallel   3. intersecting   4. parallel

5. intersecting   6. parallel   7. perpendicular   8. parallel

Write the pairs of parallel segments in each figure.

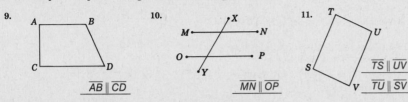

9. $\overline{AB} \parallel \overline{CD}$

10. $\overline{MN} \parallel \overline{OP}$

11. $\overline{TS} \parallel \overline{UV}$
    $\overline{TU} \parallel \overline{SV}$

Write the pairs of perpendicular segments in each figure.

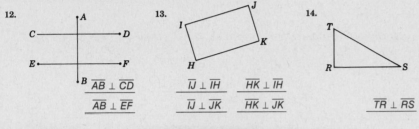

12. $\overline{AB} \perp \overline{CD}$
    $\overline{AB} \perp \overline{EF}$

13. $\overline{IJ} \perp \overline{IH}$ $\overline{HK} \perp \overline{IH}$
    $\overline{IJ} \perp \overline{JK}$ $\overline{HK} \perp \overline{JK}$

14. $\overline{TR} \perp \overline{RS}$

EXCURSION

Find the sum of the degrees of the 4 angles in a quadrilateral. First, draw a quadrilateral, cut it out and label the inside of the angles A, B, C and D. Next, cut off the 4 labeled corners and lay them side to side with the vertices touching. Use a protractor to measure the four angles. Add the degrees together. What is the sum of the degrees of the 4 angles in a quadrilateral? ___360°___

264

Correcting Common Errors

Watch for students who think that all intersecting lines are perpendicular. When they are working with intersecting lines, have them use a square corner of a piece of paper as a guide to determine whether the angles are right angles (90°) and, therefore, the lines are perpendicular.

Enrichment

Show students a way of determining if two lines are parallel. Draw this figure on the board:

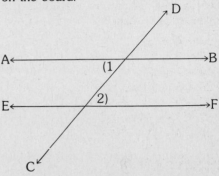

Explain that line CD is a **transversal,** crossing line AB and line EF. Point to angles 1 and 2. Explain that line AB is parallel to line EF if angle 1 equals angle 2. Give students several pairs of lines, some of which are not parallel. Have them draw transversals, measure the angles with a protractor and determine whether the lines are parallel.

Practice

Have students complete the practice exercises. Remind students of the symbols for a line (↔), a line segment (−), parallel (‖) and perpendicular (⊥) lines.

Excursion

Students will arrive at two proofs that the interior angles of a quadrilateral equal 360 degrees. When placing the vertices of the four corners together, they complete a new plane figure that requires 360 degrees. The second proof is the actual sum of the measurements.

Extra Credit   *Counting Strategies*

The Greeks in Alexandria developed the following symbols for numbers. Use the overhead projector or write these symbols on the board:

A	B	Γ	Δ	E	F	Z	H	Θ
1	2	3	4	5	6	7	8	9

I	K	Λ	M	N	Ξ	O	Π	Ϙ
10	20	30	40	50	60	70	80	90

P	Ϟ	T	Y	φ	X	Ψ	Ω	ϡ
100	200	300	400	500	600	700	800	900

Explain that the Greeks also used letters to represent numbers. Sometimes they put a line above the letter to show that they represented a number not a word. They wrote thousands by putting a slash or stroke mark before the unit symbol so that /A meant 1,000 and /B, 2,000. Tens of thousands were shown by putting a unit symbol over an M (for myriad), so that: $\binom{Z}{M}$ meant 70,000. To make larger numbers they put the symbols in a line: $\overline{YNE}$ meant 455. Give students a variety of numbers to write in the Alexandrian system.

264

Circles

pages 265-266

Objectives

To draw a circle with a compass
To label its center, radius, diameter,
  a chord, central angle and arc

Materials

square of corrugated cardboard
tack
10-inch string
sharp pencil
compass
straightedge

Mental Math

Have students round to the nearest
ten dollars and multiply:

1. $28 × 3 = ($30 × 3 = $90)
2. $15 × 2 = ($20 × 2 = $40)
3. $95 × 4 = ($100 × 4 = $400)
4. $32 × 7 = ($30 × 7 = $210)
5. $121 × 4 = ($120 × 4 = $480)
6. $87 × 5 = ($90 × 5 = $450)

Skill Review

Draw this pattern on the board.

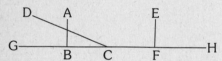

Have students find a pair of parallel
lines (AB ∥ EF), intersecting lines (AB,
(CD) and perpendicular lines (EF ⊥ GH).

Understanding Circles

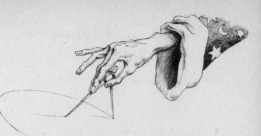

A compass can be used to draw
a circle. How many degrees are
in a circle?

To draw a circle:
1. Place the tip of the compass on a
   point.

2. Move the pencil completely around
   the tip.

The point is called the **center** of the
circle. The circle is named by the
point in the center. The distance
around a circle is called the
circumference. The segment from the
center to the circumference is called
the **radius.** Any segment connecting
two points on the circle is called a
chord. A chord through the center is
called the **diameter.** The angle formed
by the center and two radii is called a
central angle. The part of the
circumference between two points is
called an **arc.** An arc contains the
same number of degrees as its central
angle.

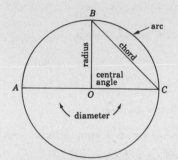

The circle is divided by the diameter
into two arcs. One arc starts at *A*,
goes through *B*, and stops at *C*. It
contains 180°. The other arc starts at
A and goes the other direction and

stops at *C*. It contains __180°__ degrees.

The complete circle has __360°__ degrees.

We say this is **circle** *O*
with **radius** $\overline{OB}$,
  diameter $\overline{AC}$,
  chord $\overline{BC}$,
  central angle ∠*BOC* and
  arc $\overgroup{BC}$.

Getting Started

Use circle *O* to answer 1 through 5.

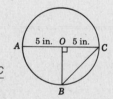

1. Name the diameter. __$\overline{AC}$__

2. The length of the diameter is __10 inches__.

3. Name one central angle that is right. __∠*AOB* or ∠*BOC*__

4. The measure of $\overgroup{AC}$ is __180°__.

5. Name the chord that is not a diameter. __$\overline{BC}$__

MCP All rights reserved

265

Teaching the Lesson

Introducing the Problem Read the problem aloud. Ask
students to follow in their texts as you explain at the board.
Reproduce the illustration on the board. Show students that
the **center** of the circle is a point equidistant from all points
along the circle. Explain that the **radius** is the distance from
the center to a point on the circle. The **diameter** is twice
the radius, or the length of a line segment from a point on
the circle, through the center, and across to a point on the
other side. Explain that the **circumference** is the distance
around the circle, like a perimeter. Show students that if
they connect two points on the circle with a straight line,
they draw a **chord.** The diameter is one specific chord
which passes through the center. The section of circle
marked by a chord is called an **arc.** The angle formed by
two radii and the center is called a **central angle.** Show
the class that the diameter is a straight central angle of 180°.

Remind them that an entire circle is made up of 360°. Have
students write the missing number of degrees in the solution
sentences. (contains 180°; complete circle has 360°)

Developing the Skill Have each student use cardboard,
string, tack and paper to draw a circle. Have them put the
tack through paper and cardboard, make a string loop, and
put the loop around the tack. Explain that if they put a
sharp pencil into the loop and swing the pencil around the
tack, leaving no slack in the string, they will draw a circle
whose radius is the length of the string loop. Have them
draw and label the center, radius, diameter, a chord, central
angle and arc.

Practice

Use circle A to answer 1 through 5.

1. $\overline{AS}$ is called the ___radius___.

2. Point A is called the ___center___.

3. $\angle NAS$ is called (a, an) ___central angle___.

4. $\overline{SM}$ is called (a, an) ___chord___.

5. $\overset{\frown}{SN}$ is called (a, an) ___arc___.

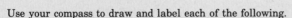

Use circle P to answer 6 through 10.

6. Name one radius. ___$\overline{PU}$ or $\overline{PT}$ or $\overline{SP}$___

7. Name one central angle. ___$\angle SPU$ or $\angle UPT$___

8. Name the diameter. ___$\overline{ST}$___

9. How long is the diameter? ___6 inches___

10. What is the measure of arc UT? ___60°___

Use your compass to draw and label each of the following.

11. Circle A with chord $\overline{MN}$.

12. Circle O with radius $\overline{OA}$.

13. Circle P with diameter $\overline{AB}$.

14. Circle R with central angle LRM.

EXCURSION

The irrational number π (pi) represents the number of times the circumference of a circle can be divided by its diameter. Thus, $\pi = \frac{c}{d}$. Use a metric measuring tape on some round objects in your classroom to find the circumference and diameter. To find π, use your calculator to divide these circumferences by their diameters and record the full decimal part for each calculation. See TE notes.

266

Correcting Common Errors

Some students may confuse radius and diameter. Have them work with partners and a 10-inch circle with the center labeled. Have them use a ruler to draw and measure a radius (5 in.) and a diameter (10 in.). Ask: How does the length of a radius compare to the length of a diameter? (It is half as long.) How does the length of a diameter compare to the length of a radius? (It is twice as long.)

Enrichment

Have students cut circles out of stiff paper. Ask them to measure the diameter of their circle, and then the circumference. One way to measure the circumference is to make a mark along the outside of the circle, put the mark on a line, and then roll the circle along the line until the mark touches down again. Have them all divide the circumference by the diameter and compare their answers. (They will all be about 3.1 or 3.2 and represent the constant ratio pi, π, more exactly 3.14.)

Practice

Have students complete the practice exercises. Remind them that line segments are labeled —, angles $\angle$ and degrees °.

Excursion

The number of decimal places in the answer will depend upon the precision of the measurements. 3.14 is the usual approximation. Pi is called irrational because its true value has an infinite decimal that is nonrepeating. The first forty-seven decimal places for pi are:
$\pi \doteq 3.14159265358979323846264338327950288419716939937$ . . . but answers will vary within a reasonable range.

Extra Credit *Applications*

Duplicate the following for students and have them use a calculator to solve.

Young Farmer Green planned to raise chickens. He started out with 23 but decided as soon as they produced chicks, he would sell the older chickens and keep the chicks until they produced chicks of their own. Each of the original 23 feathered fowl laid 10 eggs but only 7 from each chicken hatched. Each of the new chickens then laid 10 eggs but Farmer Green took 3 from each and sold them at market. All of the remaining eggs hatched and soon each of the new birds laid 5 eggs, that all hatched. This new flock of chicks each laid 3 eggs, that all hatched, grew into chickens and laid 3 eggs each, that all hatched. Even though Farmer Green had sold all of his old chickens each time their eggs hatched, he still had more chicks than he could count. Help him by calculating how many chicks he had. (Hint: Once you have the correct answer, turn your calculator upside down and you will discover where Farmer Green kept the feed for all his chickens.) (50715, on a calculator turned upside down, will read SILOS.)

266

Bisecting Lines and Angles

pages 267-268

Objective

To use a compass and straightedge to bisect line segments and angles

Materials

*chalkboard compass
compass
straightedge
ruler

Mental Math

Have students identify the mystery number:

1. $23 - n = 9$ $(n = 14)$
2. $13 - n = 5$ $(n = 8)$
3. $29 - n = 9$ $(n = 20)$
4. $52 - n = 48$ $(n = 4)$
5. $37 - n = 12$ $(n = 25)$
6. $36 - n = 15$ $(n = 21)$
7. $45 - n = 22$ $(n = 23)$

Skill Review

Draw a circle on the board. Have students label the center, a radius, diameter, chord, central angle and arc. Draw another circle and ask students to draw an obtuse central angle, an acute central angle and estimate the size of the angles. Measure the angles to see how close their estimates were.

Bisecting Segments and Angles

To **bisect** a figure is to divide it into two equal parts. How can we bisect a line segment and an angle using only a compass and a straight edge?

To bisect a line segment:

1. With your compass select a radius which is larger than half the length of $\overline{AB}$. With point A as center, construct an arc above and below $\overline{AB}$.

2. Use the same radius you used in Step 1. With point B as center, construct two arcs which intersect the arcs constructed in Step 1. Label the intersections C and D.

3. Draw $\overline{CD}$. $\overline{CD}$ bisects $\overline{AB}$. M is the **midpoint** of $\overline{AB}$.

To bisect an angle:

1. Construct an arc intersecting the rays at points M and N.

2. With M and N as center, construct two arcs intersecting in the interior of $\angle ABC$. Label the intersection D.

3. Draw $\overline{BD}$. $\overline{BD}$ bisects $\angle ABC$.

Getting Started

Use your compass and straightedge to bisect these figures.

1.

2.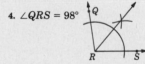

Draw each angle using your protractor. Use your compass and straightedge to bisect it. Use your protractor to check the results.

3. $\angle FGH = 20°$

4. $\angle QRS = 98°$

MCP All rights reserved

Teaching the Lesson

Introducing the Problem Use the chalkboard compass to illustrate each step as you read the sections on bisecting a line segment and bisecting an angle. Explain as you work that every time you make an arc with the compass, you are marking points that are an equal distance from the stationary end. Show that as you bisect the line you are finding two points (one above and one below the line) that are equidistant from either end. Explain that if you connect those two points, the new line will cross the original line in the center. Explain that bisecting an angle works on the same principle. You draw two arcs from points equidistant along each ray of the angle. At the point where these arcs intersect, you have found a point that is equidistant from both rays. By connecting the new point to the vertex of the angle, you will be drawing a line that bisects the angle.

Developing the Skill Explain that these constructions require only a straightedge, not a ruler, as it is the compass that finds the required points. The straightedge is necessary only to connect the new points. Point out that most straightedges are also rulers, but that they will not need to measure anything to complete the bisections.

Practice

Use your compass and straightedge to bisect each segment.

1.

2.

3.

4.
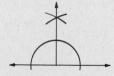

Use your compass and straightedge to bisect each angle.

5.

6.
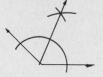

7.

8.

Draw each angle using your protractor. Use your compass and straightedge to bisect it. Use your protractor to check the results.

9. ∠ABC = 170°

10. ∠DEF = 16°

11. ∠HIJ = 100°

12. ∠MNO = 61°

268

Correcting Common Errors

Watch for students who do not place their compass points on the point where the arc intersects the rays when they are drawing the arcs to find the angle bisector. After they have drawn the first arc on the rays, have them mark the two points of intersection with a dot. Then have them place the metal tip of their compass on the dots to complete the next steps.

Enrichment

Give each student a rectangular piece of paper. Have them fold it to form a square. After cutting out the square, have them fold it on a diagonal and cut along that line.
Have them bisect the resulting right angle. Ask students what they notice about the way the angle bisector intersects the side of the triangle. (It forms two right angles.) Have them measure each angle to show that it is 90°.

Practice

Have students complete the practice problems with a compass and straightedge. Remind them of the steps needed to construct and measure an angle with a protractor.

Mixed Practice

1. 576.421 + 6,395.72 (6,972.141)
2. 11,908 − 4,396 (7,512)
3. 17.3 × 8.7 (150.51)
4. $202.44 ÷ 7 ($28.92)
5. 23 × $14.98 ($344.54)
6. 656.38 − 129.65 (526.73)
7. 1.472 ÷ 32 (0.046)
8. 3,561 + 8,195 + 308 (12,064)
9. 127.38 + 4,128.7 + 125.2 (4,381.28)
10. $3\frac{3}{8} ÷ 5\frac{1}{4} \left(\frac{9}{14}\right)$

Extra Credit   *Applications*

Have students apply their tally and graphing skills. Divide students into groups. Have each group list the different types of TV programs offered. (ex. news, situation comedy, detective) Have them conduct a poll of students and adults, tallying what types of programs are favorites. Have them graph their data in two ways: a chart showing favorite programs overall and a chart showing favorite programs of various age groups polled. Ask which graph was easier to construct. Ask which graph was the most informative. Extend the activity by compiling a graph to reflect program preferences of the class itself.

268

Problem Solving
Make a Table

pages 269-270

Objective

To solve problems by making a list or table

Materials

*overhead projector

Mental Math

Read these numbers aloud and have students identify the digit in the tenths place.

1. 23.5 (5)
2. 5.903 (9)
3. 17.03 (0)
4. 189.42 (4)
5. 100.352 (3)
6. 71.6 (6)
7. 53.24 (2)

Making a List or a Table

The greenhouse is having a problem with insects. On each spider plant there are 7 insects. On each rubber tree there are 13 insects. If there are a total of 115 insects in the greenhouse, how many spider plants are there? How many rubber trees are there?

★SEE

We want to know the number of spider plants and the number of rubber trees.

There are __7__ insects on each spider plant.

There are __13__ insects on each rubber tree.

There are __115__ insects altogether.

★PLAN

We make a table that shows the possible combinations of spider plants and rubber trees. We show the total number of insects on each type of plant. By adding the number of insects we show the total number of insects for each combination.

★DO

Number of Rubber Trees	1	2	3	4	5	6	7
Number of Insects	13	26	39	52	65	78	91
Remaining Number of Insects	102	89	76	63	50	37	22
Number of Groups of 7 Insects	14.6	12.7	10.9	9	7.1	5.3	3.1

There are __9__ spider plants and __4__ rubber trees in the greenhouse.

★CHECK

There are __9__ spider plants. $9 \times 7 = $ __63__ insects

There are __4__ rubber trees. $4 \times 13 = $ __52__ insects

$63 + 52 = $ __115__ insects.

MCP All rights reserved

269

Teaching the Lesson

Read the problem aloud. Remind students of the SEE-PLAN-DO-CHECK method for solving problems. Ask a volunteer to read the SEE section in their text. (7 insects on each spider plant; 13 on each rubber tree; 115 insects all together) Explain that to find the answer to the problem, they will have to organize the information in a table. Read the PLAN section in the book and ask students to look at the table arranged below. Explain that by trying different combinations of spider plants and rubber trees, they will find one that produces a total of 115. Suggest that students use extra paper to make their own lists of their combinations to prevent needless repitition. Have a volunteer read the solution sentence. (9 spider plants, 4 rubber trees) Ask students to work the check on the board. Explain that to check, they will multiply the number of plants by the number of insects on each, then add to see that the total is 115 insects. (9 spider plants, 63 insects; 4 rubber trees, 52 insects; 63 + 52 = 115 insects)

269

Apply

Solve these problems.

1. In a stable there are men and horses. In all, there are 22 heads and 72 feet. How many men and how many horses are in the stable?
8 men   14 horses

2. A pen and an eraser cost a dollar and a dime. The pen costs a dollar more than the eraser. How much does each cost?
$0.05 eraser $1.05 pen

3. Your heart pumps about 60 cubic centimeters of blood each time it beats. How many times would your heart have to beat to pump 6 liters of blood? (Hint: 100 cubic centimeters = 1 liter)
10 times

4. Brad has seven coins in his pocket, 4 pennies, a nickel, a dime and a quarter. What amounts of money less than 44¢ is he unable to make using one or any combination of the coins?
20¢, 21¢, 22¢, 23¢, 24¢

5. You are a contestant waiting to appear on a new game show. You know the stage will be filled with prizes priced from $1 to $500. You will be allowed to keep each prize with a price tag whose digits add up to 10. You will only have 1 minute to select your prizes. Make a list of all winning price tags. What is the most expensive prize? What is the least expensive prize?
$19 least expensive
$460 most expensive

6. People began arriving at the circus in groups. The closer that it came to showtime, the larger each group became. The first group consisted only of Joey. Each group after that had two more persons than the group that arrived before them. How many people attended the circus if altogether 10 groups came?
100 people

7. Read Problem 1 again. What if the number of heads and feet were doubled? How would this change the answer?
Double the answer.

8. Read Problem 1 again. Change the situation so that the correct answer to the problem would be 4 men and 7 horses.
See Solution Notes.

9. Henny said that 2 lines must either intersect or be parallel. Penny said that she can show 2 lines that do not intersect and are not parallel. How can she do this?
See Solution Notes.

10. Jumbo drew a triangle and showed it to Lila. He said the triangle had 2 right angles. Lila said that this was not possible. Explain why Lila is correct.
See Solution Notes.

270

Extra Credit   *Applications*

Invite a representative from a local bank to discuss savings accounts and other savings plans. Ask them to bring a sample savings account book to show how to keep track of dates, withdrawals, deposits and balances. Have them define these terms and demonstrate the math used to arrive at these figures. The teacher could then supply the students with a sample account sheet showing a list of deposits and withdrawals. Ask the students to supply correct figures in the balance column. Arrange for one of the students to open a savings account, going through each step for the class.

Solution Notes

1. Set up a table:

MEN			HORSES			TOTALS	
#	heads	feet	#	heads	feet	heads	feet
1	1	2	1	1	4	2	6
2	2	4	2	2	8	4	12
4	4	8	4	4	16	8	24

2. Set up the following table:

Eraser	Pen	Total
25¢	$1.25	$1.50
15¢	$1.15	$1.30
10¢	$1.10	$1.20
5¢	$1.05	$1.10

3. Two ways to solve the table:

Volume per Beat	Number of Beats	Total Volume
60 cc	2	120 cc
60 cc	4	240 cc . . .
60 cc	10	600 cc

Write an equation and solve for n:
$n \times 60 = (6 \times 100)$. $n \times 60 = 600$, $n = 10$.

4. Suggest a table of coins showing Brad's choices.

5. List all the possibilities: $19, $28, $37, $46, $55, $64, $73 and so on through $460.

6. Have students list groups and a running total:

Group	Total	Circus
1	1	1
2	3	4 . . .
10	19	100

Higher-Order Thinking Skills

8. Analysis: Half the original answer: there are 11 heads and 36 feet.

9. Synthesis: Henny is correct as long as he is talking about 2 lines in the same plane; Penny is correct if she is talking about 2 lines in different planes.

10. Synthesis: Lila pointed out that with 2 right angles, both rays, or sides of the triangle, would be parallel. Since parallel lines never meet, there could not be a third vertex or a traingle. Also, the sum of the angles of a triangle is 180°. Therefore, it is not possible to have two right angles in a triangle since each right angle is 90°.

270

Chapter Test

page 271

Item	Objective
1-4	Draw and label lines, line segments, rays, planes (See pages 257-258)
5-6	Draw and label parallel, intersecting, perpendicular lines (See pages 263-264)
7-8	Draw and label parts of circle (See pages 265-266)
10-11	Use protractor to measure and identify right, obtuse, acute, straight angles (See pages 259-262)
12-13	Identify rays, vertex of angles (See pages 259-260)
14-15	Bisect segments and angles (See pages 267-268)

Draw and label each figure.

1. Ray *PQ*

2. Line segment *AB*

3. Plane *STU*

4. $\overleftrightarrow{CD}$

5. Line *CD* ⊥ line *MN*

6. $\overleftrightarrow{TU} \parallel \overleftrightarrow{RS}$

7. Circle *O* with chord *ST*

8. Circle *B* with radius *BA*

Use a protractor to measure each angle, then write the word which identifies the type of angle.

9.

Measure ___90°___

Type ___right___

10.

Measure ___130°___

Type ___obtuse___

11.

Measure ___25°___

Type ___acute___

Write the names for the vertex and rays of angle *GHI*.

12. Vertex ___H___

13. Rays $\overrightarrow{HG}$
  $\overrightarrow{HI}$

Bisect segment *AB* and angle *PQR*.

14.

15.

MCP All rights reserved

271

271

Circle the letter of the correct answer.

1 17,041
 − 9,272

a 7,879
b 17,769
ⓒ 7,769
d NG

7 64.03
 + 8.7

a 72.10
b 64.703
ⓒ 72.73
d NG

2 73 × 58

ⓐ 4,234
b 4,134
c 131
d NG

8 51.2
 − 4.86

a 56.06
ⓑ 46.34
c 4.634
d NG

3 42)2,175

a 51 R3
b 51
ⓒ 51 R33
d NG

9 Round 16.71 to the nearest whole number.

a 16
ⓑ 17
c 20
d NG

4 3 hr 5 min
 − 1 hr 8 min

a 2 hr 3 min
ⓑ 1 hr 57 min
c 1 hr 7 min
d NG

10 1.36 × 100

ⓐ 136
b 100.36
c 1.3600
d NG

5 $5\frac{1}{2} + \frac{6}{7}$

ⓐ $6\frac{5}{14}$

b $6\frac{8}{14}$

c $5\frac{9}{14}$

d NG

11 0.0168 ÷ 12

a 0.014
b 0.14
ⓒ 0.0014
d NG

6 10
 − $2\frac{7}{12}$

ⓐ $7\frac{5}{12}$

b $12\frac{7}{12}$

c $8\frac{5}{12}$

d NG

12 3.2)3.36

a 1.25
b 0.105
ⓒ 1.05
d NG

☐ score

272

Cumulative Review

page 272

Item	Objective
1	Subtract two 5-digit numbers, zero in minuend (See pages 35-36)
2	Multiply two 2-digit numbers (See pages 57-58)
3	Divide a 4-digit by 2-digit number, quotient with remainder (See pages 103-106)
4	Change units of time (See pages 117-118)
5	Add mixed numbers (See pages 175-176)
6	Subtract a mixed number from whole number (See pages 181-182)
7	Add decimals (See pages 223-224)
8	Subtract decimals (See pages 225-226)
9	Round decimals to nearest whole number (See pages 229-230)
10	Multiply decimals by 1,000 (See pages 241-242)
11	Divide a decimal by a whole number, quotient with zeros (See pages 245-246)
12	Divide a decimal by tenths (See pages 247-248)

Alternate Cumulative Review

Circle the letter of the correct answer.

1 84,027
 − 56,383

ⓐ 27,644
b 27,744
c 37,644
d NG

2 96
 ×35

a 3,260
b 3,350
c 3,460
ⓓ NG

3 37)2,390

a 64 R20
ⓑ 64 R22
c 64 R32
d NG

4 There are ___ seconds in 1 day.

a 1,440
b 3,600
ⓒ 86,400
d NG

5 $6\frac{5}{6}$
 + $\frac{7}{18}$

a $6\frac{5}{18}$
ⓑ $7\frac{4}{18}$
c $7\frac{5}{18}$
d NG

6 14
 − $5\frac{9}{16}$

ⓐ $8\frac{7}{16}$
b $9\frac{7}{16}$
c $9\frac{9}{19}$
d NG

7 56.09
 + 7.4

a 56.83
b 63.13
ⓒ 63.49
d NG

8 43.2
 − 8.671

ⓐ 34.529
b 34.671
c 35.629
d NG

9 Round 76.544 to the nearest whole number.

a 54
b 76
ⓒ 77
d NG

10 8.3175
 ×1,000

a 831.75
ⓑ 8317.5
c 83.175
d NG

11 17).0459

a 0.27
b 0.027
ⓒ 0.0027
d NG

12 3.6)7.344

a 2.4
ⓑ 2.04
c 20.4
d NG

Triangles

pages 273-274

Objective

To identify and measure triangles

Materials

*three thumbtacks
*string
*triangle of heavy paper
*overhead projector

Mental Math

Have students add 3 and multiply by 2:

1. 4 (14)
2. 6 (18)
3. 10 (26)
4. 22 (50)
5. 0 (6)
6. 12 (30)
7. 100 (206)

Skill Review

Ask a student to draw a ray, RS, on the board. Have another add the ray RT to make an angle, ∠SRT. Have students estimate the size of the angle in degrees, and then measure it. (Answers will vary.)

Measuring and Identifying Triangles

A **triangle** is a 3-sided figure that also has 3 interior angles. The sum of the measures of these 3 angles is always 180 degrees. How many degrees are there in angle *ACB*?

Triangle *ABC*
or
△ *ABC*

We want to find the measurement of angle *ACB*.

Angle *CAB* measures __90__ degrees, and angle *ABC* measures __45__ degrees.

To find the measurement of angle *ACB*, we add the measurements of the two known angles and subtract the total from the sum of the interior angles.

We add __90°__ and __45°__ and subtract that sum from __180°__.

```
  90°          180°
+ 45°        - 135°
-----        ------
 135°           45°
```

Angle *ACB* measures __45__ °.

✔ There is a relationship between the angles and the sides in a triangle.

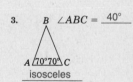

equilateral
All 3 angles are equal in measure. All 3 sides are equal in length.

isosceles
Two angles are equal in measure. The 2 sides opposite these angles are equal in length.

scalene
No angles are equal in measure. No sides are equal in length.

Getting Started

Calculate the missing angle measure. Identify the triangle as equilateral, isosceles or scalene.

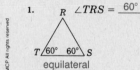

1. *R* ∠*TRS* = __60°__
   T 60° 60° *S*
   equilateral

2. ∠*XZY* = __20°__
   Z
   X 25° 135° *Y*
   scalene

3. *B* ∠*ABC* = __40°__
   A 70° 70° *C*
   isosceles

MCP All rights reserved

273

Teaching the Lesson

Introducing the Problem Read the problem aloud. Ask students to look at the triangle pictured. Explain that a triangle has 3 interior angles. This one has angles CAB, ABC and the unknown angle, ACB. Point out that the sum of the angles in a triangle is 180° no matter what the shape or size of the triangle. Have a student read the information sentences. Read the plan sentences. (add 90° and 45° and subtract sum from 180°) Have students do the addition and subtraction and read the solution sentence. (∠ACB measures 45°) Direct students' attention to the three types of triangles: **equilateral, isosceles** and **scalene.** Have a student read aloud the relationship between sides and angles for each.

Developing the Skill Use thumbtacks and string to make equilateral, isosceles and scalene triangles on the bulletin board. Remind students that **tri** means **three** and ask

what the word triangle means. (three angles) Draw a straight line on the overhead projector. Take a paper triangle, mark each of the angles with an x, and cut the angles apart. Arrange the angles along the line to show that their sum is 180°.

Have a student make a triangle, mark the corners, cut them off, and arrange them on a straight line to show this works for any triangle.

273

Calculate the missing angle measure. Identify the
triangle as equilateral, isosceles or scalene.

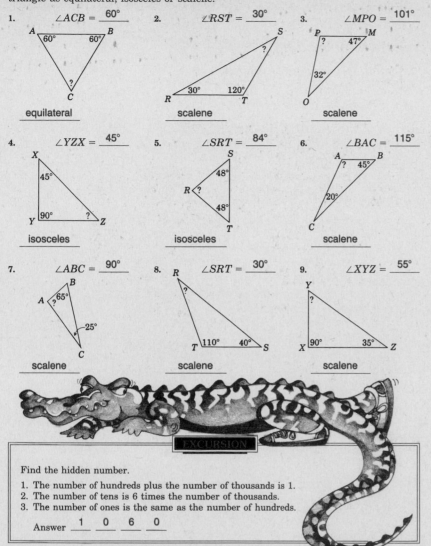

1.   ∠ACB = __60°__

equilateral

2.   ∠RST = __30°__

scalene

3.   ∠MPO = __101°__

scalene

4.   ∠YZX = __45°__

isosceles

5.   ∠SRT = __84°__

isosceles

6.   ∠BAC = __115°__

scalene

7.   ∠ABC = __90°__

scalene

8.   ∠SRT = __30°__

scalene

9.   ∠XYZ = __55°__

scalene

EXCURSION

Find the hidden number.

1. The number of hundreds plus the number of thousands is 1.
2. The number of tens is 6 times the number of thousands.
3. The number of ones is the same as the number of hundreds.

Answer __1__ __0__ __6__ __0__

274

Correcting Common Errors

Some of the students may simply subtract the measure of one of the two
given angles from 180° when they are
finding the measure of the third angle
of a triangle. Have them work with
partners and a set of triangles labeled
ABC with one of the angle measures
missing. Have them complete a chart
like that shown below to find the measure of the missing angle.

∠A	∠B	∠C	∠A + ∠B + ∠C

Enrichment

Draw this diagram on the board. Tell
students that XYZ is called an in-
scribed triangle. Explain that it is an
equilateral triangle and that O is the
center of the circle. Have students
identify the size of angles XOZ, YXO
and XYZ.

(∠XOZ = 120°, ∠YXO = 30°,
∠XYZ = 60°)

Practice

Have students complete the problems. Have them check
their answers with a protractor.

Excursion

Remind students to keep track of what place value they are
working with. Have them create similar problems of their
own for a partner to solve.

Extra Credit   *Applications*

Planning a garden can give students many opportunities to
calculate perimeters and areas. Have students develop a
plan using the following steps:

1. Choose an appropriate location for a garden.
2. Decide on the size of the garden and calculate the perimeter.
3. Choose what crops are to be grown and divide the garden into fractional sections for each crop. Calculate the
   perimeter and area for each section.
4. Read seed packet labels and determine how many seeds
   should be planted in each section and how far apart the
   seeds should be planted. Plot the plantings on paper.
5. If possible, have students prepare the soil for planting
   and plant a garden according to the plan.
6. Extend the activity by having students estimate the yield
   of the garden using information given on seed packets.

Quadrilaterals

pages 275-276

Objective

To identify and draw a parallelogram, rectangle, rhombus, square and trapezoid

Materials

*cutouts of the five quadrilaterals

Mental Math

Have students tell whether these should be measured in gallons, quarts or cups:

1. flour for a cake (cups)
2. gasoline for a car (gallons)
3. milk drunk by a 10-year-old in one day (cups or quarts)
4. paint to cover a house (gallons)
5. water to water a garden (gallons)
6. raisins to make two dozen cookies (cups)
7. lemonade for a family picnic (quarts)

Skill Review

Ask students to draw and label these plane figures: circle, triangle, square, rectangle and hexagon.

Identifying Quadrilaterals

A **quadrilateral** is a 4-sided figure. Some quadrilaterals are given special names. What special name does figure *ABCD* have?

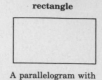

parallelogram

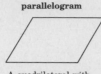

A quadrilateral with opposite sides parallel and equal in length

rectangle

A parallelogram with 4 right angles and opposite sides equal in length

rhombus

A parallelogram with 4 sides equal in length

square

A rectangle with 4 sides equal in length

trapezoid

A quadrilateral with exactly one pair of parallel sides

Figure *ABCD* has __1__ pair of parallel sides. It is called a __trapezoid__.

Getting Started

1. Write the kind of quadrilateral. Identify each kind of angle.

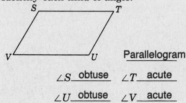

Parallelogram

∠S __obtuse__   ∠T __acute__
∠U __obtuse__   ∠V __acute__

2. Draw a trapezoid with one right angle. Label the corners *WXYZ*. Write the names of the sides.

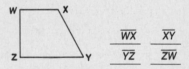

$\overline{WX}$ $\overline{XY}$
$\overline{YZ}$ $\overline{ZW}$

Complete this sentence.

3. The only figure that is not a parallelogram on this page is the __trapezoid__.

MCP All rights reserved

275

Teaching the Lesson

Introducing the Problem Read the problem aloud and have students look at the illustrations in their texts. Tell students to read the definitions of the five quadrilaterals. Remind them that parallel means two lines in a plane that never meet. Ask a student to define a right angle. (90°) Have another read the solution sentences. (ABCD has 1 pair of parallel sides, ABCD is a trapezoid.)

Developing the Skill Explain that just as tri in triangle means three, **quad** in quadrilateral means **four.** Hold up each of the quadrilateral cutouts and ask students to name and define each shape. Put this chart on the board.

Ask students to put the initial (P, R, RH, S, T) in each column that describes that figure.

opposite sides parallel	P	R	RH	S	
one pair of sides parallel					T
opposite sides equal length	P	R	RH	S	
all sides equal length			RH	S	
four right angles		R		S	

Practice

Write the kind of quadrilateral. Identify each kind of angle.

1.
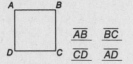

___square___

∠A ___right___   ∠B ___right___

∠D ___right___   ∠C ___right___

2.

___rectangle___

∠E ___right___   ∠F ___right___

∠G ___right___   ∠H ___right___

3.

___trapezoid___

∠J ___obtuse___   ∠K ___obtuse___

∠I ___acute___   ∠L ___acute___

4.

___square___

∠N ___right___   ∠O ___right___

∠M ___right___   ∠P ___right___

5.

___parallelogram___

∠R ___obtuse___   ∠S ___acute___

∠Q ___acute___   ∠T ___obtuse___

6.

___trapezoid___

∠X ___acute___   ∠W ___acute___

∠U ___obtuse___   ∠V ___obtuse___

Draw each figure and label the corners. Write the names of the sides.

7. square *ABCD*   8. rhombus *RSTU*   9. parallelogram *WXYZ*

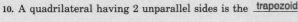

$\overline{AB}$ $\overline{BC}$ $\overline{RS}$ $\overline{ST}$ $\overline{WX}$ $\overline{XY}$

$\overline{CD}$ $\overline{AD}$ $\overline{TU}$ $\overline{UR}$ $\overline{YZ}$ $\overline{ZW}$

Complete these sentences.

10. A quadrilateral having 2 unparallel sides is the ___trapozoid___.

11. Two parallelograms that have 4 sides of equal length are the ___square___ and ___rhombus___.

12. Two parallelograms having 4 right angles are the ___rectangle___ and ___square___.

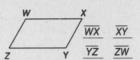

276

Correcting Common Errors

Some students may have difficulty identifying the properties of the various quadrilaterals. Have them work with partners to make and complete a chart like the one shown below.

	sides			angles	
	‖	⊥	⌞	⌝	∠
□	yes	yes	yes	no	no
▽	some	no	no	yes	yes
▱	yes	no	no	yes	yes
▭	yes	yes	yes	no	no
▱	yes	no	no	yes	yes

Enrichment

Have students make quadrilaterals using plastic straws, anchoring the corners with pins.
Ask them to try to deform the shape. Can they change its shape easily? (yes) Give them more straws and have them add struts until they have made it rigid. What kinds of figures make up the quadrilateral when it is rigid? (triangles)

Practice

Have students complete the problems. Illustrate these angles on the board for reference: right, obtuse and acute.

Extra Credit   *Biography*

Albert Einstein was one of the greatest scientists of all time. He is best known for his theory of relativity that he developed at age twenty-six. This theory helped explain how atomic energy could be controlled. In 1939, Einstein introduced President Roosevelt to the possibility of building an atomic bomb. Six years later, fearing Nazi Germany's military power, the United States produced an atomic bomb.

Einstein was born in 1879 in Germany. His creative genius was sparked at age five when his father showed him a pocket compass. From then on, Einstein felt compelled to unravel the mysteries of science. His first job after college was in a Swiss patent office. During that time he wrote three different papers which each led to the development of a new branch of physics. He then presented the now-famous formula, $E = mc^2$, representing energy equals mass times the speed of light squared. When the Nazis deprived Einstein of his property, position and citizenship in Germany, he accepted a position at the new Institute for Advanced Study in Princeton, New Jersey, where he lived until his death in 1955.

Polygons

pages 277-278

Objective

To identify regular and irregular polygons

Materials

*cutouts of regular polygons
rulers
protractors

Mental Math

Have students subtract:

1. $1\frac{1}{2} - \frac{1}{2} = (1)$
2. $3\frac{3}{4} - 1\frac{1}{4} = (2\frac{2}{4} = 2\frac{1}{2})$
3. $4\frac{1}{5} - 3 = (1\frac{1}{5})$
4. $7 - 5\frac{1}{2} = (1\frac{1}{2})$
5. $\frac{7}{8} - \frac{3}{4} = (\frac{7}{8} - \frac{6}{8} = \frac{1}{8})$
6. $1\frac{1}{3} - \frac{2}{3} = (\frac{2}{3})$
7. $\frac{1}{2} - \frac{5}{10} = (0)$

Skill Review

Have students illustrate the following on the board: point, line segment, ray, angle, radius of a circle, center of a circle, equilateral triangle and trapezoid

---

Identifying Polygons

Triangles and quadrilaterals are kinds of polygons. A **polygon** is a plane figure with sides that are line segments that meet at a vertex. Which of these figures is not a polygon?

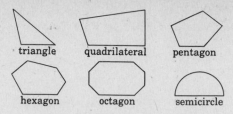

triangle   quadrilateral   pentagon

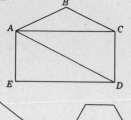

hexagon   octagon   semicircle

A polygon has straight sides. Since the ___semicircle___ has a curved side, it is not a polygon.

A **diagonal** of a polygon joins two vertices of a polygon but is not a side of the polygon. $\overline{AC}$ and $\overline{AD}$ are two diagonals of polygon $ABCDE$.

A **regular polygon** has all sides of equal length and all angles of equal measure.

triangle   square   pentagon   hexagon

Getting Started

Identify the kind of polygon. Write regular or not regular.

1.

hexagon

regular

2.

pentagon

not regular

3.

triangle

not regular

Draw all possible diagonals. Write the name of each diagonal. Then, complete the chart.

4.
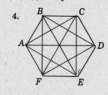

5.

$\overline{AC}$	$\overline{AD}$	$\overline{AE}$
$\overline{BD}$	$\overline{BE}$	$\overline{BF}$
$\overline{CF}$	$\overline{CE}$	$\overline{DF}$

6.

Name of figure	hexagon
Number of sides	6
Number of angles	6
Number of diagonals from one vertex	3
Total number of diagonals	9

MCP All rights reserved

277

Teaching the Lesson

Introducing the Problem Read the problem aloud and have students examine the illustration. Draw a polygon on the board and point to its sides (line segments) and its vertices. Ask a student to read the solution sentence. Have a student read the definition of a diagonal, pointing out that while the sides join two vertices, the sides are not diagonals. A diagonal must join vertices that are not adjacent. Add a diagonal to the polygon on the board. Ask another student to read the definition of a regular polygon. Have students read the name of each of the regular polygons.

Developing the Skill Draw a triangle and a square on the board. Point out that they are plane figures with line segments as sides. Explain that any plane figure with line segments as sides is a **polygon.** Remind students that a **plane figure** is a flat figure, a shape that exists in a single plane. Draw a pentagon on the board. Ask a student to give its name. (pentagon) Have another tell how many sides it has. (5) Explain that a polygon can have any number of sides. If it has 6 sides, it is called a hexagon, hex meaning six. If it has 7 sides, it is called a septagon; 8 sides, an octagon; 9 sides, a nonogon; and 10 sides, a decagon. Point out the similarity to the names of the months: September, October, November and December. (the seventh, eighth, ninth and tenth months of the Roman calendar)

Practice

Identify the kind of polygon. Write regular or not regular.

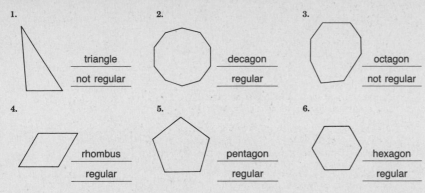

1. triangle
not regular

2. decagon
regular

3. octagon
not regular

4. 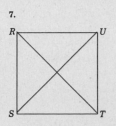 rhombus
regular

5. pentagon
regular

6. hexagon
regular

Draw all possible diagonals. Write the name of each diagonal.

7.

$\overline{RT}$
$\overline{SU}$

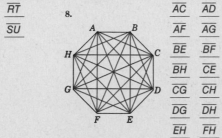

8.

$\overline{AC}$	$\overline{AD}$	$\overline{AE}$
$\overline{AF}$	$\overline{AG}$	$\overline{BD}$
$\overline{BE}$	$\overline{BF}$	$\overline{BG}$
$\overline{BH}$	$\overline{CE}$	$\overline{CF}$
$\overline{CG}$	$\overline{CH}$	$\overline{DF}$
$\overline{DG}$	$\overline{DH}$	$\overline{EG}$
$\overline{EH}$	$\overline{FH}$	

Complete the chart.

9.

Name	Number of Sides	Number of Angles	Number of Diagonals from 1 Vertex	Total Number of Diagonals
Triangle	3	3	0	0
Quadrilateral	4	4	1	2
Pentagon	5	5	2	5
Hexagon	6	6	3	9
Heptagon	7	7	4	14

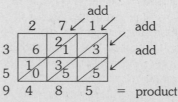

278

Correcting Common Errors

Some students may have trouble drawing and naming all the diagonals in a polygon. Have them work with partners. Give each pair a drawing of a regular hexagon labeled MNOPQR. Have them draw and name diagonals by starting with vertex M, drawing and naming all the diagonals with point M as one of the endpoints. They continue in order until they can no longer draw any more diagonals without retracing one already drawn. (They will draw segments MO, MP, MQ, NP, NQ, NR, OQ, OR, and PR.)

Enrichment

Show students how to draw regular polygons within a circle. Give students several 10-inch paper circles and a straightedge. First, having students work with you, fold one in quarters, open it, draw a line to join the creased edges to form a square.

Now, ask them to make an octagon within a circle. (fold the quartered circle so as to halve each of the right angles and connect the edges)

Practice

Have students complete the problems. Suggest that they look for patterns in the numbers of the chart in problem 9.

Mixed Practice

1. $2\frac{4}{5} \times 2\frac{3}{7}$ $\left(6\frac{4}{5}\right)$
2. $4.902 \div 3.8$ (1.29)
3. $829{,}176 + 43{,}196$ (872,372)
4. 0.15×0.07 (.0105)
5. $105{,}371 - 1{,}950$ (103,421)
6. $16 \div 1\frac{3}{4}$ $\left(9\frac{1}{7}\right)$
7. $40 \times 1{,}010$ (40,400)
8. $\frac{4}{5} + \frac{2}{3} + \frac{5}{6}$ $\left(2\frac{3}{10}\right)$
9. $12{,}662 \div 54$ (234 R26)
10. $195.73 - 107.8$ (87.93)

Extra Credit   *Numeration*

Show students this Hindu method for multiplication. Mathematicians think that it may be of Arabic origin. $271 \times 35 =$

```
              add
     2    7 ╱ 1 ╱      add
  3 │ 6 │ 2╱│ 3 │╱     add
    │   │ 1╱│   │╱
  5 │ 1╱│ 3╱│ 5 │╱
    │ 0╱│ 5╱│ 5 │
  9    4    8    5   = product
```

The factors are written along the top and side, with largest place values in the upper left corner. The product of each of the digits is written in the grid with two-digit numbers written with tens above the diagonal and ones below. Starting with the lower, right-hand digit, add all numbers along the diagonal to reach the product. Have students use this method for the problem: 254×18. (4,572)

278

Congruent Polygons

pages 279-280

Objective

To identify congruent polygons

Materials

ruler
tracing paper
straightedge
colored pencils

Mental Math

Ask students to estimate the quotient to the nearest 10:

1. $95 \div 9 = (10)$
2. $142 \div 6 = (20)$
3. $473 \div 21 = (20)$
4. $1,290 \div 102 = (10)$
5. $1,135 \div 22 = (50)$
6. $2,700 \div 52 = (50)$
7. $904 \div 27 = (30)$

Skill Review

Give each student a ruler and lined paper. Ask them to draw a triangle, square, rhombus, parallelogram, pentagon, hexagon and octagon.

Understanding Congruent Polygons

Two plane figures are **congruent** if they have the same size and shape. One figure will fit on top of the other. The parts that fit together are called **corresponding parts.** Which angle corresponds to angle ABC?

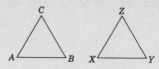

We can use tracing paper to show which parts will fit. Place the paper over triangle ABC and trace it. Slide this over triangle XYZ.
The angle that fits on angle ABC is angle __XYZ__.

Angles ABC and __XYZ__ are corresponding angles.

Corresponding Sides	Corresponding Angles
$\overline{AC}$ and $\overline{XZ}$	$\angle ABC$ and $\angle XYZ$
$\overline{CB}$ and $\overline{ZY}$	$\angle CAB$ and $\angle ZXY$
$\overline{AB}$ and $\overline{XY}$	$\angle ACB$ and $\angle XZY$

✔ The corresponding parts of congruent figures are also congruent. The symbol for "is congruent to" is ≅. **Triangle ABC is congruent to triangle XYZ is written: $\triangle ABC \cong \triangle XYZ$.**

$\overline{AC} \cong \overline{XZ}$	$\angle ABC \cong \angle XYZ$
$\overline{CB} \cong \overline{ZY}$	$\angle CAB \cong \angle ZXY$
$\overline{AB} \cong \overline{XY}$	$\angle ACB \cong \angle XZY$

Getting Started

Tell if these segments are congruent. Write Yes or No.

1. ●————————● __No__

   ●————●

Complete these statements about each set of congruent figures.

2. $\overline{AB} \cong$ __ST__
4. $\overline{DA} \cong$ __VS__
6. $\angle SVU \cong$ __∠ADC__
8. $\angle UTS \cong$ __∠CBA__

3. $\overline{AM} \cong$ __YZ__
5. $\overline{YX} \cong$ __AR__
7. $\angle RAM \cong$ __∠XYZ__
9. $\angle YZX \cong$ __∠AMR__

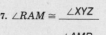

MCP All rights reserved

279

Teaching the Lesson

Introducing the Problem Read the problem aloud. Have students refer to the illustration as you explain that congruent plane figures are those that have exactly the same size and shape. Point out that the figures can be compared by looking at corresponding parts. If the figures are identical, then an angle on one will correspond exactly to an angle on the other; a side on one, to a side on the other. Give each student tracing paper and a straightedge. As you read the next section of the text, have them trace the triangle ABC and place it over triangle XYZ. Ask a student to identify the angle that corresponds to $\angle ABC$. ($\angle XYZ$) Read the solution sentence. (Angles ABC and XYZ are corresponding angles.) Using their traced figures, have students complete the table of corresponding sides and angles in their texts.

Developing the Skill Explain that congruent means the same size and shape. Draw one big and one small square on the board. Explain that while their shapes are the same, the figures are not the same size. Draw two triangles on the board; one equilateral and the other irregular, but approximately the same size. Explain that these figures, while the same size, are not the same shape. The triangles are not congruent. Draw two congruent rectangles on the board. Explain that the symbol ≅ is used to mean that two sides, angles or figures are **congruent.** Label the rectangles ABCD and EFGH. Ask students to list equal sides and angles. (AB ≅ EF, etc.)

Practice

Tell if the figures are congruent. Write Yes or No.

1.

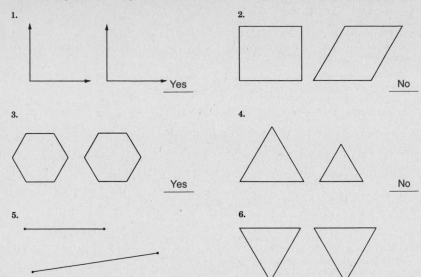

Yes

2.

No

3.

Yes

4.

No

5.

No

6.

Yes

Complete these statements about each set of congruent figures.

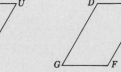

7. $\overline{AB} \cong$ _____ $\overline{LN}$

8. $\angle ABC \cong$ _____ $\angle LNM$

9. $\overline{MN} \cong$ _____ $\overline{CB}$

10. $\angle MLN \cong$ _____ $\angle CAB$

11. $\angle DGF \cong$ _____ $\angle TSV$

12. $\angle TUV \cong$ _____ $\angle DEF$

13. $\overline{ST} \cong$ _____ $\overline{GD}$

14. $\overline{GF} \cong$ _____ $\overline{SV}$

280

Correcting Common Errors

Some students may have difficulty naming the corresponding parts of congruent polygons. Have them work with partners. Give them a worksheet on which are shown pairs of labeled congruent polygons. Have them use different colored crayons to color pairs of corresponding parts the same color. After they have identified all corresponding parts by colors, have them identify them by letter names.

Enrichment

Give students a collection of wooden building blocks. Explain that these blocks have many congruent sides. Ask each student to take a block and trace the outline of one side on paper. Now have them turn the block until they find a congruent side to trace. Have them find at least five sets of congruent figures and trace each.

Practice

Have students complete the problems. Remind them that angles are labeled with the vertex between the other two points.

Mixed Practice

1. $12,204 + 38 + 6,278$ (18,520)
2. $17\frac{3}{5} + 28\frac{4}{7} \left(46\frac{6}{35}\right)$
3. $\$1,958.20 - \$671.33$ ($1,286.87)
4. $\frac{7}{12} - \frac{3}{8} \left(\frac{5}{24}\right)$
5. $50,543 \div 80$ (631 R63)
6. 25×17 (425)
7. $160.21 - 106.021$ (54.189)
8. $\frac{3}{4} \div 3 \left(\frac{1}{4}\right)$
9. $\$119.08 \times 6$ ($714.48)
10. $.592 \div 7.4$ (0.08)

Extra Credit *Probability*

Explain that finding the number of combinations of a set of objects is different from finding the number of permutations. Students already know how to find all the different possible arrangements of four differently-colored blocks. These are the permutations of the set. In this lesson they will learn to calculate the number of different combinations possible from a set of objects, for example, the number of ways of taking 2 blocks from a set of 5 different blocks. Explain that the formula for calculating the number of combinations of n objects taken r at a time, is n! divided by the product of r! and $(n - r)!$.

$$C = \frac{n!}{r! \ (n - r)!}$$

Put the following example on the board: The number of combinations of 2 books that can be taken from a set of 7 is: $7!/2! \times (7 - 2)! = 7!/(2! \times 5!) = (7 \times 6)/2 = 21$. Then have them calculate the number of different combinations of 5 playing cards that can be drawn from a deck of 52. (2,598,960)

280

Symmetry

pages 281-282

Objective

To identify and draw lines of symmetry

Materials

square paper
straightedge
*mirror
scissors

Mental Math

Have students multiply by 4:

1. $.25 ($1.00)
2. $1.50 ($6.00)
3. $10.01 ($40.04)
4. $.50 ($2.00)
5. $.39 (round to 40¢, multiply, subtract extra 4¢, $1.56)
6. $.99 ($3.96)
7. $1.19 ($4.76)

Skill Review

Have a student draw a triangle on the board and label points A, B and C. Ask another to draw a triangle DEF congruent to the first. Have students label corresponding sides.
Ask students to list corresponding angles: ∠BAC = ∠EDF, etc.

Recognizing Symmetry

If you can fold a figure so that the two parts are congruent, the figure is called a **symmetric figure.** The line where the figure is folded is called a **line of symmetry.** Name the lines of symmetry for this rectangle.

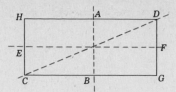

We can fold the rectangle along the dotted lines and each time make two congruent figures.

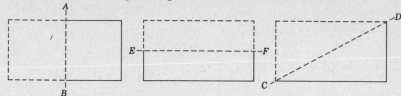

The lines of symmetry are $\overline{AB}$, $\overline{EF}$ and $\overline{CD}$.

Getting Started

Tell if the dotted line is a line of symmetry. Write Yes or No.

1.
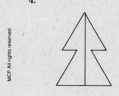
No

2.
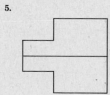
Yes

3.
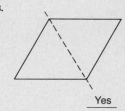
Yes

Draw all lines of symmetry for each figure.

4.
5.
6.

MCP All rights reserved

281

Teaching the Lesson

Introducing the Problem Read the problem aloud. Have students examine the rectangle. Hold up a rectangular piece of paper. Fold it in half. Show that the two halves match. Explain that the fold line is a line or **axis of symmetry.** Ask if it is possible to find another line of symmetry. (yes) Fold the paper again to show another line of symmetry. Ask a volunteer to name the lines of symmetry in the figure in their books. (AB and EF) Read the solution sentence aloud. (Lines of symmetry are AB and EF.)

Developing the Skill Give each student a piece of square paper. Ask them to fold the paper along the diagonal. Have them open the paper and trace the diagonal with a straightedge. Ask students to describe the relationship between the triangles formed by the folding. (They are congruent.) Explain that the square is symmetric about that line. Point out that this kind of symmetry is called **reflectional symmetry.** Hold a mirror along the diagonal and ask a stu-

dent to look into the mirror and tell what they see. (The entire square will seem to appear.) Explain that the diagonal is a line of reflectional symmetry because one side looks like the reflection of the other. Ask students to find two other lines of symmetry in the square by folding and tracing the lines with a straightedge. Ask each student to choose one line of symmetry, cut along the line, and superimpose one side on the other to show the pieces are congruent.

281

Tell if the dotted line is a line of symmetry. Write Yes or No.

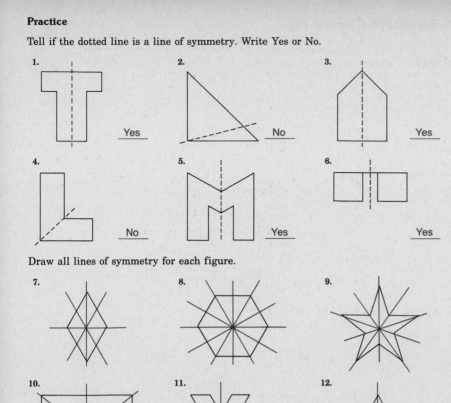

1.   Yes

2.   No

3.   Yes

4.   No

5.   Yes

6.   Yes

Draw all lines of symmetry for each figure.

7.

8.

9.

10.

11.

12.

EXCURSION

Use one half of a sheet of dark colored paper, scissors, glue and 1 full sheet of white paper to show congruence. Cut a shape out of the edge of the dark paper and flip it over onto white paper to make a reflection. Your reflections might look similar to this when completed.

282

Practice

Have students complete the practice exercises. Tell them that if they are not sure of symmetry, they can fold the page.

Excursion

Encourage students to make creative designs and glue them. Display their completed creations.

Extra Credit *Logic*

Have students solve this problem of the wise grandmother:

Two parents left their four children with their grandmother while they went shopping. To keep the children happy, they left 17 granola bars with the grandmother. The bars were to be divided according to the ages of the children.

Correcting Common Errors

Students may have difficulty drawing lines of symmetry. Have them work with partners and a sheet of paper on which are shown all upper case letters of the alphabet. Have them take turns, one letter at a time, drawing any lines of symmetry. Students should recognize that one way to test is to cut out the letter and fold it different ways to see if they can make halves match.

Enrichment

Have students fold tissue paper and cut out symmetrical patterns with scissors. Suggest that they start with a paper that has two lines of symmetry. (folded twice) Encourage them to add lines of symmetry. If they fold it once more, they will add two lines of symmetry.

The oldest, twins Bill and Beth, each were to get ⅓ of the granola bars, sister Susan was to get ⅙ of them, and Pete the youngest, was to get ⅑ of the bars. The children could not figure out how to divide the bars without cutting any apart.

They took the problem to their grandmother who reached into her cupboard, pulled out something helpful and then showed her grandchildren how to divide the bars.

What did the grandmother take from her cupboard and how many bars did each child receive?

(The grandmother pulled out another granola bar which gave her a total of 18. Each of the twins received 6 bars, Susan received 3, and Pete received 2. Having given the children the 17 bars, she returned her own to the cupboard.)

Similar Polygons

pages 283-284

Objective

To identify similar polygons

Materials

ruler
*a copy of a drawing and a reduced or enlarged copy of the same picture
*overhead projector
one-inch graph paper

Mental Math

Have students identify the next number in each series:

1. 1.3, 1.4, 1.5, . . . (1.6)
2. 2.4, 2.6, 2.8, . . . (3.0)
3. 1.1, 2.2, 3.3, . . . (4.4)
4. .5, 1.0, 1.5, . . . (2.0)
5. 1.5, 3.0, 4.5, . . . (6.0)
6. 3.9, 3.7, 3.5, . . . (3.3)
7. .7, 1.4, 2.1, . . . (2.8)

Skill Review

Have students draw and label these polygons on the board: triangle, square, trapezoid, rhombus, rectangle, pentagon, hexagon, septagon and octagon.

Identifying Similar Polygons

Similar figures have the same shape but not necessarily the same size. Which two of these rectangles are similar?

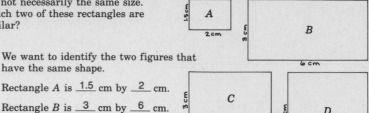

We want to identify the two figures that have the same shape.

Rectangle A is __1.5__ cm by __2__ cm.

Rectangle B is __3__ cm by __6__ cm.

Rectangle C is __3__ cm by __4__ cm.

Rectangle D is __4__ cm by __4__ cm.

✔ To be similar figures, each part of the first figure must get larger or smaller at the same rate as its corresponding part in the second figure.

Since each side of rectangle __C__ is __2__ times as large as the corresponding side of rectangle __A__,

rectangle __C__ is similar to rectangle __A__.

Getting Started

1. Which triangle is similar to triangle A? __D__

Write **Yes** or **No** to tell if the pair is similar.

2.

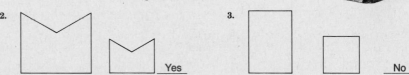

__Yes__

3. __No__

Draw a similar square with dimensions twice the size.

4.

MCP All rights reserved

283

Teaching the Lesson

Introducing the Problem Read the problem aloud and ask students to refer to the illustration in their texts. Explain that figures can have a similar shape without being the same size. Ask students to measure the sides of each rectangle with their rulers. (A is 1.5 cm by 2 cm; B is 3 cm by 6 cm; C is 3 cm by 4 cm; D is 4 cm by 4 cm) Read the next section of the text, explaining that those rectangles whose sides form the same ratio will be similar. Show students that if they compare rectangles A and C, they will notice that the sides of one are twice the length of the sides of the other. Have a student read the final sentence.

Developing the Skill Hold up the two copies of pictures, one the size of the photo and the other either reduced or enlarged. Explain that while the shapes of these two figures are the same, the sizes are different. The pictures are similar. Use the overhead projector to put a grid on the board. Within the grid draw a variety of shapes: a triangle, a square and a pentagon. Give students inch-square graph paper and ask them to transfer the shapes from the enlarged drawings on the board to the smaller scale of their paper. Explain that the shapes on the board and graph paper are similar and only the sizes will differ.

Write **Yes** or **No** to tell if the pair is similar.

1.

Yes

2.
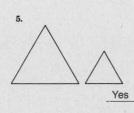
No

3.
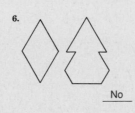
Yes

4.

Yes

5.

Yes

6.
No

7. Which rectangle is similar to rectangle A? rectangle C

A   B   C   D

8. Which triangle is similar to triangle A? triangle D

A   B   C   D

9. Draw a similar rectangle with dimensions twice the size.

284

Correcting Common Errors

Students may have difficulty identifying similar polygons. Have them work with partners, giving them rulers, paper, and the dimensions of three rectangles shown below. Have them draw the rectangles. Then have them double the dimensions and draw the corresponding similar rectangles.

1. 2 in. × 3 in. (4 in. × 6 in.)
2. 1 in. × 4 in. (2 in. × 8 in.)
3. ½ in. × 1½ in. (1 in. × 3 in.)

Have students discuss how the rectangles in each pair are similar.

Enrichment

Give each student a ruler, protractor and a sheet with these pairs of figures:

1   2   3   4
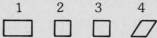

Have them measure the angles in figures 1 and 2 and the sides in figures 3 and 4. (angles in 1 = angles in 2; sides in 3 = sides in 4) Ask if either of these pairs are similar figures. (no) Have students write their own definition of similar figures. (sides must be proportional, angles must be equal)

Practice

Have students complete the practice problems. Tell them to use rulers to measure the sides of the figures.

Mixed Practice

1. $6.95 \times .03$ (.2085)
2. $207.2 \div 3.7$ (56)
3. $\$527.49 + \$895.32$ ($1,422.81)
4. $\frac{7}{9} + \frac{2}{3} + \frac{1}{6}$ $\left(1\frac{11}{18}\right)$
5. $2\frac{1}{5} \div \frac{2}{3}$ $\left(3\frac{3}{10}\right)$
6. $5,090 - 3,281$ (1,809)
7. $19\frac{4}{5} - 11$ $\left(8\frac{4}{5}\right)$
8. $\$978.12 \div 39$ ($25.08)
9. 608×957 (581,856)
10. $7\frac{1}{2} \times 3\frac{2}{3}$ $\left(27\frac{1}{2}\right)$

Extra Credit *Probability*

In a previous Extra Credit students learned how to find the number of permutations of a set of n objects. Explain that sometimes they will have a set in which some objects are identical. For example: a bag of blocks contains 2 white, 2 yellow, 1 red and 1 green. If they are to find the permutations for those 6 blocks, they will need the following formula: P = n! / (a! × b!) in which a is the number of one kind, b the number of another kind, and so on. In the example, the permutations would be 6! / (2! × 2!) or 180. Have students find the number of permutations for the letters in the word: MISSISSIPPI. (There are a total of 11 letters: 4 S's, 4 I's, 2 P's, 1 M. (11! / (4! × 4! × 2! × 1!) = 34,650)

Solid Figures

pages 285-286

Objective

To identify prisms, pyramids, cones, cylinders and spheres

Materials

*models of the solid figures
plastic straws and straight pins
wooden blocks

Mental Math

Have students add:

1. 21 + 57 = (78)
2. 102 + 70 = (172)
3. 49 + 52 = (101)
4. 64 + 25 = (89)
5. 85 + 32 = (117)
6. 75 + 24 = (99)
7. 153 + 48 = (201)

Skill Review

Remind students of the difference between plane and solid figures. Explain that space has three dimensions. Plane figures can be described in two, but solid figures require three. Have students identify examples of plane objects and solid objects. (plane: the surface of a lake, a rug on the floor; solid: a refrigerator, a can of soup)

MCP All rights reserved

Identifying Solid Figures

Prisms and pyramids are examples of **solid figures.** They are named for the shape of the bases. The sides of the figures are called **faces** and include the **bases.** The faces meet at **edges.** The edges meet at **vertices.** How many faces, edges and vertices does a rectangular prism have?

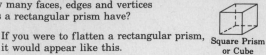
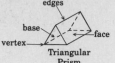

Triangular Prism   Rectangular Prism

 Square Prism or Cube

 Rectangular Pyramid

 Triangular Pyramid   Square Pyramid

If you were to flatten a rectangular prism, it would appear like this.

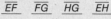

It has __6__ faces.

It has __12__ edges.

It has __8__ vertices.

Some solid figures have curved surfaces.

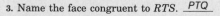

Cone   Cylinder   Sphere

Getting Started

Use these figures to answer 1 through 5.

1. What solid figure does the pencil tip suggest? __cone__

2. Name the edges of base *EFGH*.
   __EF__ __FG__ __HG__ __EH__

3. Name the face congruent to *RTS*. __PTQ__

4. Name the vertices of face *PTR*.
   __P__ __T__ __R__

Use the figures above to complete the chart.

5.

	Number of Faces	Number of Edges	Number of Vertices
Rectangular pyramid	5	8	5
Rectangular prism	6	12	8

Teaching the Lesson

Introducing the Problem Have a student read the problem aloud. Hold up a solid figure for the class. Point to a face, a base, an edge and a vertex. Explain that more than one vertex is written **vertices.** Show students a rectangular prism. Have students refer to the rectangular prism shown in their texts. Explain that this is a solid figure laid flat. Have students count the faces, edges and vertices. (6 faces, 12 edges, 8 vertices) Point to the solid, curved figures and read the names of each.

Developing the Skill Hold up each of the solid figure models and name them. Show students that a prism is a figure with two plane polygonal bases that are parallel and congruent. All the other faces are parallelograms. A pyramid, on the other hand, has a plane polygon as the base and triangles for all the other faces. Give each student straws and straight pins. Show them how to make a triangular pyramid (a tetrahedron):

Ask how they know it is a triangular pyramid. (its base is a triangle, all the other faces are triangles) Ask how many faces (4), edges (6) and vertices (4).

Practice

Write the name of the solid figure each object suggests.

1.
   cylinder

2.
   triangular prism

3.
   sphere

4.
   cube

5.
   cone

6.
   rectangular prism

Use these figures to complete 7 through 9.

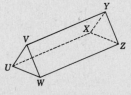

7. Name the edges of the triangular pyramid.

   $\overline{IL}$ $\overline{LJ}$ $\overline{LK}$ $\overline{IJ}$ $\overline{IK}$ $\overline{KJ}$

8. Name the faces congruent to VYZW.

   VYXU   UXZW

9. Name the vertices of UVYX.

   U   V   Y   X

Use the figures on page 285 to complete the chart.

10.

	Number of Faces	Number of Edges	Number of Vertices
Cone	2	1	1
Cylinder	3	2	0
Sphere	1	0	0
Cube	6	12	8
Triangular pyramid	4	6	4
Triangular prism	5	9	6

EXCURSION

Enlarge this pattern on a sheet of paper. Cut along the solid lines. Fold on the dotted lines and tape together to form a cube. Design your own patterns and make other solid figures out of paper. See TE notes.

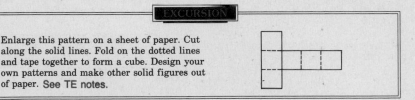

Practice

Have students complete the problems on the page. Remind them that a prism's faces are parallelograms, and pyramid faces are triangles.

Excursion

Suggest that students think of each square as either the bottom, top, front, back, left side or right side of a box. These could be labeled on the figure to determine if a side is duplicated or a side missing.

Correcting Common Errors

If some students have difficulty identifying solid figures, have them work with partners to find and name models of solid figures found in the classroom. When appropriate, have them indicate a face, a vertex, and an edge on each model.

Enrichment

Have students go to the library to look up these shapes. Ask them to draw each and fill in the following chart:

solid	number faces	number vertices	number edges
ellipsoid	(none	none	none)
pentagonal prism	(7	10	15)
hexagonal prism	(8	12	18)
octagonal prism	(10	16	24)
pentagonal pyramid	(6	6	10)
hexagonal pyramid	(7	7	12)
octagonal pyramid	(9	9	16)
regular tetrahedron	(4	4	6)

Extra Credit   *Numeration*

Show students the following series of tablets. Explain that this demonstrates the way Hindus multiplied in a very small space. Tell them that the tablets demonstrate the multiplication of 152 by 36. The series shows the same tablet in successive stages of the multiplication. Explain that the Hindus added and erased as they worked, so that the final number at the top of the tablet represents the answer:

	3	45	456	516	546	5472
36	36	36	36	36	36	36
152	152	152	152	152	152	152
A	B	C	D	E	F	G

Explain that A shows the tablet before multiplication; B - D show multiplication of 152 by 30; in E they can see that the 152 has been moved over; and in E - G the multiplication by 6 is added to the product of 152 × 30. Give students this problem to work in the same way: 121 × 35. (4,235)

Problem Solving
Make a Graph

pages 287-288

Objective

To review using tallies and bar graphs

Materials

graph paper
coin
pair of dice

Mental Math

Have students identify the larger total:

1. (1.2 + 3.0) or (2.4 + 1.5)
   (4.2 > 3.9)
2. (10.0 + 0.5) or (4.5 + 4.5)
   (10.5 > 9.0)
3. (0.6 + 0.7) or (.06 + 0.7)
   (1.3 > 0.76)
4. (1.1 + 0.9) or (1.0 + 1.1)
   (2.0 < 2.1)
5. (9.1 − 1.1) or (9.0 − 1.2) (8 > 7.8)
6. (3.5 − 2.5) or (4.7 − 2.7)
   (1.0 < 2.0)
7. (2.3 − 1.8) or (4.5 − 3.9)
   (0.5 < 0.6)

Making a Tally or Graph

Four students took a survey to find out which types of books were most popular with elementary school students in grades 3 through 6. Their results are tallied here. Make a bar graph showing the results of the survey.

	Grade 3	Grade 4	Grade 5	Grade 6
Fairy Tales	Жℋ III	IIII	Жℋ II	II
Science Fiction	Жℋ	Жℋ III	Жℋ II	Жℋ IIII
Mysteries	Жℋ Жℋ II	Жℋ II	Жℋ Жℋ I	Жℋ Жℋ Жℋ
Animal Stories	Жℋ Жℋ II	Жℋ Жℋ	Жℋ IIII	Жℋ II
Biographies	Жℋ IIII	Жℋ III	Жℋ Жℋ II	Жℋ Жℋ

★ SEE

We want to show on a bar graph the number of students who selected each kind of book. We know the results of each of the four surveys.

★ PLAN

Since the largest number of selections is 45, we choose to make the graph go from 0 to 50 with 10 selections per interval.

★ DO

Complete the graph below.

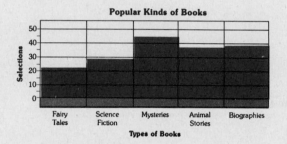

★ CHECK

We can check our work by adding again the results of all four surveys for each type of book.

Fairy Tales 8 + 4 + 7 + 2 = __21__

Science Fiction 5 + 8 + 7 + 9 = __29__

Mysteries 12 + 7 + 11 + 15 = __45__

Animal Stories 12 + 10 + 9 + 7 = __38__

Biographies 9 + 8 + 12 + 10 = __39__

MCP All rights reserved

287

Teaching the Lesson

Ask a student to read the problem aloud. Remind the class that when they take a tally, they make a single mark for each count. Show them how to cross off every five. Ask if they can tell by looking at the tally which type of book is read most. (not easily) Read the SEE section of the text. Ask one student to describe what a bar graph looks like. (numbers on the vertical axis, categories along the horizontal axis) Have a student read the PLAN and have the class look at the graph outlined in their books. Emphasize the importance of looking at the range of numbers to be illustrated. This determines the numbers to be included on the vertical scale. In the example, it runs from 0 to 50 by tens to accommodate the biggest number, 45. Have students count the tally and make a bar for each book type. Explain that to check their work, they can do the addition again and make sure that the results match the height of the bars in their graphs. Have students do each addition on the board. (fairy tales, 22; science fiction, 29; mysteries, 45; ani-mal stories, 38; biographies, 40) Draw the bar graph on the board. Ask if it is easy to tell at a glance which type of book is read most. (yes, mysteries)

287

Apply

Solve these problems.

1. Read the following sentence and tally the number of times the vowels a, e, i, o and u are used. Four score and seven years ago our fathers brought forth on this continent, a new nation, conceived in liberty and dedicated to the proposition that all men are created equal.
See Solution Notes.

2. From your tally in problem 1, make a bar graph to show the number of times each vowel was used.
See Solution Notes.

3. Toss a coin 20 times and tally the number of heads and the number of tails.
Answers will vary.

4. Create a bar graph to show the number of heads and number of tails that you recorded in problem 3.
See Solution Notes.

5. Tally the results of the entire class for problem number 3. Have each student toss a coin 20 times and record the total number of heads and tails.
Answers will vary.

6. Roll a pair of dice 36 times and tally the sums. Create a bar graph to illustrate the results. Compare your graph with those of other students.
Answers will vary.

7. A single die, or number cube, has 6 faces. Does a rectangular prism have more, fewer, or the same number of faces as the number cube?
Same number

8. Which of these solid figures has more faces, a triangular prism or a rectangular pyramid? Prove that your answer is correct.
See Solution Notes.

9. The Math Club tallied the lines of symmetry on different figures they saw in an art catalog. Does a square have more, fewer, or the same number of lines of symmetry as a rectangle that is not a square? Prove that your answer is correct.
See Solution Notes.

10. The Math Club also tallied the different kinds of angles—right, acute, or scalene—found in the art catalog. Under which of these kinds would they put a tally mark for the angle formed by the two equal sides in an isosceles right triangle?
Right angle

288

Extra Credit *Numeration*

Have students prepare 20 cards that show addition or subtraction of fractions or decimals. Tell them their card set must contain 10 pairs of problems with different operations, but matching answers. $\left(\text{ex. } \dfrac{7}{8} - \dfrac{1}{2} = \dfrac{3}{8} \text{ and } \dfrac{1}{8} + \dfrac{1}{4} = \dfrac{3}{8}\right)$

Make sure they leave the answers off. Have pairs of students shuffle their cards, and lay them face down to play Concentration. Then take turns turning over a card, solving the problem, turning over another card, and looking for the same answer. Each player keeps a match, or returns unmatched cards face down. Play continues until all cards are won. Repeat with different partners.

Solution Notes

1. Have students work in pairs, one reading the letters while the other makes the tally.
2. Tell them to arrange letters along the horizontal axis and numbers on the vertical axis on graph paper.
3. Have students work in pairs again.
4. Have them put numbers along the vertical axis and the possible outcomes along the horizontal.
5. Help students by putting each pair's coin toss results on the board. Have students add the columns of figures. Explain they will have to change the scale of the graph to have one square represent ten tosses in this bar graph.
6. Point out that this exercise is like problem 6. Have students do the tally in pairs, but have each make a bar graph of the results. Post all the graphs on the bulletin board. Ask students what they notice about the graphs.

Higher-Order Thinking Skills

7. Analysis
8. Synthesis: They both have the same number of faces, 5. Most students will draw pictures or point to models to prove their answers.
9. Synthesis: A square has more—4 in a square, 2 in a rectangle. Most students will draw pictures to prove their answers.
10. Analysis: If they draw a picture of an isosceles right triangle, most students would see that only the rays of the right angle could be congruent.

Calculators and Formulas

pages 289-290

Objective

To use a calculator to solve formulas

Materials

calculator

Mental Math

Have students find the least common denominator for these:

1. ⅓ and ⅖ (fifteenths)
2. ⅒ and ¾ (twentieths)
3. ⅗ and ½ (tenths)
4. ⅙ and ⅔ (sixths)
5. ⅐ and 3 (sevenths)
6. ½ and ⅓ (sixths)
7. ⅙ and ⅑ (eighteenths)

Skill Review

Have students use their calculators to solve:

1. $24.35 + 51.02 = (75.37)$
2. $103.7 - 26.7 = (77.0)$
3. $28.3 \times 7 = (198.1)$
4. $58.5 \div 3 = (19.5)$
5. $480.45 + 321.0 = (801.45)$
6. $55.04 - 4.32 = (50.72)$
7. $4.62 \times 1.32 = (6.0984)$
8. $8.58 \div 3.25 = (2.64)$

Calculators, Expressions and Formulas

A swimming pool in the shape of a rectangular prism is filled with water. What is the volume of the swimming pool?

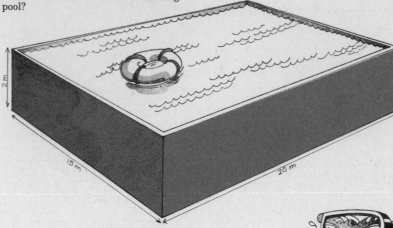

2 m 15 m 20 m

An **expression** is a mathematical sentence sometimes written with letters instead of numbers. If numbers are used to replace the letters we have **evaluated the expression.** We evaluate the expression $a \times b + c$, by replacing 12 for a, 9 for b and 56 for c. Complete this code.

12 [×] 9 [+] 56 [=] (164)

Evaluate each of these expressions by replacing 17 for a, 28 for b and 13 for c. Then compute the answers.

$$a + b - c = \underline{32} \qquad 5 \times a + c - b = \underline{70}$$

A **formula** is a special expression which helps you find particular measurements. The formula for finding volume is **length times width times height.** This is usually written as $L \times W \times H = V$, or simply $LWH = V$. To find the volume of the swimming pool we replace L by 20, W by 15 and H by 2. Complete this calculator code.

20 [×] 15 [×] 2 [=] (600)

The volume of the swimming pool is ___600___ cubic meters.

MCP All rights reserved

289

Teaching the Lesson

Introducing the Problem   Read the problem and the definition of a formula aloud. Put the formula for finding volume on the board: **L × W × H = V.** Ask a student to complete the calculator code. (20 × 15 × 2 = 600) Have a student read the solution sentence. (volume of swimming pool is 600 cubic meters) Read the definition of an expression. Explain that an **expression** can be part of a formula. Have a student complete the calculator code in the text. (12 × 9 + 56 = 164) Ask a student to read the next section of the text aloud. Have them use their calculators to evaluate the expressions given. (a + b − c = 32; 5 × a + c − b = 70)

Developing the Skill   Explain that a formula is used to describe some real situation, for example the volume of a pool or the speed of a train. Point out that an expression may or may not have a real application. Show them how to evaluate an expression, substituting a number for each letter or symbol. Ask a student to make up an expression with the letters b, h and a. (Answers will vary.) Ask another student to give two sets of values for those letters. Put the expression on the board and arrange the letters and values on the board in a chart. Have students evaluate the expression for each set of values. Explain that the same letters can be used in a formula to describe the area of a triangle. Area equals base times half the height: a = b × (½h).

Practice

Evaluate each expression when a is 25, b is 12 and c is 9.

1. $a - b + c = $ ___22___   2. $5 \times a + b = $ ___137___   3. $9 \times b - a = $ ___83___

Evaluate each expression when a is 36, b is 6 and c is 12.

4. $a \div c \times b = $ ___18___   5. $a \times b \times b = $ ___1,296___   6. $5 \times c + a \div b = $ ___16___

Apply

Write the formula. Then use it to complete each table.

7. Find the perimeter of each square where S stands for one side.

$\underline{S \times 4 = P}$

S	1	2	3	4	5	6	7	8
P	4	8	12	16	20	24	28	32

8. Find the area of each square where S stands for one side.

$\underline{S \times S = A}$

S	1	2	3	4	5	6	7	8
A	1	4	9	16	25	36	49	64

9. Find the surface area of each cube where S stands for one side of a face.

$\underline{S \times S \times 6 = A}$

S	1	2	3	4	5	6	7	8
A	6	24	54	96	150	216	294	384

10. Find the volume of each cube where E stands for one edge.

$\underline{E \times E \times E = V}$

E	1	2	3	4	5	6	7	8
V	1	8	27	64	125	216	343	512

EXCURSION

1. What happens to the perimeter of a square if each side is doubled?
   The perimeter is 2 times as great.
2. What happens to the area of a square if each side is doubled?
   The area is 4 times as great.
3. What happens to the volume of a cube if each edge is doubled?
   The volume is 8 times as great.

290

Correcting Common Errors

Some students may have difficulty using a calculator to work with formulas. Have them work with partners. Give each pair the formula: total saved = amount saved weekly times the number of weeks, or

$$T\$ = A\$ \times W.$$

Have students use their calculators to fill in the numbers missing from the following chart.

T$	A$	W
($1.00)	$0.50	2
($7.50)	$0.75	10
($11.55)	$0.55	21
($15.00)	$1.00	15
$9.50	$0.50	(19)

Enrichment

Give students this formula for finding the area of a circle:

$$A = \pi r^2$$

Explain that A stands for area, π stands for the number 3.14 and r is the radius of the circle. Show them that the expression r^2 means radius multiplied by itself or $r \times r$. Ask them to find the area of these circles:

radius	area
1. 2 in.	(12.56 sq in.)
2. 10 in.	(314 sq in.)
3. 4 cm	(50.24 sq cm)
4. 15 cm	(706.5 sq cm)

Practice

Have students complete the exercises using their calculators.

Excursion

Have students draw figures with specific measurements and test these statements for validity.

Extra Credit *Applications*

Read or duplicate the following for students, allowing them to use calculators.

Your mom gives you a shopping list. She expects you to go to two different stores, and buy each item wherever it is cheaper. Mom will give you all the money you save her, but she wants to see your calculations. Choose which item of each you would buy:

1. 20-ounce loaf of bread for 25¢ or 24-ounce loaf of bread for 29¢.(24-oz loaf)
2. 6 28-ounce cans of tomatoes for $2.67, or 2 35-ounce cans for $1.19.(6 28-oz cans)
3. 2 10-ounce cans of peas for 69¢, or 6 8-ounce cans for $1.80.(2 10-oz cans)
4. 2 dozen plastic cups for 54¢, or 50 for $1.25.(2 doz cups)
5. A 20-exposure color film for $2.43, or a 36-exposure color film for $3.84.(36 exp film)

Chapter Test

page 291

Item	Objective
1-2	Find third angle measure of triangles when two are known (See pages 273-274)
3-4	Identify squares, rectangles, parallelograms, trapezoids, rhombuses (See pages 275-276)
5-6	Identify regular and non-regular polygons (See pages 277-278)
5-6	Draw diagonals of specific polygons (See pages 277-278)
7-8	Identify congruent polygons and corresponding parts (See pages 279-280)
9	Draw lines of symmetry (See pages 281-282)
10	Identify similar polygons (See pages 283-284)
11-12	Identify solid figures and edges (See pages 285-286)

Find the missing angle measure.

1.
90°
40°
50°

2.
60°
60°
60°

Identify the kind of quadrilateral.

3.
trapezoid

4.
parallelogram

Identify the kind of polygon. Draw all possible diagonals.

5.
pentagon

6.
hexagon

7. Tell if the figures are congruent. Write Yes or No.
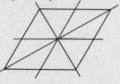
Yes

8. The triangles are congruent. Write the name of the angle which is congruent to *BCA*.

A
B   C   Y   Z
X
∠YZX

9. Draw all possible lines of symmetry.

10. Are the figures similar? Write Yes or No.
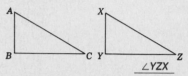
Yes

11. Identify the kind of solid figure.

cylinder

12. Write the number of edges.
8

291

MCP All rights reserved

Cumulative Review

Circle the letter of the correct answer.

1 27,915
+ 8,475

a 35,380
b 35,390
(c) 36,390
d NG

2 31,046
− 9,575

(a) 21,471
b 21,571
c 38,531
d NG

3 27 × 53

a 216
(b) 1,431
c 13,581
d NG

4 24)5,670

a 236
b 236 R4
(c) 236 R6
d NG

5 Find the volume.

2 cm
3 cm   2 cm

a 7 cm
b 12 sq cm
(c) 12 cu cm
d NG

6 $4\frac{4}{5}$
+ $3\frac{2}{3}$

a $7\frac{2}{15}$
b $7\frac{7}{15}$
c $7\frac{3}{4}$
(d) NG

7 $21\frac{1}{4}$
− $16\frac{2}{3}$

(a) $4\frac{7}{12}$
b $5\frac{7}{12}$
c $5\frac{5}{12}$
d NG

8 $2\frac{1}{2} \times 3\frac{1}{3}$

a $5\frac{1}{6}$
b $6\frac{1}{6}$
(c) $8\frac{1}{3}$
d NG

9 16.241
+ 4.79

a 20.031
b 20.931
(c) 21.031
d NG

10 16.36
− 4.788

(a) 11.572
b 11.588
c 12.428
d NG

11 1.06 × 3.6

a 48.16
b 4.816
c 4,816
(d) NG

[ ] score

292

Item	Objective
1	Add two 4-digit numbers (See pages 27-28)
2	Subtract two numbers up to 5-digits, zeros in minuend (See pages 35-36)
3	Multiply two 2-digit numbers (See pages 57-58)
4	Divide a 4-digit by 2-digit number, quotient with remainder (See pages 107-108)
5	Find the volume of rectangular solids (See pages 129-130)
6	Add two mixed numbers (See pages 175-176)
7	Subtract two mixed numbers, rename minuend (See pages 183-184)
8	Multiply two mixed numbers (See pages 197-198)
9	Add decimals (See pages 223-224)
10	Subtract decimals (See pages 225-226)
11	Multiply decimals (See pages 237-238)

Alternate Cumulative Review

Circle the letter of the correct answer.

1 1,654
+ 8,389

a 9,043
(b) 10,043
c 10,943
d NG

2 53,028
− 7,694

(a) 45,334
b 45,434
c 45,344
d NG

3 87
×19

a 1,553
(b) 1,653
c 1,663
d NG

4 44)6,871

(a) 156 R7
b 156 R8
c 156 R13
d NG

5 Find the volume of a box 4 cm by 3 cm by 3 cm.

a 12 cu cm
b 10 cu cm
c 32 cu cm
(d) NG

6 $5\frac{1}{6}$
+ $8\frac{7}{8}$

a $14\frac{1}{14}$
(b) $14\frac{1}{24}$
c $13\frac{1}{24}$
d NG

7 $46\frac{4}{5}$
− $39\frac{8}{9}$

a $6\frac{4}{5}$
b $6\frac{6}{45}$
(c) $6\frac{41}{45}$
d NG

8 $4\frac{3}{8} \times 4\frac{2}{5}$

a $18\frac{3}{4}$
(b) $19\frac{1}{4}$
c $19\frac{1}{2}$
d NG

9 23.576
+ 7.48

a 30.056
b 30.956
(c) 31.056
d NG

10 19.45
− 8.697

(a) 10.753
b 10.763
c 10.767
d NG

11 3.08
×2.4

a 73.92
b 739.2
(c) 7.392
d NG

292

Ratios

pages 293-294

Objective

To write a ratio to compare two numbers

Materials

*overhead projector
*transparent counters, 12 red and 9 blue
pieces of blue, yellow and red paper

Mental Math

Ask students to tell the time 1½ hours from:

1. noon (1:30 PM)
2. 9:30 AM (11:00 AM)
3. 5:15 PM (6:45 PM)
4. 11:30 PM (1:00 AM)
5. 2:00 AM (3:30 AM)
6. 10:30 AM (noon)
7. 1:20 PM (2:50 PM)

Skill Review

Have students reduce these fractions to lowest terms:

1. ⁴⁄₆ (⅔)
2. ²⁄₁₀ (⅕)
3. ⁶⁄₁₂ (½)
4. ³⁄₅ (³⁄₅)
5. ⁵⁄₁₀ (½)
6. ²⁄₈ (¼)
7. ⁸⁄₁₂ (⅔)
8. ²⁄₁₄ (¹⁄₇)
9. ⁵⁄₂₅ (⅕)
10. ⁴⁄₂₄ (⅙)

Writing Ratios

A **ratio** is a way of comparing two quantities. Washington has won 3 games and lost 2. The ratio of wins to losses is 3 to 2. What is the ratio of wins to total games played?

We want to express the relationship of games won to games played as a ratio.

Washington won ___3___ games.

They played ___5___ games.

The ratio of wins to games played is ___3___ to ___5___.
We can write the ratio of 3 to 5 in three ways.

$$3 \text{ to } 5 \qquad 3{:}5 \qquad \frac{3}{5}$$

Three and five are called the **terms** of the ratio. The order in which the terms are expressed is very important. 3:5 is not the same as 5:3.

Getting Started

Write each ratio in three ways. Do not simplify fractions.

1. black marbles to red marbles

$$3 \text{ to } 6 \qquad 3{:}6 \qquad \frac{3}{6}$$

2. red marbles to all marbles

$$6 \text{ to } 9 \qquad 6{:}9 \qquad \frac{6}{9}$$

3. The U.S. flag has 7 red stripes and 6 white stripes. What is the ratio of red stripes to white stripes?

$$7 \text{ to } 6 \qquad 7{:}6 \qquad \frac{7}{6}$$

4. You can buy 6 candy bars for 89¢. What is the ratio of candy bars to money?

$$6 \text{ to } 89¢ \qquad 6{:}89¢ \qquad \frac{6}{89¢}$$

Write each ratio as a fraction. Do not simplify.

5. 7 to 5 $\frac{7}{5}$

6. 4:6 $\frac{4}{6}$

7. 5 to 10 $\frac{5}{10}$

8. 3:4 $\frac{3}{4}$

293

MCP All rights reserved

Teaching the Lesson

Introducing the Problem Read the problem aloud. Have a student read the information sentence. Read the next sentences aloud and write the three forms of the ratio on the board. Continue, defining the terms of the ratio and explaining that the order of the terms is very important. Ask a student to explain why ³⁄₅ is different from ⁵⁄₃. (⁵⁄₃ is the same as 1 ²⁄₃, which is more than ³⁄₅.)

Developing the Skill Place four red and three blue transparent counters on the overhead projector. Ask students how many red and how many blue. Put the red above the blue, with a line separating the groups and write **4 to 3**. Tell students that this comparison is called a ratio. Write the ratio in its other two forms: **4:3** and ⁴⁄₃. Now arrange 8 red counters above 6 blue counters, separating the groups on the overhead with a line. Ask a student to describe the ratio of red to blue. (8 to 6) Have a volunteer write the ratio in all its forms on the board. (8 to 6, 8:6, ⁸⁄₆) Explain that when a ratio is written as a fraction, it can be read as a fraction: four thirds or eight sixths. Ask the class to compare the ratios. (⁴⁄₃ = ⁸⁄₆) Rearrange them on the overhead, blue over red, and have students write the new ratios. (3 to 4, 3:4, ¾ and 6 to 8, 6:8, ⁶⁄₈) Ask if the ratio of red to blue is the same as blue to red. (no)

Practice

Write each ratio in three ways. Do not simplify fractions.

1. red cars to black cars

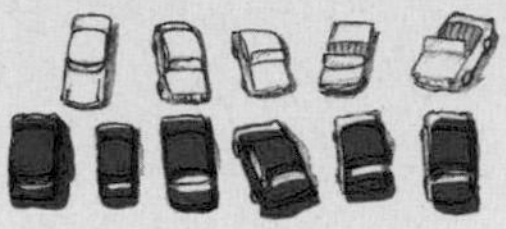

6 to 5   6:5 $\frac{6}{5}$

2. handbags to hats

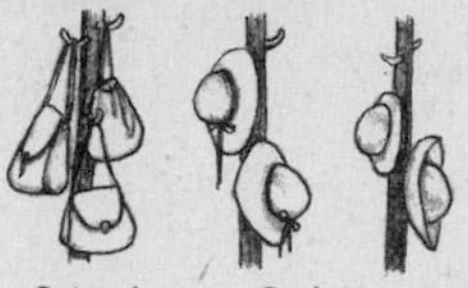

3 to 4   3:4 $\frac{3}{4}$

3. cardinals to robins

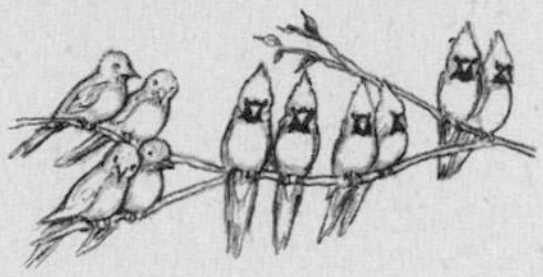

6 to 4   6:4 $\frac{6}{4}$

4. bricks to blocks

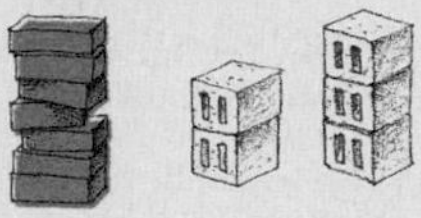

7 to 5   7:5 $\frac{7}{5}$

Write each ratio as a fraction. Do not simplify.

5. 3 to 7 $\frac{3}{7}$
6. 8 to 5 $\frac{8}{5}$
7. 6:1 $\frac{6}{1}$
8. 3 to 9 $\frac{3}{9}$
9. 10:6 $\frac{10}{6}$
10. 6 to 5 $\frac{6}{5}$
11. 4 to 8 $\frac{4}{8}$
12. 7:8 $\frac{7}{8}$

Apply

Solve these problems.

13. Rhoda got 4 hits in 7 times at bat. What is the ratio of hits to times at bat? $\frac{4}{7}$
14. George lost 3 out of 8 golf matches. What is the ratio of wins to losses? $\frac{5}{3}$
15. Lemons sell 3 for $1.00 at the grocery. What is the ratio of lemons to their cost? $\frac{3}{\$1}$
16. It took Winston 2 hours to skate 15 miles. What is the ratio of distance to time? $\frac{15}{2}$
17. Mrs. Yeager used 9 gallons of gas driving 216 miles on her weekend trip. What is the ratio of miles to gallons? $\frac{216}{9}$
18. Marcie has $1.53 in coins in her pocket. If she has 6 quarters, what is the ratio of quarters to pennies? $\frac{6}{3}$
19. What is the ratio of red stripes to stars on the U.S. flag? $\frac{7}{50}$
20. What is the ratio of inches to feet in one yard? $\frac{36}{3}$

Correcting Common Errors

Some students may not write the numbers in the proper order when they are writing ratios. Have them work with partners and a board on which 2 blue, 4 yellow, and 5 red pieces of paper are taped. Have them write each of the following ratios three ways.

1. red to blue (5 to 2, 5:2, $\frac{5}{2}$)
2. blue to yellow (2 to 4, 2:4, $\frac{2}{4}$)
3. blue to red (2 to 5, 2:5, $\frac{2}{5}$)
4. yellow to blue (4 to 2, 4:2, $\frac{4}{2}$)

Enrichment

Choose a sport for students to follow. Tell them to record one team's win : loss ratio for a month. At the end of the month have them compare the team ratios. Ask how they can tell which team has had the best season so far. (The team whose ratio fraction is greatest.) Have students list the teams in order from the one with the highest standing to the one with the lowest.

Practice

Have students complete the problems. Explain that when writing a ratio as a fraction, the first number is the numerator, the second the denominator.

Extra Credit *Applications*

Duplicate for students or write on the board: solve the problems and fill in the code that follows to find the All-Time Leading Rebounder in the NBA.

A. $\frac{1}{2} - \frac{1}{4} = (\frac{1}{4})$	B. $\frac{5}{8} - \frac{1}{4} = (\frac{3}{8})$	C. $\frac{9}{10} - \frac{3}{5} = (\frac{3}{10})$
D. $\frac{7}{9} - \frac{1}{3} = (\frac{4}{9})$	E. $\frac{5}{12} - \frac{1}{3} = (\frac{1}{12})$	F. $\frac{3}{5} - \frac{7}{15} = (\frac{2}{15})$
G. $\frac{1}{25} - \frac{1}{50} = (\frac{1}{50})$	H. $\frac{7}{15} - \frac{7}{30} = (\frac{7}{30})$	I. $\frac{7}{12} - \frac{7}{24} = (\frac{7}{24})$
J. $\frac{1}{3} - \frac{2}{9} = (\frac{1}{9})$	K. $\frac{1}{2} - \frac{1}{5} = (\frac{3}{10})$	L. $\frac{1}{2} - \frac{1}{3} = (\frac{1}{6})$
M. $\frac{1}{4} - \frac{1}{5} = (\frac{1}{20})$	N. $\frac{3}{4} - \frac{3}{7} = (\frac{9}{28})$	O. $\frac{2}{3} - \frac{1}{5} = (\frac{7}{15})$
P. $\frac{7}{8} - \frac{1}{5} = (\frac{27}{40})$	R. $\frac{1}{2} - \frac{1}{13} = (\frac{11}{26})$	S. $\frac{1}{6} - \frac{1}{9} = (\frac{1}{18})$
T. $\frac{2}{7} - \frac{1}{8} = (\frac{9}{56})$	U. $\frac{3}{4} - \frac{3}{10} = (\frac{9}{20})$	W. $\frac{7}{15} - \frac{3}{20} = (\frac{19}{60})$

(W	I	L	T)
$\frac{19}{60}$	$\frac{7}{24}$	$\frac{1}{6}$	$\frac{9}{56}$

(C	H	A	M	B	E	R	L	A	I	N)
$\frac{3}{10}$	$\frac{7}{30}$	$\frac{1}{4}$	$\frac{1}{20}$	$\frac{3}{8}$	$\frac{1}{12}$	$\frac{11}{26}$	$\frac{1}{6}$	$\frac{1}{4}$	$\frac{7}{24}$	$\frac{9}{28}$

Ratio Tables

pages 295-296

Objective

To use tables of equal ratios to solve problems

Materials

Mental Math

Have students identify the missing number:

1. $10 + n = 23$ ($n = 13$)
2. $\frac{2}{3} - n = \frac{1}{3}$ ($n = \frac{1}{3}$)
3. $n - 21 = 15$ ($n = 36$)
4. $16 + 37 = n$ ($n = 53$)
5. $52 - n = 26$ ($n = 26$)
6. $20.5 - n = 20$ ($n = 0.5$)
7. $n - 124 = 55$ ($n = 179$)

Skill Review

Dictate these ratios. Have students write each as a fraction without simplifying.

1. 3 to 10 ($\frac{3}{10}$)
2. 5 to 2 ($\frac{5}{2}$)
3. 12 to 13 ($\frac{12}{13}$)
4. 8 to 4 ($\frac{8}{4}$)
5. 2 to 3 ($\frac{2}{3}$)
6. 9 to 8 ($\frac{9}{8}$)
7. 4 to 6 ($\frac{4}{6}$)
8. 1 to 4 ($\frac{1}{4}$)

Using Ratio Tables

Manuel is running a 5-mile race. If he runs the same time for each mile, how long will it take Manuel to run the race?

Miles	1	2	3	4	5
Minutes	9	18	27	36	45

We can complete the ratio table by finding equivalent fractions.

$$\frac{1 \times 2}{9 \times 2} = \frac{2}{18}$$

$$\frac{1 \times 3}{9 \times 3} = \frac{3}{27}$$

$$\frac{1 \times 4}{9 \times 4} = \frac{4}{36}$$

$$\frac{1 \times 5}{9 \times 5} = \frac{5}{45}$$

It will take _45_ minutes for Manuel to run the race.

MCP All rights reserved

Getting Started

Complete the ratio table to find the answer.

1. One bolt costs 8¢. How much must be paid for 6 bolts?
48¢

Bolts	1	2	3	4	5	6
Cost	8¢	16¢	24¢	32¢	40¢	48¢

2. Three mints cost 15¢. How much will it cost for 12 mints?
60¢

Mints	3	6	9	12
Cost	15¢	30¢	45¢	60¢

3. Each girl in the parade is carrying a half-dozen roses. How many roses are 7 girls carrying?
42 roses

Roses	6	12	18	24	30	36	42
Girls	1	2	3	4	5	6	7

4. Walking uses about 200 calories for each 2 miles. How many calories are used in 12 miles?
1,200 calories

Calories	200	400	600	800	1,000	1,200
Miles	2	4	6	8	10	12

295

Teaching the Lesson

Introducing the Problem Read the problem aloud. Ask a student to look at the chart and tell how many minutes it took Manuel to run the first mile. (9 minutes) Write the ratio of miles to minutes for the first mile on the board. (1:9, $\frac{1}{9}$) Explain that to find how long it took to run two miles, they will write the equivalent fraction. Remind students that they can multiply any number by one and not change the value of the number. Multiply on the board while students follow in their texts: $\frac{1}{9} \times \frac{2}{2} = \frac{2}{18}$ and $\frac{1}{9} \times \frac{3}{3} = \frac{3}{27}$.
Put the race chart on the board and have students fill in missing numbers. (36, 45)

Developing the Skill Explain that apples are being sold 3 pounds for $2. Show students that the price for 6, 9 and 12 pounds can be calculated by finding equivalent fractions. Put this chart on the board:

pounds	3	6	9	12
dollars	$2			

Have students fill in the missing numbers. (4, 6, 8) Show the class how these numbers were figured: $\frac{3}{2} \times \frac{2}{2} = \frac{6}{4}$, $\frac{3}{2} \times \frac{3}{3} = \frac{9}{6}$, $\frac{3}{2} \times \frac{4}{4} = \frac{12}{8}$.
Ask why it is possible to multiply numerator and denominator by the same number and not change the ratio. (Because that is the same as multiplying by one, and any number can be multiplied by one and remain unchanged.)

Practice

Complete the ratio table to find the answer.

1. Three cards cost $2. How much does it cost for 15 cards?
$10

Cards	3	6	9	12	15
Cost	2	4	6	8	10

2. Four boys and three girls make up each team. If there are 12 girls, how many boys are playing on the teams?
16 boys

Boys	4	8	12	16
Girls	3	6	9	12

3. A recipe calling for two eggs will make seven pancakes. How many eggs will be needed for 28 pancakes?
8 eggs

Eggs	2	4	6	8
Pancakes	7	14	21	28

4. There are 5 petals and 2 leaves on each silk flower. How many petals are in a bouquet having 10 leaves?
25 petals

Petals	5	10	15	20	25
Leaves	2	4	6	8	10

5. Each sweater has 5 buttons and 3 emblems. How many emblems are on a set of identical sweaters having 40 buttons?
24 emblems

Buttons	5	10	15	20	25	30	35	40
Emblems	3	6	9	12	15	18	21	24

6. Sam walked 1 mile in 15 minutes. How long will it take him to walk 3 miles?
45 minutes

Miles	1	2	3	4
Minutes	15	30	45	60

```
EXCURSION
```

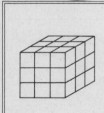

A white cube, measuring three inches on each edge, is painted red on its outer surface. When the paint is dry, it is cut into

one-inch cubes. How many little cubes will there be? __27__
How many of the little cubes will have:

1. red on 3 sides? __8__   2. red on 1 side? __6__

3. red on 2 sides? __12__   4. red on no sides? __1__

296

Correcting Common Errors

When finding equal ratios, students may not multiply both terms by the same number. They should recognize that ratios, in many ways, follow the same rules as fractions. So, for each section of the table in Exercises 1-6 that they are completing, have them write the equal ratios as equivalent fractions, circling the number that they are multiplying the numerator and denominator by. For example:

$$\frac{2}{3} \quad \frac{10}{?} \qquad \frac{2 \times ⑤}{3 \times ⑤} \quad \frac{10}{15}$$

Enrichment

Have students complete this ratio table. Explain that it expresses the ratio of pounds of raspberries to price:

pounds	.5	1.0	1.5
dollars	1.5	(3.0)	(4.5)

Have students find the price of .75 pounds ($2.25), 1.25 pounds ($3.75) and 10 pounds. ($30.00)

Practice

Have students complete all the problems using the charts as a help.

Excursion

It is helpful to draw in the one-inch cubes on the larger cube. This will help to visualize the counting.

Extra Credit   *Numeration*

Divide students into groups. Have each group research one of the following questions in a reliable source such as Adler and Adler's *Mathematics Old and New.*

1. What was the first number system?
2. Why were new number systems invented?
3. What number system do we use now?
   How does it differ from another currently in use?
4. Invent a new number system with symbols and write addition and subtraction problems using it.
5. How has the use of machines affected our counting system (from abacus to computer)?
6. How would daily life be different if our civilization had no number system? Would life be easier or harder?

296

Equal Ratios

pages 297-298

Objective

To solve equal ratio equations by finding equivalent fractions

Materials

Mental Math

Have students add 17 to each:

1. 13 (30)
2. 0.5 (17.5)
3. 101 (118)
4. 55 (72)
5. 3.75 (20.75)
6. 2 ½ (19 ½)
7. 0.035 (17.035)

Skill Review

Have students copy these fractions and tell whether they are equivalent or not:

1. ½ and ⁴⁄₈ (yes)
2. ⅔ and ¹²⁄₁₃ (no)
3. ⅘ and ¹²⁄₁₅ (yes)
4. ⅓ and ²⁄₆ (yes)
5. ¾ and ⅘ (no)
6. ½ and ⁵⁄₁₀ (yes)
7. ¾ and ⅞ (no)
8. ⅗ and ¹²⁄₂₀ (yes)

Finding Equal Ratios

Adelina and her father are making concrete. Each batch of concrete requires 9 buckets of sand. The ratio of sand to gravel is 3 to 4 parts. How much gravel is needed for each batch of concrete?

We need to find the amount of gravel needed for a batch of concrete.

There are ___9___ buckets of sand in a batch of concrete.

The ratio of sand to gravel is ___3___ to ___4___.

To find the amount of gravel in a batch, we write two equal ratios and solve for N by multiplying or dividing by the identity element.

$$\frac{\text{sand}}{\text{gravel}} \quad \frac{3}{4} = \frac{9}{N} \qquad \frac{3}{4} \times \frac{3}{3} = \frac{9}{12}$$

identity element

Each batch requires ___12___ buckets of gravel. The equation which expresses two equal ratios is called a **proportion**.

✔ We can cross multiply to see if two ratios are equal.

$$\frac{2}{3} \diagdown \frac{4}{6}$$
$$2 \times 6 = 3 \times 4$$
$$12 = 12$$

The ratios are equal. They are really a proportion.

Getting Started

Use cross multiplication to identify equal ratios. Write Yes or No.

1. $\frac{1}{2} = \frac{3}{4}$ ___No___
2. $\frac{2}{3} = \frac{10}{15}$ ___Yes___
3. $\frac{16}{24} = \frac{8}{12}$ ___Yes___

Write the missing number in each proportion.

4. $\frac{4}{5} = \frac{n}{20}$ $n = $ ___16___
5. $\frac{2}{3} = \frac{12}{n}$ $n = $ ___18___
6. $\frac{n}{8} = \frac{20}{40}$ $n = $ ___4___

MCP All rights reserved

297

Teaching the Lesson

Introducing the Problem Read the problem aloud to the class. Ask a student to complete the information sentences. Read the plan sentence aloud. Write the ratios on the board. Ask students to remember how they find equivalent fractions. (by multiplying by a fraction equal to one) Have one student come to the board and write the identity element and multiply. (¾ × ⅓ = ⁹⁄₁₂). Have another explain the meaning of the new ratio. (9 buckets of sand to 12 buckets of gravel) Read the solution sentence aloud. (requires 12 buckets gravel) Read the rest of the model. Explain that ratios can also be called **proportions**; one ratio can be proportionate to the other. Show students how to cross multiply to check to see if ratios are equal.

Developing the Skill Put this table of equal ratios on the board: ¼ = ²⁄₈ = ³⁄₁₂ = ⁴⁄₁₆ = ⁵⁄₂₀ = ⁶⁄₂₄

Point to pairs of ratios and ask students to multiply the numerator of one by the denominator of the other. Ask what they notice about these products. (They are equal.) Put this on the board to show why they are called cross products:

$$\frac{3}{12} \diagdown \frac{5}{20}$$

Remind the class how to find the identity element. In this problem, ⅔ = ⁿ⁄₆, have students cross multiply to find the mystery number. (n = 4)

297

Use cross multiplication to identify equal ratios. Write Yes or No.

1. $\frac{3}{4} = \frac{12}{16}$ _Yes_
2. $\frac{4}{5} = \frac{13}{15}$ _No_
3. $\frac{6}{36} = \frac{1}{6}$ _Yes_

4. $\frac{3}{2} = \frac{6}{4}$ _Yes_
5. $\frac{9}{2} = \frac{72}{16}$ _Yes_
6. $\frac{5}{8} = \frac{35}{54}$ _No_

7. $\frac{12}{15} = \frac{8}{10}$ _Yes_
8. $\frac{10}{15} = \frac{12}{18}$ _Yes_
9. $\frac{25}{20} = \frac{10}{8}$ _Yes_

10. $\frac{5}{7} = \frac{35}{42}$ _No_
11. $\frac{8}{24} = \frac{6}{18}$ _Yes_
12. $\frac{35}{100} = \frac{9}{25}$ _No_

Write the missing number in each proportion.

13. $\frac{3}{4} = \frac{n}{12}$ $n =$ ___9___
14. $\frac{2}{3} = \frac{n}{9}$ $n =$ ___6___
15. $\frac{n}{5} = \frac{16}{20}$ $n =$ ___4___

16. $\frac{4}{n} = \frac{12}{15}$ $n =$ ___5___
17. $\frac{6}{8} = \frac{3}{n}$ $n =$ ___4___
18. $\frac{n}{10} = \frac{70}{100}$ $n =$ ___7___

19. $\frac{n}{56} = \frac{3}{7}$ $n =$ ___24___
20. $\frac{16}{n} = \frac{2}{5}$ $n =$ ___40___
21. $\frac{9}{3} = \frac{n}{6}$ $n =$ ___18___

Apply

Write a proportion and solve.

22. The width and the length of a rectangle are in the ratio 3 to 5. If the width of the rectangle is 12, find the length.
20

23. Each quilt square uses 5 red pieces and 3 white pieces of cloth. How many red pieces are sewn in a set of quilt squares containing 18 white pieces?
30 red pieces

24. Raisins cost 23¢ for 2 boxes. Allen spent 92¢ on raisins. How many boxes of raisins did he buy?
8 boxes

25. Betsy averages 2 bites for every 5 times she casts her fishing rod. Betsy got 8 bites on her fishing trip. How many times did she cast her rod?
20 times

298

Correcting Common Errors

Some students may have difficulty deciding what numbers to multiply by when they are finding equal ratios. Have them work with partners to find the missing numbers to form sets of equal ratios, keeping in mind that, in many ways, it is just like finding equivalent fractions.

1. $\frac{2}{3} \times \frac{4}{a} = \frac{8}{b}$ ($a = 4$, $b = 12$)
2. $\frac{5}{8} \times \frac{c}{3} = \frac{15}{d}$ ($c = 3$, $d = 24$)
3. $\frac{4}{e} \times \frac{2}{2} = \frac{f}{10}$ ($e = 5$, $f = 8$)

Enrichment

Remind students that a number can be divided by one and the value will not be changed. They will remember that this is another way to find equivalent fractions. Have them find equivalent fractions:

1. $\frac{24}{30} = \frac{8}{n}$ ($n = 10$)
2. $\frac{50}{100} = \frac{n}{4}$ ($n = 2$)
3. $\frac{21}{49} = \frac{3}{n}$ ($n = 7$)
4. $\frac{15}{45} = \frac{n}{15}$ ($n = 5$)

Practice

Have students complete the problems.

Mixed Practice

1. $217.7 - 190.681$ (27.019)
2. $.00182 \div .07$ (.026)
3. $83 \times \$15.78$ ($1,309.74)
4. $1\frac{1}{4} \times 2\frac{3}{5}$ $\left(3\frac{1}{4}\right)$
5. $\$394.00 \div 8$ ($49.25)
6. $\frac{7}{15} = \frac{}{45}$ (21)
7. $1.79 \times .036$ (.06444)
8. $17\frac{3}{5} - 12\frac{1}{4}$ $\left(5\frac{7}{20}\right)$
9. $90 \times 1,275$ (114,750)
10. $\frac{5}{8} \div \frac{5}{7}$ $\left(\frac{7}{8}\right)$

Extra Credit *Geometry*

Have students make two sets of 9 cards. On each of the first nine cards, draw one of the following geometric figures: equilateral triangle, right triangle, line, trapezoid, isosceles triangle, simple closed curve, hexagon, parallelogram and circle. Write the names of the figures on the second set of cards. Place the figure cards face down between the players. Give each player an equal number of name cards, face up. Players take turns turning over one of the figure cards. If they have the name card that matches it and can do so correctly, they keep the figure card. If they cannot match the card, the figure card is returned to the bottom of the pile, face down, and the next player plays. The player collecting the greater number of figure cards is the winner. As an extension, have a student using the name cards only, pick a card, and construct the figure.

Ratios and Scale

pages 299-300

Objective

To use equal ratios to find distances on a scale drawing

Materials

*blueprints or a map
graph paper
centimeter ruler

Mental Math

Have students reduce these fractions to lowest terms:

1. ⁶⁄₈ (¾)
2. ⁶⁄₁₂ (½)
3. ³⁄₂ (1 ½)
4. ⁹⁄₄ (2 ¼)
5. ¹⁰⁄₄ (2 ½)
6. ⁴⁄₁₆ (¼)
7. ²⁴⁄₅ (4 ⅘)

Skill Review

Have students solve for n, in these equal ratio equations:

1. ¾ = ⁿ⁄₁₆ (n = 12)
2. ⅕ = ⁴⁄ₙ (n = 20)
3. ⁿ⁄₆ = ¹²⁄₃ (n = 24)
4. ¹⁰⁄ₙ = ⁵⁄₉ (n = 18)
5. ²⁰⁄₄₀ = ⁿ⁄₁₂₀ (n = 60)
6. ¹⁵⁄₄₅ = ³⁰⁄ₙ (n = 90)
7. ⁶⁄₉ = ¹⁸⁄ₙ (n = 27)
8. ⁿ⁄₃ = ⁴⁄₁₂ (n = 1)

Understanding Scale Drawings

A map is an example of a scale drawing. The scale is a ratio. Actually how far is it from Artesia to Baldwin?

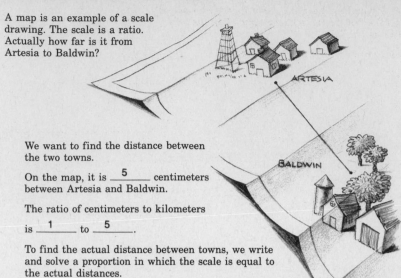

We want to find the distance between the two towns.

On the map, it is ___5___ centimeters between Artesia and Baldwin.

The ratio of centimeters to kilometers is ___1___ to ___5___.

To find the actual distance between towns, we write and solve a proportion in which the scale is equal to the actual distances.

$$\frac{cm}{km} = \frac{1}{5} = \frac{5}{n} \qquad \frac{1}{5} \times \frac{5}{5} = \frac{5}{n} \qquad n = \underline{\ 25\ }$$

It is ___25___ kilometers from Artesia to Baldwin.

Getting Started

Use the above map scale to write the distance in kilometers of the following:

1. A distance of 6 cm __30 km__
2. A distance of 10 cm __50 km__
3. A distance of 7 cm __35 km__
4. A distance of 1 cm __5 km__
5. A distance of 2 cm __10 km__
6. A distance of 9 cm __45 km__

Use the scale and a metric ruler to write the actual dimensions and area of the figure represented by this scale drawing.

7. 1 cm = 4 m $\overline{AB}$ = __16 m__
$\overline{BC}$ = __8 m__
The area is __128 sq m__.

MCP All rights reserved

299

Teaching the Lesson

Introducing the Problem Read the problem aloud. Hold the text up and indicate the scale. (1 cm = 5 km) Ask the class to use their centimeter rulers to measure the distance from Arlesia to Baldwin. (5 cm) Have a student read the information sentences. Explain that these numbers can be arranged in a proportion: 1 is to 5 as 5 is to some number, n. Put the proportion on the board. Ask students to provide the identity element (⁵⁄₅) and have a student solve the proportion. (⅕ = ⁵⁄₂₅) Ask another to interpret the new ratio and read the solution sentence. (5 km Arlesia to Baldwin)

Developing the Skill Hold up a blueprint or a map. Point out that the drawing represents an actual area much larger than the dimensions of the paper. If it is a blueprint, the house may be 30 or 40 feet long, while the blueprint is only 2 feet long. On a map, the ratio of inches to miles may be 1 inch to 10 miles or more. Explain that this allows large areas to be represented on small paper. Show students how to use a scale. Give students graph paper and ask them to draw a square that is 10 squares on a side. Write this scale on the board: 1 square to 5 cm. Ask how long each side of the square is. (5 cm × 10 = 50 cm) Have students find the length of a side using this scale: 1 square to 1 kilometer. (each side, 10 km) Ask them to find the area of the figure if the square is 1 square to 5 km. (5 km × 100 square units = 500 sq km)

Use each scale and a metric ruler to write the actual dimensions of the figures represented by these scale drawings.

1. 1 cm = 4 m

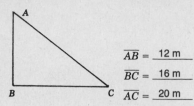

$\overline{AB}$ = __12 m__

$\overline{BC}$ = __16 m__

$\overline{AC}$ = __20 m__

2. 2 cm = 3 km

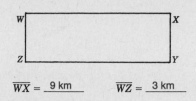

$\overline{WX}$ = __9 km__ $\overline{WZ}$ = __3 km__

3. 1 cm = 5 m

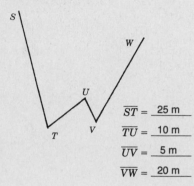

$\overline{ST}$ = __25 m__

$\overline{TU}$ = __10 m__

$\overline{UV}$ = __5 m__

$\overline{VW}$ = __20 m__

4. 1 cm = 9 km

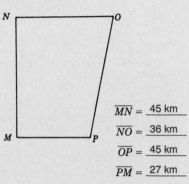

$\overline{MN}$ = __45 km__

$\overline{NO}$ = __36 km__

$\overline{OP}$ = __45 km__

$\overline{PM}$ = __27 km__

5. 1 cm = 2 m

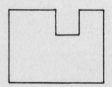

The perimeter is __32 m__.

6. 3 cm = 5 m

The area is __50 sq m__.

300

Correcting Common Errors

When students are finding distances on a scale drawing, they may write the actual distance and forget to use the scale. Have students work with partners. Have them draw a rectangle on inch-square grid paper 3 squares by 6 squares and pretend that it is a fenced corral for horses. Have them write the scale 1 in. = 10 ft. Then have them write "10 ft" above each square in the length and beside each square in the width. Have them add tens along the length and then along the width. Ask: How wide and how long is the drawing? (3 inches by 6 inches) How wide and how long is the corral? (30 feet by 60 feet)

Enrichment

Many home and craft magazines have patterns that must be transferred to one-inch graph paper before they can be used. Have students find such a pattern and bring it to class. Ask them to read the directions and find the scale. Have them choose a pattern and transfer it to inch-square paper.

Practice

Have students complete the problems on the page. Suggest that they set up each part as a ratio. For example, $\frac{1 \text{ cm}}{4 \text{ m}} = \frac{3 \text{ cm}}{12 \text{ m}}$.

Extra Credit *Applications*

Give two fractional numbers and an operation to the first student. The student will give the answer, and then give the next student that number and another fractional number and operation. The student giving the problem checks the person answering. Have students continue working in this way around the class until someone gives a wrong answer. At that point the activity starts over again. Form teams and make this a timed exercise.

If the numbers being used become too complicated, either give directions which will get the number back to workable dimensions or stop the game and begin with a new number.

Ratios as Percents

pages 301-302

Objective

To express ratios as percents

Materials

pieces of 10 × 10-square graph paper

Mental Math

Have students tell if these numbers are prime. If it is not prime, have them give the prime factors (besides 1) of the number.

1. 3 (prime)
2. 6 (not prime; factors 2, 3)
3. 1 (prime)
4. 13 (prime)
5. 14 (not prime; factors 2, 7)
6. 15 (not prime; factors 3, 5)
7. 23 (prime)

Skill Review

Have students write each fraction as a decimal:

1. $\frac{1}{10}$ (0.1)
2. $\frac{3}{100}$ (0.03)
3. $\frac{24}{100}$ (0.24)
4. $\frac{91}{100}$ (0.91)
5. $\frac{34}{10}$ (3.4)
6. $\frac{29}{1000}$ (0.029)
7. $\frac{54}{100}$ (0.54)
8. $\frac{70}{100}$ (0.70)

Expressing Ratios as Percents

A percent is a special ratio. The word **percent** means "per one hundred". The symbol for percent is %. What percent of pennies shown are heads?

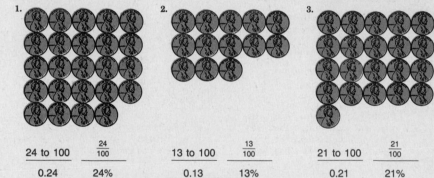

We want to express the ratio of pennies showing heads to all the pennies, as a percent.

There are ___100___ pennies altogether.

Heads are showing on ___48___ of the pennies.

To express this relationship as a percent, we first write it as a fraction and decimal. Then, to rename a decimal as a percent, we multiply it by 100.

Ratio	Fraction	Decimal	Percent
48 to 100	$\frac{48}{100}$	0.48	48%

Heads are showing on ___48___ % of the pennies.

Getting Started

Write the ratio, fraction, decimal and percent for the number of heads showing in each set of 100 coin tosses.

1.

24 to 100 $\frac{24}{100}$

0.24   24%

2.

13 to 100 $\frac{13}{100}$

0.13   13%

3.

21 to 100 $\frac{21}{100}$

0.21   21%

MCP All rights reserved

Write each number as a percent.

4. 20 out of 100
   20%

5. 66 to 100
   66%

6. $\frac{89}{100}$
   89%

7. 0.36
   36%

301

Teaching the Lesson

Introducing the Problem Have a student read the problem aloud. Write **percent** and **%** on the board. Read the information sentences. Read the plan, explaining that a ratio or fraction that has 100 as the denominator can be written as a percent. Point out that 48 heads to 100 pennies can be written $\frac{48}{100}$, 0.48 or 48%. Express the percent in this way, "Forty-eight percent of the pennies show heads." Have a student read the solution sentence. (heads showing on 48%)

Developing the Skill Explain that a percent is a special fraction whose denominator is always 100. Like a fraction, a percent describes part of a whole. Give each student three pieces of graph paper, ten squares on a side. Have them shade 25 blocks on one piece. Hold one up for the class and explain that 25 out of 100 ($\frac{25}{100}$ or 25%) of the whole piece is shaded. Write **25%** on the board and have students label their drawings. Ask them to shade 11 blocks on the next square and label it 11%, and 49 blocks on the last one, labeling it 49%. Hold up the first and ask what percentage of the blocks are not shaded. (75%) Repeat for the second (89%) and third (51%).

Write the ratio, fraction, decimal and percent for the
number of heads showing in each set of 100 coin tosses.

1.

2.

3.

| 12 to 100 | $\frac{12}{100}$ | 15 to 100 | $\frac{15}{100}$ | 7 to 100 | $\frac{7}{100}$ |
| 0.12 | 12% | 0.15 | 15% | 0.07 | 7% |

Write each number as a percent.

4. $\frac{17}{100}$
17%

5. 11:100
11%

6. 31 out of 100
31%

7. 29 to 100
29%

8. 0.12
12%

9. $\frac{36}{100}$
36%

10. $\frac{63}{100}$
63%

11. 50:100
50%

12. $\frac{37}{100}$
37%

13. 0.15
15%

14. $\frac{1}{100}$
1%

15. 0.96
96%

16. 43:100
43%

17. 100 out of 100
100%

18. 5:100
5%

19. $\frac{67}{100}$
67%

Apply

Solve these problems.

20. In a recent poll, 65 out of every
100 people surveyed thought the
president was doing a good job.
What percent thought the
president was doing a good job?
65%

21. On a test containing 100 items,
Brittany answered 87 questions
correctly. What percent did
Brittany get right? What percent
did she get wrong?
87% right   13% wrong

EXCURSION

Write five ratios equivalent to 50%.
Answers will vary but all must be equivalent to 1 to 2.
___ ___ ___ ___ ___

Correcting Common Errors

Students may have difficulty understanding how different percents are related to a whole. Have them draw a
number line ten inches long, labeling
one end 0 and the other end 1. Have
them put marks on the number line to
show tenths and label the tenths
below the line and the equivalent percents above it. Then have them locate,
mark, and label points for the following percents: 25%, 51%, 78%, and
82%.

Enrichment

Ask students to find at least ten examples of the use of percents in newspapers, magazines, television or radio.
Point out that percents are used exten-
sively to describe public opinion and
financial trends, and in advertising. Ask
students to cut out the examples or
write down those heard on television
or radio. Have them bring the examples to school to display on a percent
bulletin board.

Practice

Have students complete the practice problems. Write the
percent symbol on the board for reference.

Excursion

Have students try writing ratios showing 25%, or 1 to 4, as
an extension.

Extra Credit *Numeration*

Show students this method for finding the product of two

digits. For the product of 7 and 6: write: $\begin{array}{c}6 \\ 7\end{array} \times \begin{array}{c}4 \\ 3\end{array}$

Have students notice that the factors, 7 and 6, are written
on the left and the difference between each factor and 10
written to the right. Explain that they can find the tens digit

by subtracting 4 from 7 or 3 from 6: $\begin{array}{c}6 \\ 7\end{array} \times \begin{array}{c}4 \\ 3\end{array}$

The units digit is the product of 4 and 3. In this case the
tens digit is 3 (6 − 3 or 7 − 4), the units digit is 12. Adding
the two together: 42, 7 × 6 = 42. Have students use this
method to multiply 8 × 4 and 7 × 4.

$\left(\begin{array}{c}8 \\ 4\end{array} \times \begin{array}{c}2 \\ 6\end{array} = 20 + 12 = 32; \quad \begin{array}{c}9 \\ 6\end{array} \times \begin{array}{c}1 \\ 4\end{array} = 54\right)$

Percents as Fractions

pages 303-304

Objective

To change percents to fractions

Materials

Mental Math

Have students complete each fact family:

1. $20 \times 3 = 60$ ($3 \times 20 = 60$; $60 \div 3 = 20$; $60 \div 20 = 3$)
2. $19 + 16 = 35$
3. $52 \div 4 = 13$
4. $\frac{3}{2} \div \frac{1}{2} = 3$
5. $20 \div 8 = 2.5$

Skill Review

Have students change each expression to a percent:

1. 1:100 (1%)
2. 0.29 (29%)
3. 15 out of 100 (15%)
4. $\frac{59}{100}$ (59%)
5. 0.78 (78%)
6. 44:100 (44%)
7. 99 to 100 (99%)

Expressing Percents as Fractions

Headlines in newspapers often express number relationships in the form of percents. Express the rate that earnings have increased in the form of a fraction.

We want to write __25__ % as a fraction.

Any percent can be written as a fraction if you remember that percent means "per one hundred".

We drop the percent sign and express the number over 100. Remember we must simplify the terms if we can.

Percent	Fraction	Simplified
25%	$\frac{25}{100}$	$\frac{1}{4}$

The earnings increased by $\frac{1}{4}$.

Getting Started

Write each percent as a fraction in simplest terms.

1. 75% = $\frac{3}{4}$
2. 32% = $\frac{8}{25}$
3. 8% = $\frac{2}{25}$
4. 12% = $\frac{3}{25}$
5. 55% = $\frac{11}{20}$
6. 19% = $\frac{19}{100}$
7. 10% = $\frac{1}{10}$
8. 87% = $\frac{87}{100}$
9. 64% = $\frac{16}{25}$
10. 91% = $\frac{91}{100}$

Use the newspaper headlines to answer 11 and 12.

11. Write the employment figure as a fraction. $\frac{1}{10}$

12. Write the sales drop as a fraction. $\frac{1}{20}$

MCP All rights reserved

303

Teaching the Lesson

Introducing the Problem Read the problem aloud. Ask a student to read the headlines to the class. Read the next sentences, reminding students that percent means for every hundred, and can be written as a fraction by putting the percent over 100. Write **25% = 25/100** on the board. Ask a student to name all the factors common to 25 and 100. (5, 25) Have another reduce the fraction to lowest terms by dividing numerator and denominator by 25. (¼) Have a student read the solution sentence. (earnings increased by ¼)

Developing the Skill Put these steps for changing percents to fractions on the board:

1. **Rewrite the percent as a fraction, with a denominator of 100.**
2. **Find any factors common to numerator and denominator.**
3. **Divide both numerator and denominator by the largest common denominator, to reduce the fraction.**

Remind students that a percent is a specific fraction of a whole number that has 100 as a denominator. To change a percent to a fraction, put the percent over 100. Explain that sometimes the fraction must be simplified by dividing by 1. Help students change these percents to fractions: 10% ($\frac{10}{100} = \frac{1}{10}$); 5% ($\frac{5}{100} = \frac{1}{20}$); 34% ($\frac{34}{100} = \frac{17}{50}$).

303

Practice

Write each percent as a fraction in simplest terms.

1. $16\% = \frac{4}{25}$ 2. $4\% = \frac{1}{25}$ 3. $13\% = \frac{13}{100}$ 4. $75\% = \frac{3}{4}$

5. $28\% = \frac{7}{25}$ 6. $57\% = \frac{57}{100}$ 7. $12\% = \frac{3}{25}$ 8. $48\% = \frac{12}{25}$

9. $89\% = \frac{89}{100}$ 10. $40\% = \frac{2}{5}$ 11. $36\% = \frac{9}{25}$ 12. $62\% = \frac{31}{50}$

13. $1\% = \frac{1}{100}$ 14. $70\% = \frac{7}{10}$ 15. $8\% = \frac{2}{25}$ 16. $37\% = \frac{37}{100}$

17. $5\% = \frac{1}{20}$ 18. $14\% = \frac{7}{50}$ 19. $32\% = \frac{8}{25}$ 20. $96\% = \frac{24}{25}$

Write each percent as a fraction in simplest terms.

21.

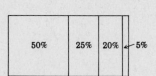

$50\% = \frac{1}{2}$ $25\% = \frac{1}{4}$

$20\% = \frac{1}{5}$ $5\% = \frac{1}{20}$

22.

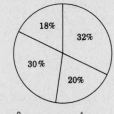

$18\% = \frac{9}{50}$ $20\% = \frac{1}{5}$

$32\% = \frac{8}{25}$ $30\% = \frac{3}{10}$

Apply

Solve these problems.

23. In Rochester, New York, 40% of the population is 35 or older. What percent of the population is younger than 35?
60%

24. Thirteen percent of the population of Rhode Island lives in rural areas. What percent of the people live in urban areas?
87%

25. Ozzie's sold chocolate and cherry shakes to the Girl Scout troop. If 74% of the troop ordered chocolate shakes, what percent ordered cherry?
26%

26. Eighteen percent of the pictures in Myles' photo album are black and white. The rest are in color. What percent of Myles' photos are in color?
82%

304

Correcting Common Errors

Some students may have difficulty expressing percents as a fraction in simplest terms. Put 40% and $\frac{40}{100}$ on the chalkboard and ask students to indicate as many factors common to the numerator and denominator as they can. (2, 5, 10, 20) Then write on the chalkboard:

$$40\% = \frac{40}{100} = \frac{2}{5}$$

Have them complete the chart below.

%	Fraction	GCF	Simplest Terms
30%	$\frac{30}{100}$	10	$\frac{3}{10}$
45%	$\frac{45}{100}$	5	$\frac{9}{20}$
84%	$\frac{84}{100}$	4	$\frac{21}{25}$

Enrichment

Have students change these percents to fractions. Suggest they make an estimate in each case and then cross multiply to check:

1. $33\frac{1}{3}\%$ $\left(\frac{1}{3}\right)$
2. $12\frac{1}{2}\%$ $\left(\frac{1}{8}\right)$
3. $11\frac{1}{9}\%$ $\left(\frac{1}{9}\right)$
4. $66\frac{2}{3}\%$ $\left(\frac{2}{3}\right)$
5. $77\frac{7}{9}\%$ $\left(\frac{7}{9}\right)$
6. $62\frac{1}{2}\%$ $\left(\frac{5}{8}\right)$

Practice

Have students complete the problems.

Mixed Practice

1. 900×500 (450,000)
2. $363 + 456 + 381 + 783$ (1,983)
3. $\frac{19}{100} = $ ____ % (19)
4. $21,850 \div 71$ (307 R53)
5. $3\frac{1}{3} \times 2\frac{1}{4}$ (15)
6. $3 \times 2,968$ (8,904)
7. 7.9×3.12 (24.648)
8. $2\frac{2}{5} \div 12\frac{1}{5}$ $\left(\frac{12}{61}\right)$
9. $72,156 - 61,042$ (11,114)
10. $16\frac{1}{8} - 8\frac{5}{6}$ $\left(7\frac{7}{24}\right)$

Extra Credit   *Applications*

Duplicate the following or write on the board:
Sarah Green is building a new house. What will it cost her to carpet an 18-foot × 13-foot living room, a 14-foot × 14-foot dining room and a 14½-foot × 3½-foot hall, at $7.50 per square yard? Figure that 10% of the material will be wasted due to cutting.
(There are 53.41666 square yards, but this equals only 90% of the material needed. The total becomes 59.351851 square yards, or $445.14.)

304

Fractions as Percents

pages 305-306

Objective

To change a fraction to a percent

Materials

Mental Math

Have students solve these equations for a = 3 and b = 5:

1. a + b = (8)
2. b − a = (2)
3. (2 × a) + b = (11)
4. a + (5 × b) = (28)
5. a × b = (15)
6. 2a × b = (30)
7. b ÷ a = ($^5/_3$ = 1$^2/_3$)

Skill Review

Have students change each percent to a fraction and reduce to lowest terms:

1. 30% ($^3/_{10}$)
2. 29% ($^{29}/_{100}$)
3. 55% ($^{11}/_{20}$)
4. 5% ($^1/_{20}$)
5. 98% ($^{49}/_{50}$)
6. 100% (1)
7. 37% ($^{37}/_{100}$)
8. 62% ($^{31}/_{50}$)

Expressing Fractions as Percents

The mathematics teacher took a poll of the favorite color of each of her students. Find the percent of the class which chose blue.

Favorite Color Survey	
Red	6
Yellow	4
Blue	8
Green	7

We want to express the part of the class which chose blue as a percent.

Blue was the favorite color of __8__ students.

There are __25__ students in the class altogether.

To express this relationship as a percent, we first write it as a fraction. We rename the fraction as a decimal by dividing the numerator by the denominator. Finally, we rename the decimal as a percent by multiplying it by 100 and affixing a percent sign.

Fraction	Decimal	Percent
$\frac{8}{25}$	$\begin{array}{r} 0.32 \\ 25)\overline{8.00} \end{array}$	0.32 × 100 = __32__%

The survey showed that __32__% of the class preferred blue.

Round all decimals to hundredths.

$\frac{1}{7}$ $\begin{array}{r} 0.142 \approx 0.14 \\ 7)\overline{1.000} \end{array}$ 14%

Getting Started

Write each fraction as a percent.

1. $\frac{1}{2}$ = __50%__   2. $\frac{1}{3}$ = __33%__   3. $\frac{3}{8}$ = __38%__   4. $\frac{4}{5}$ = __80%__

5. $\frac{3}{7}$ = __43%__   6. $\frac{9}{10}$ = __90%__   7. $\frac{3}{25}$ = __12%__   8. $\frac{4}{50}$ = __8%__

Use the favorite color survey to answer 9 and 10.

9. What percent chose red as their favorite color? __24%__

10. What percent chose green as their favorite color? __28%__

MCP All rights reserved

305

Teaching the Lesson

Introducing the Problem Read the problem aloud. Ask a student to look at the illustration and complete the information sentences. Remind students that a percent is a fraction. Put the fraction and the decimal division on the board. Read aloud, thirty-two hundredths. To rename the decimal as a percent, they will multiply by 100 and add the percent sign. Have a student multiply (.32 × 100 = 32%) and read the solution sentence. (survey showed 32% of class preferred blue) Explain that sometimes the division produces a decimal with a remainder. Remind students that they can add zeros to the right of a decimal in order to complete division. Show them how to round the quotient to hundredths. (0.142 = .14 or 14%)

Developing the Skill Put these steps for changing a fraction to a percent on the board:

1. **Divide denominator into numerator. Place decimal point to the right of the numerator, and just above it, in the quotient.**
2. **Continue division to hundredths, or to thousandths if there is a remainder.**
3. **Round quotient to hundredths** (.000 → .004, round down; .005 → .009, round up).
4. **Multiply quotient by 100 and affix % symbol.**

Follow these steps with the class to change $\frac{1}{9}$ to a percent. (11%)

305

Practice

Write each fraction as a percent.

1. $\frac{1}{5}$ = 20%
2. $\frac{2}{3}$ = 67%
3. $\frac{3}{10}$ = 30%
4. $\frac{1}{8}$ = 13%
5. $\frac{5}{6}$ = 83%
6. $\frac{3}{4}$ = 75%
7. $\frac{7}{9}$ = 78%
8. $\frac{1}{4}$ = 25%
9. $\frac{3}{25}$ = 12%
10. $\frac{4}{7}$ = 57%
11. $\frac{17}{50}$ = 34%
12. $\frac{11}{12}$ = 92%
13. $\frac{7}{8}$ = 88%
14. $\frac{14}{35}$ = 40%
15. $\frac{19}{20}$ = 95%
16. $\frac{3}{16}$ = 19%
17. $\frac{7}{40}$ = 18%
18. $\frac{3}{50}$ = 6%
19. $\frac{7}{18}$ = 39%
20. $\frac{5}{11}$ = 45%

Apply

Use the favorite team survey to answer 21 through 24.

Favorite Team Survey	
Cowboys	16
Jets	8
Bears	10
Rams	6

21. What percent voted for the Cowboys? 40%
22. What percent voted for the Jets? 20%
23. What percent voted for the Bears? 25%
24. What percent voted for the Rams? 15%

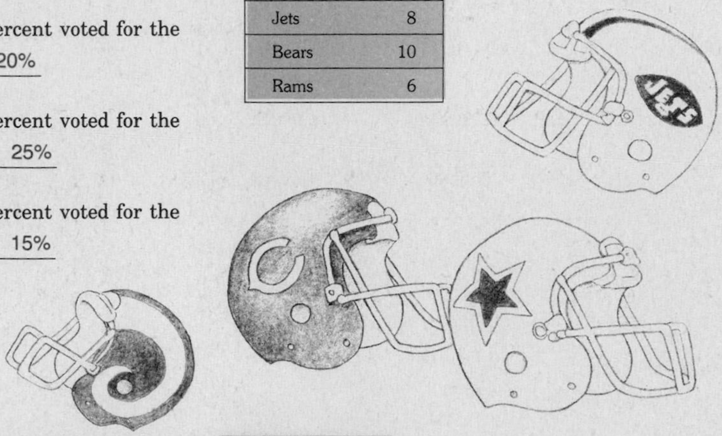

EXCURSION

A **periodic decimal** is a decimal consisting of a finite series of digits that repeat infinitely. Examples of periodic decimals are $0.33\overline{3}$ and $3.2474\overline{747}$. The bar over the digits indicates that this series of digits repeats infinitely.

Write these fractions as periodic decimals.

1. $\frac{1}{9}$ = $0.\overline{1}$
2. $\frac{2}{3}$ = $0.\overline{6}$
3. $\frac{3}{11}$ = $0.\overline{27}$

Correcting Common Errors

Some students may forget to carry out the division to one extra place when they must round to the nearest hundredth. Have them work with partners to change the following fractions to percents. Have them first show the decimal to three places after the decimal point and then the percent to the nearest whole percent.

1. 1/9 (0.111, 11%)
2. 7/8 (0.875, 88%)
3. 3/11 (0.272, 27%)

Enrichment

Have students compose a questionnaire to conduct a survey on a topic of their choice. Tell them to conduct the survey within the class and express the results as fractions, changed to percents. Ask them to illustrate the percentages with a bar graph.

Practice

Have students complete the practice problems. Remind them to round the decimal to two places if necessary.

Excursion

Have students use their calculators to find other examples of periodic decimals.

Extra Credit *Statistics*

Have students find the midrange, mode and median for the following sets of numbers:

1. 12, 16, 21, 25, 30 (range = 18, mode = none, median = 21)
2. 50, 51, 52, 54, 54, 55, 56 (range = 6, mode = 54, median = 54)
3. 101, 124, 125, 131, 131, 142 (range = 41, mode = 131, median = 128)
4. 1,240, 2,300, 2,400, 2,400, 3,210, 3,210, 4,000 (range = 2,760, mode = 2,400 and 3,210, median = 2,400)
5. ½, ⅔, ¾, ¾, 1½, 1⅔, 1¾ (range = 1¼, mode = ¾, median = ¾)

Finding Percent

Objective

To find a percent of a number

Materials

Mental Math

Ask students to compare these if a = 5 and b = 7:

1. a and b (a < b)
2. 2a and b (2a > b)
3. a × 1 and b × 1 (a × 1 < b × 1)
4. 2 + a and 2 + b (2 + a < 2 + b)
5. 2 + a and b (2 + a = b)
6. a + b and 15 (a + b < 15)

Skill Review

Have students change these percents to decimals:

1. 15% (.15)   4. 98% (.98)
2. 38% (.38)   5. 61% (.61)
3. 2% (.02)   6. 50% (.50)

Have students multiply. Remind them to count the decimal places in the factors to find decimal places in the product:

7. 142 × .025 = (3.550 = 3.55)
8. 5,600 × 0.72 = (4,032.00 = 4,032)
9. 21 × .33 = (6.93)

Finding a Percent of a Number

Mr. Hirakawa bought a new color television. He paid cash. In addition to the price of the set, Mr. Hirakawa has to pay a sales tax of 7%. How much did Mr. Hirakawa pay for the television set?

Color T.V. $450

Black & White T.V. ~ $120

Stereo $280

We are looking for the entire cost of the television set.

The television set itself cost ___$450___.

Mr. Hirakawa also paid ___7%___ sales tax. To find the total cost, we multiply the cost of the set by the sales tax rate and add that to the cost of the set.

We multiply ___$450___ by ___7%___ and add that to ___$450___.

Change the percent to a decimal.	Multiply.	Add.
7% = 0.07	$450 × 0.07 ———— $31.50	$450.00 + 31.50 ———— $481.50

Mr. Hirakawa paid a total of ___$481.50___ for the television set.

Getting Started

Write the part of each price represented by the percent.

1. 30% of $125 = ___$37.50___   2. 25% of $86 = ___$21.50___   3. 20% of $45 = ___$9___

Copy and calculate.

4. 42% of $195
   $81.90
5. 16% of $59
   $9.44
6. 4% of $38
   $1.52

Use the ad to answer 7 and 8. Add 6% sales tax to each item purchased.

7. How much does a black and white set cost?
   $127.20

8. Mr. Henry buys a stereo. He is going to make 4 payments. How much is each payment?
   $74.20

MCP All rights reserved

Teaching the Lesson

Introducing the Problem Read the problem aloud. Have a student read the information sentences. Read the plan sentences and direct students' attention to the problem worked in stages in the model. Explain that before they can multiply, they have to change the percent to a decimal. (7% = 0.07) Remind them that to find a decimal or fractional part of a whole number, they multiply the whole number by the decimal or fraction. Have a student do the multiplication on the board. ($450 × 0.07 = $31.50) Point out that the total cost of the television is the price plus the tax. Have students do that addition and ask one to read the solution sentence. (paid $481.50)

Developing the Skill Explain that finding the percent of a whole number is the same as finding a fraction or a decimal part of that number. Remind students that to find a decimal part, they multiply the whole number by a decimal; to find a fractional part, they multiply the whole number by a fraction. To find a percent, they change the percent to a decimal before multiplying. Explain that it is also possible to change a percent to a fraction and multiply. Ask a student to explain how to change a percent to a decimal. (write as hundredths, remove % sign) Have students change each of these percents to decimals and multiply by 150: 24% (36), 19% (28.5) and 80%. (120)

Practice

Write the part of each price represented by the percent.

1. 60% of $80 = $48
2. 25% of $120 = $30
3. 14% of $360 = $50.40
4. 48% of $96 = $46.08
5. 4% of $250 = $10
6. 10% of $73 = $7.30
7. 14% of $84 = $11.76
8. 61% of $13 = $7.93
9. 36% of $10 = $3.60
10. 2% of $368 = $7.36
11. 99% of $60 = $59.40
12. 86% of $65 = $55.90
13. 35% of $270 = $94.50
14. 43% of $43 = $18.49
15. 70% of $960 = $672.00
16. 50% of $472 = $236
17. 33% of $96 = $31.68
18. 1% of $100 = $1

Copy and Do

19. 16% of $236
$37.76
20. 23% of $94
$21.62
21. 38% of $375
$142.5
22. 6% of $88
$5.28
23. 65% of $795
$516.75
24. 45% of $226
$101.7
25. 12% of $400
$48
26. 3% of $115
$3.45
27. 75% of $95
$71.25
28. 50% of $320
$160
29. 87% of $636
$553.32
30. 26% of $3,425
$890.5
31. 95% of $1,200
$1,140
32. 20% of $800
$160
33. 80% of $200
$160

Apply

Solve these problems.

34. Alex took a 90 item test. He got 90% correct. How many items did Alex get correct?
81 items

35. If sales tax is 5%, what is the cost of a suit that sells for $326?
$342.30

36. Pam sells shoes for a commission. She gets to keep 8% of all she sells. How much does Pam make if she sells $475 worth of shoes?
$38

37. Roger has 240 tapes. 35% of them are country and western. Mary has 230 tapes. 40% of them are country and western. How many more country and western tapes does Mary have?
8 tapes

308

Correcting Common Errors

Some students may have difficulty keeping track of the various steps when they are finding the percent of a dollar amount. Have them write the following steps on an index card and use it as a guide when they are solving such problems.

1. change the percent to a decimal.
2. multiply by the decimal.
3. count the decimal places in the factors and make that many decimal places in the product.
4. write the dollar sign when necessary.

Enrichment

Have students work the following problems, changing each percent to a decimal and then multiplying:

1. 125% of $50 ($62.50)
2. 300% of $75 ($225.00)
3. 250% of $59 ($147.50)
4. 500% of $100 ($500.00)

Then ask students to think of times when percents greater that 100% might be used. (To indicate an increase in price, for example: the price today is 200% of the price 15 years ago.)

Practice

Have students complete all the problems. Remind them to count decimal places carefully.

Extra Credit   *Statistics*

Explain that in addition to the range, mode and median, there is also the arithmetic mean. Show students that the mean is the sum of all the numbers in the set, divided by the number of members in the set. Give them this set; 3, 4, 5, 2, 3, 4, 7. The sum = 28, the number of members in the set, 7; the mean = $^{28}/_7$ = 4.

Have students survey the class to find out how many books each student has in their desk or locker. List the results on the board and have students calculate the mean number of books in each desk or locker.

Extend the activity by using other counting problems devised by students.

308

Discount and Sale Price

Objective

To find the sale price when the rate of discount is given

Materials

*newspaper ads showing sales and discount rates

Mental Math

Have students change each fraction to a percent:

1. $^{45}/_{100}$ (45%)
2. $^{3}/_{100}$ (3%)
3. $^{15}/_{100}$ (15%)
4. $^{90}/_{100}$ (90%)
5. $^{5}/_{10}$ ($^{50}/_{100}$ = 50%)
6. $^{1}/_{10}$ ($^{10}/_{100}$ = 10%)
7. $½$ ($^{50}/_{100}$ = 50%)

Skill Review

Have students calculate these percents:

1. 25% of $50 ($12.50)
2. 30% of $180 ($54)
3. 15% of $200 ($30)
4. 66% of $90 ($59.40)
5. 33% of $4.50 ($1.49)
6. 50% of $19.00 ($9.50)
7. 75% of $125 ($93.75)

Calculating Discount and Sale Price

Store owners sometimes reduce the price of an item they wish to sell. This reduction is called a **discount**. The **rate of discount** is the percent of the original price that the customer does not pay. Tony bought a pair of skis at the big winter sale. The **list price** of the skis was originally $124. How much did Tony pay for the skis?

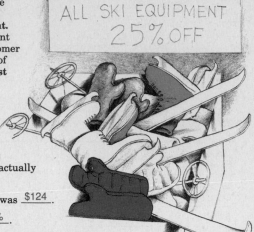

ALL SKI EQUIPMENT 25% OFF

We want to know what Tony actually paid for the skis.

The original price of the skis was $124.

The rate of discount was 25%.

To find what Tony paid, we multiply the list price by the rate of discount to get the discount. Then we subtract the discount from the list price.

We multiply $124 by 25% and subtract that

from $124.

```
  $124  ← list price          $124  ← list price
× 0.25  ← rate of discount   −  31  ← discount
   620                        $ 93  ← sale price
   248
$31.00  ← discount
```

Tony actually paid $93 for the skis.

Getting Started

Write the sale price to complete the chart.

1.

List Price	$85	$156	$260	$148	$940
Rate of Discount	10%	15%	30%	20%	5%
Sale Price	$76.50	$132.60	$182	$118.40	$893

MCP All rights reserved

309

Teaching the Lesson

Introducing the Problem Read the problem aloud. Write **discount** on the board. Have a student read the information sentences. Read the plan sentences. Explain that we use this procedure to find the amount that an item is discounted. Do the multiplication on the board. (**$124 × .25 = $31**) Indicate that $31 is the amount the skis are discounted. Show students that to find the sale price they must subtract the amount of the discount from the original price. Have a student do the subtraction on the board. ($124 − $31 = $93) Read the solution sentence aloud. (actually paid $93 for the skis)

Developing the Skill Hold up newspaper ads showing sale rates and discounts offered in local stores. Explain that in order to sell certain merchandise, merchants sometimes reduce the price by a percentage of the original price. Show students how to calculate the sale price by putting these steps on the board:

1. **change the percent to a decimal**
2. **multiply by decimal to get amount of discount**
3. **subtract discounted amount from original price**

The difference is the sale price. Work these problems with the class:
original price $80, 25% discount (sale price $60.00)
original price $175, 12% discount (sale price $154)

Practice

Write the sale price.

1. list price: $75
   rate of discount: 20%

   sale price = ___$60___

2. list price: $216
   rate of discount: 30%

   sale price = ___$151.20___

3. list price: $148
   rate of discount: 12%

   sale price = ___$130.24___

4. list price: $212
   rate of discount: 15%

   sale price = ___$180.20___

Write the sale price to complete the chart.

5.

List Price	$54	$125	$284	$635	$986	$1,865
Rate of Discount	5%	10%	25%	15%	40%	8%
Sale Price	$51.30	$112.50	$213	$539.75	$591.60	$1715.80

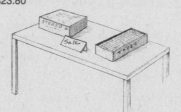

Apply

Solve these problems.

6. At the Clothes Tree Apparel Store they offered a discount rate of 5%. Mary Lou bought a jacket that was listed at $29. How much did Mary Lou actually pay for the jacket?
$27.55

7. The Favorite Foods Factory had a discount sale. Everything was on sale for 10% off. Dawn bought $48 worth of food. What did she actually pay for the food?
$43.20

8. The Super Sounds Stereo Shop held a 15% off sale. Ivan bought a stereo that cost $186. He also bought $30 worth of tapes. What did Ivan actually pay for the stereo and tapes?
$183.60

9. The Value Town Discount Store had a 20% reduction sale. Mario had saved $125 toward a new bike. The price of the bike Mario wanted was $186. How much more money does Mario still need to save to buy the bike on sale?
$23.80

310

Correcting Common Errors

Some students may forget to subtract the amount of discount from the list price when they are asked to find the sale price. As they work each problem, have them fill in information in each of the following categories.

List price	Rate of discount	Amount of discount	Sale price

Enrichment

Variety Department Store is having a final clearance. Their dresses were reduced by 30% earlier in the season, but are now an extra 40% off the already reduced price. How much will each of the dresses cost on sale if the original price was:

1. $100? ($42)
2. $55? ($23.10)
3. $79? ($33.18)
4. $150? ($63)

Practice

Have students complete the problems.

Mixed Practice

1. $3\frac{1}{2} \times 1\frac{1}{3} \left(4\frac{2}{3}\right)$
2. $112.6 - 87.709$ (24.891)
3. $\$75.98 \times 19$ ($1,443.62)
4. $1.22 \times .07$ (0.0854)
5. $47,932 \div 94$ (509 R86)
6. What fraction equals 75%? $\left(\frac{3}{4}\right)$
7. $19 - 16\frac{14}{15} \left(2\frac{1}{15}\right)$
8. $475,280 + 168,596$ (643,876)
9. $0.871 \div 13$ (0.067)
10. $60,157 - 28,341$ (31,816)

Extra Credit *Applications*

Duplicate the following or write on the board:

You can determine the height of a tall object by first measuring the shadow of the tall object and then measuring a nearby short object and its shadow. The proportion of the smaller object to its shadow will be the same as the tall object to its shadow. If a five-foot tall person casts a shadow that is 8 feet long and a tall tree casts a shadow that is 32 feet long then the proportion is:

$$8:5::32:H \text{ then } \frac{5 \times 32 = H}{8} \text{ then } \frac{5 \times 32}{8} = 20 = H$$

Have students determine the height of a tall tree or flagpole in the schoolyard using this method.

Problem Solving
Related Problems

pages 311-312

Objective

To solve problems by solving related problems first

Materials

Mental Math

Have students divide, expressing any remainder as a fraction:

1. $49 \div 8 = (6\frac{1}{8})$
2. $50 \div 10 = (5)$
3. $27 \div 8 = (3\frac{3}{8})$
4. $60 \div 7 = (8\frac{4}{7})$
5. $17 \div 3 = (5\frac{2}{3})$
6. $84 \div 9 = (9\frac{3}{9} = 9\frac{1}{3})$
7. $75 \div 25 = (3)$

Solving a Simpler but Related Problem

How many angles are there in this figure?

★ SEE

We want to find the total number of angles.

There are __5__ rays.

★ PLAN

Since there are 5 rays in this figure, we should start with a simpler problem. We should make a table of our results to see if we can find a pattern that would help us to solve the problem.

★ DO

Number of Rays	Types of Angles	Number of each Angle	Total Angles
2		1	1
3		2 } 1	3
4		3 2 1	6
5		4 3 2 1	10

MCP All rights reserved

There are __10__ different angles in this figure.

★ CHECK

There are __4__ angles.　　There are __2__ angles.

There are __3__ angles.　　There is __1__ angle.

311

Teaching the Lesson

Read the problem aloud while students examine the illustration in their texts. Have a student read the SEE section of the problem. (There are 5 rays.) Explain that although 5 is a lot to start with, they could solve the problem for fewer rays and look for a pattern in the results. Read the PLAN section of the problem and have students look at the chart in their books. Show students that in the first line, two rays are considered, one angle is formed. In the second line three rays are considered. Two single angles and one angle that includes the two smaller are possible: a total of 3. Continue, showing students the pattern that emerges. (3 + 2 + 1 for four rays; 4 + 3 + 2 + 1 for five rays) Have students complete the blanks in their books and have one read the solution sentence. (10 angles in the figure) Show the class that the CHECK consists of counting the four different types of angles, showing that there are 4 small angles, 3 angles inclusive of two smaller ones; 2 angles inclusive of three smaller ones; and 1 angle that includes all four smaller angles for a

total of 10. Explain that many problems that seem too difficult to solve can be broken down into smaller problems.

311

Apply

Solve these problems.

1. Use each of the digits from 0 to 9 to make the largest whole number possible. Then use the ten digits to make the smallest whole number possible.
9,876,543,210 largest
1,023,456,789 smallest

2. To get to its den, a fox has to go through two fences. The first fence has 2 holes in it and the second fence has 4 holes in it. How many different paths can the fox take?
8 paths

3. How long would it take you to spend one million dollars if you spent $200 a day?
5,000 days

4. How long will it take to spend a million dollars if you can spend one dollar per second?
11 days, 13 hours, 46 minutes, 40 seconds

5. If one million dollar bills are placed end to end, how far will the line of bills stretch in miles? One dollar bill is about 6 inches long.
94 miles   3,680 feet

6. In how many ways can five different flavors of ice cream be arranged on an ice cream cone? (You can only have one scoop of each flavor.)
120 ways

7. How many possible diagonals does an octagon have?
20 diagonals

8. How many squares are in this figure? (The squares may be different sizes.) 40 squares

9. Read Exercise 2 again. What if the farmer builds another fence between the two fences already there? The new fence has 1 hole in it. Now how many different paths can the fox take?
8 paths

10. Shelby and Justin picked some corn and now must shuck, or peel, the husks off the ears of corn. Shelby shucks 25% of 20 ears. Justin shucks 20% of 25 ears. Who shucked more corn?
See Solution Notes.

11. There were 2 bags of peanuts in the barn. The fox ate 50% of the peanuts in the first bag and 75% of the peanuts in the second bag. The farmer said that the fox ate 125% of his peanuts. Tell if the farmer is correct or incorrect and explain why.
Incorrect

12. Chick Little has an egg farm 2 miles outside of town. Naturally he raises hens on this farm. Some of the hens he raises are white and the rest are red. The ratio of white hens to red hens is 3 to 2. What percent of Chick Little's hens are red?
40%

312

Extra Credit *Logic*

Duplicate the following for students, How can you put 21 pigs in 4 pigpens and still have an odd number of pigs in each pen? You may put the same number of pigs in each pen, but the number in each pen must always be odd. Ask the students how can this problem be solved.

(Put 7 pigs in each of three small pens, then put a fourth pen around all of them, in case they escape the smaller pens. There is then an odd number in each of the 4 pens, with 21 in the large pen.)

Solution Notes

1. Start with the largest number possible from digits 0 through 1 (10), then 0 through 2 (210). Extrapolate to 0 through 9. (9, 876, 543, 210) Repeat for the smallest number not beginning with a zero. (1, 023, 456, 789)

2. Make a diagram and number the gaps in the fence. Have them consider hole 1 in the first fence (possible paths: 1, 1; 1, 2; 1, 3; 1, 4) then add the ways through hole 2.

4. Have students start with $1 per second up to $10 (10 sec), then up to $100 (100 sec = 1 min 40 sec), then to $1,000 (16 min 40 sec) etc.

5. Same approach as problem 4.

6. Start with two scoops arranged two ways. The pattern is 2 for 2 flavors, 3×2 for 3 flavors, $4 \times 3 \times 2$ for 4 flavors, and $5 \times 4 \times 3 \times 2 = 120$, for 5 flavors.

7. Start with diagonals for a square (2), a pentagon (5) and a hexagon (9). Confirm that the series 2, 5, 9 continues with 14 and 20 with a drawing.

8. Have students count the small squares, intermediate-sized squares (5), larger squares (4), and the figure outline itself.

Higher-Order Thinking Skills

9. Analysis: The answer is the same as before.

10. Analysis: They both shuck the same number of ears, 5 ears.

11. Synthesis: Explanations will vary but include that it is not possible to eat more than 100%.

12. Synthesis: If the ratio is 3 to 2, then 2 out of every 5 hens is red; 2 out of 5 is the same as 40 out of 100, or 40%.

312

Calculators and Interest

Objective

To use the calculator percent key

Materials

calculator with a percent key

Mental Math

Have students change each percent to a fraction and reduce if possible:

1. 50% ($^{50}/_{100}$ = ½)
2. 25% ($^{25}/_{100}$ = ¼)
3. 75% ($^{75}/_{100}$ = ¾)
4. 20% ($^{20}/_{100}$ = ⅕)
5. 30% ($^{30}/_{100}$ = $^{3}/_{10}$)
6. 100% ($^{100}/_{100}$ = 1)
7. 200% ($^{200}/_{100}$ = 2)

Skill Review

Have students work these problems on their calculators.

1. 23.4 + 15 = (38.4)
2. 59.3 − 18.4 = (40.9)
3. 14 × .95 = (13.3)
4. 21.7 ÷ .7 = (31)
5. 44.02 + 56.091 = (100.111)
6. 90 − 34.844 = (55.156)
7. 293.4 × 1.5 = (440.1)
8. 856 ÷ .02 = (42,800)

Calculators and Interest

Most calculators have a percent key. Use the % key to solve the following problem. Mr. Ivers bought a used car for $6,500. To pay for the car, he had to borrow the money. When you borrow money, interest must be paid for the loan. How much did the new car actually cost Mr. Ivers?

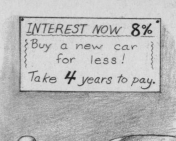

INTEREST NOW 8%
Buy a new car for less!
Take **4** years to pay.

We want to calculate the final cost of Mr. Ivers' car.

The list price of the car was __$6,500__.

The rate of interest was ___8%___ per year.

The loan was for ___4___ years.

To find the actual cost,
we find the amount of interest for 1 year,

6500 [×] 8 [%] (520)

we find the amount of interest for 4 years,

520 [×] 4 [=] (2,080)

and we find the total cost by adding the interest and the list price.

2080 [+] 6500 [=] (8,580)

The car cost Mr. Ivers __$8,580__.

We can also find the total cost with one code.

6500 [×] 8 [%] [×] 4 [+] 6500 [=] (8,580)

Find the interest and total cost of a loan of $5,000 at 9.6% for 3 years.
__$1,440__ , __$6,440__

MCP All rights reserved

313

Teaching the Lesson

Introducing the Problem Read the problem aloud. Have a student read the information sentences. Ask students to follow in their texts as you read the next section aloud. Explain that to find the actual cost, they have to calculate the amount of interest to be paid. Have students follow the code in their texts. Now have them find the interest for four years. (520 × 4 = 2,080) Explain that the total cost will be the price of the car plus the cost of the interest payments. Have students add. (2080 + 6500 = 8580) Ask a student to read the solution sentence. ($8,580) Show students how to do the problem in one series of steps. (6500 × 8% × 4 + 6500 = 8580). Have students repeat this series of steps for a loan of $5,000 at 9.6% for 3 years. (5000 × 9.6% = 480, 480 × 3 = 1440, 5000 + 1440 = 6440).

Developing the Skill The types of loan described in this lesson suggest that money is borrowed and interest owed on the full amount over the course of the loan. In this type of loan, the interest would be paid at intervals and the amount of the loan at the very end of the period. Explain that in real life, interest payments are more complicated. Usually people pay some of the money owed as well as the interest and in this way the amount on which interest is owed, changes all the time.

Practice

Use your calculator to find the part represented by the percent.

1. 60% of 380	2. 42% of $675	3. 19% of 482
228	$283.50	91.58

4. 12% of 3,765	5. 27% of 12,048	6. 6% of $16,125
451.8	3,252.96	$967.50

7. 9% of 11,214	8. 36% of $78,000	9. 2% of 29,575
1,009.26	$28,080	591.5

10. 13% of $17,214	11. 3% of $128,276	12. 14% of $308,210
$2,237.82	$3,848.28	$43,149.40

Apply

Complete the table.

13.

Loan	$8,250	$7,275	$11,940	$15,000	$15,000	$125,000
Rate of Interest	8%	9%	14%	16%	15%	11%
Years	3	5	2	4	4	20
Total Cost of Loan	$10,230	$10,548.75	$15,283.20	$24,600	$24,000	$400,000

EXCURSION

1. If $5,000 is saved at 10% for 1 year, the **simple interest** can be found by using the code 5,000 $\times$ 10 $\%$. The total in the account can be found by using the code

   5,000 $\times$ 110 $\%$. How much is in the account? __$5,500__

2. **Compound interest** is paid by most banks. The interest is paid on the original amount plus the interest earned. If 10% is compounded semi-annually, 5% is earned each 6 months. The total in the account starting with $5,000 can be found by using the code 5,000 $\times$ 105 $\%$ $\times$ 105 $\%$. How much is in the account after one year?

   __$5,512.50__

314

Correcting Common Errors

Some students may forget to press the percent key when they use their calculators to find the percent of a number. Before they use a calculator to solve a problem, have them write the calculator code—the key strokes—that they plan to use.

Enrichment

Have students research how mortgages work. (Descriptions should include that there is an initial payment. Interest is charged on what remains to be paid. The amount borrowed decreases with each payment, and so the interest payments gradually decrease.)

Practice

Have students complete the problems. Point out that they will use their calculators to find a percent of a whole number and the total cost of a loan.

Excursion

Point out that all interest, whether compounded annually, or by a fraction of a year, will be found by a multiple of 100.

Extra Credit *Probability*

Introduce the idea of **factorials** to the class. Explain that these unusual symbols are often used in probability to express the total number of ways in which an event may occur. Write **6!** on the board and tell students that this stands for the product: $1 \times 2 \times 3 \times 4 \times 5 \times 6$. (or 720) The factorial of a number, n, is the product of all the numbers up to and including n. Write on the board:

$$1! = 1$$
$$2! = 1 \times 2 = 2$$
$$3! = 1 \times 2 \times 3 = 6$$

Have students calculate the values for 4! (24), 5! (120), 7! (5,040), 8! (40,320) and 9! (362,880). Ask students to find a short way to divide 8! by 7!. (Because the factors in 8! are identical to those in 7! except for the final 8, 8! ÷ 7! = 8,)

$$\frac{1 \times 2 \times 3 \times 4 \times 5 \times 6 \times 7 \times 8}{1 \times 2 \times 3 \times 4 \times 5 \times 6 \times 7} = 8$$

Chapter Test

page 315

CHAPTER TEST

Write each ratio as a fraction. Do not simplify.

1. two to three $\frac{2}{3}$

2. five to three $\frac{5}{3}$

3. 6 to 4 $\frac{6}{4}$

4. 3:8 $\frac{3}{8}$

5. 9 out of 10 $\frac{9}{10}$

6. 8:2 $\frac{8}{2}$

Write the missing number in each proportion.

7. $\frac{4}{n} = \frac{6}{9}$

$n = 6$

8. $\frac{n}{8} = \frac{8}{16}$

$n = 4$

9. $\frac{9}{3} = \frac{n}{12}$

$n = 36$

10. $\frac{4}{8} = \frac{2}{n}$

$n = 4$

Use the scale and a metric ruler to write the actual dimensions of this figure.

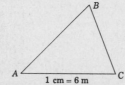

1 cm = 6 m

11. $\overline{AB}$ __24 m__

12. The perimeter of ABC is __66 m__.

Write each number as a percent.

13. $0.15 =$ __15%__ 14. $\frac{15}{100} =$ __15%__ 15. $39:100 =$ __39%__ 16. 25 out of 100 = __25%__

Write each percent as a fraction in simplest terms.

17. $30\% = \frac{3}{10}$ 18. $25\% = \frac{1}{4}$ 19. $84\% = \frac{21}{25}$ 20. $6\% = \frac{3}{50}$

Write each fraction as a percent. Round to the nearest whole-number percent, if necessary.

21. $\frac{3}{5} =$ __60%__ 22. $\frac{2}{3} =$ __67%__ 23. $\frac{1}{8} =$ __13%__ 24. $\frac{7}{25} =$ __28%__

Write the part represented by each percent.

25. 16% of 80 = __12.8__ 26. 30% of 246 = __73.8__ 27. 5% of \$235 = __\$11.75__

MCP All rights reserved

Circle the letter of the correct answer.

1 7,248
+ 29,756

  a 36,004
  b 36,994
  ⓒ 37,004
  d NG

2 54,302
− 19,658

  ⓐ 34,644
  b 34,654
  c 45,356
  d NG

3 86 × 53

  a 688
  ⓑ 4,558
  c 43,258
  d NG

4 15)7,250

  a 476
  b 477
  c 476 R1
  ⓓ NG

5 $3\frac{3}{4}$
+ $5\frac{1}{2}$

  a $8\frac{1}{4}$
  b $8\frac{2}{3}$
  ⓒ $9\frac{1}{4}$
  d NG

6 $14\frac{1}{3}$
− $9\frac{3}{4}$

  ⓐ $4\frac{7}{12}$
  b $5\frac{3}{12}$
  c $5\frac{7}{12}$
  d NG

7 $2\frac{1}{3} \div \frac{5}{9}$

  a $\frac{7}{27}$
  b $1\frac{8}{27}$
  ⓒ $4\frac{1}{5}$
  d NG

8 2.079
+ 8.16

  a 10.23
  b 10.139
  ⓒ 10.239
  d NG

9 21.2
− 8.346

  ⓐ 12.854
  b 12.946
  c 27.146
  d NG

10 3.2
× 0.06

  ⓐ 0.192
  b 1.92
  c 19.2
  d NG

11 4.96 ÷ 3.1

  a 0.16
  ⓑ 1.6
  c 16
  d NG

12 Find the measure of
∠ABC.

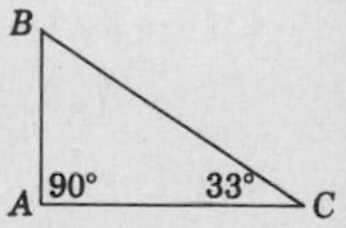

(triangle with vertex B at top, A at bottom left with 90°, C at bottom right with 33°)

  a 33°
  b 45°
  ⓒ 57°
  d NG

☐ score

316

Cumulative Review

page 316

Item	Objectives
1	Add two numbers up to 5-digits (See pages 27-28)
2	Subtract two 5-digit numbers, zero in minuend (See pages 35-36)
3	Multiply two 2-digit factors (See pages 57-58)
4	Divide a 4-digit by 2-digit number, quotient with remainder (See pages 107-108)
5	Add two mixed numbers (See pages 175-176)
6	Subtract two mixed numbers (See pages 179-180)
7	Divide a mixed number by a fraction (See pages 201-202)
8	Add decimals (See pages 223-224)
9	Subtract decimals (See pages 225-226)
10	Multiply decimals (See pages 237-238)
11	Divide a decimal by tenths (See pages 247-248)
12	Find the third angle measure of triangles when two are known (See pages 273-274)

Alternate Cumulative Review

Circle the letter of the correct answer.

1 8,694
+ 39,317

  a 47,011
  ⓑ 48,011
  c 48,911
  d NG

2 65,075
− 28,496

  ⓐ 36,579
  b 36,679
  c 36,689
  d NG

3 83
× 36

  a 2,878
  b 2,888
  ⓒ 2,988
  d NG

4 13)9427

  a 725
  b 725 R1
  c 726
  ⓓ NG

5 $16\frac{1}{3}$
+ $4\frac{3}{4}$

  a $20\frac{1}{12}$
  b 21
  ⓒ $21\frac{1}{12}$
  d NG

6 $18\frac{9}{10}$
− $7\frac{5}{6}$

  a $11\frac{1}{30}$
  ⓑ $11\frac{1}{15}$
  c $11\frac{2}{15}$
  d NG

7 $9\frac{1}{3} \div \frac{7}{14}$

  a $18\frac{13}{21}$
  b $18\frac{1}{3}$
  ⓒ $18\frac{2}{3}$
  d NG

8 4.098
+ 6.97

  a 10.968
  b 11.06
  ⓒ 11.068
  d NG

9 36.2
− 19.756

  ⓐ 16.444
  b 16.452
  c 16.558
  d NG

10 4.9
× 0.07

  ⓐ 0.343
  b 3.43
  c 34.3
  d NG

11 5.3)9.54

  a 0.18
  ⓑ 1.8
  c .18
  d NG

12 Write $\frac{6}{10}$ as a percent.

  a 6%
  ⓑ 60%
  c 66%
  d NG

316

Tallies and Bar Graphs

pages 317-318

Objective

· To use tallies and bar graphs

Materials

large-squared graph paper

Mental Math

Have students identify the larger fraction:

1. ½ or ⅓ (½)
2. ⅔ or ¼ (⅔)
3. ½ or ⁴⁄₈ (equal)
4. ⅕ or ²⁄₆ (²⁄₆)
5. ⁹⁄₁₀₀ or ¹⁄₁₀ (¹⁄₁₀)
6. ⅝ or ¾ (¾)
7. ⅜ or ¾ (¾)

Skill Review

Survey the class to see how many students are wearing blue. Have students raise their hands and keep track of the numbers on the board with a tally. Survey the class to see how many are wearing red and have each student tally those results.

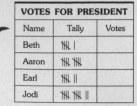

Understanding Tallies and Bar Graphs

The fifth grade class voted for president. Complete the bar graph to show the results of the election. Who won the vote?

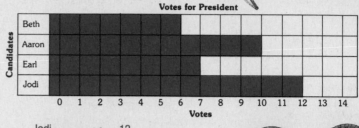

VOTES FOR PRESIDENT		
Name	Tally	Votes
Beth	~~IIII~~ I	
Aaron	~~IIII~~ ~~IIII~~	
Earl	~~IIII~~ II	
Jodi	~~IIII~~ ~~IIII~~ II	

___Jodi___ won with ___12___ votes.

Getting Started

Use the bar graph to answer these questions.

1. How many votes did Aaron receive?
   ___10___

2. How many more votes did Jodi receive than Beth? ___6___

3. How many students voted?
   ___35___

4. How many less votes did Earl get than Aaron? ___3___

Use this tally to complete the graph.

5.

Favorite Color	
Blue	~~IIII~~ IIII
Red	~~IIII~~ ~~IIII~~ ~~IIII~~ II
Green	~~IIII~~ ~~IIII~~ III

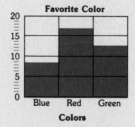

MCP All rights reserved

317

Teaching the Lesson

Introducing the Problem Read the problem aloud and ask students to look at the tally in their texts. Have students count the votes and put results in the right-hand column. Show students the bar graph that has been started. Have students use a straightedge to line up 6 along the horizontal axis with the end of Beth's bar to show that they match. Have students complete the bar graph. Suggest they use a ruler if they need help lining up the bars with the numbers. Have a student read the solution sentence. (Jodi won with 12 votes.) Ask students whether it is easier to read the results more quickly from the tally, numbers or graph. (graph)

Developing the Skill Show students how to label a graph. Explain that there are two axes in every graph: vertical and horizontal. Point out that each axis must be labeled. In the model problem the vertical axis is labeled Candidates, the horizontal, Votes. In addition, one axis will have numbers along it. Sometimes all the numbers are listed. Sometimes the graph will show every other number or every tenth number depending upon the data. Explain that before they label an axis, they will read the numbers to find the high and low. Their scale must accommodate these numbers.

317

Practice

Use this tally to complete the bar graph and answer these questions.

1.

Favorite Kind of TV Show	
Drama	IIII
Comedy	⊮ IIII
Sports	⊮ ⊮ II
Movies	⊮ III
Cartoons	⊮ ⊮ II

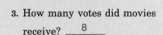

Favorite Kind of TV Show

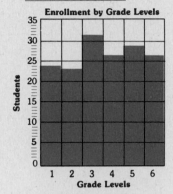

2. How many votes did comedy receive? __9__

3. How many votes did movies receive? __8__

4. How many votes were taken? __45__

5. Which shows received the most votes? sports and cartoons

Use this tally to complete the bar graph.

6.

Enrollment by Grade Levels	
1	⊮ ⊮ ⊮ ⊮ IIII
2	⊮ ⊮ ⊮ ⊮ III
3	⊮ ⊮ ⊮ ⊮ ⊮ ⊮ I
4	⊮ ⊮ ⊮ ⊮ ⊮ I
5	⊮ ⊮ ⊮ ⊮ ⊮ IIII
6	⊮ ⊮ ⊮ ⊮ ⊮ I

Enrollment by Grade Levels

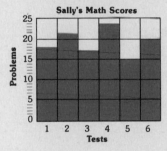

Apply

Use the given information to complete the bar graph.

7. Mr. Phillips gave 6 tests in math. Each test had 25 problems. Sally had scores of 18, 21, 17, 24, 15 and 20.

Sally's Math Scores

318

Correcting Common Errors

Some students may not draw the bars the correct length because they do not read the scale correctly and think that each square represents one. Encourage them to check the scale on the graph before they begin interpreting the bars.

Enrichment

Have students do research to find the populations of the five most populated countries in the world. (These will include China, India, former U.S.S.R. and the U.S.A. The fifth varies with the year of census.) Ask them to make a bar graph illustrating these figures. Suggest a vertical scale that shows population in millions. (100, 200, 300 million and so on)

Practice

Have students complete all the problems. Suggest that students use a straightedge to complete the bar graphs.

Extra Credit *Applications*

Duplicate or write the following on the board. Tell students to fill in the blanks in the puzzle, and the first letters reading down will name a famous mathematician. (Pythagoras)

(<u>P</u> <u>e</u> <u>r</u> <u>i</u> <u>m</u> <u>e</u> <u>t</u> <u>e</u> <u>r</u>) The distance around a rectangle.

(<u>y</u> <u>e</u> <u>a</u> <u>r</u>) 365 days make one __?__ .

(<u>t</u> <u>h</u> <u>r</u> <u>e</u> <u>e</u>) In what base does 11 mean four?

(<u>h</u> <u>a</u> <u>l</u> <u>f</u>) 9 is __?__ of 18.

(<u>a</u> <u>s</u> <u>s</u> <u>o</u> <u>c</u> <u>i</u> <u>a</u> <u>t</u> <u>i</u> <u>v</u> <u>e</u>) What law says $(3 + 2) + 4 = 3 + (2 + 4)$?

(<u>g</u> <u>r</u> <u>e</u> <u>a</u> <u>t</u> <u>e</u> <u>r</u>) > means "is __?__ than."

(<u>o</u> <u>r</u> <u>d</u> <u>e</u> <u>r</u>) 5, 9, 11, 23, 30 are written in increasing __?__ .

(<u>r</u> <u>e</u> <u>c</u> <u>i</u> <u>p</u> <u>r</u> <u>o</u> <u>c</u> <u>a</u> <u>l</u>) $\frac{2}{3}$ is the __?__ of $\frac{3}{2}$.

(<u>a</u> <u>r</u> <u>o</u> <u>u</u> <u>n</u> <u>d</u>) Circumference is the distance __?__ a circle.

(<u>s</u> <u>i</u> <u>m</u> <u>i</u> <u>l</u> <u>a</u> <u>r</u>) Triangles with equal angles are __?__ .

Mean and Median

pages 319-320

Objective

To find the mean and median of a set of numbers

Materials

Mental Math

Have students round these to the nearest thousand:

1. 32,953 (33,000)
2. 596,201 (596,000)
3. 4,452 (4,000)
4. 921 (1,000)
5. 1,421,001 (1,421,000)
6. 56,721 (57,000)
7. 206,526 (207,000)

Skill Review

Have students copy and do the following addition:

1. 21 + 59 + 36 + 42 + 25 = (183)
2. 142 + 151 + 182 + 149 + 149 = (773)
3. 255 + 143 + 229 + 196 + 202 = (1,025)
4. 15 + 13 + 17 + 17 + 14 + 15 = (91)
5. 62 + 52 + 65 + 70 + 59 = (308)

Finding the Mean and Median

Two statistics that help to understand the meaning of numbers are the mean and the median. The **mean** is the average score and the **median** is the middle score. What is the mean and median score for the Lincoln football team this year?

LINCOLN FOOTBALL TEAM	
Game	Points Scored
1	36
2	53
3	42
4	58
5	45
6	40
7	48

To find the mean,
we find the sum of the scores.

$$36 + 53 + 42 + 58 + 45 + 40 + 48 = \underline{\quad 322 \quad}$$

We divide by the number of scores.

$$\underline{\quad 322 \quad} \div \underline{\quad 7 \quad} = \underline{\quad 46 \quad}.$$

The mean score is ____46____.

To find the median,
we list the scores from lowest to highest.

36, 40, 42, 45, 48, 53, 58

We select the middle score. If there are an even number of scores, the median is the mean of the two middle scores.

The median score is ____45____.

Getting Started

Find the mean and median of each set of numbers.

1. 16, 27, 19, 23, 25

   mean ____22____

   median ____23____

2. 109, 130, 114, 106, 121, 116

   mean ____116____

   median ____115____

3. 86, 79, 105, 58, 97

   mean ____85____

   median ____86____

4. 74, 82, 68, 87, 54, 62, 66, 83

   mean ____72____

   median ____71____

5. $7.12, $7.86, $8.45, $12.81, $3.01

   mean ____$7.85____

   median ____$7.86____

6. 13,747, 11,985, 15,002

   mean ____13,578____

   median ____13,747____

MCP All rights reserved

319

Teaching the Lesson

Introducing the Problem Read the problem aloud. Explain how to find the mean while reading the accompanying section in the text. Have a student copy the scores on the board and add. (322) Have another student divide that score by the number of scores that were added. (322 ÷ 7 = 46) Explain that the mean score is 46, or the average of all the scores. Point out that this is sometimes called the **arithmetic mean.** Now explain that the median is the middle score, as you read the accompanying material in the text. Have a student list the scores on the board, arranging them from lowest to highest. Ask one student to find the middle score. (45) Read the solution sentence. (median score, 45)

Developing the Skill Put the following set on the board: **57, 88, 89, 91, 95, 98, 98.** Tell students these are sample test scores. Have them look at the scores and estimate an average score. (Answers will vary but should be around 90.) Have them then find the average by adding the scores and dividing by the number of scores. (88) Then have them find the median, or middle score. (91) Explain that the mean and median are not the same because the mean is an average, pulled down by the lowest score, 57. Take away the low score and have students find the new mean. (93)

Practice

Find the mean and median of each set of numbers.

1. 65, 70, 72, 93

mean ___75___

median ___71___

2. 145, 176, 153, 126

mean ___150___

median ___149___

3. $6.40, $2.40, $3.18, $9.85, $4.57

mean ___$5.28___

median ___$4.57___

4. 88, 96, 75, 97, 84

mean ___88___

median ___88___

5. 24, 35, 22, 29, 59, 48, 52, 43

mean ___39___

median ___39___

6. $1.18, $2.48, $1.96, $4.51, $3.12

mean ___$2.65___

median ___$2.48___

Apply

Use the table of students' heights to answer 7 through 11.

7. Who is the tallest? ___Rich___

8. Who is the shortest? ___Marcia___

9. How much taller is Diane than Tim? ___8 cm___

10. What is the mean height? ___150 cm___

11. What is the median height? ___152 cm___

Selected Students' Heights	
Pupil	**Height in cm**
Vince	152
Diane	154
Marcia	143
Tim	146
Rich	155

Complete the bar graph of the pupils' heights.

12.

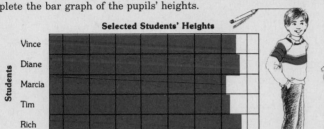

Selected Students' Heights

Students: Vince, Diane, Marcia, Tim, Rich

Height in Centimeters: 20 40 60 80 100 120 140 160

320

Correcting Common Errors

Some students may confuse mean and median. Put a number line on the chalkboard from 30 to 60. Have different volunteers come to the board and circle the following on the line: 45, 52, 39, 51, and 48. Ask students which is the middle number. (48) Mark it with an arrow. Discuss how "middle score" and "median" mean the same thing. Then have students find the average. (47) Discuss how the average, or mean, is the number that, if all the numbers were this number, the sum would be the same.

Enrichment

Have students create a set of numbers for each of these:

1. the mean of the set is higher than the median (sets will be weighted at the upper end)
2. the mean is lower than the median (sets will be weighted at the lower end)
3. the mean and median are the same

Practice

Have students complete all the problems on the page. Remind them to align columns carefully when adding.

Extra Credit *Estimation*

Duplicate or put the following on the board:
Estimate and circle the problem in each group that would give the answer.

1. 55 =
   a. 6 + 97
   b. 15 × 25
   c. 100 ÷ 25
   ⓓ 184 − 129

2. 106 =
   ⓐ 636 ÷ 6
   b. 77 + 87
   c. 136 − 68
   d. 26 × 6

3. 472 =
   a. 75 + 233 + 115
   ⓑ 1,289 − 817
   c. 174 × 3
   d. 1,860 ÷ 5

4. around 400
   a. 12 + 12
   b. 12 × 418
   ⓒ 12 × 34

Then have students check their estimations with calculators. Encourage them to create similar problems to exchange with a partner.

320

Line Graphs

pages 321-322

Objective

To interpret line graphs

Materials

graph paper

Mental Math

Have students multiply:

1. $\frac{1}{2} \times \frac{1}{3} = (\frac{1}{6})$
2. $\frac{1}{3} \times \frac{2}{3} = (\frac{2}{9})$
3. $1 \times \frac{1}{7} = (\frac{1}{7})$
4. $\frac{2}{5} \times \frac{1}{2} = (\frac{2}{10} = \frac{1}{5})$
5. $\frac{1}{3} \times \frac{1}{5} = (\frac{1}{15})$
6. $\frac{3}{4} \times \frac{1}{2} = (\frac{3}{8})$
7. $\frac{5}{6} \times \frac{1}{2} = (\frac{5}{12})$

Skill Review

Have students make a bar graph using this information:

Time to run 50 Yards

Noah	6.5 sec
Sue	7.0 sec
Amy	6.4 sec
Ron	7.1 sec
Eli	6.4 sec

(Suggest a vertical scale from 6.0 to 7.5 and divided into tenths.)

Understanding Line Graphs

The high and low average temperatures in San Francisco stay about the same throughout the year. In which months is the difference between them 20 degrees or more?

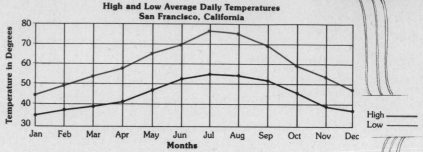

High and Low Average Daily Temperatures San Francisco, California

We want to examine the range of the high and low temperatures. To find the range, we subtract the low temperature for the month from the high temperature for the month.

January	$45° - 35° = \underline{10°}$	July	$\underline{77°} - \underline{55°} = \underline{22°}$
February	$50° - 37° = \underline{13°}$	August	$\underline{76°} - \underline{54°} = \underline{22°}$
March	$54° - 39° = \underline{15°}$	September	$\underline{70°} - \underline{52°} = \underline{18°}$
April	$58° - 41° = \underline{17°}$	October	$\underline{60°} - \underline{46°} = \underline{14°}$
May	$66° - 47° = \underline{19°}$	November	$\underline{54°} - \underline{39°} = \underline{15°}$
June	$70° - 53° = \underline{17°}$	December	$\underline{47°} - \underline{37°} = \underline{10°}$

The difference in the temperatures is 20 degrees or more during the months of ___July and August___ .

✔ In a multi-line graph, it is important to use the code provided with the graph to interpret the lines correctly.

Getting Started

Use the line graph of average daily temperatures to answer 1 and 2.

1. Between which months is the high temperature increasing the most?

   April, May

2. Between which months is the low temperature decreasing the most?

   October, November

MCP All rights reserved

321

Teaching the Lesson

Introducing the Problem Read the problem aloud and ask students to examine the graph in their texts. Have them find the correspondence between numbers in the table and those on the line graph. Show students that when the points are connected, they show a trend of rising temperatures in the summer. Explain that to understand the two lines, they have to read the code in the lower right hand corner. Have a student explain the code. (One line represents the average daily high; the other, the average daily low.) Explain that the difference between the high and low numbers is called the **range.** Have students subtract to find the range for each month, January through July. Have them read the high and low temperatures for each month, July through December, and then find the range. Read the solution sentence. (during July and August)

Developing the Skill Give students graph paper and write the following on the board showing the number of cafeteria lunches served: **Monday, 46; Tuesday, 52; Wednesday, 48; Thursday, 55; Friday, 45.** Help students make a line graph of this data, labeling the axes, finding the points, and connecting the points. Have them put the days along the horizontal axis, lunches served on the vertical axis. Show them that because the high and low numbers to be included are 55 and 45, the vertical scale should be from 40 to 60.

Practice

Use the line graph of this year's snowfall to answer 1 through 3.

This Year's Winter Snowfall

1. How much snow fell in January?

   ___10 cm___

2. How much more snow fell in February than October? ___9 cm___

3. What two months had the greatest snowfall? _Dec. and Feb._

Use the line graph of the bike sale contest to answer 4 through 7.

Six-Week Bike Sale Contest

4. How many bikes did Ben sell in the first week? ___10___

5. Which week did Ben and Frank sell a total of 26 bikes?

   Week 3 or 6

6. Who reached sales of 50 bikes first? ___Frank___

7. Who won the contest? ___Ben___

Apply

Angie recorded the temperatures each two hours during the school day. Complete this line graph showing the temperatures during school.

8.

Temperature During School	
Time	Temperature
8:00	57°
10:00	63°
12:00	73°
2:00	75°
4:00	62°

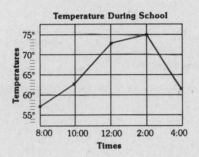

Temperature During School

9. Find the mean and median of the temperatures that Angie recorded.

   mean ___66°___ median ___63°___

322

Correcting Common Errors

Some students may not properly align the point on the graph with the point on the scale when they are interpreting a line graph. Have them use the straight edge of a ruler or piece of paper to align the point on the graph with its corresponding point on the scale.

Enrichment

Show students the Dow Jones Stock Average for 30 industrial stocks in the newspaper.
Have them make a line graph of the closing average over the course of a week. Explain that there will be listings for days the stock market is open (Monday through Friday) and that the averages are reported at the end of the day. The Dow Jones Industrial Average is also heard on the evening news.

Practice

Have students complete the practice problems.

Mixed Practice

1. $16 \div 2\frac{2}{3}$ (6)
2. $1,000 \times 358$ (358,000)
3. 2.17×5.4 (11.718)
4. $\frac{4}{5} =$ ___% (80)
5. $8 \times 71,364$ (570,912)
6. $217.28 + 16.5 + 108.109$ (341.889)
7. $35.140 \div 5$ (7.028)
8. $1,278.5 - 969.381$ (309.119)
9. $\$403.07 - \$136.26$ ($266.81)
10. $\frac{3}{5} \times \frac{10}{21}$ $\left(\frac{2}{7}\right)$

Extra Credit *Probability*

Remind students that the factorial of the number **n** is the product of all the numbers from 1 through n. Factorials can be used to find the number of ways a set of objects can be arranged. This is called the number of permutations. Explain that 3 objects can be arranged in 6 different ways. (3! = 6) Give each group of 2 students a set of colored blocks: one red, one blue and one yellow. Let them arrange them in as many ways as possible. (RBY, RYB, BYR, BRY, YBR, YRB) Now add a green block and let them show that the number of different ways the four blocks can be arranged is 4! (24). Suggest that they record each different arrangement on paper in some abbreviated way. (RYGB, RYBG, . . . for example) Now ask students how many different ways five books could be arranged on a shelf. (5! = 120)

322

Circle Graphs

pages 323-324

Objective

To interpret circle graphs representing percents

Materials

Mental Math

Have students make change for these amounts from $1.00:

1. $.50 ($.50)
2. $.25 ($.75)
3. $.35 ($.65)
4. $.79 ($.21)
5. $.58 ($.42)
6. $.49 ($.51)
7. $.99 ($.01)

Skill Review

Have students review finding a percent of a whole number. Have them round to the nearest whole number.

1. 25% of 120 (30)
2. 30% of 150 (45)
3. 21% of 75 (16)
4. 15% of 90 (14)
5. 50% of 200 (100)
6. 40% of 2,200 (880)
7. 80% of 350 (280)

Understanding Circle Graphs

Mr. Smith has $1,650 to budget for household expenses each month. How much money does Mr. Smith budget for family entertainment?

MR. SMITH'S MONTHLY BUDGET

We want to find the amount the Smiths put aside for entertainment each month.

The total monthly budget is ___$1,650___.

The percent budgeted for entertainment is ___5%___.

To find the amount to be used for entertainment, we multiply the total budget by the percent used for that purpose.

We multiply ___$1,650___ by ___0.05___.

$$\begin{array}{r} \$1,650 \\ \times\quad 0.05 \\ \hline \$82.50 \end{array}$$

The amount budgeted for entertainment is ___$82.50___.

Getting Started

Use the circle graph of Mr. Smith's monthly budget to answer 1 through 8.

1. What is the largest amount of money budgeted for? ___rent___

2. What percent is budgeted for savings? ___20%___

3. How much is budgeted for food? ___15%___

4. How much money is budgeted for rent? ___$660___

5. What percent is budgeted for food and utilities? ___23%___

6. How much more money is spent on savings than on entertainment? ___$247.50___

7. What is the sum of all the percents shown on the graph? ___100%___

8. What is the sum of all the amounts budgeted? ___$1,650___

MCP All rights reserved

323

Teaching the Lesson

Introducing the Problem Have a student read the problem aloud and ask the rest to look at the circle graph in their texts. Have a student read the information sentences. Explain that to find the amount budgeted for entertainment, they must find 5% of $1,650. This means multiplying the total by the decimal equivalent of 5%, or 0.05. Read the plan sentences. (Multiply $1,650 by 0.05.) Have a student do the multiplication on the board.

Developing the Skill Explain that a circle is often used to illustrate a whole amount. In the model problem the whole is the monthly budget. Put this graph on the board:

Total population of Pleasant Street School: 500 students

| Boys 48% | Girls 52% |

Show students that this represents the number of boys and girls in a school. Explain that to calculate the number of boys or girls, they will have to multiply the total number of students by the decimal equivalent of the percent. Ask students to list the percents and calculate the number of boys and girls. (boys: 48%, 240 students; girls: 52%, 260 students)

Practice

Enrique earns $460 each month. Use the circle graph representing his budget to answer 1 through 5.

1. What is the total of the percents shown on the graph? __100%__

2. Which item is budgeted for the most money? __savings__

Enrique's Budget

3. How much is saved each month? __$115__

4. How much more money is spent on food than clothing? __$9.20__

5. How much money is spent on entertainment and food? __$193.20__

A poll of 3,000 adults was taken to find their favorite recreation. Use the circle graph of the results to answer 6 through 10.

6. What percent chose skiing? __5%__

7. How many people chose skiing? __150__

Favorite Recreations

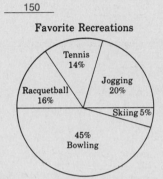

8. What was the favorite recreation? __Bowling__

9. How many more people chose racquetball than tennis? __60__

10. What fraction of the people polled chose jogging? __$\frac{1}{5}$__

EXCURSION

You want to tile a rectangular patio so that there is no space between tiles and no overlapping. Can this be done with a tile that is quadrilateral having no two sides the same length? __Yes__. To prove your answer, draw and cut out a quadrilateral with no sides equal and use it to trace copies to show the pattern of your tiling. The tile may be flipped or rotated if necessary.

Some students may answer some of the questions concerning a circle graph incorrectly because they do not compute with percents correctly. Have them write the following steps on an index card as a guide to finding the percent of a number.

1. change the percent to a decimal.
2. multiply, counting the decimal places in the factors.
3. put the decimal point in the product.

Enrichment

Circle graphs are sometimes drawn in a way that superimposes part of it on a picture that is the subject of the graph. A graph of world population could be shown within a world globe, for example.

Ask students to look in the newspaper or in magazines to find examples of such a graph.

Practice

Have students complete the practice problems. Remind them that to change a percent to a fraction, they write the percent over 100, drop the % sign and simplify if necessary.

Excursion

Have students cut out quadrilaterals in different-colored paper to test the theory and make a creative design. Display the finished products.

Extra Credit *Geometry*

Give each student a piece of heavy paper or light cardboard, a ruler, a pencil, a needle and colored thread. Have them use the ruler to draw an angle on the paper with each side ten inches long. Tell them to mark the sides in half-inch intervals, starting from the vertex and number them as shown. Have them connect like points—1 to 1, 2 to 2 and so on—with thread.

Explain that the shape resulting from this curve stitching is called a **parabola**.

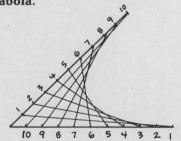

Ordered Pairs

pages 325-326

Objective

To locate and name points on a graph for ordered pairs

Materials

graph paper

Mental Math

Have students subtract:

1. $23 - 9 = (14)$
2. $58 - 18 = (40)$
3. $67 - 33 = (34)$
4. $100 - 67 = (33)$
5. $83 - 58 = (25)$
6. $75 - 24 = (51)$
7. $99 - 50 = (49)$

Skill Review

Have students draw a line graph illustrating this information:

Cartons of Milk Bought

Monday	48
Tuesday	49
Wednesday	51
Thursday	46
Friday	50

Have them find the median number (49) and the mean (49).

Graphing Ordered Pairs

Ordered pairs are used to locate points on a grid. The pair (2, 4) names the point A. We write: A(2, 4). What ordered pair names point I?

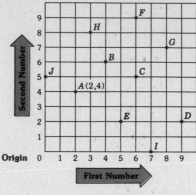

To find the ordered pair for point I, begin at the **origin** or 0. The first number tells how far to the right to go. The second number tells how far up the grid to go.

Point I is __7__ to the right and __0__ up.

The ordered pair for point I is __7, 0__.

Getting Started

Use the grid above to complete 1 through 8.

1. B(__4__, __6__)   2. D(__9__, __2__)   3. G(__8__, __7__)   4. J(__0__, __5__)

Write the letter for each ordered pair.

5. __C__ (6, 5)   6. __F__ (6, 9)   7. __E__ (5, 2)   8. __H__ (3, 8)

Locate and label each point on grid A.

9. W(5, 4)   10. X(4, 5)

11. Y(0, 3)   12. Z(7, 2)

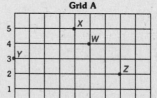

Grid A

MCP All rights reserved

325

Teaching the Lesson

Introducing the Problem Read the problem aloud and ask students to examine the illustration in their texts. Explain that **ordered pair** means that the location of the numbers within the pair makes a difference. The first number refers to a distance along the horizontal axis; the second, a distance along the vertical axis. Ask a student to give the horizontal distance for point I. (7) Ask another to read the vertical distance. (0) Read the information sentence aloud. Have a student read the solution sentence.

Developing the Skill Draw this grid on the board:

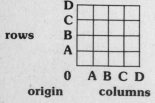

ordered pair = (column, row)

Point to different spots on the grid and ask students to name the location, listing the column and then the row. Explain that each pair of letters is an ordered pair and identifies a specific place on the grid. Point out that the same idea is used to make graphs, but each axis has numbers instead of letters. In each ordered pair, the first number refers to horizontal distance, the second to vertical distance. Together, they are called **coordinates** for a point on the graph.

Use grid X to complete 1 through 16. Write the ordered pair for each point.

1. C(_2_, _7_)   2. E(_10_, _0_)

3. K(_10_, _10_)   4. X(_1_, _1_)

5. F(_8_, _7_)   6. A(_5_, _5_)

7. M(_7_, _9_)   8. H(_0_, _4_)

9. D(_4_, _1_)   10. Z(_10_, _5_)

Write the letter for each ordered pair.

11. _G_ (9, 9)   12. _Y_ (3, 7)

13. _N_ (6, 2)   14. _I_ (3, 3)

15. _W_ (0, 8)   16. _J_ (4, 9)

17. _F_ (8, 7)   18. _L_ (9, 2)

Grid X

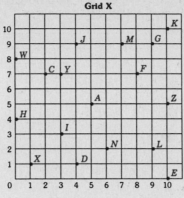

Use grid Y to complete 19 through 28. Locate and label each point on Grid Y.

19. A(2, 7)   20. B(9, 6)

21. C(0, 5)   22. D(4, 4)

23. E(7, 4)   24. F(8, 2)

25. G(1, 8)   26. H(6, 0)

27. I(3, 3)   28. J(5, 1)

Grid Y

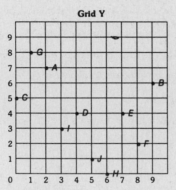

Apply

Use grid Z to complete 29 and 30.

29. Locate and label the following points on the grid: A(2, 2), B(3, 5), C(6, 5) and D(7, 2).

30. Draw $\overline{AB}$, $\overline{BC}$, $\overline{CD}$ and $\overline{DA}$ on the grid. What figure is formed?

Grid Z

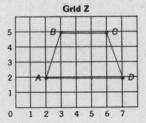

326

Correcting Common Errors

Some students may reverse "over" and "up" when graphing an ordered pair. Have them work with partners, taking turns, to graph ordered pairs that form simple patterns. For example, (4, 3), (4, 4), (4, 5), and (4, 6) lie on a vertical line; (2, 7), (3, 7), (4, 7), and (5, 7) lie on a horizontal line.

Enrichment

Give students a road map. Show them how to find a city in the index and use the letter or letter/number coordinates to find the city on the map. Ask them to choose a dozen cities and make an index to those cities, listing each city with its coordinates.

Practice

Have students complete the problems. Have them refer to the sample grid on the board.

Extra Credit *Applications*

Duplicate the following for each student: Circle the part of each problem that illustrates the term.

1. Subtrahend
   46
   −③⑦
   9

2. Multiplicand
   ㉟
   ×5
   175

3. Product
   35
   ×5
   ⑰⑤

4. Divisor
   51 ÷ ③ = 17

5. Quotient
   144 ÷ 12 = ⑫

6. Dividend
   ㉜ ÷ 8 = 4

7. Exponent
   3⁽³⁾ = 3 × 3 ×
   3 = 27

8. Numerator
   ③
   8

9. Denominator
   5
   ⑯

10. Proper Fraction
    ③   5
    ⑤   2

11. Improper Fraction
    3   ④
    8   ③

12. Mixed Number
    3   1¼   3
    8

Probability

Objective

To find probability using sets of objects

Materials

*3 red, 1 blue and 2 black counters

Mental Math

Have students find the cost:

1. 5 items at $2 each ($10)
2. 3 items at $11 each ($33)
3. 2 items at $1.50 each ($3)
4. 10 items at $2.39 each ($23.90)
5. 8 items at $3 each ($24)
6. 15 items at $4 each ($60)
7. 6 items at $3.99 each ($23.94)

Skill Review

Have students write these ratios as fractions:

1. 4 out of 10 ($\frac{4}{10}$ or $\frac{2}{5}$)
2. 3:8 ($\frac{3}{8}$)
3. 7 to 11 ($\frac{7}{11}$)
4. 10:20 ($\frac{10}{20}$ or $\frac{1}{2}$)
5. 4 to 5 ($\frac{4}{5}$)
6. 6 to 9 ($\frac{6}{9}$ or $\frac{2}{3}$)
7. 11 out of 12 ($\frac{11}{12}$)

Understanding Probability

Su Linn is removing a marble from the box. There are 12 possible outcomes of different marbles she can take. Each marble has an equally likely chance to be taken. If Su Linn selects the color marble she wants, that is called a **favorable outcome.** Since there are 3 black marbles, the chance of a favorable outcome of taking a black marble is 3 out of 12. The **probability** of a certain event taking place is the ratio of favorable outcomes to the number of possible outcomes. The probability of taking a black marble is $\frac{3}{12}$ or $\frac{1}{4}$.

We write: $P(\text{black}) = \frac{1}{4}$.

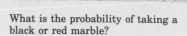

What is the probability of taking a striped marble?

There are __5__ striped marbles.

There are __12__ marbles altogether.

$$\frac{\text{favorable outcomes}}{\text{possible outcomes}} = \frac{\boxed{5}}{\boxed{12}}$$

$$P(\text{striped}) = \frac{\boxed{5}}{\boxed{12}}$$

What is the probability of taking a black or red marble?

There are __7__ black or red marbles.

There are __12__ marbles altogether.

$$\frac{\text{favorable outcomes}}{\text{possible outcomes}} = \frac{\boxed{7}}{\boxed{12}}$$

$$P(\text{black or red}) = \frac{\boxed{7}}{\boxed{12}}$$

Getting Started

Use the coins to write a ratio for each probability.

1. $P(\text{penny}) = \frac{3}{10}$
2. $P(\text{nickel}) = \frac{1}{5}$
3. $P(\text{dime}) = \frac{1}{2}$
4. $P(\text{penny or dime}) = \frac{4}{5}$
5. $P(\text{penny or nickel}) = \frac{1}{2}$
6. $P(\text{not dime}) = \frac{1}{2}$

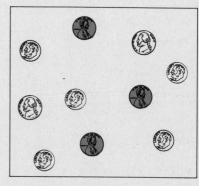

MCP All rights reserved

327

Teaching the Lesson

Introducing the Problem Read the problem aloud. Explain that probability is written P(event name), where the parenthetical description is of the desired outcome and is a ratio of favorable outcomes to total possible outcomes. Ask how many different ways there are of drawing a grey marble (5) and how many ways of drawing any marble. (12; 5 grey marbles, 12 marbles all together) Ask a student to write P(grey) on the board. ($\frac{5}{12}$) Now ask students to think about the probability of drawing a black or red marble. Ask how many ways there are to draw a black or red marble. (7, because there are a total of 7 black and red marbles) How many ways are there of drawing any marble? (12) Ask a student to write P(black or red) on the board. ($\frac{7}{12}$)

Developing the Skill Write these two definitions on the board:

$$\text{Probability} = \frac{\text{favorable outcomes}}{\text{possible outcomes}} \text{ or}$$

$$\frac{\text{specific outcome}}{\text{all outcomes}}$$

Explain that probabilities are ratios, comparing one way an event may occur to all the ways it may occur. Point out that a probability can give an idea of how likely a particular outcome is. Ask students how many ways there are of throwing a head with the toss of a penny (1), and how many possible outcomes there are to that toss. (2, head or tail) Ask the class to find P(head). ($\frac{1}{2}$)

327

Use the geometric figures to write a ratio for each probability.

1. $P(\text{triangle}) = \frac{3}{8}$

2. $P(\text{circle}) = \frac{1}{4}$

3. $P(\text{triangle or circle}) = \frac{5}{8}$

4. $P(\text{not circle}) = \frac{3}{4}$

5. $P(\text{rectangle}) = \frac{3}{8}$

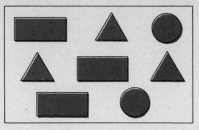

6. $P(\text{not triangle}) = \frac{5}{8}$

Use the letters to write a ratio for each probability.

7. $P(A) = \frac{2}{5}$

8. $P(B) = \frac{3}{10}$

9. $P(C) = \frac{1}{5}$

10. $P(D) = \frac{1}{10}$

11. $P(A \text{ or } B) = \frac{7}{10}$

13. $P(\text{not } C) = \frac{4}{5}$

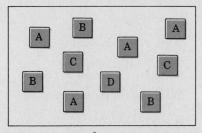

12. $P(C \text{ or } D) = \frac{3}{10}$

14. $P(A \text{ or } B \text{ or } C) = \frac{9}{10}$

Use the coins to write a ratio for each probability.

15. $P(\text{penny}) = \frac{1}{4}$

16. $P(\text{nickel}) = \frac{5}{12}$

17. $P(\text{dime or quarter}) = \frac{1}{3}$

18. $P(\text{not dime}) = \frac{5}{6}$

19. $P(\text{not quarter}) = \frac{5}{6}$

20. $P(\text{penny or quarter}) = \frac{5}{12}$

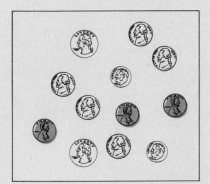

328

Correcting Common Errors

Some students may forget to count all the possibilities for a particular outcome and, as a result, always write a probability as "1 out of . . . ". When working a problem, have students first count to find all the possible outcomes and write this number. Then have them count to find all the outcomes that satisfy the given condition and write this number beside the other one. Now, tell them that they may use only the two numbers they have written to state the probability.

Enrichment

Have students describe these probabilities:

1. of drawing a heart from a deck of cards ($^{13}/_{52}$ or $\frac{1}{4}$)
2. of throwing a 3 on one die ($\frac{1}{6}$)
3. of drawing a 5 from a deck of cards ($^{4}/_{52}$ or $^{1}/_{13}$)

Practice

Have students complete the problems. Remind them that the letter or name in parentheses gives the event.

Mixed Practice

1. $500.21 - $396.56 ($103.65)
2. $13\frac{5}{9} + 47\frac{5}{6} \left(61\frac{7}{18}\right)$
3. $958 \times $3.03 ($2,902.74)
4. $\frac{5}{8}$ of 64 (40)
5. $4853 \div 93$ (52 R17)
6. 0.013×0.015 (.000195)
7. $1\frac{1}{5} \times 4\frac{1}{3} \left(5\frac{1}{5}\right)$
8. 75% of 16 (12)
9. $95 + 48 + 27 + 58$ (228)
10. $0.1728 \div 3.6$ (0.048)

Extra Credit *Probability*

Duplicate the following:

Insurance companies rely on probability theory to decide how much to charge for a policy.

Suppose you sold insurance policies to people who wanted to insure that it would not rain on their birthdays. If it did rain, they would collect $5.00. Have students list what information they need to know before writing such a rainy day policy. (Possible answers include: How many days does it rain in a year? When are those days likely to be? etc.) Have students check an almanac for weather information. Have students calculate how many people would need to buy the insurance so the company would not lose money.

328

Probability Outcomes

pages 329-330

Objective

To conduct probability experiments to determine outcomes

Materials

penny, dime and nickel
deck of cards

Mental Math

Have students multiply:

1. $2 \times 5 \times 4 = (40)$
2. $6 \times 1 \times 4 = (24)$
3. $5 \times 5 \times 2 = (50)$
4. $8 \times 5 \times 0 = (0)$
5. $2 \times 9 \times 2 = (36)$
6. $5 \times 4 \times 4 = (80)$
7. $2 \times 6 \times 5 = (60)$

Skill Review

Draw on the board: two pens, three pencils, one eraser and one paint brush.
Have students find the following probabilities:

1. P(pen) (²⁄₇)
2. P(paint brush) (¹⁄₇)
3. P(pen or pencil) (⁵⁄₇)
4. P(eraser) (¹⁄₇)

Determining Possible Outcomes

John tossed a penny and a nickel 20 times. He made a chart to show the possible outcomes of the tosses and he recorded his tosses. What ratios represent the following outcomes:

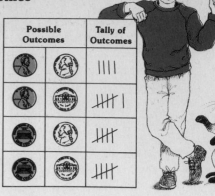

Possible Outcomes		Tally of Outcomes
(penny)	(nickel)	IIII
(penny)	(nickel)	ЖII ... I
(penny)	(nickel)	ЖII ...
(penny)	(nickel)	ЖII ...

two tails,
the penny showing heads and the nickel showing tails?

Both coins showing tails __5__

Total tosses __20__

Ratio __1 to 4__

The penny showing heads and the nickel showing tails __6__

Total tosses __20__

Ratio __3 to 10__

Getting Started

Toss a penny and a nickel 50 times and record your results. Write a simplified ratio representing each of the following:

1. Both coins show heads. _____

2. The penny shows heads and the nickel shows tails. _____

3. The penny shows tails and the nickel shows heads. _____

4. Both coins show tails. _____
Answers will vary.

Penny	Nickel	Tally
(penny)	(nickel)	
(penny)	(nickel)	
(nickel)	(penny)	
(nickel)	(penny)	

MCP All rights reserved

329

Teaching the Lesson

Introducing the Problem Read the problem aloud. Explain that there are four ways a toss might turn out. John could get penny/head and nickel/head or penny/head and nickel/tail or penny/tail and nickel/head or penny/tail and nickel/tail. Have students look at the table and ask them how many times John got penny/tail and nickel/tail. (5) Explain that the ratio of tossing two tails to total tosses is 5 to 20, or 1 to 4. Have students complete this section of their text. Ask a student to read from the chart the number of times he got penny/head with nickel/tail. (6) Have students complete this section of their text. (total tosses, 20; ratio, 6:20 or 3:10)

Developing the Skill Ask how many possible outcomes there are when tossing a coin. (2, head or tail) Flip one coin 20 times and have students keep tallies of the number of heads and of tails. Write the ratio of heads to total tosses, and the ratio of tails to total tosses. (Answers will vary.) Now add a second coin and ask how many ways the coins may fall. (four ways: head/head, head/tail, tail/head or tail/tail) Toss two different coins twenty times and have a student tally the results on the board. Ask volunteers to give the ratio of each specific result to the total tosses, 20. (Answers will vary.)

Toss three pennies 50 times. Record your results. Write a simplified ratio representing each.

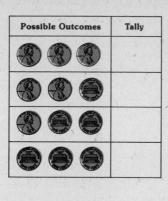

Possible Outcomes	Tally

1. 3 heads _____

2. 2 heads, 1 tail _____

3. 1 head, 2 tails _____

4. 3 tails _____

Answers will vary.

Toss 1 penny, 1 nickel and 1 dime one hundred times. Record your results.
Write a simplified ratio representing each of the following:

5. All coins show heads. _____

6. All coins show tails. _____

7. The penny shows heads.
   The nickel shows tails.
   The dime shows heads. _____

8. The dime shows heads. _____

9. The penny shows heads.
   The nickel shows tails. _____

10. The penny shows heads.
    The nickel shows tails.
    The dime shows tails. _____

11. The dime shows tails.
    The penny shows heads.
    The nickel shows heads. _____

12. The nickel shows heads.
    The other coins show tails. _____

13. The penny shows tails.
    The other coins show heads. _____
    Answers will vary.

Penny	Nickel	Dime	Tally

330

Correcting Common Errors

Some students will have difficulty understanding how probability experiments can determine different outcomes. Ask students what they think the results will be if you toss a coin 20 times. Most students are likely to say 10 heads and 10 tails. Have students work in pairs to toss a coin 20 times and record the results.

Discuss as a class how the results of the pairs tossing the coins compared with what they expected to happen.

Enrichment

Have students figure out how many possible results there are for the toss of four different coins. ($4 \times 3 \times 2 \times 1 = 24$) Suggest that they devise a shorthand for describing the different possibilities. (One way is to give each coin a place in an ordered set, and use the abbreviations H (head) and T (tail), for example: HHHH, HHHT, HHTT, HTTT, etc.) Have them toss four coins 50 times and record their results.

Practice

Have students complete all the problems. You may want students to work in pairs, with one tossing the coins and reading results to the other, who keeps a tally.

Extra Credit   *Statistics*

Bring in a bag of apples and a scale that will weigh the apples in ounces or grams. Have students work in groups and weigh each apple and record the results. Have students arrange the apples in order from the smallest to the largest. Now ask each student to find the range, the mode, the median and the mean using the data they have recorded.

Favorable Outcomes

pages 331-332

Objective

To calculate the probability of a particular event

Materials

dice
game spinner
coin

Mental Math

Have students identify the best measurement:

1. pencil: 7 ft, 7 in. or 7 mi (7 in.)
2. carton of milk: 8 oz, 8 gal or 8 qt (8 oz)
3. car: 3 oz, 30 lb or 3,000 lb (3,000 lb)
4. one month: 720 sec, 720 hr or 720 days (720 hr)

Skill Review

Have students write ratios describing the results of this experiment. Two coins were tossed a total of 25 times. The results were:

1. tail/tail ||||| || (7:25)
2. tail/head |||| (4:25)
3. head/tail ||||| | (6:25)
4. head/head ||||| ||| (8:25)

Determining Probability of Favorable Outcomes

Sammy listed the four possible outcomes when tossing a penny and a nickel. The probability of tossing a head on each coin is $\frac{1}{4}$. What is the probability of tossing one head and one tail?

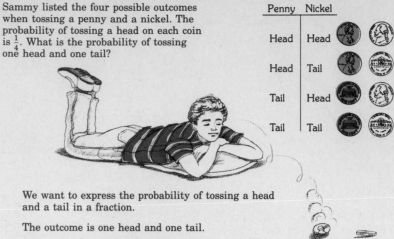

Penny	Nickel
Head	Head
Head	Tail
Tail	Head
Tail	Tail

We want to express the probability of tossing a head and a tail in a fraction.

The outcome is one head and one tail.

There are __2__ ways to get this favorable outcome.

There are __4__ possible outcomes.

$$P = \frac{\text{number of favorable outcomes}}{\text{total number of possible outcomes}}$$

$$P = \frac{2}{4} = \frac{1}{2}$$

The probability of tossing one head and one tail is $\frac{1}{2}$.

Getting Started

Write a fraction for the probability of each favorable outcome.

Activity	Possible Outcomes	Favorable Outcome	Probability
Toss a penny		1. heads	$P = \frac{1}{2}$
		2. tails	$P = \frac{1}{2}$
Spin the spinner.	1, 2, 3, 4	3. 1	$P = \frac{1}{4}$
		4. 1 or 3	$P = \frac{2}{4}$
		5. Number less than 3	$P = \frac{2}{4}$
		6. Number greater than 4	$P = \frac{0}{4}$

MCP All rights reserved

331

Teaching the Lesson

Introducing the Problem Have a student read the problem aloud. Have a student read the information sentences. Explain that the two ways of getting one head and one tail include penny/head and nickel/tail or penny/tail and nickel/head. Write the definition of the probability on the board and explain that it means that probabilities are written as fractional ratios, with the specific outcomes over the total number of outcomes. Ask students what the favorable outcome is in this case. (a head and a tail) Ask how many ways this may occur (2) and how many outcomes there are all together. (4) Write the probability of tossing a head and a tail on the board: **P(head and tail) = ²⁄₄ or ½.**

Developing the Skill Explain that they can predict the likelihood of a particular event by calculating all the ways the event can turn out in the desired way, and using that number as the numerator in a fraction that has the total possible outcomes as the denominator. Remind them of the simple coin toss, where the probability of tossing a head is ½. Show students a game spinner with 8 numbers. Ask them what the probability of spinning a 7 is. (⅛) Show students a die and ask what the probability of rolling a 2 would be (⅙); the probability of rolling a 3 or a 4. (²⁄₆ or ⅓)

Practice

Write a fraction for the probability for each favorable outcome.

Activity	Possible Outcomes	Favorable Outcomes	Probability
Spin the spinner.	1, 2, 3, 4, 5, 6, 7, 8	1. 2	$P = \frac{1}{8}$
		2. 4	$P = \frac{1}{8}$
		3. Number greater than 3	$P = \frac{5}{8}$
		4. 5 or 7	$P = \frac{1}{4}$
		5. Even number	$P = \frac{1}{2}$
		6. Number between 3 and 8	$P = \frac{1}{2}$

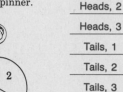

Activity	Possible Outcomes	Favorable Outcomes	Probability
Toss a dime and spin the spinner.	Heads, 1	7. Heads and a 3	$P = \frac{1}{6}$
	Heads, 2	8. Tails and a 2 or 3	$P = \frac{1}{3}$
	Heads, 3	9. Heads or tails and a 1 or a 3	$P = \frac{2}{3}$
	Tails, 1	10. Heads and an odd number	$P = \frac{1}{3}$
	Tails, 2	11. Heads and any number	$P = \frac{1}{2}$
	Tails, 3	12. Tails and a number greater than 1	$P = \frac{1}{3}$

Activity	Possible Outcomes	Favorable Outcomes	Probability
Spin two spinners.	1,1; 1,2; 1,3;	13. Both numbers are even.	$P = \frac{1}{6}$
	1,4; 2,1; 2,2;	14. Sum of the spin is 4.	$P = \frac{1}{4}$
	2,3; 2,4; 3,1;	15. Both numbers are the same.	$P = \frac{1}{4}$
	3,2; 3,3; 3,4		

332

Correcting Common Errors

When finding probability, some students may miss some of the possible outcomes because they are not listing them in an organized way. Have students work with partners to use 3 strips of white paper numbered from 1 to 3 and 3 strips of blue paper numbered 1 to 3. They are to pretend that they are selecting one white strip and one blue strip without looking. Have them write all the possible combinations that could be pairs with white number 1, then with white number 2, and finally white number 3.

Enrichment

Have students take a game that is based on drawing different cards from a pile. (examples include Candyland, Sorry or Uno) Have them sort the cards, list the different possibilities, and then calculate the probability of drawing each kind of card. (the number of that kind divided by the total number of cards) Answers will vary.

Practice

Have students complete the problems.

Mixed Practice

1. $\frac{3}{8} \times \frac{5}{9}$ $\left(\frac{5}{24}\right)$
2. $90,010 - 48,175$ $(41,835)$
3. $13\frac{3}{4} + 17\frac{5}{8} + 28\frac{5}{6}$ $\left(60\frac{5}{24}\right)$
4. $\frac{5}{9} \div 6$ $\left(\frac{5}{54}\right)$
5. $6 \times \$232.37$ $(\$1,394.22)$
6. $308.605 - 246.74$ (61.865)
7. 90% of 270 (243)
8. $9,856 \times 20$ $(197,120)$
9. $112\frac{5}{8} - 103\frac{5}{12}$ $\left(9\frac{5}{24}\right)$
10. $0.112 \div 4$ (0.028)

Extra Credit *Probability*

Another use for factorials (See page 322.) involves computing the number of different ways a few objects can be taken from a larger set. For example: license plates are made up of 5 numbers. There are ten possible digits (0 through 9) from which 5 will be drawn for each plate. Show students the formula for drawing r objects out of a set of n:

$$\text{Permutations} = \frac{n!}{(n-r)!}$$

Have students find the number of 5-digit license plates possible using the 10 numbers, 0 through 9. (30, 240; less than the total number of 5-digit numbers because no repeated digits are allowed) Have students calculate the number of 3-digit numbers that can be made from a set of 8 different digits. $[8!/(8-3)! = 8!/5! = 8 \times 7 \times 6 = 336]$

Tree Diagrams

pages 333-334

Objective

To draw tree diagrams to show possible outcomes

Materials

1 red, 1 blue and 1 yellow counter

Mental Math

Ask students to solve for n:

1. 50% + 30% + n = 100%
   (n = 20%)
2. 25% + 25% + 25% + n = 100%
   (n = 25%)
3. 10% + 10% + n = 100%
   (n = 80%)
4. 15% + 25% + n = 100%
   (n = 60%)
5. 5% + 50% + n = 100%
   (n = 45%)
6. 20% + 10% + n = 100%
   (n = 70%)

Skill Review

Give each student 1 red, 1 blue and 1 yellow counter. Have them find all the combinations of the counters, taken two at a time and illustrate their results. Explain that red + yellow is the same as yellow + red. (3 combinations: R/Y, R/B, B/Y)

Using Tree Diagrams

Shelby is getting ready for school. What possible combinations of blouses and skirts can Shelby wear?

A **tree diagram** is a graphic picture of all possible outcomes in an activity.

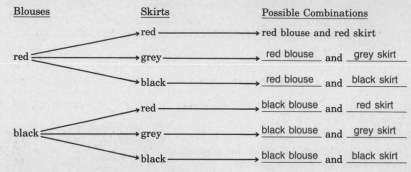

Blouses	Skirts	Possible Combinations
red	red	red blouse and red skirt
	grey	red blouse and grey skirt
	black	red blouse and black skirt
black	red	black blouse and red skirt
	grey	black blouse and grey skirt
	black	black blouse and black skirt

Getting Started

Complete the tree diagram and list all the possible combinations. Carlos is making a sandwich. He has ham, beef and chicken with wheat or rye bread to choose from. List the possible sandwich combinations.

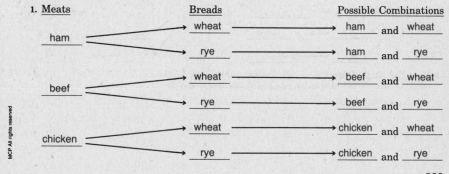

1.

Meats	Breads	Possible Combinations
ham	wheat	ham and wheat
	rye	ham and rye
beef	wheat	beef and wheat
	rye	beef and rye
chicken	wheat	chicken and wheat
	rye	chicken and rye

MCP All rights reserved

333

Teaching the Lesson

Introducing the Problem Read the problem aloud. Explain that the tree diagram is a way of organizing the information and will help them visualize the possible combinations. Point out that the first branches of the tree contain the two blouse colors. Ask the class what the second set of branches show. (choices of skirt color) Put the tree diagram on the board and show the class that there are 6 possible, different paths from one side to the other. Along each path a different combination of skirt and blouse is described. Have students come to the board and write the possible combinations to the right of the tree diagram. Ask the rest of the class to follow in their books. (red/red, red/grey, red/black; black/red, black/grey, black/black) Read the combinations aloud and ask a student to count them. (6)

Developing the Skill Explain that the tree diagram shows all the possible outcomes and allows students to organize information so that no combinations are left out. Arrange a tree diagram on the board so that it illustrates possible ways to paint a toy car where the body can be red or blue; the wheels, yellow or black.

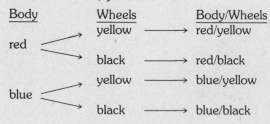

Body	Wheels	Body/Wheels
red	yellow	red/yellow
	black	red/black
blue	yellow	blue/yellow
	black	blue/black

Practice

Complete the tree diagram and list the possible combinations. Elaine is ordering lunch from a menu. She can choose vegetable, mushroom, bean or beef soup to eat with a garden or julienne salad.

1.

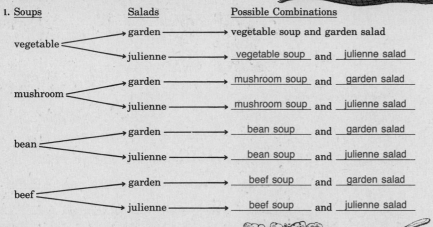

Soups	Salads	Possible Combinations
vegetable	garden	vegetable soup and garden salad
	julienne	vegetable soup and julienne salad
mushroom	garden	mushroom soup and garden salad
	julienne	mushroom soup and julienne salad
bean	garden	bean soup and garden salad
	julienne	bean soup and julienne salad
beef	garden	beef soup and garden salad
	julienne	beef soup and julienne salad

Apply

Draw a tree diagram and list all the possible combinations for each situation.

2. The class will choose a boy-girl combination to be co-chairmen of the carnival. The boy-candidates are Sal and Nate. The girls are Lois, Melissa, Theresa, Jackie and Polly.

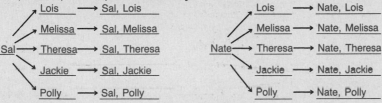

Sal	Lois → Sal, Lois		Nate	Lois → Nate, Lois	
	Melissa → Sal, Melissa			Melissa → Nate, Melissa	
	Theresa → Sal, Theresa			Theresa → Nate, Theresa	
	Jackie → Sal, Jackie			Jackie → Nate, Jackie	
	Polly → Sal, Polly			Polly → Nate, Polly	

3. Use the single letters b, c and f in combination with the double letters ad, ar and at to form three-letter words.

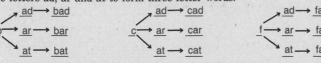

b	ad → bad	c	ad → cad
	ar → bar		ar → car
	at → bat		at → cat
f	ad → fad		
	ar → far		
	at → fat		

Correcting Common Errors

Some students might show all the possible combinations for the first choice but forget to write all the combinations for the second, third, and so on choices. To correct, have the students draw the tree diagram with all the blanks for the possible combinations before filling them in.

Enrichment

Have students use a tree diagram to solve this problem: Mike is going to a fair. He has time for only three events and is going to choose one from each category. There are 3 races: three-legged, potato sack and 1-mile. There are 2 contests: pie-eating and pole-climbing. There are 3 rides he enjoys: the ferris wheel, the roller-coaster and the bumper cars. How many combinations can he choose from and what are they? (18 possible combinations)

Practice

Have students complete all the problems. Remind them that each combination must be different.

Extra Credit *Applications*

Have students form groups and choose a country in Europe they would like to visit. Tell them to find out everything they can about that country's monetary system. Then have each of them determine the value of one item they might buy in that country, in both American money and foreign currency. (For example, in Germany, a sweater costs sixteen marks; how many American dollars would that be?) Have students reproduce or obtain money from other countries to be displayed. A local coin collector could be invited to discuss foreign coins and their values.

Problem Solving Review

pages 335-336

Objective

To review all the problem solving strategies

Materials

Mental Math

Have students find the first two common multiples of these pairs of numbers:

1. 2 and 3 (6, 12)
2. 4 and 5 (20, 40)
3. 8 and 4 (8, 16)
4. 9 and 2 (18, 36)
5. 7 and 4 (28, 56)
6. 6 and 9 (18, 36)
7. 2 and 10 (10, 20)

Review

The four-step plan can help us to be better problem solvers. A review of this plan can remind us of ways to use it.

★ SEE

We state what we want to know preferably in our own words. We state all the facts we know that will help us solve the problem.

★ PLAN

We think about the problem and the important facts and choose a plan to help us find a solution. Among the plans that will help us to solve a problem are:

Drawing a picture or a diagram
Making a model with manipulatives or on paper
Acting the problem out
Making a systematic listing or a table
Making a tally or graph
Looking for a pattern
Determining missing data
Collecting needed data
Selecting appropriate notation
Writing an open sentence
Using a formula
Guessing and checking
Working backwards
Solving a simpler but related problem
Identifying a subgoal
Restating the problem in our own words

★ DO

We carry out the plan and reach a solution to the problem.

★ CHECK

We check the problem for careless errors.
We see if the solution is reasonable.
We look for another way to solve the problem.

MCP All rights reserved

Diagram? Pattern? Data? Formula?

Teaching the Lesson

Read the entire lesson aloud to the class. Explain again the importance of reading the problem carefully and listing all the facts. Remind students that problems may have irrelevant facts. Ask students to remember the many strategies they have used to solve problems. Ask students to give examples of problems that can be solved with methods on this list. (Answers will vary.) Point out that once the SEE and PLAN sections of the problem are complete, they are ready to DO the problem, using the problem solving strategy selected. Suggest that sometimes more than one strategy may be useful. For example, it may help to draw a picture and work backwards or to solve a simpler, related problem by making a tally or a graph. Emphasize that all these plans are like tools in a tool chest, ready to be used to make a job easier. The last of the four stages is the CHECK. Remind them that this is used to make sure the plan was used correctly and to check for errors in computation. Emphasize the importance of estimating to see if the answer is reasonable.

Explain that a good way to check an answer is to find a second way to do the problem and compare the two answers.

Apply

Solve these problems.

1. In a theatre the front row has 40 seats, with each successive row containing two more seats than the row in front of it. If the last row has 100 seats, how many rows are in the theatre?
31 rows

2. Fence posts are placed in a straight line 10 feet apart. How many posts are required to support 100 feet of fence?
11 posts

3. A plane leaves Cleveland for Dallas at an average speed of 350 miles per hour. At the same time a plane leaves Dallas, flying towards Cleveland at 300 miles per hour. When the planes pass, which one is closer to Cleveland?
They are the same distance from Cleveland.

4. Fran has 12 coins. Some are nickels, some are dimes and some are quarters. How many of each coin does Fran have if the value of the coins totals $1.15?
2 quarters, 3 dimes, 7 nickels, or 1 quarter, 7 dimes, 4 nickels

5. A bag contains 4 red and 6 blue marbles. Without looking, you reach in and pick a marble, note the color, and return the marble to the bag. You do this 20 times. How many times can you expect to pick a red marble?
8 times

6. The cafeteria offers soup and sandwich for lunch. You can have tomato, bean, or noodle soup with a ham, turkey, beef, or cheese sandwich. How many choices do you have if you already decided to take the bean soup?
4 choices

7. The weather forecaster on television says there is a 40% chance of rain tomorrow. Is it more likely to rain or not rain? Explain how you decided.
See Solution Notes.

8. There are 12 cows and geese on a farm. If there are twice as many cows as there are geese, what is the ratio of cow legs to goose legs?
4:1

336

Extra Credit *Applications*

Make a jumbo size dollar bill from one large sheet of construction paper. Have students discuss the flow of money from one business and individual to another. Let students share ideas about where they become involved in this flow, such as in the lunch line, store, basketball game or fruit vending machine. Then play a game called Passing the Buck. One student takes the dollar and identifies themselves by occupation. "I am a student, and I gave this dollar to the dentist for cleaning my teeth." That student passes the buck to another student who may say, "I am the dentist who gave the dollar to a gas station attendant when I bought gas." The game continues until the buck has been passed all around the room. Emphasize that each student must come up with a new channel for the dollar. Have a student make a list of the individuals and occupations as they are suggested in the game. Discuss the importance of money skills in our everyday lives.

Solution Notes

1. Suggest students start with the first six rows. (row 1:40, row 2:42, row 3:44, row 4:46, row 5:48, row 6, 50) The increase is 10 seats for every five rows; by row 11 there are 60; row 16, 70; row 21, 80; row 26, 90; and row 31, 100.

2. This is best solved with a drawing. Have students draw posts, indicating 10 feet in between. (11 posts)

3. The planes must be the same distance from Cleveland if they are passing each other.

4. Suggest students organize the possibilities:

25¢	10¢	5¢	total coins	total $
2	0	10	12	$1.00
2	2	8	12	$1.10. . .
2	3	7		
1	7	4		

Higher-Order Thinking Skills

5. Synthesis: 4 out of 10 is the same as 8 out of 20.

6. Synthesis: The only thing you have left to choose is the sandwich, of which there are 4 kinds.

7. Synthesis: It is more likely not to rain. Explanations will differ but most will focus on the fact that 40% is a probability of $^{40}/_{100}$ or $^2/_5$, and is less than 60% or $^3/_5$, which is the probability that it will not rain.

8. Analysis: There are a variety of ways to solve this. One way is to think that the ratio of cow legs to geese legs is 4 to 2, but if there are twice as many cows as geese, then the ratio is 8 to 2, or 4 to 1.

Calculator Review

pages 337-338

Objective

To review using the calculator

Materials

calculator

Mental Math

Have students rearrange these mentally, to arrive at a multiple of 10, before finding each product:

1. $2 \times 9 \times 5 =$
   $(2 \times 5 \times 9 = 10 \times 9 = 90)$
2. $8 \times 4 \times 5 =$
   $(4 \times 5 \times 8 = 20 \times 8 = 160)$
3. $5 \times 3 \times 6 =$
   $(5 \times 6 \times 3 = 30 \times 3 = 90)$
4. $7 \times 5 \times 2 =$
   $(5 \times 2 \times 7 = 10 \times 7 = 70)$
5. $3 \times 5 \times 8 =$
   $(5 \times 8 \times 3 = 40 \times 3 = 120)$
6. $1 \times 10 \times 42 = (10 \times 42 = 420)$

Skill Review

Have students review the function keys by doing these problems on a calculator:

1. $272 + 194 = (466)$
2. $1,591 - 625 = (966)$
3. $43.2 \times 2.9 = (125.28)$
4. $15.729 \div 4.9 = (3.21)$
5. $\frac{2}{3}$ of $150 = (150 \div 3 \times 2 = 100)$
6. 4% of $\$124 = (\$4.96)$

Calculator Review

We have used a calculator to solve many consumer problems. Now let's use a calculator to have some fun.

Activity 1. Adding Numbers

Try these on a friend.
A. Find the sum of the first 12 odd numbers.
B. Find the sum of the first 12 even numbers.
C. Find the sum of the first 25 numbers.

The Long Way	The Shortcut
A. $1 + 3 + 5 + \ldots$	Count the number of numbers being added. Multiply that number by itself. $12 \times 12 = \underline{144}$
B. $2 + 4 + 6 + \ldots$	Count the number of numbers being added. Multiply that number by one more than that number. $12 \times 13 = \underline{156}$
C. $1 + 2 + 3 \ldots$	Count the number of numbers being added. Multiply that number by one more than that number and divide by 2. $25 \times 26 \div 2 = \underline{325}$

Activity 2. Finding a Pattern

Complete the statements and discover the patterns.

$3 \times 37 = 111$ and $1 + 1 + 1 = 3$
$6 \times 37 = 222$ and $\underline{2} + \underline{2} + \underline{2} = \underline{6}$
$9 \times 37 = \underline{333}$ and $\underline{3} + \underline{3} + \underline{3} = \underline{9}$
$12 \times 37 = \underline{444}$ and $\underline{4} + \underline{4} + \underline{4} = \underline{12}$

Use the patterns to find the product of 18×37. $\underline{666}$ and $\underline{6} + \underline{6} + \underline{6} = \underline{18}$

MCP All rights reserved

337

Teaching the Lesson

Activity 1: Show students a way of visualizing these problems. Write the 12 odd numbers on the board:

1 3 5 7 9 11 13 15 17 19 21 23

Make pairs of the first and last, second and eleventh, and so on, and add them: $1 + 23$, $3 + 21$, $5 + 19$, $7 + 17$, $9 + 15$ and $11 + 13$. Ask students what they notice. (Each sum is 24.) Show that the six 24s makes 144. The next problem can be worked the same way. In this case there are 6 pairs, each with a sum of 26. $(2 + 24, 4 + 22,$ and so on) $(6 \times 26 = 156)$ The last problem can also be arranged in pairs. There will be 12 pairs of 26 $(1 + 25, 2 + 24, 3 + 23, \ldots)$ and a 13 left over in the middle. $((12 \times 26) + 13 = 312 + 13 = 325)$

Activity 2: Help students see the progression of factors: 3, 6, 9, 12, to 15 and 18. The digits in the products form a pattern, too: 111, 222, 333, 444, to 555 and 666. The sum of the digits in the product of 18×37 is $(6 + 6 + 6) = 18$.

Activity 3. There is no particular pattern that will help students solve this problem. Suggest that they work in pairs to give each other ideas. Point out that in the first division, some number divided into 60 equals 6, so it is likely that $N = 9$.

Activity 4. Suggest that students write out the entire alphabet and its numerical equivalent.

Activity 5. To unravel the mystery, show students that $(3 \times 37 \times 91) = 10,101$.

Activity 3. Coded Math

Replace each letter by a number to make these problems work. The letters have the same value in both problems.
Hint: $T = 6$.

$TI\,P$		678	ULA	345
$N)\overline{TESM}$		$9)\overline{6,102}$	$\times\ EM$	$\times\ 12$
$\underline{AL}$		$\underline{5\,4}$	$\overline{TNS}$	$\overline{690}$
$I\,S$		70	$ULAS$	345
$\underline{TU}$		$\underline{63}$	$\overline{LELS}$	$\overline{4,140}$
$\overline{I\,M}$		$\overline{72}$		
$\underline{I\,M}$		$\underline{72}$		
S				

Use the same values to find

$$LATE\ +\ ME\ =\ ?$$

$$\underline{4,561}\ +\ \underline{21}\ =\ \underline{4,582}$$

Activity 4. Give more value to your name.

Give values to each of the letters of your name according to the following pattern.

ABCDE ... Z
1 2 3 4 5 ... 26

Add the values for each name. Example: Bill = 2 + 9 + 11 + 11 = 33
Pete = 16 + 5 + 20 + 5 = 46

Who has the name with the greatest value in your family?
Answers will vary.

Activity 5. It works every time.

Give your friend with a calculator these instructions.

Enter a 1-digit number without telling you what it is.
Multiply by 3.
Multiply by 37.
Multiply by 91.
Read the number.

Tell your friend the starting number by choosing the non-zero digit that is repeated in the product.

338

Extra Credit *Probability*

Ask students to guess the probability that two students in your class have the same birthday. Have students survey the class and record their birthdays. Although the calculations are beyond most fifth graders, the results are not. The probability of two birthdays being the same in a group of 23 people is slightly more than half; in a group of 25 people, 56%; in a group of 30 people, 70%; in a group of 35, 81%; in a group of 45, 94%; in a group of 50, 97% or near certainty. Of course, this seems to contrast with the fact that there are 366 possible birthdays if February 29 is included. Have students work in small groups to survey the birthdays of other classes in the school. If classes are especially small, combine them so that the probability is near certainty.

Chapter Test

page 339

Item	Objective
1	Interpret tally graph; make bar graph (See pages 317-318)
2-3	Interpret line graph (See pages 321-322)
4-5	Interpret circle graphs that use percents (See pages 323-324)
6	Locate and name points represented by ordered pairs (See pages 325-326)
7	Graph points represented by ordered pairs (See pages 325-326)
8	Find outcomes in probability (See pages 329-330)
8	Find probability of specific outcome (See pages 327-328)
9	Draw tree diagram to show possible outcomes (See pages 335-336)

339

Use the tally chart to complete problem 1.

1. Make a bar graph.

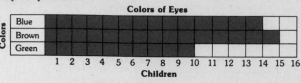

Colors of Eyes	
Blue	~~IIII~~ ~~IIII~~ IIII
Brown	~~IIII~~ ~~IIII~~ ~~IIII~~
Green	~~IIII~~ ~~IIII~~

Use the line graph to complete 2 and 3.

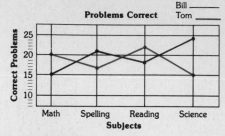

2. Who received the higher reading score? ___Tom___

3. How many more science problems did Bill get correct than Tom?
   ___9 problems___

Use the circle graph of Ed's budget to complete 4 and 5.

Savings 35%   Clothes 50%   Fun 15%

4. What percent is spent on clothes and fun? ___65%___

5. If Ed earns $62 a week, how much does he save? ___$21.70___

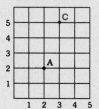

Use the grid to complete 6 and 7.

6. Write the ordered pair for *A*.
   ___(2, 2)___

7. Graph the point *C*(3, 5)

Solve these problems.

8. A penny and a quarter are tossed. List the possible outcomes of heads and tails.
   ___*H, H; H, T; T, H; T, T*___

9. Write the probability that both coins show tails. ___$\frac{1}{4}$___

MCP All rights reserved

339

Circle the letter of the correct answer.

1 3,476
+ 16,829

- a 19,305
- b 20,295
- © 20,305
- d NG

2 80,296
− 18,758

- ⓐ 61,538
- b 71,538
- c 78,542
- d NG

3 $2\frac{1}{2}$
+ $3\frac{3}{4}$

- a $5\frac{2}{3}$
- b $5\frac{1}{4}$
- © $6\frac{1}{4}$
- d NG

4 $7\frac{1}{3}$
− $4\frac{3}{4}$

- a 3
- b $3\frac{5}{12}$
- c $3\frac{7}{12}$
- ⓓ NG

5 $1\frac{1}{2} \times 5\frac{1}{3}$

- a $5\frac{1}{6}$
- ⓑ 8
- c $8\frac{1}{6}$
- d NG

6 $2\frac{1}{2} \div 3\frac{1}{2}$

- a $\frac{2}{3}$
- b $\frac{3}{7}$
- c $8\frac{1}{6}$
- ⓓ NG

7 4.2 × 36

- a 1.512
- b 15.12
- © 151.2
- d NG

8 5.2)1.716

- a 3.3
- ⓑ 0.33
- c 3
- d NG

9 Find the area.

3 cm
6 cm

- a 18 cm
- ⓑ 18 sq cm
- c 9 cm
- d NG

10 Write 75% as a simplified fraction.

- a $\frac{7}{10}$
- b $\frac{75}{100}$
- © $\frac{3}{4}$
- d NG

☐ score

340

Item	Objective
1	Add two numbers up to 5-digits (See pages 27-28)
2	Subtract two 6-digit numbers, zero in minuend (See pages 35-36)
3	Add two mixed numbers (See pages 175-176)
4	Subtract two mixed numbers, rename minuend (See pages 183-184)
5	Multiply two mixed numbers (See pages 197-198)
6	Divide two mixed numbers (See pages 201-202)
7	Multiply decimals (See pages 237-238)
8	Divide a decimal by tenths (See pages 247-248)
9	Find the area of a rectangle (See pages 127-128)
10	Express percent as a fraction in lowest terms (See pages 303-304)

Alternate Cumulative Review

Circle the letter of the correct answer.

1 5,687
+ 19,516

- a 24,203
- b 25,193
- © 25,203
- d NG

2 702,675
− 128,498

- ⓐ 574,177
- b 584,177
- c 674,177
- d NG

3 $17\frac{3}{8}$
+ $8\frac{2}{3}$

- a $25\frac{23}{24}$
- b 26
- © $26\frac{1}{24}$
- d NG

4 $352\frac{4}{5}$
− $178\frac{1}{2}$

- a $173\frac{3}{10}$
- ⓑ $174\frac{3}{10}$
- c $174\frac{2}{10}$
- d NG

5 $2\frac{4}{5} \times 1\frac{3}{7}$

- a $2\frac{34}{35}$
- b $3\frac{34}{35}$
- © 4
- d NG

6 $1\frac{3}{4} \div 2\frac{5}{6}$

- a $\frac{43}{68}$
- ⓑ $\frac{21}{34}$
- c $\frac{22}{34}$
- d NG

7 5.4
×2.9

- a 1.566
- ⓑ 15.66
- c 156.6
- d NG

8 1.8)1.746

- ⓐ 0.97
- b 9.7
- c 97
- d NG

9 Find the area of a rectangle 2 cm by 7 cm.

- a 18 cm
- ⓑ 14 sq cm
- c 9 sq cm
- d NG

10 Write the equivalent fraction for 4%.

- a $\frac{4}{10}$
- ⓑ $\frac{1}{25}$
- c $\frac{2}{5}$

340

Alternate Chapter Test

for page 21

Item	Objective
1-9	Recall basic addition and subtraction facts (See pages 1-6)
10	Add three 1-digit addends (See pages 3-4)
11-14	Identify place value in a number less than 100,000,000,000 (See pages 7-8, 11-12)
15-20	Compare and order numbers through hundred thousands (See pages 11-12)
21-24	Round numbers to the nearest 100 or 1,000 (See pages 13-14)
25-28	Read and write numbers through billions (See pages 15-16)

Add or subtract.

1. $7 + 6 = \underline{13}$ 2. $8 + 4 = \underline{12}$ 3. $18 - 9 = \underline{9}$ 4. $5 - 1 = \underline{4}$

5. $\begin{array}{r} 6 \\ +5 \\ \hline 11 \end{array}$ 6. $\begin{array}{r} 15 \\ -8 \\ \hline 7 \end{array}$ 7. $\begin{array}{r} 17 \\ -9 \\ \hline 8 \end{array}$ 8. $\begin{array}{r} 5 \\ +0 \\ \hline 5 \end{array}$ 9. $\begin{array}{r} 8 \\ -0 \\ \hline 8 \end{array}$ 10. $\begin{array}{r} 3 \\ 5 \\ +7 \\ \hline 15 \end{array}$

Write the place value of the underlined digit.

11. 736,921   12. 45,728   13. 814,653   14. 506,492

    hundreds   ones   tens   hundred
                                                thousands

Write < or > in the circle.

15. $72 < 82$ 16. $493 < 498$ 17. $254 > 155$

18. $8,732 > 8,372$ 19. $76,917 > 67,917$ 20. $387,469 < 387,520$

Round to the nearest hundred.   Round to the nearest thousand.

21. 1,250   22. 7,829   23. 89,716   24. 27,365
    1,300   7,800   90,000   27,000

Write in standard form.

25. thirty-five million, three hundred sixty-two thousand, seven
    35,362,007

26. six hundred fifty-five billion, eighty-two million, four thousand, sixty-nine
    655,082,004,069

Write in words.

27. 62,010,020 _____ sixty-two million, ten thousand, twenty _____

28. 30,100,000,000 _____ thirty billion, one hundred million _____

MCP All rights reserved

341

Add.

1. 65 + 26 —— 91	2. 37 + 59 —— 96	3. 464 + 28 —— 492	4. $5.18 + 1.79 —— $6.97
5. 5,876 + 4,769 ——— 10,645	6. 24,318 + 59,678 ——— 83,996	7. 347,569 + 622,983 ——— 970,552	8. 82,576 34,158 + 68,943 ——— 185,677

Estimate each sum after rounding to the greatest common place value.

9. 592   600
+ 286 + 300
————
     900
	10. 3,650 4,000
	+ 6,505 + 7,000
	—————
	      11,000
		11. 12,866 13,000
		+ 9,447 + 9,000
		—————
		      22,000
			12. 68,241 68,000
			+ 3,875 + 4,000
			—————
			      72,000

13. 278   300
+ 256 + 300
————
     600
	14. 9,027 9,000
	+ 3,700 + 4,000
	—————
	      13,000
		15. 65,321 65,000
		+ 2,189 + 2,000
		—————
		      67,000
			16. 39,610 40,000
			+ 5,089 + 5,000
			—————
			      45,000

Subtract.

17. 82 − 36 —— 46	18. 539 − 42 —— 497	19. 784 − 591 —— 193	20. 6,074 − 983 ——— 5,091
21. 9,815 − 7,286 ——— 2,529	22. 18,603 − 9,845 ——— 8,758	23. $190.07 − 85.68 ——— $104.39	24. 324,787 − 59,948 ——— 264,839

Estimate each difference after rounding to the greatest common place value.

25. 743   700
− 250 − 300
————
     400
	26. 6,460 6,000
	− 1,758 − 2,000
	—————
	      4,000
		27. 16,492 16,000
		− 9,537 − 10,000
		—————
		      6,000
			28. 98,748 99,000
			− 7,355 − 7,000
			—————
			      92,000

29. 951   1,000
− 297 − 300
————
     700
	30. 3,695 4,000
	− 1,099 − 1,000
	—————
	      3,000
		31. 92,232 92,000
		− 6,712 − 7,000
		—————
		      85,000
			32. 37,406 40,000
			− 19,588 − 20,000
			—————
			      20,000

33. 549   500
− 376 − 400
————
     100
	34. 6,158 6,000
	− 2,892 − 3,000
	—————
	      3,000
		35. 87,406 90,000
		− 29,029 − 30,000
		—————
		      60,000
			36. 64,162 64,000
			− 3,872 − 4,000
			—————
			      60,000

342

Alternate Chapter Test

for page 43

Item	Objective
1-4	Add two numbers with sums less than 1,000, one regrouping (See pages 23-24)
5	Add two or more numbers less than 10,000 (See pages 25-26)
6-8	Add two or more numbers less than 1,000,000 (See pages 27-28)
9-16	Estimate sums by rounding to nearest 100 or 1,000 and adding (See pages 29-30)
17-19	Subtract two numbers up to 3 digits (See pages 31-32)
20-23	Subtract up to 4-digit numbers, zeros in the minuend (See pages 33-34)
24	Subtract two numbers less than 1,000,000 (See pages 35-36)
25-36	Estimate differences by rounding to nearest 100 or 1,000 and subtracting (See pages 37-38)

Alternate Chapter Test

for page 69

Item	Objective
1-6	Recall basic multiplication facts (See pages 45-46)
7	Multiply 2-digit by 1-digit factors (See pages 53-54)
8-9	Multiply up to 6-digits by 1-digit factor (See pages 55-56)
10	Multiply money by 1-digit factor (See pages 55-56)
11-14	Multiply two 2-digit factors (See pages 57-58)
15-18	Multiply up to 5-digits by 2-digit number; estimate product of two numbers (See pages 51-52, 59-60)
19-22	Multiply two 3-digit numbers; estimate product of two numbers (See pages 51-52, 63-64)
23-31	Identify least common multiple (See pages 47-48)
32-40	Identify even or odd numbers (See page 48)

Multiply. Check by estimation.

1.
$$\begin{array}{r} 5 \\ \times\ 9 \\ \hline 45 \end{array}$$

2.
$$\begin{array}{r} 3 \\ \times\ 0 \\ \hline 0 \end{array}$$

3.
$$\begin{array}{r} 8 \\ \times\ 6 \\ \hline 48 \end{array}$$

4.
$$\begin{array}{r} 7 \\ \times\ 7 \\ \hline 49 \end{array}$$

5.
$$\begin{array}{r} 9 \\ \times\ 4 \\ \hline 36 \end{array}$$

6.
$$\begin{array}{r} 3 \\ \times\ 8 \\ \hline 24 \end{array}$$

7.
$$\begin{array}{r} 48 \\ \times\ 4 \\ \hline 192 \end{array}$$

8.
$$\begin{array}{r} 327 \\ \times\ 9 \\ \hline 2{,}943 \end{array}$$

9.
$$\begin{array}{r} 2{,}137 \\ \times\ 4 \\ \hline 8{,}548 \end{array}$$

10.
$$\begin{array}{r} \$15.69 \\ \times\ 8 \\ \hline \$125.52 \end{array}$$

11.
$$\begin{array}{r} 26 \\ \times\ 75 \\ \hline 1{,}950 \end{array}$$

12.
$$\begin{array}{r} 48 \\ \times\ 39 \\ \hline 1{,}872 \end{array}$$

13.
$$\begin{array}{r} 60 \\ \times\ 70 \\ \hline 4{,}200 \end{array}$$

14.
$$\begin{array}{r} 98 \\ \times\ 52 \\ \hline 5{,}096 \end{array}$$

15.
$$\begin{array}{r} 297 \\ \times\ 53 \\ \hline 15{,}741 \end{array}$$

16.
$$\begin{array}{r} 1{,}804 \\ \times\ 62 \\ \hline 111{,}848 \end{array}$$

17.
$$\begin{array}{r} \$69.73 \\ \times\ 80 \\ \hline \$5{,}578.40 \end{array}$$

18.
$$\begin{array}{r} 2{,}912 \\ \times\ 43 \\ \hline 125{,}216 \end{array}$$

19.
$$\begin{array}{r} 685 \\ \times\ 319 \\ \hline 218{,}515 \end{array}$$

20.
$$\begin{array}{r} 206 \\ \times\ 724 \\ \hline 149{,}144 \end{array}$$

21.
$$\begin{array}{r} \$5.27 \\ \times\ 418 \\ \hline \$2{,}202.86 \end{array}$$

22.
$$\begin{array}{r} 230 \\ \times\ 761 \\ \hline 175{,}030 \end{array}$$

Write the least common multiple of each pair of numbers.

23. 3 and 8 __24__   24. 16 and 20 __80__   25. 3 and 5 __15__

26. 8 and 16 __16__   27. 7 and 8 __56__   28. 5 and 11 __55__

29. 4 and 6 __12__   30. 3 and 13 __39__   31. 10 and 11 __110__

Write even or odd for each number.

MCP All rights reserved

32. 41 __odd__   33. 534 __even__   34. 89 __odd__

35. 605 __odd__   36. 320 __even__   37. 467 __odd__

38. 108 __even__   39. 752 __even__   40. 263 __odd__

343

Divide and check.

     3
1. 4)$\overline{12}$ 2. 8)$\overline{8}$ 3. 6)$\overline{36}$ 4. 1)$\overline{7}$ 5. 9)$\overline{72}$

1. $\quad 3 \atop 4)\overline{12}$ 2. $\quad 1 \atop 8)\overline{8}$ 3. $\quad 6 \atop 6)\overline{36}$ 4. $\quad 7 \atop 1)\overline{7}$ 5. $\quad 8 \atop 9)\overline{72}$

6. $\quad 0 \atop 5)\overline{0}$ 7. $\quad 8\,R2 \atop 5)\overline{42}$ 8. $\quad 9\,R5 \atop 6)\overline{59}$ 9. $\quad 6\,R1 \atop 4)\overline{25}$

10. $\quad 7\,R4 \atop 7)\overline{53}$ 11. $\quad 13 \atop 6)\overline{78}$ 12. $\quad 13\,R3 \atop 7)\overline{94}$ 13. $\quad \$0.64 \atop 5)\overline{\$3.20}$

14. $\quad 22 \atop 8)\overline{176}$ 15. $\quad 136\,R3 \atop 4)\overline{547}$ 16. $\quad 104\,R2 \atop 6)\overline{626}$ 17. $\quad 397\,R4 \atop 6)\overline{2,386}$

18. $\quad \$63.59 \atop 5)\overline{\$317.95}$ 19. $\quad 12,073 \atop 8)\overline{96,584}$ 20. $\quad 1,607\,R6 \atop 7)\overline{11,255}$ 21. $\quad 3,827 \atop 2)\overline{7,654}$

Write the product of primes for each composite number.

22. 32 = $\underline{2 \times 2 \times 2 \times 2 \times 2}$ 23. 50 = $\underline{\quad 2 \times 5 \times 5 \quad}$

Write the greatest common factor for each pair of numbers.

24. 12 and 16 $\underline{\quad\quad 4 \quad\quad}$ 25. 32 and 60 $\underline{\quad\quad 4 \quad\quad}$

Find the average for each set of numbers.

26. 95, 47 71   27. 182, 234, 361 259   28. 15, 10, 11, 13, 16 13

344

Alternate Chapter Test

for page 95

Item	Objective
1-5	Recall basic division facts (See pages 71-72)
6-8	Basic facts to find 1-digit quotients, remainders (See pages 77-78)
9-11	Divide 2-digit by 1-digit number, quotient with or without remainder (See pages 79-80)
12-14	Divide 3-digit number by 1-digit number with or without remainder (See pages 81-86)
15-21	Divide 4- and 5-digit numbers by 1-digit number with or without remainder (See pages 87-90)
22-23	Find prime factors for composite number (See pages 75-76)
24-25	Find greatest common factor (See pages 73-74)
26-28	Find averages (See pages 91-92)

Alternate Chapter Test

for page 115

Item	Objective
1-2	Divide 2- or 3-digit number by multiple of 10, quotient with or without remainder (See pages 97-98)
3-9	Divide 2- or 3-digit number by 2-digit number, quotient with or without remainder (See pages 101-102)
10-16	Divide 4-digit number by 2-digit number to get 2-digit quotient with or without remainder (See pages 103-104)
17-25	Divide 4- or 5-digit number by 2-digit number to get 3-digit quotient with or without remainder (See pages 107-110)

Divide.

1. $30)\overline{210}$ 7

2. $40)\overline{345}$ 8 R25

3. $16)\overline{99}$ 6 R3

4. $19)\overline{80}$ 4 R4

5. $28)\overline{254}$ 9 R2

6. $57)\overline{459}$ 8 R3

7. $33)\overline{180}$ 5 R15

8. $82)\overline{600}$ 7 R26

9. $41)\overline{984}$ 24

10. $64)\overline{1,216}$ 19

11. $36)\overline{1,908}$ 53

12. $27)\overline{2,052}$ 76

13. $73)\overline{3,066}$ 42

14. $95)\overline{5,912}$ 62 R22

15. $58)\overline{5,193}$ 89 R31

16. $84)\overline{3,192}$ 38

17. $26)\overline{\$145.86}$ \$5.61

18. $49)\overline{32,240}$ 657 R47

19. $74)\overline{67,137}$ 907 R19

20. $31)\overline{\$249.86}$ \$8.06

21. $54)\overline{16,362}$ 303

22. $76)\overline{8,292}$ 109 R8

23. $48)\overline{34,752}$ 724

24. $36)\overline{\$248.04}$ \$6.89

25. $29)\overline{14,561}$ 502 R3

MCP All rights reserved

345

345

Rename these measurements.

1. 6 hours 37 minutes = __397__ minutes

2. 2 hours 3 minutes = __7,380__ seconds

3. 3 feet 7 inches = __43__ inches

4. 107 feet = __35__ yards __2__ feet

5. 85 ounces = __5__ pounds __5__ ounces

6. 8 gallons = __32__ quarts

7. 5 kilometers = __5,000__ meters

8. 3,000 milliliters = __3__ liters

Solve these problems.

9. Find the area of a square that is 23 yards on each side.
529 square yards

10. Find the volume of a box that is 32 feet long, 13 feet wide, and 8 feet high.
3,328 cubic feet

Complete these sentences.

11. There are usually __28__ days in February.

12. When it is 1:00 PM in Chicago, it is __9:00__ AM in Honolulu.

Find the perimeter.

13.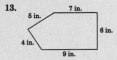

P = __31 in.__

14.

P = __36 cm__

Add or subtract.

15. 8 ft 6 in.
   + 4 ft 7 in.
   ‾‾‾‾‾‾‾‾‾‾‾
    13 ft 1 in.

16. 9 yd 3 ft
   − 8 yd 5 ft
   ‾‾‾‾‾‾‾‾‾‾‾
      1 ft

Circle the best estimate.

17. A footstool is about __?__ high.

25 mm (25 cm) 25 m

18. An elephant weighs about __?__.

1,000 g (1,000 kg)

Alternate Chapter Test

for page 141

Item	Objective
1-8	Rename units of customary and metric measures (See pages 117-118, 123-124, 131-132, 135-138)
9	Find area of rectangles (See pages 127-128)
10	Find volume of rectangular solids (See pages 129-130)
11-12	Answer questions about time (See pages 117-120)
13-14	Find perimeter of simple figures (See pages 125-126)
15-16	Add, subtract customary units of length (See pages 123-124)
17-18	Choose appropriate units of length (See pages 133-136)

Alternate Chapter Test

for page 163

Item	Objective
1-4	Find equivalent fractions by multiplying (See pages 147-148)
5-12	Reduce fractions to lowest terms (See pages 149-150)
13-16	Compare and order fractions (See pages 151-152)
17-24	Change mixed numbers to fractions (See pages 153-154)
25-32	Divide by a whole number, quotient as mixed number (See pages 155-156)
33-40	Change improper fractions to whole or mixed numbers (See pages 157-158)

Write the equivalent fraction.

1. $\frac{3}{4} = \frac{12}{16}$ 2. $\frac{6}{7} = \frac{18}{21}$ 3. $\frac{5}{9} = \frac{10}{18}$ 4. $\frac{2}{8} = \frac{10}{40}$

Write each fraction in simplest terms.

5. $\frac{4}{8} = \frac{1}{2}$ 6. $\frac{15}{20} = \frac{3}{4}$ 7. $\frac{6}{30} = \frac{1}{5}$ 8. $\frac{15}{25} = \frac{3}{5}$

9. $\frac{21}{28} = \frac{3}{4}$ 10. $\frac{24}{40} = \frac{3}{5}$ 11. $\frac{18}{20} = \frac{9}{10}$ 12. $\frac{45}{56} = \frac{45}{56}$

Write < or > in the circle.

13. $\frac{4}{6} \gtrdot \frac{5}{8}$ 14. $\frac{9}{12} \lessdot \frac{7}{9}$ 15. $\frac{3}{5} \gtrdot \frac{8}{20}$ 16. $\frac{9}{10} \gtrdot \frac{7}{8}$

Write each mixed number as an improper fraction.

17. $7\frac{4}{5} = \frac{39}{5}$ 18. $4\frac{5}{8} = \frac{37}{8}$ 19. $5\frac{6}{11} = \frac{61}{11}$ 20. $9\frac{3}{16} = \frac{147}{16}$

21. $2\frac{5}{6} = \frac{17}{6}$ 22. $3\frac{7}{9} = \frac{34}{9}$ 23. $6\frac{1}{10} = \frac{61}{10}$ 24. $8\frac{3}{7} = \frac{59}{7}$

Write each quotient as a mixed number. Simplify if necessary.

25. $4\overline{)33}\ \ 8\frac{1}{4}$ 26. $9\overline{)238}\ \ 26\frac{4}{9}$ 27. $42\overline{)301}\ \ 7\frac{1}{6}$ 28. $12\overline{)640}\ \ 53\frac{1}{3}$

29. $16\overline{)360}\ \ 22\frac{1}{2}$ 30. $13\overline{)295}\ \ 22\frac{9}{13}$ 31. $35\overline{)702}\ \ 20\frac{2}{35}$ 32. $17\overline{)156}\ \ 9\frac{3}{17}$

Rename each improper fraction as a whole or mixed number.

33. $\frac{36}{12} = 3$ 34. $\frac{25}{10} = 2\frac{1}{2}$ 35. $\frac{32}{8} = 4$ 36. $\frac{56}{11} = 5\frac{1}{11}$

37. $\frac{81}{9} = 9$ 38. $\frac{63}{2} = 31\frac{1}{2}$ 39. $\frac{56}{6} = 9\frac{1}{3}$ 40. $\frac{39}{9} = 4\frac{1}{3}$

MCP All rights reserved

347

Add or subtract. Simplify if necessary.

1. $\dfrac{3}{7}$

   $+\dfrac{2}{7}$

   $\dfrac{5}{7}$

2. $\dfrac{4}{9}$

   $+\dfrac{2}{9}$

   $\dfrac{2}{3}$

3. $\dfrac{9}{10}$

   $-\dfrac{6}{10}$

   $\dfrac{3}{10}$

4. $\dfrac{13}{5}$

   $-\dfrac{7}{5}$

   $1\dfrac{1}{5}$

5. $\dfrac{4}{5}$

   $+\dfrac{1}{4}$

   $1\dfrac{1}{20}$

6. $\dfrac{1}{2}$

   $+\dfrac{3}{7}$

   $\dfrac{13}{14}$

7. $\dfrac{8}{9}$

   $-\dfrac{1}{3}$

   $\dfrac{5}{9}$

8. $\dfrac{5}{6}$

   $-\dfrac{3}{4}$

   $\dfrac{1}{12}$

9. $5\dfrac{5}{6}$

   $+8\dfrac{4}{9}$

   $14\dfrac{5}{18}$

10. $9\dfrac{3}{5}$

    $+9\dfrac{2}{3}$

    $19\dfrac{4}{15}$

11. $7\dfrac{3}{4}$

    $+4\dfrac{4}{7}$

    $12\dfrac{9}{28}$

12. $3\dfrac{7}{8}$

    $+7\dfrac{3}{5}$

    $11\dfrac{19}{40}$

13. $8\dfrac{4}{9}$

    $-3\dfrac{5}{12}$

    $5\dfrac{1}{36}$

14. $20\dfrac{13}{16}$

    $-4\dfrac{5}{8}$

    $16\dfrac{3}{16}$

15. $15\dfrac{10}{17}$

    $-7\dfrac{8}{17}$

    $8\dfrac{2}{17}$

16. $18\dfrac{2}{3}$

    $-11\dfrac{1}{4}$

    $7\dfrac{5}{12}$

17. 5

    $-4\dfrac{5}{6}$

    $\dfrac{1}{6}$

18. $10\dfrac{9}{10}$

    $-7\dfrac{2}{5}$

    $3\dfrac{1}{2}$

19. $13\dfrac{5}{7}$

    $-8\dfrac{7}{8}$

    $4\dfrac{47}{56}$

20. $9\dfrac{7}{15}$

    $-8\dfrac{7}{10}$

    $\dfrac{23}{30}$

Rename as mixed numbers.

21. $36 = \underline{35\dfrac{10}{10}}$

22. $11\dfrac{3}{5} = 10\dfrac{8}{5}$

23. $7 = \underline{6\dfrac{6}{6}}$

24. $12\dfrac{1}{7} = 11\dfrac{8}{7}$

Simplify these mixed numbers.

25. $7\dfrac{11}{5} = \underline{9\dfrac{1}{5}}$

26. $18\dfrac{12}{16} = \underline{18\dfrac{3}{4}}$

27. $5\dfrac{13}{6} = \underline{7\dfrac{1}{6}}$

28. $12\dfrac{81}{90} = 12\dfrac{9}{10}$

348

Alternate Chapter Test

for page 189

Item	Objective
1-2	Add fractions with like denominators (See pages 165-166)
3-4	Subtract fractions with like denominators (See pages 167-168)
5-6	Add fractions with unlike denominators (See pages 171-172)
7-8	Subtract fractions with unlike denominators (See pages 173-174)
9-12	Add two mixed numbers (See pages 175-176)
13-16	Subtract two mixed numbers (See pages 179-180)
17-20	Subtract mixed numbers with renaming (See pages 181-184)
21-24	Rename whole numbers as mixed numbers (See pages 181-184)
25-28	Simplify mixed numbers (See pages 177-178)

Alternate Chapter Test

for page 211

Write the number of each fractional part.

1. $\frac{3}{4}$ of 20 = __15__
2. $\frac{1}{6}$ of 42 = __7__
3. $\frac{4}{7}$ of 21 = __12__
4. $\frac{1}{9}$ of 270 = __30__

5. $\frac{1}{5}$ of \$15 = __\$3__
6. $\frac{3}{4}$ of 45 = __$33\frac{3}{4}$__
7. $\frac{7}{8}$ of \$112 = __\$98__
8. $\frac{2}{3}$ of 111 = __74__

9. $\frac{2}{9}$ of 369 = __82__
10. $\frac{1}{4}$ of \$192 = __\$48__
11. $\frac{5}{9}$ of \$252 = __\$140__
12. $\frac{1}{6}$ of 498 = __83__

13. $\frac{7}{10}$ of 340 = __238__
14. $\frac{3}{7}$ of \$364 = __\$156__
15. $\frac{8}{8}$ of 632 = __632__
16. $\frac{2}{5}$ of \$900 = __\$360__

Multiply. Simplify if necessary.

17. $\frac{1}{6} \times \frac{3}{10} = \frac{1}{20}$
18. $\frac{4}{5} \times \frac{5}{6} = \frac{2}{3}$
19. $\frac{2}{5} \times \frac{7}{12} = \frac{7}{30}$
20. $\frac{3}{8} \times \frac{8}{9} = \frac{1}{3}$

21. $4\frac{1}{5} \times 10 = 42$
22. $5\frac{1}{2} \times \frac{7}{8} = 4\frac{13}{16}$
23. $7\frac{1}{2} \times 4\frac{2}{3} = 35$
24. $6\frac{2}{3} \times 2\frac{1}{7} = 14\frac{2}{7}$

25. $6\frac{1}{3} \times \frac{1}{2} = 3\frac{1}{6}$
26. $3\frac{1}{7} \times \frac{1}{4} = \frac{11}{14}$
27. $\frac{3}{8} \times 2\frac{5}{6} = 1\frac{1}{16}$
28. $\frac{5}{6} \times 3\frac{2}{5} = 2\frac{5}{6}$

29. $7\frac{3}{4} \times 1\frac{1}{3} = 10\frac{1}{3}$
30. $2\frac{1}{9} \times 1\frac{2}{3} = 3\frac{14}{27}$
31. $4\frac{1}{8} \times 3\frac{1}{3} = 13\frac{3}{4}$
32. $11\frac{1}{2} \times 1\frac{3}{4} = 20\frac{1}{8}$

Write the reciprocal.

33. $\frac{2}{8}$ $\frac{8}{2}$
34. $\frac{3}{4}$ $\frac{4}{3}$
35. 10 $\frac{1}{10}$

36. $6\frac{1}{2}$ $\frac{2}{13}$
37. $\frac{5}{15}$ $\frac{15}{5}$
38. $3\frac{1}{3}$ $\frac{3}{10}$

39. 5 $\frac{1}{5}$
40. $7\frac{3}{7}$ $\frac{7}{52}$
41. $\frac{12}{7}$ $\frac{7}{12}$

42. $8\frac{3}{4}$ $\frac{4}{35}$
43. $\frac{1}{9}$ 9
44. $10\frac{3}{5}$ $\frac{5}{53}$

Divide. Simplify if necessary.

45. $\frac{1}{4} \div \frac{1}{5}$ $1\frac{1}{4}$
46. $\frac{3}{4} \div \frac{3}{8}$ 2

47. $\frac{7}{8} \div \frac{4}{9}$ $1\frac{31}{32}$
48. $\frac{5}{9} \div \frac{2}{3}$ $\frac{5}{6}$

49. $6 \div 2\frac{1}{5}$ $2\frac{8}{11}$
50. $2\frac{5}{8} \div 3$ $\frac{7}{8}$

51. $4\frac{2}{3} \div 3\frac{1}{4}$ $1\frac{17}{39}$
52. $2\frac{3}{4} \div 1\frac{1}{8}$ $2\frac{4}{9}$

MCP All rights reserved

Write the decimal.

1. $6\frac{1}{10} =$ ___6.1___

2. $5\frac{2}{100} =$ ___5.02___

3. $\frac{7}{1000} =$ ___0.007___

4. fifty-two hundredths = ___0.52___

5. one and two thousandths = ___1.002___

6. seven and two tenths = ___7.2___

7. sixteen thousandths = ___0.016___

Write the place value of each red digit.

8. 84.76<u>2</u>
   hundredths

9. 9<u>8</u>4.6
   tens

10. 5.9<u>0</u>3
    hundredths

11. 7.69<u>5</u>
    thousandths

Write <, = or > in the circle.

12. 725.31 ⊚> 725.3

13. 45.5 ⊚= 45.50

14. 0.012 ⊚< 0.021

15. 6.02 ⊚> 6.018

Add.

16.
```
  279.38
+ 514.7
--------
  794.08
```

17.
```
  16.94
+  1.907
-------
 18,847
```

18.
```
   967.483
 + 125.469
----------
 1,092,952
```

19.
```
    8.06
   34.233
 +  7.645
---------
   49.938
```

Subtract.

20.
```
  72.395
- 16.286
--------
  56.109
```

21.
```
   4.073
-  0.98
-------
   3.093
```

22.
```
   17
 -  4.95
--------
   12.05
```

23.
```
  347.65
- 88.471
--------
 259.179
```

Round to the nearest tenth.

24. 823.48 ___823.5___

25. 27.550 ___27.6___

26. 64.794 ___64.8___

27. 6.23 ___6.2___

Round to the nearest hundredth.

28. 64.983 ___64.98___

29. 537.026 ___537.03___

30. 57.059 ___57.06___

31. 3.444 ___3.44___

Alternate Chapter Test

for page 233

Item	Objective
1-7	Change mixed numbers and decimal words to equivalent decimal numbers (See pages 213-214)
8-11	Identify place value from thousands through thousandths (See pages 215-220)
12-15	Compare, order decimals (See pages 221-222)
16-19	Add decimals (See pages 223-224)
20-23	Subtract decimals (See pages 225-226)
24-27	Round decimals to nearest tenth (See pages 229-230)
28-31	Round decimals to nearest hundredth (See pages 229-230)

Alternate Chapter Test

for page 255

Item	Objective
1-4	Multiply decimals (See pages 237-238)
5-7	Multiply decimals that need additional zeros written in product (See pages 239-240)
8	Multiply decimals by powers of 10 (See pages 241-242)
9-12	Divide a decimal by whole number (See pages 243-244)
13-16	Divide a decimal by whole number, quotient with zeros (See pages 245-246)
17-20	Divide a decimal by tenths (See pages 247-248)
21-24	Divide a decimal, round quotient to nearest tenth (See pages 249-250)

Multiply.

1. 7.5
    × 2.3
    17.25

2. 4.63
    × 0.8
    3.704

3. 52.9
    × 1.6
    84.64

4. 3.84
    × 0.72
    2.7648

5. 0.7
    × 0.1
    0.07

6. 0.08
    × 2.7
    0.216

7. 0.0006
    ×   9
    0.0054

8. 0.005
    × 100
    0.5

Divide.

9. $\dfrac{0.34}{7)2.38}$

10. $\dfrac{\$4.85}{9)\$43.65}$

11. $\dfrac{2.16}{36)77.76}$

12. $\dfrac{0.957}{28)26.796}$

13. $\dfrac{0.007}{6)0.042}$

14. $\dfrac{0.013}{42)0.546}$

15. $\dfrac{0.059}{3)0.177}$

16. $\dfrac{0.087}{33)2.871}$

17. $\dfrac{17.3}{0.5)8.65}$

18. $\dfrac{3.9}{2.2)8.58}$

19. $\dfrac{0.54}{1.4)0.756}$

20. $\dfrac{0.08}{6.7)0.536}$

Divide. Round the quotient to the nearest tenth.

21. $\dfrac{0.5}{7)3.15}$

22. $\dfrac{0.6}{9)5.67}$

23. $\dfrac{0.7}{1.4)0.938}$

24. $\dfrac{0.9}{9.7)8.8076}$

MCP All rights reserved

351

351

Alternate Chapter Test

for page 271

Item	Objective
1-4	Draw and label lines, line segments, rays, planes (See pages 257-258)
5-6	Draw and label parallel, intersecting, perpendicular lines (See pages 263-264)
7-8	Draw and label parts of circle (See pages 265-266)
10-11	Use protractor to measure and identify right, obtuse, acute, straight angles (See pages 259-262)
12-13	Identify rays, vertex of angles (See pages 259-260)
14-15	Bisect segments and angles (See pages 267-268)

Draw and label each figure.

1. line *ST*

2. ray *LM*

3. plane *ABC*

4. $\overline{XY}$

5. $\overleftrightarrow{FD} \parallel \overleftrightarrow{JK}$

6. line *PQ* ⊥ line *RS*

7. Circle *E* with arc *CD*

8. Circle *N* with diameter *TU*

Use a protractor to measure each angle, then write the word which identifies the type of angle.

9.

Measure ___25°___

Type ___acute___

10.

Measure ___90°___

Type ___right___

11.

Measure ___115°___

Type ___obtuse___

Write the names for the vertex and rays of angle *STU*.

12. Vertex ___T___

13. Rays ___TS___
___TU___

Bisect segment *EF* and angle *LMN*.

14.

15.

Alternate Chapter Test

for page 291

Item	Objective
1-2	Find third angle measure of triangles when two are known (See pages 273-274)
3-4	Identify squares, rectangles, parallelograms, trapezoids, rhombuses (See pages 275-276)
5-6	Identify regular and non-regular polygons (See pages 277-278)
5-6	Draw diagonals of specific polygons (See pages 277-278)
7-8	Identify congruent polygons and corresponding parts (See pages 279-280)
9	Draw lines of symmetry (See pages 281-282)
10	Identify similar polygons (See pages 283-284)
11-12	Identify solid figures and edges (See pages 285-286)

Find the missing angle measure.

1.

2.

_55°_   _60°_

Identify the kind of quadrilateral.

3.

4.

parallelogram   trapezoid

Identify the kind of polygon. Draw all possible diagonals.

5.

square

6.

hexagon

7. Tell if the figures are congruent. Write Yes or No.

Yes

8. The parallelgrams are congruent. Write the name of the angle which is congruent to *OPM*.

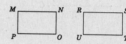

TUR

9. Draw all possible lines of symmetry.

10. Are the figures similar? Write Yes or No.

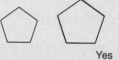

Yes

11. Identify the kind of solid figure.

rectangular prism

12. Write the number of edges.

_9_

MCP All rights reserved

353

353

Write each ratio as a fraction. Do not simplify.

1. three to five $\frac{3}{5}$

2. two to four $\frac{2}{4}$

3. 8 to 7 $\frac{8}{7}$

4. 5 out of 9 $\frac{5}{9}$

5. 1:4 $\frac{1}{4}$

6. 10:3 $\frac{10}{3}$

Write the missing number in each proportion.

7. $\frac{3}{n} = \frac{6}{8}$

8. $\frac{12}{8} = \frac{n}{4}$

9. $\frac{2}{6} = \frac{7}{n}$

10. $\frac{n}{5} = \frac{6}{15}$

$n = 4$

$n = 6$

$n = 21$

$n = 2$

Use the scale and a metric rule to write the actual dimensions of this figure.

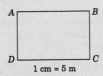

1 cm = 5 m

11. The length of AB is $\underline{15\ m}$

12. The perimeter of ABCD is $\underline{50\ m}$.

Write each number as a percent.

13. 0.36 = $\underline{36\%}$

14. $\frac{40}{100}$ = $\underline{40\%}$

15. 28 out of 100 = $\underline{28\%}$

16. 75:100 = $\underline{75\%}$

Write each percent as a fraction in simplest terms.

17. 80% = $\frac{4}{5}$

18. 14% = $\frac{7}{50}$

19. 92% = $\frac{23}{25}$

20. 7% = $\frac{7}{100}$

Write each fraction as a percent. Round to the nearest whole-number percent, if necessary.

21. $\frac{3}{20}$ = $\underline{15\%}$

22. $\frac{5}{6}$ = $\underline{83\%}$

23. $\frac{3}{8}$ = $\underline{38\%}$

24. $\frac{11}{25}$ = $\underline{44\%}$

Write the part represented by each percent.

25. 15% of 90 = $\underline{13.5}$

26. 20% of 75 = $\underline{15}$

27. 6% of $430 = $\underline{\$25.80}$

Alternate Chapter Test

page 315

Item	Objective
1-2	Write a ratio as a fraction (See pages 293-294)
3-6	Write a ratio as a fraction (See pages 293-294)
7-10	Solve equal ratio equations (See pages 297-298)
11-12	Use equal ratios to find distances on scale drawing (See pages 299-300)
13	Express a decimal as percent (See pages 301-302)
14	Express a fraction as percent (See pages 301-302, 305-306)
15-16	Express a ratio as percent (See pages 301-302)
17-20	Express percents as fractions in lowest terms (See pages 303-304)
21-24	Express fractions as percents, round to nearest whole percent (See pages 305-306)
25-27	Find percent of a number (See pages 307-308)

Alternate Chapter Test

for page 339

Item	Objective
1	Interpret tally graph; make bar graph (See pages 317-318)
2-3	Interpret line graph (See pages 321-322)
4-5	Interpret circle graphs that use percents (See pages 323-324)
6	Locate and name points represented by ordered pairs (See pages 325-326)
7	Graph points represented by ordered pairs (See pages 325-326)
8	Find outcomes in probability (See pages 329-330)
9	Find probability of specific outcome (See pages 327-328)

Use the tally chart to complete problem 1.

1. Make a bar graph.

Car Sales	
Mustang	JHT JHT I
Camero	JHT JHT IIII
Firebird	JHT II

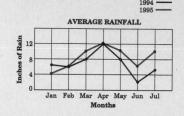

Use the line graph to complete 2 and 3.

2. What month had the highest average rainfall? __April__

3. In what months did 1994 have more rain than the same months in 1995? __January__

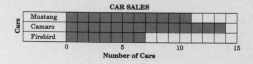

Use the circle graph of a poll of 34,650 adults' choices of favorite sports to complete 4 and 5.

4. What percent chose golf? __20%__

5. How many people chose baseball? __13,860__

Use the grid to complete 6 and 7.

6. Give the ordered pair of x. __(4,5)__

7. Graph the point Y (1,4)

Solve these problems.

8. Three dimes are tossed. List the possible outcomes.
__HHH, THH, THT, TTH, HTT, HTH, HHT, TTT__

9. Write the probability that all 3 dimes show heads. __$\frac{1}{8}$__

MCP All rights reserved

355

355

Glossary

Acute angle   An angle which measures less than 90°.

Addend   A number that is added to another number.
   In 3 + 4 = 7, 3 and 4 are both addends.

Angle   The figure made by two straight lines that meet at one endpoint or vertex.

Arc   A part of a curved line as in a circle.

Area   The measure of a surface surrounded by a boundary.
   The shaded part of the square is its area.

Average   The number obtained by adding two or more quantities and dividing by the number of quantities added.
   The average of 2, 5, and 11 is 6;
   2 + 5 + 11 = 18; 18 ÷ 3 = 6.

Bar graph   A representation of numerical facts using lengths of bars to show information.

Base (of an exponent)   The number that is raised to a power.
   base $\longrightarrow 5^2 \longleftarrow$ power

Base (of geometric figure)   A side or face in a figure.

Bisect   To divide into two equal parts.

Calculator code   The order for pressing keys on a calculator to solve an equation.

Centimeter (cm)   A metric unit of length.
   100 centimeters = 1 meter

Central angle   An angle whose vertex is the center of a circle.

central angle →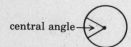

Chord   A line segment that joins two points on a circle.

$\overline{AB}$ is a chord

Circle   A plane figure bounded by a curved line made up of points all the same distance from the center.

Circle graph   A representation of numerical facts using parts or sections of a circle to show information.

Circumference   The distance around a circle.

Clear-entry key   The calculator key that cancels the last entry without erasing the previous entries.

Clear key   The calculator key that erases all entries and returns the screen to zero.

Composite number   A whole number greater than 1 which has more than 2 factors.
   The factors of the composite
   12 are 1, 2, 3, 4, 6 and 12.

Cone   A solid figure with a circle for its base and a curved surface forming to a point.

Congruent   A word that describes figures, sides or angles having the same size and shape.

Constant key   The equal key on a calculator. It remembers the last operation and number entered.

Cube   A solid figure with 6 equal, square sides.

Customary units   Standard measures of length, weight, volume and capacity.
   Inches, miles, pounds, cubic feet and ounces are examples of customary units.

Cylinder   A solid figure with two congruent circular bases and a curved rectangular region.

Decimal   A fractional part that uses place value and a decimal point to show tenths, hundredths and so on.
   0.6 is the decimal equivalent for the fraction $\frac{3}{5}$.

© MCP, All rights reserved

Denominator   The number below the line in a fraction.

In $\frac{3}{5}$, 5 is the denominator.

Diagonal   A segment which connects two vertices of a polygon but is not a side.

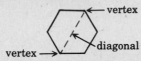

Diameter   A line or chord passing through the center of a circle.

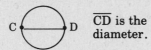

$\overline{CD}$ is the diameter.

Difference   The answer in a subtraction problem.
In $14 - 2 = 12$, 12 is the difference.

Discount   An amount of money saved when an original price is lowered.
To find the discount of $\frac{3}{4}$ off \$12, multiply

12 by 3 and divide by 4. The discount is \$9.

Dividend   The number that is being divided in a division problem.
In $42 \div 7 = 6$, 42 is the dividend.

Divisor   The number that is being divided into the dividend.
In $42 \div 7 = 6$, 7 is the divisor.

Edge   A segment that is the side of a face on a solid figure.

Equilateral triangle   A triangle with 3 equal sides.

Equivalent fractions   Fractions that name the same number.

$\frac{3}{4}$ and $\frac{9}{12}$ are equivalent fractions
because both name $\frac{3}{4}$.

Even Number   A whole number that is divisible by two:
2, 4, 6, 8, 10, 12 . . . are even numbers.

Expanded form   A number written as the sum of its place values.
426 is $400 + 20 + 6$ or
$(4 \times 100) + (2 \times 10) + (6 \times 1)$.

Exponent   A raised number that tells how many times the base number is to be used as a factor.

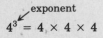

$4^3 = 4 \times 4 \times 4$

Expression   A mathematical sentence sometimes written with letters instead of numbers.
$a + b = c$ is an expression.

Face   A plane figure making up part of a solid figure.

Fact family   The set of 4 related facts having the same 3 numbers in their equations.

$$\begin{array}{cccc} 2 & 3 & 3 & 2 \\ \times 3 & \times 2 & 2\overline{)6} & 3\overline{)6} \\ \hline 6 & 6 \end{array}$$

or

$$\begin{array}{cccc} 5 & 4 & 9 & 9 \\ +4 & +5 & -4 & -5 \\ \hline 9 & 9 & 5 & 4 \end{array}$$

Factor   A number to be multiplied.
In $2 \times 3 = 6$, both 2 and 3 are factors.

Formula   A general rule expressed using symbols.

Graphing   Drawing a picture of relationships among numbers and quantities.

Greater than   A comparison of two numbers with the number of greater value written first.
$10 > 5$, $\frac{7}{8} > \frac{3}{4}$

Greatest common factor (GCF)   The largest number that is a common factor of two or more numbers.
$12 = 3 \times 4$
$15 = 3 \times 5$ 3 is the GCF of 12 and 15.

Grouping property   When the grouping of 3 or more addends or factors is changed, the sum or product remains the same.

$(2 + 5) + 1 = 2 + (5 + 1)$

or

$(5 \times 3) \times 2 = 5 \times (3 \times 2)$

Hexagon   A plane figure with 6 straight sides and 6 angles.

Identity property   Any factor multiplied by one equals the original factor. Or, any number added to zero is that number.
$7 \times 1 = 7; 7 + 0 = 7$

Improper fraction   A fraction whose numerator is larger in value than the denominator.
$\frac{6}{5}$ and $\frac{14}{3}$ are improper fractions.

Intersect To meet and cross over at a point.
Line AB intersects
line CD at point P.

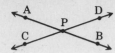

Isosceles triangle A triangle with 2 equal sides.

Kilogram (kg) A metric unit of weight.
1 kilogram = 1,000 grams

Kilometer (km) A metric unit of length.
1 kilometer = 1,000 meters

Least common multiple (LCM) The smallest number that is a common multiple of two or more numbers.
The LCM of 4 and 6 is 12.

Less than A comparison of two numbers with the number of lesser value written first.
$3 < 10$, $\frac{1}{8} < \frac{7}{8}$

Line A set of points whose straight path extends indefinitely in opposite directions.

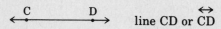
line CD or $\overleftrightarrow{CD}$

Line graph A representation of numerical facts using points and lines on a grid to show information.

Line of symmetry A line which equally divides a figure to produce a mirror image.

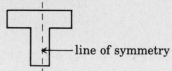
line of symmetry

Line segment A part of a line having two endpoints.

A————————B   segment AB or $\overline{AB}$

Liter (L) A basic metric unit of liquid measure.
1 liter = 1,000 milliliters

Mean A number representing the average of a group of numbers.

Median The middle number in a series of numbers.
5, 9, 17, 31, 50
↑
median

Meter (m) A basic metric unit of length.
1 meter = 100 centimeters

Metric units Measures of length, weight, volume and capacity based on the decimal system.
Meters, grams and liters are basic metric units.

Midpoint The middle point on a line segment.

Milliliter (mL) A metric unit of liquid measure.
1 milliliter = $\frac{1}{1000}$ liter

Minuend A number or quantity from which another is subtracted.
In $18 - 5 = 13$, 18 is the minuend.

Mixed number A fractional number greater than 1 that is written as a whole number and a fraction.
$5\frac{2}{3}$ is a mixed number.

Multiple The product of any given number and a whole number.
$10 \times 3 = 30$, $10 \times 5 = 50$
30 and 50 are multiples of 10.

Numerator The number above the line in a fraction.
In $\frac{3}{5}$, 3 is the numerator.

Obtuse angle An angle which measures between 90° and 180°.

Octagon A plane figure with 8 sides and 8 angles.

Odd number A whole number that is not divisible by two.
3, 5, 7, 9, 11, 13 are odd numbers.

Open sentence A mathematical sentence using a letter for a missing number.

Order property The order of addends or factors does not change the sum or product.
$5 + 7 = 7 + 5$
$3 \times 4 = 4 \times 3$

Ordered pair Two numbers that define one point on a grid; the first number names the distance across, and the second names the distance up.

Origin The point on a grid represented by the ordered pair 0,0.

Parallel lines Lines in the same plane that do not intersect.

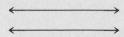

© MCP, All rights reserved

Parallelogram A quadrilateral having two pairs of opposite, congruent, parallel sides.

Pentagon A plane figure with 5 straight sides and 5 angles.

Percent A word meaning hundredths.
37 percent is written 37%
and means 0.37 or $\frac{37}{100}$.

Perimeter The distance around a shape that is the sum of the lengths of all of its sides.
The perimeter of this rectangle
is equal to 10 units.

Period Each group of 3 digits in a base-ten numeral. A comma is used to separate periods.
thousands
 period
1, 345, 752

Perpendicular Lines that form right angles where they intersect.

Pi (π) The ratio of the circumference of a circle to its diameter, approximately 3.14.

Place value The value of a digit depends upon its position in a numeral.

Plane A flat surface having infinite length and width.

Point A location in space.
• B   point B

Polygon A closed plane figure having three or more angles or sides.

Prime factor A factor that is a prime number.
The prime factors for 60 = 2 × 2 × 3 × 5.

Prime number A counting number greater than one whose only factors are itself and 1.
1 × 17 = 17
1 × 3 = 3   17 and 3 are prime numbers.

Probability A number which tells how likely it is that a certain event will happen.

Product The answer to a multiplication problem.
In 4 × 5 = 20, 20 is the product.

Product of primes The prime factors which equal a composite number when multiplied.
Product of primes   Composite
2 × 3 × 5 =   30

Proportion An equation showing that two ratios are equal.
$\frac{a}{b} = \frac{c}{d}$; then a × d = b × c

Quadilateral A polygon with 4 line segments joined to make 4 angles.

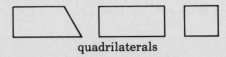

quadrilaterals

Quotient The answer to a division problem.
In 63 ÷ 7 = 9, 9 is the quotient.

Radius A segment whose endpoints are the center of the circle and a point on the circle.

Ratio A comparison of two quantities.
The ratio of 3 to 4 can be written $\frac{3}{4}$.

Ray A part of a line having one endpoint.
E   F   ray EF or $\overrightarrow{EF}$

Reciprocal When the product of two numbers is 1, they are called reciprocals of each other.
$\frac{5}{8}$ and $\frac{8}{5}$ are reciprocals.
4 and $\frac{1}{4}$ are reciprocals.

Remainder The number left over in a division problem.

$$\begin{array}{r} 16\ R4 \\ 6\overline{)100} \\ \underline{6\ \ } \\ 40 \\ \underline{36} \\ 4 \end{array}$$

In 6)100   4 is the remainder.

Rhombus A parallelogram with all sides congruent.

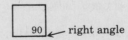

rhombus

Right angle An angle which measures exactly 90°.
In this square, all four angles are right angles.

90 ← right angle

Rounding Estimating a number's value by raising or lowering any of its place values.
To round to the nearest ten, look at the ones digit. If it is 4 or less, the tens digit stays the same, and the ones digit is replaced by zero. If the ones digit is 5 or more, the tens digit is raised by one, and the ones digit is replaced by zero. 34 rounded to the nearest 10 is 30, but 35 rounded to the nearest 10 is 40.

Scale drawing A representation of an actual object using proportional measurements.

Scalene triangle A triangle with no sides the same length and no angles the same measure.

Semicircle A half circle.

Similar figures Plane figures that have the same shape but not necessarily the same size or position.
  Figures A and B are similar.

Simplest terms A fraction or mixed number whose numerator and denominator cannot be divided by any common factor other than 1.

simplest form	simplest form
$\frac{12}{36} = \frac{1}{3}$	$\frac{34}{6} = 5\frac{4}{6} = 5\frac{2}{3}$

Simplify To rename a fraction as an equivalent fraction or mixed number whose numerator and denominator cannot be divided by any common factor other than 1.

simplest form	simplest form
$\frac{12}{36} = \frac{1}{3}$	$\frac{36}{10} = 3\frac{6}{10} = 3\frac{3}{5}$

Also, to rename an improper fraction as an equivalent whole number.

simplest form
$\frac{35}{7} = 5$

Solid figure A figure that is in more than one plane.

cube   pyramid   cylinder

Sphere A solid, round figure having a surface equally distant from its center at all points.

Standard form A number written using the symbols 0 through 9 in place-value form.
  4,036 is in standard form.

Statistics Numerical facts selected and compiled to present information.

Straight angle An angle which measures 180°.

<--------------------->

Subtrahend The number that is subtracted from the minuend.
  In 18 − 5 = 13, 5 is the subtrahend.

Sum The answer to an addition problem.
  In 8 + 9 = 17, 17 is the sum.

Symmetry A relationship between equal halves of a figure having the same size, shape and position.

Tally Marks used to count by fives.
  ‖‖‖ ‖‖‖ ‖‖‖ = 13

Terms The numerator and the denominator of a fraction.

Trapezoid A quadrilateral having one pair of parallel sides.

Trapezoid

Vertex (pl. vertices) The point at which two sides of an angle, two sides of a plane figure, or three or more sides of a solid figure meet.

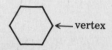← vertex

Volume The number of cubic units needed to fill a solid figure.
  The volume of this cube is 8 cubic units.

Zero property of addition and multiplication If an addend is zero, the sum is the non-zero addend. If a factor is zero, the product is zero.

Addend   Factor
  ↓   ↓
5 + 0 = 5   and   2 × 0 = 0

Zero property of division Zero can never be a divisor. Also, if a dividend is zero, the quotient will be zero.

© MCP. All rights reserved

TABLE OF MEASURES
Metric System

Metric Prefixes

Prefix	Multiplication Factor
kilo	1,000
hecto	100
deka	10
deci	0.1 or 1/10
centi	0.01 or 1/100
milli	0.001 or 1/1000

Common Equivalents

	Unit	Symbol	Relationship
Length	Kilometer	km	1 km = 1,000 m
	meter	m	1 m = 10 dm
			100 cm
			1,000 mm
	decimeter	dm	1 dm = 0.1 m
			10 cm
	centimeter	cm	1 cm = 0.01 m
			10 mm
	millimeter	mm	1 mm = 0.001 m
Mass	kilogram	kg	1 kg = 1,000 g
	gram	g	1 g = 1,000 mg
			0.001 kg
	milligram	mg	1 mg = 0.001 g
	metric ton	t	1 t = 1,000 kg
Capacity	liter	L	1 L = 1,000 mL
	milliliter	mL	1 mL = 0.001 L
Volume	cubic centimeter	cm^3	$1\ cm^3 = 1\ mL$
	cubic decimeter	dm^3	$1\ dm^3 = 1\ L$
	cubic meter	m^3	$1\ m^3 = 1,000\ L$

Temperature

Water freezes at 0° Celsius (C)

Water boils at 100° Celsius (C)

TABLE OF MEASURES
Customary System

Common Equivalents

	Unit	Symbol	Relationship
Length	foot	ft	1 ft = 12 inches (in.)
	yard	yd	1 yd = 3 ft 36 in.
	mile	mi	1 mi = 5,280 ft 1,760 yd
Weight	pound	lb	1 lb = 16 ounces (oz)
	ton	T	1 T = 2,000 lb
Liquid Measure	tablespoon	tbs	1 tbs = 3 teaspoons (tsp)
	fluid ounce	fl oz	1 fl oz = 2 tbs
	cup	c	1 c = 8 fl oz
	pint	pt	1 pt = 2 c 16 fl oz
	quart	qt	1 qt = 2 pt 32 fl oz
	gallon	gal	1 gal = 4 qt 8 pt
Dry Measure	quart	qt	1 qt = 2 pt
	peck	pk	1 pk = 8 qt
	bushel	bu	1 bu = 4 pk

Temperature

Water freezes at 32° Fahrenheit (F)
Water boils at 212° Fahrenheit (F)

Common Fraction/Decimal Equivalents

1/8 = 0.125	1/2 = 0.5
1/4 = 0.25	3/4 = 0.75
3/8 = 0.375	1/5 = 0.20
1/20 = 0.05	7/20 = 0.35

© MCP, All rights reserved

Time Equivalents

Unit	Symbol	Relationship
minute	min	1 min = 60 seconds (sec)
hour	h	1 h = 60 min
day	d	1 d = 24 h
week	wk	1 wk = 7 d
month	mo	1 mo = approximately 4 wk 28, 29, 30 or 31 d
year	yr	1 yr = 12 mo 365 d 366 d in a leap year
decade		10 yr
century		100 yr

Roman Numeral Equivalents

I = 1	VI = 6	XI = 11	L = 50	CD = 400
II = 2	VII = 7	XIX = 19	LX = 60	D = 500
III = 3	VIII = 8	XX = 20	XC = 90	CM = 900
IV = 4	IX = 9	XXX = 30	C = 100	M = 1,000
V = 5	X = 10	XL = 40	CC = 200	$\bar{V}$ = 5,000

Measurement Formulas

Measurement	Formula	Method
Circumference of a circle	$C = D\pi$	Multiply the diameter by 3.1416.
Perimeter of a square	$P = 4S$	Multiply the length of one side by 4.
Perimeter of a rectangle	$P = 2(L + W)$	Multiply the sum of the length and width by 2.
Perimeter of a triangle	$P = S_1 + S_2 + S_3$	Add the length of the 3 sides.
Area of a rectangle	$A = LW$	Multiply the length by the width.
Area of a circle	$A = R^2\pi$	Multiply the square of the radius by 3.1416.
Area of a square	$A = S^2$	Multiply one side by itself.
Area of a trapezoid	$A = \frac{1}{2}A(B + B)$	Add the length of the two parallel sides, multiply by the altitude and divide by 2.
Area of a triangle	$A = \frac{1}{2}(AB)$	Multiply the altitude by the base and divide by 2.
Volume of a cube	$V = S^3$	Use the length of one edge as a factor 3 times.
Volume of a rectangular prism	$V = LWH$	Multiply the length by the width by the height.

Index

A

Addition
  column, 25–26
  customary units, 123–124, 131–132
  decimals, 223–224, 227–228
  estimating, 29–30
  fact families, 1–2
  facts, 1–5
  fractions, 165–166, 171–172
  greater numbers, 27–28
  mixed numbers, 175–178, 185–186
  properties, 3–4
  renaming mixed numbers, 177–178
  solving for n, 3–4
  two- and three-digit numbers, 23–24
  unlike denominators, 171–172
  whole numbers, 23–30

Angles
  bisecting, 267–268
  estimating, 261–262
  identifying, 259–260
  measuring, 261–262

Area, 127–128

Averages, 91–92, 113–114

C

Calculator
  addition, 19–20, 41–42
  averages, 113–114
  codes, 19–20
  expressions, 289–290
  formulas, 289–290
  interest, 313–314
  inventory, 67–68
  rates, 253–254
  review, 337–338
  sale price, 209–210
  savings accounts, 41–42
  subtraction, 19–20, 41–42
  unit prices, 161–162

Capacity, 137–138

Centimeters, 133–134

Circles, 265–266

Comparing
  decimals, 221–222
  fractions, 151–152
  numbers, 9–12, 15–16

Cubic units, 129–130

Customary measurement
  capacity, 131–132
  length, 121–126
  weight, 131–132

D

Decimals
  adding, 223–224, 227–228
  comparing, 221–222
  dividing
    by decimals, 247–248
    by whole numbers, 243–244
    rounding quotients, 249–250
    zeros in quotient, 245–246
  hundredths, 215–216
  multiplying
    by decimals, 237–238
    by whole numbers, 235–236
    multiples of ten, 241–242
    zeros in product, 239–240
  periodic, 306
  place value, 213–220
  rounding, 229–230
  subtracting, 225–228
  tenths, 213–214
  thousandths, 217–218
  writing, 213–220

Division
  averages, 91–92
  deciding where to start, 83
  decimals
    by decimals, 247–248
    by whole numbers, 243–246
    rounding quotients, 249–250
    zeros in quotient, 245–246
  estimating quotients, 101–102
  fact families, 71
  facts, 71–72
  factors
    greatest common, 73–74, 149–150
    primes, 75–76
    trees, 75–76
  fractions, 201–206
  larger numbers, 87–88, 107–110
  mixed numbers, 203–206
  multiples of 10, 97–98
  one-digit quotients, 77–78, 99–102
  properties, 71
  quotients
    as mixed numbers, 155–156
    decimal, 243–250
    estimating, 101–102
    one-digit, 77–78, 99–102
    three-digit, 81–82
    two-digit, 79–80, 103–106
    with zeros, 85–86, 109–110, 245–246
  remainders, 77–90, 155–156
  short division, 89
  two-digit divisors, 97–110

E

Estimation
  differences, 37–38
  one-digit quotients, 101–102
  products, 51–52
  sums, 29–30
  two-digit quotients, 103–106

F

Feet, 123–124

Fractions
  adding
    like denominators, 165–166
    mixed numbers, 175–178, 185–186, 205–206
    unlike denominators, 171–172, 175–178
  as percents, 305–306
  comparing, 151–152
  dividing, 201–206
  equivalent, 145–148
  finding fractional parts, 191–192
  improper, 153–154, 157–158, 177–178
  mixed numbers, 153–158, 175–186, 195–198, 200, 203–206
  multiplying, 147–148, 191–198, 205–206
  quotients, 155–156
  reciprocals, 199–200
  renaming, 157–158
  reviewing operations, 205–206
  simplifying, 149–150
  subtracting
    from whole numbers, 181–182
    like denominators, 167–168
    mixed numbers, 179–186, 205–206
    unlike denominators, 173–174, 179–180, 183–186, 205–206
    with renaming, 181–186
  sums, 177–178
  writing, 143–144

Fundamental Theorem of Counting, 200

G

Gallons, 131–132

Geometry
  angles, 259–262
  circles, 265–266
  lines
    definition, 257
    intersecting, 263–264

© MCP, All rights reserved

R

Ratios
  as percents, 301–302
  definition, 293
  equal, 297–298
  tables, 295–296
  writing, 293–294

Reciprocals, 199–200

Renaming
  customary units, 123–124,
    131–132
  improper fractions, 157–
    158
  in multiplication, 53–54
  in subtracting mixed numbers,
    183–184
  mixed numbers, 153–154
  mixed numbers in sums, 177–
    178

Rounding
  decimals, 229–230
  estimating, 29–30, 37–38
  numbers, 13–14, 29–30, 37–38
  quotients, 249–250

S

Savings accounts, 41–42

Scale drawings, 299–300

Subtraction
  customary units, 123–124
  decimals, 225–228
  estimating, 37–38
  fact families, 1–2
  facts, 1–4, 6
  fractions, 167–168, 173–174,
    179–186
  greater numbers, 35–36
  minuends
    two- and three-digit, 31–
      32
    with zeros, 33–34
  mixed numbers, 179–186
  properties, 3–4
  renaming mixed numbers,
    183–184
  solving for n, 3–4
  unlike denominators, 173–174,
    179–186
  whole numbers, 31–38

Symmetry, 281–282

T

Tallies, 317–318

Time, 117–120

Time zones, 119–120

Tree diagrams, 333–334

Triangles, 273–274, 277–278

V

Volume, 129–130

Y

Yards, 123–130

Z

Zeros
  in minuends, 33–34
  in multiplication, 63–64
  in quotients, 85–86, 109–110,
    245–246

© MCP. All rights reserved